S0-AGE-512

Seeing Like a State

Seeing Like a State

How Certain Schemes to Improve the Human Condition Have Failed

James C. Scott

A VERITAS PAPERBACK

Yale UNIVERSITY PRESS
New Haven and London

Veritas paperback edition, 2020

Copyright © 1998 by Yale University.
All rights reserved.
This book may not be reproduced, in whole or in part, including illustrations, in any form
(beyond that copying permitted by Sections 107 and 108 of the U.S. Copyright Law and
except by reviewers for the public press), without written permission from the publishers.

Originally published in 1998 by Yale University Press.
Designed by James J. Johnson and set in Aster type by Running Feet Books, Durham, NC.
Printed in the United States of America

The Library of Congress has catalogued the hardcover edition as follows:

Scott, James C.
  Seeing like a state : how certain schemes to improve the human condition have failed /
James C. Scott.
      p. cm.—(Yale agrarian studies) (The Yale ISPS series)
      Includes bibliographical references and index.
      ISBN 0-300-07016-0 (cloth : alk. paper)
      ISBN 13: 978-0-300-07815-2 (pbk.: alk. paper)
      1. Central planning—Social aspects. 2. Social engineering. 3. Authoritarianism.
I. Title. II. Series. III. Series: The Yale ISPS series.
HD87.5.S365   1998
338.9—dc21   97-26556

Veritas Paperback Edition ISBN: 978-0-300-24675-9

A catalogue record for this book is available from the British Library.

10 9 8 7 6 5 4 3 2

For Louise, again, always

OWEN: What is happening?

YOLLAND: I'm not sure. But I'm concerned about my part in it. It's an eviction of sorts.

OWEN: We're making a six-inch map of the country. Is there something sinister in that?

YOLLAND: Not in . . .

OWEN: And we're taking place names that are riddled with confusion and . . .

YOLLAND: Who's confused? Are the people confused?

OWEN: And we're standardising those names as accurately and as sensitively as we can.

YOLLAND: Something is being eroded.

—Brian Friel, *Translations* 2.1

Contents

Acknowledgments

This book has been longer in the making than I would care to admit. It would be nice to be able to claim that it just took that long to think it through. Nice, but not truthful. A nearly fatal combination of malingering and administrative chores accounts for part of the delay. For the rest, the scope of the book simply expanded, in an academic version of Parkinson's Law, to fill all the space that I would give to it. Finally, I had to call an arbitrary halt or else start thinking of it as a life's work.

The scope of the book together with the time it took to complete it explain the long list of intellectual debts I have accumulated along the way. A full accounting of them would be interminable except for the fact that I realize some of my creditors would just as soon not be associated with the final product. Though I shall not implicate them here, I owe them nonetheless. Instead of turning my argument in the direction they urged, I took their criticisms to heart by fortifying my case so that it would better answer their objections. My other intellectual creditors, having failed to disavow the final product in advance, will be named here and, it is to be hoped, implicated.

Some of my debts are to institutions. I spent the 1990–91 academic year at the Wissenschaftskolleg zu Berlin as a recipient of their hospitality and largesse. The temptation of living for a time in Berlin, just a year after the Wall came down, proved irresistible. After physically laboring for six weeks on an ex-collective farm on the Mecklenburg Plain in eastern Germany (an alternative that I dreamed up to avoid sitting for six weeks in Goethe Institute classes with pimply teenagers), I hurled myself at the German language, Berlin, and my German colleagues. My research hardly advanced in any formal sense, but I realize that many fruitful lines of inquiry opened up then. I want particularly to thank Wolf Lepenies, Reinhard Prasser, Joachim Nettlebeck, Barbara Sanders, Barbara Golf, Christine Klohn, and Gerhard Riedel for their many kindnesses. The intellectual boon companionship of Georg Elwert, my local patron saint, as well as that of Shalini Randeria, Gabor Klaniczay, Christoph Harbsmeier, Barbara Lane, Mitchell Ash, Juan Linz, Jochen Blaschke, Arthur von Mehren, Akim von Oppen, Hans Luther, Carola Lenz, Gerd Spittler, Hans Medick, and Alf Lüdke opened my eyes to lines of inquiry that proved formative. Only the great efforts and unfailing friendship of Heinz Lechleiter and Ursula Hess brought my German to a (barely) tolerable level.

At various stages in the laborious preparation of this book, I had the privilege of making extended visits to institutions filled with large-spirited but skeptical colleagues. My good luck was that they so often made a project of straightening me out. They might not be satisfied with the final result, but I'll bet that they can see their influence at work. At the Ecole des Hautes Etudes en Sciences Sociales, Marseille, I especially want to thank my patron, Jean-Pierre Olivier de Sardan, Thomas Bierschenk, and their colleagues in the staff seminar. Living in Le Vieux Panier and working every day in the magnificent atmosphere of La Vielle Charité were unforgettable experiences. At the Humanities Research Centre at the Australian National University in Canberra, I had the benefit of an unmatched crowd of humanists and Asian specialists looking over my shoulder. Thanks go in particular to Graeme Clark, director, and Iain McCalman, associate director, who invited me, and to Tony Reid and David Kelly, who organized the conference, "Ideas of Freedom in Asia," which was the premise of my visit. Tony Milner and Claire Milner, Ranajit Guha (my guru) and Mechthild Guha, Bob Goodin and Diane Gibson, Ben Tria Kerkvliet and Melinda Tria, Bill Jenner, Ian Wilson, and John Walker in various ways made my stay convivial and intellectually rewarding.

This book would definitely have been much longer in the making were it not for the fact that Dick Ohmann and Betsy Traube invited me to spend the academic year of 1994–95 as a fellow of the Center for Humanities at Wesleyan University. My colleagues there and our weekly seminars together were intellectually bracing, thanks in large part to Betsy Traube's capacity to frame each paper brilliantly. The center's ideal combination of solitude and a staff that could not have been more helpful allowed me to finish a first draft of the entire manuscript. I am enormously grateful to Pat Camden and Jackie Rich for their inexhaustible fund of kindnesses. The astute insights of Betsy Traube and Khachig

Tololyan mark this work in many ways. Thanks also to Bill Cohen, Peter Rutland, and Judith Goldstein.

I would not have had the leisure for reflection and writing in 1994–95 had it not been for generous grants from the Harry Frank Guggenheim Foundation (Research for Understanding and Reducing Violence, Aggression, and Dominance) and a John D. and Catherine T. MacArthur Foundation Peace and Security Program Fellowship. But for their confidence in my work and their assistance, which made possible a respite from all administrative and teaching chores, I wouldn't have had a prayer of finishing this study when I did.

Finally, I want to thank my colleagues in the Netherlands and at the Amsterdam School for Social Science Research for the opportunity of visiting there in order to give the Sixth Annual W. F. Wertheim Lecture: Jan Breman, Bram de Swaan, Hans Sonneveld, Otto van den Muijzenberg, Anton Blok, Rod Aya, Roseanne Rutten, Johan Goudsblom, Jan-Willem Duyvendak, Ido de Haan, Johan Heilbron, Jose Komen, Karin Peperkamp, Niels Mulder, Frans Hüsken, Ben White, Jan Nederveen Pieterse, Franz von Benda-Beckmann, and Keebet von Benda-Beckmann. Having Wim Wertheim there to offer advice and criticism was a great privilege for me, for I have admired his many contributions to social science theory and Southeast Asian studies. I learned at least as much from the thesis-writing graduate students in my seminar there as they learned from me; Talja Potters and Peer Smets were kind enough to read my chapter on urban planning and provide searching critiques.

There are a good many scholars whose writings opened up new perspectives for me or provided outstanding analyses of issues that I could not have hoped to study so comprehensively on my own. Some of them have not seen this work, some of them I have never met, and some of them would probably want to disown what I have written. Nevertheless, I will venture to acknowledge my heavy intellectual debts to them all: Edward Friedman, Ben Anderson, Michael Adas, Teodor Shanin, James Ferguson, and Zygmunt Bauman. I could not have written the chapter on the high-modernist city without taking shameless advantage of the insights of James Holston's fine book on Brasília. The chapter on Soviet collectivization and its connection with industrial agriculture in the United States leans heavily on the work of Sheila Fitzpatrick and Deborah Fitzgerald. I thank Sheila Fitzpatrick for her searching comments, only a few of which are adequately reflected in the finished chapter.

The elaboration of the concept of mētis I owe to Marcel Detienne and Jean-Pierre Vernant. Although our terminology differs, Stephen

Marglin and I had, unbeknownst to one another, been taking separate trains to roughly the same destination. Thanks to the Rockefeller Foundation, Marglin organized a conference, "The Greening of Economics," in Bellagio, Italy, where I had my first opportunity to present some of my initial ideas, and Marglin's work on episteme and techne as well as his work on agriculture have influenced my thinking. Stephen Gudeman's perceptive comments, Frédérique Apffel Marglin's work on "variolation," and Arun Agrawal's work and commentary have helped to shape my sense of practical knowledge. Chapter 8, which is about agriculture, bears the distinct marks of all that I have learned from the work of Paul Richards and from Jan Douwe van der Ploeg. I am an amateur as an Africanist, and the chapter on *ujamaa* villages in Tanzania owes a great deal to Joel Gao Hiza, who wrote a brilliant senior honors thesis on the subject while at Yale University and who generously shared his voluminous research materials. (He is now finishing a thesis in anthropology at the University of California at Berkeley.) Bruce McKim, Ron Aminzade, Goran Hyden, David Sperling, and Allen Isaacman read the chapter on Tanzania and saved me from some blunders; some undoubtedly remain despite their efforts. Birgit Müller's fine analysis of the role of "fixers and traders" in the East German factory economy before unification helped me to understand the symbiotic relationship between planned order and informal arrangements.

Larry Lohmann and James Ferguson read an early draft of the manuscript and made comments that clarified my thinking enormously and prevented some serious missteps. A few other good friends offered to read all or part of the manuscript, in spite of its forbidding length. Those who rolled their eyes when offering or whose body language suggested mixed feelings, I avoided burdening. The few who genuinely wanted to read it, or whose feigned interest was completely convincing, in every case provided a set of comments that shaped the book in important ways. I owe an enormous debt and my warmest thanks to Ron Herring, Ramachandra Guha, Zygmunt Bauman, K. Sivaramakrishnan, Mark Lendler, Allan Isaacman, and Peter Vandergeest.

A great many thoughtful colleagues made useful criticisms or brought to my attention work that contributed to improvements in the argument and evidence. They include Arjun Appadurai, Ken Alder, Gregory Kasza, Daniel Goldhagen, Erich Goldhagen, Peter Perdue, Esther Kingston-Mann, Peter Sahlins, Anna Selenyi, Doug Gallon, and Jane Mansbridge. I also thank Sugata Bose, Al McCoy, Richard Landes, Gloria Raheja, Kiren Aziz Chaudhry, Jess Gilbert, Tongchai Winichakul, Dan Kelliher, Dan Little, Jack Kloppenberg, Tony Gulielmi, Robert Evenson, and Peter Sahlins. Others who kindly contributed are Adam

Ashforth, John Tehranian, Michael Kwass, Jesse Ribot, Ezra Suleiman, Jim Boyce, Jeff Burds, Fred Cooper, Ann Stoler, Atul Kohli, Orlando Figes, Anna Tsing, Vernon Ruttan, Henry Bernstein, Michael Watts, Allan Pred, Witoon Permpongsacharoen, Gene Ammarell, and David Feeny.

For the past five years the Program in Agrarian Studies at Yale has been for me the site of a broad, interdisciplinary education in rural life and a major source of intellectual companionship. The program has given me more that I can imagine ever giving back. Virtually every page of this book can be traced to one or another of the wide-ranging encounters fostered by the program. I will forgo mentioning fifty or so postdoctoral fellows who have visited for a year, but all of them have contributed in large and small ways to this enterprise. We invited them to join us because we admired their work, and they have never disappointed us. The chief of the Program in Agrarian Studies, Marvel Kay Mansfield, has been the heart and soul of the success of Agrarian Studies and every other enterprise with which I have been associated at Yale. This is not the first occasion I have acknowledged my debt to her; it has only grown with time. Nor could Agrarian Studies have thrived as it has without the initiative of K. Sivaramakrishnan, Rick Rheingans, Donna Perry, Bruce McKim, Nina Bhatt, and Linda Lee.

My intellectual debts to colleagues at Yale defy accounting. Those with whom I have taught—Bill Kelly, Helen Siu, Bob Harms, Angelique Haugerud, Nancy Peluso, John Wargo, Cathy Cohen, and Lee Wandel—have, in practice, taught me. Other Yale colleagues whose fingerprints can be found on this manuscript include Ian Shapiro, John Merriman, Hal Conklin, Paul Landau, Enrique Meyer, Dimitri Gutas, Carol Rose, Ben Kiernan, Joe Errington, Charles Bryant, and Arvid Nelson, a visiting fellow who is completing a thesis on forestry in East Germany and who was an exceptional source of information on the history of scientific forestry in Germany. The graduate students in my seminar, "Anarchism," and in a jointly taught seminar, "The Comparative Study of Agrarian Societies," read several draft chapters of the manuscript, pulling them to pieces in ways that forced me to rethink more than a few issues.

I have been blessed with research assistants who turned what began as wild goose chases into serious quests. Without their imagination and work I would have learned little about the invention of permanent last names, the physical layout of new villages, and language planning. Here is my chance to thank Kate Stanton, Cassandra Moseley, Meredith Weiss, John Tehranian, and Allan Carlson for their superb work. I owe Cassandra Moseley not only thanks but an apology, because all her fine work on the Tennessee Valley Authority resulted in a chapter that I reluctantly cut in order to keep the book within reasonable bounds. It will find another home, I trust.

Yale University Press has been good to me in more ways than one. I want to thank particularly John Ryden; Judy Metro; my editor, Charles Grench; and the best manuscript editor I have ever worked with, Brenda Kolb.

Several variants of chapter 1, each with some material from later chapters, have appeared elsewhere: "State Simplifications: Nature, Space, and People," Occasional Paper No. 1, Department of History, University of Saskatchewan, Canada, November 1994; "State Simplifications," *Journal of Political Philosophy* 4, no. 2 (1995): 1–42; "State Simplifications: Nature, Space, and People," in Ian Shapiro and Russell Hardin, eds., *Political Order*, vol. 38 of *Nomos* (New York: New York University Press, 1996): 42–85; "Freedom *Contra* Freehold: State Simplification, Space, and People in Southeast Asia," in David Kelly and Anthony Reid, eds., *Freedom in Asia* (forthcoming); "State Simplifications: Some Applications to Southeast Asia," Sixth Annual W. F. Wertheim Lecture, Centre for Asian Studies, Amsterdam, June 1995; and "State Simplifications and Practical Knowledge," in Stephen Marglin and Stephen Gudeman, eds., *People's Economy, People's Ecology* (forthcoming).

I'd like to kick the habit of writing books, at least for a while. If there were a detox unit or an analog to the nicotine patch for serial offenders, I think I would sign up for treatment. My habit has already cost me more precious time than I care to admit. The problem with book writing and other addictions is that the resolve to quit is greatest during withdrawal, but as the painful symptoms recede, the craving is apt to return. Louise and our children, Mia, Aaron, and Noah, would, I know, be only too happy to have me committed until I was "clean." I'm trying. God knows I'm trying.

Seeing Like a State

Introduction

This book grew out of an intellectual detour that became so gripping that I decided to abandon my original itinerary altogether. After I had made what appeared to be an ill-considered turn, the surprising new scenery and the sense that I was headed for a more satisfying destination persuaded me to change my plans. The new itinerary, I think, has a logic of its own. It might even have been a more elegant trip had I possessed the wit to conceive of it at the outset. What does seem clear to me is that the detour, although along roads that were bumpier and more circuitous than I had foreseen, has led to a more substantial place. It goes without saying that the reader might have found a more experienced guide, but the itinerary is so peculiarly off the beaten track that, if you're headed this way, you have to settle for whatever local tracker you can find.

A word about the road not taken. Originally, I set out to understand why the state has always seemed to be the enemy of "people who move around," to put it crudely. In the context of Southeast Asia, this promised to be a fruitful way of addressing the perennial tensions between mobile, slash-and-burn hill peoples on one hand and wet-rice, valley kingdoms on the other. The question, however, transcended regional geography. Nomads and pastoralists (such as Berbers and Bedouins), hunter-gatherers, Gypsies, vagrants, homeless people, itinerants, runaway slaves, and serfs have always been a thorn in the side of states. Efforts to permanently settle these mobile peoples (sedentarization) seemed to be a perennial state project — perennial, in part, because it so seldom succeeded.

The more I examined these efforts at sedentarization, the more I came to see them as a state's attempt to make a society legible, to arrange the population in ways that simplified the classic state functions of taxation, conscription, and prevention of rebellion. Having begun to think in these terms, I began to see legibility as a central problem in statecraft. The premodern state was, in many crucial respects, partially blind; it knew precious little about its subjects, their wealth, their landholdings and yields, their location, their very identity. It lacked anything like a detailed "map" of its terrain and its people. It lacked, for the most part, a measure, a metric, that would allow it to "translate" what it knew into a common standard necessary for a synoptic view. As a result, its interventions were often crude and self-defeating.

It is at this point that the detour began. How did the state gradually get a handle on its subjects and their environment? Suddenly, processes as disparate as the creation of permanent last names, the standardization of weights and measures, the establishment of cadastral surveys and population registers, the invention of freehold tenure, the standardization of language and legal discourse, the design of cities, and the organization of transportation seemed comprehensible as attempts at legibility and simplification. In each case, officials took exceptionally complex, illegible, and local social practices, such as land tenure customs or naming customs, and created a standard grid whereby it could be centrally recorded and monitored.

The organization of the natural world was no exception. Agriculture is, after all, a radical reorganization and simplification of flora to suit man's goals. Whatever their other purposes, the designs of scientific forestry and agriculture and the layouts of plantations, collective farms, ujamaa villages, and strategic hamlets all seemed calculated to make the terrain, its products, and its workforce more legible —and hence manipulable—from above and from the center.

A homely analogy from beekeeping may be helpful here. In premodern times the gathering of honey was a difficult affair. Even if bees were housed in straw hives, harvesting the honey usually meant driving off the bees and often destroying the colony. The arrangement of brood chambers and honey cells followed complex patterns that varied from hive to hive—patterns that did not allow for neat extractions. The modern beehive, in contrast, is designed to solve the beekeeper's problem. With a device called a "queen excluder," it separates the brood chambers below from the honey supplies above, preventing the queen from laying eggs above a certain level. Furthermore, the wax cells are arranged neatly in vertical frames, nine or ten to a box, which enable the easy extraction of honey, wax, and propolis. Extraction is made possible by observing "bee space"—the precise distance between the frames that the bees will leave open as passages rather than bridging the frames by building intervening honeycomb. From the beekeeper's point of view, the modern hive is an orderly, "legible" hive allowing the beekeeper to inspect the condition of the colony and the queen, judge its honey production (by weight), enlarge or contract the size of the hive by standard units, move it to a new location, and, above all, extract just enough honey (in temperate climates) to ensure that the colony will overwinter successfully.

I do not wish to push the analogy further than it will go, but much of early modern European statecraft seemed similarly devoted to rationalizing and standardizing what was a social hieroglyph into a legible and administratively more convenient format. The social simplifications thus introduced not only permitted a more finely tuned system of taxation and conscription but also greatly enhanced state capacity. They made possible quite discriminating interventions of every kind, such as public-health measures, political surveillance, and relief for the poor.

These state simplifications, the basic givens of modern statecraft, were, I began to realize, rather like abridged maps. They did not successfully represent the actual activity of the society they depicted, nor were they intended to; they represented only that slice of it that interested the official observer. They were, moreover, not just maps. Rather, they were maps that, when allied with state power, would enable much of the reality they depicted to be remade. Thus a state cadastral map created to designate taxable property-holders does not merely describe a system of land tenure; it creates such a system through its ability to give its categories the force of law. Much of the first chapter is intended to convey how thoroughly society and the environment have been refashioned by state maps of legibility.

This view of early modern statecraft is not particularly original. Suitably modified, however, it can provide a distinctive optic through which a number of huge development fiascoes in poorer Third World nations and Eastern Europe can be usefully viewed.

But "fiasco" is too lighthearted a word for the disasters I have in mind. The Great Leap Forward in China, collectivization in Russia, and compulsory villagization in Tanzania, Mozambique, and Ethiopia are among the great human tragedies of the twentieth century, in terms of both lives lost and lives irretrievably disrupted. At a less dramatic but far more common level, the history of Third World development is littered with the debris of huge agricultural schemes and new cities (think of Brasília or Chandigarh) that have failed their residents.

It is not so difficult, alas, to understand why so many human lives have been destroyed by mobilized violence between ethnic groups, religious sects, or linguistic communities. But it is harder to grasp why so many well-intended schemes to improve the human condition have gone so tragically awry. I aim, in what follows, to provide a convincing account of the logic behind the failure of some of the great utopian social engineering schemes of the twentieth century.

I shall argue that the most tragic episodes of state-initiated social engineering originate in a pernicious combination of four elements. All four are necessary for a full-fledged disaster. The first element is the administrative ordering of nature and society—the transformative state simplifications described above. By themselves, they are the unremarkable tools of modern statecraft; they are as vital to the maintenance of our welfare and freedom as they are to the designs of a would-be modern despot. They undergird the concept of citizenship and the provision of social welfare just as they might undergird a policy of rounding up undesirable minorities.

The second element is what I call a high-modernist ideology. It is best conceived as a strong, one might even say muscle-bound, version of the self-confidence about scientific and technical progress, the expansion of production, the growing satisfaction of human needs, the mastery of nature (including human nature), and, above all, the rational design of social order commensurate with the scientific understanding of natural laws. It originated, of course, in the West, as a by-product of unprecedented progress in science and industry.

High modernism must not be confused with scientific practice. It was fundamentally, as the term "ideology" implies, a faith that borrowed, as it were, the legitimacy of science and technology. It was, accordingly, uncritical, unskeptical, and thus unscientifically optimistic about the possibilities for the comprehensive planning of human settlement and production. The carriers of high modernism tended to see rational order in remarkably visual aesthetic terms. For them, an efficient, rationally organized city, village, or farm was a city that *looked* regimented and orderly in a geometrical sense. The carriers of high modernism, once their plans miscarried or were thwarted, tended to retreat to what I call miniaturization: the creation of a more easily controlled micro-order in model cities, model villages, and model farms.

High modernism was about "interests" as well as faith. Its carriers, even when they were capitalist entrepreneurs, required state action to realize their plans. In most cases, they were powerful officials and heads of state. They tended to prefer certain forms of planning and social organization (such as huge dams, centralized communication and transportation hubs, large factories and farms, and grid cities), because these forms fit snugly into a high-modernist view and also answered their political interests as state officials. There was, to put it mildly, an elective affinity between high modernism and the interests of many state officials.

Like any ideology, high modernism had a particular temporal and social context. The feats of national economic mobilization of the belligerents (especially Germany) in World War I seem to mark its high tide. Not surprisingly, its most fertile social soil was to be found among planners, engineers, architects, scientists, and technicians whose skills and status it celebrated as the designers of the new order. High-modernist faith was no respecter of traditional political boundaries; it could be found across the political spectrum from left to right but particularly among those who wanted to use state power to bring about huge, utopian changes in people's work habits, living patterns, moral conduct, and worldview. Nor was this utopian vision dangerous in and of itself. Where it animated plans in liberal parliamentary societies and where the planners therefore had to negotiate with organized citizens, it could spur reform.

Only when these first two elements are joined to a third does the combination become potentially lethal. The third element is an authoritarian state that is willing and able to use the full weight of its coercive power to bring these high-modernist designs into being. The most fertile soil for this element has typically been times of war, revolution, depression, and struggle for national liberation. In such situations, emergency conditions foster the seizure of emergency powers and frequently delegitimize the previous regime. They also tend to give rise to elites who repudiate the past and who have revolutionary designs for their people.

A fourth element is closely linked to the third: a prostrate civil society that lacks the capacity to resist these plans. War, revolution, and economic collapse often radically weaken civil society as well as make the populace more receptive to a new dispensation. Late colonial rule, with its social engineering aspirations and ability to run roughshod over popular opposition, occasionally met this last condition.

In sum, the legibility of a society provides the capacity for large-scale social engineering, high-modernist ideology provides the desire, the authoritarian state provides the determination to act on that desire, and an incapacitated civil society provides the leveled social terrain on which to build.

I have not yet explained, the reader will have noted, why such high-modernist plans, backed by authoritarian power, actually failed. Accounting for their failure is my second purpose here.

Designed or planned social order is necessarily schematic; it always ignores essential features of any real, functioning social order. This truth is best illustrated in a work-to-rule strike, which turns on the fact that any production process depends on a host of informal practices and improvisations that could never be codified. By merely following the rules meticulously, the workforce can virtually halt production. In the same fashion, the simplified rules animating plans for, say, a city, a village, or a collective farm were inadequate as a set of instructions for creating a functioning social order. The formal scheme was parasitic on informal processes that, alone, it could not create or maintain. To the degree that the formal scheme made no allowance for these processes or actually suppressed them, it failed both its intended beneficiaries and ultimately its designers as well.

Much of this book can be read as a case against the *imperialism* of high-modernist, planned social order. I stress the word "imperialism" here because I am emphatically not making a blanket case against either bureaucratic planning or high-modernist ideology. I am, however, making a case against an imperial or hegemonic planning mentality that excludes the necessary role of local knowledge and know-how.

Throughout the book I make the case for the indispensable role of practical knowledge, informal processes, and improvisation in the face of unpredictability. In chapters 4 and 5, I contrast the high-modernist views and practices of city planners and revolutionaries with critical views emphasizing process, complexity, and open-endedness. Le Corbusier and Lenin are the protagonists, with Jane Jacobs and Rosa Luxemburg cast as their formidable critics. Chapters 6 and 7 contain accounts of Soviet collectivization and Tanzanian forced villagization, which illustrate how schematic, authoritarian solutions to production and social order inevitably fail when they exclude the fund of valuable knowledge embodied in local practices. (An early draft contained a case study of the Tennessee Valley Authority, the United States' high-modernist experiment and the granddaddy of all regional development projects. It was reluctantly swept aside to shorten what is still a long book.)

Finally, in chapter 9 I attempt to conceptualize the nature of practical knowledge and to contrast it with more formal, deductive, epistemic knowledge. The term *mētis*, which descends from classical Greek and denotes the knowledge that can come only from practical experience, serves as a useful portmanteau word for what I have in mind.

Here I should also acknowledge my debt to anarchist writers (Kropotkin, Bakunin, Malatesta, Proudhon) who consistently emphasize the role of mutuality as opposed to imperative, hierarchical coordination in the creation of social order. Their understanding of the term "mutuality" covers some, but not all, of the same ground that I mean to cover with "mētis."

Radically simplified designs for social organization seem to court the same risks of failure courted by radically simplified designs for natural environments. The failures and vulnerability of monocrop commercial forests and genetically engineered, mechanized monocropping mimic the failures of collective farms and planned cities. At this level, I am making a case for the resilience of both social and natural diversity and a strong case about the limits, in principle, of what we are likely to know about complex, functioning order. One could, I think, successfully turn this argument against a certain kind of reductive social science. Having already taken on more than I could chew, I leave this additional detour to others, with my blessing.

In trying to make a strong, paradigmatic case, I realize that I have risked displaying the hubris of which high modernists are justly accused. Once you have crafted lenses that change your perspective, it is a great temptation to look at everything through the same spectacles. I do, however, want to plead innocent to two charges that I do not think a careful reading would sustain. The first charge is that my argument is uncritically admiring of the local, the traditional, and the customary. I understand that the practical knowledge I describe is often inseparable from the practices of domination, monopoly, and exclusion that offend the modern liberal sensibility. My point is not that practical knowledge is the product of some mythical, egalitarian state of nature. Rather, my point is that formal schemes of order are untenable without some elements of the practical knowledge that they tend to dismiss. The second charge is that my argument is an anarchist case against the state itself. The state, as I make abundantly clear, is the vexed institution that is the ground of both our freedoms and our unfreedoms. My case is that certain kinds of states, driven by utopian plans and an authoritarian disregard for the values, desires, and objections of their subjects, are indeed a mortal threat to human well-being. Short of that draconian but all too common situation, we are left to weigh judiciously the benefits of certain state interventions against their costs.

As I finished this book, I realized that its critique of certain forms of state action might seem, from the post–1989 perspective of capitalist triumphalism, like a kind of quaint archaeology. States with the pretensions and power that I criticize have for the most part vanished or have drastically curbed their ambitions. And yet, as I make clear in examining scientific farming, industrial agriculture, and capitalist markets in general, large-scale capitalism is just as much an agency of homogenization, uniformity, grids, and heroic simplification as the state is, with the difference being that, for capitalists, simplification must pay. A market necessarily reduces quality to quantity via the price mechanism and promotes standardization; in markets, money talks, not people. Today, global capitalism is perhaps the most powerful force for homogenization, whereas the state may in some instances be the defender of local difference and variety. (In *Enlightenment's Wake*, John Gray makes a similar case for liberalism, which he regards as self-limiting because it rests on cultural and institutional capital that it is bound to undermine.) The "interruption," forced by widespread strikes, of France's structural adjustments to accommodate a common European currency is perhaps a straw in the wind. Put bluntly, my bill of particulars against a certain kind of state is by no means a case for politically unfettered market coordination as urged by Friedrich Hayek and Milton Friedman. As we shall see, the conclusions that can be drawn from the failures of modern projects of social engineering are as applicable to market-driven standardization as they are to bureaucratic homogeneity.

Part 1

State Projects of

Legibility and Simplification

1 Nature and Space

Would it not be a great satisfaction to the king to know at a designated moment every year the number of his subjects, in total and by region, with all the resources, wealth & poverty of each place; [the number] of his nobility and ecclesiastics of all kinds, of men of the robe, of Catholics and of those of the other religion, all separated according to the place of their residence? . . . [Would it not be] a useful and necessary pleasure for him to be able, in his own office, to review in an hour's time the present and past condition of a great realm of which he is the head, and be able himself to know with certitude in what consists his grandeur, his wealth, and his strengths?
—Marquis de Vauban, *proposing an annual census to Louis XIV in 1686*

Certain forms of knowledge and control require a narrowing of vision. The great advantage of such tunnel vision is that it brings into sharp focus certain limited aspects of an otherwise far more complex and unwieldy reality. This very simplification, in turn, makes the phenomenon at the center of the field of vision more legible and hence more susceptible to careful measurement and calculation. Combined with similar observations, an overall, aggregate, synoptic view of a selective reality is achieved, making possible a high degree of schematic knowledge, control, and manipulation.

The invention of scientific forestry in late eighteenth-century Prussia and Saxony serves as something of a model of this process.[1] Although the history of scientific forestry is important in its own right, it is used here as a metaphor for the forms of knowledge and manipulation characteristic of powerful institutions with sharply defined interests, of which state bureaucracies and large commercial firms are perhaps the outstanding examples. Once we have seen how simplification, legibility, and manipulation operate in forest management, we can then explore how the modern state applies a similar lens to urban planning, rural settlement, land administration, and agriculture.

The State and Scientific Forestry: A Parable

I [Gilgamesh] would conquer in the Cedar Forest. . . . I will set my hand to it and will chop down the Cedar.
—*Epic of Gilgamesh*

The early modern European state, even before the development of scientific forestry, viewed its forests primarily through the fiscal lens of revenue needs. To be sure, other concerns—such as timber for ship-building, state construction, and fuel for the economic security of its subjects—were not entirely absent from official management. These concerns also had heavy implications for state revenue and security.[2] Exaggerating only slightly, one might say that the crown's interest in forests was resolved through its fiscal lens into a single number: the revenue yield of the timber that might be extracted annually.

The best way to appreciate how heroic was this constriction of vision is to notice what fell outside its field of vision. Lurking behind the number indicating revenue yield were not so much forests as commercial wood, representing so many thousands of board feet of saleable timber and so many cords of firewood fetching a certain price. Missing, of course, were all those trees, bushes, and plants holding little or no potential for state revenue. Missing as well were all those parts of trees, even revenue-bearing trees, which might have been useful to the population but whose value could not be converted into fiscal receipts. Here I have in mind foliage and its uses as fodder and thatch; fruits, as food for people and domestic animals; twigs and branches, as bedding, fencing, hop poles, and kindling; bark and roots, for making medicines and for tanning; sap, for making resins; and so forth. Each species of tree—indeed, each part or growth stage of each species—had its unique properties and uses. A fragment of the entry under "elm" in a popular seventeenth-century encyclopedia on aboriculture conveys something of the vast range of practical uses to which the tree could be put.

> Elm is a timber of most singular use, especially whereby it may be continually dry, or wet, in extremes; therefore proper for water works, mills, the ladles and soles of the wheel, pumps, aqueducts, ship planks below the water line, . . . also for wheelwrights, handles for the single handsaw, rails and gates. Elm is not so apt to rive [split] . . . and is used for chopping blocks, blocks for the hat maker, trunks and boxes to be covered with leather, coffins and dressers and shovelboard tables of great length; also for the carver and those curious workers of fruitage, foliage, shields, statues and most of the ornaments appertaining to the orders of architecture. . . . And finally . . . the use of the very leaves of this tree, especially the female, is not to be despised, . . . for they will prove of great relief to cattle in the winter and scorching summers when hay and fodder is dear. . . . The green leaf of the elms contused heals a green wound or cut, and boiled with the bark, consolidates bone fractures.[3]

In state "fiscal forestry," however, the actual tree with its vast number of possible uses was replaced by an abstract tree representing a volume of lumber or firewood. If the princely conception of the forest was still utilitarian, it was surely a utilitarianism confined to the direct needs of the state.

From a naturalist's perspective, nearly everything was missing from the state's narrow frame of reference. Gone was the vast majority of flora: grasses, flowers, lichens, ferns, mosses, shrubs, and vines. Gone, too, were reptiles, birds, amphibians, and innumerable species of insects. Gone were most species of fauna, except those that interested the crown's gamekeepers.

From an anthropologist's perspective, nearly everything touching on human interaction with the forest was also missing from the state's tunnel vision. The state did pay attention to poaching, which impinged on its claim to revenue in wood or its claim to royal game, but otherwise it typically ignored the vast, complex, and negotiated social uses of the forest for hunting and gathering, pasturage, fishing, charcoal making, trapping, and collecting food and valuable minerals as well as the forest's significance for magic, worship, refuge, and so on.[4]

If the utilitarian state could not see the real, existing forest for the (commercial) trees, if its view of its forests was abstract and partial, it was hardly unique in this respect. Some level of abstraction is necessary for virtually all forms of analysis, and it is not at all surprising that the abstractions of state officials should have reflected the paramount fiscal interests of their employer. The entry under "forest" in Diderot's *Encyclopédie* is almost exclusively concerned with the *utilité publique* of forest products and the taxes, revenues, and profits that they can be made to yield. The forest as a habitat disappears and is replaced by the forest as an economic resource to be managed efficiently and profitably.[5] Here, fiscal and commercial logics coincide; they are both resolutely fixed on the bottom line.

The vocabulary used to organize nature typically betrays the overriding interests of its human users. In fact, utilitarian discourse replaces the term "nature" with the term "natural resources," focusing on those aspects of nature that can be appropriated for human use. A comparable logic extracts from a more generalized natural world those flora or fauna that are of utilitarian value (usually marketable commodities) and, in turn, reclassifies those species that compete with, prey on, or otherwise diminish the yields of the valued species. Thus, plants that are valued become "crops," the species that compete with them are stigmatized as "weeds," and the insects that ingest them are stigmatized as "pests." Thus, trees that are valued become "timber," while species that compete with them become "trash" trees or "underbrush." The same logic applies to fauna. Highly valued animals become "game" or "livestock," while those animals that compete with or prey upon them become "predators" or "varmints."

The kind of abstracting, utilitarian logic that the state, through its officials, applied to the forest is thus not entirely distinctive. What is distinctive about this logic, however, is the narrowness of its field of vision, the degree of elaboration to which it can be subjected, and above all, as we shall see, the degree to which it allowed the state to impose that logic on the very reality that was observed.[6]

Scientific forestry was originally developed from about 1765 to 1800, largely in Prussia and Saxony. Eventually, it would become the basis of forest management techniques in France, England, and the United States and throughout the Third World. Its emergence cannot be understood outside the larger context of the centralized state-making initiatives of the period. In fact, the new forestry science was a subdiscipline of what was called cameral science, an effort to reduce the fiscal management of a kingdom to scientific principles that would allow systematic planning.[7] Traditional domainal forestry had hitherto simply divided the forest into roughly equal plots, with the number of plots coinciding with the number of years in the assumed growth cycle.[8] One plot was cut each year on the assumption of equal yields (and value) from plots of equal size. Because of poor maps, the uneven distribution of the most valuable large trees (*Hochwald*), and very approximate cordwood (*Bruststaerke*) measures, the results were unsatisfactory for fiscal planning.

Careful exploitation of domainal forests was all the more imperative in the late eighteenth century, when fiscal officials became aware of a growing shortage of wood. Many of the old-growth forests of oak, beech, hornbeam, and linden had been severely degraded by planned and unplanned felling, while the regrowth was not as robust as hoped. The prospect of declining yields was alarming, not merely because it threatened revenue flows but also because it might provoke massive poaching by a peasantry in search of firewood. One sign of this concern were the numerous state-sponsored competitions for designs of more efficient woodstoves.

The first attempt at more precise measurements of forests was made by Johann Gottlieb Beckmann on a carefully surveyed sample plot. Walking abreast, several assistants carried compartmentalized boxes with color-coded nails corresponding to five categories of tree sizes, which they had been trained to identify. Each tree was tagged with the appropriate nail until the sample plot had been covered. Because each assistant had begun with a certain number of nails, it was a simple matter to subtract the remaining nails from the initial total and arrive at an inventory of trees by class for the entire plot. The sample plot had been carefully chosen for its representativeness, allowing the foresters to then calculate the timber and, given certain price assumptions, the revenue yield of the whole forest. For the forest scientists (*Forstwissenschaftler*) the goal was always to "deliver the greatest possible *constant* volume of wood."[9]

The effort at precision was pushed further as mathematicians worked from the cone-volume principle to specify the volume of saleable wood contained by a standardized tree (*Normalbaum*) of a given size-class. Their calculations were checked empirically against the actual volume of wood in sample trees.[10] The final result of such calculations was the development of elaborate tables with data organized by tree size and age under specified conditions of normal growth and maturation. By radically narrowing his vision to commercial wood, the state forester had, with his tables, paradoxically achieved a synoptic view of the entire forest.[11] This restriction of focus reflected in the tables was in fact the only way in which the whole forest could be taken in by a single optic. Reference to these tables coupled with field tests allowed the forester to estimate closely the inventory, growth, and yield of a given forest. In the regulated, abstract forest of the forstwissenschaftler, calculation and measurement prevailed, and the three watchwords, in modern parlance, were "minimum diversity," the "balance sheet," and "sustained yield." The logic of the state-managed forest science was virtually identical with the logic of commercial exploitation.[12]

The achievement of German forestry science in standardizing techniques for calculating the sustainable yield of commercial timber and hence revenue was impressive enough. What is decisive for our purposes, however, was the next logical step in forest management. That step was to attempt to create, through careful seeding, planting, and cutting, a forest that was easier for state foresters to count, manipulate, measure, and assess. The fact is that forest science and geometry, backed by state power, had the capacity to transform the real, diverse, and chaotic old-growth forest into a new, more uniform forest that closely resembled the administrative grid of its techniques. To this end, the underbrush was cleared, the number of species was reduced (often to monoculture), and plantings were done simultaneously and in straight rows on large tracts. These management practices, as Henry Lowood observes, "produced the monocultural, even-age forests that eventually transformed the Normalbaum from abstraction to reality. The German forest became the archetype for imposing on disorderly nature the neatly arranged constructs of science. Practical goals had encouraged mathematical utilitarianism, which seemed, in turn, to promote geometric perfection as the outward sign of the well-managed forest; in turn the rationally ordered arrangements of trees offered new possibilities for controlling nature."[13]

The tendency was toward regimentation, in the strict sense of the word. The forest trees were drawn up into serried, uniform ranks, as it were, to be measured, counted off, felled, and replaced by a new rank and file of lookalike conscripts. As an army, it was also designed hierarchically from above to fulfill a unique purpose and to be at the disposition of a single commander. At the limit, the forest itself would not even have to be seen; it could be "read" accurately from the tables and maps in the forester's office.

1. Mixed temperate forest, part managed, part natural regeneration

2. One aisle of a managed poplar forest in Tuscany

How much easier it was to manage the new, stripped-down forest. With stands of same-age trees arranged in linear alleys, clearing the underbrush, felling, extraction, and new planting became a far more routine process. Increasing order in the forest made it possible for forest workers to use written training protocols that could be widely applied. A relatively unskilled and inexperienced labor crew could adequately carry out its tasks by following a few standard rules in the new forest environment. Harvesting logs of relatively uniform width and length not only made it possible to forecast yields successfully but also to market homogeneous product units to logging contractors and timber merchants.[14] Commercial logic and bureaucratic logic were, in this instance, synonymous; it was a system that promised to maximize the return of a single commodity over the long haul and at the same time lent itself to a centralized scheme of management.

The new legible forest was also easier to manipulate experimentally. Now that the more complex old-growth forest had been replaced by a forest in which many variables were held constant, it was a far simpler matter to examine the effects of such variables as fertilizer applications, rainfall, and weeding, on same-age, single-species stands. It was the closest thing to a forest laboratory one could imagine at the time.[15] The very simplicity of the forest made it possible, for the first time, to assess novel regimens of forest management under nearly experimental conditions.

Although the geometric, uniform forest was intended to facilitate management and extraction, it quickly became a powerful aesthetic as well. The visual sign of the well-managed forest, in Germany and in the many settings where German scientific forestry took hold, came to be the regularity and neatness of its appearance. Forests might be inspected in much the same way as a commanding officer might review his troops on parade, and woe to the forest guard whose "beat" was not sufficiently trim or "dressed." This aboveground order required that underbrush be removed and that fallen trees and branches be gathered and hauled off. Unauthorized disturbances—whether by fire or by local populations—were seen as implicit threats to management routines. The more uniform the forest, the greater the possibilities for centralized management; the routines that could be applied minimized the need for the discretion necessary in the management of diverse old-growth forests.

The controlled environment of the redesigned, scientific forest promised many striking advantages.[16] It could be synoptically surveyed by the chief forester; it could be more easily supervised and harvested according to centralized, long-range plans; it provided a steady, uniform commodity, thereby eliminating one major source of revenue fluctuation; and it created a legible natural terrain that facilitated manipulation and experimentation.

This utopian dream of scientific forestry was, of course, only the *immanent* logic of its techniques. It was not and could not ever be realized in practice. Both nature and the human factor intervened. The existing topography of the landscape and the vagaries of fire, storms, blights, climatic changes, insect populations, and disease conspired to thwart foresters and to shape the actual forest. Also, given the insurmountable difficulties of policing large forests, people living nearby typically continued to graze animals, poach firewood and kindling, make charcoal, and use the forest in other ways that prevented the foresters' management plan from being fully realized.[17] Although, like all utopian schemes, it fell well short of attaining its goal, the critical fact is that it did partly succeed in stamping the actual forest with the imprint of its designs.

The principles of scientific forestry were applied as rigorously as was practicable to most large German forests throughout much of the nineteenth century. The Norway spruce, known for its hardiness, rapid growth, and valuable wood, became the bread-and-butter tree of commercial forestry. Originally, the Norway spruce was seen as a restoration crop that might revive overexploited mixed forests, but the commercial profits from the first rotation were so stunning that there was little effort to return to mixed forests. The monocropped forest was a disaster for peasants who were now deprived of all the grazing, food, raw materials, and medicines that the earlier forest ecology had afforded. Diverse old-growth forests, about three-fourths of which were broadleaf (deciduous) species, were replaced by largely coniferous forests in which Norway spruce or Scotch pine were the dominant or often only species.

In the short run, this experiment in the radical simplification of the forest to a single commodity was a resounding success. It was a rather long short run, in the sense that a single crop rotation of trees might take eighty years to mature. The productivity of the new forests reversed the decline in the domestic wood supply, provided more uniform stands and more usable wood fiber, raised the economic return of forest land, and appreciably shortened rotation times (the time it took to harvest a stand and plant another).[18] Like row crops in a field, the new softwood forests were prodigious producers of a single commodity. Little wonder that the German model of intensive commercial forestry became standard throughout the world.[19] Gifford Pinchot, the second chief forester of the United States, was trained at the French forestry school at Nancy, which followed a German-style curriculum, as did most U.S. and European forestry schools.[20] The first forester hired by the British to assess and manage the great forest resources of India and Burma was Dietrich Brandes, a German.[21] By the end of the nineteenth century, German forestry science was hegemonic.

The great simplification of the forest into a "one-commodity machine" was precisely the step that allowed German forestry science to become a rigorous technical and commercial discipline that could be codified and taught. A condition of its rigor was that it severely bracketed, or assumed to be constant, all variables except those bearing directly on the yield of the selected species and on the cost of growing and extracting them. As we shall see with urban planning, revolutionary theory, collectivization, and rural resettlement, a whole world lying "outside the brackets" returned to haunt this technical vision.

In the German case, the negative biological and ultimately commercial consequences of the stripped-down forest became painfully obvious only after the *second* rotation of conifers had been planted. "It took about one century for them [the negative consequences] to show up clearly. Many of the pure stands grew excellently in the first generation but already showed an amazing retrogression in the second generation. The reason for this is a very complex one and only a simplified explanation can be given. . . . Then the whole nutrient cycle got out of order and eventually was nearly stopped. . . . Anyway, the drop of one or two site classes [used for grading the quality of timber] during two or three generations of pure spruce is a well known and frequently observed fact. This represents a production loss of 20 to 30 percent."[22]

A new term, *Waldsterben* (forest death), entered the German vocabulary to describe the worst cases. An exceptionally complex process involving soil building, nutrient uptake, and symbiotic relations among fungi, insects, mammals, and flora—which were, and still are, not entirely understood—was apparently disrupted, with serious consequences. Most of these consequences can be traced to the radical simplicity of the scientific forest.

Only an elaborate treatise in ecology could do justice to the subject of what went wrong, but mentioning a few of the major effects of simplification will illustrate how vital many of the factors bracketed by scientific forestry turned out to be. German forestry's attention to formal order and ease of access for management and extraction led to the clearing of underbrush, deadfalls, and snags (standing dead trees), greatly reducing the diversity of insect, mammal, and bird populations so essential to soil-building processes.[23] The absence of litter and woody biomass on the new forest floor is now seen as a major factor leading to thinner and less nutritious soils.[24] Same-age, same-species forests not only created a far less diverse habitat but were also more vulnerable to massive storm-felling. The very uniformity of species and age among, say, Norway spruce also provided a favorable habitat to all the "pests" which were specialized to that species. Populations of these pests built up to epidemic proportions, inflicting losses in yields and large outlays for fertilizers, insecticides, fungicides, or rodenticides.[25] Apparently the first rotation of Norway spruce had grown exceptionally well in large part because it was living off (or mining) the long-accumulated soil capital of the diverse old-growth forest that it had replaced. Once that capital was depleted, the steep decline in growth rates began.

As pioneers in scientific forestry, the Germans also became pioneers in recognizing and attempting to remedy many of its undesirable consequences. To this end, they invented the science of what they called "forest hygiene." In place of hollow trees that had been home to woodpeckers, owls, and other tree-nesting birds, the foresters provided specially designed boxes. Ant colonies were artificially raised and implanted in the forest, their nests tended by local schoolchildren. Several species of spiders, which had disappeared from the monocropped forest, were reintroduced.[26] What is striking about these endeavors is that they are attempts to work around an impoverished habitat still planted with a single species of conifers for production purposes.[27] In this case, "restoration forestry" attempted with mixed results to create a *virtual* ecology, while denying its chief sustaining condition: diversity.

The metaphorical value of this brief account of scientific production forestry is that it illustrates the dangers of dismembering an exceptionally complex and poorly understood set of relations and processes in order to isolate a single element of instrumental value. The instrument, the knife, that carved out the new, rudimentary forest was the razor-sharp interest in the production of a single commodity. Everything that interfered with the efficient production of the key commodity was implacably eliminated. Everything that seemed unrelated to efficient production was ignored. Having come to see the forest as a commodity, scientific forestry set about refashioning it as a commodity machine.[28] Utilitarian simplification in the forest was an effective way of maximizing wood production in the short and intermediate term. Ultimately, however, its emphasis on yield and paper profits, its relatively short time horizon, and, above all, the vast array of consequences it had resolutely bracketed came back to haunt it.[29]

Even in the realm of greatest interest—namely, the production of wood fiber—the consequences of not seeing the forest for the trees sooner or later became glaring. Many were directly traceable to the basic simplification imposed in the interest of ease of management and economic return: monoculture. Monocultures are, as a rule, more fragile and hence more vulnerable to the stress of disease and weather than polycultures are. As Richard Plochmann expresses it, "One further drawback, which is typical of all pure plantations, is that the ecology of the natural plant associations became unbalanced. Outside of the natural habitat, and when planted in pure stands, the physical condition of the single tree weakens and resistance against enemies decreases."[30] Any unmanaged forest may experience stress from storms, disease, drought, fragile soil, or severe cold. A diverse, complex forest, however, with its many species of trees, its full complement of birds, insects, and mammals, is far more resilient—far more able to withstand and recover from such injuries—than pure stands. Its very diversity and complexity help to inoculate it against devastation: a windstorm that fells large, old trees of one species will typically spare large trees of other species as well as small trees of the same species; a blight or insect attack that threatens, say, oaks may leave lindens and hornbeams unscathed. Just as a merchant who, not knowing what conditions her ships will face at sea, sends out scores of vessels with different designs, weights, sails, and navigational aids stands a better chance of having much of her fleet make it to port, while a merchant who stakes everything on a single ship design and size runs a higher risk of losing everything, forest biodiversity acts like an insurance policy. Like the enterprise run by the second merchant, the simplified forest is a more vulnerable system, especially over the long haul, as its effects on soil, water, and "pest" populations become manifest. Such dangers can only partly be checked by the use of artificial fertilizers, insecticides, and fungicides. Given the fragility of the simplified production forest, the massive outside intervention that was required to establish it—we might call it the administrators' forest—is increasingly necessary in order to sustain it as well.[31]

Social Facts, Raw and Cooked

> Society must be remade before it can be the object of quantification. Categories of people and things must be defined, measures must be interchangeable; land and commodities must be conceived as represented by an equivalent in money. There is much of what Weber called rationalization in this, and also a good deal of centralization.
> —Theodore M. Porter, *"Objectivity as Standardization"*

The administrators' forest cannot be the naturalists' forest. Even if the ecological interactions at play in the forest were known, they would constitute a reality so complex and variegated as to defy easy shorthand description. The intellectual filter necessary to reduce the complexity to manageable dimensions was provided by the state's interest in commercial timber and revenue.

If the natural world, however shaped by human use, is too unwieldy in its "raw" form for administrative manipulation, so too are the actual social patterns of human interaction with nature bureaucratically indigestible in their raw form. No administrative system is capable of representing *any* existing social community except through a heroic and greatly schematized process of abstraction and simplification. It is not simply a question of capacity, although, like a forest, a human community is surely far too complicated and variable to easily yield its secrets to bureaucratic formulae. It is also a question of purpose. State agents have no interest—nor should they—in describing an entire social reality, any more than the scientific forester has an interest in describing the ecology of a forest in detail. Their abstractions and simplifications are disciplined by a small number of objectives, and until the nineteenth century the most prominent of these were typically taxation, political control, and conscription. They needed only the techniques and understanding that were adequate to these tasks. As we shall see, here are some instructive parallels between the development of modern "fiscal forestry" and modern forms of taxable property in land. Premodern states were no less concerned with tax receipts than are modern states. But, as with premodern state forestry, the taxation techniques and reach of the premodern state left much to be desired.

Absolutist France in the seventeenth century is a case in point.[32] Indirect taxes—excise levies on salt and tobacco, tolls, license fees, and the sale of offices and titles—were favored forms of taxation; they were easy to administer and required little or nothing in the way of information about landholding and income. The tax-exempt status of the nobility and clergy meant that a good deal of the landed property was not taxed at all, transferring much of the burden to wealthy commoner farmers and the peasantry. Common land, although it was a vitally important subsistence resource for the rural poor, yielded no revenue either. In the eighteenth century, the physiocrats would condemn all common property on two presumptive grounds: it was inefficiently exploited, and it was fiscally barren.[33]

What must strike any observer of absolutist taxation is how wildly variable and unsystematic it was. James Collins has found that the main direct land tax, the *taille*, was frequently not paid at all and that no community paid more than one-third of what they were assessed.[34] The result was that the state routinely relied on exceptional measures to overcome shortfalls in revenue or to pay for new expenses, particularly military campaigns. The crown exacted "forced loans" (*rentes, droits aliénés*) in return for annuities that it might or might not honor; it sold offices and titles (*vénalités d'offices*); it levied exceptional hearth taxes (*fouages extraordinaires*); and, worst of all, it billeted troops directly in communities, often ruining the towns in the process.[35]

The billeting of troops, a common form of fiscal punishment, is to modern forms of systematic taxation as the drawing and quartering of would-be regicides (so strikingly described by Michel Foucault at the beginning of *Discipline and Punish*) is to modern forms of systematic incarceration of criminals. Not that there was a great deal of choice involved. The state simply lacked both the information and the administrative grid that would have allowed it to exact from its subjects a reliable revenue that was more closely tied to their actual capacity to pay. As with forest revenue, there was no alternative to rough-and-ready calculations and their corresponding fluctuations in yields. Fiscally, the premodern state was, to use Charles Lindblom's felicitous phrase, "all thumbs and no fingers"; it was incapable of fine tuning.

Here is where the rough analogy between forest management and taxation begins to break down. In the absence of reliable information about sustainable timber yield, the state might either inadvertently overexploit its resources and threaten future supply or else fail to realize the level of proceeds the forest might sustain.[36] The trees themselves, however, were not political actors, whereas the taxable subjects of the crown most certainly were. They signaled their dissatisfaction by flight, by various forms of quiet resistance and evasion, and, in extremis, by outright revolt. A reliable format for taxation of subjects thus depended not just on discovering what their economic conditions were but also on trying to judge what exactions they would vigorously resist.

How were the agents of the state to begin measuring and codifying, throughout each region of an entire kingdom, its population, their landholdings, their harvests, their wealth, the volume of commerce, and so on? The obstacles in the path of even the most rudimentary knowledge of these matters were enormous. The struggle to establish uniform weights and measures and to carry out a cadastral mapping of landholdings can serve as diagnostic examples. Each required a large, costly, long-term campaign against determined resistance. Resistance came not only from the general population but also from local power-holders; they were frequently able to take advantage of the administrative incoherence produced by differing interests and missions within the ranks of officialdom. But in spite of the ebbs and flows of the various campaigns and their national peculiarities, a pattern of adopting uniform measurements and charting cadastral maps ultimately prevailed.

Each undertaking also exemplified a pattern of relations between local knowledge and practices on one hand and state administrative routines on the other, a pattern that will find echoes throughout this book. In each case, local practices of measurement and landholding were "illegible" to the state in their raw form. They exhibited a diversity and intricacy that reflected a great variety of purely local, not state, interests. That is to say, they could not be assimilated into an administrative grid without being either transformed or reduced to a convenient, if partly fictional, shorthand. The logic behind the required shorthand was provided, as in scientific forestry, by the pressing material interests of rulers: fiscal receipts, military manpower, and state security. In turn, this shorthand functioned, as did Beckmann's Normalbäume, as not just a description, however inadequate. Backed by state power through records, courts, and ultimately coercion, these state fictions transformed the reality they presumed to observe, although never so thoroughly as to precisely fit the grid.

Forging the Tools of Legibility: Popular Measures, State Measures

Nonstate forms of measurement grew from the logic of local practice. As such, they shared some generic features despite their bewildering variety—features that made them an impediment to administrative uniformity. Thanks to the synthesis of the medievalist Witold Kula, the reasoning that animated local practices of measurement may be set out fairly succinctly.[37]

Most early measures were human in scale. One sees this logic at work in such surviving expressions as a "stone's throw" or "within earshot" for distances and a "cartload," a "basketful," or a "handful" for volume. Given that the size of a cart or basket might vary from place to place and that a stone's throw might not be precisely uniform from person to person, these units of measurement varied geographically and temporally. Even measures that were apparently fixed might be deceptive. The *pinte* in eighteenth-century Paris, for example, was equivalent to .93 liters, whereas in Seine-en-Montagne it was 1.99 liters and in Precy-sous-Thil, an astounding 3.33 liters. The *aune*, a measure of length used for cloth, varied depending on the material (the unit for silk, for instance, was smaller than that for linen), and across France there were at least seventeen different aunes.[38]

Local measures were also relational or "commensurable."[39] Virtually any request for a judgment of measure allows a range of responses depending on the context of the request. In the part of Malaysia with which I am most familiar, if one were to ask "How far is it to the next village?" a likely response would be "Three rice-cookings." The answer assumes that the questioner is interested in how much time it will take to get there, not how many miles away it is. In varied terrain, of course, distance in miles is an utterly unreliable guide to travel time, especially when the traveler is on foot or riding a bicycle. The answer also expresses time not in minutes—until recently, wristwatches were rare—but in units that are locally meaningful. Everyone knows how long it takes to cook the local rice. Thus an Ethiopian response to a query about how much salt is required for a dish might be "Half as much as to cook a chicken." The reply refers back to a standard that everyone is expected to know. Such measurement practices are irreducibly local, inasmuch as regional differences in, say, the type of rice eaten or the preferred way of cooking chicken will give different results.

Many local units of measurement are tied practically to particular activities. Marathi peasants, as Arjun Appadurai notes, express the desired distance between the onion sets they plant in terms of handbreadths. When one is moving along a field row, the hand is, well, the most handy gauge. In similar fashion, a common measure for twine or rope is the distance between the thumb and elbow because this corresponds with how it is wrapped and stored. As with setting onions, the process of measuring is embedded in the activity itself and requires no separate operation. Such measurements, moreover, are often approximate; they are only as exact as the task at hand requires.[40] Rainfall may be said to be abundant or inadequate if the context of the query implies an interest in a particular crop. And a reply in terms of inches of rainfall, however accurate, would also fail to convey the desired information; it ignores such vital matters as the timing of the rain. For many purposes, an apparently vague measurement may communicate more valuable information than a statistically exact figure. The cultivator who reports that his rice yield from a plot is anywhere between four and seven baskets is conveying more accurate information, when the focus of attention is on the variability of the yield, than if he reported a ten-year statistical average of 5.6 baskets.

There is, then, no single, all-purpose, correct answer to a question implying measurement unless we specify the relevant local concerns that give rise to the question. Particular customs of measurement are thus situationally, temporally, and geographically bound.

Nowhere is the particularity of customary measurement more evident than with cultivated land. Modern abstract measures of land by surface area—so many hectares or acres—are singularly uninformative figures to a family that proposes to make its living from these acres. Telling a farmer only that he is leasing twenty acres of land is about as helpful as telling a scholar that he has bought six kilograms of books. Customary measures of land have therefore taken a variety of forms corresponding to those aspects of the land that are of greatest practical interest. Where land was abundant and manpower or draftpower scarce, the most meaningful gauge of land was often the number of days required to plow or to weed it. A plot of land in nineteenth-century France, for example, would be described as representing so many *morgen* or *journals* (days of work) and as requiring a specific kind of work (*homée*, *bechée*, *fauchée*). How many morgen were represented by a field of, say, ten acres could vary greatly; if the land were rocky and steeply pitched, it might require twice as much labor to work than if it were rich bottomland. The morgen would also differ from place to place depending on the strength of local draftpower and the crops sown, and it would differ from time to time as technology (plow tips, yokes, harnesses) affected the work a man could accomplish in a day.

Land might also be evaluated according to the amount of seed required to sow it. If the soil were very good, a field would be densely sown, whereas poor land would be more lightly seeded. The amount of seed sown to a field is in fact a relatively good proxy for average yield, as the sowing is done in anticipation of average growing conditions, while the actual seasonal yield would be more variable. Given a particular crop regimen, the amount of seed sown would indicate roughly how productive a field had been, although it would reveal little about how arduous the land was to cultivate or how variable the harvests were. But the average yield from a plot of land is itself a rather abstract figure. What most farmers near the subsistence margin want to know above all is whether a particular farm will meet their basic needs reliably. Thus small farms in Ireland were described as a "farm of one cow" or a "farm of two cows" to indicate their grazing capacity to those who lived largely by milk products and potatoes. The physical area a farm might comprise was of little interest compared to whether it would feed a particular family.[41]

To grasp the prodigious variety of customary ways of measuring land, we would have to imagine literally scores of "maps" constructed along very different lines than mere surface area. I have in mind the sorts of maps devised to capture our attention with a kind of fun-house effect in which, say, the size of a country is made proportional to its population rather than its geographical size, with China and India looming menacingly over Russia, Brazil, and the United States, while Libya, Australia, and Greenland virtually disappear. These types of customary maps (for there would be a great many) would construct the landscape according to units of work and yield, type of soil, accessibility, and ability to provide subsistence, none of which would necessarily accord with surface area. The measurements are decidedly *local, interested, contextual,* and *historically specific.* What meets the subsistence needs of one family may not meet the subsistence needs of another. Factors such as local crop regimens, labor supply, agricultural technology, and weather ensure that the standards of evaluation vary from place to place and over time. Directly apprehended by the state, so many maps would represent a hopelessly bewildering welter of local standards. They definitely would not lend themselves to aggregation into a single statistical series that would allow state officials to make meaningful comparisons.

The Politics of Measurement

Thus far, this account of local measurement practices risks giving the impression that, although local conceptions of distance, area, volume, and so on were different from and more varied than the unitary abstract standards a state might favor, they were nevertheless aiming at objective accuracy. That impression would be false. Every act of measurement was an act marked by the play of power relations. To understand measurement practices in early modern Europe, as Kula demonstrates, one must relate them to the contending interests of the major estates: aristocrats, clergy, merchants, artisans, and serfs.

A good part of the politics of measurement sprang from what a contemporary economist might call the "stickiness" of feudal rents. Noble and clerical claimants often found it difficult to increase feudal dues directly; the levels set for various charges were the result of long struggle, and even a small increase above the customary level was viewed as a threatening breach of tradition.[42] Adjusting the measure, however, represented a roundabout way of achieving the same end. The local lord might, for example, lend grain to peasants in smaller baskets and insist on repayment in larger baskets. He might surreptitiously or even boldly enlarge the size of the grain sacks accepted for milling (a monopoly of the domain lord) and reduce the size of the sacks used for measuring out flour; he might also collect feudal dues in larger baskets and pay wages in kind in smaller baskets. While the formal custom governing feudal dues and wages would thus remain intact (requiring, for example, the same number of sacks of wheat from the harvest of a given holding), the actual transaction might increasingly favor the lord.[43] The results of such fiddling were far from trivial. Kula estimates that the size of the bushel (*boisseau*) used to collect the main feudal rent (taille) increased by one-third between 1674 and 1716 as part of what was called the *réaction féodale*.[44]

Even when the unit of measurement—say, the bushel—was apparently agreed upon by all, the fun had just begun. Virtually everywhere in early modern Europe were endless micropolitics about how baskets might be adjusted through wear, bulging, tricks of weaving, moisture, the thickness of the rim, and so on. In some areas the local standards for the bushel and other units of measurement were kept in metallic form and placed in the care of a trusted official or else literally carved into the stone of a church or the town hall.[45] Nor did it end there. How the grain was to be poured (from shoulder height, which packed it somewhat, or from waist height?), how damp it could be, whether the container could be shaken down, and, finally, if and how it was to be leveled off when full were subjects of long and bitter controversy. Some arrangements called for the grain to be heaped, some for a "half-heap," and still others for it to be leveled or "striked" (*ras*). These were not trivial matters. A feudal lord could increase his rents by 25 percent by insisting on receiving wheat and rye in heaped bushels.[46] If, by custom, the bushel of grain was to be striked, then a further micropolitics erupted over the strickle. Was it to be round, thereby packing in grain as it was rolled across the rim, or was it to be sharp-edged? Who would apply the strickle? Who could be trusted to keep it?

A comparable micropolitics, as one might expect, swirled around the unit of land measurement. A common measure of length, the ell, was used to mark off the area to be plowed or weeded as a part of feudal labor dues. Once again, the lengths and widths in ells were "sticky," having been established through long struggle. It was tempting for a lord or overseer to try raising labor dues indirectly by increasing the length of the ell. If the attempt were successful, the formal rules of corvée labor would not be violated, but the amount of work extracted would increase. Perhaps the stickiest of all measures before the nineteenth century was the price of bread. As the most vital subsistence good of premodern times, it served as a kind of cost-of-living index, and its cost was the subject of deeply held popular customs about its relationship to the typical urban wage. Kula shows in remarkable detail how bakers, afraid to provoke a riot by directly violating the "just price," managed nevertheless to manipulate the size and weight of the loaf to compensate to some degree for changes in the price of wheat and rye flour.[47]

Statecraft and the Hieroglyphics of Measurement

Because local standards of measurement were tied to practical needs, because they reflected particular cropping patterns and agricultural technology, because they varied with climate and ecology, because they were "an attribute of power and an instrument of asserting class privilege," and because they were "at the center of bitter class struggle," they represented a mind-boggling problem for statecraft.[48] Efforts to simplify or standardize measures recur like a leitmotif throughout French history—their reappearance a sure sign of previous failure. More modest attempts to simply codify local practices and create conversion tables were quickly overtaken and rendered obsolete by changes on the ground. The king's ministers were confronted, in effect, with a patchwork of local measurement codes, each of which had to be cracked. It was as if each district spoke its own dialect, one that was unintelligible to outsiders and at the same time liable to change without notice. Either the state risked making large and potentially damaging miscalculations about local conditions, or it relied heavily on the advice of local trackers—the nobles and clergy in the Crown's confidence—who, in turn, were not slow to take full advantage of their power.

The illegibility of local measurement practices was more than an administrative headache for the monarchy. It compromised the most vital and sensitive aspects of state security. Food supply was the Achilles heel of the early modern state; short of religious war, nothing so menaced the state as food shortages and the resulting social upheavals. Without comparable units of measurement, it was difficult if not impossible to monitor markets, to compare regional prices for basic commodities, or to regulate food supplies effectively.[49] Obliged to grope its way on the basis of sketchy information, rumor, and self-interested local reports, the state often responded belatedly and inappropriately. Equity in taxation, another sensitive political issue, was beyond the reach of a state that found it difficult to know the basic comparative facts about harvests and prices. A vigorous effort to collect taxes, to requisition for military garrisons, to relieve urban shortages, or any number of other measures might, given the crudeness of state intelligence, actually provoke a political crisis. Even when it did not jeopardize state security, the Babel of measurement produced gross inefficiencies and a pattern of either undershooting or overshooting fiscal targets.[50] No effective central monitoring or controlled comparisons were possible without standard, fixed units of measurement.

Simplification and Standardization of Measurement

> The conquerors of our days, peoples or princes, want their empire to possess a unified surface over which the superb eye of power can wander without encountering any inequality which hurts or limits its view. The same code of law, the same measures, the same rules, and if we could gradually get there, the same language; that is what is proclaimed as the perfection of the social organization. . . . The great slogan of the day is *uniformity*.
> —Benjamin Constant, *De l'esprit de conquête*

If scientific forestry's project of creating a simplified and legible forest encountered opposition from villagers whose usage rights were being challenged, the political opposition to standard and legible units of measurement was even more refractory. The power to establish and impose local measures was an important feudal prerogative with material consequences which the aristocracy and clergy would not willingly surrender. Testimony to their capacity to thwart standardization is evident in the long series of abortive initiatives by absolutist rulers who tried to insist on some degree of uniformity. The very particularity of local feudal practices and their impenetrability to would-be centralizers helped to underwrite the autonomy of local spheres of power.

Three factors, in the end, conspired to make what Kula calls the "metrical revolution" possible. First, the growth of market exchange encouraged uniformity in measures. Second, both popular sentiment and Enlightenment philosophy favored a single standard throughout France. Finally, the Revolution and especially Napoleonic state building actually enforced the metric system in France and the empire.

Large-scale commercial exchange and long-distance trade tend to promote common standards of measurement. For relatively small-scale trade, grain dealers could transact with several suppliers as long as they knew the measure each was using. They might actually profit from their superior grasp of the profusion of units, much as smugglers take advantage of small differences in taxes and tariffs. Beyond a certain point, however, much of commerce is composed of long chains of transactions, often over great distances, between anonymous buyers and sellers. Such trade is greatly simplified and made legible by standard weights and measures. Whereas artisanal products were typically made by a single producer according to the desires of a particular customer and carried a price specific to that object, the mass-produced commodity is made by no one in particular and is intended for any purchaser at all. In a sense, the virtue of the mass commodity is its reliable uniformity. In proportion, then, as the volume of commerce grew and the goods exchanged became increasingly standardized (a ton of wheat, a dozen plow tips, twenty cart wheels), there was a growing tendency to accept widely agreed upon units of measurement. Officials and physiocrats alike were convinced that uniform measures were the precondition for creating a national market and promoting rational economic action.[51]

The perennial state project of unifying measures throughout the kingdom received a large degree of popular support in the eighteenth century, thanks to the réaction féodale. Aiming to maximize the return on their estates, owners of feudal domains, many of them arrivistes, achieved their goal in part by manipulating units of measurement. This sense of victimization was evident in the *cahiers* of grievances prepared for the meeting of the Estates General just before the Revolution. The cahiers of the members of the Third Estate consistently called for equal measures (although this was hardly their main grievance), whereas the cahiers of the clergy and nobility were silent, presumably indicating their satisfaction with the status quo on this issue. The following petition from Brittany is typical of the way in which an appeal for unitary measures could be assimilated to devotion to the Crown: "We beg them [the king, his family, and his chief minister] to join with us in checking the abuses being perpetrated by tyrants against that class of citizens which is kind and considerate and which, until this day has been unable to present its very grievances to the very foot of the throne, and now we call on the King to mete out justice, and *we express our most sincere desire for but one king, one law, one weight, and one measure.*"[52]

For centralizing elites, the universal meter was to older, particularistic measurement practices as a national language was to the existing welter of dialects. Such quaint idioms would be replaced by a new universal gold standard, just as the central banking of absolutism had swept away the local currencies of feudalism. The metric system was at once a means of administrative centralization, commercial reform, and cultural progress. The academicians of the revolutionary republic, like the royal academicians before them, saw the meter as one of the intellectual instruments that would make France "revenue-rich, militarily potent, and *easily administered.*"[53] Common measures, it was supposed, would spur the grain trade, make land more productive (by permitting easier comparisons of price and productivity), and, not incidentally, lay the groundwork for a national tax code.[54] But the reformers also had in mind a genuine cultural revolution. "As mathematics was the language of science, so would the metric system be the language of commerce and industry," serving to unify and transform French society.[55] A rational unit of measurement would promote a rational citizenry.

The simplification of measures, however, depended on that other revolutionary political simplification of the modern era: the concept of a uniform, homogeneous citizenship. As long as each estate operated within a separate legal sphere, as long as different categories of people were unequal in law, it followed that they might also have unequal rights with respect to measures.[56] The idea of equal citizenship, the abstraction of the "unmarked" citizen, can be traced to the Enlightenment and is evident in the writings of the Encyclopedists.[57] For the Encyclopedists, the cacophony among measurements, institutions, inheritance laws, taxation, and market regulations was the great obstacle to the French becoming a single people. They envisioned a series of centralizing and rationalizing reforms that would transform France into a national community where the same codified laws, measures, customs, and beliefs would everywhere prevail. It is worth noting that this project promotes the concept of *national* citizenship—a national French citizen perambulating the kingdom and encountering exactly the same fair, equal conditions as the rest of his compatriots. In place of a welter of incommensurable small communities, familiar to their inhabitants but mystifying to outsiders, there would rise a single national society perfectly legible from the center. The proponents of this vision well understood that what was at stake was not merely administrative convenience but also the transformation of a people: "The uniformity of customs, viewpoints, and principles of action will, inevitably, lead to a greater community of habits and predispositions."[58] The abstract grid of equal citizenship would create a new reality: the French citizen.

The homogenization of measures, then, was part of a larger, emancipatory simplification. At one stroke the equality of all French people before the law was guaranteed by the state; they were no longer mere subjects of their lords and sovereign but bearers of inalienable rights as citizens.[59] All the previous "natural" distinctions were now "denaturalized" and nullified, at least in law.[60] In an unprecedented revolutionary context where an entirely new political system was being created from first principles, it was surely no great matter to legislate uniform weights and measures. As the revolutionary decree read: "The centuries old dream of the masses of only one just measure has come true! The Revolution has given the people the meter."[61]

Proclaiming the universal meter was far simpler than ensuring that it became the daily practice of French citizens. The state could insist on the exclusive use of its units in the courts, in the state school system, and in such documents as property deeds, legal contracts, and tax codes. Outside these official spheres, the metric system made its way only very slowly. In spite of a decree for confiscating *toise* sticks in shops and replacing them with meter sticks, the populace continued to use the older system, often marking their meter sticks with the old measures. Even as late as 1828 the new measures were more a part of *le pays légal* than of *le pays réel*. As Chateaubriand remarked, "Whenever you meet a fellow who, instead of talking *arpents*, *toises*, and *pieds*, refers to hectares, meters, and centimeters, rest assured, the man is a prefect."[62]

Land Tenure: Local Practice and Fiscal Shorthand

The revenue of the early modern state came mainly from levies on commerce and land, the major sources of wealth. For commerce, this implied an array of excise taxes, tolls and market duties, licensing fees, and tariffs. For landed wealth, this meant somehow attaching every parcel of taxable property to an individual or an institution responsible for paying the tax on it. As straightforward as this procedure seems in the context of the modern state, its achievement was enormously difficult for at least two reasons. First, the actual practices of customary land tenure were frequently so varied and intricate as to defy any one-to-one equation of taxpayer and taxable property. And second, as was the case with standardizing measurement, there were social forces whose interests could only be damaged by the unified and transparent set of property relations desired by the state's fiscal agents. In the end, the centralizing state succeeded in imposing a novel and (from the center) legible property system, which, as had the work of the scientific foresters, not only radically abridged the practices that the system described but at the same time transformed those practices to align more closely with their shorthand, schematic reading.

An Illustration

> *Negara mawi tata, desa mawi cara* (The capital has its order, the village its customs).
> —*Javanese proverb*

A hypothetical case of customary land tenure practices may help demonstrate how difficult it is to assimilate such practices to the barebones schema of a modern cadastral map. The patterns I will describe are an amalgam of practices I have encountered in the literature of or in the course of fieldwork in Southeast Asia, and although the case is hypothetical, it is not unrealistic.

Let us imagine a community in which families have usufruct rights to parcels of cropland during the main growing season. Only certain crops, however, may be planted, and every seven years the usufruct land is redistributed among resident families according to each family's size and its number of able-bodied adults. After the harvest of the main-season crop, all cropland reverts to common land where any family may glean, graze their fowl and livestock, and even plant quickly maturing, dry-season crops. Rights to graze fowl and livestock on pastureland held in common by the village is extended to all local families, but the number of animals that can be grazed is restricted according to family size, especially in dry years when forage is scarce. Families not using their grazing rights can give them to other villagers but not to outsiders. Everyone has the right to gather firewood for normal family needs, and the village blacksmith and baker are given larger allotments. No commercial sale from village woodlands is permitted.

Trees that have been planted and any fruit they may bear are the property of the family who planted them, no matter where they are now growing. Fruit fallen from such trees, however, is the property of anyone who gathers it. When a family fells one of its trees or a tree is felled by a storm, the trunk belongs to the family, the branches to the immediate neighbors, and the "tops" (leaves and twigs) to any poorer villager who carries them off. Land is set aside for use or leasing out by widows with children and dependents of conscripted males. Usufruct rights to land and trees may be let to anyone in the village; the only time they may be let to someone outside the village is if no one in the community wishes to claim them.

After a crop failure leading to a food shortage, many of these arrangements are readjusted. Better-off villagers are expected to assume some responsibility for poorer relatives—by sharing their land, by hiring them, or by simply feeding them. Should the shortage persist, a council composed of heads of families may inventory food supplies and begin daily rationing. In cases of severe shortages or famine, the women who have married into the village but have not yet borne children will not be fed and are expected to return to their native village. This last practice alerts us to the inequalities that often prevail in local customary tenure; single women, junior males, and anyone defined as falling outside the core of the community are clearly disadvantaged.

This description could be further elaborated. It is itself a simplification, but it does convey some of the actual complexity of property relations in contexts where local customs have tended to prevail. To describe the usual practices in this fashion, as if they were laws, is itself a distortion. Customs are better understood as a living, negotiated tissue of practices which are continually being adapted to new ecological and social circumstances—including, of course, power relations. Customary systems of tenure should not be romanticized; they are usually riven with inequalities based on gender, status, and lineage. But because they are strongly local, particular, and adaptable, their plasticity can be the source of microadjustments that lead to shifts in prevailing practice.

Imagine a lawgiver whose only concern was to respect land practices. Imagine, in other words, a written system of positive law that attempted to represent this complex skein of property relations and land tenure. The mind fairly boggles at the clauses, sub-clauses, and sub-sub-clauses that would be required to reduce these practices to a set of regulations that an administrator might understand, never mind enforce. And even if the practices could be codified, the resulting code would necessarily sacrifice much of their plasticity and subtle adaptability. The circumstances that might provoke a new adaptation are too numerous to foresee, let alone specify, in a regulatory code. That code would in effect freeze a living process. Changes in the positive code designed to reflect evolving practice would represent at best a jerky and mechanical adaptation.

And what of the *next* village, and the village after that? Our hypothetical code-giver, however devilishly clever and conscientious, would find that the code devised to fit one set of local practices would not travel well. Each village, with its own particular history, ecology, cropping patterns, kinship alignments, and economic activity, would require a substantially new set of regulations. At the limit, there would be at least as many legal codes as there were communities.

Administratively, of course, such a cacophony of local property regulations would be a nightmare. The nightmare is experienced not by those whose particular practices are being represented but by those state officials who aspire to a uniform, homogeneous, national administrative code. Like the "exotic" units of weights and measures, local land tenure practice is perfectly legible to all who live within it from day to day. Its details may often be contested and far from satisfactory to all its practitioners, but it is completely familiar; local residents have no difficulty in grasping its subtleties and using its flexible provisions for their own purposes. State officials, on the other hand, cannot be expected to decipher and then apply a new set of property hieroglyphs for each jurisdiction. Indeed, the very concept of the modern state presupposes a vastly simplified and uniform property regime that is legible and hence manipulable from the center.

My use of the term "simple" to describe modern property law, whose intricacies provide employment to armies of legal professionals, will seem grossly misplaced. It is surely the case that property law has in many respects become an impenetrable thicket for ordinary citizens. The use of the term "simple" in this context is thus both relative and perspectival. Modern freehold tenure is tenure that is mediated through the state and therefore readily decipherable only to those who have sufficient training and a grasp of the state statutes.[63] Its relative simplicity is lost on those who cannot break the code, just as the relative clarity of customary tenure is lost on those who live outside the village.

The fiscal or administrative goal toward which all modern states aspire is to measure, codify, and simplify land tenure in much the same way as scientific forestry reconceived the forest. Accommodating the luxuriant variety of customary land tenure was simply inconceivable. The historical solution, at least for the liberal state, has typically been the heroic simplification of individual freehold tenure. Land is owned by a legal individual who possesses wide powers of use, inheritance, or sale and whose ownership is represented by a uniform deed of title enforced through the judicial and police institutions of the state. Just as the flora of the forest were reduced to Normalbäume, so the complex tenure arrangements of customary practice are reduced to freehold, transferrable title. In an agrarian setting, the administrative landscape is blanketed with a uniform grid of homogeneous land, each parcel of which has a legal person as owner and hence taxpayer. How much easier it then becomes to assess such property and its owner on the basis of its acreage, its soil class, the crops it normally bears, and its assumed yield than to untangle the thicket of common property and mixed forms of tenure.

The crowning artifact of this mighty simplification is the cadastral map. Created by trained surveyors and mapped to a given scale, the cadastral map is a more or less complete and accurate survey of all landholdings. Since the driving logic behind the map is to create a manageable and reliable format for taxation, the map is associated with a property register in which each specified (usually numbered) lot on the map is linked to an owner who is responsible for paying its taxes. The cadastral map and property register are to the taxation of land as the maps and tables of the scientific forester were to the fiscal exploitation of the forest.

The Code Rural *That Almost Was*

The rulers of postrevolutionary France confronted a rural society that was a nearly impenetrable web of feudal *and* revolutionary practices. It was inconceivable that they could catalogue its complexities, let alone effectively eliminate them, in the short run. Ideologically, for example, their commitment to equality and liberty was contradicted by customary rural contracts like those used by craft guilds, which still employed the terms "master" (*maître*) and "servant" (*serviteur*). As rulers of a new nation—not a kingdom—they were likewise offended by the absence of an overall legal framework for social relations. For some, a new civil code covering all Frenchmen seemed as if it would be sufficient.[64] But for bourgeois owners of rural property who, along with their noble neighbors, had been threatened by the local uprisings of the Revolution and La Grand Peur and, more generally, by the aggressiveness of an emboldened and autonomous peasantry, an explicit *code rural* seemed necessary to underwrite their security.

In the end, no postrevolutionary rural code attracted a winning coalition, even amid a flurry of Napoleonic codes in nearly all other realms. For our purposes, the history of the stalemate is instructive. The first proposal for a code, which was drafted between 1803 and 1807, would have swept away most traditional rights (such as common pasturage and free passage through others' property) and essentially recast rural property relations in the light of bourgeois property rights and freedom of contract.[65] Although the proposed code prefigured certain modern French practices, many revolutionaries blocked it because they feared that its hands-off liberalism would allow large landholders to recreate the subordination of feudalism in a new guise.[66]

A reexamination of the issue was then ordered by Napoleon and presided over by Joseph Verneilh Puyrasseau. Concurrently, Deputé Lalouette proposed to do precisely what I supposed, in the hypothetical example, was impossible. That is, he undertook to systematically gather information about all local practices, to classify and codify them, and then to sanction them by decree. The decree in question would become the code rural. Two problems undid this charming scheme to present the rural populace with a rural code that simply reflected its own practices. The first difficulty was in deciding which aspects of the literally "infinite diversity" of rural production relations were to be represented and codified.[67] Even in a particular locality, practices varied greatly from farm to farm and over time; any codification would be partly arbitrary and artificially static. To codify local practices was thus a profoundly political act. Local notables would be able to sanction their preferences with the mantle of law, whereas others would lose customary rights that they depended on. The second difficulty was that Lalouette's plan was a mortal threat to all the state centralizers and economic modernizers for whom a legible, national property regime was the precondition of progress. As Serge Aberdam notes, "The Lalouette project would have brought about exactly what Merlin de Douai and the bourgeois, revolutionary jurists always sought to avoid."[68] Neither Lalouette's nor Verneilh's proposed code was ever passed, because they, like their predecessor in 1807, seemed to be designed to strengthen the hand of the landowners.

The Illegibility of Communal Tenure

The premodern and early modern state, as we have noted, dealt more with communities than with individuals when it came to taxes. Some apparently individual taxes, such as the notorious Russian "soul tax," which was collected from all subjects, were actually paid directly by the communities or indirectly through the nobles whose subjects they were. Failure to deliver the required sum usually led to collective punishment.[69] The only agents of taxation who regularly reached to the level of the household and its cultivated fields were the local nobility and clergy in the course of collecting feudal dues and the religious tithe. For its part, the state had neither the administrative tools nor the information to penetrate to this level.

The limitations on state knowledge were partly due to the complexity and variability of local production. This was not the most important reason, however. The collective form of taxation meant that it was generally in the interest of local officials to misrepresent their situation in order to minimize the local tax and conscription burden. To this end, they might minimize the local population, systematically understate the acreage under cultivation, hide new commercial profits, exaggerate crop losses after storms and droughts, and so on.[70] The point of the cadastral map and land register was precisely to eliminate this fiscal feudalism and rationalize the fiscal take of the state. Just as the scientific forester needed an inventory of trees to realize the commercial potential of the forest, so the fiscal reformer needed a detailed inventory of landownership to realize the maximum, sustainable revenue yield.[71]

Assuming that the state had the will to challenge the resistance of the local nobles and elites and the financial resources to undertake a full cadastral survey (which was both time-consuming and expensive), it faced other obstacles as well. In particular, some communal forms of tenure simply could not be adequately represented in cadastral form. Rural living in seventeenth- and early eighteenth-century Denmark, for example, was organized by *ejerlav*, whose members had certain rights for using local arable, waste, and forest land. It would have been impossible in such a community to associate a household or individual with a particular holding on a cadastral map. The Norwegian large farm (*gard*) posed similar problems. Each household held rights to a given proportion of the value (*skyld*) of the farm, not to the plot of land; none of the joint owners could call a specific part of the farm his own.[72] Although it was possible to estimate the arable land of each community and, making some assumptions about crop yields and subsistence needs, arrive at a plausible tax burden, these villagers derived a substantial part of their livelihood from the commons by fishing, forestry, collecting resin, hunting, and making charcoal. Monitoring this kind of income was almost impossible. Nor would crude estimates of the value of the commons solve the problem, for the inhabitants of nearby villages often shared one another's commons (even though the practice was outlawed). The mode of production in such communities was simply incompatible with the assumption of individual freehold tenure implicit in a cadastral map. It was claimed, although the evidence is not convincing, that common property was less productive than freehold property.[73] The state's case against communal forms of land tenure, however, was based on the correct observation that it was fiscally illegible and hence fiscally less productive. Rather than trying, like the hapless Lalouette, to bring the map into line with reality, the historical resolution has generally been for the state to impose a property system in line with its fiscal grid.

As long as common property was abundant and had essentially no fiscal value, the illegibility of its tenure was no problem. But the moment it became scarce (when "nature" became "natural resources"), it became the subject of property rights in law, whether of the state or of the citizens. The history of property in this sense has meant the inexorable incorporation of what were once thought of as free gifts of nature: forests, game, wasteland, prairie, subsurface minerals, water and watercourses, air rights (rights to the air above buildings or surface area), breathable air, and even genetic sequences, into a property regime. In the case of common-property farmland, the imposition of freehold property was clarifying not so much for the local inhabitants — the customary structure of rights had always been clear enough to them — as it was for the tax official and the land speculator. The cadastral map added documentary intelligence to state power and thus provided the basis for the synoptic view of the state and a supralocal market in land.[74]

An example may help to clarify the process of installing a new, more legible property regime. The case of two prerevolutionary Russian villages provides a nearly textbook example of state attempts to create individual tenure in keeping with its convictions about agricultural growth and administrative order. Most of rural Russia, even after the emancipation of 1861, was a model of fiscal illegibility. Communal forms of tenure prevailed, and the state had little or no knowledge of who cultivated which strips of land or what their yields and income were.

Novoselok village had a varied economy of cultivation, grazing, and forestry, whereas Khotynitsa village was limited to cultivation and some grazing (figures 3 and 4). The complex welter of strips was designed to ensure that each village household received a strip of land in every ecological zone. An individual household might have as many as ten to fifteen different plots constituting something of a representative sample of the village's ecological zones and microclimates. The distribution spread a family's risks prudently, and from time to time the land was reshuffled as families grew or shrunk.[75]

It was enough to make the head of a cadastral surveyor swim. At first glance it seems as if the village itself would need a staff of professional surveyors to get things right. But in practice the system, called interstripping, was quite simple to those who lived it. The strips of land

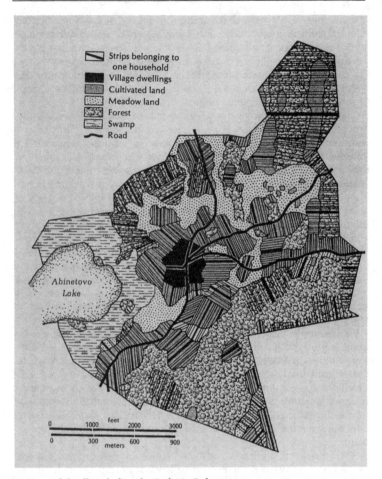

Strips belonging to
one household
Village dwellings
Cultivated land
Meadow land
Forest
Swamp
Road

*Abinetovo
Lake*

feet
0   1000   2000   3000
0   300   600   900
meters

3. Novoselok village before the Stolypin Reform

were generally straight and parallel so that a readjustment could be made by moving small stakes along just one side of a field, without having to think of areal dimensions. Where the other end of the field was not parallel, the stakes could be shifted to compensate for the fact that the strip lay toward the narrower or wider end of the field. Irregular fields were divided, not according to area, but according to yield. To the eye—and certainly to those involved in cadastral mapping—the pattern seemed convoluted and irrational. But to those familiar with it, it was simple enough and worked admirably for their purposes.

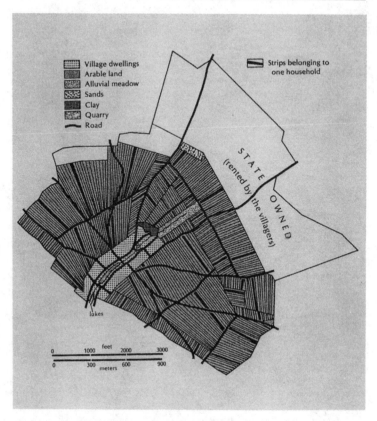

Village dwellings
Arable land
Alluvial meadow
Sands
Clay
Quarry
Road

Strips belonging to
one household

STATE OWNED
(rented by the villagers)

lakes

feet
0   1000   2000   3000
0   300   600   900
meters

4. Khotynitsa village before the Stolypin Reform

The dream of state officials and agrarian reformers, at least since emancipation, was to transform the open-field system into a series of consolidated, independent farmsteads on what they took to be the western European model. They were driven by the desire to break the hold of the community over the individual household and to move from collective taxation of the whole community to a tax on individual landholders. As in France, fiscal goals were very much connected to reigning ideas of agricultural progress. Under Count Sergei Witte and Petr Stolypin, as George Yaney notes, plans for reform shared a common vision of how things were and how they needed to be: "First tableau: poor peasants, crowded together in villages, suffering from hunger, running into each other with their plows on their tiny strips. Second tableau: agriculture specialist agent leads a few progressive

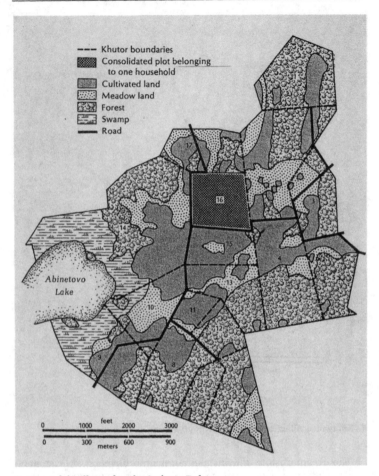

5. Novoselok village after the Stolypin Reform

peasants off to new lands, leaving those remaining more room. Third tableau: departing peasants, freed from restraints of strips, set up khutor [integral farmsteads with dwellings] on new fields and adapt latest methods. Those who remain, freed of village and family restraints, plunge into a demand economy—all are richer, more productive, the cities get fed, and the peasants are not proletarianized."[76] It was abundantly clear that the prejudicial attitude toward interstripping was based as much on the autonomy of the Russian village, its illegibility to outsiders, and prevailing dogma about scientific agriculture as it was

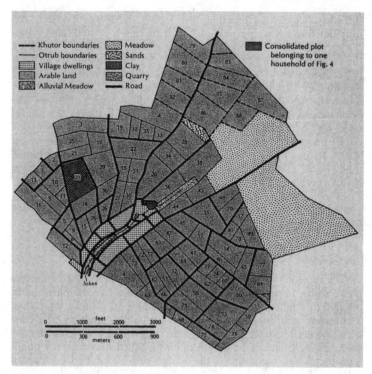

Legend:
- — — — Khutor boundaries
- ——— Otrub boundaries
- Village dwellings
- Arable land
- Alluvial Meadow
- Meadow
- Sands
- Clay
- Quarry
- — Road
- Consolidated plot belonging to one household of Fig. 4

6. Khotynitsa village after the Stolypin Reform

on hard evidence.[77] The state officials and agrarian reformers reasoned that, once given a consolidated, private plot, the peasant would suddenly want to get rich and would organize his household into an efficient workforce and take up scientific agriculture. The Stolypin Reform therefore went forward, and cadastral order was brought to both villages in the wake of the reform (figures 5 and 6).

In Novoselok village, seventeen independent farmsteads (*khutor*) were created in a way that aimed to give each household a share of meadow, arable, and forest. In Khotynitsa village, ten khutor were created as well as seventy-eight farms (*otrub*), whose owners continued to dwell in the village center. As a cadastral matter, the new farms were mappable, easily legible from above and outside, and, since each was owned by an identifiable person, assessable.

Taken alone, the maps shown in figures 5 and 6 are misleading. Such model villages suggest efficient cadastral teams working their way diligently through the countryside and turning open-field chaos into tidy little farms. Reality was something else. In fact, the dream of orderly, rectangular fields was approximated only on newly settled land, where the surveyor faced little geographical or social resistance.[78] Elsewhere, the reformers were generally thwarted, despite tremendous pressure to produce integral farms. There were unauthorized consolidations, although they were forbidden; there were also "paper consolidations," in which the new farmers continued to farm their strips as before.[79] The best evidence that the agricultural property system had in fact not become legible to central tax officials was the immensely damaging procurement policies pursued by the czarist government during World War I. No one knew what a reasonable levy on grain or draft animals might be; as a result, some farmers were ruined, while others managed to hoard grain and livestock.[80] The same experience of forced procurement without adequate knowledge of landholdings and wealth was repeated again after the October Revolution during the period of War Communism.[81]

The Cadastral Map as Objective Information for Outsiders

The value of the cadastral map to the state lies in its abstraction and universality. In principle, at least, the same objective standard can be applied throughout the nation, regardless of local context, to produce a complete and unambiguous map of all landed property. The completeness of the cadastral map depends, in a curious way, on its abstract sketchiness, its lack of detail—its thinness. Taken alone, it is essentially a geometric representation of the borders or frontiers between parcels of land. What lies inside the parcel is left blank—unspecified—since it is not germane to the map plotting itself.

Surely many things about a parcel of land are far more important than its surface area and the location of its boundaries. What kind of soil it has, what crops can be grown on it, how hard it is to work, and how close it is to a market are the first questions a potential buyer might ask. These are questions a tax assessor would also want to ask. From a capitalist perspective, the physical dimensions of land are beside the point. But these other qualities can become relevant (especially to the state) only after the terrain to which they apply has been located and measured. And unlike identifying location and dimension, identifying these qualities involves judgments that are complex, susceptible to fraud, and easily overtaken by events. Crop rotations and yields may change, new tools or machines may transform cultivation, and markets may shift. The cadastral survey, by contrast, is precise, schematic, general, and uniform. Whatever its other defects, it is the precondition of a tax regime that comprehensively links every patch of land with its owner—the taxpayer.[82] In this spirit, the survey for a 1807 Dutch land tax (inspired by Napoleonic France) stressed that all surveyors were to use the same measurements, surveyors' instruments were to be periodically inspected to ensure conformity, and all maps were to be drawn up on a uniform scale of 1:2,880.[83]

Land maps in general and cadastral maps in particular are designed to make the local situation legible to an outsider. For purely local purposes, a cadastral map was redundant. Everyone knew who held, say, the meadow by the river, the value of the fodder it yielded, and the feudal dues it carried; there was no need to know its precise dimensions. A substantial domain might have the kind of prose map, or *terrier*, that one finds in old deeds ("from the large oak tree, north 120 feet to the river bank, thence . . ."), with a notation about the holder's obligations to the domain. One imagines such a document proving valuable to a young heir, new to the management of a domain. But a proper map seems to have come into use especially when a brisk market in land developed. The Netherlands was thus a leader in land mapping because of its early commercialization and because each speculator who invested in the draining of land by windmill wanted to know in advance precisely what plot of the newly opened land he would be entitled to. The map was especially crucial to the new bourgeois owners of landed estates, for it allowed them to survey a large territory at a glance. Its miniaturization helped it to serve as an aide-mémoire when the property consisted of many small parcels or the owner was not intimately familiar with the terrain.

As early as 1607, an English surveyor, John Norden, sold his services to the aristocracy on the premise that the map was a substitute for the tour of inspection: "A plot rightly drawne by true information, discribeth so the lively image of a manor, and every branch and member of the same, as the lord sitting in his chayre, may see what he hath, and where and how he lyeth, and in whole use and occupation of every particular is upon suddaine view."[84] A national tax administration requires the same logic: a legible, bureaucratic formula which a new official can quickly grasp and administer from the documents in his office.

What Is Missing in This Picture?

Administrative man recognizes that the world he perceives is a drastically simplified model of the buzzing, blooming confusion that constitutes the real world. He is content with the gross simplification because he believes that the real world is mostly empty—that most of the facts of the real world have no great relevance to any particular situation he is facing and that most significant chains of causes and consequences are short and simple.
—Herbert Simon

Isaiah Berlin, in his study of Tolstoy, compared the hedgehog, who knew "one big thing," to the fox, who knew many things. The scientific forester and the cadastral official are like the hedgehog. The sharply focused interest of the scientific foresters in commercial lumber and that of the cadastral officials in land revenue constrain them to finding clear-cut answers to one question. The naturalist and the farmer, on the other hand, are like the fox. They know a great many things about forests and cultivable land. Although the forester's and cadastral official's range of knowledge is far narrower, we should not forget that their knowledge is systematic and synoptic, allowing them to see and understand things a fox would not grasp.[85] What I want to emphasize here, however, is how this knowledge is gained at the expense of a rather static and myopic view of land tenure.

The cadastral map is very much like a still photograph of the current in a river. It represents the parcels of land as they were arranged and owned at the moment the survey was conducted. But the current is always moving, and in periods of major social upheaval and growth, a cadastral survey may freeze a scene of great turbulence.[86] Changes are taking place on field boundaries; land is being subdivided or consolidated by inheritance or purchase; new canals, roads, and railways are being cut; land use is changing; and so forth. Inasmuch as these particular changes directly affect tax assessments, there are provisions for recording them on the map or in a title register. The accumulation of annotations and marginalia at some point render the map illegible, whereupon a more up-to-date but still static map must be drawn and the process repeated.

No operating land-revenue system can stop at the mere identification of parcel and ownership. Other schematic facts, themselves static, must be created to arrive at some judgment of a sustainable tax burden. Land may be graded by soil class, how well it is watered, what crops are grown on it, and its presumed average yield, which is often checked by sample crop-cuttings. These facts are themselves changing, or they are averages that may mask great variation. Like the still photo of the cadastral map, they grow more unrealistic with time and must be reexamined.

These state simplifications, like all state simplifications, are always far more static and schematic than the actual social phenomena they presume to typify. The farmer rarely experiences an average crop, an average rainfall, or an average price for his crops. Much of the long history of rural tax revolts in early modern Europe and elsewhere can be illuminated by the lack of fit between an unyielding fiscal claim, on one hand, and an often wildly fluctuating capacity of the rural population to meet that claim, on the other.[87] And yet, even the most equitable, well-intentioned cadastral system cannot be uniformly administered except on the basis of stable units of measurement and calculation. It can no more reflect the actual complexity of a farmer's experience than the scientific forester's schemes can reflect the complexity of the naturalist's forest.[88]

Governed by a practical, concrete objective, the cadastral lens also ignored anything lying outside its sharply defined field of vision. This was reflected in a loss of detail in the survey itself. Surveyors, one recent Swedish study found, made the fields more geometrically regular than they in fact were. Ignoring small jogs and squiggles made their job easier and did not materially affect the outcome.[89] Just as the commercial forester found it convenient to overlook minor forest products, so the cadastral official tended to ignore all but the main commercial use of a field. The fact that a field designated as growing wheat or hay might also be a significant source of bedding straw, gleanings, rabbits, birds, frogs, and mushrooms was not so much unknown as ignored lest it needlessly complicate a straightforward administrative formula.[90] The most significant instance of myopia, of course, was that the cadastral map and assessment system considered only the dimensions of the land and its value as a productive asset or as a commodity for sale. Any value that the land might have for subsistence purposes or for the local ecology was bracketed as aesthetic, ritual, or sentimental values.

Transformation and Resistance

> The cadastral map is an instrument of control which both reflects and consolidates the power of those who commission it. . . . The cadastral map is partisan: where knowledge is power, it provides comprehensive information to be used to the advantage of some and the detriment of others, as rulers and ruled were well aware in the tax struggles of the 18th and 19th centuries. Finally, the cadastral map is active: in portraying one reality, as in the settlement of the new world or in India, it helps obliterate the old.
> —Roger J. P. Kain and Elizabeth Baigent, *The Cadastral Map*

The shorthand formulas through which tax officials must apprehend reality are not mere tools of observation. By a kind of fiscal Heisenberg principle, they frequently have the power to transform the facts they take note of.

The door-and-window tax established in France under the Directory and abolished only in 1917 is a striking case in point.[91] Its originator must have reasoned that the number of windows and doors in a dwelling was proportional to the dwelling's size. Thus a tax assessor need not enter the house or measure it but merely count the doors and windows. As a simple, workable formula, it was a brilliant stroke, but it was not without consequences. Peasant dwellings were subsequently designed or renovated with the formula in mind so as to have as few openings as possible. While the fiscal losses could be recouped by raising the tax per opening, the long-term effects on the health of the rural population lasted for more than a century.

The novel state-imposed form of land tenure was far more revolutionary than a door-and-window tax. It established a whole new institutional nexus. However simple and uniform the new tenure system was to an administrator, it flung villagers willy-nilly into a world of title deeds, land offices, fees, assessments, and applications. They faced powerful new specialists in the form of land clerks, surveyors, judges, and lawyers whose rules of procedure and decisions were unfamiliar.

Where the new tenure system was a colonial imposition—that is, where it was totally unfamiliar, where it was imposed by alien conquerors using an unintelligible language and institutional context, and where local practices bore no resemblance to freehold tenure—the consequences were far-reaching. The permanent settlement in India, for example, created a new class who, because they paid the taxes on the land, became full owners with rights of inheritance and sale where none had existed earlier.[92] At the same time, literally millions of cultivators, tenants, and laborers lost their customary rights of access to the land and its products. Those in the colonies who first plumbed the mysteries of the new tenure administration enjoyed unique opportunities. Thus the Vietnamese *secrétaires* and *interprètes* who served as intermediaries between the French officials in the Mekong Delta and their Vietnamese subjects were in a position to make great fortunes. By concentrating on the legal paperwork, such as title deeds, and the appropriate fees, they occasionally became landlords to whole villages of cultivators who had imagined they had opened common land free for the taking. The new intermediaries, of course, might occasionally use their knowledge to see their compatriots safely through the new legal thicket. Whatever their conduct, their fluency in a language of tenure specifically designed to be legible and transparent to administrators, coupled with the illiteracy of the rural population to whom the new tenure was indecipherable, brought about a momentous shift in power relations.[93] What was simplifying to an official was mystifying to most cultivators.

Freehold title and standard land measurement were to central taxation and the real-estate market what central bank currency was to the marketplace.[94] By the same token, they threatened to destroy a great deal of local power and autonomy. It is no wonder, then, that they should have been so vigorously resisted. In the eighteenth-century European context, any general cadastral survey was by definition a gambit of centralization; the local clergy and nobility were bound to see both their own taxing powers and the exemptions they enjoyed menaced. Commoners were likely to see it as a pretext for an additional local tax. Jean-Baptiste Colbert, the great "centralizer" of absolutism, proposed to conduct a national cadastral survey of France, but he was thwarted in 1679 by the combined opposition of the aristocracy and clergy. After the Revolution more than a century later, the radical François-Noël Babeuf, in his "Projet de cadastre perpetuel," dreamed of a perfectly egalitarian land reform in which everyone would get an equal parcel.[95] He too was thwarted.

We must keep in mind not only the capacity of state simplifications to transform the world but also the capacity of the society to modify, subvert, block, and even overturn the categories imposed upon it. Here it is useful to distinguish what might be called facts on paper from facts on the ground. As Sally Falk Moore and many others have emphasized, the land-office records may serve as the basis for taxation, but they may have little to do with the actual rights to the land. Paper owners may not be the effective owners.[96] Russian peasants, as we saw, might register a "paper" consolidation while continuing to interstrip. Land invasions, squatting, and poaching, if successful, represent the exercise of de facto property rights which are not represented on paper. Certain land taxes and tithes have been evaded or defied to the point where they have become dead letters.[97] The gulf between land tenure facts on paper and facts on the ground is probably greatest at moments of social turmoil and revolt. But even in more tranquil times, there will always be a shadow land-tenure system lurking beside and beneath the official account in the land-records office. We must never assume that local practice conforms with state theory.

All centralizing states recognized the value of a uniform, comprehensive cadastral map. Carrying out the mapmaking, however, was another matter. As a rule of thumb, cadastral mapping was earlier and more comprehensive where a powerful central state could impose itself on a relatively weak civil society. Where, by contrast, civil society was well organized and the state relatively weak, cadastral mapping was late, often voluntary, and fragmentary. Thus Napoleonic France was mapped much earlier than England, where the legal profession managed for a long time to stymie this threat to its local, income-earning function. It followed from the same logic that conquered colonies ruled by fiat would often be cadastrally mapped before the metropolitan nation that ordered it. Ireland may have been the first. After Cromwell's conquest, as Ian Hacking notes, "Ireland was completely surveyed for land, buildings, people, and cattle under the directorship of William Petty, in order to facilitate the rape of that nation by the English in 1679."[98]

Where the colony was a thinly populated settler-colony, as in North America or Australia, the obstacles to a thorough, uniform cadastral grid were minimal. There it was a question less of mapping preexisting patterns of land use than of surveying parcels of land that would be given or sold to new arrivals from Europe and of ignoring indigenous peoples and their common-property regimes.[99] Thomas Jefferson, with

7. The survey landscape, Castleton, North Dakota

an eye trained by Enlightenment rationalism, imagined dividing the United States west of the Ohio River into "hundreds"—squares measuring ten miles by ten miles—and requiring settlers to take the parcels of land as so designated.

The geometrical clarity of Jefferson's proposal was not merely an aesthetic choice; he claimed that irregular lots facilitated fraud. To reinforce his case, he cited the experience of Massachusetts, where actual landholdings were 10 percent to 100 percent greater than what had been granted by deed.[100] Not only did the regularity of the grid create legibility for the taxing authority, but it was a convenient and cheap way to package land and market it in homogeneous units. The grid facilitated the commoditization of land as much as the calculation of taxes and boundaries. Administratively, it was also disarmingly simple. Land could be registered and titled from a distance by someone who possessed virtually no local knowledge.[101] Once it was in place, the scheme had some of the impersonal, mechanical logic of the foresters' tables. But in practice, land titling in Jefferson's plan (which was modified by Congress to provide for rectangular lots and townships that were thirty-six square miles) did not always follow the prescribed pattern.

The Torrens system of land titling, developed in Australia and New Zealand in the 1860s, provided a lithographed, presurveyed grid representing allotments that were registered to settlers on a first-come, first-served basis. It was the quickest and most economical means yet devised to sell land, and it was later adopted in many British colonies. The more homogeneous and rigid the geometric grid, however, the more likely it was to run afoul of the natural features of the nonconforming landscape. The possibilities for surprises was nicely captured in this satirical verse from New Zealand.

> Now the road through Michael's section
>   though it looked well on the map
> For the use it was intended
>   wasn't really worth a rap
> And at night was not unlikely
>   to occasion some mishap.
>
> It was nicely planned on paper
>   and was ruled without remorse
> Over cliffs, and spurs and gullies
>   with a straight and even course
> Which precluded locomotion
>   on part of man or horse.[102]

The cadastral survey was but one technique in the growing armory of the utilitarian modern state.[103] Where the premodern state was content with a level of intelligence sufficient to allow it to keep order, extract taxes, and raise armies, the modern state increasingly aspired to "take in charge" the physical and human resources of the nation and make them more productive. These more positive ends of statecraft required a much greater knowledge of the society. And an inventory of land, people, incomes, occupations, resources, and deviance was the logical place to begin. "The need for the increasingly bureaucratic state to organize itself and control its resources gave an impulse to the collection of vital and other statistics; to forestry and rational agriculture; to surveying and exact cartography; and to public hygiene and climatology."[104]

Although the purposes of the state were broadening, what the state wanted to know was still directly related to those purposes. The nineteenth-century Prussian state, for example, was very much interested in the ages and sexes of immigrants and emigrants but not in their religions or races; what mattered to the state was keeping track of possible draft dodgers and maintaining a supply of men of military age.[105] The state's increasing concern with productivity, health, sanitation, education, transportation, mineral resources, grain production, and investment was less an abandonment of the older objectives of statecraft than a broadening and deepening of what those objectives entailed in the modern world.

2 Cities, People, and Language

And the Colleges of the Cartographers set up a Map of the Empire which had the size of the Empire itself and coincided with it point by point. . . . Succeeding generations understood that this Widespread Map was Useless, and not without Impiety they abandoned it to the Inclemencies of the Sun and the Winters.

—Suarez Miranda, *Viajes de varones prudentes (1658)*

An aerial view of a town built during the Middle Ages or the oldest quarters (*medina*) of a Middle Eastern city that has not been greatly tampered with has a particular look. It is the look of disorder. Or, to put it more precisely, the town conforms to no overall abstract form. Streets, lanes, and passages intersect at varying angles with a density that resembles the intricate complexity of some organic processes. In the case of a medieval town, where defense needs required walls and perhaps moats, there may be traces of inner walls superseded by outer walls, much like the growth rings of a tree. A representation of Bruges in about 1500 illustrates the pattern (figure 8). What definition there is to the city is provided by the castle green, the marketplace, and the river and canals that were (until they silted up) the lifeblood of this textile-trading city.

The fact that the layout of the city, having developed without any overall design, lacks a consistent geometric logic does not mean that it was at all confusing to its inhabitants. One imagines that many of its cobbled streets were nothing more than surfaced footpaths traced by repeated use. For those who grew up in its various quarters, Bruges would have been perfectly familiar, perfectly legible. Its very alleys and lanes would have closely approximated the most common daily movements. For a stranger or trader arriving for the first time, however, the town was almost certainly confusing, simply because it lacked a repetitive, abstract logic that would allow a newcomer to orient herself. The cityscape of Bruges in 1500 could be said to privilege local knowledge over outside knowledge, including that of external political authori-

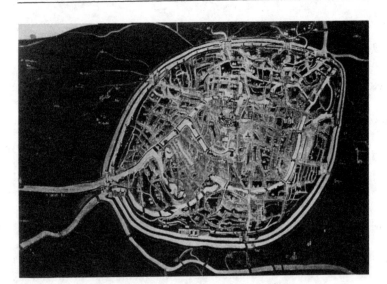

8. Bruges circa 1500, from a painting in the Town Hall, Bruges

ties.[1] It functioned spatially in much the same way a difficult or unintelligible dialect would function linguistically. As a semipermeable membrane, it facilitated communication within the city while remaining stubbornly unfamiliar to those who had not grown up speaking this special geographic dialect.

Historically, the relative illegibility to outsiders of some urban neighborhoods (or of their rural analogues, such as hills, marshes, and forests) has provided a vital margin of political safety from control by outside elites. A simple way of determining whether this margin exists is to ask if an outsider would have needed a local guide (a native tracker) in order to find her way successfully. If the answer is yes, then the community or terrain in question enjoys at least a small measure of insulation from outside intrusion. Coupled with patterns of local solidarity, this insulation has proven politically valuable in such disparate contexts as eighteenth- and early nineteenth-century urban riots over bread prices in Europe, the Front de Libération Nationale's tenacious resistance to the French in the Casbah of Algiers,[2] and the politics of the bazaar that helped to bring down the Shah of Iran. Illegibility, then, has been and remains a reliable resource for political autonomy.[3]

Stopping short of redesigning cities in order to make them more legible (a subject that we shall soon explore), state authorities endeavored to map complex, old cities in a way that would facilitate policing and control. Most of the major cities of France were thus the subject of careful military mapping (*reconnaissances militaires*), particularly after the Revolution. When urban revolts occurred, the authorities wanted to be able to move quickly to the precise locations that would enable them to contain or suppress the rebellions effectively.[4]

States and city planners have striven, as one might expect, to overcome this spatial unintelligibility and to make urban geography transparently legible from without. Their attitude toward what they regarded as the higgledy-piggledy profusion of unplanned cities was not unlike the attitude of foresters to the natural profusion of the unplanned forest. The origin of grids or geometrically regular settlements may lie in a straightforward military logic. A square, ordered, formulaic military camp on the order of the Roman *castra* has many advantages. Soldiers can easily learn the techniques of building it; the commander of the troops knows exactly in which disposition his subalterns and various troops lie; and any Roman messenger or officer who arrives at the camp will know where to find the officer he seeks. On a more speculative note, a far-flung, polyglot empire may find it symbolically useful to have its camps and towns laid out according to formula as a stamp of its order and authority. Other things being equal, the city laid out according to a simple, repetitive logic will be easiest to administer and to police.

Whatever the political and administrative conveniences of a geometric cityscape, the Enlightenment fostered a strong aesthetic that looked with enthusiasm on straight lines and visible order. No one expressed the prejudice more clearly than Descartes: "These ancient cities that were once mere *straggling* villages and have become in the course of time great cities are commonly quite *poorly laid out* compared to those *well-ordered towns that an engineer lays out on a vacant plane* as it suits his fancy. And although, upon considering one-by-one the buildings in the former class of towns, one finds as much art or more than one finds in the latter class of towns, still, upon seeing how the buildings are arranged—*here a large one, there a small one*—and how *they make the streets crooked and uneven*, one will say that *it is chance more than the will of some men using their reason that has arranged them thus*."[5]

Descartes's vision conjures up the urban equivalent of the scientific forest: streets laid out in straight lines intersecting at right angles, buildings of uniform design and size, the whole built according to a single, overarching plan.

The elective affinity between a strong state and a uniformly laid out city is obvious. Lewis Mumford, the historian of urban form, locates the modern European origin of this symbiosis in the open, legible baroque style of the Italian city-state. He claims, in terms that Descartes would have found congenial, "It was one of the triumphs of the baroque mind to organize space, to make it continuous, reduce it to measure and order."[6] More to the point, the baroque redesigning of medieval cities—with its grand edifices, vistas, squares, and attention to uniformity, proportion, and perspective—was intended to reflect the grandeur and awesome power of the prince. Aesthetic considerations frequently won out over the existing social structure and the mundane functioning of the city. "Long before the invention of bulldozers," Mumford adds, "the Italian military engineer developed, through his professional specialization in destruction, a bulldozing habit of mind: one that sought to clear the ground of encumbrances, so as to make a clear beginning on its own inflexible mathematical lines."[7]

The visual power of the baroque city was underwritten by scrupulous attention to the military security of the prince from internal as well as external enemies. Thus both Alberti and Palladio thought of main thoroughfares as military roads (viae militaires). Such roads had to be straight, and, in Palladio's view, "the ways will be more convenient if they are made everywhere equal: that is to say that there will be *no part in them where armies may not easily march*."[8]

There are, of course, many cities approximating Descartes's model. For obvious reasons, most have been planned from the ground up as new, often utopian cities.[9] Where they have not been built by imperial decrees, they have been designed by their founding fathers to accommodate more repetitive and uniform squares for future settlement.[10] A bird's-eye view of central Chicago in the late nineteenth century (William Penn's Philadelphia or New Haven would do equally well) serves as an example of the grid city (figure 9).

From an administrator's vantage point, the ground plan of Chicago is nearly utopian. It offers a quick appreciation of the ensemble, since the entirety is made up of straight lines, right angles, and repetitions.[11] Even the rivers seem scarcely to interrupt the city's relentless symmetry. For an outsider—or a policeman—finding an address is a comparatively simple matter; no local guides are required. The knowledge of local citizens is not especially privileged vis-à-vis that of outsiders. If, as is the case in upper Manhattan, the cross streets are consecutively numbered and are intersected by longer avenues, also consecutively numbered, the plan acquires even greater transparency.[12] The aboveground order of a grid city facilitates its underground order in the layout of water pipes, storm drains, sewers, electric cables, natural

9. Map of downtown Chicago, circa 1893

gas lines, and subways—an order no less important to the administrators of a city. Delivering mail, collecting taxes, conducting a census, moving supplies and people in and out of the city, putting down a riot or insurrection, digging for pipes and sewer lines, finding a felon or conscript (providing he is at the address given), and planning public transportation, water supply, and trash removal are all made vastly simpler by the logic of the grid.

Three aspects of this geometric order in human settlement bear emphasis. The first is that the order in question is most evident, not at street level, but rather from above and from outside. Like a marcher in a parade or like a single riveter in a long assembly line, a pedestrian in the middle of this grid cannot instantly perceive the larger design of the city. The symmetry is either grasped from a representation—it is in fact what one would expect if one gave a schoolchild a ruler and a blank piece of paper—or from the vantage point of a helicopter hovering far above the ground: in short, a God's-eye view, or the view of an absolute ruler. This spatial fact is perhaps inherent in the process of urban or architectural planning itself, a process that involves miniaturization and scale models upon which patron and planner gaze down, exactly as if they were in a helicopter.[13] There is, after all, no other way of visually imagining what a large-scale construction project will look like when it is completed except by a miniaturization of this kind. It follows, I believe, that such plans, which have the scale of toys, are judged for their sculptural properties and visual order, often from a perspective that no or very few human observers will ever replicate.

The miniaturization imaginatively achieved by scale models of cities or landscapes was practically achieved with the airplane. The mapping tradition of the bird's-eye view, evident in the map of Chicago, was no longer a mere convention. By virtue of its great distance, an aerial view resolved what might have seemed ground-level confusion into an apparently vaster order and symmetry. It would be hard to exaggerate the importance of the airplane for modernist thought and planning. By offering a perspective that flattened the topography as if it were a canvas, flight encouraged new aspirations to "synoptic vision, rational control, planning, and spatial order."[14]

A second point about an urban order easily legible from outside is that the grand plan of the ensemble has no necessary relationship to the order of life as it is experienced by its residents. Although certain state services may be more easily provided and distant addresses more easily located, these apparent advantages may be negated by such perceived disadvantages as the absence of a dense street life, the intrusion of hostile authorities, the loss of the spatial irregularities that foster coziness, gathering places for informal recreation, and neighborhood feeling. The formal order of a geometrically regular urban space is just that: formal order. Its visual regimentation has a ceremonial or ideological quality, much like the order of a parade or a barracks. The fact that such order works for municipal and state authorities in administering the city is no guarantee that it works for citizens. Provisionally, then, we must remain agnostic about the relation between formal spatial order and social experience.

The third notable aspect of homogeneous, geometrical, uniform property is its convenience as a standardized commodity for the market. Like Jefferson's scheme for surveying or the Torrens system for titling open land, the grid creates regular lots and blocks that are ideal for buying and selling. Precisely because they are abstract units detached from any ecological or topographical reality, they resemble a kind of currency which is endlessly amenable to aggregation and fragmentation. This feature of the grid plan suits equally the surveyor, the planner, and the real-estate speculator. Bureaucratic and commercial logic, in this instance, go hand in hand. As Mumford notes, "The beauty of this mechanical pattern, from the commercial standpoint, should be plain. This plan offers the engineer none of those special problems that irregular parcels and curved boundary lines present. An office boy could figure out the number of square feet involved in a street opening or in a sale of land: even a lawyer's clerk could write a description of the necessary deed of sale, merely by filling in with the proper dimensions the standard document. With a T-square and a triangle, finally, the municipal engineer could, without the slightest training as either an architect or a sociologist, 'plan' a metropolis, with its standard lots, its standard blocks, its standard width streets. . . . The very absence of more specific adaptation to landscape or to human purpose only increased, by its very indefiniteness, *its general usefulness for exchange*."[15]

The vast majority of Old World cities are, in fact, some historical amalgam of a Bruges and a Chicago. Although more than one politician, dictator, and city planner have devised plans for the total recasting of an existing city, these dreams came at such cost, both financial and political, that they have rarely left the drawing boards. Piecemeal planning, by contrast, is far more common. The central, older core of many cities remains somewhat like Bruges, whereas the newer outskirts are more likely to exhibit the marks of one or more plans. Sometimes, as in the sharp contrast between old Delhi and the imperial capital of New Delhi, the divergence is formalized.

Occasionally, authorities have taken draconian steps to retrofit an existing city. The redevelopment of Paris by the prefect of the Seine, Baron Haussmann, under Louis Napoleon was a grandiose public works program stretching from 1853 to 1869. Haussmann's vast scheme absorbed unprecedented amounts of public debt, uprooted tens of thousands of people, and could have been accomplished only by a single executive authority not directly accountable to the electorate.

The logic behind the reconstruction of Paris bears a resemblance to the logic behind the transformation of old-growth forests into scientific forests designed for unitary fiscal management. There was the same emphasis on simplification, legibility, straight lines, central management, and a synoptic grasp of the ensemble. As in the case of the forest, much of the plan was achieved. One chief difference, however, was that Haussmann's plan was devised less for fiscal reasons than for its impact on the conduct and sensibilities of Parisians. While the plan did create a far more legible fiscal space in the capital, this was a byproduct of the desire to make the city more governable, prosperous, healthy, and architecturally imposing.[16] The second difference was, of course, that those uprooted by the urban planning of the Second Empire could, and did, strike back. As we shall see, the retrofitting of Paris foreshadows many of the paradoxes of authoritarian high-modernist planning that we will soon examine in greater detail.

The plan reproduced in figure 10 shows the new boulevards constructed to Haussmann's measure as well as the prerevolutionary inner

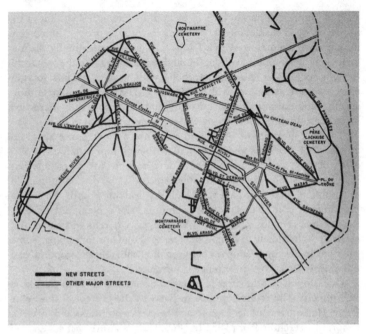

10. Map of Paris, 1870, showing the principal new streets built between 1850 and 1870

boulevards, which were widened and straightened.[17] But the retrofit, seen merely as a new street map, greatly underestimates the transformation. For all the demolition and construction required, for all the new legibility added to the street plan, the new pattern bore strong traces of an accommodation with "old-growth" Paris. The outer boulevards, for example, follow the line of the older customs (*octroi*) wall of 1787. But Haussmann's scheme was far more than a traffic reform. The new legibility of the boulevards was accompanied by changes that revolutionized daily life: new aqueducts, a much more effective sewage system, new rail lines and terminals, centralized markets (Les Halles), gas lines and lighting, and new parks and public squares.[18] The new Paris created by Louis Napoleon became, by the turn of the century, a widely admired public works miracle and shrine for would-be planners from abroad.

At the center of Louis Napoleon's and Haussmann's plans for Paris lay the military security of the state. The redesigned city was, above all, to be made safe against popular insurrections. As Haussmann wrote, "The order of this Queen-city is one of the main pre-conditions of general [public] security."[19] Barricades had gone up nine times in the twenty-five years before 1851. Louis Napoleon and Haussmann had seen the revolutions of 1830 and 1848; more recently, the June Days and resistance to Louis Napoleon's coup represented the largest insurrection of the century. Louis Napoleon, as a returned exile, was well aware of how tenuous his hold on power might prove.

The geography of insurrection, however, was not evenly distributed across Paris. Resistance was concentrated in densely packed, working-class *quartiers*, which, like Bruges, had complex, illegible street plans.[20] The 1860 annexation of the "inner suburbs" (located between the customs wall and the outer fortifications and containing 240,000 residents) was explicitly designed to gain mastery over a *ceinture sauvage* that had thus far escaped police control. Haussmann described this area as a "dense belt of suburbs, given over to twenty different administrations, built at random, covered by an inextricable network of narrow and tortuous public ways, alleys, and dead-ends, where a nomadic population without any real ties to the land [property] and without any effective surveillance, grows at a prodigious speed."[21] Within Paris itself, there were such revolutionary *foyers* as the Marais and especially the Faubourg Saint-Antoine, both of which had been determined centers of resistance to Louis Napoleon's coup d'état.

The military control of these insurrectionary spaces—spaces that had not yet been well mapped—was integral to Haussmann's plan.[22] A series of new avenues between the inner boulevards and the customs wall was designed to facilitate movement between the barracks on the outskirts of the city and the subversive districts. As Haussmann saw it, his new roads would ensure multiple, direct rail and road links between each district of the city and the military units responsible for order there.[23] Thus, for example, new boulevards in northeastern Paris allowed troops to rush from the Courbevoie barracks to the Bastille and then to subdue the turbulent Faubourg Saint-Antoine.[24] Many of the new rail lines and stations were located with similar strategic goals in mind. Where possible, insurrectionary quartiers were demolished or broken up by new roads, public spaces, and commercial development. Explaining the need for a loan of 50 million francs to begin the work, Léon Faucher emphasized state security needs: "The interests of public order, no less than those of salubrity, demand that a wide swath be cut as soon as possible across this district of barricades."[25]

The reconstruction of Paris was also a necessary public-health measure. And here the steps that the hygienists said would make Paris more healthful would at the same time make it more efficient economically and more secure militarily. Antiquated sewers and cesspools, the droppings of an estimated thirty-seven thousand horses (in 1850), and the unreliable water supply made Paris literally pestilential. The city had the highest death rate in France and was most susceptible to virulent epidemics of cholera; in 1831, the disease killed 18,400 people, including the prime minister. And it was in those districts of revolutionary resistance where, because of crowding and lack of sanitation, the rates of mortality were highest.[26] Haussmann's Paris was, for those who were not expelled, a far healthier city; the greater circulation of air and water and the exposure to sunlight reduced the risk of epidemics just as the improved circulation of goods and labor (healthier labor, at that) contributed to the city's economic well-being. A utilitarian logic of labor productivity and commercial success went hand in hand with strategic and public-health concerns.

The politico-aesthetic tastes of the driving force behind the transformation of Paris, Louis Napoleon himself, were also decisive. When Haussmann was appointed prefect of the Seine, Louis Napoleon handed him a map that provided for the central market, the Bois de Bologne, and many of the streets eventually built. There is no doubt that Louis Napoleon's plans drew heavily from the ideas of the Saint Simonists in their visionary journal *Le globe* and from the model urban communities sketched by Fourier and Cabet.[27] Their grandiose designs appealed to his own determination to have the new grandeur of the capital city serve as testimony to the grandeur of the regime.

As happens in many authoritarian modernizing schemes, the political tastes of the ruler occasionally trumped purely military and functional concerns. Rectilinear streets may have admirably assisted the mobilization of troops against insurgents, but they were also to be flanked by elegant facades and to terminate in imposing buildings that would impress visitors.[28] Uniform modern buildings along the new boulevards may have represented healthier dwellings, but they were often no more than facades. The zoning regulations were almost exclusively concerned with the visible surfaces of buildings, but behind the facades, builders could build crowded, airless tenements, and many of them did.[29]

The new Paris, as T. J. Clark has observed, was intensely visualized: "Part of Haussmann's purpose was to give modernity a shape, and he seemed at the time to have a measure of success in doing so; he built a set of forms in which the city appeared to be visible, even intelligible: Paris, to repeat the formula, was becoming a spectacle."[30]

Legibility, in this case, was achieved by a much more pronounced segregation of the population by class and function. Each fragment of Paris increasingly took on a distinctive character of dress, activity, and wealth—bourgeois shopping district, prosperous residential quarter, industrial suburb, artisan quarter, bohemian quarter. It was a more easily managed and administered city and a more "readable" city because of Haussmann's heroic simplifications.

As in most ambitious schemes of modern order, there was a kind of evil twin to Haussmann's spacious and imposing new capital. The hierarchy of urban space in which the rebuilt center of Paris occupied pride of place presupposed the displacement of the urban poor toward the periphery.[31] Nowhere was this more true than in Belleville, a popular working-class quarter to the northeast which grew into a town of sixty thousand people by 1856. Many of its residents had been disinherited by Haussmann's demolitions; some called it a community of outcasts. By the 1860s, it had become a suburban equivalent of what the Faubourg Saint-Antoine had been earlier—an illegible, insurrectionary *foyer*. "The problem was not that Belleville was not a community, but that it became the sort of community which the bourgeoisie feared, which the police could not penetrate, which the government could not regulate, where the popular classes, with all their unruly passions and political resentments, held the upper hand."[32] If, as many claim, the Commune of Paris in 1871 was partly an attempt to reconquer the city ("la reconquete de la Ville par la Ville")[33] by those exiled to the periphery by Haussmann, then Belleville was the geographical locus of that sentiment. The Communards, militarily on the defensive in late May 1871, retreated toward the northeast and Belleville, where, at the Belleville town hall, they made their last stand. Treated as a den of revolutionaries, Belleville was subjected to a brutal military occupation.

Two diagnostic ironies marked the suppression of the Commune. The first was that the strategic design of Haussmann was triumphant. The boulevards and rail lines that the Second Empire had hoped would foil a popular insurrection had proved their value. "Thanks to Haussmann, the Versailles army could move in one fell swoop from the Place du Chateau d'eau to Belleville."[34] The second irony was that, just as the Faubourg Saint-Antoine had been effaced by Haussmann's demolitions, so too was much of the newly offending quarter obliterated by the building of the Eglise Sacré Coeur, built "in the guilty town . . . as restitution made on the site of the crime."[35]

The Creation of Surnames

Some of the categories that we most take for granted and with which we now routinely apprehend the social world had their origin in state projects of standardization and legibility. Consider, for example, something as fundamental as permanent surnames.

A vignette from the popular film *Witness* illustrates how, when among strangers, we do rely on surnames as key navigational aids.[36] The detective in the film is attempting to locate a young Amish boy who may have witnessed a murder. Although the detective has a surname to go on, he is thwarted by several aspects of Amish traditionalism, including the antique German dialect spoken by the Amish. His first instinct is, of course, to reach for the telephone book—a list of proper names and addresses—but the Amish don't have telephones. Furthermore, he learns, the Amish have a very small number of last names. His quandary reminds us that the great variety of surnames and given names in the United States allows us to identify unambiguously a large number of individuals whom we may never have met. A world without such names is bewildering; indeed, the detective finds Amish society so opaque that he needs a native tracker to find his way.

Customary naming practices throughout much of the world are enormously rich. Among some peoples, it is not uncommon for individuals to have different names during different stages of life (infancy, childhood, adulthood) and in some cases after death; added to these are names used for joking, rituals, and mourning and names used for interactions with same-sex friends or with in-laws. Each name is specific to a certain phase of life, social setting, or interlocutor. A single individual will frequently be called by several different names, depending on the stage of life and the person addressing him or her. To the question "What is your name?" which has a more unambiguous answer in the contemporary West, the only plausible answer is "It depends."[37]

For the insider who grows up using these naming practices, they are both legible and clarifying. Each name and the contexts of its use convey important social knowledge. Like the network of alleys in Bruges, the assortment of local weights and measures, and the intricacies of customary land tenure, the complexity of naming has some direct and often quite practical relations to local purposes. For an outsider, however, this byzantine complexity of names is a formidable obstacle to understanding local society. Finding someone, let alone situating him or her in a kinship network or tracing the inheritance of property, becomes a major undertaking. If, in addition, the population in question has reason to conceal its identity and its activities from external authority, the camouflage value of such naming practices is considerable.

The invention of permanent, inherited patronyms was, after the administrative simplification of nature (for example, the forest) and space (for example, land tenure), the last step in establishing the necessary preconditions of modern statecraft. In almost every case it was a state project, designed to allow officials to identify, unambiguously, the majority of its citizens. When successful, it went far to create a legible people.[38] Tax and tithe rolls, property rolls, conscription lists, censuses, and property deeds recognized in law were inconceivable without some means of fixing an individual's identity and linking him or her to a kin group. Campaigns to assign permanent patronyms have typically taken place, as one might expect, in the context of a state's exertions to put its fiscal system on a sounder and more lucrative footing. Fearing, with good reason, that an effort to enumerate and register them could be a prelude to some new tax burden or conscription, local officials and the population at large often resisted such campaigns.

If permanent surnames were largely a project of official legibility, then they should have appeared earliest in those societies with precocious states. China provides a striking example.[39] By roughly the fourth century B.C. (although the exact timing and comprehensiveness are in dispute), the Qin dynasty had apparently begun imposing surnames on much of its population and enumerating them for the purposes of taxes, forced labor, and conscription.[40] This initiative may well have been the origin of the term "laobaixing," meaning, literally, "the old one hundred surnames," which in modern China has come to mean "the common people." Before this, the fabled Chinese patrilineage, while established among ruling houses and related lines, was absent among commoners. They did not have surnames, nor did they even imitate elite practices in this respect. The assigning of patronyms by family was integral to state policy promoting the status of (male) family heads, giving them legal jurisdiction over their wives, children, and juniors and, not incidentally, holding them accountable for the fiscal obligations of the entire family.[41] This (Qin) policy required registering the entire population, after which the "hodgepodge of terms by which people were called were all classified as *hsing* [surname], to be passed down to their patrilineal descendants indefinitely."[42] On this account, both the establishment of permanent patronyms and the creation of the patrilineal family itself can be attributed to early state simplification.

Until at least the fourteenth century, the great majority of Europeans did not have permanent patronymics.[43] An individual's name was typically his given name, which might well suffice for local identification. If something more were required, a second designation could be added, indicating his occupation (in the English case, smith, baker), his geographical location (hill, edgewood), his father's given name, or a personal characteristic (short, strong). These secondary designations were not permanent surnames; they did not survive their bearers, unless by chance, say, a baker's son went into the same trade and was called by the same second designation.

We can learn something about the creation of permanent patronyms in Europe by the documentation left behind from the failed census (*catasto*) of the Florentine state in 1427.[44] The catasto was an audacious attempt to rationalize the state's revenues and military strength by specifying its subjects and their wealth, residences, landholdings, and ages.[45] Close study of these records demonstrates, first, that, as in the Chinese case, state initiative created new surnames rather than simply recording existing surnames. It is thus often impossible to know whether a state-recorded surname has any social existence outside the role of the text in which it is inscribed. Second, the variable imposition of permanent surnames within a territory—in this case Tuscany— serves as a rough-and-ready gauge of state capacity.

Family names in early fifteenth-century Tuscany were confined to a very few powerful, property-owning lineages (such as the Strozzi). For such lineages, a surname was a way of achieving social recognition as a "corporate group," and kin and affines adopted the name as a way of claiming the backing of an influential lineage. Beyond this narrow segment of society and a small urban patriciate that copied its practices, there were no permanent family names.

How, in this case, was the catasto office to pinpoint and register an individual, let alone his location, his property, and his age? When making his declaration, a typical Tuscan provided not only his own given name but those of his father and perhaps his grandfather as well, in quasi-biblical fashion (Luigi, son of Giovanni, son of Paolo). Given the limited number of baptismal names and the tendency of many families to repeat names in alternate generations, even this sequence might not suffice for unambiguous identification. The subject might then add his profession, his nickname, or a personal characteristic. There is no evidence that any of these designations was a permanent patronym, although this exercise and others like it might have eventually served to crystallize surnames, at least for documentary purposes. In the final analysis, the Florentine state was inadequate to the administrative feat intended by the catasto. Popular resistance, the noncompliance of many local elites, and the arduousness and cost of the census exercise doomed the project, and officials returned to the earlier fiscal system.

What evidence we have suggests that second names of any kind became rarer as distance from the state's fiscal reach increased. Whereas one-third of the households in Florence declared a second name, the proportion dropped to one-fifth for secondary towns and to one-tenth in the countryside. It was not until the seventeenth century that family names crystallized in the most remote and poorest areas of Tuscany— the areas that would have had the least contact with officialdom.

A comparable connection between state building and the invention of permanent patronyms exists for fourteenth- and fifteenth-century England. As in Tuscany, in England only wealthy aristocratic families tended to have fixed surnames. In the English case such names referred typically to families' places of origin in Normandy (for example, Baumont, Percy, Disney) or to the places in England that they held in fief from William the Conqueror (for example, Gerard de Sussex). For the rest of the male population, the standard practice of linking only father and son by way of identification prevailed.[46] Thus, William Robertson's male son might be called Thomas Williamson (son of William), while Thomas's son, in turn, might be called Henry Thompson (Thomas's son). Note that the grandson's name, by itself, bore no evidence of his grandfather's identity, complicating the tracing of descent through names alone. A great many northern European surnames, though now permanent, still bear, like a fly caught in amber, particles that echo their antique purpose of designating who a man's father was (Fitz–, O'–, –sen, –son, –s, Mac–, –vich).[47] At the time of their establishment, last names often had a kind of local logic to them: John who owned a mill became John Miller; John who made cart wheels became John Wheelwright; John who was physically small became John Short. As their male descendants, whatever their occupations or stature, retained the patronyms, the names later assumed an arbitrary cast.

The development of the personal surname (literally, a name added to another name, and not to be confused with a permanent patronym) went hand in hand with the development of written, official documents such as tithe records, manorial dues rolls, marriage registers, censuses, tax records, and land records.[48] They were necessary to the successful conduct of any administrative exercise involving large numbers of people who had to be individually identified and who were not known personally by the authorities. Imagine the dilemma of a tithe or capitation-tax collector faced with a male population, 90 percent of whom bore just six Christian names (John, William, Thomas, Robert, Richard, and Henry). Some second designation was absolutely essential for the records, and, if the subject suggested none, it was invented for him by the recording clerk. These second designations and the rolls of names that they generated were to the legibility of the population what uniform measurement and the cadastral map were to the legibility of real property. While the subject might normally prefer the safety of anonymity, once he was forced to pay the tax, it was then in his interest to be accurately identified in order to avoid paying the same tax twice. Many of these fourteenth-century surnames were clearly nothing more than administrative fictions designed to make a population fiscally legible. Many of the subjects whose "surnames" appear in the documents were probably unaware of what had been written down, and, for the great majority, the surnames had no social existence whatever outside the document.[49] Only on very rare occasions does one encounter an entry, such as "William Carter, tailor," that implies that we may be dealing with a permanent patronym.

The increasing intensity of interaction with the state and statelike structures (large manors, the church) exactly parallels the development of permanent, heritable patronyms. Thus, when Edward I clarified the system of landholding, establishing primogeniture and hereditary copyhold tenure for manorial land, he provided a powerful incentive for the adoption of permanent patronyms. Taking one's father's surname became, for the eldest son at least, part of a claim to the property on the father's death.[50] Now that property claims were subject to state validation, surnames that had once been mere bureaucratic fantasies took on a social reality of their own. One imagines that for a long time English subjects had in effect two names—their local name and an "official," fixed patronym. As the frequency of interaction with impersonal administrative structures increased, the official name came to prevail in all but a man's intimate circle. Those subjects living at a greater distance, both socially and geographically, from the organs of state power, as did the Tuscans, acquired permanent patronyms much later. The upper classes and those living in the south of England thus acquired permanent surnames before the lower classes and those living in the north did. The Scottish and Welsh acquired them even later.[51]

State naming practices, like state mapping practices, were inevitably associated with taxes (labor, military service, grain, revenue,) and hence aroused popular resistance. The great English peasant rising of 1381 (often called the Wat Tyler Rebellion) is attributed to an unprecedented decade of registrations and assessments of poll taxes.[52] For English as well as for Tuscan peasants, a census of all adult males could not but appear ominous, if not ruinous.

The imposition of permanent surnames on colonial populations offers us a chance to observe a process, telescoped into a decade or less, that in the West might have taken several generations. Many of the same state objectives animate both the European and the colonial exercises, but in the colonial case, the state is at once more bureaucratized and less tolerant of popular resistance. The very brusqueness of colonial naming casts the purposes and paradoxes of the process in sharp relief.

Nowhere is this better illustrated than in the Philippines under the Spanish.[53] Filipinos were instructed by the decree of November 21, 1849, to take on permanent Hispanic surnames. The author of the decree was Governor (and Lieutenant General) Narciso Claveria y Zaldua, a meticulous administrator as determined to rationalize names as he had been determined to rationalize existing law, provincial boundaries, and the calendar.[54] He had observed, as his decree states, that Filipinos generally lacked individual surnames, which might "distinguish them by families," and that their practice of adopting baptismal names drawn from a small group of saints' names resulted in great "confusion." The remedy was the *catalogo*, a compendium not only of personal names but also of nouns and adjectives drawn from flora, fauna, minerals, geography, and the arts and intended to be used by the authorities in assigning permanent, inherited surnames. Each local official was to be given a supply of surnames sufficient for his jurisdiction, "taking care that the distribution be made by letters [of the alphabet]."[55] In practice, each town was given a number of pages from the alphabetized catalogo, producing whole towns with surnames beginning with the same letter. In situations where there has been little in-migration in the past 150 years, the traces of this administrative exercise are still perfectly visible across the landscape: "For example, in the Bikol region, the entire alphabet is laid out like a garland over the provinces of Albay, Sorsogon, and Catanduanes which in 1849 belonged to the single jurisdiction of Albay. Beginning with *A* at the provincial capital, the letters *B* and *C* mark the towns along the coast beyond Tabaco to Tiwi. We return and trace along the coast of Sorsogon the letters *E* to *L;* then starting down the Iraya Valley at Daraga with *M*, we stop with *S* to Polangui and Libon, and finish the alphabet with a quick tour around the island of Catanduanes."[56]

The confusion for which the decree is the antidote is largely that of the administrator and the tax collector. Universal last names, they believe, will facilitate the administration of justice, finance, and public order as well as make it simpler for prospective marriage partners to calculate their degree of consanguinity.[57] For a utilitarian state builder of Claveria's temper, however, the ultimate goal was a complete and legible list of subjects and taxpayers. This is abundantly clear from the short preamble to the decree: "In view of the extreme usefulness and practicality of this measure, the time has come to issue a directive for the formation of a civil register [formerly a clerical function], which may not only fulfill and ensure the said objectives, but may also serve as a basis for the statistics of the country, guarantee the collection of taxes, the regular performance of personal services, and the receipt of payment for exemptions. It likewise provides exact information of the movement of the population, thus avoiding unauthorized migrations, hiding taxpayers, and other abuses."[58]

Drawing on the accurate lists of citizens throughout the colony, Claveria envisioned each local official constructing a table of eight columns specifying tribute obligations, communal labor obligations, first name, surname, age, marital status, occupation, and exemptions. A ninth column, for updating the register, would record alterations in status and would be submitted for inspection every month. Because of their accuracy and uniformity, these registers would allow the state to compile the precise statistics in Manila that would make for fiscal efficiency. The daunting cost of assigning surnames to the entire population and building a complete and discriminating list of taxpayers was justified by forecasting that the list, while it might cost as much as twenty thousand pesos to create, would yield one hundred thousand or two hundred thousand pesos in continuing annual revenue.

What if the Filipinos chose to ignore their new last names? This possibility had already crossed Claveria's mind, and he took steps to make sure that the names would stick. Schoolteachers were ordered to forbid their students to address or even know one another by any name except the officially inscribed family name. Those teachers who did not apply the rule with enthusiasm were to be punished. More efficacious perhaps, given the minuscule school enrollment, was the proviso that forbade priests and military and civil officials from accepting any document, application, petition, or deed that did not use the official surnames. All documents using other names would be null and void.

Actual practice, as one might expect, fell considerably short of Claveria's administrative utopia of legible and regimented taxpayers. The continued existence of such non-Spanish surnames as Magsaysay or Macapagal suggests that part of the population was never mustered for this exercise. Local officials submitted incomplete returns or none at all. And there was another serious problem, one that Claveria had foreseen but inadequately provided for. The new registers rarely recorded, as they were supposed to, the previous names used by the registrants. This meant that it became exceptionally difficult for officials to trace back property and taxpaying to the period before the transformation of names. The state had in effect blinded its own hindsight by the very success of its new scheme.

With surnames, as with forests, land tenure, and legible cities, actual practice never achieved anything like the simplified and uniform perfection to which its designers had aspired. As late as 1872, an attempt at taking a census proved a complete fiasco, and it was not tried again until just before the revolution of 1896. Nevertheless, by the twentieth century, the vast majority of Filipinos bore the surnames that Claveria had dreamed up for them. The increasing weight of the state in people's lives and the state's capacity to insist on its rules and its terms ensured that.

Universal last names are a fairly recent historical phenomenon. Tracking property ownership and inheritance, collecting taxes, maintaining court records, performing police work, conscripting soldiers, and controlling epidemics were all made immeasurably easier by the clarity of full names and, increasingly, fixed addresses. While the utilitarian state was committed to a complete inventory of its population, liberal ideas of citizenship, which implied voting rights and conscription, also contributed greatly to the standardization of naming practices. The legislative imposition of permanent surnames is particularly clear in the case of Western European Jews who had no tradition of last names. A Napoleonic decree "concernant les Juifs qui n'ont pas de nom de famille et de prenoms fixes," in 1808, mandated last names.[59] Austrian legislation of 1787, as part of the emancipation process, required Jews to choose last names or, if they refused, to have fixed last names chosen for them. In Prussia the emancipation of the Jews was contingent upon the adoption of surnames.[60] Many of the immigrants to the United States, Jews and non-Jews alike, had no permanent surnames when they set sail. Very few, however, made it through the initial paperwork without an official last name that their descendants carry still.

The process of creating fixed last names continues in much of the Third World and on the "tribal frontiers" of more developed countries.[61] Today, of course, there are now many other state-impelled standard designations that have vastly improved the capacity of the state to identify an individual. The creation of birth and death certificates, more specific addresses (that is, more specific than something like "John-on-the-hill"), identity cards, passports, social security numbers, photographs, fingerprints, and, most recently, DNA profiles have superseded the rather crude instrument of the permanent surname. But the surname was a first and crucial step toward making individual citizens officially legible, and along with the photograph, it is still the first fact on documents of identity.

The Directive for a Standard, Official Language

The great cultural barrier imposed by a separate language is perhaps the most effective guarantee that a social world, easily accessible to insiders, will remain opaque to outsiders.[62] Just as the stranger or state official might need a local guide to find his way around sixteenth-century Bruges, he would need a local interpreter in order to understand and be understood in an unfamiliar linguistic environment. A distinct language, however, is a far more powerful basis for autonomy than a complex residential pattern. It is also the bearer of a distinctive history, a cultural sensibility, a literature, a mythology, a musical past.[63] In this respect, a unique language represents a formidable obstacle to state knowledge, let alone colonization, control, manipulation, instruction, or propaganda.

Of all state simplifications, then, the imposition of a single, official language may be the most powerful, and it is the precondition of many other simplifications. This process should probably be viewed, as Eugen Weber suggests in the case of France, as one of domestic colonization in which various foreign provinces (such as Brittany and Occitanie) are linguistically subdued and culturally incorporated.[64] In the first efforts made to insist on the use of French, it is clear that the state's objective was the legibility of local practice. Officials insisted that every legal document—whether a will, document of sale, loan instrument, contract, annuity, or property deed—be drawn up in French. As long as these documents remained in local vernaculars, they were daunting to an official sent from Paris and virtually impossible to bring into conformity with central schemes of legal and administrative standardization. The campaign of linguistic centralization was assured of some success since it went hand in hand with an expansion of state power. By the late nineteenth century, dealing with the state was unavoidable for all but a small minority of the population. Petitions, court cases, school documents, applications, and correspondence with officials were all of necessity written in French. One can hardly imagine a more effective formula for immediately devaluing local knowledge and privileging all those who had mastered the official linguistic code. It was a gigantic shift in power. Those at the periphery who lacked competence in French were rendered mute and marginal. They were now in need of a local guide to the new state culture, which appeared in the form of lawyers, *notaires*, schoolteachers, clerks, and soldiers.[65]

A cultural project, as one might suspect, lurked behind the linguistic centralization. French was seen as the bearer of a national civilization; the purpose of imposing it was not merely to have provincials digest the Code Napoleon but also to bring them Voltaire, Racine, Parisian newspapers, and a national education. As Weber provocatively puts it, "There can be no clearer expression of imperialist sentiment, a white man's burden of Francophony, whose first conquests were to be right at home."[66] Where the command of Latin had once defined participation in a wider culture for a small elite, the command of standard French now defined full participation in French culture. The implicit logic of the move was to define a hierarchy of cultures, relegating local languages and their regional cultures to, at best, a quaint provincialism. At the apex of this implicit pyramid was Paris and its institutions: ministries, schools, academies (including the guardian of the language, l'Académie Française). The relative success of this cultural project hinged on both coercion and inducements. "It was centralization," says Alexandre Sanguinetti, "which permitted the making of France despite the French, or in the midst of their indifference. . . . France is a deliberate political construction for whose creation the central power has never ceased to fight."[67] Standard (Parisian) French and Paris were not only focal points of power; they were also magnets. The growth of markets, physical mobility, new careers, political patronage, public service, and a national educational system all meant that facility in French and connections to Paris were the paths of social advancement and material success. It was a state simplification that promised to reward those who complied with its logic and to penalize those who ignored it.

The Centralization of Traffic Patterns

The linguistic centralization impelled by the imposition of Parisian French as the official standard was replicated in a centralization of traffic. Just as the new dispensation in language made Paris the hub of communication, so the new road and rail systems increasingly favored movement to and from Paris over interregional or local traffic. State policy resembled, in computer parlance, a "hardwiring" pattern that made the provinces far more accessible, far more legible, to central authorities than even the absolutist kings had imagined.

Let us contrast, in an overly schematic way, a relatively uncentralized network of communication, on one hand, with a relatively centralized network, on the other. If mapped, the uncentralized pattern would be the physical image of the actual movements of goods and people along routes *not* created by administrative fiat. Such movements would not be random; they would reflect both the ease of travel

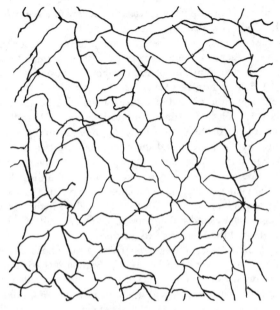

11. Paths created by use and topography

along valleys, by watercourses, and around defiles and also the location of important resources and ritual sites. Weber captures the wealth of human activities that animate these movements across the landscape: "They served professional pursuits, like the special trails followed by glassmakers, carriers or sellers of salt, potters, or those that led to forges, mines, quarries, and hemp fields, or those along which flax, hemp, linen, and yarn were taken to market. There were pilgrimage routes and procession trails."[68]

If we can imagine, for the sake of argument, a place where physical resources are evenly distributed and there are no great physical barriers to movement (such as mountains or swamps), then a map of paths in use might form a network resembling a dense concentration of capillaries (figure 11). The tracings would, of course, never be entirely random. Market towns based on location and resources would constitute small hubs, as would religious shrines, quarries, mines, and other important sites.[69] In the French case as well, the network of roads would have long reflected the centralizing ambitions of local lords and the nation's monarchs. The point of this illustrative idealization, however, is to depict a landscape of communication routes that is only

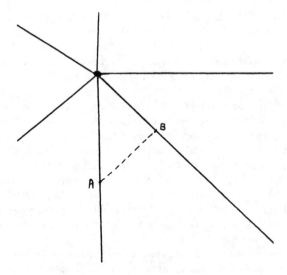

12. Centralized traffic hub

lightly marked by state centralization. It would resemble in many ways the cityscape of late fourteenth-century Bruges, shown earlier.

Beginning with Colbert, the state-building modernizers of France were bent on superimposing on this pattern a carefully planned grid of administrative centralization.[70] Their scheme, never entirely realized, was to align highways, canals, and ultimately rail lines to radiate out from Paris like the spokes of a wheel (figure 12). The similarity between this grid and the *tire-aire* of the well-managed state forest as conceived by Colbert was not accidental. They were both devised to maximize access and to facilitate central control. And the kind of simplification involved was, again, entirely relative to location. For an official at the hub, it was now much easier to go to A or to B along the new routes. The layout was designed "to serve the government and the cities and lacking a network of supporting thoroughfares had little to do with popular habit or need. Administrative highways, a historian of the center called them, [were] made for troops to march on and for tax revenues to reach the treasury."[71] For anyone wanting to travel or move goods between A and B, however, things were not so simple. Just as all documents had to "pass through" the official legal language, so too did much of the commercial traffic have to pass through the capital.

The driving intellectual force behind this *esprit géométrique* was, and has remained, the renowned engineers of the Corps des Ponts et

Chaussées.[72] Victor Legrand, the director of Ponts et des Chaussees, was the originator of the *belle idée* of seven grand lines of junction linking Paris to points from the Atlantic to the Mediterranean. His plan became known as the Legrand Star and was proposed first for canals and then, with greater effect, for railroads (among them the Gare du Nord and Gare de l'Est).[73]

As a centralizing aesthetic, the plan defied the canons of commercial logic or cost-effectiveness. The first phase of the grid, the line from Paris east to Strasbourg and the frontier, ran straight through the plateau of Brie rather than following the centers of population along the Marne. By refusing to conform to the topography in its quest of geometric perfection, the railway line was ruinously expensive compared to English or German railroads. The army had also adopted the Ponts et Chaussees logic, believing that direct rail lines to the borders would be militarily advantageous. They were proven tragically wrong in the Franco-Prussian War of 1870–71.[74]

This retrofitting of traffic patterns had enormous consequences, most of which were intended: linking provincial France and provincial French citizens to Paris and to the state and facilitating the deployment of troops from the capital to put down civil unrest in any department in the nation. It was aimed at achieving, for the military control of the nation, what Haussmann had achieved in the capital itself. It thus empowered Paris and the state at the expense of the provinces, greatly affected the economics of location, expedited central fiscal and military control, and severed or weakened lateral cultural and economic ties by favoring hierarchical links. At a stroke, it marginalized outlying areas in the way that official French had marginalized local dialects.

Conclusion

Officials of the modern state are, of necessity, at least one step—and often several steps—removed from the society they are charged with governing. They assess the life of their society by a series of typifications that are always some distance from the full reality these abstractions are meant to capture. Thus the foresters' charts and tables, despite their synoptic power to distill many individual facts into a larger pattern, do not quite capture (nor are they meant to) the real forest in its full diversity. Thus the cadastral survey and the title deed are a rough, often misleading representation of actual, existing rights to land use and disposal. The functionary of any large organization "sees" the human activity that is of interest to him largely through the simplified approximations of documents and statistics: tax proceeds, lists of taxpayers, land records, average incomes, unemployment numbers, mortality rates, trade and productivity figures, the total number of cases of cholera in a certain district.

These typifications are indispensable to statecraft. State simplifications such as maps, censuses, cadastral lists, and standard units of measurement represent techniques for grasping a large and complex reality; in order for officials to be able to comprehend aspects of the ensemble, that complex reality must be reduced to schematic categories. The only way to accomplish this is to reduce an infinite array of detail to a set of categories that will facilitate summary descriptions, comparisons, and aggregation. The invention, elaboration, and deployment of these abstractions represent, as Charles Tilly has shown, an enormous leap in state capacity—a move from tribute and indirect rule to taxation and direct rule. Indirect rule required only a minimal state apparatus but rested on local elites and communities who had an interest in withholding resources and knowledge from the center. Direct rule sparked widespread resistance and necessitated negotiations that often limited the center's power, but for the first time, it allowed state officials direct knowledge of and access to a previously opaque society.

Such is the power of the most advanced techniques of direct rule, that it discovers new social truths as well as merely summarizing known facts. The Center for Disease Control in Atlanta is a striking case in point. Its network of sample hospitals allowed it to first "discover"—in the epidemiological sense—such hitherto unknown diseases as toxic shock syndrome, Legionnaires' disease, and AIDS. Stylized facts of this kind are a powerful form of state knowledge, making it possible for officials to intervene early in epidemics, to understand economic trends that greatly affect public welfare, to gauge whether their policies are having the desired effect, and to make policy with many of the crucial facts at hand.[75] These facts permit discriminating interventions, some of which are literally lifesaving.

The techniques devised to enhance the legibility of a society to its rulers have become vastly more sophisticated, but the political motives driving them have changed little. Appropriation, control, and manipulation (in the nonpejorative sense) remain the most prominent. If we imagine a state that has no reliable means of enumerating and locating its population, gauging its wealth, and mapping its land, resources, and settlements, we are imagining a state whose interventions in that society are necessarily crude. A society that is relatively opaque to the state is thereby insulated from some forms of finely tuned state interventions, both welcomed (universal vaccinations) and resented (personal income taxes). The interventions it does experience will typically be mediated by local trackers who know the society from inside and who are likely to interpose their own particular interests. Without this mediation—and often with it—state action is likely to be inept, greatly overshooting or undershooting its objective.

An illegible society, then, is a hindrance to any effective intervention by the state, whether the purpose of that intervention is plunder or public welfare. As long as the state's interest is largely confined to grabbing a few tons of grain and rounding up a few conscripts, the state's ignorance may not be fatal. When, however, the state's objective requires changing the daily habits (hygiene or health practices) or work performance (quality labor or machine maintenance) of its citizens, such ignorance can well be disabling. A thoroughly legible society eliminates local monopolies of information and creates a kind of national transparency through the uniformity of codes, identities, statistics, regulations, and measures. At the same time it is likely to create new positional advantages for those at the apex who have the knowledge and access to easily decipher the new state-created format.

The discriminating interventions that a legible society makes possible can, of course, be deadly as well. A sobering instance is wordlessly recalled by a map produced by the City Office of Statistics of Amsterdam, then under Nazi occupation, in May 1941 (figure 13).[76] Along with lists of residents, the map was the synoptic representation that guided the rounding up of the city's Jewish population, sixty-five thousand of whom were eventually deported.

The map is titled "The Distribution of Jews in the Municipality." Each dot represents ten Jews, a scheme that makes the heavily Jewish districts readily apparent. The map was compiled from information obtained not only through the order for people of Jewish extraction to register themselves but also through the population registry ("exceptionally comprehensive in the Netherlands")[77] and the business registry. If one reflects briefly on the kind of detailed information on names, addresses, and ethnic backgrounds (determined perhaps by names in the population registry or by declaration) and the cartographic exactitude required to produce this statistical representation, the contribution of legibility to state capacity is evident. The Nazi authorities of course, supplied the murderous purpose behind the exercise, but the legibility provided by the Dutch authorities supplied the means to its efficient implementation.[78] That legibility, I should emphasize, merely amplifies the capacity of the state for discriminating interventions—a capacity that in principle could as easily have been deployed to feed the Jews as to deport them.

13. Map produced by the City Office of Statistics of Amsterdam and entitled "The Distribution of Jews in the Municipality (May 1941)"

Legibility implies a viewer whose place is central and whose vision is synoptic. State simplifications of the kind we have examined are designed to provide authorities with a schematic view of their society, a view not afforded to those without authority. Rather like U.S. highway patrolmen wearing mirrored sunglasses, the authorities enjoy a quasi-monopolistic picture of selected aspects of the whole society. This privileged vantage point is typical of all institutional settings where command and control of complex human activities is paramount. The monastery, the barracks, the factory floor, and the administrative bureaucracy (private or public) exercise many statelike functions and often mimic its information structure as well.

State simplifications can be considered part of an ongoing "project of legibility," a project that is never fully realized. The data from which such simplifications arise are, to varying degrees, riddled with inaccuracies, omissions, faulty aggregations, fraud, negligence, political distortion, and so on. A project of legibility is immanent in any statecraft that aims at manipulating society, but it is undermined by intrastate rivalries, technical obstacles, and, above all, the resistance of its subjects.

State simplifications have at least five characteristics that deserve emphasis. Most obviously, state simplifications are observations of only those aspects of social life that are of official interest. They are *interested*, utilitarian facts. Second, they are also nearly always written (verbal or numerical) *documentary* facts. Third, they are typically *static* facts.[79] Fourth, most stylized state facts are also *aggregate* facts. Aggregate facts may be impersonal (the density of transportation networks) or simply a collection of facts about individuals (employment rates, literacy rates, residence patterns). Finally, for most purposes, state officials need to group citizens in ways that permit them to make a collective assessment. Facts that can be aggregated and presented as averages or distributions must therefore be *standardized* facts. However unique the actual circumstances of the various individuals who make up the aggregate, it is their sameness or, more precisely, their differences along a standardized scale or continuum that are of interest.

The process by which standardized facts susceptible to aggregation are manufactured seems to require at least three steps. The first, indispensable step is the creation of common units of measurement or coding. Size classes of trees, freehold tenure, the metric system for measuring landed property or the volume of grain, uniform naming practices, sections of prairie land, and urban lots of standard sizes are among the units created for this purpose. In the next step, each item or instance falling within a category is counted and classified according to the new unit of assessment. A particular tree reappears as an instance of a certain size class of tree; a particular plot of agricultural land reappears as coordinates in a cadastral map; a particular job reappears as an instance of a category of employment; a particular person reappears bearing a name according to the new formula. Each fact must be recuperated and brought back on stage, as it were, dressed in a new uniform of official weave—as part of "a series in a total classificatory grid."[80] Only in such garb can these facts play a role in the culmination of the process: the creation of wholly new facts by aggregation, following the logic of the new units. One arrives, finally, at synoptic facts that are useful to officials: so many thousands of trees in a given size class, so many thousands of men between the ages of eighteen and thirty-five, so many farms in a given size class, so many students whose surnames begin with the letter A, so many people with tuberculosis. Combining several metrics of aggregation, one arrives at quite subtle, complex, heretofore unknown truths, including, for example, the distribution of tubercular patients by income and urban location.

To call such elaborate artifacts of knowledge "state simplifications" risks being misleading. They are anything but simple-minded, and they are often wielded with great sophistication by officials. Rather, the term "simplification" is meant in two quite specific senses. First, the knowledge that an official needs must give him or her a synoptic view of the ensemble; it must be cast in terms that are replicable across many cases. In this respect, such facts must lose their particularity and reappear in schematic or simplified form as a member of a class of facts.[81] Second, in a meaning closely related to the first, the grouping of synoptic facts necessarily entails collapsing or ignoring distinctions that might otherwise be relevant.

Take, for example, simplifications about employment. The working lives of many people are exceptionally complex and may change from day to day. For the purposes of official statistics, however, being "gainfully employed" is a stylized fact; one is or is not gainfully employed. Also, available characterizations of many rather exotic working lives are sharply restricted by the categories used in the aggregate statistics.[82] Those who gather and interpret such aggregate data understand that there is a certain fictional and arbitrary quality to their categories and that they hide a wealth of problematic variation. Once set, however, these thin categories operate unavoidably as if all similarly classified cases were in fact homogeneous and uniform. All Normalbäume in a given size range are the same; all soil in a defined soil class is statistically identical; all autoworkers (if we are classifying by industry) are alike; all Catholics (if we are classifying by religious faith) are alike. There is, as Theodore Porter notes in his study of mechanical objectivity, a "strong incentive to prefer precise and standardizable measures to highly accurate ones," since accuracy is meaningless if the identical procedure cannot reliably be performed elsewhere.[83]

To this point, I have been making a rather straightforward, even banal point about the simplification, abstraction, and standardization that are necessary for state officials' observations of the circumstances of some or all of the population. But I want to make a further claim, one analogous to that made for scientific forestry: the modern state, through its officials, attempts with varying success to create a terrain and a population with precisely those standardized characteristics that will be easiest to monitor, count, assess, and manage. The utopian, immanent, and continually frustrated goal of the modern state is to reduce the chaotic, disorderly, constantly changing social reality beneath it to something more closely resembling the administrative grid of its observations. Much of the statecraft of the late eighteenth and nineteenth centuries was devoted to this project. "In the period of movement from tribute to tax, from indirect rule to direct rule, from subordination to assimilation," Tilly remarks, "states generally worked to homogenize their populations and break down their segmentation by imposing common languages, religions, currencies, and legal systems, as well as promoting the construction of connected systems of trade, transportation, and communication."[84]

As the scientific forester may dream of a perfectly legible forest planted with same-aged, single-species, uniform trees growing in straight lines in a rectangular flat space cleared of all underbrush and poachers,[85] so the exacting state official may aspire to a perfectly legible population with registered, unique names and addresses keyed to grid settlements; who pursue single, identifiable occupations; and all of whose transactions are documented according to the designated formula and in the official language. This caricature of society as a military parade ground is overdrawn, but the grain of truth that it embodies may help us understand the grandiose plans we will examine later.[86] The aspiration to such uniformity and order alerts us to the fact that modern statecraft is largely a project of internal colonization, often glossed, as it is in imperial rhetoric, as a "civilizing mission." The builders of the modern nation-state do not merely describe, observe, and map; they strive to shape a people and landscape that will fit their techniques of observation.[87]

This tendency is perhaps one shared by many large hierarchical organizations. As Donald Chisholm, in reviewing the literature on administrative coordination, concludes, "central coordinating schemes do work effectively under conditions where the task environment is known and unchanging, where it can be treated as a closed system."[88] The more static, standardized, and uniform a population or social space is, the more legible it is, and the more amenable it is to the techniques of state officials. I am suggesting that many state activities aim at transforming the population, space, and nature under their jurisdiction into the closed systems that offer no surprises and that can best be observed and controlled.

State officials can often make their categories stick and impose their simplifications, because the state, of all institutions, is best equipped to insist on treating people according to its schemata. Thus categories that may have begun as the artificial inventions of cadastral surveyors, census takers, judges, or police officers can end by becoming categories that organize people's daily experience precisely because they are embedded in state-created institutions that structure that experience.[89] The economic plan, survey map, record of ownership, forest management plan, classification of ethnicity, passbook, arrest record, and map of political boundaries acquire their force from the fact that these synoptic data are the points of departure for reality as state officials apprehend and shape it. In dictatorial settings where there is no effective way to assert another reality, fictitious facts-on-paper can often be made eventually to prevail on the ground, because it is on behalf of such pieces of paper that police and army are deployed.

These paper records are the operative facts in a court of law, in an administrative dossier, and before most functionaries. In this sense, there are virtually no other facts for the state than those that are contained in documents standardized for that purpose. An error in such a document can have far more power—and for far longer—than can an unreported truth. If, for example, you want to defend your claim to real property, you are normally obliged to defend it with a document called a property deed, and to do so in the courts and tribunals created for that purpose. If you wish to have any standing in law, you must have a document that officials accept as evidence of citizenship, be that document a birth certificate, passport, or identity card. The categories used by state agents are not merely means to make their environment legible; they are an authoritative tune to which most of the population must dance.

Part 2

Transforming Visions

3 Authoritarian High Modernism

> Then, as this morning on the dock, again I saw, as if for the first time in my life, the impeccably straight streets, the glistening glass of the pavement, the divine parallelepipeds of the transparent dwellings, the square harmony of the grayish blue rows of Numbers. And it seemed to me that not past generations, but I myself, had won a victory over the old god and the old life.
> —Eugene Zamiatin, *We*

> Modern science, which displaced and replaced God, removed that obstacle [limits on freedom]. It also created a vacancy: the office of the supreme legislator-cum-manager, of the designer and administrator of the world order, was now horrifyingly empty. It had to be filled or else. . . . The emptiness of the throne was throughout the modern era a standing and tempting invitation to visionaries and adventurers. The dream of an all-embracing order and harmony remained as vivid as ever, and it seemed now closer than ever, more than ever within human reach. It was now up to mortal earthlings to bring it about and to secure its ascendancy.
> —Zygmunt Bauman, *Modernity and the Holocaust*

All the state simplifications that we have examined have the character of maps. That is, they are designed to summarize precisely those aspects of a complex world that are of immediate interest to the mapmaker and to ignore the rest. To complain that a map lacks nuance and detail makes no sense unless it omits information necessary to its function. A city map that aspired to represent every traffic light, every pothole, every building, and every bush and tree in every park would threaten to become as large and as complex as the city that it depicted.[1] And it certainly would defeat the purpose of mapping, which is to abstract and summarize. A map is an instrument designed for a purpose. We may judge that purpose noble or morally offensive, but the map itself either serves or fails to serve its intended use.

In case after case, however, we have remarked on the apparent power of maps to transform as well as merely to summarize the facts that they portray. This transformative power resides not in the map, of course, but rather in the power possessed by those who deploy the perspective of that particular map.[2] A private corporation aiming to maximize sustainable timber yields, profit, or production will map its world according to this logic and will use what power it has to ensure that the logic of its map prevails. The state has no monopoly on utilitarian simplifications. What the state does at least aspire to, though, is a monopoly on the legitimate use of force. That is surely why, from the seventeenth century until now, the most transformative maps have been those invented and applied by the most powerful institution in society: the state.

Until recently, the ability of the state to impose its schemes on society was limited by the state's modest ambitions and its limited capacity. Although utopian aspirations to a finely tuned social control can be traced back to Enlightenment thought and to monastic and military practices, the eighteenth-century European state was still largely a machine for extraction. It is true that state officials, particularly under absolutism, had mapped much more of their kingdoms' populations, land tenures, production, and trade than their predecessors had and that they had become increasingly efficient in pumping revenue, grain, and conscripts from the countryside. But there was more than a little irony in their claim to absolute rule. They lacked the consistent coercive power, the fine-grained administrative grid, or the detailed knowledge that would have permitted them to undertake more intrusive experiments in social engineering. To give their growing ambitions full rein, they required a far greater hubris, a state machinery that was equal to the task, and a society they could master. By the mid–nineteenth century in the West and by the early twentieth century elsewhere, these conditions were being met.

I believe that many of the most tragic episodes of state development in the late nineteenth and twentieth centuries originate in a particularly pernicious combination of three elements. The first is the aspiration to the administrative ordering of nature and society, an aspiration that we have already seen at work in scientific forestry, but one raised to a far more comprehensive and ambitious level. "High modernism" seems an appropriate term for this aspiration.[3] As a faith, it was shared by many across a wide spectrum of political ideologies. Its main carriers and exponents were the avant-garde among engineers, planners, technocrats, high-level administrators, architects, scientists, and visionaries. If one were to imagine a pantheon or Hall of Fame of high-modernist figures, it would almost certainly include such names as Henri Comte de Saint-Simon, Le Corbusier, Walther Rathenau, Robert McNamara, Robert Moses, Jean Monnet, the Shah of Iran, David Lilienthal, Vladimir I. Lenin, Leon Trotsky, and Julius Nyerere.[4] They envisioned a sweeping, rational engineering of all aspects of social life in order to improve the human condition. As a conviction, high modernism was not the exclusive property of any political tendency; it had both right- and left-wing variants, as we shall see. The second element is the unrestrained use of the power of the modern state as an instrument for achieving these designs. The third element is a weakened or prostrate civil society that lacks the capacity to resist these plans. The ideology of high modernism provides, as it were, the desire; the modern state provides the means of acting on that desire; and the incapacitated civil society provides the leveled terrain on which to build (dis)utopias.

We shall return shortly to the premises of high modernism. But here it is important to note that many of the great state-sponsored calamities of the twentieth century have been the work of rulers with grandiose and utopian plans for their society. One can identify a high-modernist utopianism of the right, of which Nazism is surely the diagnostic example.[5] The massive social engineering under apartheid in South Africa, the modernization plans of the Shah of Iran, villagization in Vietnam, and huge late-colonial development schemes (for example, the Gezira scheme in the Sudan) could be considered under this rubric.[6] And yet there is no denying that much of the massive, state-enforced social engineering of the twentieth century has been the work of progressive, often revolutionary elites. Why?

The answer, I believe, lies in the fact that it is typically progressives who have come to power with a comprehensive critique of existing society and a popular mandate (at least initially) to transform it. These progressives have wanted to use that power to bring about enormous changes in people's habits, work, living patterns, moral conduct, and worldview.[7] They have deployed what Václav Havel has called "the armory of holistic social engineering."[8] Utopian aspirations per se are not dangerous. As Oscar Wilde remarked, "A map of the world which does not include Utopia is not worth even glancing at, for it leaves out the one country at which Humanity is always landing."[9] Where the utopian vision goes wrong is when it is held by ruling elites with no commitment to democracy or civil rights and who are therefore likely to use unbridled state power for its achievement. Where it goes brutally wrong is when the society subjected to such utopian experiments lacks the capacity to mount a determined resistance.

What is high modernism, then? It is best conceived as a strong (one might even say muscle-bound) version of the beliefs in scientific and technical progress that were associated with industrialization in Western Europe and in North America from roughly 1830 until World War I. At its center was a supreme self-confidence about continued linear progress, the development of scientific and technical knowledge, the expansion of production, the rational design of social order, the growing satisfaction of human needs, and, not least, an increasing control over nature (including human nature) commensurate with scientific understanding of natural laws.[10] *High* modernism is thus a particularly sweeping vision of how the benefits of technical and scientific progress might be applied—usually through the state—in every field of human activity.[11] If, as we have seen, the simplified, utilitarian *descriptions* of state officials had a tendency, through the exercise of state power, to bring the facts into line with their representations, then one might say that the high-modern state began with extensive *prescriptions* for a new society, and it intended to impose them.

It would have been hard not to have been a modernist of some stripe at the end of the nineteenth century in the West. How could one fail to be impressed—even awed—by the vast transformation wrought by science and industry?[12] Anyone who was, say, sixty years old in Manchester, England, would have witnessed in his or her lifetime a revolution in the manufacturing of cotton and wool textiles, the growth of the factory system, the application of steam power and other astounding new mechanical devices to production, remarkable breakthroughs in metallurgy and transportation (especially railroads), and the appearance of cheap mass-produced commodities. Given the stunning advances in chemistry, physics, medicine, math, and engineering, anyone even slightly attentive to the world of science would have almost come to expect a continuing stream of new marvels (such as the internal combustion engine and electricity). The unprecedented transformations of the nineteenth century may have impoverished and marginalized many, but even the victims recognized that something revolutionary was afoot. All this sounds rather naive today, when we are far more sober about the limits and costs of technological progress and have acquired a postmodern skepticism about any totalizing discourse. Still, this new sensibility ignores both the degree to which modernist assumptions prevail in our lives and, especially, the great enthusiasm and revolutionary hubris that were part and parcel of high modernism.

The Discovery of Society

The path from description to prescription was not so much an inadvertent result of a deep psychological tendency as a deliberate move. The point of the Enlightenment view of legal codes was less to mirror the distinctive customs and practices of a people than to create a cultural community by codifying and generalizing the most rational of those customs and suppressing the more obscure and barbaric ones.[13] Establishing uniform standards of weight and measurement across a kingdom had a greater purpose than just making trade easier; the new standards were intended both to express and to promote a new cultural unity. Well before the tools existed to make good on this cultural revolution, Enlightenment thinkers such as Condorcet were looking ahead to the day when the tools would be in place. He wrote in 1782: "Those sciences, created almost in our own days, the object of which is man himself, the direct goal of which is the happiness of man, will enjoy a progress no less sure than that of the physical sciences, and this idea so sweet, that our descendants will surpass us in wisdom as in enlightenment, is no longer an illusion. In meditating on the nature of the moral sciences, one cannot help seeing that, as they are based like physical sciences on the observation of fact, they must follow the same method, acquire a language equally exact and precise, attaining the same degree of certainty."[14] The gleam in Condorcet's eye became, by the mid–nineteenth century, an active utopian project. Simplification and rationalization previously applied to forests, weights and measures, taxation, and factories were now applied to the design of society as a whole.[15] Industrial-strength social engineering was born. While factories and forests might be planned by private entrepreneurs, the ambition of engineering whole societies was almost exclusively a project of the nation-state.

This new conception of the state's role represented a fundamental transformation. Before then, the state's activities had been largely confined to those that contributed to the wealth and power of the sovereign, as the example of scientific forestry and cameral science illustrated. The idea that one of the central purposes of the state was the improvement of all the members of society—their health, skills and education, longevity, productivity, morals, and family life—was quite novel.[16] There was, of course, a direct connection between the old conception of the state and this new one. A state that improved its population's skills, vigor, civic morals, and work habits would increase its tax base and field better armies; it was a policy that any enlightened sovereign might pursue. And yet, in the nineteenth century, the welfare of the population came increasingly to be seen, not merely as a means to national strength, but as an end in itself.

One essential precondition of this transformation was the discovery of society as a reified object that was separate from the state and that could be scientifically described. In this respect, the production of statistical knowledge about the population—its age profiles, occupations, fertility, literacy, property ownership, law-abidingness (as demonstrated by crime statistics)—allowed state officials to characterize the population in elaborate new ways, much as scientific forestry permitted the forester to carefully describe the forest. Ian Hacking explains how a suicide or homicide rate, for example, came to be seen as a characteristic of a people, so that one could speak of a "budget" of homicides that would be "spent" each year, like routine debits from an account, although the particular murderers and their victims were unknown.[17] Statistical facts were elaborated into social laws. It was but a small step from a simplified description of society to a design and manipulation of society, with its improvement in mind. If one could reshape nature to design a more suitable forest, why not reshape society to create a more suitable population?

The scope of intervention was potentially endless. Society became an object that the state might manage and transform with a view toward perfecting it. A progressive nation-state would set about engineering its society according to the most advanced technical standards of the new moral sciences. The existing social order, which had been more or less taken by earlier states as a given, reproducing itself under the watchful eye of the state, was for the first time the subject of active management. It was possible to conceive of an artificial, engineered society designed, not by custom and historical accident, but according to conscious, rational, scientific criteria. Every nook and cranny of the social order might be improved upon: personal hygiene, diet, child rearing, housing, posture, recreation, family structure, and, most infamously, the genetic inheritance of the population.[18] The working poor were often the first subjects of scientific social planning.[19] Schemes for improving their daily lives were promulgated by progressive urban and public-health policies and instituted in model factory towns and newly founded welfare agencies. Subpopulations found wanting in ways that were potentially threatening—such as indigents, vagabonds, the mentally ill, and criminals—might be made the objects of the most intensive social engineering.[20]

The metaphor of gardening, Zygmunt Bauman suggests, captures much of this new spirit. The gardener—perhaps a landscape architect specializing in formal gardens is the most appropriate parallel—takes a natural site and creates an entirely designed space of botanical order. Although the organic character of the flora limits what can be achieved, the gardener has enormous discretion in the overall arrangement and in training, pruning, planting, and weeding out selected plants. As an untended forest is to a long-managed scientific forest, so untended nature is to the garden. The garden is one of man's attempts to impose his own principles of order, utility, and beauty on nature.[21] What grows in the garden is always a small, consciously selected sample of what *might* be grown there. Similarly, social engineers consciously set out to design and maintain a more perfect social order. An Enlightenment belief in the self-improvement of man became, by degrees, a belief in the perfectibility of social order.

One of the great paradoxes of social engineering is that it seems at odds with the experience of modernity generally. Trying to jell a social world, the most striking characteristic of which appears to be flux, seems rather like trying to manage a whirlwind. Marx was hardly alone in claiming that the "constant revolutionizing of production, uninterrupted disturbance of all social relations, everlasting uncertainty and agitation, distinguish the bourgeois epoch from all earlier times."[22] The experience of modernity (in literature, art, industry, transportation, and popular culture) was, above all, the experience of disorienting speed, movement, and change, which self-proclaimed modernists found exhilarating and liberating.[23] Perhaps the most charitable way of resolving this paradox is to imagine that what these designers of society had in mind was roughly what designers of locomotives had in mind with "streamlining." Rather than arresting social change, they hoped to design a shape to social life that would minimize the friction of progress. The difficulty with this resolution is that state social engineering was inherently authoritarian. In place of multiple sources of invention and change, there was a single planning authority; in place of the plasticity and autonomy of existing social life, there was a fixed social order in which positions were designated. The tendency toward various forms of "social taxidermy" was unavoidable.

The Radical Authority of High Modernism

> The real thing is that this time we're going to get science applied to social problems and backed by the whole force of the state, just as war has been backed by the whole force of the state in the past.
> —C. S. Lewis, *That Hideous Strength*

The troubling features of high modernism derive, for the most part, from its claim to speak about the improvement of the human condition with the authority of scientific knowledge and its tendency to disallow other competing sources of judgment.

First and foremost, high modernism implies a truly radical break with history and tradition. Insofar as rational thought and scientific laws could provide a single answer to every empirical question, nothing ought to be taken for granted. All human habits and practices that were inherited and hence not based on scientific reasoning—from the structure of the family and patterns of residence to moral values and forms of production—would have to be reexamined and redesigned. The structures of the past were typically the products of myth, superstition, and religious prejudice. It followed that scientifically designed schemes for production and social life would be superior to received tradition.

The sources of this view are deeply authoritarian. If a planned social order is better than the accidental, irrational deposit of historical practice, two conclusions follow. Only those who have the scientific knowledge to discern and create this superior social order are fit to rule in the new age. Further, those who through retrograde ignorance refuse to yield to the scientific plan need to be educated to its benefits or else swept aside. Strong versions of high modernism, such as those held by Lenin and Le Corbusier, cultivated an Olympian ruthlessness toward the subjects of their interventions. At its most radical, high modernism imagined wiping the slate utterly clean and beginning from zero.[24]

High-modernist ideology thus tends to devalue or banish politics. Political interests can only frustrate the social solutions devised by specialists with scientific tools adequate to their analysis. As individuals, high modernists might well hold democratic views about popular sovereignty or classical liberal views about the inviolability of a private sphere that restrained them, but such convictions are external to, and often at war with, their high-modernist convictions.

Although high modernists came to imagine the refashioning of social habits and of human nature itself, they began with a nearly limitless ambition to transform nature to suit man's purposes—an ambition that remained central to their faith. How completely the utopian possibilities gripped intellectuals of almost every political persuasion is captured in the paean to technical progress of the *Communist Manifesto*, where Marx and Engels write of the "subjection of nature's forces to man, machinery, and the application of chemistry to agriculture and industry, steam navigation, railways, electric telegraphs, clearing of whole continents for cultivation, canalization of rivers, whole populations conjured out of the ground."[25] In fact, this promise, made plausible by capitalist development, was for Marx the point of departure for socialism, which would place the fruits of capitalism at the service of the working class for the first time. The intellectual air in the late nineteenth century was filled with proposals for such vast engineering projects as the Suez Canal, which was completed in 1869 with enormous consequences for trade between Asia and Europe. The pages of *Le globe*, the organ of utopian socialists of Saint-Simon's persuasion, featured an endless stream of discussions about massive projects: the construction of Panama Canal, the development of the United States, far-reaching schemes for energy and transportation. This belief that it was man's destiny to tame nature to suit his interests and preserve his safety is perhaps the keystone of high modernism, partly because the success of so many grand ventures was already manifest.[26]

Once again the authoritarian and statist implications of this vision are clear. The very scale of such projects meant that, with few exceptions (such as the early canals), they demanded large infusions of monies raised through taxes or credit. Even if one could imagine them being financed privately in a capitalist economy, they typically required a vast public authority empowered to condemn private property, relocate people against their will, guarantee the loans or bonds required, and coordinate the work of the many state agencies involved. In a statist society, be it Louis Napoleon's France or Lenin's Soviet Union, such power was already built into the political system. In a nonstatist society, such tasks have required new public authorities or "superagencies" having quasi-governmental powers for sending men to the moon or for constructing dams, irrigation works, highways, and public transportation systems.

The temporal emphasis of high modernism is almost exclusively on the future. Although any ideology with a large altar dedicated to progress is bound to privilege the future, high modernism carries this to great lengths. The past is an impediment, a history that must be transcended; the present is the platform for launching plans for a better future. A key characteristic of discourses of high modernism and of the public pronouncements of those states that have embraced it is a heavy reliance on visual images of heroic progress toward a totally transformed future.[27] The strategic choice of the future is freighted with consequences. To the degree that the future is known and achievable— a belief that the faith in progress encourages—the less future benefits are discounted for uncertainty. The practical effect is to convince most high modernists that the certainty of a better future justifies the many short-term sacrifices required to get there.[28] The ubiquity of five-year plans in socialist states is an example of that conviction. Progress is objectified by a series of preconceived goals—largely material and quantifiable—which are to be achieved through savings, labor, and investments in the interim. There may, of course, be no alternative to planning, especially when the urgency of a single goal, such as winning a war, seems to require the subordination of every other goal. The immanent logic of such an exercise, however, implies a degree of certainty about the future, about means-ends calculations, and about the meaning of human welfare that is truly heroic. That such plans have often had to be adjusted or abandoned is an indication of just how heroic are the assumptions behind them.

In this reading, high modernism ought to appeal greatly to the classes and strata who have most to gain—in status, power, and wealth—from its worldview. And indeed it is the ideology par excellence of the bureaucratic intelligentsia, technicians, planners, and engineers.[29] The position accorded to them is not just one of rule and privilege but also one of responsibility for the great works of nation building and social transformation. Where this intelligentsia conceives of its mission as the dragging of a technically backward, unschooled, subsistence-oriented population into the twentieth century, its self-assigned cultural role as educator of its people becomes doubly grandiose. Having a historic mission of such breadth may provide a ruling intelligentsia with high morale, solidarity, and the willingness to make (and impose) sacrifices. This vision of a great future is often in sharp contrast to the disorder, misery, and unseemly scramble for petty advantage that the elites very likely see in their daily foreground. One might in fact speculate that the more intractable and resistant the real world faced by the planner, the greater the need for utopian plans to fill, as it were, the void that would otherwise invite despair. The elites who elaborate such plans implicitly represent themselves as exemplars of the learning and progressive views to which their compatriots might aspire. Given the ideological advantages of high modernism as a discourse, it is hardly surprising that so many postcolonial elites have marched under its banner.[30]

Aided by hindsight as it is, this unsympathetic account of high-modernist audacity is, in one important respect, grossly unfair. If we put the development of high-modernist beliefs in their historical context, if we ask who the enemies of high modernism actually were, a far more sympathetic picture emerges. Doctors and public-health engineers who did possess new knowledge that could save millions of lives were often thwarted by popular prejudices and entrenched political interests. Urban planners who could in fact redesign urban housing to be cheaper, more healthful, and more convenient were blocked by real-estate interests and existing tastes. Inventors and engineers who had devised revolutionary new modes of power and transportation faced opposition from industrialists and laborers whose profits and jobs the new technology would almost certainly displace.

For nineteenth-century high modernists, the scientific domination of nature (including human nature) was emancipatory. It "promised freedom from scarcity, want and the arbitrariness of natural calamity," David Harvey observes. "The development of rational forms of social organization and rational modes of thought promised liberation from the irrationalities of myth, religion, superstition, release from the arbitrary use of power as well as from the dark side of our human natures."[31] Before we turn to later versions of high modernism, we should recall two important facts about their nineteenth-century forebears: first, that virtually every high-modernist intervention was undertaken in the name of and with the support of citizens seeking help and protection, and, second, that we are all beneficiaries, in countless ways, of these various high-modernist schemes.

Twentieth-Century High Modernism

The idea of a root-and-branch, rational engineering of entire social orders in creating realizable utopias is a largely twentieth-century phenomenon. And a range of historical soils have seemed particularly favorable for the flourishing of high-modernist ideology. Those soils include crises of state power, such as wars and economic depressions, and circumstances in which a state's capacity for relatively unimpeded planning is greatly enhanced, such as the revolutionary conquest of power and colonial rule.

The industrial warfare of the twentieth century has required unprecedented steps toward the total mobilization of the society and the economy.[32] Even quite liberal societies like the United States and Britain became, in the context of war mobilization, directly administered societies. The worldwide depression of the 1930s similarly propelled liberal states into extensive experiments in social and economic planning in an effort to relieve economic distress and to retain popular legitimacy. In the cases of war and depression, the rush toward an administered society has an aspect of *force majeure* to it. The postwar rebuilding of a war-torn nation may well fall in the same category.

Revolution and colonialism, however, are hospitable to high modernism for different reasons. A revolutionary regime and a colonial regime each disposes of an unusual degree of power. The revolutionary state has defeated the ancien régime, often has its partisans' mandate to remake the society after its image, *and* faces a prostrate civil society whose capacity for active resistance is limited.[33] The millennial expectations commonly associated with revolutionary movements give further impetus to high-modernist ambitions. Colonial regimes, particularly late colonial regimes, have often been sites of extensive experiments in social engineering.[34] An ideology of "welfare colonialism" combined with the authoritarian power inherent in colonial rule have encouraged ambitious schemes to remake native societies.

If one were required to pinpoint the "birth" of twentieth-century high modernism, specifying a particular time, place, and individual—

in what is admittedly a rather arbitrary exercise, given high modernism's many intellectual wellsprings—a strong case can be made for German mobilization during World War I and the figure most closely associated with it, Walther Rathenau. German economic mobilization was the technocratic wonder of the war. That Germany kept its armies in the field and adequately supplied long after most observers had predicted its collapse was largely due to Rathenau's planning.[35] An industrial engineer and head of the great electrical firm A.E.G (Allgemeine Elektricitäts-Gesellschaft), which had been founded by his father, Rathenau was placed in charge of the Office of War Raw Materials (Kriegsrohstoffabteilung).[36] He realized that the planned rationing of raw materials and transport was the key to sustaining the war effort. Inventing a planned economy step by step, as it were, Germany achieved feats—in industrial production, munitions and armament supply, transportation and traffic control, price controls, and civilian rationing—that had never before been attempted. The scope of planning and coordination necessitated an unprecedented mobilization of conscripts, soldiers, and war-related industrial labor. Such mobilization fostered the idea of creating "administered mass organizations" that would encompass the entire society.[37]

Rathenau's faith in pervasive planning and in rationalizing production had deep roots in the intellectual connection being forged between the physical laws of thermodynamics on one hand and the new applied sciences of work on the other. For many specialists, a narrow and materialist "productivism" treated human labor as a mechanical system which could be decomposed into energy transfers, motion, and the physics of work. The simplification of labor into isolated problems of mechanical efficiencies led directly to the aspiration for a scientific control of the entire labor process. Late nineteenth-century materialism, as Anson Rabinbach emphasizes, had an equivalence between technology and physiology at its metaphysical core.[38]

This productivism had at least two distinct lineages, one of them North American and the other European. An American contribution came from the influential work of Frederick Taylor, whose minute decomposition of factory labor into isolable, precise, repetitive motions had begun to revolutionize the organization of factory work.[39] For the factory manager or engineer, the newly invented assembly lines permitted the use of unskilled labor and control over not only the pace of production but the whole labor process. The European tradition of "energetics," which focused on questions of motion, fatigue, measured rest, rational hygiene, and nutrition, also treated the worker notionally as a machine, albeit a machine that must be well fed and kept in good working order. In place of worker*s*, there was an abstract, standardized worker with uniform physical capacities and needs. Seen initially as a way of increasing wartime efficiency at the front and in industry, the Kaiser Wilhelm Institut für Arbeitsphysiologie, like Taylorism, was based on a scheme to rationalize the body.[40]

What is most remarkable about both traditions is, once again, how widely they were believed by educated elites who were otherwise poles apart politically. "Taylorism and technocracy were the watchwords of a three-pronged idealism: the elimination of economic and social crisis, the expansion of productivity through science, and the reenchantment of technology. The vision of society in which social conflict was eliminated in favor of technological and scientific imperatives could embrace liberal, socialist, authoritarian, and even communist and fascist solutions. Productivism, in short, was politically promiscuous."[41]

The appeal of one or another form of productivism across much of the right and center of the political spectrum was largely due to its promise as a technological "fix" for class struggle. If, as its advocates claimed, it could vastly increase worker output, then the politics of redistribution could be replaced by class collaboration, in which both profits and wages could grow at once. For much of the left, productivism promised the replacement of the capitalist by the engineer or by the state expert or official. It also proposed a single optimum solution, or "best practice," for any problem in the organization of work. The logical outcome was some form of slide-rule authoritarianism in the interest, presumably, of all.[42]

A combination of Rathenau's broad training in philosophy and economics, his wartime experience with planning, and the social conclusions that he thought were inherent in the precision, reach, and transforming potential of electric power allowed him to draw the broadest lessons for social organization. In the war, private industry had given way to a kind of state socialism; "gigantic industrial enterprises had transcended their ostensibly private owners and all the laws of property."[43] The decisions required had nothing to do with ideology; they were driven by purely technical and economic necessities. The rule of specialists and the new technological possibilities, particularly huge electric power grids, made possible a new social-industrial order that was both centralized and locally autonomous. During the time when war made necessary a coalition among industrial firms, technocrats, and the state, Rathenau discerned the shape of a progressive peacetime society. Inasmuch as the technical and economic requirements for reconstruction were obvious and required the same sort of collaboration in all countries, Rathenau's rationalist faith in planning had an internationalist flavor. He characterized the modern era as a "new machine order . . . [and] a consolidation of the world into an unconscious association of constraint, into an uninterrupted community of production and harmony."[44]

The world war was the high-water mark for the political influence of engineers and planners. Having seen what could be accomplished in extremis, they imagined what they could achieve if the identical energy and planning were devoted to popular welfare rather than mass destruction. Together with many political leaders, industrialists, labor leaders, and prominent intellectuals (such as Philip Gibbs in England, Ernst Jünger in Germany, and Gustave Le Bon in France), they concluded that only a renewed and comprehensive dedication to technical innovation and the planning it made possible could rebuild the European economies and bring social peace.[45]

Lenin himself was deeply impressed by the achievements of German industrial mobilization and believed that it had shown how production might be socialized. Just as Lenin believed that Marx had discovered immutable social laws akin to Darwin's laws of evolution, so he believed that the new technologies of mass production were scientific laws and not social constructions. Barely a month before the October 1917 revolution, he wrote that the war had "accelerated the development of capitalism to such a tremendous degree, converting monopoly capitalism into *state*-monopoly capitalism, that *neither* the proletariat *nor* the revolutionary petty-bourgeois democrats *can* keep within the limits of capitalism."[46] He and his economic advisers drew directly on the work of Rathenau and Mollendorf in their plans for the Soviet economy. The German war economy was for Lenin "the ultimate in modern, large-scale capitalist techniques, planning and organization"; he took it to be the prototype of a socialized economy.[47] Presumably, if the state in question were in the hands of representatives of the working class, the basis of a socialist system would exist. Lenin's vision of the future looked much like Rathenau's, providing, of course, we ignore the not so small matter of a revolutionary seizure of power.

Lenin was not slow to appreciate how Taylorism on the factory floor offered advantages for the socialist control of production. Although he had earlier denounced such techniques, calling them the "scientific extortion of sweat," by the time of the revolution he had become an enthusiastic advocate of systematic control as practiced in Germany. He extolled "the principle of discipline, organization, and harmonious cooperation based upon the most modern, mechanized industry, the most rigid system of accountability and control."[48]

The Taylor system, the last word of capitalism in this respect, like all capitalist progress, is a combination of the subtle brutality of bourgeois exploitation and a number of its great scientific achievements in the fields of analysing mechanical motions during work, the elimination of superfluous and awkward motions, the working out of correct methods of work, the introduction of the best system of accounting and control, etc. The Soviet Republic must at all costs adopt all that is valuable in the achievements of science and technology in this field. . . . We must organize in Russia the study and teaching of the Taylor system and systematically try it out and adapt it to our purposes.[49]

By 1918, with production falling, he was calling for rigid work norms and, if necessary, the reintroduction of hated piecework. The first All-Russian Congress for Initiatives in Scientific Management was convened in 1921 and featured disputes between advocates of Taylorism and those of energetics (also called ergonomics). At least twenty institutes and as many journals were by then devoted to scientific management in the Soviet Union. A command economy at the macrolevel and Taylorist principles of central coordination at the microlevel of the factory floor provided an attractive and symbiotic package for an authoritarian, high-modernist revolutionary like Lenin.

Despite the authoritarian temptations of twentieth-century high modernism, they have often been resisted. The reasons are not only complex; they are different from case to case. While it is not my intention to examine in detail all the potential obstacles to high-modernist planning, the particular barrier posed by liberal democratic ideas and institutions deserves emphasis. Three factors seem decisive. The first is the existence and belief in a private sphere of activity in which the state and its agencies may not legitimately interfere. To be sure, this zone of autonomy has had a beleaguered existence as, following Mannheim, more heretofore private spheres have been made the object of official intervention. Much of the work of Michel Foucault was an attempt to map these incursions into health, sexuality, mental illness, vagrancy, or sanitation and the strategies behind them. Nevertheless, the idea of a private realm has served to limit the ambitions of many high modernists, through either their own political values or their healthy respect for the political storm that such incursions would provoke.

The second, closely related factor is the private sector in liberal political economy. As Foucault put it: unlike absolutism and mercantilism, "political economy announces the unknowability for the sovereign of the totality of economic processes and, as a consequence, the *impossibility of an economic sovereignty*."[50] The point of liberal political economy was not only that a free market protected property and created wealth but also that the economy was far too complex for it ever to be managed in detail by a hierarchical administration.[51]

The third and by far most important barrier to thoroughgoing high-modernist schemes has been the existence of working, representative institutions through which a resistant society could make its influence felt. Such institutions have thwarted the most draconian features of high-modernist schemes in roughly the same way that publicity and mobilized opposition in open societies, as Amartya Sen has argued, have prevented famines. Rulers, he notes, do not go hungry, and they are unlikely to learn about and respond readily to curb famine unless their institutional position provides strong incentives. The freedoms of speech, of assembly, and of the press ensure that widespread hunger will be publicized, while the freedoms of assembly and elections in representative institutions ensure that it is in the interest of elected officials' self-preservation to prevent famine when they can. In the same fashion, high-modernist schemes in liberal democratic settings must accommodate themselves sufficiently to local opinion in order to avoid being undone at the polls.

But high modernism, unimpeded by liberal political economy, is best grasped through the working out of its high ambitions and its consequences. It is to this practical terrain in urban planning and revolutionary discourse that we now turn.

4 The High-Modernist City: An Experiment and a Critique

> No one, wise Kuublai, knows better than you that the city must never be confused with the words that describe it.
> —Italo Calvino, *Invisible Cities*

> Time is a fatal handicap to the baroque conception of the world: its mechanical order makes no allowances for growth, change, adaptation, and creative renewal. In short, a baroque plan was a block achievement. It must be laid out at a stroke, fixed and frozen forever, as if done overnight by Arabian nights genii. Such a plan demands an architectural despot, working for an absolute ruler, who will live long enough to complete their own conceptions. To alter this type of plan, to introduce fresh elements of another style, is to break its esthetic backbone.
> —Lewis Mumford, *The City in History*

In Mumford's epigraph to this chapter, his criticism is directed at Pierre-Charles L'Enfant's Washington in particular and at baroque urban planning in general.[1] Greatly amplified, Mumford's criticism could be applied to the work and thought of the Swiss-born French essayist, painter, architect, and planner Charles-Edouard Jeanneret, who is better known by his professional name, Le Corbusier. Jeanneret was the embodiment of high-modernist urban design. Active roughly between 1920 and 1960, he was less an architect than a visionary planner of planetary ambitions. The great majority of his gargantuan schemes were never built; they typically required a political resolve and financial wherewithal that few political authorities could muster. Some monuments to his expansive genius do exist, the most notable of which are perhaps Chandigarh, the austere capital of India's Punjab, and L'Unité d'Habitation, a large apartment complex in Marseilles, but his legacy is most apparent in the logic of his unbuilt megaprojects. At one time or another he proposed city-planning schemes for Paris, Algiers, São Paulo, Rio de Janeiro, Buenos Aires, Stockholm, Geneva, and Barcelona.[2] His early politics was a bizarre combination of Sorel's revolutionary syndicalism and Saint-Simon's utopian modernism, and he designed both in Soviet Russia (1928–36)[3] and in Vichy for Marshal Philippe Pétain. The key manifesto of modern urban planning, the Athens charter of the Congrés Internationaux d'Architecture Moderne (CIAM), faithfully reflected his doctrines.

Le Corbusier embraced the huge, machine-age, hierarchical, centralized city with a vengeance. If one were looking for a caricature—a Colonel Blimp, as it were, of modernist urbanism—one could hardly do better than to invent Le Corbusier. His views were extreme but influential, and they were representative in the sense that they celebrated the logic implicit in high modernism. In his daring, his brilliance, and his consistency, Le Corbusier casts the high-modernist faith in sharp relief.[4]

Total City Planning

In *The Radiant City (La ville radieuse)*, published in 1933 and republished with few changes in 1964, Le Corbusier offers the most complete exposition of his views.[5] Here as elsewhere, Le Corbusier's plans were self-consciously immodest. If E. F. Schumacher made the case for the virtue of smallness, Le Corbusier asserted, in effect, "Big is beautiful." The best way to appreciate the sheer extravagance of his reach is to look briefly at three of his designs. The first is the core idea behind his Plan Voisin for central Paris (figure 14); the second, a new "business city" for Buenos Aires (figure 15); and the last, a vast housing scheme for about ninety thousand residents in Rio de Janeiro (figure 16).

In their magnitude, these plans speak for themselves. No compromise is made with the preexisting city; the new cityscape completely supplants its predecessor. In each case, the new city has striking sculptural properties; it is designed to make a powerful visual impact as a *form*. That impact, it is worth noting, can be had only from a great distance. Buenos Aires is pictured as if seen from many miles out to sea: a view of the New World "after a two-week crossing," writes Le Corbusier, adopting the perspective of a modern-day Christopher Columbus.[6] Rio is seen at several miles remove, as if from an airplane. What we behold is a six-kilometer-long highway elevated one hundred meters and enclosing a continuous ribbon of fifteen-story apartments. The new city literally towers over the old. The plan for a city of 3 million in Paris is seen from far above and outside, the distance emphasized by dots representing vehicles on the major avenue as well as by a small airplane and what appears to be a helicopter. None of the plans makes any reference to the urban history, traditions, or aesthetic tastes of the place in which it is to be located. The cities depicted, however striking, betray no context; in their neutrality, they could be anywhere at all. While astoundingly high construction costs may explain why none of these projects was ever adopted, Le Corbusier's refusal to make any appeal to local pride in an existing city cannot have helped his case.

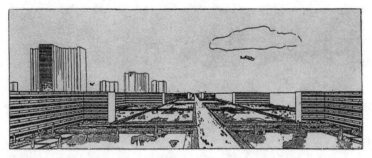

14. Le Corbusier's Plan Voisin for Paris, a city of 3 million people

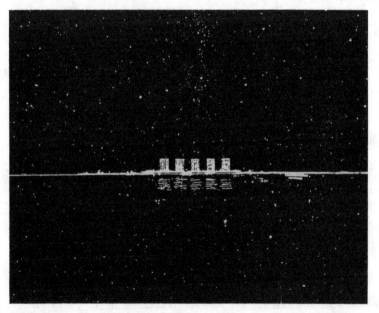

15. Le Corbusier's plan for the "business city" of Buenos Aires, as if seen from an approaching ship

16. Le Corbusier's plan for roads and housing in Rio de Janeiro

Le Corbusier had no patience for the physical environment that centuries of urban living had created. He heaped scorn on the tangle, darkness, and disorder, the crowded and pestilential conditions, of Paris and other European cities at the turn of the century. Part of his scorn was, as we shall see, on functional and scientific grounds; a city that was to become efficient and healthful would indeed have had to demolish much of what it had inherited. But another source of his scorn was aesthetic. He was visually offended by disarray and confusion. And the disorder he wished to correct was not so much a disorder at ground level but a disorder that was a function of distance, a bird's-eye view.[7] His mixed motives are nicely captured in his judgment on small rural properties as seen from the air (figure 17). "From airplanes, a look down on infinitely subdivided, *incongruously shaped* plots of land. The more modern machinery develops, the more land is chopped up into tiny holdings that render the miraculous promise of machinery useless. The result is waste: inefficient, individual scrabbling."[8] The purely formal order was at least as important as the accommodation with the machine age. "Architecture," he insisted, "is the art above all others which achieves a state of platonic grandeur, mathematical order, speculation, the perception of harmony that lies in emotional relationships."[9]

Formal, geometric simplicity and functional efficiency were not two distinct goals to be balanced; on the contrary, formal order was a precondition of efficiency. Le Corbusier set himself the task of inventing the ideal industrial city, in which the "general truths" behind the machine age would be expressed with graphic simplicity. The rigor and unity of this ideal city required that it make as few concessions as possible to the history of existing cities. "We must refuse to afford even the slightest concession to what is: to the mess we are in now," he wrote. "There is no solution to be found there." Instead, his new city would preferably rise on a cleared site as a single, integrated urban composi-

17. Aerial view of Alsace, circa 1930, from Le Corbusier's *La ville radieuse*

tion. Le Corbusier's new urban order was to be a lyrical marriage between Cartesian pure forms and the implacable requirements of the machine. In characteristically bombastic terms, he declared, "We claim, in the name of the steamship, the airplane, and the automobile, the right to health, logic, daring, harmony, perfection."[10] Unlike the existing city of Paris, which to him resembled a "porcupine" and a "vision of Dante's Inferno," his city would be an "organized, serene, forceful, airy, ordered entity."[11]

Geometry and Standardization

It is impossible to read much of Le Corbusier or to see many of his architectural drawings without noticing his love (mania?) for simple, repetitive lines and his horror of complexity. He makes a personal commitment to austere lines and represents that commitment as an essential characteristic of human nature. In his own words, "an infinity of combinations is possible when innumerable and diverse elements are brought together. But the human mind loses itself and becomes fatigued by such a labyrinth of possibilities. Control becomes impossible. The spiritual failure that must result is disheartening. . . . Reason . . . is an unbroken straight line. Thus, in order to save himself from this chaos, in order to provide himself with a bearable, acceptable framework for his existence, one productive of human well-being and control, man has projected the laws of nature into a system that is a manifestation of the human spirit itself: geometry."[12]

When Le Corbusier visited New York City, he was utterly taken by the geometric logic of midtown Manhattan. The clarity of what he called the "skyscraper machines" and the street plan pleased him: "The streets are at right angles to each other and the mind is liberated."[13] Elsewhere Le Corbusier answered what he saw as the criticism of those who were nostalgic for the variety of the existing city—in this case, Paris. People may complain, he noted, that in reality streets intersect at all sorts of angles and that the variations are infinite. "But," he replied, "that's precisely the point. *I eliminate all those things. That's my starting point. . . . I insist on right-angled intersections.*"[14]

Le Corbusier would have liked to endow his love of straight lines and right angles with the authority of the machine, of science, and of nature. Neither the brilliance of his designs nor the heat of his polemic, however, could succeed in justifying this move. The machines to which he most adoringly referred—the locomotive, the airplane, and the automobile—embody rounder or more elliptical shapes than right angles (the teardrop being the most streamlined of shapes). As for science, *any* shape is geometrical: the trapezoid, the triangle, the circle. If sheer simplicity or efficiency was the criterion, why not prefer the circle or sphere—as the minimum surface enclosing the maximum space—to the square or the rectangle? Nature, as Le Corbusier claimed, might be mathematical, but the complex, intricate, "chaotic" logic of living forms has only recently been understood with the aid of computers.[15] No, the great architect was expressing no more, and no less, than an aesthetic ideology—a strong taste for classic lines, which he also considered to be "Gallic" lines: "sublime straight lines, and oh, sublime French rigor."[16] It was *one* powerful way of mastering space. What's more, it provided a legible grid that could be easily grasped at a glance and that could be repeated in every direction, ad infinitum. As a practical matter, of course, a straight line was often impractical and ruinously expensive. Where the topography was irregular, building a straight, flat avenue without daunting climbs and descents would require great feats of digging and leveling. Le Corbusier's kind of geometry was rarely cost effective.

He took his utopian scheme for an abstract, linear city to impressive lengths. He foresaw that the industrialization of the construction trades would lead to a welcome standardization. He foresaw, too, the prefabrication of houses and office blocks, whose parts were built at factories and then assembled at the building sites. The sizes of all elements would be standardized, with multiples of standard sizes allowing for unique combinations determined by the architect. Door frames, windows, bricks, roof tiles, and even screws would all conform to a uniform code. The first manifesto of CIAM in 1928 called for the new standards to be legislated by the League of Nations, which would develop a universal technical language to be compulsorily taught throughout the world. An international convention would "normalize" the various standard measurements for domestic equipment and appliances.[17] Le Corbusier made efforts to practice what he preached. His design for the mammoth Palace of Soviets (never built) was intended to appeal to Soviet high modernism. The building, he claimed, would establish precise and universal new standards for all buildings—standards that would cover lighting, heating, ventilation, structure, and aesthetics and that would be valid in all latitudes for all needs.[18]

The straight line, the right angle, and the imposition of international building standards were all determined steps in the direction of simplification. Perhaps the most decisive step, however, was Le Corbusier's lifelong insistence on strict functional separation. Indicative of this doctrine was the second of fourteen principles he enunciated at the beginning of La ville radieuse, namely, "the death of the street." What he meant by this was simply the complete separation of pedestrian traffic from vehicle traffic and, beyond that, the segregation of slow-from fast-moving vehicles. He abhorred the mingling of pedestrians and vehicles, which made walking unpleasant and impeded the circulation of traffic.

The principle of functional segregation was applied across the board. Written by Le Corbusier and his brother Pierre, the final report for the second meeting of CIAM, in 1929, began with an assault on traditional housing construction: "The poverty, the inadequacy of traditional techniques have brought in their wake a confusion of powers, *an artificial mingling of functions*, only indifferently related to one another. . . . We must find and apply new methods . . . lending themselves naturally to standardization, industrialization, Taylorization. . . . If we persist in the present methods by which the two functions [arrangement and furnishing versus construction; circulation versus structure] are mingled and interdependent, then we will remain petrified in the same immobility."[19]

Outside the apartment block, the city itself was an exercise in planned functional segregation—an exercise that became standard urban-planning doctrine until the late 1960s. There would be separate zones for workplaces, residences, shopping and entertainment centers, and monuments and government buildings. Where possible, work zones were to be further subdivided into office buildings and factories. Le Corbusier's insistence on an urban plan in which each district had one and only one function was evident in his first act after taking over the planning of Chandigarh, his only built city. He replaced the housing that had been planned for the city center with an "acropolis of monuments" on a 220-acre site at a great distance from the nearest residences.[20] In his Plan Voisin for Paris, he separated what he called *la ville*, which was for dwelling, and the business center, which was for working. "These are two distinct functions, consecutive and not simultaneous, representative of two distinct and categorically separate areas."[21]

The logic of this rigid segregation of functions is perfectly clear. It is far easier to plan an urban zone if it has just one purpose. It is far easier to plan the circulation of pedestrians if they do not have to compete with automobiles and trains. It is far easier to plan a forest if its sole purpose is to maximize the yield of furniture-grade timber. When two purposes must be served by a single facility or plan, the trade-offs become nettlesome. When several or many purposes must be considered, the variables that the planner must juggle begin to boggle the mind. Faced with such a labyrinth of possibilities, as Le Corbusier noted, "the human mind loses itself and becomes fatigued."

The segregation of functions thus allowed the planner to think with greater clarity about efficiency. If the only function of roads is to get automobiles from *A* to *B* quickly and economically, then one can compare two road plans in terms of relative efficiency. This logic is eminently reasonable inasmuch as this is precisely what we have in mind when we build a road from *A* to *B*. Notice, however, that the clarity is achieved by bracketing the many other purposes that we may want roads to serve, such as affording the leisure of a touristic drive, providing aesthetic beauty or visual interest, or enabling the transfer of heavy goods. Even in the case of roads, narrow criteria of efficiency ignore other ends that are not trivial. In the case of the places that people call home, narrow criteria of efficiency do considerably greater violence to human practice. Le Corbusier calculates the air (*la respiration exacte*), heat, light, and space people need as a matter of public health. Starting with a figure of fourteen square meters per person, he reckons that this could be reduced to ten square meters if such activities as food preparation and laundering were communal. But here the criteria of efficiency that may apply to a road can hardly do justice to a home, which is variously used as a place for work, recreation, privacy, sociability, education, cooking, gossip, politics, and so on. Each of these activities, moreover, resists being reduced to criteria of efficiency; what is going on in the kitchen when someone is cooking for friends who have gathered there is not merely "food preparation." But the logic of efficient planning from above for large populations requires that each of the values being maximized be sharply specified and that the number of values being maximized simultaneously be sharply restricted—preferably to a single value.[22] The logic of Le Corbusier's doctrine was to carefully delineate urban space by use and function so that single-purpose planning and standardization were possible.[23]

Rule by the Plan, the Planner, and the State

The first of Le Corbusier's "principles of urbanism," before even "the death of the street," was the dictum "The Plan: Dictator."[24] It would be difficult to exaggerate the emphasis that, like Descartes, Le Corbusier placed on making the city the reflection of a single, rational plan. He greatly admired Roman camps and imperial cities for the overall logic of their layouts. He returned repeatedly to the contrast between the existing city, which is the product of historical chance, and the city of the future, which would be consciously designed from start to finish following scientific principles.

The centralization required by Le Corbusier's doctrine of the Plan (always capitalized in his usage) is replicated by the centralization of the city itself. Functional segregation was joined to hierarchy. His city was a "monocephalic" city, its centrally located core performing the "higher" functions of the metropolitan area. This is how he described the business center of his Plan Voisin for Paris: "From its offices come the commands that put the world in order. In fact, the skyscrapers are the *brain* of the city, *the brain of the whole country*. They embody the work of elaboration and command on which all activities depend. Everything is concentrated there: the tools that conquer time and space—telephones, telegraphs, radios, the banks, trading houses, the organs of decision for the factories: finance, technology, commerce."[25]

The business center issues commands; it does not suggest, much less consult. The program of high-modernist authoritarianism at work here stems in part from Le Corbusier's love of the order of the factory. In condemning the "rot" (*la pourriture*) of the contemporary city, its houses, and its streets, he singles out the factory as the sole exception. There, a single rational purpose structures both the physical layout and the coordinated movements of hundreds. The Van Nelle tobacco factory in Rotterdam is praised in particular. Le Corbusier admires its austerity, its floor-to-ceiling windows on each floor, the order in the work, and the apparent contentment of the workers. He finishes with a hymn to the authoritarian order of the production line. "There is a hierarchical scale, famously established and respected," he admiringly observes of the workers. "They accept it so as to manage themselves like a colony of worker-bees: order, regularity, punctuality, justice and paternalism."[26]

The scientific urban planner is to the design and construction of the city as the entrepreneur-engineer is to the design and construction of the factory. Just as a single brain plans the city and the factory, so a single brain directs its activity—from the factory's office and from the city's business center. The hierarchy doesn't stop there. The city is the brain of the whole society. "The great city commands everything: peace, war, work."[27] Whether it is a matter of clothing, philosophy, technology, or taste, the great city dominates and colonizes the provinces: the lines of influence and command are exclusively from the center to the periphery.[28]

There is no ambiguity to Le Corbusier's view of how authority relations should be ordered: hierarchy prevails in every direction. At the apex of the pyramid, however, is not a capricious autocrat but rather a modern philosopher-king who applies the truths of scientific understanding for the well-being of all.[29] It is true, naturally, that the master planner, in his not infrequent bouts of megalomania, imagines that he alone has a monopoly on the truth. In a moment of personal reflection in *The Radiant City*, for example, Le Corbusier declares: "I drew up plans [for Algiers], after analyses, after calculations, with imagination, with poetry. The plans were prodigiously true. They were incontrovertible. They were breathtaking. They expressed all the splendor of modern times."[30] It is not, however, the excess of pride that concerns us here but the sort of implacable authority Le Corbusier feels entitled to claim on behalf of universal scientific truths. His high-modernist faith is nowhere so starkly—or so ominously—expressed as in the following, which I quote at length:

> The despot is not a man. It is the *Plan. The correct, realistic, exact plan,* the one that will provide your solution once the problem has been posited clearly, in its entirety, in its indispensable harmony. *This plan has been drawn up well away from the frenzy in the mayor's office or the town hall, from the cries of the electorate or the laments of society's victims.* It has been drawn up by serene and lucid minds. It has taken account of nothing but human truths. It has ignored all current regulations, all existing usages, and channels. It has not considered whether or not it could be carried out with the constitution now in force. It is a biological creation destined for human beings and capable of realization by modern techniques.[31]

The wisdom of the plan sweeps away all social obstacles: the elected authorities, the voting public, the constitution, and the legal structure. At the very least, we are in the presence of a dictatorship of the planner; at most, we approach a cult of power and remorselessness that is reminiscent of fascist imagery.[32] Despite the imagery, Le Corbusier sees himself as a technical genius and demands power in the name of his truths. Technocracy, in this instance, is the belief that the human problem of urban design has a unique solution, which an expert can discover and execute. Deciding such technical matters by politics and bargaining would lead to the wrong solution. As there is a single, true answer to the problem of planning the modern city, no compromises are possible.[33]

Throughout his career, Le Corbusier is clearly aware that his kind of root-and-branch urban planning requires authoritarian measures. "A Colbert is required," he declares to his French reading public in an early article entitled "Toward a Machine Age Paris."[34] On the title page of his major work, one finds the words, "This work is Dedicated to Authority." Much of Le Corbusier's career as a would-be public architect can be read as a quest for a "Prince" (preferably an authoritarian one) who would anoint him as the court's Colbert. He exhibited designs for the League of Nations, lobbied the Soviet elite to accept his new plan for Moscow, and did what he could to get himself appointed as regulator of planning and zoning for the whole of France and to win the adoption of his plan for the new Algiers. Finally, under the patronage of Jawaharlal Nehru, he built a provincial capital at Chandigarh in India. Although Le Corbusier's own political affiliations in France were firmly anchored on the right,[35] he would clearly have settled for any state authority that would give him a free hand. He was appealing to logic rather than politics when he wrote, "Once his [the scientific planner's] calculations are finished, he is in a position to say—and he does say: *It shall be thus!*"[36]

What captivated Le Corbusier about the Soviet Union was not so much its ideology as the prospect that a revolutionary, high-modernist state might prove hospitable to a visionary planner. After building the headquarters of the Central Union of Consumer Cooperatives (Centrosoyuz),[37] he proposed, in plans prepared in only six weeks, a vast design for the rebuilding of Moscow in line with what he thought were Soviet aspirations to create an entirely new mode of living in a classless society. Having seen Sergey Eisenstein's film about the peasantry and technology, *The General Line*, Le Corbusier was utterly taken with its celebration of tractors, centrifuge creamers, and huge farms. He referred to it often in his plan to work a comparable transformation of Russia's urban landscape.

Stalin's commissars found his plans for Moscow as well as his project for the Palace of Soviets too radical.[38] The Soviet modernist El Lissitzky attacked Le Corbusier's Moscow as a "city of nowhere, . . . [a city] that is neither capitalist, nor proletarian, nor socialist, . . . a city on paper, extraneous to living nature, located in a desert through which not even a river must be allowed to pass (since a curve would contradict the style)."[39] As if to confirm El Lissitzky's charge that he had designed a "city of nowhere," Le Corbusier recycled his design virtually intact—aside from removing all references to Moscow—and presented it as *La ville radieuse*, suitable for central Paris.

The City as a Utopian Project

Believing that his revolutionary urban planning expressed universal scientific truths, Le Corbusier naturally assumed that the public, once they understood this logic, would embrace his plan. The original manifesto of CIAM called for primary school students to be taught the elementary principles of scientific housing: the importance of sunlight and fresh air to health; the rudiments of electricity, heat, lighting, and sound; the right principles of furniture design; and so on. These were matters of science, not of taste; instruction would create, in time, a clientele worthy of the scientific architect. Whereas the scientific forester could, as it were, go right to work on the forest and shape it to his plan, the scientific architect was obliged to first train a new clientele that would "freely" choose the urban life that Le Corbusier had planned for them.

Any architect, I imagine, supposes that the dwellings she designs will contribute to her clients' happiness rather than to their misery. The difference lies in how the architect understands happiness. For Le Corbusier, "*human happiness already exists* expressed in terms of numbers, of mathematics, of properly calculated designs, plans in which the cities can already be seen."[40] He was certain, at least rhetorically, that since his city was the rational expression of a machine-age consciousness, modern man would embrace it wholeheartedly.[41]

The kinds of satisfactions that the citizen-subject of Le Corbusier's city would experience, however, were not the pleasures of personal freedom and autonomy. They were the pleasures of fitting logically into a rational plan: "Authority must now step in, patriarchal authority, the authority of a father concerned for his children. . . . We must build places where mankind will be reborn. When the collective functions of the urban community have been organized, then there will be individual liberty for all. Each man will live in an ordered relation to the whole."[42] In the Plan Voisin for Paris, the place of each individual in the great urban hierarchy is spatially coded. The business elite (*industrials*) will live in high-rise apartments at the core, while the subaltern classes will have small garden apartments at the periphery. One's status can be directly read from one's distance from the center. But, like everyone in a well-run factory, everyone in the city will have the "collective pride" of a team of workers producing a perfect product. "The worker who does only a part of the job understands the role of his labor; the machines that cover the floor of the factory are examples to him of power and clarity, and *make him part of a work of perfection to which his simple spirit never dared to aspire*."[43] Just as Le Corbusier was perhaps most famous for asserting that "the home is a machine for living," so he thought of the planned city as a large, efficient machine with many closely calibrated parts. He assumed, therefore, that the citizens of his city would accept, with pride, their own modest role in a noble, scientifically planned urban machine.

By his own lights Le Corbusier was planning for the basic needs of his fellow men—needs that were ignored or traduced in the existing city. Essentially, he established them by stipulating an abstract, simplified human subject with certain material and physical requirements. This schematic subject needed so many square meters of living space, so much fresh air, so much sunlight, so much open space, so many essential services. At this level, he designed a city that was indeed far more healthful and functional than the crowded, dark slums against which he railed. Thus he spoke of "punctual and exact respiration," of various formulas for determining optimal sizes for apartments; he insisted on apartment skyscrapers to allow for park space and, above all, for efficient traffic circulation.

The Le Corbusian city was designed, first and foremost, as a workshop for production. Human needs, in this context, were scientifically stipulated by the planner. Nowhere did he admit that the subjects for whom he was planning might have something valuable to say on this matter or that their needs might be plural rather than singular. Such was his concern with efficiency that he treated shopping and meal preparation as nuisances that would be discharged by central services like those offered by well-run hotels.[44] Although floor space was provided for social activities, he said almost nothing about the actual social and cultural needs of the citizenry.

High modernism implies, as we have seen, a rejection of the past as a model to improve upon and a desire to make a completely fresh start. The more utopian the high modernism, the more thoroughgoing its implied critique of the existing society. Some of the most vituperative prose of *The Radiant City* was directed at the misery, confusion, "rot," "decay," "scum," and "refuse" of the cities that Le Corbusier wanted to transcend. The slums he showed in pictures were labeled "shabby" or, in the case of the French capital, "history, historic and tubercular Paris." He deplored both the conditions of the slums and the people they had created. "How many of those five million [those who came from the countryside to make their fortune] are simply a dead weight on the city, an obstacle, a black clot of misery, of failure, of human garbage?"[45]

His objection to the slums was twofold. First, they failed aesthetically to meet his standards of discipline, purpose, and order. "Is there anything," he asked rhetorically, "more pitiful than an undisciplined crowd?" Nature, he added, is "all discipline" and will "sweep them away" even if nature operates by a logic "contrary to the interests of mankind."[46] Here he signals that the founders of the modern city must be prepared to act ruthlessly. The second danger of the slums was that, besides being noisy, dangerous, dusty, dark, and disease-ridden, they harbored a potential revolutionary menace to the authorities. He understood, as Haussmann had, that crowded slums were and had always been an obstacle to efficient police work. Switching back and forth between Louis XIV's Paris and imperial Rome, Le Corbusier wrote: "From the huddle of hovels, from the depths of grimy lairs (in Rome—the Rome of the Caesars—the plebes lived in an inextricable chaos of abutting and warren-like skyscrapers), there sometimes came the hot gust of rebellion; the plot would be hatched in the *dark recesses of an accumulated chaos in which any kind of police activity was extremely difficult.* . . . St. Paul of Tarsus was impossible to arrest while he stayed in the slums, and the words of his Sermons were passed like wildfire from mouth to mouth."[47]

In case they were wondering, Le Corbusier's potential bourgeois backers and their representatives could rest assured that his legible, geometric city would facilitate police work. Where Haussmann managed to retrofit the baroque city of absolutism, Le Corbusier proposed to clear the decks completely and replace the center of Haussmann's city with one built with control and hierarchy in mind.[48]

A Textbook Case of High-Modernist Architecture

Le Corbusier's intellectual influence on architecture was out of all proportion to the actual structures he built. Not even the Soviet Union was quite up to his sweeping ambition. It is as an exemplar, a textbook case, of the key elements of high-modernist planning—often exaggerated—that he belongs in this analysis. His commitment to what he called the "total efficiency and total rationalization" of a new machine-age civilization was uncompromising.[49] Although he was obliged to deal with nation-states, his vision was universal. As he put it, "city planning everywhere, universal city planning, total city planning."[50] His actual plans for Algiers, Paris, and Rio were, as we have seen, on a scale that was virtually without precedent. Le Corbusier was influenced, as were others of his generation, by the spectacle of total military mobilization in World War I. "Let's make our plans," he urged, "plans on a scale with twentieth century events, plans equally as big as Satan's [war]. . . . Big! Big!"[51]

The visual, aesthetic component of his bold plans was central. Clean, smooth lines were something he associated with the "all-business" leanness of the machine. He was positively lyrical about the beauty of the machine and its products. And houses, cities, and agrovilles could also "emerge properly equipped, glitteringly new, from the factory, from the workshop, faultless products of smoothly humming machines."[52]

Integral, finally, to Le Corbusier's ultramodernism was his repudiation of tradition, history, and received taste. After explaining the origin of the traffic congestion in contemporary Paris, he warned against temptations to reform. "We must refuse even the slightest consideration to *what is:* to the mess we are in now." He emphasized, "There is no solution to be found here."[53] Instead, he insisted, we must take a "blank piece of paper," a "clean tablecloth," and start new calculations from zero. It was in this context that he was drawn to the USSR and to the ambitious rulers of developing countries. There, he hoped, he would not be cramped by the "grotesquely inadequate sites" available in the West, where it was possible to practice only what he called an "*orthopedic architecture.*"[54] The long-established cities of the West, their traditions, their interest groups, their slow-moving institutions, and their complex legal and regulatory structures could only shackle the dreams of a high-modernist Gulliver.

Brasília: The High-Modernist City Built—Almost

> Cities also believe they are the work of the mind or of chance, but neither the one nor the other suffices to hold up their walls.
> —Italo Calvino, *Invisible Cities*

No utopian city gets built precisely as designed by its prophet-architect. Just as the scientific forester is foiled by the vagaries of unpredictable nature and by the divergent purposes of both his employers and those who have access to the forest, so the urban planner must contend with the tastes and financial means of his patrons as well as the resistance of builders, workers, and residents. Even so, Brasília is about the closest thing we have to a high-modernist city, having been built more or less along the lines set out by Le Corbusier and CIAM. Thanks to an excellent book by James Holston, *The Modernist City: An Anthropological Critique of Brasília*,[55] it is possible to analyze both the logic of the plan for Brasília and the extent of its realization. An appreciation of the slippage between what Brasília meant for its originators on one hand and for its residents on the other will in turn pave the way (no pun intended) for Jane Jacob's thoroughgoing critique of modern urban planning.

The idea of a new capital in the interior predates even the independence of Brazil.[56] Its realization, however, was the pet project of Juscelino Kubitschek, the populist president from 1956 to 1961, who promised Brazilians "fifty years of progress in five" and a future of self-sustaining economic growth. In 1957 Oscar Niemeyer, who had already been named the chief architect for public buildings and housing prototypes, organized a design competition that was won, on the basis of very rough sketches, by Lucio Costa. Costa's idea—for it was no more than that—was of a "monumental axis" to define the center of the city, which consisted of terraced embankments describing an arc intersected in its center by a straight avenue, and of a triangle to define the city's limits (figure 18).

Both architects were working within the doctrines of CIAM and Le Corbusier. Niemeyer, a longtime member of the Brazilian Communist Party, was also influenced by the Soviet version of architectural modernism. After the design competition, construction began almost immediately on an empty site on the Central Plateau in the state of Goiás, nearly 1000 kilometers from Rio de Janeiro and the coast and 1620 kilometers from the Pacific Ocean in the northeast. It was indeed a new city in the wilderness. No "orthopedic" compromises were necessary now that the planners had, thanks to Kubitschek, who made Brasília his top priority, a "clean tablecloth." The state planning agency controlled all the land at the site, so there were no private-property owners with whom to negotiate. The city was then designed from the ground up, according to an elaborate and unified plan. Housing, work, recreation, traffic, and public administration were each spatially segregated as Le Corbusier would have insisted. Inasmuch as Brasília was itself a single-function, strictly administrative capital, the planning itself was greatly simplified.

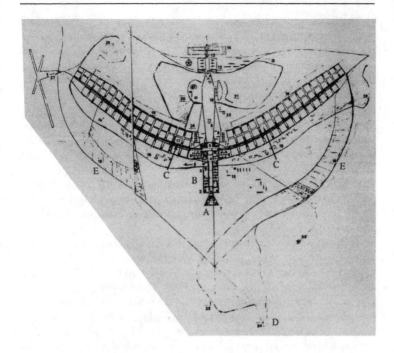

18. The Costa plan of 1957, showing *A*, the Plaza of the Three Powers; *B*, the ministries; *C*, superquadra residential zones; *D*, the president's residence; and *E*, single-family housing

Brasília as the Negation (or Transcendence) of Brazil

Brasília was conceived of by Kubitschek and by Costa and Niemeyer as a city of the future, a city of development, a realizable utopia. It made no reference to the habits, traditions, and practices of Brazil's past or of its great cities, São Paulo, Salvador, and Rio de Janeiro. As if to emphasize the point, Kubitschek called his own residence in Brasília the Dawn Palace. "What else will Brasília be," he asked, "if not the dawn of a new day for Brazil?"[57] Like the Saint Petersburg of Peter the Great, Brasília was to be an exemplary city, a center that would transform the lives of the Brazilians who lived there—from their personal habits and household organization to their social lives, leisure, and work. The goal of making over Brazil and Brazilians necessarily implied a disdain for what Brazil had been. In this sense, the whole point of the new capital was to be a manifest contrast to the corruption, backwardness, and ignorance of the old Brazil.

The great crossroads that was the plan's point of departure has been variously interpreted as a symbol of Christ's cross or an Amazonian bow. Costa, however, referred to it as a "monumental axis," the same term that Le Corbusier used to describe the center of many of his urban plans. Even if the axis represented a small attempt to assimilate Brasília in some way to its national tradition, it remained a city that could have been anywhere, that provided no clue to its own history, unless that history was the modernist doctrine of CIAM. It was a state-imposed city invented to project a new Brazil to Brazilians and to the world at large. And it was a state-imposed city in at least one other sense: inasmuch as it was created to be a city for civil servants, many aspects of life that might otherwise have been left to the private sphere were minutely organized, from domestic and residential matters to health services, education, child care, recreation, commercial outlets, and so forth.

If Brasília was to be Brazil's urban future, what was Brazil's urban past and present? What, precisely, was the new capital intended to negate? A large part of the answer can be inferred from Le Corbusier's second principle of the new urbanism: "the death of the street." Brasília was designed to eliminate the street and the square as places for public life. Although the elimination of local bairro loyalties and rivalries may not have been planned, they were also a casualty of the new city.

The public square and the crowded "corridor" street had been venues of civic life in urban Brazil since colonial days. As Holston explains, this civic life took two forms. In the first, which had been sponsored by the church or state, ceremonial or patriotic processions and rituals were typically held in the principal square of the town.[58] The second form encompassed a nearly inexhaustible range of popular uses of all the town squares. Children might play there; adults might simply shop, stroll and run into acquaintances, meet friends for a meal or coffee, play cards or chess, enjoy the social diversions of seeing and being seen. The point is that the square, as a confluence of streets and a sharply enclosed, framed space, become what Holston aptly calls a "public visiting room."[59] As a public room, the square is distinguished by its accessibility to all social classes and the great variety of activities it accommodates. Barring state proscriptions, it is a flexible space that enables those who use it to use it for *their* mutual purposes. The square or the busy street attracts a crowd precisely because it provides an animated scene—a scene in which thousands of unplanned, informal, improvised encounters can take place simultaneously. The street was the spatial focus for public life outside the usually cramped family dwelling.[60] The colloquialism for "I'm going downtown" was "I'm going to the street." As the focus for sociability, these spaces were also crucial sites for the development of public opinion as well as for "bairro nationalism," which could take institutional form in sports teams, bands, patron-saint celebrations, festival groups, and so on. It goes without saying that the street or the public square, under the right circumstances, could also become the site of public demonstrations and riots directed against the state.

A mere glance at the scenes of Brasília, juxtaposed to the urban Brazil that we have been describing, shows at once how radical is the transformation. There are no streets in the sense of public gathering places; there are only roads and highways to be used exclusively by motorized traffic (compare figures 19 and 20).

There *is* a square. But what a square! The vast, monumental Plaza of the Three Powers, flanked by the Esplanade of the Ministries, is of such a scale as to dwarf even a military parade (compare figures 21 and 22, and figures 23 and 24). In comparison, Tiananmen Square and the Red Square are positively cozy and intimate. The plaza is best seen, as are many of Le Corbusier's plans, from the air (as in figure 24). If one were to arrange to meet a friend there, it would be rather like trying to meet someone in the middle of the Gobi desert. And if one did meet up with one's friend, there would be nothing to do. Functional simplification demands that the rationale for the square as a public visiting room be designed out of Brasília. This plaza is a symbolic center for the state; the only activity that goes on around it is the work of the ministries. Whereas the vitality of the older square depended on the mix of residence, commerce, and administration in its catchment area, those who work in the ministries must drive to their residences and then again to the separate commercial centers of each residential area.

One striking result of Brasília's cityscape is that virtually all the public spaces in the city are officially designated public spaces: the stadium, the theater, the concert hall, the planned restaurants. The smaller, unstructured, informal public spaces—sidewalk cafés, street corners, small parks, neighborhood squares—do not exist. Paradoxically, a great deal of nominally open space characterizes this city, as it does Le Corbusier's city plans. But that space tends to be "dead" space, as in the Plaza of the Three Powers. Holston explains this by showing how CIAM doctrines create sculptural masses widely separated by large voids, an inversion of the "figure-ground" relations in older cities. Given our perceptual habits, these voids in the modernist city seem to be not inviting public spaces but boundless, empty spaces that are avoided.[61] One could fairly say that the effect of the plan was to design out all those unauthorized locations where casual encounters could

19. Residential street in the neighborhood Barra Funda, São Paulo, 1988

20. Residential access way L1 in Brasília, 1980

21. Largo do Pelourinho, with the museum of the city and the former slave market, São Salvador, 1980

22. The Plaza of the Three Powers, with the museum of the city and Planalto Palace, Brasília, 1980

23. The Praça de Sé, São Paulo, 1984

24. The Plaza of the Three Powers and the Esplanade of the Ministries, Brasília, 1981

occur and crowds could gather spontaneously. The dispersal and functional segregation meant that meeting someone virtually required a plan.

Costa and Niemeyer were not only banishing the street and the square from their utopian city. They believed that they were also banishing crowded slums, with their darkness, disease, crime, pollution, traffic jams and noise, and lack of public services. There were definite advantages to beginning with an empty, bulldozed site belonging to the state. At least the problems of land speculation, rent gouging, and property-based inequalities that beset most planners could be circumvented. As with Le Corbusier and Haussmann, there was an emancipating vision here. The best and most current architectural knowledge about sanitation, education, health, and recreation could be made part of the design. Twenty-five square meters of green space per resident reached the UNESCO-designed ideal. And as with any utopian plan, the design of Brasília reflected the social and political commitments of the builders and their patron, Kubitschek. All residents would have similar housing; the sole difference would be the number of units they were allotted. Following the plans of progressive European and Soviet architects, the planners of Brasília grouped the apartment buildings into what were called *superquadra* in order to facilitate the development of a collective life. Each superquadra (roughly 360 apartments housing 1,500–2,500 residents) had its own nursery and elementary school; each grouping of four superquadra had a secondary school, a cinema, a social club, sports facilities, and a retail sector.

Virtually all the needs of Brasília's future residents were reflected in the plan. It is just that these needs were the same abstract, schematic needs that produced the formulas for Le Corbusier's plans. Although it was surely a rational, healthy, rather egalitarian, state-created city, its plans made not the slightest concession to the desires, history, and practices of its residents. In some important respects, Brasília is to São Paulo or Rio as scientific forestry is to the unplanned forest. Both plans are highly legible, planned simplifications devised to create an efficient order that can be monitored and directed from above. Both plans, as we shall see, miscarry in comparable respects. Finally, both plans change the city and the woods to conform to the simple grid of the planner.

Living in Brasília

Most of those who have moved to Brasília from other cities are amazed to discover "that it is a city without crowds." People complain that Brasília lacks the bustle of street life, that it has none of the busy street corners and long stretches of storefront facades that animate a sidewalk for pedestrians. For them, it is almost as if the founders of Brasília, rather than having planned a city, have actually planned to prevent a city. The most common way they put it is to say that Brasília "lacks street corners," by which they mean that it lacks the complex intersections of dense neighborhoods comprising residences and public cafés and restaurants with places for leisure, work, and shopping. While Brasília provides well for some human needs, the functional separation of work from residence and of both from commerce and entertainment, the great voids between superquadra, and a road system devoted exclusively to motorized traffic make the disappearance of the street corner a foregone conclusion. The plan did eliminate traffic jams; it also eliminated the welcome and familiar pedestrian jams that one of Holston's informants called "the point of social conviviality."[62]

The term *brasilite*, meaning roughly Brasíl(ia)-itis, which was coined by the first-generation residents, nicely captures the trauma they experienced.[63] As a mock clinical condition, it connotes a rejection of the standardization and anonymity of life in Brasília. "They use the term *brasilite* to refer to their feelings about a daily life without the pleasures—the distractions, conversations, flirtations, and little rituals—of outdoor life in other Brazilian cities."[64] Meeting someone normally requires seeing them either at their apartment or at work. Even if we allow for the initial simplifying premise of Brasília's being an administrative city, there is nonetheless a bland anonymity built into the very structure of the capital. The population simply lacks the small accessible spaces that they could colonize and stamp with the character of their activity, as they have done historically in Rio and São Paulo. To be sure, the inhabitants of Brasília haven't had much time to modify the city through their practices, but the city is designed to be fairly recalcitrant to their efforts.[65]

"Brasilite," as a term, also underscores how the built environment affects those who dwell in it. Compared to life in Rio and São Paulo, with their color and variety, the daily round in bland, repetitive, austere Brasília must have resembled life in a sensory deprivation tank. The recipe for high-modernist urban planning, while it may have created formal order and functional segregation, did so at the cost of a sensorily impoverished and monotonous environment—an environment that inevitably took its toll on the spirits of its residents.

The anonymity induced by Brasília is evident from the scale and exterior of the apartments that typically make up each residential superquadra (compare figures 25 and 26). For superquadra residents, the two most frequent complaints are the sameness of the apartment blocks and the isolation of the residences ("In Brasília, there is only house and work").[66] The facade of each block is strictly geometric and egalitarian. Nothing distinguishes the exterior of one apartment from another; there are not even balconies that would allow residents to add distinctive touches and create semipublic spaces. Part of the disorientation arises from the fact that apartment dwelling—especially, perhaps, this form of apartment dwelling—fails to accord with deeply embedded conceptions of home. Holston asked a class of nine-year-old children, most of whom lived in superquadra, to draw a picture of "home." Not one drew an apartment building of any kind. All drew, instead, a traditional freestanding house with windows, a central door, and a pitched roof.[67] The superquadra blocks, by contrast, resist the stamp of individuality, while the glass walls on their exteriors infringe on the sense of private space in the home.[68] Concerned with the overall aesthetic of the plan, the architects erased not only the external display of status distinctions but also much of the visual play of difference. Just as the general design of the city militates against an autonomous public life, so the design of the residential city militates against individuality.

The disorienting quality of Brasília is exacerbated by architectural repetition and uniformity. Here is a case where what seems like rationality and legibility to those working in administration and urban services seems like mystifying disorder for the ordinary residents who must navigate the city. Brasília has few landmarks. Each commercial quarter or superquadra cluster looks roughly like any other. The sectors of the city are designated by an elaborate set of acronyms and abbreviations that are nearly impossible to master, except from the global logic of the center. Holston notes the irony between macro-order and micro-confusion: "Thus, while the topologies of total order produce an unusual, abstract awareness of the plan, practical knowledge of the city actually decreases with the imposition of systematic rationality."[69] From the perspective of the planners of a utopian city, whose goal is more to change the world than to accommodate it, however, the shock and disorientation occasioned by life in Brasília may be part of its didactic purpose. A city that merely pandered to existing tastes and habits would not be doing its utopian job.

Unplanned Brasília

From the beginning, Brasília failed to go precisely as planned. Its master builders were designing for a new Brazil and for new Brazil-

25. Residential area along Rua Tiradentes in Ouro Preto, 1980

26. A superquadra apartment block in Brasília, 1980

ians—orderly, modern, efficient, and under their discipline. They were thwarted by contemporary Brazilians with different interests and the determination to have them heard. Somehow, it was assumed that the huge workforce (more than sixty thousand strong) would respond to the call to build the city and then quietly leave it to the administrators for whom it was intended. The construction workers, moreover, had not been adequately planned for. Kubitschek accorded top priority to finishing Brasília as quickly as possible. Although most construction laborers routinely worked overtime, the population at the building site quickly outstripped the temporary housing allotted to them in what was called the Free City. They soon squatted on additional land on which they built makeshift houses; in cases where whole families migrated to Brasília (or farmed there), the houses they erected were sometimes quite substantial.

The "pioneers" of Brasília were collectively called "*bandeirantes* of the twentieth century," after the adventurers who had first penetrated the interior. The label was intended as a compliment, inasmuch as Kubitschek's Brasília was also a symbolic conquest of the interior in a nation that had historically clung to the shoreline. At the outset, however, the manual laborers attracted to Brasília were derogatorily called *candangos*. A candango was "a man without qualities, without culture, a vagabond, lower-class, lowbrow."[70] Kubitschek changed that. He used the building of Brasília, which was, after all, devised to transform Brazil, in order to transform the candangos into the proletarian heroes of the new nation. "Future interpreters of Brazilian Civilization," he declared, "must dwell with astonishment before the bronzed rigors of this anonymous titan, who is the candango, the obscure and formidable hero of the construction of Brasília. . . . While the skeptics laughed at the intended utopia of the new city that I prepared to build, the candangos shouldered the responsibility."[71] Taking full advantage of the rhetorical space thus provided them, the candangos insisted on having their own patch of the utopian city. They organized to defend their land, to demand urban services, and to be given secure title. In the end, by 1980, 75 percent of the population of Brasília lived in settlements that had never been anticipated, while the planned city had reached less than half of its projected population of 557,000. The foothold the poor gained in Brasília was not just a result of the beneficence of Kubitschek and his wife, Doña Sara. Political structure played a key role as well. Squatters were able to mobilize, protest, and be heard by virtue of a reasonably competitive political system. Neither Kubitschek nor other politicians could possibly ignore the opportunity to cultivate a political clientele who might vote as a bloc.

The unplanned Brasília—that is, the real, existing Brasília—was quite different from the original vision. Instead of a classless administrative city, it was a city marked by stark spatial segregation according to social class. The poor lived on the periphery and commuted long distances to the center, where much of the elite lived and worked. Many of the rich also created their own settlements with individual houses and private clubs, thereby replicating the affluent lifestyles found elsewhere in Brazil. The unplanned Brasílias—that of the rich and that of the poor—were not merely a footnote or an accident; one could say that the cost of this kind of order and legibility at the center of the plan virtually required that it be sustained by an unplanned Brasília at the margins. The two Brasílias were not just different; they were symbiotic.

Radically transforming an entire nation of Brazil's size and diversity—let alone in only five years—was all but inconceivable. One senses that Kubitschek, like many rulers with great ambitions for their countries, despaired of a direct assault on all Brazil and all Brazilians and turned to the more plausible task of creating from zero a utopian model. Raised on a new site, in a new place, the city would provide a transforming physical environment for its new residents—an environment minutely tailored to the latest dictates regarding health, efficiency, and rational order. As the progressive city would evolve from a unitary, integrated plan on land owned entirely by the state, with all contracts, commercial licenses, and zoning in the hands of the planning agency (Novacap), the conditions seemed favorable for a successful "utopian miniaturization."

How successful was Brasília as a high-modernist, utopian space? If we judge it by the degree to which it departs from cities in older, urban Brazil, then its success was considerable. If we judge it by its capacity either to transform the rest of Brazil or to inspire a love of the new way of life, then its success was minimal. The real Brasília, as opposed to the hypothetical Brasília in the planning documents, was greatly marked by resistance, subversion, and political calculation.

Le Corbusier at Chandigarh

Since Le Corbusier did not design Brasília, it may seem like guilt by association to blame him for its manifest failings. Two considerations, however, justify the connection. The first is that Brasília was faithfully built according to CIAM doctrines elaborated mostly by Le Corbusier. Second, Le Corbusier did in fact play a major role in designing another capital city that reflected precisely the human problems encountered in Brasília.

27. The *chowk*, or piazza, that Le Corbusier designed for Chandigarh's city center

Chandigarh, the new capital of the Punjab, was half planned when the architect in charge, Matthew Nowicki, suddenly died.[72] Nehru, in search of a successor, invited Le Corbusier to finish the design and supervise the construction. The choice was in keeping with Nehru's own high-modernist purpose: namely, the promotion of modern technology in a new capital that would dramatize the values that the new Indian elite wished to convey.[73] Le Corbusier's modifications of Nowicki's and Albert Mayer's original plan were all in the direction of monumentalism and linearity. In place of large curves, Le Corbusier substituted rectilinear axes. At the center of the capital, he inserted a huge monumental axis not unlike those in Brasília and in his plan for Paris.[74] In place of crowded bazaars cramming as many goods and people as possible into small spaces, he substituted huge squares that today stand largely empty (figure 27).

Whereas road crossings in India had typically served as public gathering places, Le Corbusier shifted the scale and arranged the zoning in order to prevent animated street scenes from developing. Notes one recent observer: "On the ground, the scale is so large and the width between meeting streets so great that one sees nothing but vast stretches of concrete paving with a few lone figures here and there. The small-scale street trader, the hawker or the rehris (barrows) have been banned from the city center, so that even where sources of interest and activity could be included, if only to reduce the concreted barrenness and authority of the *chowk*, these are not utilized."[75]

As in Brasília, the effort was to transcend India as it existed and to present Chandigarh's citizens—largely administrators—with an image of their own future. As in Brasília, the upshot was another unplanned city at the periphery and the margins, one that contradicted the austere order at the center.

The Case Against High-Modernist Urbanism: Jane Jacobs

Jane Jacobs's book *The Death and Life of Great American Cities* was written in 1961 against a high tide of modernist, functional urban planning. Hers was by no means the first criticism of high-modernist urbanism, but it was, I believe, the most carefully observed and intellectually grounded critique.[76] As the most comprehensive challenge to contemporary doctrines of urban planning, it sparked a debate, the reverberations of which are still being felt. The result, some three decades later, has been that many of Jacobs's views have been incorporated into the working assumptions of today's urban planners. Although what she called her "attack on current city planning and rebuilding" was concerned primarily with American cities, she located Le Corbusier's doctrines, as applied abroad and at home, at the center of her field of fire.

What is remarkable and telling about Jacobs's critique is its unique perspective. She begins at street level, with an ethnography of microorder in neighborhoods, sidewalks, and intersections. Where Le Corbusier "sees" his city initially from the air, Jacobs sees her city as a pedestrian on her daily rounds would. Jacobs was also a political activist involved in many campaigns against proposals for zoning changes, road building, and housing development that she thought ill-advised.[77] It was all but inconceivable that a radical critique, grounded in this fashion, could ever have originated from within the intellectual circle of urban planners.[78] Her novel brand of everyday urban sociology applied to the design of cities was simply too far removed from the orthodox educational routines of urban planning schools at the time.[79] An examination of her critique from the margins serves to underline many of the failings of high modernism.

Visual Order Versus Experienced Order

A formative insight in Jacobs's argument is that there is no necessary correspondence between the tidy look of geometric order on one hand and systems that effectively meet daily needs on the other. Why should we expect, she asks, that well-functioning built environments or social arrangements will satisfy purely visual notions of order and regularity? To illustrate the conundrum, she refers to a new housing project in East Harlem that sported, conspicuously, a rectangular lawn. The lawn was the object of general contempt by the residents. It was even taken as an insult by those who had been forcibly relocated and now lived in a project among strangers where it was impossible to get a newspaper or a cup of coffee or to borrow fifty cents.[80] The apparent order of the lawn seemed cruelly emblematic of a more keenly felt disorder.

A fundamental mistake that urban planners made, Jacobs claims, was to infer *functional* order from the duplication and regimentation of building forms: that is, from purely visual order. Most complex systems, on the contrary, do not display a surface regularity; their order must be sought at a deeper level. "To see complex systems of functional order as order, and not as chaos, takes understanding. The leaves dropping from the trees in the autumn, the interior of an airplane engine, the entrails of a rabbit, the city desk of a newspaper, all appear to be chaos if they are seen without comprehension. Once they are seen as systems of order, they actually look different." At this level one could say that Jacobs was a "functionalist," a word whose use was banned in Le Corbusier's studio. She asked, What function does this structure serve, and how well does it serve it? The "order" of a thing is determined by the purpose it serves, not by a purely aesthetic view of its surface order.[81] Le Corbusier, by contrast, seemed to have firmly believed that the most efficient forms would *always* have a classical clarity and order. The physical environments Le Corbusier designed and built had, as did Brasília, an overall harmony and simplicity of form. For the most part, however, they failed in important ways as places where people would want to live and work.

It was this failure of the general urban planning models that so preoccupied Jacobs. The planners' conception of a city accorded neither with the actual economic and social functions of an urban area nor with the (not unrelated) individual needs of its inhabitants. Their most fundamental error was their entirely aesthetic view of order. This error drove them to the further error of rigidly segregating functions. In their eyes, mixed uses of real estate—say, stores intermingled with apartments, small workshops, restaurants, and public buildings—created a kind of visual disorder and confusion. The great advantage of single uses—one shopping area, one residential area—was that it made possible the monofunctional uniformity and visual regimentation that they sought. As a planning exercise, it was of course vastly easier to plan an area zoned for a single use than one zoned for several. Minimizing the number of uses and hence the number of variables to be juggled thus combined with an aesthetic of visual order to argue for a single-use doctrine.[82] The metaphor that comes to mind in this connection is that of an army drawn up on the parade ground as opposed to an army engaged in combat with the enemy. In the first case is a tidy visual order created by units and ranks drawn up in straight lines. But it is an army doing nothing, an army on display. An army at war will not display the same orderly arrangement, but it will be, in Jacobs's terms, an army doing what it was trained to do. Jacobs thinks she knows the roots of this penchant for abstract, geometric order from above: "Indirectly through the utopian tradition, and directly through the more realistic doctrine of art by imposition, modern city planning has been burdened from its beginnings with the unsuitable aim of converting cities into disciplined works of art."[83]

Recently, Jacobs notes, the statistical techniques and input-output models available to planners had become far more sophisticated. They were encouraged to attempt such ambitious feats of planning as massive slum clearance now that they could closely calculate the budget, materials, space, energy, and transportation needs of a rebuilt area. These plans continued to ignore the social costs of moving families "like grains of sand, or electrons, or billiard balls."[84] The plans were also based on notoriously shaky assumptions, and they treated systems of complex order as if they could be simplified by numerical techniques, regarding shopping, for example, as a purely mathematical issue involving square footage for shopping space and traffic management as an issue of moving a certain number of vehicles in a given time along a certain number of streets of a given width. These were indeed formidable technical problems, but, as we shall see, the real issues involved much more besides.

The Functional Superiority of Cross-Use and Complexity

The establishment and maintenance of social order in large cities are, as we have increasingly learned, fragile achievements. Jacobs's view of social order is both subtle and instructive. *Social* order is not the result of the architectural order created by T squares and slide rules. Nor is social order brought about by such professionals as policemen, nightwatchmen, and public officials. Instead, says Jacobs, "the public peace—the sidewalk and street peace—of cities . . . is kept by an intricate, almost unconscious network of voluntary controls and standards among the people themselves, and enforced by the people themselves." The necessary conditions for a safe street are a clear demarcation between public space and private space, a substantial number of people who are watching the street on and off ("eyes on the street"), and fairly continual, heavy use, which adds to the quantity of eyes on the street.[85] Her example of an area where these conditions were met is Boston's North End. Its streets were thronged with pedestrians throughout the day owing to the density of convenience and grocery stores, bars, restaurants, bakeries, and other shops. It was a place where people came to shop and stroll and to watch others shop and stroll. The shopkeepers had the most direct interest in watching the sidewalk: they knew many people by name, they were there all day, and their businesses depended on the neighborhood traffic. Those who came and went on errands or to eat or drink also provided eyes on the street, as did the elderly who watched the passing scene from their apartment windows. Few of these people were friends, but a good many were acquaintances who did recognize one another. The process is powerfully cumulative. The more animated and busier the street, the more interesting it is to watch and observe; all these unpaid observers who have some familiarity with the neighborhood provide willing, informed surveillance.

Jacobs recounts a revealing incident that occurred on her mixed-use street in Manhattan when an older man seemed to be trying to cajole an eight- or nine-year-old girl to go with him. As Jacobs watched this from her second-floor window, wondering if she should intervene, the butcher's wife appeared on the sidewalk, as did the owner of the deli, two patrons of a bar, a fruit vendor, and a laundryman, and several other people watched openly from their tenement windows, ready to frustrate a possible abduction. No "peace officer" appeared or was necessary.[86]

Another instance of informal urban order and services is instructive. Jacobs explains that when a friend used their apartment while she and her husband were away or when they didn't want to wait up for a late-arriving visitor, they would leave the key to their apartment with the deli owner, who had a special drawer for such keys and who held them for the friends.[87] She noted that every nearby mixed-use street had someone who played the same role: a grocer, candy-store owner, barber, butcher, dry cleaner, or bookshop owner. This is one of the many public functions of private business.[88] These services, Jacobs notes, are not the outgrowth of any deep friendship; they are the result of people being on what she calls "sidewalk terms" with others. And these are services that could not plausibly be provided by a public institution. Having no recourse to the face-to-face politics of personal reputation that underwrites social order in small rural communities, the city relies on the density of people who are on sidewalk terms with one another to maintain a modicum of public order. The web of familiarity and acquaintanceship enabled a host of crucial but often invisible public amenities. A person didn't think twice about asking someone to hold one's seat at the theater, to watch a child while one goes to the restroom, or to keep an eye on a bike while one ducks into a deli to buy a sandwich.

Jacobs's analysis is notable for its attention to the microsociology of public order. The agents of this order are all nonspecialists whose main business is something else. There are no formal public or voluntary organizations of urban order here—no police, no private guards or neighborhood watch, no formal meetings or officeholders. Instead, the order is embedded in the logic of daily practice. What's more, Jacobs argues, the formal public institutions of order function successfully *only* when they are undergirded by this rich, informal public life. An urban space where the police are the sole agents of order is a very dangerous place. Jacobs admits that each of the small exchanges of informal public life—nodding hello, admiring a newborn baby, asking where someone's nice pears come from—can be seen as trivial. "But the sum is not trivial at all," she insists. "The sum of each casual, public contact at a local level—most of it fortuitous, most of it associated with errands, all of it metered by the person concerned and not thrust upon him by anyone—is a feeling for the public identity of people, a web of public respect and trust, and a resource in time of personal or neighborhood need. The absence of this trust is a disaster to a city street. Its cultivation cannot be institutionalized. And above all, *it implies no private commitments*."[89] Where Le Corbusier began with formal, architectural order from above, Jacobs begins with informal, social order from below.

Diversity, cross-use, and complexity (both social and architectural) are Jacobs's watchwords. The mingling of residences with shopping areas and workplaces makes a neighborhood more interesting, more convenient, and more desirable—qualities that draw the foot traffic that in turn makes the streets relatively safe. The whole logic of her case depends on the creation of the crowds, diversity, and conveniences that define a setting where people will want to be. In addition, a high volume of foot traffic stimulated by an animated and colorful neighborhood has economic effects on commerce and property values, which are hardly trivial. The popularity of a district and its economic success go hand in hand. Once created, such places will attract activities that most planners would have specially sequestered elsewhere. Rather than play in the large parks created for that purpose, many children prefer the sidewalks, which are safer, more eventful, and more convenient to the comforts available in stores and at home.[90] Understanding the magnetic effect of the busy street over more specialized settings is no more difficult than understanding why the kitchen is typically the busiest room in a house. It is the most versatile setting—a place of food and drink, of cooking and eating, and hence of socialization and exchange.[91]

What are the conditions of this diversity? That a district have mixed primary uses, Jacobs suggests, is the most vital factor. Streets and blocks should be short in order to avoid creating long barriers to pedestrians and commerce.[92] Buildings should ideally be of greatly varying age and condition, thereby making possible different rental terms and the varied uses that accompany them. Each of these conditions, not surprisingly, violates one or more of the working assumptions of orthodox urban planners of the day: single-use districts, long streets, and architectural uniformity. Mixed primary uses, Jacobs explains, are synergistic with diversity and density.

Take, for example, a small restaurant in a single-use district—say, the financial district of Wall Street. Such a restaurant must make virtually all its profit between 10 A.M. and 3 P.M., the hours when office workers take their midmorning coffee breaks and lunch breaks before commuting home at the end of the day, leaving the street silent. The restaurant in a mixed-use district, on the other hand, has potential clients passing by throughout the day and into the night. It may therefore stay open for more hours, benefiting not only its own business but also that of nearby specialized shops, which might be economically marginal in a single-use district but which become going concerns in a lively mixed-use area. The very jumble of activities, buildings, and people—the apparent *disorder* that offended the aesthetic eye of the planner—was for Jacobs the sign of dynamic vitality: "Intricate minglings of different uses are not a form of chaos. On the contrary they represent a complex and highly developed form of order."[93]

While Jacobs makes a convincing case for mixed use and complexity by examining the micro-origins of public safety, civic trust, visual interest, and convenience, there is a larger argument to be made for cross-use and diversity. Like the diverse old-growth forest, a richly differentiated neighborhood with many kinds of shops, entertainment centers, services, housing options, and public spaces is, virtually by definition, a more resilient and durable neighborhood. Economically, the diversity of its commercial "bets" (everything from funeral parlors and public services to grocery stores and bars) makes it less vulnerable to economic downturns. At the same time its diversity provides many opportunities for economic growth in upturns. Like monocropped forests, single-purpose districts, although they may initially catch a boom, are especially susceptible to stress. The diverse neighborhood is more sustainable.

I think that a "woman's eye," for lack of a better term, was essential to Jacobs's frame of reference. A good many men, to be sure, were insightful critics of high-modernist urban planning, and Jacobs refers to many of their writings. Nevertheless, it is difficult to imagine her argument being made in quite the same way by a man. Several elements of her critique reinforce this impression. First, she experiences the city as far more than a setting for the daily trek to and from work and the acquisition of goods and services. The eyes with which she sees the street are, by turns, those of shoppers running errands, mothers pushing baby carriages, children playing, friends having coffee or a bite to eat, lovers strolling, people looking from their windows, shopkeepers dealing with customers, old people sitting on park benches.[94] Work is not absent from her account, but her attention is riveted on the quotidian in the street as it appears around work and outside of work. A concern with public space puts both the interior of the home and the office as factory outside her purview. The activities that she observes so carefully, from taking a walk to window-shopping, are largely activities that do not have a single purpose or that have no conscious purpose in the narrow sense.

Compare this perspective with most of the key elements in high-modernist urban planning. Such plans all but require forms of simplification that strip human activity to a sharply defined single purpose. In orthodox planning, such simplifications underlie the strict functional segregation of work from domicile and both from commerce. The matter of transportation becomes, for Le Corbusier and others, the single problem of how to transport people (usually in automobiles) as quickly and economically as possible. The activity of shopping becomes a question of providing adequate floor space and access for a certain quantity of shoppers and goods. Even the category of entertainment was split up into specified activities and segregated into playgrounds, athletic fields, theaters, and so on.

Thus, the second result of Jacobs's having a woman's eye is her realization that a great deal of human activity (including, by all means, work) is pursued for a wide range of goals and satisfactions. An amiable lunch with co-workers may be the most significant part of the day for a jobholder. Mothers pushing baby carriages may also be talking to friends, doing errands, getting a bite to eat, and looking for a book at the local bookstore or library. In the course of these activities, still another "purpose" might arise, unbidden. The man or woman driving to work may not just be driving to work. He or she may care about the scenery or companionship along the way and the availability of coffee near the parking lot. Jacobs herself was an enormously gifted "eye on the street," and she wrote in full recognition of the great variety of human purposes embedded in any activity. The purpose of the city is to accommodate and abet this rich diversity and not to thwart it. And the persistent failure of urban-planning doctrines to do so, she suggested, had something to do with gender.[95]

Authoritarian Planning as Urban Taxidermy

For Jacobs, the city as a social organism is a living structure that is constantly changing and springing surprises. Its interconnections are so complex and dimly understood that planning always risks unknowingly cutting into its living tissue, thereby damaging or killing vital social processes. She contrasts the "art" of the planner to the practical conduct of daily life: "A city cannot be a work of art. . . . In relation to the inclusiveness and literally endless intricacy of life, art is arbitrary, symbolic, and abstracted. That is its value and the source of its own kind of order and coherence. . . . The results of such profound confusion between art and life are neither life nor art. They are taxidermy. In its place, taxidermy can be a useful and decent craft. However, it goes too far when the specimens put on display are exhibitions of dead, stuffed cities."[96] The core of Jacobs's case against modern city planning was that it placed a static grid over this profusion of unknowable possibilities. She condemned Ebenezer Howard's vision of the garden city because its planned segregation presumed that farmers, factory workers, and businessmen would remain fixed and distinct castes. Such a presumption failed to respect or provide for the "spontaneous self-diversification" and fluidity that were the main features of the nineteenth-century city.[97]

Urban planners' great penchant for massive schemes of slum clearance was attacked on the same grounds. Slums were the first foothold of poor migrants to the city. As long as these areas were reasonably stable, the economy relatively strong, and people and businesses not starved for credit, the slums could, given time, manage to "unslum" themselves. Many already had. Planners frequently destroyed "unslumming slums" because these areas violated their doctrines of "layout, use, ground coverage, mixture and activities"[98]—not to mention the land speculation and security concerns behind much "urban renewal."

From time to time Jacobs stands back from the infinite and changing variety of American cities to express a certain awe and humility: "Their intricate order—a manifestation of the freedom of countless numbers of people to make and carry out countless plans—is in many ways a great wonder. We ought not to be reluctant to make this living collection of interdependent uses, this freedom, this life, more understandable for what it is, nor so unaware that we do not know what it is."[99] The magisterial assumption behind the doctrines of many urban planners—that they know what people want and how people should spend their time—seems to Jacobs shortsighted and arrogant. They assumed, or at least their plans assumed, that people preferred open spaces, visual (zoned) order, and quiet. They assumed that people wanted to live in one place and work in another. Jacobs believes they were mistaken, and most important, she is prepared to argue from close daily observation at street level rather than stipulating human wishes from above.

The logic behind the spatial segregation and single-use zoning of the urban planners that Jacobs criticized was at once aesthetic, scientific, and practical. As an aesthetic matter, it led to the visual regularity—even regimentation—that a sculptural view of the ensemble required. As a scientific matter it reduced the number of unknowns for which the planner had to find a solution. Like simultaneous equations in algebra, too many unknowns in urban planning rendered any solution problematic or else required heroic assumptions. The problem the planner faced was analogous to that of the forester. One modern solution to the forester's dilemma was to borrow a management technique called optimum control theory, whereby the sustained timber yield could be successfully predicted by few observations and a parsimonious formula. It goes without saying that optimum control theory was simplest where more variables could be turned into constants. Thus a single-species, same-age forest planted in straight lines on a flat plain with consistent soil and moisture profiles yielded simpler and more accurate optimum control formulas. Compared to uniformity, diversity is always more difficult to design, build, and control. When Ebenezer Howard approached town planning as a simple, two-variable problem of relating housing needs to the quantity of jobs in a closed system, he was both temporally and functionally operating "scientifically" within those self-imposed limits. Formulas for green space, light, schools, and square meters per capita did the rest.

In urban planning as in forestry, it is a short step from parsimonious assumptions to the practice of shaping the environment so that it satisfies the simplifications required by the formula. The logic of planning for the shopping needs of a given population serves as an example. Once planners applied the formula for a certain number of square feet of commercial space, parceled out among such categories as food and clothing, they realized that they would then have to make these shopping centers monopolistic within their areas, lest nearby competitors draw away their clientele. The whole point was to legislate the formula, thereby guaranteeing the shopping center a monopoly of its catchment area.[100] Rigid, single-use zoning is, then, not just an aesthetic measure. It is an indispensable aid to scientific planning, and it can also be used to transform formulas posing as observations into self-fulfilling prophesies.

The radically simplified city, provided it is viewed from above, is also practical and efficient. The organization of services—electricity, water, sewage, mail—is simplified both below and above ground. Single-use districts, by virtue of the repetition of functionally similar apartments or offices, are simpler to produce and build. Le Corbusier looked forward to a future when all the components of such buildings would be industrially prefabricated.[101] Zoning along these lines also produces a city that is, district by district, both more uniform aesthetically and more "orderly" functionally. A single activity or narrow band of activities is appropriate to each district: work in the business district, family life in the residential quarter, shopping and entertainment in the commercial district. As a police matter, this functional segregation minimizes unruly crowds and introduces as much regimentation into the movement and conduct of the population as physical planning alone can encourage.

Once the desire for comprehensive urban planning is established, the logic of uniformity and regimentation is well-nigh inexorable. Cost effectiveness contributes to this tendency. Just as it saves a prison trouble and money if all prisoners wear uniforms of the same material, color, and size, every concession to diversity is likely to entail a corresponding increase in administrative time and budgetary cost. If the planning authority does not need to make concessions to popular desires, the one-size-fits-all solution is likely to prevail.[102]

Against the planners' eye and formulas, Jacobs juxtaposes her own. Her aesthetic, she would claim, is pragmatic and street level, an aesthetic that has as its reference the experienced working order of the city for the people who live there. She asks, What physical environments draw people, facilitate circulation, promote social exchange and contact, and satisfy both utilitarian and nonutilitarian needs? This perspective leads her to many judgments. Short blocks are preferable to long blocks because they knit together more activities. Large truck depots or filling stations that break the continuity of pedestrian interest are to be avoided. To be kept to a minimum are huge roads and vast, forbidding open spaces that operate as visual and physical barriers. There is a logic here, but it is not an a priori visual logic, nor is it a purely utilitarian logic narrowly conceived. Rather, it is a standard of evaluation that springs from how satisfactorily a given arrangement meets the social and practical desires of urban dwellers as those needs are revealed in their actual activity.

Planning for the Unplanned

The historic diversity of the city—the source of its value and magnetism—is an unplanned creation of many hands and long historical practice. Most cities are the outcome, the vector sum, of innumerable small acts bearing no discernible overall intention. Despite the best efforts of monarchs, planning bodies, and capitalist speculators, "most city diversity is the creation of incredible numbers of different people and different private organizations, with vastly different ideas and purposes, planning and contriving outside the formal framework of public action."[103] Le Corbusier would have agreed with this description of the existing city, and it was precisely what appalled him. It was just this cacophony of intentions that was responsible for the clutter, ugliness, disorder, and inefficiencies of the unplanned city. Looking at the same social and historical facts, Jacobs sees reason to praise them: "Cities have the capability of providing something for everybody, only because, and only when, they are created by everybody."[104] She is no free-market libertarian, however; she understands clearly that capitalists and speculators are, willy-nilly, transforming the city with their commercial muscle and political influence. But when it comes to urban public policy, she thinks planning ought not to usurp this unplanned city: "The main responsibility of city planning and design should be to develop, insofar as public policy and action can do so, cities that are congenial places for this great range of unofficial plans, ideas, and opportunities to flourish."[105] Whereas Le Corbusier's planner is concerned with the overall form of the cityscape and its efficiency in moving people from point to point, Jacobs's planner consciously makes room for the unexpected, small, informal, and even nonproductive human activities that constitute the vitality of the "lived city."

Jacobs is more aware than most urban planners of the ecological and market forces continually transforming the city. The succession of harbors, railroads, and highways as means of moving people and goods had already marked the rise and decline of sections of the city. Even the successful, animated neighborhoods that Jacobs so prizes were, she recognizes, becoming victims of their own success. Areas were "colonized" by urban migrants because land values, and hence rents, were cheap. As an area became more desirable to live in, its rents rose and its local commerce changed, the new businesses often driving out the original pioneers who had helped transform it. The nature of the city was flux and change; a successful neighborhood could not be frozen and preserved by the planners. A city that was extensively planned would inevitably diminish much of the diversity that is the hallmark of great towns. The best a planner can hope for is to modestly enhance rather than impede the development of urban complexity.

For Jacobs, how a city develops is something like how a language evolves. A language is the joint historical creation of millions of speakers. Although all speakers have some effect on the trajectory of a language, the process is not particularly egalitarian. Linguists, grammarians, and educators, some of them backed by the power of the state, weigh in heavily. But the process is not particularly amenable to a dictatorship, either. Despite the efforts toward "central planning," language (especially its everyday spoken form) stubbornly tends to go on its own rich, multivalent, colorful way. Similarly, despite the attempts by urban planners toward designing and stablizing the city, it escapes their grasp; it is always being reinvented and inflected by its inhabitants.[106] For both a large city and a rich language, this openness, plasticity, and diversity allow them to serve an endless variety of purposes—many of which have yet to be conceived.

The analogy can be pressed further. Like planned cities, planned languages are indeed possible. Esperanto is one example; technical and scientific languages are another, and they are quite precise and powerful means of expression within the limited purposes for which they were designed. But language per se is not for only one or two purposes. It is a general tool that can be bent to countless ends by virtue of its adaptability and flexibility. The very history of an inherited language helps to provide the range of associations and meanings that sustain its plasticity. In much the same way, one could plan a city from zero. But since no individual or committee could ever completely encompass the purposes and lifeways, both present and future, that animate its residents, it would necessarily be a thin and pale version of a complex city with its own history. It will be a Brasília, Saint Petersburg, or Chandigarh rather than a Rio de Janeiro, Moscow, or Calcutta. Only time and the work of millions of its residents can turn these thin cities into thick cities. The grave shortcoming of a planned city is that it not only fails to respect the autonomous purposes and subjectivity of those who live in it but also fails to allow sufficiently for the contingency of the interaction between its inhabitants and what that produces.

Jacobs has a kind of informed respect for the novel forms of social order that emerge in many city neighborhoods. This respect is reflected in her attention to the mundane but meaningful human connections in a functioning neighborhood. While recognizing that no urban neighborhood can ever be, or should be, static, she stresses the minimal degree of continuity, social networks, and "street-terms" acquaintanceship required to knit together an urban locality. "If self-government in the place is to work," she muses, "underlying any float of population must be a continuity of people who have forged neighborhood networks. These networks are a city's irreplaceable social capital. Whenever the capital is lost, from whatever cause, the [social] income from it disappears, never to return until and unless new capital is slowly and chancily accumulated."[107] It follows from this vantage point that even in the case of slums, Jacobs was implacably opposed to the wholesale slum-clearance projects that were so much in vogue when she was writing. The slum might not have much social capital, but what it did have was something to build on, not destroy.[108] What keeps Jacobs from becoming a Burkean conservative, celebrating whatever history has thrown up, is her emphasis on change, renewal, and invention. To try to arrest this change (although one might try to modestly influence it) would be not only unwise but futile.

Strong neighborhoods, like strong cities, are the product of complex processes that cannot be replicated from above. Jacobs quotes with approval Stanley Tankel, a planner who made the rarely heard case against large-scale slum clearance in these terms: "The next step will require great humility, since we are now so prone to confuse great building projects with great social achievements. We will have to admit that it is beyond the scope of anyone's imagination to create a community. We must learn to cherish the communities we have, they are hard to come by. 'Fix the buildings, but leave the people.' 'No relocation outside the neighborhood.' These must be the slogans if public housing is to be popular."[109] In fact, the political logic of Jacobs's case is that while the planner cannot create a functioning community, a functioning community can, within limits, improve its own condition. Standing the planning logic on its head, she explains how a reasonably strong neighborhood can, in a democratic setting, fight to create and maintain good schools, useful parks, vital urban services, and decent housing.

Jane Jacobs was writing against the major figures still dominating the urban planning landscape of her day: Ebenezer Howard and Le Corbusier. To some of her critics she has seemed a rather conservative figure, extolling the virtues of community in poor neighborhoods that many were anxious to leave and ignoring the degree to which the city was already being "planned," not by popular initiative or by the state but by developers and financiers with political connections. There is some justice to these points of view. For our purposes, however, there is little doubt that she has put her finger on the central flaws of hubris in high-modernist urban planning. The first flaw is the presumption that planners can safely make most of the predictions about the future that their schemes require. We know enough by now to be exceptionally skeptical about forecasting from current trends in fertility rates, urban migration, or the structure of employment and income. Such predictions have often been wildly wrong. As for wars, oil embargoes, weather, consumer tastes, and political eruptions, our capacity for prediction is practically nil. Second, thanks in part to Jacobs, we now know more about what constitutes a satisfactory neighborhood for the people who live in it, but we still know precious little about how such communities can be fostered and maintained. Working from formulas about density, green space, and transportation may produce narrowly efficient outcomes, but it is unlikely to result in a desirable place to live. Brasília and Chandigarh, at a minimum, demonstrate this.

It is not a coincidence that many of the high-modernist cities actually built—Brasília, Canberra, Saint Petersburg, Islamabad, Chandigarh, Abuja, Dodoma, Ciudad Guayana[110]—have been administrative capitals. Here at the center of state power, in a completely new setting, with a population consisting largely of state employees who have to reside there, the state can virtually stipulate the success of its planning grid. The fact that the business of the city is state administration already vastly simplifies the task of planning. Authorities do not have to contend, as did Haussmann, with preexisting commercial and cultural centers. And because the authorities control the instruments of zoning, employment, housing, wage levels, and physical layout, they can bend the environment to the city. These urban planners backed by state power are rather like tailors who are not only free to invent whatever suit of clothes they wish but also free to trim the customer so that he fits the measure.

Urban planners who reject "taxidermy," Jacobs claims, must nevertheless invent a kind of planning that encourages novel initiatives and contingencies, foreclosing as few options as possible, and that fosters the circulation and contact out of which such initiatives arise. To illustrate the diversity of urban life, Jacobs lists more than a dozen uses which have been served over the years by the center for the arts in Louisville: stable, school, theater, bar, athletic club, blacksmith's forge, factory, warehouse, artists' studio. She then asks, rhetorically, "Who could anticipate or provide for such a succession of hopes and services?" Her answer is simple: "Only an unimaginative man would think he could; only an arrogant man would want to."[111]

5 The Revolutionary Party: A Plan and a Diagnosis

Feeling, Comrade C, is a mass element, but thought is organization. Comrade Lenin said that organization is the highest of all of us.
—Andrei Platonov, *Chevengur*

Communism was modernity's most devout, vigorous and gallant champion. . . . It was under communist . . . auspices that the audacious dream of modernity, freed from obstacles by the merciless and omnipotent state, was pushed to its radical limits: grand designs, unlimited social engineering, huge and bulky technology, total transformation of nature.
—Zygmunt Bauman, *"Living Without an Alternative"*

Lenin's design for the construction of the revolution was in many ways comparable to Le Corbusier's design for the construction of the modern city. Both were complex endeavors that had to be entrusted to the professionalism and scientific insight of a trained cadre with full power to see the plan through. And just as Le Corbusier and Lenin shared a broadly comparable high modernism, so Jane Jacobs's perspective was shared by Rosa Luxemburg and Aleksandra Kollontay, who opposed Lenin's politics. Jacobs doubted both the possibility and the desirability of the centrally planned city, and Luxemburg and Kollontay doubted the possibility and desirability of a revolution planned from above by the vanguard party.

Lenin: Architect and Engineer of Revolution

Lenin, if we judge him from his major writings, was a convinced high modernist. The broad lines of his thought were quite consistent; whether he was writing about revolution, industrial planning, agricultural organization, or administration, he focused on a unitary scientific answer that was known to a trained intelligentsia and that ought to be followed. The Lenin of practice was, of course, something else again. His capacity for sensing the popular mood in fashioning Bolshevik propaganda, for beating a tactical retreat when it seemed prudent, and for striking boldly to seize the advantage was more relevant than his high modernism to his success as a revolutionary. It is Lenin as a high modernist, however, with whom we are primarily concerned.

The major text for the elaboration of Lenin's high-modernist views of revolution is *What Is to Be Done?*[1] High modernism was integral to the central purpose of Lenin's argument: to convince the Russian left that only a small, selected, centralized, professional cadre of revolutionaries could bring about a revolution in Russia. Written in 1903, well before the "dress rehearsal" revolution of 1905, this view was never entirely abandoned, even under totally different circumstances in 1917 between the February overthrow of the czar and the Bolshevik seizure of power in October, when he wrote *State and Revolution*. I shall compare Lenin's view in these two works and in his writings on agriculture with Rosa Luxemburg's "Mass-Strike, Party, and Trade Unions," written in reply to *What Is to Be Done?* and with the writings of Aleksandra Kollontay, an important figure in what was called the Workers' Opposition, a group within the Bolshevik party who criticized many of Lenin's policies after the revolution.

The Lenin of What Is to Be Done?

Lenin's choice of the title *What Is to Be Done?* has great significance. It was also the title of an exceptionally popular novel by Nicholas Chernyshevsky, in which a "new man" of the intelligentsia set about destroying the old order and then ruling autocratically to establish a social utopia. It had been the favorite book of Lenin's adored older brother, Alexander, who had been executed in 1887 for a plot against the czar's life. Even after Lenin became a Marxist, it was still his favorite book: "I became acquainted with the works of Marx, Engels, and Plekhanov, but it was only Chernyshevsky who had an overwhelming influence on me."[2] The idea that superior knowledge, authoritarian instruction, and social design could transform society pervades both works.

Certain metaphors suffuse Lenin's analysis of the link between the vanguard party and the workers in *What Is to Be Done?* They set the tone of the work and limit what can be said within its confines. These metaphors center on the classroom and the barracks.[3] The party and its local agitators and propagandists function as schoolteachers capable of raising merely economic complaints to the level of revolutionary political demands, or they function as officers in a revolutionary army who deploy their troops to best advantage. In their roles as teachers, the vanguard party and its newspaper develop a pedagogical style that is decidedly authoritarian. The party analyzes the many and varied popular grievances and, at the right time, "dictate[s] a positive programme of action" that will contribute to a "universal political struggle."[4] In fact, Lenin complained, the party's activists have been woefully inadequate. It is not enough to call the movement a "vanguard," he insisted. "We must act in such a way that *all other units of the army* shall see us, and be obliged to admit that we are the vanguard." The goal of the vanguard party is to train willing but "backward" proletarians in revolutionary politics so that they may be inducted into an army that will "collect and utilize every grain of even rudimentary protest," thereby creating a disciplined revolutionary army.[5]

In keeping with these metaphors, the "masses" in general and the working class in particular become "the body," while the vanguard party is "the brain." The party is to the working class as intelligence is to brute force, deliberation to confusion, a manager to a worker, a teacher to a student, an administrator to a subordinate, a professional to an amateur, an army to a mob, or a scientist to a layman. A brief explanation of how these metaphors work will help situate Lenin's own version of high-modern, albeit revolutionary, politics.

Lenin realized, of course, that the revolutionary project depended on popular militancy and spontaneous protest. The problem of relying solely on popular action from below, however, was that such action was scattered and sporadic, making easy pickings for the czarist police. If we think of popular action as incendiary political material, the role of the vanguard party was to concentrate and aim this explosive charge so that its detonation could bring down the regime. The vanguard party "merged the *elemental* destructive force of a crowd with the *conscious* destructive force of the organization of revolutionists."[6] It was the thinking organ of the revolution, ensuring that the otherwise diffuse brute force of the masses was effectively used.

The logic of this perspective led Lenin to think of the vanguard party as a would-be general staff to a vast but undisciplined army of raw recruits already in combat. The more unruly the army, the greater the need for a small, cohesive general staff. To his competitors on the left (the Economists), who argued that ten wise men could easily be grabbed by the police, whereas one hundred fools (the revolutionary crowd) could not be stopped, Lenin replied, "Without the 'dozen' of tried and talented leaders (and talented men are not born by hundreds), professionally trained, schooled by long experience and working in perfect harmony, no class in modern society is capable of conducting a determined struggle."[7]

Lenin's analogies to military organization were not just colorful figures of speech; they were how he thought about most aspects of party organization. He wrote of "tactics" and "strategy" in a straightforwardly military style. Only a general staff is capable of deploying its revolutionary forces in accord with an overall battle plan. Only a general staff can see the entire battlefield and anticipate enemy movements. Only a general staff would have the "flexibility . . . to adapt itself immediately to the most diverse and rapidly changing conditions of struggle," the "ability to renounce an open fight against overwhelming and concentrated forces, and yet capable of taking advantage of the awkwardness and immobility of the enemy and of attacking at a time and a place where he least expects attack."[8] The earlier failures of social democrat revolutionaries could, he insisted, be attributed precisely to the absence of organization, planning, and coordination that a general staff could provide. These "young warriors," who had "marched to battle with astonishingly primitive equipment and training," were "like peasants from the plough, snatching up a club." Their "immediate and complete defeat" was a foregone conclusion "because these open conflicts were not the result of a systematic and carefully thought-out and gradually prepared plan for a prolonged and stubborn struggle."[9]

Part of the necessity for strict discipline arose from the fact that the enemies of revolution were better armed and more sophisticated. This explains why "freedom of criticism" among the revolutionary forces could only favor opportunists and the ascendancy of bourgeois values. Once again Lenin seized on a military analogy to drive the point home: "We are marching in a compact group along a precipitous and difficult path, firmly holding each other by the hand. We are surrounded on all sides by enemies, and are under their almost constant fire. We have combined voluntarily, especially for the purpose of fighting the enemy and not to retreat into the adjacent marsh," that is, freedom of criticism.[10]

The relationship envisioned by Lenin between the vanguard party and its rank and file is perhaps best exemplified by the terms "mass" or "masses." Although the terms became standard in socialist parlance, they are heavy with implications. Nothing better conveys the impression of mere quantity and number without order than the word "masses." Once the rank and file are so labeled, it is clear that what they chiefly add to the revolutionary process are their weight in numbers and the kind of brute force they can represent if firmly directed. The impression conveyed is of a huge, formless, milling crowd without any cohesion—without a history, without ideas, without a plan of action. Lenin was all too aware, of course, that the working class does have its own history and values, but this history and these values will lead the working class in the wrong direction unless they are replaced by the historical analysis and advanced revolutionary theory of scientific socialism.

Thus the vanguard party not only is essential to the tactical cohesion of the masses but also must literally do their thinking for them. The party functions as an executive elite whose grasp of history and dialectical materialism allows it to devise the correct "war aims" of the class struggle. Its authority is based on its scientific intelligence. Lenin quoted the "profoundly true and important utterances by Karl Kautsky," who said that the proletariat cannot aspire to "modern socialist consciousness" on its own because it lacks the "profound scientific knowledge" required to do so: "The vehicles of science are not the proletariat, but the *bourgeois intelligentsia*."[11]

This is the core of Lenin's case against spontaneity. There are only two ideologies: bourgeois and socialist. Given the pervasiveness and historical power of bourgeois ideology, the spontaneous development of the working class will always lead to the triumph of bourgeois ideology. In Lenin's memorable formulation, "the working class, exclusively by its own effort, is able to develop only trade-union consciousness."[12] Social democratic consciousness, in contrast, must come from outside, that is, from the socialist intelligentsia. The vanguard party is depicted as conscious, scientific, and socialist in the full sense and is contrasted with the masses who are, by extension, unconscious, prescientific, and in constant danger of absorbing bourgeois values. Lenin's stern admonitions about indiscipline—"to deviate from it [socialist ideology] in the slightest degree means strengthening bourgeois ideology"[13]—leave the impression of a general staff whose tight control is the only counterweight to a force of conscripts who might at any moment disband and wander off.

Another metaphor occasionally replaces those of the army and classroom in Lenin's discourse. It is the image of a bureaucratic or industrial enterprise in which only the executives and engineers can see the larger purposes of the organization. Lenin appeals to something like a division of labor in revolutionary work, where the executive has a monopoly on the advanced theory without which revolution is impossible. Resembling factory owners and engineers who design rational plans for production, the vanguard party possesses a scientific grasp of revolutionary theory that makes it uniquely able to guide the entire proletarian struggle for emancipation. It was a bit too early, in 1903, for Lenin to refer to the assembly lines of mass production to make his point, but he appropriated the next best analogy from the building industry. "Pray tell me," he proposed. "When a brick layer lays bricks in various parts of an *enormous structure*, the like of which has never been seen before, is it a 'paper' line that he uses to help him find the correct place to place each brick, to indicate to him the ultimate goal of the work as a whole, to enable him to use not only every brick but even every piece of brick, which, joining with the bricks placed before and after it, forms a complete and all embracing line? And are we not now passing through a period in our party life, when we have bricks and bricklayers, but we lack the guiding line, visible to all, by which to guide our movements?"[14] What the party has is the blueprint of the entire new structure, which its scientific insight has made possible. The role of the workers is to follow that part of the blueprint allotted to them in the confidence that the architects of revolution know what they are doing.

The analogy to the division of labor in modern capitalist production has implications roughly parallel to those of the military metaphor. Both, for example, require authoritarian methods and central control. Thus Lenin wrote of the party's need "to distribute the thousand-and-one minute *functions* of their organizational work," complained of "technical defects," and called for the unification of "all these tiny fractions into one whole." As he concluded, "specialization necessarily presupposes centralization, and in its turn imperatively calls for it."[15]

It is surely a great paradox of *What Is to Be Done?* that Lenin takes a subject—promoting revolution—that is inseparable from popular anger, violence, and the determination of new political *ends* and transforms it into a discourse on technical specialization, hierarchy, and the efficient and predictable organization of *means*. Politics miraculously disappears from within the revolutionary ranks and is left to the elite of the vanguard party, much as industrial engineers might discuss, among themselves, how to lay out a factory floor. The vanguard party is a machine to produce a revolution. There is no need for politics within the party inasmuch as the science and rationality of the socialist intelligentsia require instead a technically necessary subordination; the party's judgments are not subjective and value laden but objective and logically inevitable.

Lenin extends this line of reasoning to his characterization of the revolutionary elite. They are not mere revolutionaries; they are "professional revolutionists." He insists on the full meaning of the term "professional": someone who is an experienced, full-time, trained revolutionist. This small, secret, disciplined, professional cadre is specifically contrasted to workers' organizations, which are large, public, and established according to trades. The two are never to be confused. Thus, to the analogy of the factory manager vis-à-vis the worker, Lenin adds that of the professional vis-à-vis the apprentice or amateur. It is assumed that those in the second category will defer to those in the first on the basis of their greater technical knowledge and experience.

Just as Le Corbusier imagines that the public will acquiesce to the knowledge and calculations of the master architect, so Lenin is confident that a sensible worker will want to place himself under the authority of professional revolutionists.

Let us return, finally, to the metaphor of the schoolroom where the vanguard party is the teacher and the masses are the pupils. Lenin is hardly unique in his use of this analogy. His was a pedagogical age in general, and reading circles for workers and schools for socialist militants were common, especially in Germany, where Rosa Luxemburg taught at the Socialist Party's school in Berlin. Although the imagery of the schoolroom may have been commonplace, Lenin's particular use of it to characterize socialist training bears emphasis. A tremendous amount of Lenin's thought and prose was devoted to "socialist instruction" broadly understood. He was preoccupied with how militants might be trained, the role of the party newspaper, *Iskra*, and the content of speeches, manifestos, and slogans. But Lenin's socialist schoolroom is fraught with danger. His constant fear is that the teachers will lose control of the students and be swamped by the pervasive influence of narrow economic demands, legislative reforms, and purely local concerns. The classroom metaphor is inherently hierarchical, but Lenin's main worry is that his socialist teachers will succumb and "go native." Lurking near the surface of Lenin's writings is a powerful cultural judgment, which is evident here in a representative passage.

> Our very first and most imperative duty is to help to train working-class revolutionists who will be on the same level *in regard to party activity* as intellectual revolutionists (we emphasize the words "in regard to party activity" because although it is necessary, it is not so easy and not so imperative to bring workers up to the level of intellectuals in other respects). Therefore attention must be devoted *principally* to the task of *raising* the workers to the level of revolutionists, but without, in doing so, necessarily *degrading* ourselves to the level of the "labor masses" as the Economists wish to do, or necessarily to the level of the average worker, as [the newspaper] *Svoboda* desires to do.[16]

The dilemma for the party is how to train revolutionists who will be close to the workers (and perhaps of worker backgrounds themselves) but who will not be absorbed, contaminated, and weakened by the political and cultural backwardness of the workers. Some of Lenin's worries have to do with his conviction at the time that the Russian working class and most of its socialist intelligentsia were woefully backward compared to their German counterparts. In *What Is to Be Done?* German social democracy and the German trade-union movement function repeatedly as the model, in terms of which Russia is found wanting. But the principle behind Lenin's concerns transcends national differences; it stems from the sharply delineated, functional roles that the party and the working class each played. Class consciousness, in the final analysis, is an objective truth carried solely by the ideologically enlightened who direct the vanguard party.[17]

However contrary to Newton's first law of motion, the central idea informing Lenin's logic is that the party will be an "unmoved mover." An intimate association with the working class is absolutely necessary to the task of propaganda and agitation, but it must be a closeness that will never threaten the hierarchy of knowledge, influence, and power. If professional revolutionists are to be effective leaders, they require the kind of detailed understanding and knowledge of the workers that successful teachers need of their students, military officers need of their troops, or production managers need of their workforce. It is knowledge for the purpose of achieving goals set by an elite. The relationship depicted is so asymmetrical that one is even tempted to compare it to the relation that a craftsman has to his raw material. A woodworker or a mason must know his inert materials well in order to realize his designs. In Lenin's case, the relative inertness of the material being shaped is implied by the global imagery of "the masses" or "the proletariat." Once these flattened terms are used, it becomes difficult to examine the enormous differences in history, political experience, organizational skills, and ideology (not to mention religion, ethnicity, and language) that exist within the working class.

There is still another contingent and Russia-centered reason why Lenin might have insisted on a small, disciplined, and secret cadre of revolutionists. They were, after all, operating in an autocracy, under the noses of the czarist secret police. After commenting favorably on the openness of competition for office within the German Social Democratic Party, where, owing to certain political and press freedoms, all candidates' public records were known, he exclaimed, "Try to put this picture in the frame of our autocracy!"[18] Where a revolutionary must conceal his identity, under pain of arrest, such openly democratic methods were impossible. The revolutionaries in Russia must, Lenin argued, adapt their tactics to those of their enemy—the political police. If this were the only argument Lenin made for secrecy and iron discipline, then it could be treated as an incidental tactical concession to local conditions. But it was not. The secrecy of the party was designed to prevent contamination from below as much as arrest and exile. There is no other way to interpret passages like the following: "If such an organization [a secret body of 'tried' revolutionists] existed on a firm theoretical basis, and possessed a Social-Democratic journal, we would have *no reason to fear that the movement will be diverted from its path by the numerous 'outside' elements that will be attracted to it.*"[19]

How would the movement be diverted? Lenin had chiefly two potential dangers in mind. The first was the danger of spontaneity, which makes the tactical coordination of revolutionary pressure impossible. The second was, of course, the virtually inevitable ideological diversion of the working class toward trade unionism and legislative reform. Since authentic, revolutionary class consciousness could never develop autonomously within the working class, it followed that the actual political outlook of workers was always a threat to the vanguard party.

It is perhaps for these reasons that when Lenin wrote of propaganda and agitation, it was a one-way transmission of information and ideas that he had in mind. His unrelenting emphasis on a party newspaper fit nicely into this context. A newspaper, even more than "agitation" before heckling or sullen crowds, creates a decidedly one-sided relationship.[20] The organ is a splendid way to diffuse instructions, explain the party line, and rally the troops. Like its successor, the radio, the newspaper is a medium better suited to sending messages than to receiving them.

On many occasions, Lenin and his colleagues took the threat of contamination more literally and spoke in metaphors drawn from the science of hygiene and the germ theory of disease. Thus it became possible to talk of "petit-bourgeois bacilli" and "infection."[21] The shift in imagery was not far-fetched, for Lenin did want to keep the party in an environment that was as sterile and germ-free as possible lest the party contract one of the many diseases lurking outside.[22]

Lenin's general treatment of the working class in *What Is to Be Done?* is strongly reminiscent of Marx's famous depiction of the smallholding French peasantry as a "sack of potatoes"—just so many "homologous" units lacking any overall structure or cohesion. This premise shapes in turn the role of the vanguard party. The trick is to change a formless, sporadic, fragmented, and localized anger among the masses into an organized force with purpose and direction. Just as the force of a powerful magnet aligns a chaos of thousands of iron filings, so the party's leadership is expected to turn a crowd into a political army. At times it is hard to know what the masses actually bring to the revolutionary project beyond the raw material they represent. Lenin's catalogue of the functional roles that the party assumes is quite comprehensive: "We must go among all classes of people as *theoreticians*, as *propagandists*, as *agitators*, and as *organizers*."[23] The inference to be drawn from this list is that the revolutionists are to provide knowledge, opinion, the urge and direction to action, and organizational structure. Given this unidirectional flow of intellectual, social, and cultural services from above, it is hard to imagine what role the masses could have had beyond being mustered up.

Lenin conceived of a division of revolutionary labor that resembled what came to be the expectation (if rarely the practice) of Communist parties both in and out of power. The central committee made all the crucial decisions about tactics and strategy, while the mass organizations and trade unions affiliated with the party served as "transmission belts" for instructions. If we consider the vanguard party, as Lenin did, to be a machine for bringing about the revolution, then we see that the vanguard party's relation to the working class is not much different from a capitalist entrepreneur's relation to the working class. The working class is necessary to production; its members must be trained and instructed, and the efficient organization of their work must be left to professional specialists. The ends of the revolutionist and the capitalist are, of course, utterly different, but the problem of *means* that confronts each is similar and is similarly resolved. The problem of the factory manager is how to deploy so many factory "hands" (interchangeable units all) for the purpose of efficient production. The problem of the scientific socialist party is how to efficiently deploy the masses in order to hasten the revolution. Such organizational logic seems more appropriate to factory production, which involves steady routines, known technologies, and daily wages, than to the decidedly nonroutine, high-stakes endeavor of revolution. Nevertheless, it was the model of organization that structured much of Lenin's argument.

To grasp the picture of Lenin's utopian hopes for the vanguard party, one might relate it to the "mass exercises" that were enormously popular among both reactionary (mobilizing) and left-wing movements of the turn of the century. Set in huge stadiums or on parade grounds, they involved thousands of young men and women trained to move in unison. The more complicated their maneuvers, which were often set to rhythmic music, the more impressive the spectacle. In 1891, at the Second National Congress of Sokol, a Czech gymnastic and physical fitness organization promoting nationalism, no fewer than seventeen thousand Czechs gave an elaborate display of coordinated movement.[24] The whole idea of mass exercises was to create a striking exhibition of order, training, and discipline from above, one that would awe participants and spectators alike with its display of disciplined power. Such spectacles assumed and required a single centralized authority, which planned and executed the display.[25] It is little wonder that the new mass-mobilization parties of all stripes should have found public exhibitions of this kind compatible with their organizational ideology. Lenin was far too realistic to imagine that the Russian social democrats would ever resemble anything this coherent and disciplined. Nevertheless, it was clearly the model of centralized coordination to which he aspired and thus the yardstick by which he measured his achievements.

Lenin and Le Corbusier, notwithstanding the great disparity in their training and purpose, shared some basic elements of the high-modernist outlook. While the scientific pretensions of each may seem implausible to us, they both believed in the existence of a master science that served as the claim to authority of a small planning elite. Le Corbusier believed that the scientific truths of modern construction and efficient design entitled him to replace the discordant, chaotic historical deposit of urbanism with a utopian city. Lenin believed that the science of dialectical materialism gave the party unique insight into the revolutionary process and entitled it to claim the leadership of an otherwise disorganized and ideologically misled working class. Both were convinced that their scientific knowledge provided correct, unitary answers to how cities should be designed and how revolutions might be brought to fruition. Their confidence in their method meant that neither the science of designing cities nor that of designing revolutions had much to learn from the existing practices and values of their intended beneficiaries. On the contrary, each looked forward to refashioning the human material that came under their purview. Both, of course, had the improvement of the human condition as their ultimate goal, and both attempted to attain it with methods that were profoundly hierarchical and authoritarian. In the writings of both men, metaphors of the military and the machine pervaded; for Le Corbusier, the house and city were machines for living, and for Lenin, the vanguard party was a machine for revolution. Appeals to centralized forms of bureaucratic coordination—especially the factory and the parade ground—creep naturally into their prose.[26] They were, to be sure, among the most far-reaching and grandiose figures of high modernism, but they were at the same time representative.

Theory and Practice: The Revolutions of 1917

A detailed account of the two Russian Revolutions of 1917 (February and, above all, October) would take us too far afield. What is possible, however, is to sketch briefly some of the principal ways in which the actual revolutionary process resembled little the organizational doctrines advocated in *What Is to Be Done?* The high-modernist scheme for revolution was no more borne out in practice than were high-modernist plans for Brasília and Chandigarh borne out in practice.

The most discordant fact about the Russian Revolution was that it was not to any significant degree brought about by the vanguard party, the Bolsheviks. What Lenin did succeed brilliantly in doing was in capturing the revolution once it was an accomplished fact. As Hannah Arendt succinctly put it, "The Bolsheviks found power lying in the street, and picked it up."[27] E. H. Carr, who wrote one of the earliest and most complete studies of the revolutionary period, concluded that "the contribution of Lenin and the Bolsheviks to the overthrow of czarism was negligible" and that indeed "Bolshevism succeeded to an empty throne." Nor was Lenin the prescient commander in chief who could see the strategic situation clearly. In January 1917, a month before the February Revolution, he wrote disconsolately, "We of the older generation may not see the decisive battles of the coming revolution."[28]

The Bolsheviks, on the eve of the revolution, did have a modest working-class base, especially among the unskilled in Moscow and Saint Petersburg, but Social Revolutionaries, Mensheviks, anarchists, and unaffiliated workers predominated. What is more, the workers who were affiliated with the Bolsheviks were rarely amenable to anything like the hierarchical control envisioned in *What Is to Be Done?*

Lenin's aspiration for revolutionary practice was that the Bolsheviks would come to form a tight, disciplined, command-and-control structure. Nothing could have been further from actual experience. In all but one crucial respect, the revolution of 1917 was very much like the miscarried revolution of 1905. Workers in revolt took over the factories and seized municipal power, while in the countryside, the peasantry began seizing land and attacking the gentry and tax officials. Neither of these activities, either in 1905 or in 1917, was brought about by the Bolsheviks or any other revolutionary vanguard. The workers, who spontaneously formed soviets to run each factory in 1917, disregarded at will the instructions of their own Executive Committee of Soviets, not to mention the Bolsheviks. For their part, the peasantry took the opportunity created by a political vacuum at the center to restore communal control over land and enact their local concept of justice. Most of the peasants had not even heard of the Bolsheviks, let alone presumed to act on their orders.

What must forcefully strike any reader of accounts of the detailed events of late October 1917 is the utter confusion and localized spontaneity that prevailed.[29] The very idea of centralized coordination in this political environment was implausible. In the course of battle, as military historians and astute observers have always understood, the command structure typically falters. Generals lose contact with their troops and are unable to follow the rapidly changing tides of battle; the commands the generals do issue are likely to be irrelevant by the time they reach the battlefield.[30] In Lenin's case, the command-and-control structure could hardly falter, as it had never existed in the first place. Ironically, Lenin himself was out of step with the party's leadership (many of whom were behind bars) and was criticized on the eve of the Revolution as a reckless putschist.

The new element in 1917 that made a revolutionary outcome far more likely than it had been in 1905 was World War I—specifically, the military collapse of the Russian offensive in Austria. Soldiers by the thousands threw down their weapons to return to the cities or to seize land in the countryside. The provisional government of Aleksandr Kerensky had little or nothing in the way of coercive resources to deploy in its defense. It is in this sense that the Bolsheviks "succeeded to an empty throne," although Lenin's small military uprising of October 24 proved a crucial stroke. What followed in the years until 1921 is best described as the *reconquest*, now by the fledgling Bolshevik state, of Russia. The reconquest was not simply a civil war against the "Whites"; it was also a war against the autonomous forces that had seized local power in the revolution.[31] It involved, first and foremost, a long struggle to destroy the independent power of the soviets and to impose piecework, labor control, and the abrogation of the right to strike on the workers. In the countryside, the Bolshevik state gradually imposed political control (in place of communal power), grain deliveries, and, eventually, collectivization on the peasantry.[32] The process of Bolshevik state making entailed a great deal of violence against its erstwhile beneficiaries, as the uprisings of Kronstadt, Tambov, and the Maknovchina in the Ukraine attested.

The model for the vanguard party depicted so sharply in *What Is to Be Done?* is an impressive example of executive command and control. Applied to the actual revolutionary process, however, it is a pipe dream, bearing hardly any relation to the facts. Where the model is descriptively accurate, alas, is in the exercise of state authority after the revolutionary seizure of power. As it turned out, the structure of power that Lenin hoped would characterize the making of the revolution was more closely approximated by the long-lived "dictatorship of the proletariat." And in this case, of course, the workers and peasants did not consent to the structure of power; the state imposed it as a matter of imperative coordination.

Since the revolutionary victors get to write the official history of how they achieved power, it matters little, in one sense, how snugly their account fits the historical facts. Because most citizens come to believe the neatly packaged account, whether or not it is accurate, it further enhances their confidence in the clairvoyance, determination, and power of their revolutionary leaders. The standard "just so" story of the revolutionary process is perhaps the ultimate state simplification. It serves a variety of political and aesthetic purposes, which in turn help to account for the form it assumes. Surely, in the first instance, the inheritors of the revolutionary state have a vested interest in representing themselves as the prime animators of the historical outcome. Such an account emphasizes their indispensable role as leaders and missionaries, and in the case of Lenin, it accorded best with the stated organizational ideology of the Bolsheviks. The authorized histories of revolutions, as Milovan Djilas points out, "describe the revolution as if it were the fruit of the previously planned action of its leaders."[33] No cynicism or mendacity need be involved. It is perfectly natural for leaders and generals to exaggerate their influence on events; that is the way the world looks from where they sit, and it is rarely in the interest of their subordinates to contradict their picture.

After seizing state power, the victors have a powerful interest in moving the revolution out of the streets and into the museums and schoolbooks as quickly as possible, lest the people decide to repeat the experience.[34] A schematic account highlighting the decisiveness of a handful of leaders reinforces their legitimacy; its emphasis on cohesion, uniformity, and central purpose makes it seem inevitable and therefore, it is to be hoped, permanent. The slighting of autonomous popular action serves the additional purpose of implying that the working class is incapable of acting on its own without outside leadership.[35] The account is likely to take the opportunity to identify enemies outside and inside the revolution, singling out appropriate targets of hatred and suppression.

The standard account promoted by revolutionary elites is buttressed by the way in which the historical process itself "naturalizes" the world, erasing evidence of its contingency. Those who fought in "The Russian Revolution" discovered this fact about themselves only later, when the revolution was an accomplished fact. In the same way, none of the historical participants in, say, World War I or the Battle of the Bulge, not to mention the Reformation or the Renaissance, knew at the time that they were participating in anything that could be so summarily described. And because things *do* turn out in a certain way after all, with certain patterns or causes that are clear in retrospect, it is not surprising that the outcome should sometimes seem inevitable. Everyone forgets that it might all have turned out quite differently.[36] In that forgetting, another step in naturalizing the revolutionary triumph has been taken.[37]

When victors such as Lenin get to impose their theories of revolution, not so much on the revolutionary events themselves, but on the postrevolutionary official story, the narrative typically stresses the agency, purpose, and genius of the revolutionary leadership and minimizes contingency.[38] The final irony, then, was that the official story of the Bolshevik Revolution was made, for more than sixty years, to conform closely to the utopian directions outlined in *What Is to Be Done?*

The Lenin of State and Revolution

The later Lenin of *State and Revolution* is often juxtaposed to the Lenin of *What Is to Be Done?* to demonstrate a substantial shift in his view of the relationship between the vanguard party and the masses. Without a doubt, much of Lenin's tone in the pamphlet, written at breakneck speed in August and September of 1917—after the February Revolution and just before the October Revolution—is difficult to square with the text of 1903. There were important tactical reasons why, in 1917, Lenin might have wanted to encourage as much autonomous popular revolutionary action as possible. He and other Bolsheviks were concerned that many workers, now masters of their factories, and many Russian urbanites would lose their revolutionary ardor, allowing Kerensky's provisional government to gain control and block the Bolsheviks. For Lenin's revolutionaries, everything depended on destabilizing the Kerensky regime, even if the crowds were not at all under Bolshevik discipline. No wonder that, even in early November, before the Bolsheviks had consolidated power, Lenin sounded very much like the anarchists: "Socialism is not created by orders from above. State bureaucratic automatism is alien to its spirit; socialism is alive, creative—the creation of the popular masses themselves."[39]

While *State and Revolution* has an egalitarian and utopian tone that echoes Marx's picture of Communism, what is striking for our purpose is the degree to which Lenin's high-modernist convictions still pervade the text. First, Lenin leaves no doubt that the application of state coercive power is the only way to build socialism. He openly avows the need for violence after the seizure of power: "The proletariat needs state power, the centralized organization of force, the organization of violence, . . . for the purpose of *guiding* the great mass of the population—the peasantry, the petite bourgeoisie, the semi-proletarians—in the work of organizing Socialist economy."[40] Once again Marxism provides the ideas and training that alone create a brain for the working masses: "By educating a workers' party, Marxism educates the vanguard of the proletariat, capable of assuming power and leading the whole people to Socialism, of directing and organizing the new order, of being teacher, guide and leader of all the toiling and exploited in the task of building up their social life without the bourgeoisie and against the bourgeoisie."[41] The assumption is that the social life of the working class will be organized either by the bourgeoisie or by the vanguard party, but never by members of the working class themselves.

At the same time, Lenin waxes eloquent about a new society in which politics will have disappeared and in which virtually anyone could be entrusted with the administration of things. The models for Lenin's optimism were precisely the great human machines of his time: industrial organizations and large bureaucracies. In his picture, the growth of capitalism has built a nonpolitical technostructure that rolls along of its accord: "Capitalist culture has *created* large-scale production, factories, railways, the postal service, telephones, etc., and *on this basis* the great majority of functions of the old 'state power' have become so simplified and can be reduced to such simple operations of registration, filing, and checking that they would be quite within the reach of every literate person, and it will be possible to perform them for working men's wages, which circumstance can (and must) strip those functions of every shadow of privilege and every appearance of official grandeur."[42] Lenin conjures up a vision of the perfect technical rationality of modern production. Once the "simple operations" appropriate to each niche in the established division of labor are mastered, there is quite literally nothing more to discuss. The revolution ousts the bourgeoisie from the bridge of this "ocean liner," installs the vanguard party, and sets a new course, but the jobs of the vast crew are unchanged. Lenin's picture of the technical structure, it should be noted, is entirely static. The forms of production are either set or, if they do change, the changes cannot require skills of a different order.

The utopian promise of this capitalist-created state of affairs is that anyone could take part in the administration of the state. The development of capitalism had produced massive, socialized, bureaucratic apparatuses as well as the "training and *disciplining* of millions of workers."[43] Taken together, these huge, centralized bureaucracies were the key to the new world. Lenin had seen them at work in the wartime mobilization of Germany under Rathenau's guiding hand. Science and the division of labor had spawned an institutional order of technical expertise in which politics and quarrels were beside the point. Modern production provided the basis of a technically necessary dictatorship. "In regard to . . . the importance of individual dictatorial powers,"

Lenin observed, "it must be said that large-scale machine industry—which is precisely . . . the foundation of socialism[—] . . . calls for absolute and strict *unity of will*, which directs the joint labours of hundreds, thousands and tens of thousands of people. . . . But how can strict unity of will be ensured? By thousands subordinating their will to the will of one. . . . We must learn to combine the public-meeting democracy of the working people—turbulent, surging, overflowing its banks like a spring flood—with iron discipline while at work, with *unquestioning obedience* to the will of a single person, the Soviet leader, while at work."[44]

In this respect, Lenin joins many of his capitalist contemporaries in his enthusiasm for Fordist and Taylorist production technology. What was rejected by Western trade unions of the time as a "de-skilling" of an artisanal workforce was embraced by Lenin as the key to rational state planning.[45] There is, for Lenin, a single, objectively correct, efficient answer to all questions of how to rationally design production or administration.[46]

Lenin goes on to imagine, in a Fourierist vein, a vast national syndicate that will virtually run itself. He sees it as a technical net whose mesh will confine workers to the appropriate routines by its rationality and the discipline of habit. In a chillingly Orwellian passage—a warning, perhaps, to anarchist or lumpen elements who might resist its logic—Lenin indicates how remorseless the system will be: "Escape from this national accounting will inevitably become increasingly difficult . . . and will probably be accompanied by such swift and severe punishment (for the armed workers are men of practical life, not sentimental intellectuals and they will scarcely allow anyone to trifle with them), that very soon the *necessity* of observing the simple, fundamental rules of social life in common will have become a *habit*."[47]

Except for the fact that Lenin's utopia is more egalitarian and is set in the context of the dictatorship of the proletariat, the parallels with Le Corbusier's high modernism are conspicuous. The social order is conceived as a vast factory or office—a "smoothly humming machine," as Le Corbusier would have put it, in which "each man would live in an ordered relation to the whole." Neither Lenin nor Le Corbusier were unique in sharing this vision, although they were exceptionally influential. The parallels serve as a reminder of the extent to which much of the socialist left as well as the right were in thrall to the template of modern industrial organization. Comparable utopias, a "dream of authoritarian, military, egalitarian, bureaucratic socialism which was openly admiring of Prussian values," could be found in Marx, in Saint-Simon, and in the science fiction that was widely popular in Russia at the time, especially a translation of Edward Bellamy's *Looking Backward*.[48] High modernism was politically polymorphous; it could appear in any political disguise, even an anarchist one.

The Lenin of The Agrarian Question

In order to clinch the argument for Lenin's consistently high-modernist stance, we need only turn to his writings on agriculture, a field in which high-modernist views were hotly contested. Most of our evidence can be drawn from a single work, *The Agrarian Question*, written between 1901 and 1907.[49]

This text was an unremitting condemnation of small-scale family farming and a celebration of the gigantic, highly mechanized forms of modern agriculture. For Lenin it was not just a question of aesthetics of scale but a question of historical inevitability. The difference between low-technology family farming and large-scale, mechanized farming was precisely the difference between the hand-operated looms of cottage-industry weavers on one hand and the mechanized looms of large textile factories on the other. The first mode of production was simply doomed. Lenin's analogy was borrowed from Marx, who frequently used it as a way of saying that the hand loom gives you feudalism and the power loom gives you capitalism. So suggestive was this imagery that Lenin fell back on it in other contexts, claiming, for example, in *What Is to Be Done?* that his opponents, the Economists, were using "handicraft methods," whereas the Bolsheviks operated as professional (modern, trained) revolutionaries.

Peasant forms of production—not to mention the peasants themselves—were, for Lenin, hopelessly backward. They were mere historical vestiges that would undoubtedly be swept away, as the cottage-industry weavers had been, by the agrarian equivalent of large-scale machine industry. "Two decades have passed," he wrote, "and machinery has driven the small producer from still another of his last refuges, as if telling those who have ears to hear and eyes to see that the economist must always look forward, towards technical progress, or else be left behind at once, for he who will not look ahead turns his back on history; there is not and there cannot be any middle path."[50] Here and in other writings Lenin denounced all the cultivation and social practices associated with the customary, communal, three-field system of land allotments that still pertained in much of Russia. In this case, the idea of common property prevented the full development of capitalism, which, in turn, was a condition of revolution. "Modern agricultural technique," he concluded, "demands that *all* the conditions of the ancient, conservative, barbarous, ignorant, and pauper methods of economy on peasant allotments be transformed. The three-field system, the primitive implements, the patriarchical impecuniosity of the tiller, the routine methods of stock breeding and crass naive ignorance of the conditions and requirements of the market must all be thrown overboard."[51]

The suitability of a logic drawn from manufacturing and applied to agriculture, however, was very much contested. Any number of economists had carried out detailed studies of labor allocation, production, and expenditures for rural producer households. While some were perhaps ideologically committed to developing a case for the productive efficiency of small property, they had a wealth of empirical evidence that had to be confronted.[52] They argued that the nature of much agricultural production meant that the economic returns of mechanization were minimal when compared to the returns of intensification (which focused on manuring, careful breeding, and so on). The returns to scale as well, they argued, were minimal or negative beyond the average acreage of the family farm. Lenin might have taken these arguments less seriously had they all been based on Russian data, where the backwardness of rural infrastructure impeded mechanization and commercial production. But most of the data came from Germany and Austria, comparatively developed countries, where the small farmers in question were highly commercialized and responsive to market forces.[53]

Lenin set out to refute the data purporting to show the efficiency or competitiveness of family agriculture. He exploited the inconsistencies of their empirical evidence and introduced data from other scholars, both Russian and German, to make the case against them. Where the evidence seemed unassailable, Lenin claimed that the small farmers who did survive managed to do so only by starving and overworking themselves, their wives and children, their cows, and their plow animals. Whatever profits the small farms produced were the consequence of overwork and underconsumption. Although such patterns of "auto-exploitation" were not uncommon within peasant families, Lenin's evidence was not completely convincing. For his (and Marx's) understanding of modes of production, the survival of artisanal handiwork and small farming had to be an incidental anachronism. We have since learned how efficient and tenacious small-scale production can be, but Lenin was in no doubt about what the future held. "This inquiry demonstrates the technical superiority of large-scale production in agriculture . . . [and] the overwork and underconsumption of the small peasant and his transformation into a regular or day-labourer for the landlord. . . . The facts prove incontestably that under the capitalist system the position of the small peasant in agriculture is in every way analogous to that of the handicraftsman in industry."[54]

The Agrarian Question also allows us to appreciate an additional facet of Lenin's high modernism: his celebration of the most modern technology and, above all, electricity.[55] He was famous for claiming that "Communism is Soviet Power plus the Electrification of the whole countryside." Electricity had, for him and for most other high modernists, a nearly mythical appeal. That appeal had to do, I think, with the unique qualities of electricity as a form of power. Unlike the mechanisms of steam power, direct waterpower, and the internal combustion engine, electricity was *silent*, precise, and well-nigh invisible. For Lenin and many others, electricity was magical. Its great promise for the modernization of rural life was that, once transmission lines were laid down, power could be delivered over long distances and was instantly available wherever it was needed and in the quantity required. Lenin imagined, incorrectly, that it would replace the internal combustion engine in most farm operations. "Machinery powered by electricity runs more smoothly and precisely, and for that reason it is more convenient to use in thrashing, ploughing, milking, cutting fodder."[56] By placing power within reach of an entire people, the state could eliminate what Marx termed the "idiocy of rural life."

Electrification was, for Lenin, the key to breaking the pattern of petit-bourgeois landholding and hence the only way to extirpate "the roots of capitalism" in the countryside, which was "the foundation, the basis, of the internal enemy." The enemy "depends on small-scale production, and there is only one way of undermining it, namely, to place the economy of the country, including agriculture, on a new technical basis, that of modern large-scale production. Only electricity provides that basis."[57]

Much of the attraction of electricity for Lenin had to do with its perfection, its mathematical precision. Man's work and even the work of the steam-driven plow or threshing machine were imperfect; the operation of an electric machine, in contrast, seemed certain, precise, and continuous. Electricity was also, it should be added, centralizing.[58] It produced a visible network of transmission lines emanating from a central power station from which the flow of power was generated, distributed, and controlled. The nature of electricity suited Lenin's utopian, centralizing vision perfectly. A map of electric lines from the generating plant would look like the spokes of a centralized transportation hub like Paris (see chapter 1), except that the direction of flow was one way. Transmission lines blanketed the nation with power in a way that overcame geography. Electricity equalized access to an essential part of the modern world and, not incidentally, brought light—both literally and culturally—to the *narod* (literally, the "dark people").[59] Finally, electricity allowed and indeed required planning and calculation. The way that electricity worked was very much the way that Lenin hoped the power of the socialist state would work.

For Lenin, much the same developmental logic applied to the top elite of the vanguard party, the factory, and the farm. Professionals, technicians, and engineers would replace amateurs as leaders. Centralized authority based on science would prevail. As with Le Corbusier, the degree of functional specificity within the organization, the degree of order provided by routines and the substitutability of units, and the extent of mechanization were all yardsticks of superior efficiency and rationality. In the case of farms and factories, the larger and more capital intensive they were, the better. One can already glimpse in Lenin's conception of agriculture the mania for machine-tractor stations, the establishment of large state farms and eventual collectivization (after Lenin's death), and even the high-modernist spirit that would lead to such vast colonization schemes as Khrushchev's Virgin Lands initiative. At the same time, Lenin's views have a strong Russian lineage. They bear a family resemblance to Peter the Great's project for Saint Petersburg and to the huge model military colonies set up by Alexei Arakcheev with the patronage of Alexander I in the early nineteenth century—both designed to drag Russia into the modern world.

By focusing on Lenin's high-modernist side, we risk simplifying an exceptionally complex thinker whose ideas *and* actions were rich with crosscurrents. During the revolution he was capable of encouraging the communal seizure of land, autonomous action, and the desire of rural Soviets "to learn from their own mistakes."[60] He decided, at the end of a devastating civil war and a grain-procurement crisis, to shelve collectivization and encourage small-scale production and petty trade. Some have suggested that in his last writings he was more favorably disposed to peasant farming and, it is speculated, would not have forced through the brutal collectivization that Stalin ordered in 1929.

Despite the force of these qualifications, there is little reason, I think, to believe that Lenin ever abandoned the core of his high-modernist convictions.[61] This is apparent even in how he phrases his tactical retreat following the Kronstadt uprising in 1921 and the continuing urban food crisis: "Until we have remolded the peasant, . . . *until large-scale machinery has recast him*, we must assure him of the possibility of running his economy without restrictions. We must find forms of coexistence with the small farmer, . . . *since the remaking of the small farmer,* the reshaping of his whole psychology and all his habits, is a task requiring generations."[62] If this is a tactical retreat, the acknowledgment that the transformation of the peasants will take generations does not exactly sound like the words of a general who expects to resume the offensive soon. On the other hand, Lenin's faith in mechanization as the key to the transformation of a recalcitrant human nature is undiminished. There is a new modesty—the fruit of effective peasant resistance—about how tortuous and long the path to a modern, socialized agriculture will be, but the vista, once the journey is made, looks the same.

Luxemburg: Physician and Midwife to the Revolution

Rosa Luxemburg was more than merely a contemporary of Lenin. She was an equally committed revolutionary and Marxist who was assassinated, along with Karl Liebknecht, in Berlin in 1919 at the behest of her less revolutionary allies on the left. Although Jane Jacobs was a critic of Le Corbusier and high-modernist urban planning in general, Le Corbusier had almost certainly never heard of Jacobs before he died. Lenin, on the other hand, had met Luxemburg. They wrote largely for the same audience and in the knowledge of each other's opinions, and indeed Luxemburg specifically refuted Lenin's arguments about the vanguard party and its relation to the proletariat in a revolutionary setting. We will chiefly be concerned with the essays in which Luxemburg most directly confronts Lenin's high-modernist views: "Organizational Questions of Russian Social Democracy" (1904), "Mass-Strike, Party, and Trade Unions" (1906), and her posthumously published "The Russian Revolution" (written in 1918, first published in 1921, after the Kronstadt uprising).

Luxemburg differed most sharply with Lenin in her relative faith in the autonomous creativity of the working class. Her optimism in "Mass-Strike, Party, and Trade Unions" is partly due to the fact that it was written, unlike *What Is to Be Done?* after the object lesson of worker militancy provided by the 1905 revolution. Luxemburg was especially struck by the massive response of the Warsaw proletariat to the revolution of 1905. On the other hand, "Organizational Questions of Russian Social Democracy" was written before the events of 1905 and in direct reply to *What Is to Be Done?* This essay was a key text in the refusal of the Polish party to place itself under the central discipline of the Russian Social Democratic Party.[63]

In emphasizing the differences between Lenin and Luxemburg,

we must not overlook the ideological common ground they took for granted. They shared, for example, Marxist assumptions about the contradictions of capitalist development and the inevitability of revolution. They were both enemies of gradualism and of anything more than tactical compromises with nonrevolutionary parties. Even at the strategic level, they both argued for the importance of a vanguard party on the grounds that the vanguard party was more likely to see the whole situation (the "totality"), whereas most workers were more likely to see only their local situation and their particular interests. Neither Lenin nor Luxemburg had what might be called a sociology of the party. That is, it did not occur to them that the intelligentsia of the party might have interests that did not coincide with the workers' interests, however defined. They were quick to see a sociology of trade-union bureaucracies but not a sociology of the revolutionary Marxist party.

Luxemburg, in fact, was not above using the metaphor of the factory manager, as did Lenin, to explain why the worker might be wise to follow instructions in order to contribute to a larger result not immediately apparent from where he stood. Where the difference arises, however, is in the lengths to which this logic is pursued. For Lenin, the totality was exclusively in the hands of the vanguard party, which had a virtual monopoly of knowledge. He imagined an all-seeing center—an eye in the sky, as it were—which formed the basis for strictly hierarchical operations in which the proletariat became mere foot soldiers or pawns. For Luxemburg, the party might well be more farsighted than the workers, but it would nevertheless be constantly surprised and taught new lessons by those whom it presumed to lead.

Luxemburg viewed the revolutionary process as being far more complex and unpredictable than did Lenin, just as Jacobs saw the creation of successful urban neighborhoods as being far more complex and mysterious than did Le Corbusier. The metaphors Luxemburg used, as we shall see, were indicative. Eschewing military, engineering, and factory parallels, she wrote more frequently of growth, development, experience, and learning.[64]

The idea that the vanguard party could either order or prohibit a mass strike, the way a commander might order his soldiers to the front or confine them to barracks, struck Luxemburg as ludicrous. Any attempt to so engineer a strike was both unrealistic and morally inadmissible. She rejected the instrumentalism that underlay this view. "Both tendencies [ordering or prohibiting a mass strike] proceed from the same, pure anarchist [sic] notion that the mass strike is merely a technical means of struggle which can be 'decided' or 'forbidden' at pleasure, according to one's knowledge and conscience, a kind of pocket-knife which one keeps clasped in his packet, 'ready for all emergencies,' or decides to unclasp and use."[65] A general strike, or a revolution for that matter, was a complex social event involving the wills and knowledge of many human agents, of which the vanguard party was only one element.

Revolution as a Living Process

Luxemburg looked on strikes and political struggles as dialectical, historical processes. The structure of the economy and the workforce helped to shape, but never determine, the options available. Thus, if industry was small scale and geographically scattered, strikes would typically be small and scattered as well. Each set of strikes, however, forced changes in the structure of capital. If workers won higher wages, for example, the increases might provoke consolidations in the industry, mechanization, and new patterns of supervision, all of which would influence the character of the next round of strikes. A strike would also, of course, teach the workforce new lessons and alter the character of its cohesion and leadership.[66] This insistence on process and human agency served Luxemburg as a warning against a narrow view of tactics. A strike or a revolution was not simply an end toward which tactics and command ought to be directed; the process leading to it was at the same time shaping the character of the proletariat. *How* the revolution was made mattered as much as whether it was made at all, for the process itself had heavy consequences.

Luxemburg found Lenin's desire to turn the vanguard party into a military general staff for the working class to be both utterly unrealistic and morally distasteful. His hierarchical logic ignored the inevitable autonomy of the working class (singly and in groups), whose own interests and actions could never be machine-tooled into strict conformity. What is more, even if such discipline were conceivable, by imposing it the party would deprive itself of the independent, creative force of a proletariat that was, after all, the subject of the revolution. Against Lenin's aspiration for control and order Luxemburg juxtaposed the inevitably disorderly, tumultuous, and living tableau of large-scale social action. "Instead of a fixed and hollow scheme of sober political action executed with a prudent plan decided by the highest committees," she wrote, in what was a clear reference to Lenin, "we see a vibrant part of life in flesh and blood which cannot be cut out of the larger frame of the revolution: The mass strike is bound by a thousand veins to all parts of the revolution."[67] When contrasting her understanding to Lenin's, she consistently reached for metaphors from complex, organic processes, which cannot be arbitrarily carved up without threatening the vitality of the organism itself. The idea that a rational, hierarchical executive committee might deploy its proletarian troops as it wished not only was irrelevant to real political life but was also dead and hollow.[68]

In her refutation of *What Is to Be Done?* Luxemburg made clear that the cost of centralized hierarchy lay in the loss of creativity and initiative from below: "The 'discipline' Lenin has in mind is by no means only implanted in the proletariat by the factory, but equally by the barracks, by the modern bureaucracy, by the entire mechanism of the centralized bourgeois state apparatus. . . . The ultracentrism advocated by Lenin is permeated in its very essence by the sterile spirit of a *nightwatchman* (*Nachtwachtergeist*) rather than by a positive and creative spirit. He concentrated mostly on *controlling* the party, not on *fertilizing* it, on *narrowing* it down, not *developing* it, on *regimenting* and not *unifying* it."[69]

The core of the disagreement between Lenin and Luxemburg is caught best in the figures of speech they each use. Lenin comes across as a rigid schoolmaster with quite definite lessons to convey—a schoolmaster who senses the unruliness of his pupils and wants desperately to keep them in line for their own good. Luxemburg sees that unruliness as well, but she takes it for a sign of vitality, a potentially valuable resource; she fears that an overly strict schoolmaster will destroy the pupils' enthusiasm and leave a sullen, dispirited classroom where nothing is really learned. She argues elsewhere, in fact, that the German Social Democrats, by their constant efforts at close control and discipline, have demoralized the German working class.[70] Lenin sees the possibility that the pupils might influence a weak, timorous teacher and deplores it as a dangerous counterrevolutionary step. Luxemburg, for whom the classroom bespeaks a genuine collaboration, implicitly allows for the possibility that the teacher might just learn some valuable lessons from the pupils.

Once Luxemburg began thinking of the revolution as analogous to a complex natural process, she concluded that the role of a vanguard party was inevitably limited. Such processes are far too complicated to be well understood, let alone directed or planned in advance. She was deeply impressed by the autonomous popular initiatives taken all over Russia after the shooting of the crowd before the Winter Palace in 1905. Her description, which I quote at length, invokes metaphors from nature to convey her conviction that centralized control is an illusion.

As the Russian Revolution [1905] shows to us, the mass strike is such a changeable phenomenon that it reflects in itself all phases of political and economic struggle, all stages and moments of the revolution. Its applicability, its effectiveness, and the moments of its origin change continually. It suddenly opens new, broad perspectives of revolution just where it seemed to have come to a narrow pass; and it disappoints where one thought he could reckon on it in full certitude. Now it flows like a broad billow over the whole land, now it divides itself into a gigantic net of thin streams; now it bubbles forth from under the ground like a fresh spring, now it trickles flat along the ground. . . . All [forms of popular struggle] run through one another, next to each other, across one another, flow in and over one another; it is an eternal, moving, changing sea of appearances.[71]

The mass strike, then, was not a tactical invention of the vanguard party to be used at the appropriate moment. It was, rather, the "living pulse-beat of the revolution and at the same time its most powerful driving-wheel, . . . the phenomenal form of the proletarian struggle in the revolution."[72] From Luxemburg's perspective, Lenin must have seemed like an engineer with hopes of damming a wild river in order to release it at a single stroke in a massive flood that would be the revolution. She believed that the "flood" of the mass strike could not be predicted or controlled; its course could not be much affected by professional revolutionists, although they could, as Lenin actually did, ride that flood to power. Luxemburg's understanding of the revolutionary process, curiously enough, provided a better description of how Lenin and the Bolsheviks came to power than did the utopian scenario in *What Is to Be Done?*

A grasp of political conflict as process allowed Luxemburg to see well beyond what Lenin considered to be failures and dead ends. Writing of 1905, she emphasized that "after every foaming wave of political action a fructifying deposit remains from which a thousand stalks of economic struggle shoot forth."[73] The analogy she drew to organic processes conveyed both their autonomy and their vulnerability. To extract from the living tissue of the proletarian movement a particular kind of strike for instrumental use would threaten the whole organism. With Lenin in mind she wrote, "If the contemplative theory proposes the artificial dissection of the mass strike to get at the 'pure political mass strike,' then by this dissection, as with any other, it will not perceive the phenomenon in its living essence, but will kill it all together."[74] Luxemburg, then, saw the workers' movement in much the same light as Jacobs saw the city: as an intricate social organism whose origin, dynamics, and future were but dimly understood. To nevertheless intervene and dissect the workers' movement was to kill it, just as carving up the city along strict functional lines produced a lifeless, taxidermist's city.

If Lenin approached the proletariat as an engineer approached his raw materials, with a view toward shaping them to his purposes, Luxemburg approached the proletariat as a physician would. Like any patient, the proletariat had its own constitution, which limited the kind of interventions that could be made. The physician needed to respect the patient's constitution and assist according to its potential strengths and weaknesses. Finally, the autonomy and history of the patient would inevitably influence the outcome. The proletariat could not be reshaped from the ground up and fitted neatly into a predetermined design.

But the major, recurrent theme of Luxemburg's criticism of Lenin and the Bolsheviks generally was that their dictatorial methods and their mistrust of the proletariat made for bad educational policy. It thwarted the development of the mature, independent working class that was necessary to the revolution and to the creation of socialism. Thus she attacked both the German and Russian revolutionists for substituting the ego of the vanguard party for the ego of the proletariat—a substitution that ignored the fact that the objective was to *create* a self-conscious workers' movement, not just to use the proletariat as instruments. Like a confident and sympathetic guardian, she anticipated false steps as part of the learning process. "However, the nimble acrobat," she charged, referring to the Social Democratic Party, "fails to see that the true subject to whom this role of director falls is the collective ego of the working class which insists on its right to make its own mistakes and learn the historical dialectic by itself. Finally, we must frankly admit to ourselves that the errors made by a truly revolutionary labor movement are historically infinitely more fruitful and valuable than the infallibility of the best of all possible 'central committees.' "[75]

Nearly fifteen years later, a year after the October 1917 Bolshevik seizure of power, Luxemburg was attacking Lenin in precisely the same terms. Her warnings, so soon after the revolution, about the direction in which the dictatorship of the proletariat was headed seem prophetic.

She believed that Lenin and Trotsky had completely corrupted a proper understanding of the dictatorship of the proletariat. To her, it meant rule by the *whole* proletariat, which required the broadest political freedoms for all workers (though not for enemy classes) so that they could bring their influence and wisdom to bear on the building of socialism. It did not mean, as Lenin and Trotsky assumed, that a small circle of party leaders would exercise dictatorial power merely in the name of the proletariat. Trotsky's proposal that the constituent assembly not convene because circumstances had changed since its election struck Luxemburg as a cure that was worse than the disease. Only an active public life could remedy the shortcomings of representative bodies. By concentrating absolute power in so few hands, the Bolsheviks had "blocked up the fountain of political experience and the source of this rising development [the attaining of higher stages of socialism] by their suppression of public life."[76]

Beneath this dispute was not just a difference in tactics but a fundamental disagreement about the nature of socialism. Lenin proceeded as if the road to socialism were already mapped out in detail and the task of the party were to use the iron discipline of the party apparatus to make sure that the revolutionary movement kept to that road. Luxemburg, on the contrary, believed that the future of socialism was to be discovered and worked out in a genuine collaboration between workers and their revolutionary state. There were no "ready-made prescriptions" for the realization of socialism, nor was there "a key in any socialist party program or textbook."[77] The openness that characterized a socialist future was not a shortcoming but rather a sign of its superiority, as a dialectical process, over the cut-and-dried formulas of utopian socialism. The creation of socialism was "new territory. A thousand problems—only experience is capable of correcting and opening new ways. Only unobstructed, effervescing life falls into a thousand new forms and *improvisations*, brings to light creative force, itself corrects all mistaken attempts."[78] Lenin's use of decrees and terror and what Luxemburg called the "dictatorial force of the factory overseer" deprived the revolution of this popular creative force and experience. Unless the working class as a whole participated in the political process, she added ominously, "socialism will be decreed from behind a few official desks by a dozen intellectuals."[79]

Looking ahead, so soon after the revolution, to the closed and authoritarian political order Lenin was constructing, Luxemburg's predictions were chilling but accurate: "But with the repression of political life in the land as a whole, life in the soviets must also become crippled. Without general elections, without unrestricted freedom of the press and assembly, without a free struggle of opinion, life dies out in every public institution. . . . Public life gradually falls asleep. . . . In reality only a dozen outstanding heads [party leaders] do the leading and an elite of the working class is invited to applaud the speeches of the leaders, and to approve proposed resolutions unanimously—at bottom then, a clique affair, . . . a dictatorship in the bourgeois sense."[80]

Aleksandra Kollontay and the Workers' Opposition to Lenin

Aleksandra Kollontay was in effect the local voice of a Luxemburgian critique among the Bolsheviks after the revolution. A revolutionary activist, the head of the women's section of the Central Committee (Zhenotdel), and, by early 1921, closely associated with the Workers' Opposition, Kollontay was a thorn in Lenin's side. He regarded the sharply critical pamphlet she wrote just before the Tenth Party Congress in 1921 as a nearly treasonous act. The Tenth Party Congress opened just as the suppression of the workers' and sailors' revolt in Kronstadt was being organized and in the midst of the Makno uprising in the Ukraine. To attack the party leadership at such a perilous moment was a treacherous appeal to "the base instincts of the masses."

There was a direct connection between Luxemburg and her Russian colleague. Kollontay had been deeply impressed by reading Luxemburg's *Social Reform or Revolution* early in the century and had actually met Luxemburg at a socialist meeting in Germany. While Kollontay's pamphlet echoed most of Luxemburg's criticisms of centralized, authoritarian socialist practice, its historical context was distinctive. Kollontay was making her case as part of the Workers' Opposition argument for an all-Russian congress of producers, freely elected from the trade unions, which would direct production and industrial planning. Alexander Shlyiapnikov, a close ally of Kollontay, and other trade unionists were alarmed at the increasingly dominant role of technical specialists, the bureaucracy, and the party center and the exclusion of workers' organizations. During the civil war, martial-law techniques of management were perhaps understandable. But now that the civil war was largely won, the direction of socialist construction seemed at stake. Kollontay brought to her case for trade-union co-management of industry a wealth of practical experience acquired in the frustrating job of negotiating with state organs on behalf of working women who had organized creches and canteens. In the end, the Workers' Opposition was outlawed and Kollontay was silenced, but not before leaving behind a prophetic legacy of criticism.[81]

Kollontay's pamphlet attacked the party state, which she compared to an authoritarian schoolteacher, in much the same terms used by Luxemburg. She complained, above all, that the relationship between the central committee and the workers had become a stark one-way relationship of command. The trade unions were seen as a mere "connecting link" or transmission belt of the party's instructions to the workers; unions were expected to "bring up the masses" in exactly the way a schoolteacher whose curriculum and lesson plans are mandated from above passes those lessons on to pupils. She castigated the party for its out-of-date pedagogical theory, which left no room for the potential originality of the students. "When one begins to turn over the pages of the stenographic minutes and speeches made by our prominent leaders, one is astonished by the unexpected manifestation of their pedagogical activities. Every author of the thesis proposes the most perfect system of bringing up the masses. But all these systems of 'education' lack provisions for freedom of experiment, for training and for expression of creative abilities by those who are to be taught. In this respect also all our pedagogues are behind the times."[82]

There is some evidence that Kollontay's work on behalf of women had a direct bearing on her case for the Workers' Opposition. Just as Jacobs was afforded a different view of how the city functioned by virtue of her additional roles as housewife and mother, so Kollontay saw the party from the vantage point of an advocate for women whose work was rarely taken seriously. She accused the party of denying women opportunities in organization of "creative tasks in the sphere of production and development of creative abilities" and of confining them to the "restricted tasks of home economics, household duties, etc."[83] Her experience of being patronized and condescended to as a representative of the women's section seems directly tied to her accusation that the party was also treating the workers as infants rather than as autonomous, creative adults. In the same passage as her charge that the party thought women fit only for home economics, she mocked Trotsky's praise for the workers at a miner's congress, who had voluntarily replaced shop windows, as showing that he wanted to limit them to mere janitorial tasks.

Like Luxemburg, Kollontay believed that the building of socialism could not be accomplished by the Central Committee alone, however farseeing it might be. The unions were not mere instruments or transmission belts in the building of socialism; they were to a great extent the subjects and the creators of a socialist mode of production. Kollontay put the fundamental difference succinctly: *"The Workers' Opposition sees in the unions the managers and creators of the communist economy, whereas Bukharin, together with Lenin and Trotsky, leave to them only the role of schools of communism and no more."*[84]

Kollontay shared Luxemburg's conviction that the practical experience of industrial workers on the factory floor was indispensable knowledge that the experts and technicians needed. She did not want to minimize the role of specialists and officials; they were vital, but they could do their job effectively only in a genuine collaboration with the trade unions and workers. Her vision of the form this collaboration might take closely resembles that of an agricultural extension service and farmers to whose needs the service is closely tied. That is, technical centers concerned with industrial production would be established throughout Russia, but the tasks they addressed and the services they provided would be directly responsive to the demands of the producers.[85] The experts would serve the producers rather than dictating to them. To this end Kollontay proposed that a host of specialists and officials, who had no practical factory experience and who had joined the party after 1919, be dismissed—at least until they had done some manual labor.

She clearly saw, as did Luxemburg, the social and psychological consequences of frustrating the independent initiatives of workers. Arguing from concrete examples—workers procuring firewood, establishing a dining hall, and opening a nursery—she explained how they were thwarted at every turn by bureaucratic delay and pettifoggery: "Every independent thought or initiative is treated as a 'heresy,' as a violation of party discipline, as an attempt to infringe on the prerogatives of the center, which must 'foresee' everything and 'decree' everything and anything." The harm done came not just from the fact that the specialists and bureaucrats were more likely to make bad decisions. The attitude had two other consequences. First, it reflected a "distrust towards the creative abilities of the workers," which was unworthy of the "professed ideals of our party." Second, and most important, it smothered the morale and creative spirit of the working class. In their frustration at the specialists and officials, "the workers became cynical and said, 'let [the] officials themselves take care of us.'" The end result was an arbitrary, myopic layer of officials presiding over a dispirited workforce putting in a "bad-faith" day on the factory floor.[86]

Kollontay's point of departure, like Luxemburg's, is an assumption about what *kinds* of tasks are the making of revolutions and the creating of new forms of production. For both of them, such tasks are voyages in uncharted waters. There may be some rules of thumb, but there can be no blueprints or battle plans drawn up in advance; the numerous unknowns in the equation make a one-step solution inconceivable. In more technical language, such goals can be approached only by a stochastic process of successive approximations, trial and error, experiment, and learning through experience. The kind of knowledge required in such endeavors is not deductive knowledge from first principles but rather what Greeks of the classical period called *mētis*, a concept to which we shall return. Usually translated, inadequately, as "cunning," *mētis* is better understood as the kind of knowledge that can be acquired only by long practice at similar but rarely identical tasks, which requires constant adaptation to changing circumstances. It is to this kind of knowledge that Luxemburg appealed when she characterized the building of socialism as "new territory" demanding "improvisation" and "creativity." It is to this kind of knowledge that Kollontay appealed when she insisted that the party leaders were not infallible, that they needed the "everyday experience" and "practical work of the basic class collectives" of those "who actually produce and organize production at the same time."[87] In an analogy that any Marxist would recognize, Kollontay asked whether it was conceivable that the cleverest feudal estate managers could have invented early capitalism by themselves. Of course not, she answered, because their knowledge and skills were directly tied to feudal production, just as the technical specialists of her day had learned their lessons within a capitalist framework. There was simply no precedent for the future now being forged.

Echoing, for rhetorical effect, a sentiment that both Luxemburg and Lenin had uttered, Kollontay claimed that "it is impossible to decree communism. It can be created only in the process of practical research, through mistakes, perhaps, but only by the creative powers of the working class itself." While specialists and officials had a collaborative role of vital importance, "only those who are directly bound to industry can introduce into it animating innovations."[88]

For Lenin, the vanguard party is a machine for making a revolution and then for building socialism—tasks whose main lines have, it is assumed, already been worked out. For Le Corbusier, the house is a machine for living, and the city planner is a specialist whose knowledge shows him how a city must be built. For Le Corbusier, the people are irrelevant to *the process* of city planning, although the result is designed with their well-being and productivity in mind. Lenin cannot make the revolution without the proletariat, but they are seen largely as troops to be deployed. The goals of revolution and scientific socialism are, of course, also for the benefit of the working class. Each of these schemes implies a single, unitary answer discoverable by specialists and hence a command center, which can, or ought to, impose the correct solution.

Kollontay and Luxemburg, in contrast, take the tasks at hand to be unknowable in advance. Given the uncertainty of the endeavor, a plurality of experiments and initiatives will best reveal which lines of attack are fruitful and which are barren. The revolution and socialism will fare best, as will Jacobs's city, when they are joint productions between technicians and gifted, experienced amateurs. Above all, there is no strict distinction between means and ends. Luxemburg's and

Kollontay's vanguard party is not producing a revolution or socialism in the straightforward sense that a factory produces, say, axles. Thus the vanguard party cannot be adequately judged, as a factory might, by its output—by how many axles of a certain quality it makes with a given labor force, capitalization, and so on—no matter how it goes about producing that result. Also, the vanguard party of Luxemburg and Kollontay is at the same time producing a certain kind of working class—a creative, conscious, competent, and empowered working class—that is the precondition of its achieving any of its other goals. Put positively, the way the trip is made matters at least as much as the destination. Put negatively, a vanguard party can achieve its revolutionary results in ways that defeat its central purpose.

Part 3

The Social Engineering of Rural

Settlement and Production

Legibility is a condition of manipulation. Any substantial state intervention in society—to vaccinate a population, produce goods, mobilize labor, tax people and their property, conduct literacy campaigns, conscript soldiers, enforce sanitation standards, catch criminals, start universal schooling—requires the invention of units that are visible. The units in question might be citizens, villages, trees, fields, houses, or people grouped according to age, depending on the type of intervention. Whatever the units being manipulated, they must be organized in a manner that permits them to be identified, observed, recorded, counted, aggregated, and monitored. The degree of knowledge required would have to be roughly commensurate with the depth of the intervention. In other words, one might say that the greater the manipulation envisaged, the greater the legibility required to effect it.

It was precisely this phenomenon, which had reached full tide by the middle of the nineteenth century, that Proudhon had in mind when he declared, "To be ruled is to be kept an eye on, inspected, spied on, regulated, indoctrinated, sermonized, listed and checked off, estimated, appraised, censured, ordered about. . . . To be ruled is at every operation, transaction, movement, to be noted, registered, counted, priced, admonished, prevented, reformed, redressed, corrected."[1]

From another perspective, what Proudhon was deploring was in fact the great achievement of modern statecraft. How hard-won and tenuous this achievement was is worth emphasizing. Most states, to speak broadly, are "younger" than the societies that they purport to administer. States therefore confront patterns of settlement, social relations, and production, not to mention a natural environment, that have evolved largely independent of state plans.[2] The result is typically a diversity, complexity, and unrepeatability of social forms that are relatively opaque to the state, often purposely so. Consider, for a moment, the patterns in such urban settlements as Bruges or the *medina* of an old Middle Eastern city touched on earlier (see chapter 2). Each city, each quarter, each neighborhood is unique; it is the historical vector sum of millions of designs and activities. While its form and function surely have a logic, that logic is not derived from any single, overall plan. Its complexity defies easy mapping. Any map, moreover, would be spatially and temporally limited. The map of a single neighborhood would provide little guidance to the unique intricacies of the next neighborhood, and a description that was satisfactory today would be inadequate in a few years.

If the state's goals are minimal, it may not need to know much about the society. Just as a woodsman who takes only an occasional load of firewood from a large forest need have no detailed knowledge of that forest, so a state whose demands are confined to grabbing a few carts of grain and the odd conscript may not require a very accurate or detailed map of the society. If, however, the state is ambitious—if it wants to extract as much grain and manpower as it can, short of provoking a famine or a rebellion, if it wants to create a literate, skilled, and healthy population, if it wants everyone to speak the same language or worship the same god—then it will have to become both far more knowledgeable and far more intrusive.

How does the state get a handle on the society? Here and in the next two chapters, I am especially concerned with the logic behind large-scale attempts to redesign rural life and production from above. Seen from the center, the royal court or the seat of state, this process has often been described as a "civilizing process."[3] I prefer to see it as an attempt at domestication, a kind of social gardening devised to make the countryside, its products, and its inhabitants more readily identifiable and accessible to the center. Certain elements of these efforts at domestication seem, if not universal, at least very common, and they may be termed "sedentarization," "concentration," and "radical simplification" of both settlement and cultivation.

We shall examine in some detail two notorious schemes of agrarian simplification—collectivization in Soviet Russia and ujamaa villages in Tanzania—searching both for the larger political logic of their design and for the reasons behind their manifold failures as schemes of production. First, however, it may help to provide a schematic illustration of this process from the history of Southeast Asia, which reveals a great continuity of purpose that joins the projects of the precolonial, colonial, and independence regimes together with the modern state's progressive capacity to realize these projects of planned settlement and production.

The demography of precolonial Southeast Asia was such that control of land per se, unless it was a strategically vital estuary, strait, or pass, was seldom decisive in state building. Control of the population—roughly five persons per square kilometer in 1700—mattered far more. The key to successful statecraft was typically the ability to attract and hold a substantial, productive population within a reasonable radius of the court. Given the relative sparseness of the population and the ease of physical flight, the control of arable land was pointless unless there was a population to work it. The precolonial kingdom thus trod a narrow path between a level of taxes and corvée exactions that would sustain a monarch's ambitions and a level that would precipitate wholesale flight. Precolonial wars were more often about rounding up captives and settling them near the central court than asserting a territorial claim. A growing, productive population settled in the ambit of a monarch's capital was a more reliable indicator of a kingdom's power than its physical extent.

The precolonial state was thus vitally interested in the sedentarization of its population—in the creation of permanent, fixed settlements. The greater the concentration of people, providing that they produced an economic surplus, the greater the ease of appropriating grain, labor, and military service. At the crudest level, this determinist geographical logic is nothing more than an application of standard theories of location. As Johann Heinrich von Thünen, Walter Christaller, and G. William Skinner have amply demonstrated, the economics of movement, other things being equal, tend to produce recurring geographical patterns of market location, crop specialization, and administrative structure.[4] The political appropriation of labor and grain tends to obey much the same locational logic, favoring population concentration rather than dispersion and reflecting a logic of appropriation based on transportation costs.[5] In this context, much of the classical literature on statecraft is preoccupied with the techniques of attracting and holding a population in an environment where they can flee to the nearby frontier or settle under the wing of another nearby prince. The expression "to vote with one's feet" had a literal meaning in much of Southeast Asia.[6]

Traditional Thai statecraft hit on a novel technique for minimizing flight and attaching commoners to the state or to their noble lords. The

Thai devised a system of tattoos for literally marking commoners with symbols making it clear who "belonged" to whom. Such tattooing is evidence that exceptional measures were required to identify and fix a subject population inclined to vote with its feet. So common was physical flight that a large number of bounty hunters made a living coursing the forests in search of runaways to return to their lawful owners.[7] Similar problems beset the estates of Roman Catholic friars in the early years of Spain's dominion in the Philippines. The Tagalogs who were resettled and organized for supervised production on the Latin American model frequently fled the harsh labor regime. They were known as *remontados*, that is, peasants who had gone "back up to the hills," where they enjoyed more autonomy.

More generally, for precolonial and colonial Southeast Asia, it might be helpful to think in terms of state spaces and nonstate spaces. In the first, to put it crudely, the subject population was settled rather densely in quasi-permanent communities, producing a surplus of grain (usually of wet rice) and labor which was relatively easily appropriated by the state. In the second, the population was sparsely settled, typically practiced slash-and-burn or shifting cultivation, maintained a more mixed economy (including, for example, polyculture or reliance on forest products), and was highly mobile, thereby severely limiting the possibilities for reliable state appropriation. State spaces and nonstate spaces were not merely preexisting ecological and geographical settings that encouraged or discouraged the formation of states. A major objective of would-be rulers was to *create* and then expand state spaces by building irrigation works, capturing subjects in wars, forcing settlement, codifying religions, and so on. The classical state envisaged a concentrated population, within easy range, producing a steady supply of easily transportable, storable grain and tribute and providing a surplus of manpower for security, war, and public works.

Edmund Leach's perceptive effort to understand the frontiers of Burma implicitly followed this logic in its reconstruction of the traditional Burmese polity. He suggested that we look at the precolonial Burmese state not as a physically contiguous territory, as we would in the context of modern states, but as a complex patchwork that followed an entirely different logic. We should picture the kingdom, he insisted, in terms of horizontal slices through the topography. Following this logic, Burma was, in practice, a collection of *all* the sedentary, wet-rice producers settled in valleys within the ambit of the court center. These would be, in the terms suggested above, the state spaces. The next horizontal stratum of the landscape from, say, five hundred feet to fifteen hundred feet would, given its different ecology, contain inhabitants who practiced shifting cultivation, were more widely scattered, and were therefore less promising subjects of appropriation. They were not an integral part of the kingdom, although they might regularly send tribute to the central court. Still higher elevations would constitute yet other ecological, political, and cultural zones. What Leach proposed, in effect, is that we consider all relatively dense, wet-rice settlements within range of the capital as "the kingdom" and the rest, even if relatively close to the capital, as "nonstate spaces."[8]

The role of statecraft in this context becomes that of maximizing the productive, settled population in such state spaces while at the same time drawing tribute from, or at least neutralizing, the nonstate spaces.[9] These stateless zones have always played a potentially subversive role, both symbolically and practically. From the vantage point of the court, such spaces and their inhabitants were the exemplars of rudeness, disorder, and barbarity against which the civility, order, and sophistication of the center could be gauged.[10] Such spaces, it goes without saying, have served as refuges for fleeing peasants, rebels, bandits, and the pretenders who have often threatened kingdoms.

Of course, the ecology of different elevations is only one among many factors that might characterize nonstate spaces. They also appear to share one or more of the following distinctive features: they are relatively impenetrable (wild, trackless, labyrinthine, inhospitable); their population is dispersed or migratory; and they are unpromising sites for surplus appropriation.[11] Thus marshes and swamps (one thinks of the now beleaguered Marsh Arabs on the Iraqi-Iranian border), ever-shifting deltas and estuaries, mountains, deserts (favored by nomadic Berbers and Bedouins), and the sea (home to the so-called sea gypsies of southern Burma), and, more generally, the frontier have all served as "nonstate spaces" in the sense that I have been using the term.[12]

Contemporary development schemes, whether in Southeast Asia or elsewhere, require the creation of state spaces where the government can reconfigure the society and economy of those who are to be "developed." The transformation of peripheral nonstate spaces into state spaces by the modern, developmentalist nation-state is ubiquitous and, for the inhabitants of such spaces, frequently traumatic. Anna Lowenhaupt Tsing's sensitive account of the attempts of the Indonesian state to capture, as it were, the nomadic Meratus hill peoples of Kalimantan describes a striking case in point. The Meratus live, as she notes, in an area that, "so far, has eluded the clarity and visibility required for model development schemes." As migratory hunter-gatherers who at the same time practice shifting cultivation, who live in constantly changing kinship units, who are widely dispersed over a demanding terrain, and who are, in Indonesian eyes, pagans, the Meratus are a tough case for development. Indonesian officials have tried, in their desultory fashion, to concentrate the Meratus in planned villages near the main roads. The implicit goal was to create a fixed, concentrated population that officials in charge of the management of isolated populations could see and instruct when touring the district.[13] Meratus immobility was the precondition of state supervision and development, whereas much of the identity of the Meratus as a people depended on "unhampered mobility."[14]

The inaccessibility of the Meratus was, in state-development parlance and in the eyes of government officials, an index of their lamentable backwardness. They were described by their would-be civilizers as "not yet arranged" or "not yet ordered" (*belum di-ator*), as "not yet brought to religion" (*belum berugama*), and their cultivation practices were described as "disorderly agriculture" (*pertanian yang tidak teratur*). For their part, the Meratus grasped the essentials of what the government had in mind for them. They had been asked to settle along the main tracks through the forest, one local leader observed, "so the government can see the people." The clustered houses they were asked to settle in were meant, they believed, to "look good if the government came to visit."[15] Cast in a discourse of development, progress, and civilization, the plans of the Indonesian state for the Meratus peoples are at the same time a synoptic project of legibility and concentration.

It is in the context of actual rebellion where the effort to create and sharply distinguish state spaces from nonstate spaces is carried to its logical conclusion. The nature of military threat requires clearly defined and easily monitored and patrolled state spaces, such as forts, forced settlements, or internment camps. Modern examples of this can be found in the so-called new villages in Malaya during the Emergency following World War II, which were designed particularly to sequester a Chinese smallholder and rubber-tapping population and prevent it from providing manpower, food, cash, and supplies to a largely Chinese guerrilla force in the hinterland beyond. In an arrangement later copied in the "strategic hamlets" in Vietnam, the reluctant residents were lodged in identical, numbered houses arrayed in straight lines.[16] The population's movement in and out was strictly monitored. They were one short step away from the concentration camps built in wartime to create and maintain a legible, bounded, *concentrated* state space and seal it off as completely as possible from the outside. Here, direct control and discipline are more important than appropriation. In recent times there have been unprecedented efforts to reclaim nonstate space for the state. In any case, that is one way to characterize the massive use of Agent Orange to defoliate large sections of forest during the Vietnam War, thus render the forest legible and safe (for government forces, that is).

The concept of state spaces, suitably modified for the context of a market economy, can also help us to resolve an apparent paradox in colonial agrarian policy in Southeast Asia. How do we explain the decided colonial preference for plantation agriculture over smallholder production? The grounds for the choice can certainly not have been efficiency. For almost any crop one can name, with the possible exception of sugarcane,[17] smallholders have been able historically to out-compete larger units of production. Time and time again, the colonial states found, small producers, owing to their low fixed costs and flexible use of family labor, could consistently undersell state-managed or private-sector plantations.

The paradox is largely resolved, I believe, if we consider the "efficiencies" of the plantation as a unit of taxation (both taxes on profits and various export levies), of labor discipline and surveillance, and of political control. Take, for example, rubber production in colonial Malaya. At the beginning of the rubber boom in the first decade of the twentieth century, British officials and investors no doubt believed that rubber produced by estates, which had better planting stock, better scientific management, and more available labor, would prove more efficient and profitable than rubber produced by smallholders.[18] When they discovered they were wrong, however, officials persisted in systematically favoring rubber estates at some considerable cost to the overall economy of the colony. The infamous Stevenson scheme in Malaya during the worldwide depression was a particularly blatant attempt to preserve the failing estate sector of the rubber industry by limiting smallholder production. Without it, most estates would have perished.

The fact that, in protecting the estate sector, the colonizers were also protecting the interests of their countrymen and those of metropolitan investors was only one factor in explaining their policy. If it were the main reason, one would expect the policy to lapse with the country's independence. As we shall shortly see, it did not. The plantations, although less efficient than smallholders as producers, were far more convenient as units of taxation. It was easier to monitor and tax large, publicly-owned businesses than to do so for a vast swarm of small growers who were here today and gone tomorrow and whose landholdings, production, and profits were illegible to the state. But because plantations specialized in a single crop, it was a simple matter to assess their production and profits. A second advantage of estate rubber production was that it typically provided centralized forms of residence and labor that were far more amenable to central political and administrative control. Estates were, in a word, far more legible communities than were the Malay *kampung*, which had its own history, leadership, and mixed economy.

A comparable logic can be usefully applied to the establishment of federal land schemes in independent Malaysia. Why did the Malaysian state elect to establish large, costly, bureaucratically monitored settlements in the 1960s and 1970s when the frontier was already being actively pioneered by large-scale voluntary migration? Pioneer settlement cost the state virtually nothing and had historically created viable household enterprises that grew and marketed cash crops. As an economic proposition, the huge rubber and palm oil concerns established by the government made little sense. They were enormously costly to set up, the capital expenditure per settler being far beyond what a rational businessman would have invested.

Politically and administratively, however, the advantages of these large, centrally planned, and centrally run government schemes were manifold. At a time when the attempted revolution of the Malayan Communist Party was still fresh in the minds of the country's Malay rulers, planned settlements had some of the advantages of strategic hamlets. They were laid out according to a simple grid pattern and were immediately legible to an outside official. The house lots were numbered consecutively, and the inhabitants were registered and monitored far more closely than in open frontier areas. Malaysian settlers could be, and were, carefully selected for age, skills, and political reliability; villagers in the state of Kedah, where I worked in the late 1970s, understood that if they wanted to be selected for a settlement scheme, they needed a recommendation from a local politician of the ruling party.

The administrative and economic situation of the Malaysian settlers was comparable to that of the "company towns" of early industrialization, where everyone worked at comparable jobs, were paid by the same boss, lived in company housing, and shopped at the same company store. Until the plantation crops were mature, the settlers were paid a wage. Their production was marketed through state channels, and they could be dismissed for any one of a large number of infractions against the rules established by the scheme's officials. The economic dependency and direct political control meant that such schemes could regularly be made to produce large electoral majorities for the ruling party. Collective protest was rare and could usually be snuffed out by the sanctions available to the administrators. It goes without saying that the settlements of the Federal Land Development Authority (FELDA) allowed the state to control the mix of export crops, to monitor production and processing, and to set producer prices in order to generate revenue.

The publicly stated rationale for planned settlement schemes was almost always couched in the discourse of orderly development and social services (such as the provision of health clinics, sanitation, adequate housing, education, clean water, and infrastructure). The public rhetoric was not intentionally insincere; it was, however, misleadingly silent about the manifold ways in which orderly development of this kind served important goals of appropriation, security, and political hegemony that could not have been met through autonomous frontier settlement. FELDA schemes were "soft" civilian versions of the new villages created as part of counterinsurgency policy. The dividend they paid was less an economic return than a dividend in expanding state spaces.

State plans of sedentarization and planned settlement have rarely gone as anticipated—in Malaysia or elsewhere. Like the scientific forest or the grid city, the targets of development have habitually escaped the fine-tuned control aspired to by their inventors. But we must never overlook the fact that the effect of these schemes, however inflected by local practice, lies as much in what they replace as in the degree to which they live up to their own rhetoric.

The concentration of population in planned settlements may not create what state planners had in mind, but it has almost always disrupted or destroyed prior communities whose cohesion derived mostly from nonstate sources. The communities thus superseded—however objectionable they may have been on normative grounds—were likely to have had their own unique histories, social ties, mythology, and capacity for joint action. Virtually by definition, the state-designated settlement must start from the beginning to build its own sources of cohesion and joint action. A new community is thus, also by definition, a community demobilized, and hence a community more amenable to control from above and outside.[19]

6 Soviet Collectivization, Capitalist Dreams

The master builders of Soviet society were rather more like Niemeyer designing Brasília than Baron Haussmann retrofitting Paris. A combination of defeat in war, economic collapse, and a revolution had provided the closest thing to a bulldozed site that a state builder ever gets. The result was a kind of ultrahigh modernism that in its audacity recalled the utopian aspects of its precursor, the French Revolution.

This is not the place, nor am I the most knowledgeable guide, for an extensive discussion of Soviet high modernism.[1] What I aim to do, instead, is to emphasize the cultural and aesthetic elements in Soviet high modernism. This will in turn pave the way for an examination of an illuminating point of direct contact between Soviet and American high modernism: the belief in huge, mechanized, industrial farms.

In certain vital respects, Soviet high modernism is not a sharp break from Russian absolutism. Ernest Gellner has argued that of the two facets of the Enlightenment—the one asserting the sovereignty of the individual and his interests, the other commending the rational authority of experts—it was the second that spoke to rulers who wanted their "backward" states to catch up. The Enlightenment arrived in Central Europe, he concludes, as a "centralizing rather than a liberating force."[2]

Strong historical echoes of Leninist high modernism can thus be found in what Richard Stites calls the "administrative utopianism" of the Russian czars and their advisers in the eighteenth and nineteenth centuries. This administrative utopianism found expression in a succession of schemes to organize the population (serfs, soldiers, workers, functionaries) into institutions "based upon hierarchy, discipline, reg-imentation, strict order, rational planning, a geometrical environment, and a form of welfarism."[3] Peter the Great's Saint Petersburg was the urban realization of this vision. The city was laid out according to a strict rectilinear and radial plan on completely new terrain. Its straight boulevards were, by design, twice as wide as the tallest building, which was, naturally, at the geometric center of the city. The buildings them-selves reflected function and hierarchy, as the facade, height, and ma-terial of each corresponded to the social class of its inhabitants. The city's physical layout was in fact a legible map of its intended social structure.

Saint Petersburg had many counterparts, urban and rural. Under Catherine the Great, Prince Grigory Potemkin established a whole se-ries of model cities (such as Ekaterinoslav) and model rural settlements. The next two czars, Paul and Alexander I, inherited Catherine's passion for Prussian order and efficiency.[4] Their adviser, Alexei Arakcheev, es-tablished a model estate on which peasants wore uniforms and fol-lowed elaborate instructions on upkeep and maintenance, to the point of carrying "punishment books" inscribed with records of their viola-tions. This estate was made the basis of a far bolder plan for a network of widely scattered, self-sufficient military colonies, which by the late 1820s included 750,000 people. This attempt to create a new Russia, in contrast to the disorder, mobility, and flux of a frontier society, quickly succumbed to popular resistance, corruption, and inefficiency. Long before the Bolsheviks took power, in any case, the historical landscape was littered with the wreckage of many miscarried experiments in au-thoritarian social planning.

Lenin and his confederates could implement their high-modernist plans starting from nearly zero. The war, the revolution, and the subse-quent famine had gone a long way toward dissolving the prerevolu-tionary society, particularly in the cities. A general collapse of industrial production had provoked a vast exodus from the cities and a virtual re-gression to a barter economy. The ensuing four-year civil war further dissolved existing social ties as well as schooling the hard-pressed Bol-sheviks in the methods of "war Communism"—requisitions, martial law, coercion.

Working on a leveled social terrain and harboring high-modernist ambitions in keeping with the distinction of being the pioneers of the first socialist revolution, the Bolsheviks thought big. Nearly everything they planned was on a monumental scale, from cities and individual buildings (the Palace of Soviets) to construction projects (the White Sea Canal) and, later, the great industrial projects of the first Five-Year

Plan (Magnitogorsk), not to mention collectivization. Sheila Fitz-patrick has appropriately called this passion for sheer size "giganto-mania."[5] The economy itself was conceived as a well-ordered machine, where everyone would simply produce goods of the description and quantity specified by the central state's statistical bureau, as Lenin had foreseen.

A transformation of the physical world was not, however, the only item on the Bolshevik agenda. It was a cultural revolution that they sought, the creation of a new person. Members of the secular intelli-gentsia were the most devoted partisans of this aspect of the revolu-tion. Campaigns to promote atheism and to suppress Christian rituals were pressed in the villages. New "revolutionary" funeral and mar-riage ceremonies were invented amidst much fanfare, and a ritual of "Octobering" was encouraged as an alternative to baptism.[6] Cremation —rational, clean, economical—was promoted. Along with this secu-larization came enormous and widely popular campaigns to promote education and literacy. Architects and social planners invented new communal living arrangements designed to supersede the bourgeois family pattern. Communal food, laundry, and child-care services promised to free women from the traditional division of labor. Hous-ing arrangements were explicitly intended to be "social condensers."

The "new man"—the Bolshevik specialist, engineer, or functionary—came to represent a new code of social ethics, which was sometimes simply called *kultura*. In keeping with the cult of technology and sci-ence, kultura emphasized punctuality, cleanliness, businesslike direct-ness, polite modesty, and good, but never showy, manners.[7] It was this understanding of kultura and the party's passion for the League of Time, with its promotion of time consciousness, efficient work habits, and clock-driven routine, that were so brilliantly caricatured in Eu-gene Zamiatin's novel *We* and that later became the inspiration for George Orwell's *1984*.

What strikes an outside observer of this revolution in culture and architecture is its emphasis on public form—on getting the visual and aesthetic dimensions of the new world straight. One can perhaps see this best in what Stites calls the "festivals of mustering" organized by the cultural impresario of the early Soviet state, Anatoly Lunacharsky.[8] In the outdoor dramas he produced, the revolution was reenacted on a scale that must have seemed as large as the original, with cannons, bands, searchlights, ships on the river, four thousand actors, and thirty-five thousand spectators.[9] Whereas the actual revolution had all the usual messiness of reality, the reenactment called for military pre-cision, and the various actors were organized by platoon and mobilized with semaphore and field telephones. Like mass exercises, the public spectacle gave a retroactive order, purpose, and central direction to the events, which were designed to impress the spectator, not to reflect the historical facts.[10] If one can see in Arakcheev's military colonies an attempt to prefigure, to represent, a wished-for order, then perhaps Lunacharsky's staged revolution can be seen as a representation of the wished-for relationship between the Bolsheviks and the proletarian crowd. Little effort was spared to see that the ceremony turned out right. When Lunacharsky himself complained that churches were being demolished for the May Day celebrations, Lazar Kaganivich, the city boss of Moscow, replied, "And *my* aesthetics demand that the demonstration processions from the six districts of Moscow should all pour into Red Square at the same time."[11] In architecture, public manners, urban design, and public ritual, the emphasis on a visible, rational, disciplined social facade seemed to prevail.[12] Stites suggests that there is some inverse relation between this public face of order and purpose and the near anarchy that reigned in society at large: "As in the case of all such utopias, its organizers described it in rational, symmetrical terms, in the mathematical language of planning, control figures, statistics, projections and precise commands. As in the vision of military colonies, which the utopian plan faintly resembled, its rational facade barely obscured the oceans of misery, disorder, chaos, corruption and whimsicality that went with it."[13]

One possible implication of Stites's assertion is that, in some circumstances, what I call the miniaturization of order may be substituted for the real thing. A facade or a small, easily managed zone of order and conformity may come to be an end in itself; the representation may usurp the reality. Miniatures and small experiments have, of course, an important role in studying larger phenomena. Model aircraft built to scale and wind tunnels are essential steps in the design of new airplanes. But when the two are confused—when, say, the general mistakes the parade ground for the battlefield itself—the consequences are potentially disastrous.

A Soviet-American Fetish: Industrial Farming

Before plunging into a discussion of the practice and logic of Soviet collectivization, we should recognize that the rationalization of farming on a huge, even national, scale was part of a faith shared by social engineers and agricultural planners throughout the world.[14] And they were conscious of being engaged in a common endeavor. Like the architects of the Congrés Internationaux d'Architecture Moderne, they kept in touch through journals, professional conferences, and exhibitions. The connections were strongest between American agronomists and their Russian colleagues—connections that were not entirely broken even during the Cold War. Working in vastly different economic and political environments, the Russians tended to be envious of the level of capitalization, particularly in mechanization, of American farms while the Americans were envious of the political scope of Soviet planning. The degree to which they were working together to create a new world of large-scale, rational, industrial agriculture can be judged by this brief account of their relationship.

The high tide of enthusiasm for applying industrial methods to agriculture in the United States stretched roughly from 1910 to the end of the 1930s. Agricultural engineers, a new specialty, were the main carriers of this enthusiasm; influenced by currents in their parent discipline, industrial engineering, and most particularly by the doctrines of the prophet of time-motion studies, Frederick Taylor, they reconceptualized the farm as a "food and fiber factory."[15] Taylorist principles of scientifically measuring work processes in order to break them down into simple, repetitive motions that an unskilled worker could learn quickly might work well enough on the factory floor,[16] but their application to the variegated and nonrepetitive requirements of growing crops was questionable. Agricultural engineers therefore turned to those aspects of farm operation that might be more easily standardized. They tried to rationalize the layout of farm buildings, to standardize machinery and tools, and to promote the mechanization of major grain crops.

The professional instincts of the agricultural engineers led them to try to replicate as much as possible the features of the modern factory. This impelled them to insist on enlarging the scale of the typical small farm so that it could mass-produce standard agricultural commodities, mechanize its operation, and thereby, it was thought, greatly reduce the unit cost of production.[17]

As we shall see later, the industrial model was applicable to some, but not all, of agriculture. It was nonetheless applied indiscriminately as a creed rather than a scientific hypothesis to be examined skeptically. The modernist confidence in huge scale, centralization of production, standardized mass commodities, and mechanization was so hegemonic in the leading sector of industry that it became an article of faith that the same principles would work, pari passu, in agriculture.

Many efforts were made to put this faith to the test. Perhaps the most audacious was the Thomas Campbell "farm" in Montana, begun —or, perhaps I should say, founded—in 1918.[18] It was an industrial farm in more than one respect. Shares were sold by prospectuses describing the enterprise as an "industrial opportunity"; J. P. Morgan, the financier, helped to raise $2 million from the public. The Montana Farming Corporation was a monster wheat farm of ninety-five thousand acres, much of it leased from four Native American tribes. Despite the private investment, the enterprise would never have gotten off the ground without help and subsidies from the Department of Interior and the United States Department of Agriculture (USDA).

Proclaiming that farming was about 90 percent engineering and only 10 percent agriculture, Campbell set about standardizing as much of his operation as possible. He grew wheat and flax, two hardy crops that needed little if any attention between planting and harvest time.[19] The land he farmed was the agricultural equivalent of the bulldozed site of Brasília. It was virgin soil, with a natural fertility that would eliminate the need for fertilizer. The topography also vastly simplified matters: it was flat, with no forests, creeks, rocks, or ridges that would impede the smooth course of machinery over its surface. In other words, the selection of the simplest, most standardized crops and the leasing of something very close to a blank agricultural space were calculated to favor the application of industrial methods. In the first year Campbell bought thirty-three tractors, forty binders, ten threshing machines, four combines, and one hundred wagons; he employed about fifty men most of the year, but hired as many as two hundred during the peak season.[20]

This is not the place to chronicle the fortunes of the Montana Farming Corporation, and in any event Deborah Fitzgerald has done so splendidly.[21] Suffice it to note that a drought in the second year and the elimination of a government support for prices the following year led to a collapse that cost J. P. Morgan $1 million. The Campbell farm faced other problems besides weather and prices: soil differences, labor turnover, the difficulty of finding skilled, resourceful workers who would need little supervision. Although the corporation struggled on until Campbell's death in 1966, it provided no evidence that industrial farms were superior to family farms in efficiency and profitability. The advantages industrial farms did have over smaller producers were of another kind. Their very size gave them an edge in access to credit, political influence (relevant to taxes, support payments, and the avoidance of foreclosure), and marketing muscle. What they gave away in agility and quality labor they often made up for in their considerable political and economic clout.

Many large industrial farms managed along scientific lines were established in the 1920s and 1930s.[22] Some of them were the stepchildren of depression foreclosures that left banks and insurance companies holding many farms they could not sell. Such "chain farms," consisting of as many as six hundred farmsteads organized into one integrated operation (one farm to farrow pigs, say, and another to feed them out, along the lines of contemporary "contract farming" for poultry), were quite common, and buying into them was a speculative investment.[23] They proved no more competitive to the family farm than did Campbell's corporation. In fact, they were so highly capitalized that they were vulnerable to unfavorable credit markets and lower farm gate prices, given their high fixed costs in payroll and interest. The family farm could, by contrast, more easily tighten its belt and move into a subsistence mode.

The most striking proposal designed to reconcile the American small-property regime with huge economies of scale and scientific, centralized management was that of Mordecai Ezekial and Sherman Johnson in 1930. They outlined a "national farming corporation" that would incorporate all farms. It would be vertically integrated and centralized and "could move raw farming materials through the individual farms of the country, could establish production goals and quotas, distribute machinery, labor and capital, and move farm products from one region to another for processing and use. Bearing a striking resemblance to the industrial world, this organizational plan was a sort of gigantic conveyor belt."[24] Ezekial was no doubt influenced by his recent tour of Russian collective farms as well as by the plight of the depression-stricken economy. Johnson and Ezekial were hardly alone in calling for centralized industrial farming on a massive scale, not just as a response to economic crisis but as a matter of confidence in an ineluctable high-modernist future. The following expression of that confidence is fairly representative: "Collectivization is posed by history and economics. Politically, the small farmer or peasant is a drag on progress. Technically, he is as antiquated as the small machinists who once put automobiles together by hand in little wooden sheds. The Russians have been the first to see this clearly, and to adapt themselves to historical necessity."[25]

Behind these admiring references to Russia was less a specifically political ideology than a shared high-modernist faith. That faith was reinforced by something on the order of an improvised, high-modernist exchange program. A great many Russian agronomists and engineers came to the United States, which they regarded as the Mecca of industrial farming. Their tour of American agriculture nearly always included a visit to Campbell's Montana Farming Corporation and to M. L. Wilson, who in 1928 headed the Department of Agricultural Economics at Montana State University and later became a high-level official in the Department of Agriculture under Henry Wallace. The Russians were so taken with Campbell's farm that they said they would provide him with 1 million acres if he would come to the Soviet Union and demonstrate his farming methods.[26]

Traffic in the other direction was just as brisk. The Soviet Union had hired thousands of American technicians and engineers to help in the design of various elements of Soviet industrial production, including the production of tractors and other farm machinery. By 1927, the Soviet Union had also purchased twenty-seven thousand American tractors. Many of the American visitors, such as Ezekial, admired Soviet state farms, which by 1930 offered the promise of collectivized agriculture on a massive scale. The Americans were impressed not just by the sheer size of the state farms but also by the fact that technical specialists—agronomists, economists, engineers, statisticians—were, it seemed, developing Russian production along rational, egalitarian lines. The failure of the Western market economy in 1930 reinforced the attractiveness of the Soviet experiment. Visitors traveling in either direction returned to their own country thinking that they had seen the future.[27]

As Deborah Fitzgerald and Lewis Feuer argue, the attraction that collectivization held for American agricultural modernizers had little to do with a belief in Marxism or an affinity for Soviet life.[28] "Rather it was because the Soviet idea of growing wheat on an industrial scale and in an industrial fashion was similar to American ideas about the direction American agriculture should take."[29] Soviet collectivization represented, to these American viewers, an enormous demonstration project without the political inconveniences of American institutions; "that is, the Americans viewed the giant Soviet farms as huge experiment stations on which Americans could try out their most radical ideas for increasing agricultural production, and, in particular, wheat production. Many of the things they wished to learn more about simply could not be tried in America, partly because it would cost too much, partly because no suitable large farmsite was available, and partly because many farmers and farm laborers would be alarmed at the implications of this experimentation."[30] The hope was that the Soviet experiment would be to American industrial agronomy more or less what the Tennessee Valley Authority was to be to American regional planning: a proving ground and a possible model for adoption.

Although Campbell did not accept the Soviet offer of a vast demonstration farm, others did. M. L. Wilson, Harold Ware (who had extensive experience in the Soviet Union), and Guy Riggin were invited to plan a huge mechanized wheat farm of some 500,000 acres of virgin land. It would be, Wilson wrote to a friend, the largest mechanized wheat farm in the world. They planned the entire farm layout, labor force, machinery needs, crop rotations, and lockstep work schedule in a Chicago hotel room in two weeks in December 1928.[31] The fact that they imagined that such a farm *could* be planned in a Chicago hotel room underlines their presumption that the key issues were abstract, technical interrelationships that were context-free. As Fitzgerald perceptively explains: "Even in the U.S., those plans would have been optimistic, actually, because they were based on an unrealistic idealization of nature and human behavior. And insofar as the plans represented what the Americans would do if they had millions of acres of flat land, lots of laborers, and a government commitment to spare no expense in meeting production goals, *the plans were designed for an abstract, theoretical kind of place*. This agricultural place, which did not correspond to America, Russia, or any other actual location, obeyed the laws of physics and chemistry, recognized no political or ideological stance."[32]

The giant *sovkhoz*, named Verblud, which they established near Rostov-on-Don, one thousand miles south of Moscow, comprised 375,000 acres that were to be sown to wheat. As an economic proposition, it was an abject failure, although in the early years it did produce large quantities of wheat. The detailed reasons for the failure are of less interest for our purposes than the fact that most of them could be summarized under the rubric of *context*. It was the specific context of this specific farm that defeated them. The farm, unlike the plan, was not a hypothecated, generic, abstract farm but an unpredictable, complex, and particular farm, with its own unique combination of soils, social structure, administrative culture, weather, political strictures, machinery, roads, and the work skills and habits of its employees. As we shall see, it resembled Brasília in being the kind of failure typical of ambitious high-modernist schemes for which local knowledge, practice, and context are considered irrelevant or at best an annoyance to be circumvented.

Collectivization in Soviet Russia

> What we have here isn't a mechanism, it's people living here. You can't get them squared around until they get themselves arranged. I used to think of the revolution as a steam engine, but now I see that it's not.
> —Andrei Platonov, *Chevengur*

The collectivization of Soviet agriculture was an extreme but diagnostic case of authoritarian high-modernist planning. It represented an unprecedented transformation of agrarian life and production, and it was imposed by all the brute force at the state's disposal. The officials who directed this massive change, moreover, were operating in relative ignorance of the ecological, social, and economic arrangements that underwrote the rural economy. They were flying blind.

Between early 1930 and 1934, the Soviet state waged a virtual war in the countryside. Realizing that he could not depend on the rural Soviets to "liquidate the *kulaks*" and collectivize, Stalin dispatched twenty-five thousand battle-tested, urban Communists and proletarians with full powers to requisition grain, arrest resistors, and collectivize. He was convinced that the peasantry was trying to bring down the Soviet state. In reply to a personal letter from Mikhail Sholokhov (author of *And Quiet Flows the Don*) alerting him to the fact that peasants along the Don were on the verge of starvation, Stalin replied, "The esteemed grain growers of your district (and not only of your district alone) carried on an 'Italian strike' (*ital'ianka*), sabotage!, and were not loathe to leave the workers and the Red Army without bread. That the sabotage was quiet and outwardly harmless (without bloodshed) does not change the fact that the esteemed grain growers waged what was virtually a 'quiet' war against Soviet power. A war of starvation, dear comrade Sholokhov."[33]

The human costs of that war are still in dispute, but they were undeniably grievous. Estimates of the death toll alone, as a result of the "dekulakization" and collectivization campaigns and the ensuing famine, range from a "modest" 3 or 4 million to, as some current Soviet figures indicate, more than 20 million. The higher estimates have, if anything, gained more credibility as new archival material has become available. Behind the deaths rose a level of social disruption and violence that often exceeded that of the civil war immediately following the revolution. Millions fled to the cities or to the frontier, the infamous gulag was vastly enlarged, open rebellion and famine raged in much of the countryside, and more than half of the nation's livestock (and draft power) was slaughtered.[34]

By 1934, the state had "won" its war with the peasantry. If ever a war earned the designation "Pyrrhic victory," this is the one. The *sovkhoz* (state farms) and *kolkhoz* (collective farms) failed to deliver on any of the specifically socialist goals envisioned by Lenin, Trotsky, Stalin, and most Bolsheviks. They were an evident failure in raising the level of grain production or of producing cheap and abundant foodstuffs for an urban, industrializing workforce. They failed to become the technically efficient and innovative farms that Lenin had anticipated. Even in the realm of electrification, Lenin's touchstone of modernization, only one in twenty-five collective farms had electricity by the eve of World War II. By no measure had the collectivization of agriculture created "new men and women" in the countryside or abolished the cultural difference between the country and the city. For the next half-century, the yields per hectare of many crops were stagnant or actually inferior to the levels recorded in the 1920s or the levels reached before the Revolution.[35]

At another level, collectivization was, in a curious state-centric way, a qualified success. Collectivization proved a rough-and-ready instrument for the twin goals of traditional statecraft: appropriation and political control. Though the Soviet kolkhoz may have failed badly at generating huge surpluses of foodstuffs, it served well enough as a means whereby the state could determine cropping patterns, fix real rural wages, appropriate a large share of whatever grain was produced, and politically emasculate the countryside.[36]

The great achievement, if one can call it that, of the Soviet state in the agricultural sector was to take a social and economic terrain singularly unfavorable to appropriation and control and to create institutional forms and production units far better adapted to monitoring, managing, appropriating, and controlling from above. The rural society that the Soviet state inherited (and for a time encouraged) was one in which the allies of the czarist state, the great landlords and the aristocratic officeholders, had been swept away and been replaced by smallholding and middle peasants, artisans, private traders, and all sorts of mobile laborers and lumpen elements.[37] Confronting a tumultuous, footloose, and "headless" (acephalous) rural society which was hard to control and which had few political assets, the Bolsheviks, like the scientific foresters, set about redesigning their environment with a few simple goals in mind. They created, in place of what they had inherited, a new landscape of large, hierarchical, state-managed farms whose cropping patterns and procurement quotas were centrally mandated and whose population was, by law, immobile. The system thus devised served for nearly sixty years as a mechanism for procurement and control at a massive cost in stagnation, waste, demoralization, and ecological failure.

That collectivized agriculture persisted for sixty years was a tribute less to the plan of the state than to the improvisations, gray markets, bartering, and ingenuity that partly compensated for its failures. Just as an "informal Brasília," which had no legitimate place in official plans, arose to make the city viable, so did a set of informal practices lying outside the formal command economy—and often outside Soviet law as well—arise to circumvent some of the colossal waste and inefficiencies built into the system. Collectivized agriculture, in other words, never quite operated according to the hierarchical grid of its production plans and procurements.

What seems clear, in the brief account that follows, is that collectivization per se cannot be laid solely at the feet of Stalin, though he bore much responsibility for its exceptional speed and brutality.[38] A collectivized agriculture was always part of the Bolshevik map of the future, and the great procurement struggles of the late 1920s could hardly have had any other outcome in the context of the decision to pursue forced-draft industrialization. The party's high-modernist faith in great collectivist schemes survived long after the desperate improvisations of the early 1930s. That faith, which claimed to be both aesthetic and scientific, is clearly visible in a much later agrarian high-modernist dream: namely, Khrushchev's virgin lands scheme, launched well after Stalin's death and after his crimes during collectivization had been publicly denounced. What is remarkable is how long these beliefs and structures prevailed, in spite of the evidence of their manifold failings.

Round One: The Bolshevik State and the Peasantry

> It sometimes seems to me that if I could persuade everyone to say "systematize" each time he wanted to say "liberate" and to say "mobilization" every time he wanted to say "reform" or "progress" I would not have to write long books about government-peasant interaction in Russia.
> —George Yaney, *The Urge to Mobilize*

In the particular book quoted above, Yaney was writing about prerevolutionary Russia, but he could just as easily have been writing about the Bolshevik state. Until 1930, the continuities between the rural policy of the Leninist state and its czarist predecessor are more striking than their differences. There is the same belief in reform from above and in large, modern, mechanized farms as the key to productive agriculture. There is also, alas, the same high level of ignorance about a very complex rural economy coupled, disastrously, with heavy-handed raids on the countryside to seize grain by force. Although the continuities persisted even after the institutional revolution of 1930, what is new about the all-out drive to collectivize is the revolutionary state's willingness to completely remake the institutional landscape of the agrarian sector, and at whatever cost.

The new Bolshevik state faced a rural society that was significantly more opaque, resistant, autonomous, and hostile than the one encountered by the czarist bureaucracy. If the czarist officials had provoked massive defiance and evasion in their "crude Muscovite tribute-collecting methods" during World War I,[39] there was every reason to suspect that the Bolsheviks would have an even harder time squeezing grain from the countryside.

If much of the countryside was hostile to the Bolsheviks, the sentiment was abundantly reciprocated. For Lenin, as we have seen, the Land Decree, which gave to the peasants the land that they had seized, had been a strategic maneuver designed to buy rural quiescence while power was consolidated; he had no doubt that peasant smallholdings must eventually be abolished in favor of large, socialized farms. For Trotsky, the sooner what he called "the Russia of icons and cockroaches" was transformed and "urbanized," the better. And for many of the newly urbanized, rank-and-file Bolsheviks, the abolition of the "dark and backward peasant world" was a "vital part of their own emerging personal and working-class identity."[40]

The peasantry was virtually terra incognita to the Bolsheviks. At the time of the revolution, the party had throughout Russia a grand total of 494 "peasant" members (most of them probably rural intelligentsia).[41] Most villagers had never seen a Communist, although they may well have heard of the Bolshevik decree confirming peasant ownership of the land that had been seized. The only revolutionary party with any rural following was the Social Revolutionaries, whose populist roots tended to make them unsympathetic to Lenin's authoritarian outlook.

The effects of the revolutionary process itself had rendered rural society more opaque and hence more difficult to tax. There had already been a sweeping seizure of land, dignified, retrospectively, by the inappropriate term "land reform." In fact, after the collapse of the offensive into Austria during the war and the subsequent mass desertions, much of the land of the gentry and church, as well as "crown land," had been absorbed by the peasantry. Rich peasants cultivating independent farmsteads (the "separators" of the Stolypin reforms) were typically forced back into the village allotments, and rural society was in effect radically compressed. The very rich had been dispossessed, and many of the very poor became smallholders for the first time in their lives. According to one set of figures, the number of landless rural laborers in Russia dropped by half, and the average peasant holding increased by 20 percent (in the Ukraine, by 100 percent). A total of 248 million acres was confiscated, almost always by local initiative, from large and small landlords and added to peasant holdings, which now averaged about 70 acres per household.[42]

From the perspective of a tax official or a military procurement unit, the situation was nearly unfathomable. The land-tenure status in each village had changed dramatically. Prior landholding records, if they existed at all, were entirely unreliable as a guide to current land claims. Each village was unique in many respects, and, even if it could in principle have been "mapped," the population's mobility and military turmoil of the period all but guaranteed that the map would have been made obsolete in six months or sooner. The combination, then, of smallholdings, communal tenure, and constant change, both spatial and temporal, operated as an impenetrable barrier to any finely tuned tax system.

Two additional consequences of the revolution in the countryside compounded the difficulties of state officials. Before 1917, large peasant farms and landlord enterprises had produced nearly three-fourths of the grain marketed for domestic use and export. It was this sector of the rural economy that had fed the cities. Now it was gone. The bulk of the remaining cultivators were consuming a much larger share of their own yield. They would not surrender this grain without a fight. The new, more egalitarian distribution of land meant that extracting anything like the czarist "take" in grain would bring the Bolsheviks in conflict with the subsistence needs of small and middle peasants.[43]

The second and perhaps decisive consequence of the revolution was that it had greatly enhanced the determination and capacity of peasant communities to resist the state. Every revolution creates a temporary power vacuum when the power of the ancien regime has been destroyed but the revolutionary regime has not yet asserted itself throughout the territory. Inasmuch as the Bolsheviks were largely urban and found themselves fighting an extended civil war, the power vacuum in much of the countryside was unusually pronounced. It was the first time, as Orlando Figes reminds us, that the villages, although in straitened circumstances, were free to organize their own affairs.[44] As we have seen, the villagers typically forced out or burned out the gentry, seized the land (including rights to common land and forests), and forced the separators back into the communes. The villages tended to behave as autonomous republics, well disposed to the Reds as long as they confirmed the local "revolution," but strongly resistant to forced levies of grain, livestock, or men from any quarter. In this situation, the fledgling Bolshevik state, arriving as it often did in the form of military plunder, must have been experienced by the peasantry as a reconquest of the countryside by the state—as a brand of colonization that threatened their newly won autonomy.

Given the political atmosphere in rural Russia, even a government having detailed knowledge of the agricultural economy, a local base of support, and a knack for diplomatic tact would have confronted great difficulties. The Bolsheviks lacked all three. A tax system based on income or wealth was possible only with a valid cadastral map and an up-to-date census, neither of which existed. Farm income, moreover, varied greatly with regard to yields and prices from year to year, so any income tax would have had to have been exceptionally sensitive to these conditions in local harvests. Not only did the new state lack the basic information it needed to govern efficiently, it had also largely destroyed the czarist state apparatus of local officials, gentry, and specialists in finance and agronomy who had managed, however inadequately, to collect taxes and grain during the war. Above all, the Bolsheviks generally lacked the village-level native trackers who could have helped them to find their way in a hostile and confusing environment. The village soviets that were supposed to play this role were typically headed by villagers loyal to local interests rather than to the center. An alternative organ, the Committee of the Rural Poor (*kombedy*), which purported to represent the rural proletariat in local class struggles, was either successfully coopted by the village or locked in often violent conflict with the village soviet.[45]

The inscrutability of the mir to most Bolshevik officials was not simply a result of their urban social origins and the admitted complexity of village affairs. It was also the product of a conscious local strategy, one that had demonstrated its protective value in earlier conflicts with the gentry and the state. The local commune had a long history of underreporting its arable land and overreporting its population in order to appear as poor and untaxable as possible.[46] As a result of such deception in the census of 1917, the arable land in Russia had been underestimated by about 15 percent. Now, in addition to the woodland, pastures, and open land that the peasantry had earlier converted into cropland without reporting it, they had an interest in hiding much of the land they had just seized from the landlords and the gentry. Village committees did, of course, keep records for allocating allotment land, organizing communal plow teams, fixing grazing schedules, and so on, but none of these records was made available either to officials or to the kombedy. A popular saying of the period captures the situation nicely: the peasant "owned by decree" (that is, the Land Decree) but "lived secretly."

How did the hard-pressed state find its way in this labyrinth? Where possible, the Bolsheviks did try to establish large state farms or collective farms. Many of these were "Potemkin collectives" designed merely to give cover of legitimacy to existing practices. But where they were not a sham, they revealed the political and administrative attractiveness of a radical simplification of the landholding and taxpaying unit in the countryside. Yaney's summary of the logic entailed is impeccable.

> From a technical point of view it was infinitely easier to plough up large units of land without regard for individual claims than it was to identify each family allotment, measure its value in the peasants' traditional terms, and then painfully transpose it from scattered strips into a consolidated farm. Then, too, a capital city administrator could not help but prefer to supervise and tax large productive units and not have to deal with separate farmers. . . . The collective had a dual appeal to authentic agrarian reformers. They represented a social ideal for rhetorical purposes, and at the same time they seemed to simplify the technical problems of land reform and state control.[47]

In the turmoil of 1917–21, not many such agrarian experiments were possible, and those that were attempted generally failed badly. They were, however, a straw in the wind for the full collectivization campaign a decade later.

Unable to remake the rural landscape, the Bolsheviks turned to the same methods of forced tribute under martial law that had been used by their czarist predecessors during the war. The term "martial law," however, conveys an orderliness that was absent from actual practice. Armed bands (*otriady*)—some authorized and others formed spontaneously by hungry townsmen—plundered the countryside during the grain crisis of spring and summer 1918, securing whatever they could. Insofar as grain procurement quotas were set at all, they were "purely mechanical accounting figures originating from an unreliable estimate of arable and assuming a good harvest." They were, from the beginning, "fictional and unfulfillable."[48] The procurement of grain looked more like plunder and theft than delivery and purchase. Over 150 distinct uprisings, by one estimate, erupted against the state's grain seizures. Since the Bolsheviks had, in March 1918, renamed themselves the Communist Party, many of the rebels claimed to be for the Bolsheviks and the Soviets (whom they associated with the Land Decree) and against the Communists. Lenin, referring to the peasant uprisings in Tambov, the Volga, and the Ukraine, declared that they posed more of a threat than all the Whites put together. Desperate peasant resistance had in fact all but starved the cities out of existence,[49] and in early 1921, the party, for the first time, turned its guns on its own rebellious sailors and workers in Kronstadt. At this point the beleaguered party beat a tactical retreat, abandoning War Communism and inaugurating the New Economic Policy (NEP), which condoned free trade and small property. As Figes notes, "Having defeated the White Army, backed by eight Western powers, the Bolshevik government surrendered before its own peasants."[50] It was a hollow victory. The deaths from the hunger and epidemics of 1921–22 nearly equaled the toll claimed by World War I and the civil war combined.

Round Two: High Modernism and Procurement

The conjunction of a high-modernist faith in what agriculture should look like in the future and a more immediate crisis of state appropriation helped to spark the all-out drive to collectivization in the winter of 1929–30. In focusing on just these two issues, we must necessarily leave to others (and they are a multitude) the gripping issues of the human costs of collectivization, the struggle with the "right" opposition led by Bukharin, and whether Stalin intended to liquidate Ukrainian culture as well as many Ukrainians.

There is no doubt that Stalin shared Lenin's faith in industrial agriculture. The aim of collectivization, he said in May 1928, was "to transfer from small, backward, and fragmented peasant farms to consolidated, big, public farms, provided with machines, equipped with the data of science, and capable of producing the greatest quantity of grain for the market."[51]

This dream had been deferred in 1921. There had been some hope that a gradually expanding collective sector in the 1920s could provide as much as one-third of the country's grain needs. Instead, the collectivized sector (both the state farms and the collective farms), which absorbed 10 percent of the labor force, produced a dismal 2.2 percent of gross farm production.[52] When Stalin decided on a crash industrialization program, it was clear that the existing socialist agricultural sector could not provide either the food for a rapidly growing urban workforce or the grain exports necessary to finance the imported technology needed for industrial growth. The middle and rich peasants, many of them newly prosperous since the New Economic Policy, had the grain he needed.

Beginning in 1928, the official requisition policy put the state on a collision course with the peasantry. The mandated delivery price of grain was one-fifth of the market price, and the regime returned to using police methods as peasant resistance stiffened.[53] When the procurements faltered, those who refused to deliver what was required (who, along with anyone else opposing collectivization, were called kulaks, regardless of their economic standing) were arrested for deportation or execution, and all their grain, equipment, land, and livestock were seized and sold. The orders sent to those directly in charge of grain procurement specified that they were to arrange meetings of poor peasants to make it seem as if the initiative had come from below. It was in the context of this war over grain, and not as a carefully planned policy initiative, that the decision to force "total" (*sploshnaia*) collectivization was made in late 1929. Scholars who agree on little else are in accord on this point: the overriding purpose of collectivization was to ensure the seizure of grain. Fitzpatrick begins her study of the collectives with this assertion: "The main purpose of collectivization was to increase state grain procurements and reduce the peasants' ability to withhold grain from the market. This purpose was obvious to peasants from the start, since the collectivization drive of the winter of 1929–30 was the culmination of more than two years of bitter struggle between the peasants and the state over grain procurements."[54] Robert Conquest concurs: "The collective farms were essentially a chosen mechanism for extracting grain and other products."[55]

It appears that this was also how the vast majority of the peasantry saw it, judging from their determined resistance and what we know of their views. The seizure of grain threatened their survival. The peasant depicted in Andrei Platonov's novel about collectivization sees how the seizure of grain negates the earlier land reform: "It's a sly business. First you hand over the land, and then you take away the grain, right down to the last kernel. You can choke on land like that! The muzhik doesn't have anything left from the land except the horizon. Who are you fooling?"[56] At least as threatening was the loss of what little margin of social and economic autonomy the peasantry had achieved since the revolution. Even poor peasants were afraid of collectivization, because "it would involve giving up one's land and implements and working with other families, under orders, not temporarily, as in the army, but forever—it means the barracks for life."[57] Unable to rely on any significant rural support, Stalin dispatched twenty-five thousand "plenipotentiaries" (party members) from the towns and factories "to destroy the peasant commune and replace it by a collective economy subordinate to the state," whatever the cost.[58]

Authoritarian High-Modernist Theory and the Practice of Serfdom

If the move to "total" collectivization was directly animated by the party's determination to seize the land and the crops sown on it once and for all, it was a determination filtered through a high-modernist lens. Although the Bolsheviks might disagree about means, they did think they knew exactly what modern agriculture should look like in the end; their understanding was as much visual as scientific. Modern agriculture was to be large in scale, the larger the better; it was to be highly mechanized and run hierarchically along scientific, Taylorist principles. Above all, the cultivators were to resemble a highly skilled and disciplined proletariat, not a peasantry. Stalin himself, before practical failures discredited a faith in colossal projects, favored collective farms ("grain factories") of 125,000 to 250,000 acres, as in the American-assisted scheme described earlier.[59]

The utopian abstraction of the vision was matched, on the ground, by wildly unrealistic planning. Given a map and a few assumptions about scale and mechanization, a specialist could devise a plan with little reference to local knowledge and conditions. A visiting agricultural official wrote back to Moscow from the Urals in March 1930 to complain that, "on the instruction of the Raion Executive Committee, twelve agronomists have been sitting for twenty days composing an operational-production plan for the non-existent raion commune without ever leaving their offices or going out into the field."[60] When another bureaucratic monstrosity in Velikie Lukie in the west proved unwieldy, the planners simply reduced the scale without sacrificing abstraction. They divided the 80,000-hectare scheme into thirty-two equal squares of 2,500 hectares each, with one square constituting a kolkhoz. "The squares were drawn on a map without any reference to actual villages, settlements, rivers, hills, swamps or other demographic and topological characteristics of the land."[61]

Semiotically, we cannot understand this modernist vision of agriculture as an isolated ideological fragment. It is always seen as the negation of the existing rural world. A kolkhoz is meant to replace a mir or village, machines to replace horse-drawn plows and hand labor, proletarian workers to replace peasants, scientific agriculture to replace folk tradition and superstition, education to replace ignorance and *malokulturnyi*, and abundance to replace bare subsistence. Collectivization was meant to spell the end of the peasantry and its way of life. The introduction of a socialist economy entailed a cultural revolution as well; the "dark" narod, the peasants who were perhaps the great remaining, intractable threat to the Bolshevik state, were to be replaced by rational, industrious, de-Christianized, progressive-thinking kolkhoz workers.[62] The scale of collectivization was intended to efface the peasantry and its institutions, thereby narrowing the gulf between the rural and urban worlds. Underlying the whole plan, of course, was the assumption that the great collective farms would operate like factories in a centralized economy, in this case fulfilling state orders for grain and other agricultural products. As if to drive the point home, the state confiscated roughly 63 percent of the entire harvest in 1931.

From a central planner's perspective, one great advantage of collectivization is that the state acquired control over how much of each crop was sown. Starting with the state's needs for grains, meat, dairy products, and so on, the state could theoretically build those needs into its instructions to the collective sector. In practice, the sowing plans imposed from above were often wholly unreasonable. The land departments, which prepared the plans, knew little about the crops they were mandating, the inputs needed to grow them locally, or local soil conditions. Nevertheless, they had quotas to fill, and fill them they did. When, in 1935, A. Iakovlev, the head of the Central Committee's agricultural department, called for collective farms to be managed by "permanent cadres" who "genuinely knew their fields," he implied that the present incumbents did not.[63] We catch a glimpse of the disasters from the Great Purges of 1936–37, when a certain amount of peasant criticism of kolkhoz officials was briefly encouraged in order to detect "wreckers." One kolkhoz was instructed to plow meadows and open land, without which they could not have fed their livestock. Another received sowing orders that doubled the previous acreage allotted for hay fields by taking in private plots and quicksands.[64]

The planners clearly favored monoculture and a far-reaching, strict division of labor. Entire regions, and certainly individual *kolkhozy*, were increasingly specialized, producing only, say, wheat, livestock, cotton, or potatoes.[65] In the case of livestock production, one kolkhoz would produce fodder for beef cattle or hogs while another would raise and breed them. The logic behind kolkhoz and regional specialization was roughly comparable to the logic behind functionally specific urban zones. Specialization reduced the number of variables that agronomists had to consider; it also increased the administrative routinization of work and hence the power and knowledge of central officials.

Procurement followed a comparable centralizing logic. Starting with the needs of the plan and a usually unreliable estimate of the harvest, a series of quotas for every oblast, *raion*, and kolkhoz was mechanically derived. Each kolkhoz then claimed that its quota was impossible to fulfill and appealed to have it lowered. Actually meeting a quota, they knew from bitter experience, only raised the ante for the next round of procurements. In this respect collective farmers were in a more precarious situation than industrial workers, who still received their wages and ration cards whether or not the factory met its quota. For the *kolkhozniki*, however, meeting the quota might mean starvation. Indeed, the great famine of 1933–34 can only be called a collectivization and procurement famine. Those who were tempted to make trouble risked running afoul of a more grisly quota: the one for kulaks and enemies of the state.

For much of the peasantry, the authoritarian labor regime of the kolkhoz seemed not only to jeopardize their subsistence but to revoke many of the freedoms they had won since their emancipation in 1861. They compared collectivization to the serfdom their grandparents remembered. As one early sovkhoz worker put it, "The *sovkhozy* are always forcing the peasant to work; they make the peasants weed their fields. And they don't even give us bread or water. What will come of all this? It's like *barschina* [feudal labor dues] all over again."[66] The peasants began to say that the acronym for the All-Union Communist Party—VKP—stood for *vtoroe krepostnoe pravo,* or "second serfdom."[67] The parallel was not a mere figure of speech; the resemblances to serfdom were remarkable.[68] The kolkhoz members were required to work on the state's land at least half-time for wages, in cash or kind, that were derisory. They depended largely on their own small private plots to grow the food they needed (other than grain), although they had little free time to cultivate their gardens.[69] The quantity to be delivered and price paid for kolkhoz produce was set by the state. The kolkhozniki owed annual corvée labor dues for roadwork and cartage. They were obliged to hand over quotas of milk, meat, eggs, and so on from their private plots. The collective's officials, like feudal masters, were wont to use kolkhoz labor for their private sidelines and had, in practice if not in law, the arbitrary power to insult, beat, or deport the peasants. As they were under serfdom, they were legally immobilized. An internal passport system was reintroduced to clear the cities of "undesirable and unproductive residents" and to make sure that the peasantry did not flee. Laws were passed to deprive the peasantry of the firearms they used for hunting. Finally, the kolkhozniki living outside the village nucleus (khutor dwellers), often on their old farmsteads, were forcibly relocated, beginning in 1939. This last resettlement affected more than half a million peasants.

The resulting labor rules, property regime, and settlement pattern did in fact resemble a cross between plantation or estate agriculture on one hand and feudal servitude on the other.

As a vast, state-imposed blueprint for revolutionary change, collectivization was at least as notable for what it destroyed as for what it built. The initial intent of collectivization was not just to crush the resistance of well-to-do peasants and grab their land; it was also to dismantle the social unit through which that resistance was expressed: the mir. The peasant commune had typically been the vehicle for organizing land seizures during the revolution, for orchestrating land use and grazing, for managing local affairs generally, and for opposing procurements.[70] The party had every reason to fear that if the collectives were based on the traditional village, they would simply reinforce the basic unit of peasant resistance. Hadn't the village soviets quickly escaped the state's control? Huge collectives, then, had the decided advantage of bypassing village structures altogether. They could be run by a board consisting of cadres and specialists. If the giant kolkhoz was then divided into sections, one specialist could be named manager of each, "*like the bailiffs in the old days'* [of serfdom] as [one] . . . report wryly noted."[71] Eventually, except in frontier areas, practical considerations prevailed and a majority of the kolkhozy coincided roughly with the earlier peasant commune and its lands.

The kolkhoz was not, however, just window dressing hiding a traditional commune. Almost everything had changed. All the focal points for an autonomous public life had been eliminated. The tavern, rural fairs and markets, the church, and the local mill disappeared; in their places stood the kolkhoz office, the public meeting room, and the school. Nonstate public spaces gave way to the state spaces of government agencies, albeit local ones.

The concentration, legibility, and centralization of social organization and production can be seen in the map of the state farm at Verchnyua Troitsa (Upper Trinity) in Tver Oblast (figure 28).[72] Much of the old village has been removed from the center and relocated on the outskirts (legend reference 11).[73] Two-story apartment houses containing sixteen flats each have been clustered near the center (legend references 13, 14, 15; see also figure 29), while the local administration and trade center, school, and community building, all public institutions run by the state, lie close to the center of the new grid. Even allowing for the exaggerated formalism of the map, the state farm is a far cry from the sprawl and autonomous institutional order of the precollectivized village; a photograph showing the old-style housing and a lane illustrates the stark visual contrast (see figure 30).

Compared to Haussmann's retrofitting of the physical geography of Paris to make it legible and to facilitate state domination, the Bolsheviks' retrofitting of rural Russia was far more thoroughgoing. In place of an opaque and often obstinate mir, it had fashioned a legible kolkhoz. In place of myriad small farms, it had created a single, local economic unit.[74] With the establishment of hierarchical state farms, a quasi-autonomous petite bourgeoisie was replaced with dependent employees. In place, therefore, of an agriculture in which planting, harvesting, and marketing decisions were in the hands of individual households, the party-state had built a rural economy where all these decisions would be made centrally. In place of a peasantry that was

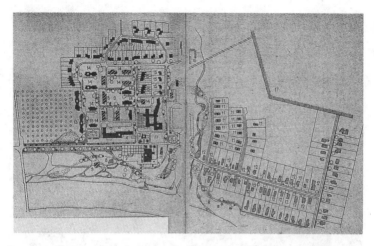

28. Plan of the state farm at Verchnyua Troitsa (Upper Trinity) in Tver Oblast, showing the following sites: *1*, community center; *2*, monument; *3*, hotel; *4*, local administration and trade center; *5*, school; *6*, kindergarten; *7–8*, museums; *9*, shop; *10*, bathhouse; *11*, old wooden house moved from new construction area; *12*, old village; *13–15*, two- and three-story houses; *16*, garage (private); and *17*, agricultural sites (farm, storage, water tower, and so on)

29. At Verchnyua Troitsa, one of the new village's two-story houses, each containing sixteen flats

30. Houses along a lane in the old village at Verchnyua Troitsa

technically independent, it had created a peasantry that was directly dependent on the state for combines and tractors, fertilizer, and seeds. In place of a peasant economy whose harvests, income, and profits were well-nigh indecipherable, it had created units that were ideal for simple and direct appropriation. In place of a variety of social units with their own unique histories and practices, it had created homologous units of accounting that could all be fitted into a national administrative grid. The logic was not unlike the management scheme at McDonald's: modular, similarly designed units producing similar products, according to a common formula and work routine. Units can easily be duplicated across the landscape, and the inspectors coming to assess their operations enter legible domains which they can evaluate with a single checklist.

Any comprehensive assessment of sixty years of collectivization would require both archival material only now becoming available and abler hands than my own. What must strike even a casual student of collectivization, however, is how it largely failed in *each* of its high-modernist aims, despite huge investments in machinery, infrastructure, and agronomic research. Its successes, paradoxically, were in the domain of traditional statecraft. The state managed to get its hands on enough grain to push rapid industrialization, even while contending with staggering inefficiencies, stagnant yields, and ecological devastation.[75] The state also managed, at great human cost, to eliminate the social basis of organized, public opposition from the rural population. On the other hand, the state's capacity for realizing its vision of large, productive, efficient, scientifically advanced farms growing high-quality products for market was virtually nil.

The collectives that the state had created manifested in some ways the facade of modern agriculture without its substance. The farms *were* highly mechanized (by world standards), and they *were* managed by officials with degrees in agronomy and engineering. Demonstration farms really did achieve large yields, although often at prohibitive costs.[76] But in the end none of this could disguise the many failures of Soviet agriculture. Only three sources of these failures are noted here, because they will concern us later.[77] First, having taken from the peasants both their (relative) independence and autonomy as well as their land and grain, the state created a class of essentially unfree laborers who responded with all the forms of foot-dragging and resistance practiced by unfree laborers everywhere. Second, the unitary administrative structure and imperatives of central planning created a clumsy machine that was utterly unresponsive to local knowledge or to local conditions. Finally, the Leninist political structure of the Soviet Union gave agriculture officials little or no incentive to adapt to, or negotiate with, its rural subjects. The very capacity of the state to essentially reenserf rural producers, dismantle their institutions, and impose its will, in the crude sense of appropriation, goes a long way toward explaining the state's failure to realize anything but a simulacrum of the highmodernist agriculture that Lenin so prized.

State Landscapes of Control and Appropriation

Drawing on the history of Soviet collectivization, I shall now venture a few more frankly speculative ideas about the institutional logic of authoritarian high modernism. Then I shall suggest a way of grasping why such massive social bulldozing may have worked tolerably well for some purposes but failed dismally for others—an issue to which we shall return in later chapters.

The headlong drive to collectivization was animated by the shortterm goal of seizing enough grain to push rapid industrialization.[78] Threats and violence had worked, up to a point, for the harvests of 1928 and 1929, but each annual turn of the screw elicited more evasion and resistance from the peasantry. The bitter fact was that the Soviet state faced an exceptionally diverse population of commune-based smallholders whose economic and social affairs were nearly unintelligible to the center. These circumstances offered some strategic advantages to a peasantry waging a quiet guerrilla war (punctuated by open revolt) against state claims. The state, under the existing property regime, could only look forward to a bruising struggle for grain each year, with no assurance of success.

Stalin chose this moment to strike a decisive blow. He imposed a designed and legible rural landscape that would be far more amenable to appropriation, control, and central transformation. The social and economic landscape he had in mind was of course the industrial model of advanced agriculture—large, mechanized farms run along factory lines and coordinated by state planning.

It was a case of the "newest state" meeting the "oldest class" and attempting to remake it into some reasonable facsimile of a proletariat. Compared to the peasantry, the proletariat was already relatively more legible as a class, and not just because of its central place in Marxist theory. The proletariat's work regimen was regulated by factory hours and by man-made techniques of production. In the case of new industrial projects like the great steel complex at Magnitogorsk, the planners could start virtually from zero, as with Brasília. The peasants, on the other hand, represented a welter of small, individual household enterprises. Their settlement pattern and social organization had a historical logic far deeper than that of the factory floor.

One purpose of collectivization was to destroy these economic and social units, which were hostile to state control, and to force the peasantry into an institutional straitjacket of the state's devising. The new institutional order of collective farms would now be compatible with the state's purposes of appropriation and directed development. Given the quasi–civil war conditions of the countryside, the solution was as much a product of military occupation and "pacification" as of "socialist transformation."[79]

It is possible, I believe, to say something more generally about the "elective affinity" between authoritarian high modernism and certain institutional arrangements.[80] What follows is rather crude and provisional, but it will serve as a point of departure. High-modernist ideologies embody a doctrinal preference for certain social arrangements. *Authoritarian* high-modernist *states*, on the other hand, take the next step. They attempt, and often succeed, in imposing those preferences on their population. Most of the preferences can be deduced from the criteria of legibility, appropriation, and centralization of control. To the degree that the institutional arrangements can be readily monitored and directed from the center and can be easily taxed (in the broadest sense of taxation), then they are likely to be promoted. The implicit goals behind these comparisons are not unlike the goals of premodern statecraft.[81] Legibility, after all, is a prerequisite of appropriation as well as of authoritarian transformation. The difference, and it is a crucial one, lies in the wholly new scale of ambition and intervention entertained by high modernism.

The principles of standardization, central control, and synoptic legibility to the center could be applied to many other fields; those noted in the accompanying table are only suggestive. If we were to apply them to education, for example, the most illegible educational system would be completely informal, nonstandardized instruction determined entirely by local mutuality. The most legible educational system would resemble Hippolyte Taine's description of French education in the nineteenth century, when "the Minister of Education could pride himself, just by looking at his watch, which page of Virgil all schoolboys of the Empire were annotating at that exact moment."[82] A more exhaustive table would replace the dichotomies with more elaborate continua (open commons landholding, for example, is less legible and taxable than closed commons landholding, which in turn is less legible than private freeholding, which is less legible than state ownership). It is no coincidence that the more legible or appropriable form can more read-

Legibility of Social Groups, Institutions, and Practices

	Illegible	Legible
Settlements	• Temporary encampments of hunter-gatherers, nomads, slash-and-burn cultivators, pioneers, and gypsies	• Permanent villages, estates, and plantations of sedentary peoples
	• Unplanned cities and neighborhoods: Bruges in 1500, medina of Damascus, Faubourg Saint-Antoine, Paris, in 1800	• Planned grid cities and neighborhoods: Brasília, Chicago
Economic units	• Small property, petite bourgeoisie	• Large property
	• Small peasant farms	• Large farms
	• Artisanal production	• Factories (proletariat)
	• Small shops	• Large commercial establishments
	• Informal economy, "off the books"	• Formal economy, "on the books"
Property regimes	• Open commons, communal property	• Collective farms
	• Private property	• State property
	• Local records	• National cadastral survey
Technical and resource organizations		
Water	• Local customary use, local irrigation societies	• Centralized dam, irrigation control
Transportation	• Decentralized webs and networks	• Centralized hubs
Energy	• Cow pats and brushwood gathered locally or local electric generating stations	• Large generating stations in urban centers
Identification	• Unregulated local naming customs	• Permanent patronyms
	• No state documentation of citizens	• National system of identification cards, documents, or passports

ily be converted into a source of rent—either as private property or as the monopoly rent of the state.

The Limits of Authoritarian High Modernism

When are high-modernist arrangements likely to work and when are they likely to fail? The abject performance of Soviet agriculture as an efficient producer of foodstuffs was, in retrospect, "overdetermined" by many causes having little to do with high modernism per se: the radically mistaken biological theories of Trofim Lysenko, Stalin's obsessions, conscription during World War II, and the weather. And it is apparent that centralized high-modernist solutions can be the most efficient, equitable, and satisfactory for many tasks. Space exploration, the planning of transportation networks, flood control, airplane manufacturing, and other endeavors may require huge organizations minutely coordinated by a few experts. The control of epidemics or of pollution requires a center staffed by experts receiving and digesting standard information from hundreds of reporting units.

On the other hand, these methods seem singularly maladroit at such tasks as putting a really good meal on the table or performing surgery. This issue will be addressed at length in chapter 8, but some valuably suggestive evidence can be gleaned from Soviet agriculture. If we think of particular crops, it is apparent that collective farms were successful at growing some crops, especially the major grains: wheat, rye, oats, barley, and maize. They were notably inefficient at turning out other products, especially fruits, vegetables, small livestock, eggs, dairy products, and flowers. Most of these crops were supplied from the minuscule private plots of the kolkhoz members, even at the height of collectivization.[83] The systematic differences between these two categories of crops helps to explain why their institutional setting might vary.

Let us take wheat as an example of what I will call a "proletarian crop" and compare it with red raspberries, which I think of as the ultimate "petit-bourgeois crop." Wheat lends itself to extensive large-scale farming and mechanization. One might say that wheat is to collectivized agriculture what the Norway spruce is to centrally managed, scientific forestry. Once planted, it needs little care until harvest, when a combine can cut and thresh the grain in one operation and then blow it into trucks bound for granaries or into railroad cars. Relatively sturdy in the ground, wheat remains sturdy once harvested. It is relatively easy to store for extended periods with only small losses to spoilage. The red raspberry bush, on the other hand, requires a particular soil to be fruitful; it must be pruned annually; it requires more than one picking, and it is virtually impossible to pick by machine. Once packed, raspberries last only a few days under the best conditions. They will spoil within hours if packed too tightly or if stored at too high a temperature. At virtually every stage the raspberry crop needs delicate handling and speed, or all is lost.

Little wonder, then, that fruits and vegetables—petit-bourgeois crops—were typically not grown as kolkhoz crops but rather as sidelines produced by individual households. The collective sector in effect ceded such crops to those who had the personal interest, incentive, and horticultural skills to grow them successfully. Such crops can, in principle, be grown by huge centralized enterprises as well, but they must be enterprises that are elaborately attentive to the care of the crops and to the care of the labor that tends them. Even where such crops are grown on large farms, the farms tend to be family enterprises of smaller size than wheat farms and are insistent on a stable, knowledgeable workforce. In these situations, the small family enterprise has, in the terms of neoclassical economics, a comparative advantage.

Another way in which wheat production is different from raspberry production is that the growing of wheat involves a modest number of routines that, because the grain is robust, allow some slack or play. The crop will take some abuse. Raspberry growers, because successful cultivation of their crop is complex and the fruit is delicate, must be adaptive, nimble, and exceptionally attentive. Successful raspberry growing requires, in other words, a substantial stock of local knowledge and experience. These distinctions will prove germane to the Tanzanian example, to which we now turn, and later to our understanding of local knowledge.

7 Compulsory Villagization in Tanzania: Aesthetics and Miniaturization

The ujamaa village campaign in Tanzania from 1973 to 1976 was a massive attempt to permanently settle most of the country's population in villages, of which the layouts, housing designs, and local economies were planned, partly or wholly, by officials of the central government. We shall examine the Tanzanian experience for three reasons. First, the campaign was by most accounts the largest forced resettlement scheme undertaken in independent Africa up to that time; at least 5 million Tanzanians were relocated.[1] Second, documentation of the villagization process is abundant, thanks to the international interest in the experiment and the relatively open character of Tanzanian political life. Finally, the campaign was undertaken largely as a development and welfare project and not, as has often been the case, as part of a plan of punitive appropriation, ethnic cleansing, or military security (as in South Africa's forced removals and homeland schemes under apartheid). Compared with Soviet collectivization, the ujamaa village campaign was a case of large-scale social engineering by a relatively benign and weak state.

Many other large-scale resettlement schemes can be subjected to much the same analysis. If, in the Tanzanian case, Chinese and Russian models as well as Marxist-Leninist rhetoric play an important ideological role, we should not imagine that these were the only sources of inspiration for such schemes.[2] We could as easily have examined the huge forced removals under apartheid policies in South Africa, which were far more brutal and economically destructive. We could also have analyzed any number of the many large-scale capitalist schemes for production, often requiring substantial population movements, that have been undertaken with international assistance in poor countries.[3] Julius Nyerere, Tanzania's head of state, viewed the permanent resettlement in ways that were strikingly continuous with colonial policy, as we shall see, and his ideas about both mechanization and economies of scale in agriculture were part and parcel of international development discourse at the time. That discourse of modernization was, in turn, heavily influenced by the model of the Tennessee Valley Authority, the development of capital-intensive agriculture in the United States, and the lessons of economic mobilization from World War II.[4]

In contrast to Soviet collectivization, Tanzanian villagization was not conceived as an all-out war of appropriation. Nyerere made a point of warning against the use of administrative or military coercion, insisting that no one should be forced, against his or her will, into the new villages. And in fact the disruptions and inhumanities of Nyerere's program, however serious for its victims, were not in the same league as those inflicted by Stalin. Even so, the ujamaa campaign was coercive and occasionally violent. It proved, moreover, a failure, ecologically as well as economically.

Even in this "softer" version of authoritarian high modernism, certain family resemblances stand out. The first is the logic of "improvement." As in the "unimproved" forest, the existing patterns of settlement and social life in Tanzania were illegible and resistant to the narrow purposes of the state. Only by radically simplifying the settlement pattern was it possible for the state to efficiently deliver such development services as schools, clinics, and clean water. Mere administrative convenience was hardly the only objective of state officials, and that is our second point. The thinly veiled subtext of villagization was also to reorganize human communities in order to make them better objects of political control and to facilitate the new forms of communal farming favored by state policy. In this context, there are striking parallels between what Nyerere and Tanzanian African National Union (TANU) envisioned and the program of agriculture and settlement initiated by the colonial regimes in East Africa. The parallels suggest that we have stumbled across something generic about the projects of the modern developmentalist state.

Beyond this second criterion of bureaucratic management, however, lay a third resemblance that had nothing directly to do with efficiency. As in the Soviet case, there was also, I believe, a powerful aesthetic dimension. Certain visual representations of order and efficiency, although they may have made eminent sense in some original context, are detached from their initial moorings. High-modernist plans tend to "travel" as an abbreviated visual image of efficiency that is less a scientific proposition to be tested than a quasi-religious faith in a visual sign or representation of order. As Jacobs suggested, they may substitute an apparent visual order for the real thing. The fact that they look right becomes more important than whether they work; or, better put, the assumption is that if the arrangement looks right, it will also, ipso facto, function well. The importance of such representations is manifested in a tendency to miniaturize, to create such microenvironments of apparent order as model villages, demonstration projects, new capitals, and so on.

Finally, like Soviet collectives, ujamaa villages were economic and ecological failures. For ideological reasons, the designers of the new society had paid virtually no attention to the local knowledge and practices of cultivators and pastoralists. They had also forgotten the most important fact about social engineering: its efficiency depends on the response and cooperation of real human subjects. If people find the new arrangement, however efficient in principle, to be hostile to their dignity, their plans, and their tastes, they can *make* it an inefficient arrangement.

Colonial High-Modernist Agriculture in East Africa

> For the colonial state did not merely aspire to create, under its control, a human landscape of perfect visibility; the condition of this visibility was that everyone, everything, had (as it were) a serial number.
> —Benedict Anderson, *Imagined Communities*

Colonial rule has always been meant to be profitable for the colonizer. This implied, in a rural society, stimulating cultivation for the market. A variety of such means as head taxes payable in cash or in valuable crops, private-sector plantations, and the encouragement of white settlers were deployed to this end. Beginning during World War II and especially after it, the British in East Africa turned to planning large-scale development projects and mobilizing the required labor. A straw in the wind was the conscription of nearly thirty thousand laborers for work on plantations (particularly sisal plantations) during the war. Postwar schemes, although they often had prewar precedents, were far more ambitious: a gigantic groundnut (peanut) scheme; various rice, tobacco, cotton, and cattle schemes; and, above all, elaborate soil-conservation plans mandating a strict regimen of practices. Resettlement and mechanization were integral parts of many schemes.[5] The vast majority of these projects were neither popular nor successful. In fact, one of the standard explanations for the successes of TANU in the countryside was precisely the widespread popular resentment against colonial agricultural policy—particularly forced conservation measures and such livestock regulations as destocking and cattle dipping.[6]

The most searching account of the logic underlying these schemes of "welfare colonialism" is William Beinert's study of neighboring Malawi (then Nyasaland).[7] Although the ecology is different in Malawi, the broad lines of its agricultural policy varied little from that attempted elsewhere in British East Africa. For our purposes, what is most striking is the degree to which the assumptions of the colonial regime matched those of the independent, and far more legitimate, socialist state of Tanzania.

The point of departure for colonial policy was a complete faith in what officials took for "scientific agriculture" on one hand and a nearly total skepticism about the actual agricultural practices of Africans on the other. As a provincial agricultural officer in the Shire (Tchiri) Valley put it, "The African has neither the training, skill, nor equipment to diagnose his soil erosion troubles nor can he plan the remedial measures, which are based on scientific knowledge, and this is where I think we rightly come in."[8] Although the officer's sentiment was no doubt perfectly sincere, one cannot fail to note how it justified, at the same time, the importance and authority of agricultural experts over mere practitioners.

In keeping with the planning ideology of the time, the experts were inclined to propose elaborate projects—a "total development scheme," a "comprehensive land usage scheme."[9] But there were enormous obstacles to imposing a complicated and draconian set of regulations on a population of cultivators well aware of environmental constraints and convinced of the logic of their own farming practices. Pushing ahead autocratically only courted protest and evasion. It was in just such contexts that the strategy of resettlement was so appealing. Opening new land or repurchasing the estates of white settlers allowed officials to start from scratch with compact village sites and consolidated individual plots. The newly recruited settlers could then be relocated to a prepared, legible site replacing the scattered residences and complex tenure patterns found elsewhere. The more the planners filled in the details—that is, the more that huts were built or specified, sites demarcated, fields cleared and plowed, and plants selected (and sometimes sown)—the greater the chance of controlling the scheme and keeping it to its designed form.

The planning of the lower Shire Valley along these lines, Beinert makes clear, was not an entirely scientific exercise. The scheme's designers were deploying a set of technical beliefs associated with modern agriculture, very few of which had been verified in the context of local conditions. They were also deploying a set of aesthetic and visual standards, some of them obviously originating in the temperate West, which had come to symbolize an ordered and productive agriculture.[10] They were driven by what Beinert called the "technical imagination of what might be possible."

> In the case of ridging and bunding in the lower river, the imagination had an almost pictorial quality: they looked forward to a valley of regular fields, neatly ridged, between long straight contour bunds, below a line of storm drains topped by forests. It was a rectangular contoured order which would render the environment susceptible to control, facilitate technical transformation of, and controls over, peasant agriculture and, perhaps, accord with their sense of planned beauty. It was this solution which would make adequate production possible. But driven by their technical conviction and imagination, they were unresponsive to the effects of their interventions on peasant society and peasant culture.[11]

Aesthetic order in the agricultural and forest landscape was replicated in the human geography as well.[12] A series of model villages, spread evenly across the rectangular grid of fields and linked by roads, would become the center of technical and social services. The fields themselves were so arrayed as to facilitate the dryland rotational farming built into the scheme. In fact, the Shire Valley project was to be a miniature version of the Tennessee Valley Authority, complete with dams along the river and sites indicated for capital-intensive processing plants. A three-dimensional model, along the lines of an architect's model of a new town, was constructed to show, in miniature, what the whole project would look like when completed.[13]

The plans for human settlement and land use in the lower Shire Valley "failed almost completely." The reasons for their failure presage the fiasco of the ujamaa villages. Local cultivators, for example, resisted the generic colonial solution to soil erosion: ridging. As later research showed, in this context their resistance was both economically and ecologically sound. Ridging on sandy soil was unstable, tending to create larger erosion gullies in the rainy season, and ridging caused the soil to dry out quickly during the dry season, encouraging white ants to attack the roots of crops. Would-be settlers hated the regimentation of the government schemes; a "model settlement with communal farming" drew no voluntary migrants and had to be converted into a government maize farm using wage labor. The prohibitions on farming the settlement's rich marshland (*dimba*) deterred volunteers. Later, officials conceded that they, and not the peasants, had been mistaken in this respect.

The lower Shire Valley project miscarried for two larger reasons that are crucial to our understanding of the limits of high-modernist planning. The first is that the planners operated with a model of the agricultural environment that was standardized for the entire valley. It was precisely this assumption that made it possible to specify the generic, and apparently permanent, solution of a particular dryland rotation for all cultivators. The solution was a static, freeze-frame answer to a dynamic and variegated valley environment. In contrast, the peasants possessed a flexible repertoire of strategies depending on the timing and extent of the floods, the microlocal soil compositions, and so on—strategies that were to some degree unique to each farmer, each plot of land, and to each growing season. The second reason behind the failure was that the planners also operated with a standardized model of the cultivators themselves, assuming that all peasants would desire roughly the same crop mix, techniques, and yields. Such an assumption completely ignored key variables, such as family size and composition, sideline occupations, gender divisions of labor, and culturally conditioned needs and tastes. The fact was that each family had its own particular mix of resources and goals that would affect its agricultural strategy year by year in ways that the overall plan did not provide for. As a plan, it was both aesthetically pleasing to its inventors and also precise and consistent within its own strict parameters. As a scheme for development, however, it was the kind of environmental and social taxidermy that doomed it almost from the start. Ironically, successful, voluntary, pioneer settlement outside the government's purview and without any financial assistance continued apace. This disorderly, illegible, but more productive settlement was castigated as squatting and severely reproved, although without much practical effect.

The abject failure of the ambitious groundnuts scheme in Tanganyika just after World War II is also instructive as a dress rehearsal for massive villagization.[14] The joint venture between the United African Company (a subsidiary of Unilever) and the colonial state proposed the clearing of no fewer than 3 million acres of bush that would, when cultivated, yield more than half a million tons of peanuts to be converted to cooking oil for export. The scheme was conceived during the postwar high tide of faith in the economic prowess of a command economy joined to large capitalist firms. By 1950, when less than 10 percent of the acreage had been cleared and not as many nuts had been grown as seeds had been sown, the project was abandoned.

The reasons for the failure were legion. In development circles, in fact, the groundnuts scheme is one of a handful of legendary failures cited as examples of what not to do. At least two of the ingredients of this disaster relate to the failure of the lower Shire Valley project and to the later disaster of large-scale villagization. First, the design for the scheme was narrowly agronomic and abstract. Very general figures for the tractor hours needed to clear land, the amounts of fertilizer and pesticide needed to attain a given yield per acre, and so forth were applied to the new terrain. No detailed mapping of soils, rainfall patterns, or topography and certainly no experimental trials had been undertaken. Field reconnaissance was allotted a mere nine weeks, much of it conducted from the air! The general figures proved wildly erroneous precisely because they were heedless of the particularities of the locality: clayey soil that compacted in the dry season, irregular rainfall, crop diseases for which there were no resistant plant varieties, inappropriate machinery for the soil and terrain.

The second fatal premise in the design of the scheme was its "blind faith in machinery and large-scale operation."[15] The project's founder, Frank Samuel, had a motto: "No operation will be performed by hand for which mechanical equipment is available."[16] The scheme was essentially a quasi-military operation perhaps derived from wartime experience and designed to be technically self-contained. The plan's level of abstraction resembles that of the Soviet collective wheat farm laid out by Wilson, Ware, and Riggin in their Chicago hotel room in 1928 (see chapter 6). The groundnuts scheme intentionally bypassed African smallholders in order to create a colossal industrial farm under European management. As such, the project might have reflected relative factor prices on, say, the plains of Kansas, but surely not in Tanganyika. Had it succeeded in growing peanuts in any quantities, it would have grown them on grossly uneconomic terms. Capitalist high modernism of the utopian kind that inspired the groundnuts scheme was no more appropriate to Tanzania than would be the template of villagization and collectivist, socialist production that inspired Nyerere.

Villages and "Improved" Farming in Tanzania Before 1973

The vast majority of the Tanzanian rural population was, in terms of legibility and appropriation, outside the reach of the state. At independence, an estimated 11 out of 12 million rural dwellers lived "scattered" across the landscape. With the exception of densely settled areas in the cool, wet highlands where substantial amounts of coffee and tea were grown and marketed, much of the population practiced subsistence farming or pastoralism. Much of what they did sell was offered at local markets largely outside the ambit of state supervision and taxation. The objective of colonial agricultural policy and also of the independent state of Tanzania (and seconded, early on, by the World Bank) was to assemble more of the population into fixed, permanent settlements and to promote forms of agriculture that would yield a greater marketable surplus, especially for export.[17] Whether these policies took the form of private ventures or socialized agriculture, they were strategies designed, as Goran Hyden has said, "to capture the peasantry."[18] The nationalist regime of TANU was, of course, much more legitimate than its colonial predecessor. But we should not forget that much of the popularity of TANU in rural areas rested on its endorsement of resistance to the onerous and mandatory agricultural regulations of the colonial state.[19] As in Russia, the peasantry had taken advantage of the interregnum at independence to ignore or defy policies declared in the capital.

At the outset, villagization was a central goal of Nyerere and of TANU. The purpose of village formation was at this stage threefold: the delivery of services; the creation of a more productive, modern agriculture; and the encouragement of communal, socialist forms of cooperation. Nyerere outlined the importance of village living as early as 1962, in his inaugural address to Tanzania's parliament.

> And if you ask me why the government wants us to live in villages, the answer is just as simple: unless we do we shall not be able to provide ourselves with the things we need to develop our land and to raise our standard of living. We shall not be able to use tractors; we shall not be able to provide schools for our children; we shall not be able to build hospitals, or have clean drinking water; it will be quite impossible to start small village industries, and instead we shall have to go on depending on the towns for all our requirements; and if we had a plentiful supply of electric power we should never be able to connect it up to each isolated homestead.[20]

By 1967, in a major policy statement called "Socialism and Rural Development," Nyerere elaborated on the specifically socialist aspect of the campaign for village living. It was clear to him that if the present pattern of capitalist development continued, Tanzania would eventually develop a class of wealthy "kulak" (the Russian term then in vogue in TANU circles) farmers who would reduce their neighbors to the status of wage laborers. Ujamaa villages (that is, socialist cooperatives) would set the rural economy on a different path. "What is here being proposed," Nyerere explained, "is that we in Tanzania should move from being a nation of individual peasant producers who are gradually adopting the incentives and ethics of the capitalist system. Instead we should gradually become a nation of ujamaa villages where the people co-operate directly in small groups and where these small groups co-operate together for joint enterprises."[21]

For Nyerere, village living, development services, communal agriculture, and mechanization were a single indissoluble package. Farmers who were scattered hither and yon could not easily be educated or treated for common illnesses, could not learn the techniques of modern agriculture, could not even cooperate, unless they first moved to villages. He declared: "The first and absolutely essential thing to do, therefore, if we want to be able to start using tractors for cultivation, is to begin living in *proper* villages. . . . We shall not be able to use tractors [if we have no villages]."[22] Modernization required, above all, physical concentration into standardized units that the state might service and administer. Little wonder that electrification and tractors, those emblems of development, were on the tip of Nyerere's tongue as well as Lenin's.[23] There is, I believe, a powerful aesthetic of modernization at play here. A modern population must live in communities with a certain physical layout—not just villages, but *proper* villages.

Nyerere, unlike Stalin, at first insisted that the creation of ujamaa villages be gradual and completely voluntary. He imagined that a few families would move their houses to be closer together and would plant their crops nearby, after which they might open a communal plot. Success would attract others. "Socialist communities cannot be established by compulsion," he declared. They "can only be established with willing members; the task of leadership and of Government is not to try and force this kind of development, but to explain, encourage, and participate."[24] Later on, in 1973, having gauged the general resistance to villagization on government terms, Nyerere would change his mind. By then the seeds of coercion had been sown, by a politicized, authoritarian bureaucracy and also by Nyerere's underlying conviction that the peasants did not know what was good for them. Thus, immediately after disavowing "compulsion" in the sentence just quoted, Nyerere concedes, "It may be possible—*and sometimes necessary*—to insist on all farmers in a given area growing a certain acreage of a particular crop until they realize that this brings them a more secure living, and then do not have to be *forced* to grow it."[25] If the peasants could not be persuaded to act in their own interest, they might have to be coerced. This logic was a replication of that in the 1961 World Bank report associated with Tanganyika's first five-year plan. That report was laced with the era's standard discourse about having to overcome the habits and superstitions of a backward and obstinate peasantry. The report also doubted whether persuasion alone would get the job done. While its authors hoped that "social emulation, cooperation, and the expansion of community development services" would transform attitudes, they warned darkly that "where incentives, emulation and propaganda are ineffective, enforcement or coercive measures of an appropriate sort will be considered."[26]

Scores of village settlements and cultivation schemes were initiated in the 1960s. Despite their great variety—some were joint ventures between the state and foreign firms, some were government or parastatal schemes, and others were spontaneous popular initiatives—most were judged to be failures and closed down, either by decree or by attrition. Three aspects of these schemes seem especially relevant to understanding the all-out villagization campaign that began in 1973.

The first was a penchant for creating pilot schemes. In itself this approach made sense, since policy makers could learn what would work and what would not before embarking on more ambitious plans. Many such schemes, however, became showpiece demonstration farms absorbing huge amounts of scarce equipment, funds, and personnel. For a time, a few of these precious miniatures of progress and modernization were maintained. One influential scheme involving a mere three hundred settlers managed to acquire four bulldozers, nine tractors, a field car, seven lorries, a maize mill, an electric generator, and a cadre of about fifteen administrators and specialists, 150 laborers, and twelve artisans.[27] It was, after a fashion, a successful example of a modern farm, providing that one overlooked its truly legendary inefficiency and the fact that it was irrelevant to the Tanzanian situation.

The second aspect prefiguring the Tanzanian experience was that, given single-party rule, an authoritarian administrative tradition, and a dictator (albeit a rather benevolent one)[28] who wanted results, the normal bureaucratic pathologies were exaggerated. Sites for new settlements were often chosen, not by economic logic, but by finding "blank spots" on the map (preferably near roads) where the settlers might be dumped.[29] In the West Lake (west of Lake Victoria) region (1970), a member of Parliament and five technical specialists descended briefly to design a four-year plan (1970–1974) for all ujamaa villages in the region. They were obviously under great pressure to please their superiors by promising huge increases in cultivation and production which were "utterly unrealistic and completely out of touch with any possible development in the village."[30] The plans were promulgated without any real consultation and were based on abstract assumptions about machine use, days of labor, rates of land clearance, and a new crop regimen, not unlike the groundnut scheme or the Soviet collective hatched in a Chicago hotel room.

Finally, where the pressure was greatest to create new villages, TANU activists and officials ignored Nyerere's advice against compulsion. Thus, when he decided in 1970 that the entire population of

Dodoma (a drought-prone region in central Tanzania) should be relocated to ujamaa villages within fourteen months, officials sprang into action. Relying on everyone's sharp memories of a regional famine in 1969, the officials let it be understood that only those dwelling in ujamaa villages would ever receive famine relief. Those who already lived in ujamaa villages with fewer than the stipulated minimum of 250 families were often forced to amalgamate with another settlement to reach the required size. Communal plots were built into the new settlements, as were, in theory, labor regulations and cropping schedules. When an agricultural officer insisted that there be no discussion of the official decision to enlarge one village's communal field to 170 acres, absorbing the adjacent private plots, he was thrown out of the village meeting in a rare open revolt. An M.P. who sided with the village was barred from running again and placed under surveillance, while the district's TANU chairman, who did likewise, was removed and placed under house arrest. Dodoma was a preview of what was to come.

Lest there be any doubt that villagization meant central control and not simply village formation and communal farming, the sorry fate of the Ruvuma Development Association (RDA) settled the matter.[31] The RDA was an umbrella organization representing fifteen communal villages scattered over one hundred miles in the Songea, a remote and poor district in the southwestern part of the country. Unlike most ujamaa villages, these were the spontaneous creation of young local militants in TANU. They began in 1960, long before Nyerere's policy declaration of 1967, with each village inventing its own forms of communal enterprise. Early on, Nyerere singled out one of the villages, Litowa, heralding it as a place where he could send people to see rural socialism in action.[32] Its school, milling cooperative, and marketing association were the envy of neighboring villages. Given the high level of patronage and financial backing the villagers attracted, it is hard to tell how economically sound their enterprises were. They did, however, anticipate Nyerere's declared policy of local control and nonauthoritarian cooperation. The villagers were, on the other hand, independent and assertive vis-à-vis the state. Having won over many of the local party officials and having pioneered village cooperation on their own, they were not about to let themselves simply be absorbed into bureaucratic party routines. When each family in these villages was ordered to grow one acre of fire-cured tobacco, a crop they considered to be labor-intensive and without profit, they openly protested through their organization. In 1968, following a high-level visit by TANU's central committee, the RDA was officially banned as an illegal organization, its assets seized, and its functions assumed by the party and bureaucracy.[33]

Although it put into practice Nyerere's espoused goals, its refusal to fit into the centralized scheme of the party was fatal.

"To Live in Villages Is an Order"

With his order of December 1973,[34] Nyerere ended a period of villagization marked by sporadic but unauthorized coercion and put the entire machinery of the state behind compulsory, universal villagization.[35] Whatever restraining influence that his public disavowal of the use of force had provided was now nullified; it was replaced by the desire of the party and bureaucracy to produce the quick results he wanted. Villagization was, after all, for their own benefit, as Juma Mwapachu, an official in charge of forced settlement in the district of Shinyanga, explained. "The 1974 Operation [Planned] Villages was not to be a matter of persuasion but of coercion. As Nyerere argued, the move had to be compulsory because Tanzania could not sit back seeing the majority of its people leading a 'life of death.' The State, had, therefore, to take the role of the 'father' in ensuring that its people chose a better and more prosperous life for themselves."[36] New villages and communal farming had been an official policy priority at least since 1967, but the results had been a disappointment. Now it was time to insist on village living, Nyerere claimed, as the only way to promote development and increased production. The official term employed after 1973 was "planned" villages (not "ujamaa" villages), presumably to distinguish them both from the communal-production regime of ujamaa villages, which had failed, and from the unplanned settlements and homesteads in which Tanzanians now resided.

The actual campaign was called *Operation* Planned Villages, conjuring in the popular mind images of military operations. And so it was. The operational plan specified, by the book, a six-phase sequence: "educate [or "politicize"] the people, search for a suitable site, inspect the location, plan the village and demarcate the land clearly, train the officials in the methodology of ujamaa, and resettlement."[37] The sequence was both inevitable and involuntary. Given the "crash" nature of the campaign, educating the people did not mean asking their consent; it meant telling them that they had to move and why it was in their best interest. The pace was, moreover, double-quick. The dress rehearsal in Dodoma in 1970 had allowed planning teams one day per village plan; the new campaign stretched the planning apparatus even thinner.

Nor was the speed of the operation a mere by-product of administrative haste. The planners felt that the shock of lightning-quick settlement would have a salutary effect. It would rip the peasantry from their traditional surroundings and networks and would put them down in entirely new settings where, it was hoped, they could then be more readily remade into modern producers following the instructions of experts.[38] In a larger sense, of course, the purpose of forced settlement is always disorientation and then reorientation. Colonial schemes for state farms or private plantations, as well as the many plans to create a class of progressive yeoman farmers, operated on the assumption that revolutionizing the living arrangements and working environments of people would transform them fundamentally. Nyerere was fond of contrasting the loose, autonomous work rhythms of traditional cultivators with the tight-knit, interdependent discipline of the factory.[39] Densely settled villages with cooperative production would move the Tanzanian population toward that ideal.

Rural Tanzanians were understandably reluctant to move into new communities planned by the state. Their past experience, whether before independence or after, warranted their skepticism. As cultivators and pastoralists, they had developed patterns of settlement and, in many cases, patterns of periodic movements that were finely tuned adaptations to an often stingy environment which they knew exceptionally well. The state-mandated movement threatened to destroy the logic of this adaptation. Administrative convenience, not ecological considerations, governed the selection of sites; they were often far from fuelwood and water, and their population often exceeded the carrying capacity of the land. As one specialist foresaw: "Unless villagization can be coupled with infrastructural inputs to create a novel technology to master the environment, the nucleated settlement pattern may, by itself, be counter-productive in economic terms and destructive of the ecological balance maintained under the traditional settlement pattern. Nucleated settlement will mean over-crowding . . . with people and domestic animals and the accompanying soil erosion, gully formation, and dust bowls which are common features in situations where the human initiative has suddenly overtaxed the carrying capacity of the land."[40]

Given the resistance of the population and the bureaucratic-military imperative of a crash program, violence was inevitable. Threats were all but universal. Those slated to move were again told that famine relief would be accorded only to those who moved peacefully. The militia and the army were mobilized to provide transport and to compel compliance. People were told that if they did not pull down their houses and load them into the government trucks, the authorities would pull down the houses. In order to prevent those forcibly moved from returning, many homes were burned. Typical of the reports that came out of Tanzania was the following description by a student in the poor region of Kigoma: "Force and brutality was used. The police were the ones empowered together with some government officials. For example at Katanazuza in Kalinzi, . . . the police had to take charge physically. In some areas where peasants refused to pack their belongings and board the Operation lorries and trucks, their houses were destroyed through burning or pulling them down. House destruction was witnessed in Nyange village. It became a routine order of the day. And the peasants had unconditionally to shift. It was a forceful villagization in some villages."[41] When the peasantry realized that open resistance was dangerous and probably futile, they saved what they could, often fleeing the new village at the first opportunity.[42]

Such incentives as clinics, piped water, and schools were offered to those who went peacefully. Sometimes they did, although they tried to insist on a written contract with officials and to require that the new services promised them be established *before* they moved. Positive inducements were, apparently, more typical of the early, voluntary phase of villagization than the later, compulsory phase. A few regions were little affected; officials there simply designated many existing settlements as planned villages and left it at that. There was both an economic and political logic to the exclusions. Wealthy, densely settled areas such as West Lake and Kilimanjaro were largely spared for three reasons: farmers there were already living in populous villages; their undisturbed productivity in cash crops was vital for state revenues and foreign exchange; and the groups residing in these areas were overrepresented among the bureaucratic elite. Some critics suggested that the higher the proportion of government officials from an area, the later (and more desultory) its villagization.[43]

When Nyerere learned exactly how thin was the fiction of persuasion and how widespread were the brutalities, he expressed his dismay. He decried the failure to compensate peasants for their destroyed huts and allowed that some officials had moved people to unsuitable locations that lacked water or sufficient arable land. "Despite our official policies and despite all our democratic institutions, some leaders do not listen to the people," he admitted. "They find it much easier to tell people what to do."[44] But it was "absurd to pretend that these cases were typical of villagization,"[45] let alone to call off the campaign. Nyerere wanted local authorities to be knowledgeable, close to the people, and persuasive in putting across state policy; he did not, any more than Lenin did, want them to obey the people's wishes. Not surprisingly, the sources agree that virtually all village meetings were one-way affairs of lectures, explanations, instructions, scoldings, promises, and warnings. The assembled villagers were expected to be what Sally Falk Moore has appropriately called "ratifying bodies public," giving populist legitimacy to decisions made elsewhere.[46] Far from achieving this populist legitimacy, the villagization campaign created only an alienated, skeptical, demoralized, and uncooperative peasantry for which Tanzania would pay a huge price, both financially and politically.[47]

A Streamlined People and Their Crops

The planned new villages followed both a bureaucratic logic and an aesthetic logic. Nyerere and his planners had a visual idea of just how a modern village should look. Such visual ideas become powerful tropes. Take the word "streamline," for example. "Streamlining" has become a powerful image for modern forms, conveying economy, sleekness, efficiency, and minimal friction or resistance. Politicians and administrators hasten to cash in on the symbolic capital behind the term by declaring that they will streamline this agency or that corporation, allowing the audience's visual imagination to fill in the details of a bureaucratic equivalent of a sleek locomotive or jet. Thus it is that a term that has a specific, contextual meaning in one field (aerodynamics) comes to be generalized to subjects where its meaning is more visual and aesthetic than scientific. Above all, as we shall see, the aesthetic of the new village was a negation of the past. First, however, to the administrative logic.

What greeted Nyerere when he visited new villages in the district of Shinyanga (northwest Tanzania) in early 1975 was fairly typical of bureaucratic haste and insensibility.[48] Some of the villages were laid out as "one long street of houses stretching for miles like the wagons of a locomotive."[49] It appeared to Nyerere that this was a crude case of simply "dumping" the settlers. But such linear villages did have a curious logic behind them. Administrators had a penchant for locating new villages along the major roads, where they could be most easily reached and monitored.[50] Roadside siting rarely made economic sense; it did, on the other hand, demonstrate how the goal of extending the state's control over the peasantry often trumped the state's other goal of raising agricultural production. As Stalin had learned, a captured peasantry was not necessarily a productive peasantry.

The visual aesthetics of how a proper new village should look combined elements of administrative regularity, tidiness, and legibility linked to an overall Cartesian order. This was the modern administrative village, and it was implicitly associated with a modern, disciplined, and productive peasantry. One astute observer, sympathetic to the aims of villagization, noted the overall effect. "The new approach," he explained, "was more in line with bureaucratic thinking and with what a bureaucracy can do effectively: enforced movement of the peasants into new 'modern' settlements, i.e., settlements with houses placed close together, in straight lines, along the roads, and with the fields outside the nucleated village, organized in block farms, each block containing the villager's individual plots, but with only one type of crop, and readily accessible for control by the agricultural extension officer and eventual cultivation by government tractors."[51]

As the exercise of village creation was repeated, the administrative image of the modern village became increasingly codified, a known protocol that almost any bureaucrat could reproduce. "The first response of the West Lake leaders, when they were called upon to implement ujamaa in the Region, was to think of resettlement. Creating new settlements had several advantages. They were highly visible, and easy to organize right from the beginning in the orderly, nice looking way preferred by bureaucrats with the houses and shambas [gardens, farms] in straight lines, etc."[52] Reconstructing the historical lineage of this composite picture of modern rural life would be fascinating, although tangential to our purposes. No doubt it owes something to colonial policy and hence to the look of the modern European rural landscape, and we also know that Nyerere was impressed with what he saw on his trips to the Soviet Union and to China. What is significant, however, is that the modern planned village in Tanzania was essentially a point-by-point negation of existing rural practice, which included shifting cultivation and pastoralism; polycropping; living well off the main roads; kinship and lineage authority; small, scattered settlements with houses built higgledy-piggledy; and production that was dispersed and opaque to the state. The logic of this negation seemed often to prevail over sound ecological or economic considerations.

Communal Farming and Intensive Production

Collecting Tanzanians into villages was seen from the very beginning as a necessary step in establishing completely new forms of agricultural production in which the state would play the major role. The first five-year plan was explicit.

> Although the improvement approach [as opposed to the transformation approach] can contribute to increasing production in . . . zones [with low and irregular rainfall], it cannot in all events give rise to very sub-

stantial results because of the dispersal of the farm producers, the impoverishment of the soils by the practice of bush burning and considerable difficulties in marketing products. The policy which Government has decided to pursue with respect to all these zones consists in *re-grouping* and *re-settling* farmers on the most favorable soil, installing there a system of private or collective ownership and introducing *supervised crop rotation and mixed farming* that would permit the maintenance of soil fertility.[53]

The population concentrated in planned villages would, by degrees, grow cash crops (as specified by the agricultural experts) on communal fields with state-supplied machinery. Their housing, their local administration, their agricultural practices, and, most important, their workdays would be overseen by state authorities.

The forced villagization campaign itself had such a disastrous effect on agricultural production that the state was in no position to press ahead immediately with full-scale communal farming. Huge imports of food were necessary from 1973 through 1975.[54] Nyerere declared that the 1.2 billion shillings spent for food imports would have bought one cow for every Tanzanian family. Roughly 60 percent of the new villages were located on semiarid land unsuitable for permanent cultivation, requiring peasants to walk long distances to reach viable plots. The chaos of the move itself and the slow process of adapting to a new ecological setting meant further disruptions of production.[55]

Until 1975, the state's effort to control production outside its own state schemes took the classic colonial form: laws mandating that each household grow certain crops on a minimum number of acres. A variety of fines and penalties were deployed to enforce these measures. In one region, officials announced that no one would be allowed to go to market or ride a bus unless he could prove that he was cultivating the required seven and one-half acres of land. In another case, famine relief was withheld until each villager had planted one acre of cassava in accordance with the minimum acreage law.[56] One major source of the conflict leading to the dissolution of the Ruvuma ujamaa villages was the forced cultivation of fire-cured tobacco at what the villagers took to be confiscatory prices. As the colonizers had understood long before, forced cultivation of this kind could be successfully imposed only on a peasantry that was physically concentrated and therefore able to be monitored and, if necessary, disciplined.[57]

The next step was regulated, communal production.[58] This form of cultivation was anticipated in the Villages and Ujamaa Villages Act (1975), which established "village collective farms" and required village authorities to draw up annual work plans and production targets.

In practice, the size of each communal field and its production plan were typically set by an agricultural field officer (who was eager to please his superiors) and the village chief, with little or no wider consultation.[59] The result was a labor plan that bore no relation to the seasonal supply of local labor, let alone the peasants' own goals. Work on the collective village farm was experienced as little different from corvee labor. Villagers had no choice in the matter, and it was rare for their work to yield a profit. Even though extension agents were directed to devote their efforts exclusively to the communal fields, the crops were often unsuitable, the soil infertile, the seed and fertilizer late to arrive, and the promised tractor with plow nowhere in sight. These shortcomings, plus the provision that any profit (a very rare event) from the communal field could be counted as revenue for the village committee, meant that the work was deeply resented.

In theory, the system of political and labor control was thorough and inescapable. Villages were divided into sections (*mitaa*) and each section into several cells (*mashina*, made up of ten households). The residential order was replicated on the communal fields. Each section was responsible for the cultivation of a segment of the communal field, and within that segment, each cell was responsible for a corresponding fragment. Again in theory, the cell leader was responsible for labor mobilization and surveillance.[60] Structurally, then, the parallels in the residential and labor-disciplinary hierarchies were designed to make them perfectly transparent and legible to the authorities.

In practice, the system broke down quickly. The areas actually under communal cultivation were typically far smaller than the figures officially reported.[61] Most section and village authorities were content to go through the motions when it came to communal cultivation. And they were reluctant to impose fines on their neighbors who neglected the labor rules in order to tend to their all-important private plots.

As a response to such pervasive foot-dragging, many communal fields were divided up, and each household was made responsible for cultivating, say, half an acre.[62] It was no longer necessary to coordinate labor for working a single large field, and the responsibility for cultivation, and hence sanctions, could now be pinpointed. The new system resembled the colonial forced cultivation system, with one difference: the plots were physically consolidated for easier supervision. Still, the absence of any appreciable return from this labor meant that each household focused on its private holding and treated the communal plot as an onerous residual activity, despite occasional official warnings that the priorities should be inverted.[63] The disparity in yields naturally reflected the disparity in attention.

The aim of Tanzanian rural policy from 1967 through the early 1980s was to reconfigure the rural population into a form that would allow the state to impose its development agenda and, in the process, to control the work and production of cultivators. Nowhere is this more explicit than in the document for the third five-year plan (1978): "In the rural sector, the Party has had great success in resettling the rural peasantry in villages *where it is now possible to identify able-bodied individuals able to work* and also to identify the acreage available for agricultural purposes. . . . The plan intends to make sure that in every workplace, rural or urban, *our implementing organs set specific work targets each year.* . . . The village government will see to it that all Party policies in respect of development programmes are adhered to."[64] In case the purpose of visibility and control was doubted, the plan went on to explain that agricultural development "in our present conditions" calls for "setting up work timetables and production targets."[65] Communal farms (now called village government farms) were mandated. But as Henry Bernstein notes, with the incomplete collectivization of land and the unwillingness to resort to truly draconian enforcement measures, these communal farms were bound to founder.[66]

The underlying premise of Nyerere's agrarian policy, for all its rhetorical flourishes in the direction of traditional culture, was little different from that of colonial agrarian policy. That premise was that the practices of African cultivators and pastoralists were backward, unscientific, inefficient, and ecologically irresponsible. Only close supervision, training, and, if need be, coercion by specialists in scientific agriculture could bring them and their practices in line with a modern Tanzania. They were the problem to which the agricultural experts were the solution.

It was precisely the assumption, to quote a Tanzanian civil servant, of a "traditional outlook and unwillingness to change"[67] that *required* the entire series of agricultural schemes, from ujamaa villages to forced relocation to the supervised cultivation launched by the colonial and the independent regimes. This view of the peasantry permeates the 1964 World Bank report and the first Tanganyikan five-year plan. Although the plan notes that "significant inroads have been made into the conservatism of the rural population, who as they become organized into co-operatives, respond encouragingly,"[68] it argues that more extensive measures are called for. Thus the 1964 plan declares: "How to overcome the *destructive conservatism of the people*, and generate the drastic agrarian reforms which must be effected if the country is to survive is one of the most difficult problems the political leaders of Tanzania have to face."[69]

Nyerere entirely agreed with the majority of the extension officials, who believed that their job was to "overcome [the farmers'] apathy and attachment to outmoded practices."[70] He and the World Bank saw eye-to-eye in having the first plan provide for sixty new settlement schemes in which farmers who followed the rules would receive land. There is no mistaking this picture of a willfully ignorant and less than diligent class of cultivators in Nyerere's first broadcast as prime minister in 1961: "If you have cotton unpicked on your shamba, if you have cultivated half an acre less than you could cultivate, if you are letting the soil run needlessly off your land, or if your shamba is full of weeds, if you deliberately ignore the advice given you by the agricultural experts, then you are a traitor in the battle."[71]

The logical counterpart to the lack of faith of the ordinary cultivator was the hyperfaith of the agricultural experts and the "blind faith in machines and large scale operations."[72] Just as the planned village was a vast "improvement" in legibility and control over past settlement practices, the planned agriculture offered by the experts was, in its legibility and order, an "improvement" on the infinite variety and muddle of smallholdings and their existing techniques.[73] In the new villages, the settlers' private plots (*shambas*) were generally mapped out by surveyors and were trim, square or rectangular plots of equal size, placed side by side in straight rows (figure 31). Their design followed the same logic as the segmented communal plots: a logic of clarity and administrative ease rather than agronomic sense. Thus when a scheme for tea cultivation was begun, the smallholders were required to plant their tea in a single block "because it was easier for the extension staff to work tea that was planted in the same place."[74]

The order of the fields was replicated in the order of the plants within the fields. Tanzanian farmers often planted two or more crops together in the same field (a technique variously called polycropping, intercropping, or relay cropping). In the coffee-growing areas, for example, coffee was often interplanted with bananas, beans, and other annuals. For most agronomists, this practice was anathema. As one dissenting specialist explained, "The agricultural extension service has been encouraging farmers to plant *pure-stand* coffee and considering this practice the *sine qua non* of modern farming."[75] If the crop were bananas, the banana trees must also be in pure stands. Agricultural field officers judged their accomplishments by whether each crop under their supervision was planted in straight, properly spaced rows and was not mixed with any other cultigen.[76] Like large-scale mechanized farming, monocropping had a scientific rationale *in particular contexts*, but extension officers often promoted monocropping uncritically as an article

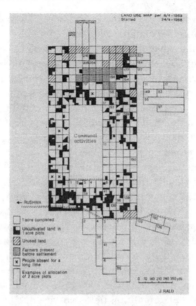

31. Plan for a ujamaa village: Makazi
Mapya, Omulunazi, Rushwa, Tanzania

of faith in the catechism of modern farming. While empirical evidence was even then mounting in favor of the ecological soundness and productivity of some intercropping regimes, the faith continued unabated. What is clear, however, is that monocropping and row planting vastly facilitate the work of administrators and agronomists. Both techniques facilitate inspection and calculations of acreage and yield; they greatly simplify field trials by minimizing the number of variables at play in any one field; they streamline the job of extension recommendations and the supervision of cultivation; and, finally, they simplify control of the harvest. The simplified and legible field crop offers to state agricultural officers many of the same advantages that the "stripped-down" commercial forest offered to scientific foresters and revenue officers.

Bureaucratic Convenience, Bureaucratic Interests

Authoritarian social engineering is apt to display the full range of standard bureaucratic pathologies. The transformations it wishes to effect cannot generally be brought about without applying force or without treating nature and human subjects as if they were functions in a few administrative routines. Far from being regrettable anomalies, these behavioral by-products are inherent in high-modernist campaigns of this kind. I am purposely ignoring here the more obvious inhumanities that are inevitable whenever great power is placed in the hands of largely unaccountable state authorities who are under pressure from above to produce results despite popular resistance. Instead, I stress two key elements of the bureaucratic response typified by the ujamaa village campaign: first, the civil servants' inclination to reinterpret the campaign so that it called for results that they could more easily deliver, and second, their disposition to reinterpret the campaign in line with what was in their corporate interests.

The first tendency was most readily apparent in the displacement of goals toward strictly quantitative criteria of performance. What might be called a "substantive ujamaa village," whose residents had freely consented to move, had agreed on how to manage a communal plot, and were productive farmers managing their own local affairs (Nyerere's initial vision), was replaced by a "notional ujamaa village," an integer that could be added to an avalanche of statistics. Thus party cadres and civil servants, in showing how much they had accomplished, emphasized the numbers of people moved, new villages created, house lots and communal fields surveyed, wells drilled, areas cleared and plowed, tons of fertilizer delivered, and TANU branches set up. No matter if a given ujamaa village was not much more than a few truckloads of angry peasants and their belongings, unceremoniously dumped at a site marked off with a few surveyors' stakes; it still counted as one ujamaa village to the officials' credit. In addition, a pettifogging aesthetics might prevail over substance. The desire to have all the houses in a planned village perfectly aligned, which was presumably linked to easy surveying and the desire to please the inspecting officials, might require that a house be dismantled in order to move it a scant fifty feet to the surveyor's line.[77]

The "productivity of the political apparatus" was judged by numerical results that permitted aggregation and, perhaps more important, comparisons.[78] And when officials realized that their futures depended on producing impressive figures quickly, a process of competitive emulation was unleashed. One official described the atmosphere that caused him to abandon an initial strategy of selective implementation and to plunge ahead.

> This [strategy] was found to be unworkable, for two main reasons. First, there was a competitive attitude (particularly between regions) with all its political overtones. Here was a moment for self-aggrandizement by proving ability to mobilize a rural population wholesale. Reports were coming in from Mara Region that they were about to complete their op-

eration when we had not started at all. Top party officials were heralding and positively reinforcing the achievements of resettlement in Geita
District. Who, in such circumstances, would have wished to lag behind?
Political leaders therefore called for quick measures to complete the resettlement exercise in a short time. Such a rushed exercise caused problems, of course, in the form of poorly planned villages.[79]

Nyerere, necessarily perceiving the campaign largely through sets
of statistics and self-congratulatory official reports, exacerbated the
competitive atmosphere. His glowing report to TANU was a delirium of
numbers, targets, and percentages.[80]

> Consider, for example, the question of villagization. In my report to the
> 1973 TANU Conference I was able to say that 2,028,164 people were liv-
> ing in villages. Two years later, in June 1975, I reported to the next TANU
> Conference that approximately 9,100,000 people were living in village
> communities. Now there are about 13,065,000 people living together in
> 7,684 villages. This is a tremendous achievement. It is an achievement
> of TANU and Government leaders in cooperation with the people of Tan-
> zania. It means that something like 70% of our people have moved
> their homes in the space of about three years.[81]

The second, and surely most ominous, deflection of the ujamaa
campaign brought off by state authorities was to see that its implementation systematically served to underwrite their status and power.
As Andrew Coulson has perceptively noted, in the actual process of
creating new villages, the administrators and party officials (themselves competitors) effectively evaded all those policies that would
have diminished their privileges and power while exaggerating those
that reinforced their corporate sway. Thus such ideas as allowing small
ujamaa villages like Ruvuma to operate free of government interference (before 1968), pupils' involvement in decision making in schools
(1969), workers' participation in management (1969–70), and the
power to elect village councils and leadership (1973–75) were all hon-
ored in the breach.[82] High-modernist social engineering is ideal soil
for authoritarian pretensions, and Tanzanian officialdom made the
most of this chance to consolidate its position.[83]

The Idea of a "National Plantation"

Villagization was meant to radically concentrate Tanzania's peasantry in order to regiment it politically and economically. If it worked,
it would transform the dispersed, autonomous, and illegible populations
that had thus far eluded most of the state policies they found onerous.
The planners pictured, instead, a population settled in government-

designed villages under tight administrative control, planting communal fields in which pure-stand crops were grown according to state specifications. If we allow for the continued existence of substantial private plots and the (related) weakness of labor control, the whole scheme came perilously close to looking like a vast, albeit noncontiguous, state plantation. What a neutral observer might have taken as a new form of servitude, however benevolent, was largely unquestioned by the elites, for the policy sailed under the banner of "development."

It seems incredible, in retrospect, that any state could proceed with so much hubris and so little information and planning to the dislocation of so many million lives. It seems, again in retrospect, a wild and irrational scheme which was bound to fail both the expectations of its planners and the material and social needs of its hapless victims.

The inhumanities of compulsory villagization were magnified by the deeply ingrained authoritarian habits of the bureaucracy and by the pell-mell rush of the campaign. To concentrate on such administrative and political shortcomings, however, is to miss the point. Even if the campaign had been granted more time, more technical skill, and a better "bedside manner," the party-state could not possibly have assembled and digested the information necessary to make a fundamentally schematic plan succeed. The existing economic activity and physical movement of the Tanzanian rural population were the consequences of a mind-bogglingly complex, delicate, and pliable set of adaptations to their diverse social and material environment.[84] As in the customary land-tenure arrangements examined in chapter 1, these adaptations defy administrative codification because of their endless local variability, their elaboration, and their plasticity in the face of new conditions. If land tenure defies codification, then, it stands to reason that the connections structuring the entire material and social life of each particular group of peasants would remain largely opaque to both specialists and administrators.

Under the circumstances, wholesale, by-the-book resettlement made a havoc of peasant lives. Only a few of the most obvious ecological failures of villagization will serve to illustrate the pattern of ignorance. Peasants were forcibly moved from annually flooded lands that were vital to their cropping regime and shifted to poor soils on high ground. They were, as we have seen, moved to all-weather roads where the soil was unfamiliar or unsuitable for the crops envisaged. Village living placed cultivators far from their fields, thus thwarting the crop watching and pest control that more dispersed homesteads made possible. The concentration of livestock and people often had the unfortunate consequence of encouraging cholera and livestock epidemics. For the highly mobile Maasai and other pastoralists, the scheme of creating ujamaa ranches by herding cattle to a single location was an unmitigated disaster for range conservation and pastoral livelihoods.[85]

The failure of ujamaa villages was almost guaranteed by the high-modernist hubris of planners and specialists who believed that they alone knew how to organize a more satisfactory, rational, and productive life for their citizens. It should be noted that they did have something to contribute to what could have been a more fruitful development of the Tanzanian countryside. But their insistence that they had a monopoly on useful knowledge and that they impose this knowledge set the stage for disaster.

Settling people into supervised villages was emphatically *not* uniquely the brainchild of the nationalist elites of independent Tanzania. Villagization had a long colonial history in Tanzania and elsewhere, as program after program was devised to concentrate the population. The same techno-economic vision was shared, until very late in the game, by the World Bank, United States Agency for International Development (USAID), and other development agencies contributing to Tanzanian development.[86] However enthusiastic they were in spearheading their campaign, the political leaders of Tanzania were more consumers of a high-modernist faith that had originated elsewhere much earlier than they were producers.

What was perhaps distinctive about the Tanzanian scheme was its speed, its comprehensiveness, and its intention to deliver such collective services as schools, clinics, and clean water. Although considerable force was applied in seeing the scheme through, even then its consequences were not nearly as brutal or irremediable as those of Soviet collectivization.[87] The Tanzanian state's relative weakness and unwillingness to resort to Stalinist methods[88] as well as the Tanzanian peasants' tactical advantages, including flight, unofficial production and trade, smuggling, and foot-dragging, combined to make the practice of villagization far less destructive than the theory.[89]

The "Ideal" State Village: Ethiopian Variation

The pattern of compulsory villagization in Ethiopia uncannily resembles that of Russia in its coerciveness and Tanzania in its ostensible rationale. Beyond the obvious shared socialist terrain and official visits by Ethiopian officials to Tanzania to observe its program in action,[90] there seems to be a deeper affinity at work between the assertion of state authority in the countryside, on one hand, and the results in terms of process and actual physical plans, on the other. The continuity of

Nyerere's plans with those of the colonizers is obvious in the Tanzanian case. In Ethiopia, which was never colonized, resettlement can be seen as a century-old project of the imperial dynasty to subjugate non-Amharic-speaking peoples and, more generally, to bring fractious provinces under central control.

Although the Marxist revolutionary elite that seized power in early 1974 resorted to forced settlement at an early stage, its leader, Lieutenant Colonel Mengistu Haile Mariam and the Dergue—the shadowy ruling body of the revolutionary regime—did not call for full-scale villagization until 1985. The policy anticipated the eventual resettlement of all 33 million rural Ethiopians. Echoing Nyerere, Mengistu declared, "The scattered and haphazard habitation and livelihood of Ethiopian peasants cannot build socialism. . . . Insofar as efforts are dispersed and livelihood is individual, the results are only hand-to-mouth existence amounting to fruitless struggle and drudgery, which cannot build a prosperous society."[91] The other explanations for village settlement were no different from those given in Tanzania: concentration would bring services to scattered populations, permit state-designed social production (producer cooperatives), and allow mechanization and political education.[92]

Socialism and its precondition, villagization, were virtually Mengistu's way of saying "modern." In his justification for massive resettlement, he decried Ethiopia's reputation as "a symbol of backwardness and a valley of ignorance." He called on Ethiopians to "rally together to free farming from the ugly forces of nature." Finally, he condemned pastoralism per se, praising villagization as a way "to rehabilitate our nomad society."[93]

The pace of resettlement, however, was far more brutal in Ethiopia, inadvertently helping to lay the groundwork for the subsequent rebellions that brought down the regime. By March 1986, a scant year into the operation, the regime claimed that 4.6 million peasants had been settled in 4,500 villages.[94] Only three months were allotted between the first "agitation and propaganda" (read, "command") and the move itself—often over huge distances. All accounts suggest that many of the new settlements received almost nothing in the way of services and had more of the aspect of a penal colony than of a functioning village.

Forced villagization in the Arsi region was apparently planned directly from the center in Addis Ababa, with little or no local participation. There was a strict template which local surveyors and administrators were ordered to follow. The plan was carefully replicated in each location, inasmuch as this was not a regime inclined to tolerate local improvisation. "But the local recruits learned their jobs well, for the villages and their 1,000 [square] meter compounds, carefully marked by pegs and sod cuts, have followed the geometric grid pattern required by the guidelines. In fact, some villages have been too rigidly laid out; for example, one farmer had to move his large, well-constructed *tukul* [traditional thatched house] some 20 feet so that it would be 'in line' with all the other buildings in its row."[95]

The close alignment between theory and practice can be seen by comparing the layout of a government plan for an ideal village with an aerial photograph of a new village (figures 32 and 33). Notice the central location of all key government functions. A standardizing, round-number, bureaucratic mentality is obvious from the fact that each village was expected to have one thousand inhabitants and each compound one thousand square meters.[96] If every village had the same population and the same land allotment, a single model could simply be applied everywhere; no local knowledge would be required. The identical disposition of land in each settlement would make it that much easier for the authorities to send out general directives, to monitor crop production, and to control the harvest through the new Agricultural Marketing Corporation (AMC). The generic plan was particularly convenient for the hard-pressed surveyors, precisely because it bore no relation whatever to local ecological, economic, or social patterns. In order to facilitate the uniform design of the cookie-cutter villages, the planning officials were directed to choose flat, cleared sites and to insist on straight roads and similar, numbered houses.[97]

The objects of this exercise in geometry were under no illusions about its purpose. When they were finally free to talk, refugees in Somalia told their interviewers that the new settlement pattern was devised to control dissidence and rebellion, to prevent people from leaving, to "make it easier to watch the people," to control the crops, to register possessions and livestock, and (in Wollega) to "allow them to take our boys to war more easily."[98]

In "model producer cooperatives," standardized housing was provided: square, tin-roofed houses (*chika bets*). Elsewhere, traditional housing (*tukuls*) were disassembled and reconstructed in the rigidly stipulated order. As in Russia, all the private shops, tea houses, and small trading establishments were abolished, leaving only such state spaces as the village's mass organization and peasant association offices, literacy shed, health clinic, or state cooperative shop as public gathering places. In contrast to the Tanzanian experience, the Ethiopian campaign had a much stronger military component, as peasants were moved great distances with a view to military pacification and political emasculation.[99] Needless to say, the draconian conditions of Ethiopian

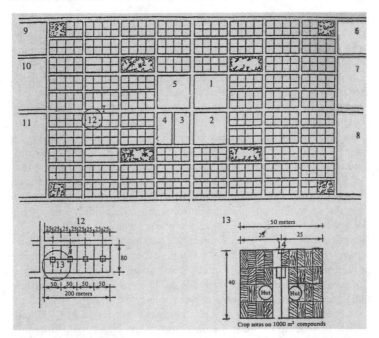

32. A government plan for a standard socialist village, Arsi region, Ethiopia. The layout shows *1*, a mass organization office; *2*, a kindergarten; *3*, a health clinic; *4*, a state cooperative shop; *5*, peasant association office; *6*, reserve plots; *7*, a primary school; *8*, a sports field; *9*, a seed-multiplication center; *10*, a handicrafts center; and *11*, an animal-breeding station. Detail *12* depicts an enlargement of compound sites, and detail *13* is an enlargement of two sites, showing the neighborhood latrine at *14*.

villagization meant that it was even more destructive of peasant livelihoods and of the environment than its Tanzanian counterpart.[100]

A full appreciation of the toll of forced resettlement in Ethiopia extends far beyond the standard reports of starvation, executions, deforestation, and failed crops. The new settlements nearly always failed their inhabitants as human communities and as units of food production. The very fact of massive resettlement nullified a precious legacy of local agricultural and pastoral knowledge and, with it, some thirty to forty thousand functioning communities, most of them in regions that had regularly produced food surpluses.

A typical cultivator in Tigray, a location singled out for harsh measures, planted an average of fifteen crops a season (such cereal crops

33. Aerial view of a resettlement site in southwestern Ethiopia, 1986

as teff, barley, wheat, sorghum, corn, millet; such root crops as sweet potatoes, potatoes, onions; some legumes, including horsebeans, lentils, and chickpeas; and a number of vegetable crops, including peppers, okra, and many others).[101] It goes without saying that the farmer was familiar with each of several varieties of any crop, when to plant it, how deeply to sow it, how to prepare the soil, and how to tend and harvest it. This knowledge was *place specific* in the sense that the successful growing of any variety required local knowledge about rainfall and soils, down to and including the peculiarities of each plot the farmer cultivated.[102] It was also place specific in the sense that much of this knowledge stored in the collective memory of the locality: an oral archive of techniques, seed varieties, and ecological information.

Once the farmer was moved, often to a vastly different ecological setting, his local knowledge was all but useless. As Jason Clay emphasizes, "Thus, when a farmer from the highlands is transported to settlement camps in areas like Gambella, he is instantly transformed from an agricultural expert to an unskilled, ignorant laborer, completely dependent for his survival on the central government."[103] Resettlement was far more than a change in scenery. It took people from a setting in which they had the skills and resources to produce many of their own basic needs and hence the means of a reasonably self-sufficient independence. It then transferred them to a setting where these skills were of little or no avail. Only in such circumstances was it possible for camp officials to reduce migrants to mendicants whose obedience and labor could be exacted for subsistence rations.

Although the drought that coincided with forced migration in Ethiopia was real enough, much of the famine to which international aid agencies responded was a product of the massive resettlement.[104] The destruction of social ties was almost as productive of famine as were the crop failures induced by poor planning and ignorance of the new agricultural environment. Communal ties, relations with kin and affines, networks of reciprocity and cooperation, local charity and dependence had been the principal means by which villagers had managed to survive periods of food shortage in the past. Stripped of these social resources by indiscriminate deportations, often separated from their immediate family and forbidden to leave, the settlers in the camps were far more vulnerable to starvation than they had been in their home regions.

The immanent logic, never achieved, of the Dergue's rural policy is telling. If implemented successfully, rural Ethiopians would have been permanently settled along the main roads in large, legible villages, where uniform, numbered houses would have been set in a grid centered on the headquarters of the peasant association (that is, the party), where the chairman, his deputies, and the militia maintained their posts. Designated crops would have been grown collectively, with machinery, on flat fields laid out uniformly by state surveyors and then harvested for delivery to state agencies for distribution and sale abroad. Labor would have been closely supervised by experts and cadres. Intended to modernize Ethiopian agriculture and, not incidentally, to strengthen the control of the Dergue, the policy was literally fatal to hundreds of thousands of cultivators and, finally, to the Dergue itself.

Conclusion

In quiet and untroubled times, it seems to every administrator that it is only by his efforts that the whole population under his rule is kept going, and in this consciousness of being indispensable every administrator finds the chief reward of his labor and efforts. While the sea of history remains calm the ruler-administrator in his frail bark, holding it with a boat hook to the ship of the people and himself moving, naturally imagines that his efforts move the ship he is holding on to. But as soon as a storm arises and the sea begins to heave and the ship to move, such a delusion is no longer possible. The ship moves independently with its own enormous motion, the boat hook no longer reaches the moving vessel, and suddenly the administrator, instead of appearing a ruler and a source of power, becomes an insignificant, useless, feeble man.
—Leo Tolstoy, *War and Peace*

The conflict between the officials and specialists actively planning the future on one hand and the peasantry on the other has been billed by the first group as a struggle between progress and obscurantism, rationality and superstition, science and religion. Yet it is apparent from the high-modernist schemes we have examined that the "rational" plans they imposed were often spectacular failures. As units of production, as human communities, or as a means of delivering services, the planned villages failed the people they were intended, sometimes sincerely, to serve. In the long run they even failed their originators as units of growing appropriation or as a way of securing the loyalty of the rural population, although they may have still served effectively, in the short run at least, as a way of detaching a population from its customary social network and thus thwarting collective protest.

High Modernism and the Optics of Power

If the plans for villagization were so rational and scientific, why did they bring about such general ruin? The answer, I believe, is that such plans were not scientific or rational in any meaningful sense of those terms. What these planners carried in their mind's eye was a certain aesthetic, what one might call a visual codification of modern rural production and community life. Like a religious faith, this visual codification was almost impervious to criticism or disconfirming evidence. The belief in large farms, monocropping, "proper" villages, tractor-plowed fields, and collective or communal farming was an aesthetic conviction undergirded by a conviction that this was the way in which the world was headed—a teleology.[105] For all but a handful of specialists, these were not empirical hypotheses derived from particular contexts in the temperate West that would have to be carefully examined in practice. In a given historical and social context—say, wheat growing by farmers breaking new ground on the plains of Kansas—many elements of this faith might have made sense.[106] As a faith, however, it was generalized and applied uncritically in widely divergent settings with disastrous results.

If the proverbial man from Mars were to stumble on the facts here, he could be forgiven if he were confused about exactly who was the empiricist and who was the true believer. Tanzanian peasants had, for example, been readjusting their settlement patterns and farming practices in accordance with climate changes, new crops, and new markets with notable success in the two decades before villagization. They seemed to have an eminently empirical, albeit cautious, outlook on their own practices. By contrast, specialists and politicians seemed to be in the unshakable grip of a quasi-religious enthusiasm made even more potent in being backed by the state.

This was not just any faith. It had a direct relation to the status and interests of its bearers. Because the bearers of this visual codification saw themselves as self-conscious modernizers of their societies, their vision required a sharp and morally loaded contrast between what looked modern (tidy, rectilinear, uniform, concentrated, simplified, mechanized) and what looked primitive (irregular, dispersed, complicated, unmechanized). As the technical and political elite with a monopoly on modern education, they used this visual aesthetic of progress to define their historic mission and to enhance their status.

Their modernist faith was self-serving in other respects as well. The very idea of a national plan, which would be devised at the capital and would then reorder the periphery after its own image into quasi-military units obeying a single command, was profoundly centralizing. Each unit at the periphery was tied not so much to its neighboring settlement as to the command center in the capital; the lines of communication rather resembled the converging lines used to organize perspective in early Renaissance paintings. "The convention of perspective . . . centers everything in the eye of the beholder. It is like a beam from a lighthouse—only instead of travelling outward, appearances travel in. The conventions called those appearances reality. Perspective makes the single eye the center of the visible world. Everything converges on the eye as to the vanishing point of infinity. The visible world is arranged for the spectator as the universe was once thought to be arranged for God."[107]

The image of čoordination and authority aspired to here recalls that of mass exercises—thousands of bodies moving in perfect unison according to a meticulously rehearsed script. When such coordination is achieved, the spectacle may have several effects. The demonstration of mass coordination, its designers hope, will awe spectators and participants with its display of powerful cohesion. The awe is enhanced by the fact that, as in the Taylorist factory, only someone outside and above the display can fully appreciate it as a totality; the individual participants at ground level are small molecules within an organism whose brain is elsewhere. The image of a nation that might operate along these lines is enormously flattering to elites at the apex—and, of course, demeaning to a population whose role they thus reduce to that of ciphers. Beyond impressing observers, such displays may, in the short run at least, constitute a reassuring self-hypnosis which serves to reinforce the moral purpose and self-confidence of the elites.[108]

The modernist visual aesthetic that animated planned villages has a curiously static quality to it. It is rather like a completed picture that cannot be improved upon.[109] Its design is the result of scientific and technical laws, and the implicit assumption is that, once built, the task then becomes one of maintaining its form. The planners aim to have each new village look like the last. Like a Roman military commander entering a new camp, the official arriving from Dar es Salaam would know exactly where everything could be found, from the TANU head-quarters to the peasant association and the health clinic. Every field and every house would also, in principle, be nearly identical and lo-cated according to an overall scheme. To the degree that this vision had been realized in practice, it would have made absolutely no con-nections to the particularities of place and time. It would be a view from nowhere. Instead of the unrepeatable variety of settlements closely adjusted to local ecology and subsistence routines and instead of the constantly changing local response to shifts in demography, cli-mate, and markets, the state would have created thin, generic villages that were uniform in everything from political structure and social stratification to cropping techniques. The number of variables at play would be minimized. In their perfect legibility and sameness, these vil-lages would be ideal, substitutable bricks in an edifice of state plan-ning. Whether they would *function* was another matter.

The Failure of Grids

> Ideas cannot digest reality.
> —Jean-Paul Sartre

It is far easier for would-be reformers to change the formal struc-ture of an institution than to change its practices. Redesigning the lines and boxes in an organizational chart is simpler than changing how that organization in fact operates. Changing the rules and regula-tions is simpler than eliciting behavior that conforms to them.[110] Re-designing the physical layout of a village is simpler than transforming its social and productive life. For obvious reasons, political elites—particularly authoritarian high-modernist elites—typically begin with changes in the formal structure and rules. Such legal and statutory changes are the most accessible and the easiest to rearrange.

Anyone who has worked in a formal organization—even a small one strictly governed by detailed rules—knows that handbooks and written guidelines fail utterly in explaining how the institution goes successfully about its work. Accounting for its smooth operation are nearly endless and shifting sets of implicit understandings, tacit coordinations, and practical mutualities that could never be successfully captured in a written code. This ubiquitous social fact is useful to employees and labor unions. The premise behind what are tellingly called work-to-rule strikes is a case in point. When Parisian taxi drivers want to press a point on the municipal authorities about regulations or fees, they sometimes launch a work-to-rule strike. It consists merely in following meticulously all the regulations in the *Code routier* and thereby bringing traffic throughout central Paris to a grinding halt. The drivers thus take tactical advantage of the fact that the circulation of traffic is possible *only* because drivers have mastered a set of practices that have evolved outside, and often in contravention, of the formal rules.

Any attempt to completely plan a village, a city, or, for that matter, a language is certain to run afoul of the same social reality. A village, city, or language is the jointly created, partly unintended product of many, many hands. To the degree that authorities insist on replacing this ineffably complex web of activity with formal rules and regulations, they are certain to disrupt the web in ways that they cannot possibly foresee.[111] This point is most frequently made by such proponents of laissez-faire as Friedrich Hayek, who are fond of pointing out that a command economy, however sophisticated and legible, cannot begin to replace the myriad, rapid, mutual adjustments of functioning markets and the price system.[112] In this context, however, the point applies in important ways to the even more complex patterns of social interaction with the material environment that we call a city or a village. Cities with a long history may be called "deep" or "thick" cities in the sense that they are the historical product of a vast number of people from all stations (including officialdom) who are long gone. It is possible, of course, to build a new city or a new village, but it will be a "thin" or "shallow" city, and its residents will have to begin (perhaps from known repertoires) to make it work in spite of the rules. In cases like Brasília or Tanzania's planned villages, one can understand why state planners may prefer a freshly cleared site and a "shocked" population moved abruptly to the new setting in which the planners' influence is maximized. The alternative is to reform in situ an existing, functioning community that has more social resources for resisting and refashioning the transformation planned for it.

The thinness of artificially designed communities can be compared to the thinness of artificially designed languages.[113] Communities planned at a single stroke—Brasília or the planned village in Tanzania or Ethiopia—are to older, unplanned communities as Esperanto is to, say, English or Burmese. One can in fact design a new language that in many respects is more logical, simpler, more universal, and less irreg-

ular and that would technically lend itself to more clarity and precision. This was, of course, precisely the objective of Esperanto's inven-
tor, Lazar Zamenhof, who also imagined that Esperanto, which was
also known as international language, would eliminate the parochial
nationalisms of Europe.[114] Yet it is also perfectly obvious why Esperanto, which lacked a powerful state to enforce its adoption, failed
to replace the existing vernaculars or dialects of Europe. (As social linguists are fond of saying, "A national language is a dialect with an
army.") It was an exceptionally thin language, without any of the resonances, connotations, ready metaphors, literature, oral history, idioms, and traditions of practical use that any socially embedded language already had. Esperanto has survived as a kind of utopian
curiosity, a very thin dialect spoken by a handful of intelligentsia who
have kept its promise alive.

The Miniaturization of Perfection and Control

The pretense of authoritarian high-modernist schemes to discipline
virtually everything within their ambit is bound to encounter intractable resistance. Social inertia, entrenched privileges, international
prices, wars, environmental change, to mention only a few factors, ensure that the results of high-modernist planning will look substantially
different from what was originally imagined. Such is even the case
where, as in Stalinist collectivization, the state devotes great resources
to enforcing a high degree of formal compliance with its directives.
Those who have their hearts set on realizing such plans cannot fail to
be frustrated by stubborn social realities and material facts.

One response to this frustration is a retreat to the realm of appearances and miniatures—to model cities and Potemkin villages, as it
were.[115] It is easier to build Brasília than to fundamentally transform
Brazil and Brazilians. The effect of this retreat is to create a small, relatively self-contained, utopian space where high-modernist aspirations
might more nearly be realized. The limiting case, where control is maximized but impact on the external world is minimized, is in the museum or the theme park.[116]

This miniaturization of perfection, I think, has a logic all its own,
in spite of its implicit abandonment of large-scale transformations.
Model villages, model cities, military colonies, show projects, and demonstration farms offer politicians, administrators, and specialists an opportunity to create a sharply defined experimental terrain in which the
number of rogue variables and unknowns are minimized. If, of course,
such experiments make it successfully from the pilot stage to general

application, then they are a perfectly rational form of policy planning. There are advantages to miniaturization. The constriction of focus makes possible a far higher degree of social control and discipline. By concentrating the material and personnel resources of the state at a single point, miniaturization can approximate the architecture, layout, mechanization, social services, and cropping patterns that its vision calls for. Small islands of order and modernity, as Potemkin well understood, are politically useful to officials who want to please their superiors with an example of what they can accomplish. If their superiors are sufficiently closeted and misinformed, they may mistake, as Catherine the Great apparently did with Potemkin's convincing scenery, the exemplary instance for the larger reality.[117] The effect is to banish at one place and one time, in a kind of high-modernist version of Versailles and Le Petit Trianon, the larger loss of control.

The visual aesthetic of miniaturization seems significant as well. Just as the architectural drawing, the model, and the map are ways of dealing with a larger reality that is not easily grasped or manageable in its entirety, the miniaturization of high-modernist development offers a visually complete example of what the future looks like.

Miniaturization of one kind or another is ubiquitous. It is tempting to wonder whether the human tendency to miniaturization—to create "toys" of larger objects and realities that cannot so easily be manipulated—does not also have a bureaucratic equivalent. Yi-fu Tuan has brilliantly examined how we miniaturize, and thereby domesticate, the larger phenomena that are outside our control, often with benign intentions. Under this elastic rubric, he includes bonsai, bonseki, and gardens (a miniaturization of the plant world) along with dolls and dollhouses, toy locomotives, toy soldiers and weapons of war, and "living toys" in the form of specially bred fish and dogs.[118] While Tuan concentrates on more or less playful domestication, something of the same desire for control and mastery can also, it would seem, operate on the larger scale of bureaucracies. Just as *substantive* goals, the achievement of which are hard to measure, may be supplanted by thin, notional statistics—the number of villages formed, the number of acres plowed—so may they also be supplanted by microenvironments of modernist order.

Capital cities, as the seat of the state and of its rulers, as the symbolic center of (new) nations, and as the places where often powerful foreigners come, are most likely to receive close attention as veritable theme parks of high-modernist development. Even in their contemporary secular guises, national capitals retain something of the older tradition of being sacred centers for a national cult. The symbolic power of high-modernist capitals depends not, as it once did, on how well they represent a sacred past but rather on how fully they symbolize the utopian aspirations that rulers hold for their nations. As ever, to be sure, the display is meant to exude power as well as the authority of the past or of the future.

Colonial capitals were fashioned with these functions in mind. The imperial capital of New Delhi, designed by Edwin Lutyens, was a stunning example of a capital intended to overawe its subjects (and perhaps its own officials) with its scale and its grandeur, with its processional axes for parades demonstrating military power and its triumphal arches. *New* Delhi was naturally intended as a negation of what then became *Old* Delhi. One central purpose of the new capital was captured nicely by the private secretary to George V in a note about the future residence of the British viceroy. It must, he wrote, be "conspicuous and commanding," not dominated by the structures of past empires or by the features of the natural landscape. "We must now let [the Indian] see for the first time the power of Western science, art, and civilization."[119] Standing at its center for a ceremonial occasion, one might forget for a moment that this tiny gem of imperial architecture was all but lost in a vast sea of Indian realities which either contradicted it or paid it no heed.

A great many nations, some of them former colonies, have built entirely new capitals rather than compromise with an urban past that their leaders were determined to transcend; one thinks of Brazil, Pakistan, Turkey, Belize, Nigeria, the Ivory Coast, Malawi, and Tanzania.[120] Most were built following the plans of Western or Western-trained architects, even when they attempted to incorporate references to vernacular building traditions. As Lawrence Vale points out, many new capitals seem intended as completed and self-contained objects. No subtraction, addition, or modification is contemplated—only admiration. And in their strategic use of hills and elevation, of complexes set behind walls or water barriers, of finely graded structural hierarchy reflecting function and status, they also convey an impression of hegemony and domination which was unlikely to prevail beyond the city limits.[121]

Nyerere planned a new capital, Dodoma, that was to be somewhat different. The ideological commitments of the regime were to be expressed in an architecture that was purposely *not* monumental. Several interconnected settlements would undulate with the landscape, and the modest scale of the buildings would eliminate the need for elevators and air conditioning. Dodoma was very definitely, however, intended to be a utopian space that both represented the future and explicitly negated Dar es Salaam. The master plan for Dodoma condemned Dar as a "dominant focus of development, . . . the antithesis of what Tanzania is aiming for, and is growing at a pace, which if not checked, will damage the city as a humanist habitat and Tanzania as an egalitarian socialist-state."[122] While planning villages for everyone else whether they liked it or not, the rulers also designed for themselves a new symbolic center incorporating, not by accident, I think, a hilltop refuge amidst manicured, orderly surroundings.

If the intractable difficulties of transforming existing cities can lead to the temptation to erect a model capital city, so can the difficulties of transforming existing villages prompt a retreat into miniaturization. One major variant of this tendency was the creation of carefully controlled production environments by frustrated colonial extension officers. Coulson notes the logic involved: "If a farmer could not be forced, or persuaded, the only alternatives were to ignore them altogether and go for mechanized agriculture controlled by outsiders (as in the Groundnuts Scheme, or on settler farms controlled by Europeans), or to take them right away from the traditional surroundings, to settlement schemes where in return for receiving land they might perhaps agree to follow the instructions of the agricultural staff."[123]

Still another variant was the attempt to distill out of the general population a cadre of progressive farmers who would then be mobilized to practice modern agriculture. Such policies were followed in elaborate detail in Mozambique and were important in colonial Tanzania as well.[124] When the state confronted a "brick wall of peasant conservatism," notes a 1956 document from the Tanganyika Department of Agriculture, it became necessary "to withdraw the effort from some portions so as to concentrate on small selected points, a procedure which has come to be known as the 'focal-point approach.'"[125] In their desire to isolate the small sector of the agricultural population that they thought would respond to scientific agriculture, the extension agents frequently overlooked other realities that bore directly on their substantive mission—realities that were under their nose but not under their aegis. Pauline Peters thus describes an effort in Malawi to depopulate a rural area of all but those whom the agricultural authorities had designated "master farmers." Extension agents were attempting to create a microlandscape of "neatly-bounded, mixed-farming lot[s] based on rotation of single-stand crops which would replace the scattered, multi-cropped farming they considered backward. In the meantime, they entirely ignored an autonomous and general rush to plant tobacco—the very transformation they were trying to bring about by force."[126]

The planned city, the planned village, and the planned language (not to mention the command economy) are, we have emphasized, likely to be thin cities, villages, and languages. They are thin in the sense that they cannot reasonably plan for anything more than a few schematic aspects of the inexhaustibly complex activities that characterize "thick" cities and villages. One all-but-guaranteed consequence of such thin planning is that the planned institution generates an unofficial reality—a "dark twin"—that arises to perform many of the various needs that the planned institution fails to fulfill. Brasília, as Holston showed, engendered an "unplanned Brasília" of construction workers, migrants, and those whose housing and activities were necessary but were not foreseen or were precluded by the plan. Nearly every new, exemplary capital city has, as the inevitable accompaniment of its official structures, given rise to another, far more "disorderly" and complex city *that makes the official city work*—that is virtually a condition of its existence. That is, the dark twin is not just an anomaly, an "outlaw reality"; it represents the activity and life without which the official city would cease to function. The outlaw city bears the same relation to the official city as the Parisian taxi drivers' actual practices bear to the *Code routier*.

On a more speculative note, I imagine that the greater the pretense of and insistence on an officially decreed micro-order, the greater the volume of nonconforming practices necessary to sustain that fiction. The most rigidly planned economies tend to be accompanied by large "underground, 'gray,' informal," economies that supply, in a thousand ways, what the formal economy fails to supply.[127] When this economy is ruthlessly suppressed, the cost has often been economic ruin and starvation (the Great Leap Forward and the Cultural Revolution in China; the autarkic, moneyless economy of Pol Pot's Cambodia). Efforts to force a country's inhabitants to maintain permanent, fixed residences tend to produce large, illegal, undocumented populations in urban areas where they have been forbidden to go.[128] The insistence on a rigid visual aesthetic at the core of the capital city tends to produce settlements and slums teeming with squatters who, as often as not, sweep the floors, cook the meals, and tend the children of the elites who work in the decorous, planned center.[129]

8 Taming Nature:
An Agriculture of Legibility
and Simplicity

Yes, enumerate the carriage parts—
Still not a carriage.

When you begin making decisions and cutting it up
    rules and names appear
And once names appear, you should know when to stop.
—*Tao-te-ching*

The necessarily simple abstractions of large bureaucratic institutions, as we have seen, can never adequately represent the actual complexity of natural or social processes. The categories that they employ are too coarse, too static, and too stylized to do justice to the world that they purport to describe.

For reasons that will become apparent, state-sponsored high-modernist agriculture has recourse to abstractions of the same order. The simple "production and profit" model of agricultural extension and agricultural research has failed in important ways to represent the complex, supple, negotiated objectives of real farmers and their communities. That model has also failed to represent the space in which farmers plant crops—its microclimates, its moisture and water movement, its microrelief, and its local biotic history. Unable to effectively represent the profusion and complexity of real farms and real fields, high-modernist agriculture has often succeeded in radically simplifying those farms and fields so they can be more directly apprehended, controlled, and managed. I emphasize the *radical* simplification of agricultural high modernism because agriculture is, even in its most rudimentary, neolithic forms, inevitably a process of simplifying the floral profusion of nature.[1] How else are we to understand the process by which man has encouraged certain species of flora that he found useful and discouraged others that he found a nuisance?

The logic behind the radical simplification of the field is almost precisely identical to the logic behind the radical simplification of the forest. In fact, a simplified agriculture, which was developed earlier, served as the model for scientific forestry. The guiding idea was the maximization of the crop yield or profit.[2] The forests were reconceptualized as "timber farms" in which a single species of tree was planted in straight rows and harvested like a crop when it was "mature." The preconditions of such simplifications were the existence of a commodity market and competitive pressure, on states as well as on entrepreneurs, to maximize profits or revenue. In the monocropped field and single-species forest alike, the innumerable other members of the biotic community were ignored unless they had some direct bearing on the health and yield of the species to be harvested. Such narrowing of attention to a single outcome—invariably the one of most commercial or fiscal interest—confers an analytical power that allows foresters and agronomists to track carefully the influence of other factors on this single dependent variable. Within its ambit, there is no denying the extraordinary power of this approach to increase yields. As we shall see, however, this potent but narrow perspective is troubled both by certain inevitable blind spots and by phenomena that lie outside its restricted field of vision. To continue the metaphor, this narrowness in turn means that production agronomy is occasionally blindsided by factors outside its analytical focus and is forced, by the resulting crisis, to take a broader perspective.

The question we shall address in this chapter is why a model of modern, scientific agriculture that has apparently been successful in the temperate, industrializing West has so often foundered in the Third World. In spite of these indifferent results, the model has been pressed by colonial modernizers, independent states, and international agencies. In Africa, where the results have been particularly sobering, an agronomist with great experience has claimed that "one of the crucial lessons of the past fifty years or so of ecological research focused on African agriculture is that the 'dramatic modernization' option has a track record so poor that a return to slower and more incremental approaches must now be given serious and sustained attention."[3]

We will not be much concerned in this discussion with the particular reasons that made this scheme or that cropping plan fail. To be sure, the familiar bureaucratic pathologies as well as openly predatory practices have often greatly compounded these failures. My claim, however, is that the origin of these failures can be traced to a deeper level; these were, in other words, systemic failures and would have occurred under the best assumptions about administrative efficiency and probity.

At least four elements seem to be at work in these systemic failures. The first two are linked to the historical origin and institutional nexus of high-modernist agriculture. First, given their discipline's origin in the temperate, industrializing West, the bearers of modernism in agricultural planning inherited a series of unexamined assumptions about cropping and field preparation that turned out to work badly in other contexts. Second, given the presumptions about expertise embodied in modernist agricultural planning, the actual schemes were continually bent to serve the power and status of officials and of the state organs they controlled.[4]

The third element, however, operates at a deeper level: it is the systematic, cyclopean shortsightedness of high-modernist agriculture that courts certain forms of failure. Its rigorous attention to productionist goals casts into relative obscurity all the outcomes lying outside the immediate relationship between farm inputs and yields. This means that both long-term outcomes (soil structure, water quality, land-tenure relations) and third-party effects, or what welfare economists call "externalities," receive little attention until they begin to affect production.

Finally, the very strength of scientific agricultural experimentation—its simplifying assumptions and its ability to isolate the impact of a single variable on total production—is incapable of dealing adequately with certain forms of complexity. It tends to ignore, or discount, agricultural practices that are not assimilable to its techniques.

Lest there be any misunderstanding about my purpose here, I want to emphasize that this is not a general offensive against modern agronomic science, let alone an attack on the culture of scientific research. Modern agronomic science, with its sophisticated plant breeding, plant pathology, analysis of plant nutrition, soil analysis, and technical virtuosity, is responsible for creating a fund of technical knowledge that is by now being used in some form by even the most traditional cultivators. My purpose, rather, is to show how the *imperial pretensions* of agronomic science—its inability to recognize or incorporate knowledge created outside its paradigm—sharply limited its utility to many cultivators. Whereas farmers, as we shall see, seem pragmatically alert to knowledge coming from *any* quarter should it serve their purposes, modern agricultural planners are far less receptive to other ways of knowing.

Varieties of Agricultural Simplification

Early Agriculture

Cultivation is simplification. Even the most cursory forms of agriculture typically produce a floral landscape that is less diverse than an unmanaged landscape. The crops that mankind has cultivated have, when fully domesticated, become dependent for their survival upon the management of cultivators—such activities as making a clearing, burning brush, breaking the soil, weeding, pruning, manuring. Strictly speaking, a crop in the field is not an artificial landscape, inasmuch as all fauna, not excluding human beings, modify their environment in the course of food gathering. What is certain, however, is that most of *Homo sapiens*'s cultivars have been so adapted to their altered landscape that they have become "'biological monsters'" which could not survive in the wild.[5]

Millennia of variation and conscious human selection have favored cultivars that are systematically different from their wild and weedy cousins.[6] Our convenience has led us to prefer plants that have large seeds and are easy to germinate, have more blossoms and hence more fruit, and whose fruits are more easily threshed or shelled. Cultivated maize thus has a few large ears with large kernels whereas wild or semidomesticated maizes have very small cobs with small kernels. The difference is most starkly captured by the contrast between the huge, seed-laden commercial sunflower and its diminutive woodland relative.

Beyond the question of the harvest itself, of course, cultivators have also selected for scores of other properties: texture, flavor, color, storage quality, aesthetic value, grinding and cooking qualities, and so on. The breadth of human purposes has led not to a single, ideal cultivar of each species but rather to a great many varieties, each distinctive in some important way. Thus we have the varieties of barley grown for porridge, for bread, for beer, and for feeding livestock; and thus "sweet sorghum for chewing, white-seeded types for bread, small, dark, red-seeded types for beer, and strong-stemmed, fibrous types for house-construction and basketry."[7]

The greatest selection pressure, however, came from the dominant anxiety of cultivators: that they not starve. This most basic of existential concerns also led to a great variety of cultivars, termed the "landraces" of the various crops. Landraces are genetically variable populations that respond differently to different soil conditions, levels of moisture, temperature, sunlight, diseases and pests, microclimates, and so forth. Over time, traditional cultivators, operating as experienced applied botanists, have developed literally thousands of landraces of a single species. A working knowledge of many, if not all, of these landraces provided cultivators with enormous flexibility in the face of environmental factors that they could not control.[8]

For our purposes, the long development of so many landraces is significant in at least two respects. First, while early farmers were transforming and simplifying their natural environment, they also had a surpassing interest in fostering a certain kind of diversity. A combination of their wide interests and their concern about the food supply impelled them to select and protect many landraces. The genetic variability of the crops they grew provided some built-in insurance against drought, flooding, plant diseases, pests, and the seasonal vagaries of climate.[9] A pathogen might affect one landrace but not another; some landraces would do well in a drought, others in wet conditions; some would do well in clayey soil, others in sandy soil. Placing a large number of prudent bets, finely tuned to microlocal conditions, the cultivator maximized the dependability of a tolerable harvest.

The variety of landraces is significant in another sense. *All* modern crops of any economic significance are the product of landraces. Until about 1930 all scientific crop breeding was essentially a process of selection from among the existing landraces.[10] Landraces and their wild progenitors and "escapes" represent the "germ plasm" or seed-stock capital upon which modern agriculture is based. In other words, as James Boyce has put it, modern varieties and traditional agriculture are complements, not substitutes.[11]

Twentieth-Century Agriculture

Modern, industrial, scientific farming, which is characterized by monocropping, mechanization, hybrids, the use of fertilizers and pesticides, and capital intensiveness, has brought about a level of standardization into agriculture that is without historical precedent. Far beyond mere monocropping on the model of scientific forestry explored earlier, this simplification has entailed a genetic narrowing fraught with consequences that we are only beginning to comprehend.

One of the basic sources of increasing uniformity in crops arises from the intense commercial pressures to maximize profits in a competitive mass market. Thus the effort to increase planting densities in order to stretch the productivity of land encouraged the adoption of varieties that would tolerate crowding. Greater planting densities have, in turn, intensified the use of commercial fertilizers and therefore the selection of subspecies known for high fertilizer (especially nitrogen) uptake and response. At the same time, the growth of great supermarket chains, with their standardized routines of shipping, packaging, and display, has inexorably led to an emphasis on uniformity of size, shape, color, and "eye appeal."[12] The result of these pressures was to concentrate on the small number of cultivars that met these criteria while abandoning others.

The production of uniformity in the field is best grasped, however, through the logic of mechanization. As factor prices in the West have, since at least 1950, favored the substitution of farm machinery for hired labor, the farmer has sought cultivars that were compatible with mechanization. That is, he selected crops whose architecture did not interfere with tractors or sprayers, which ripened uniformly, and which could be picked in a "once-over" pass of the machine.

Given the techniques of hybridization being developed at roughly the same time, it was but a short step to creating new crop varieties bred explicitly for mechanization. "Genetic variability," as Jack Ralph Kloppenberg notes, "is the enemy of mechanization."[13] In the case of corn, hybridization—the progeny of two inbred lines—produces a field of the genetically identical individuals that are ideal for mechanization. Varieties developed with machinery in mind were available as early as 1920, when Henry Wallace joined forces with a manufacturer of harvesting equipment to cultivate his new, stiff-stalked variety with a strong shank connecting the ear to the stalk. An entire field of plant breeding, termed "phytoengineering," was thus born in order to adapt the natural world to machine processing. "Machines are not made to harvest crops," noted two proponents of phytoengineering. "In reality, crops must be designed to be harvested by machine."[14] Having been adapted to the cultivated field, the crop was now adapted to mechanization. The "machine-friendly" crop was bred to incorporate a series of characteristics that made it easier to harvest it mechanically. Among the most important of these characteristics were resilience, a concentrated fruit set, uniformity of plant size and architecture, uniformity of fruit shape and size, dwarfing (in the case of tree crops especially), and fruits that easily break away from the plant.[15]

The development of the "supermarket tomato" by G. C. (Jack) Hanna at the University of California at Davis in the late 1940s and 1950s is an early and diagnostic case.[16] Spurred by the wartime shortage of field labor, researchers set about inventing a mechanical harvester *and* breeding the tomato that would accommodate it. The tomato plants eventually bred for the job were hybrids of low stature and uniform maturity that produced similarly sized fruits with thick walls, firm flesh, and no cracks; the fruits were picked green in order to avoid being bruised by the grasp of the machinery and were artificially ripened by ethylene gas during transport. The results were the small, uniform winter tomatoes, sold four to a package, which dominated supermarket shelves for several decades. Taste and nutritional quality were secondary to machine compatibility. Or to put it more charitably, the breeders did what they could to develop the best tomato within the very sharp constraints of mechanization.

The imperatives of maximizing profits and hence, in this case, of mechanizing the harvest worked powerfully to transform and simplify both the field and the crop. Relatively inflexible, nonselective machines work best in flat fields with identical plants growing uniform fruits of perfectly even maturity. Agronomic science was deployed to approximate this ideal: large, finely graded fields; uniform irrigation and nutrients to regulate growth; liberal use of herbicides, fungicides, and insecticides to maintain uniform health; and, above all, plant breeding to create the ideal cultivar.

The Unintended Consequences of Simplification

Reviewing the history of major crop epidemics, beginning with the Irish potato famine in 1850, a committee of the United States National Research Council concluded: "These encounters show clearly that crop mono-culture and genetic uniformity invite epidemics. All that is needed is the arrival on the scene of a parasite that can take advantage of the vulnerability. If the crop is uniformly vulnerable, so much the better for the parasite. In this way virus diseases have devastated sugar beets with 'yellows,' peaches with yellows, potatoes with leaf roll and X and Y viruses, cocoa with swollen shoot, clover with sudden death, sugarcane with mosaic, and rice with hoja blanca."[17] After a corn leaf blight had devastated much of the 1970 corn crop, the committee had been convened in order to consider the genetic vulnerability of all major crops. One of the pioneer breeders of hybrid corn, Donald Jones, had foreseen the problems that the loss of genetic diversity might bring: "Genetically uniform pure line varieties are very productive and highly desirable when environmental conditions are favorable and the varieties are well-protected from pests of all kinds. When these external factors are not favorable, the result can be disastrous . . . due to some new virulent parasite."[18]

The logic of epidemiology in crops is relatively straightforward in principle. All plants have some resistance to pathogens; otherwise they and the pathogen (if it preyed upon only that plant) would disappear. At the same time, all plants are genetically vulnerable to certain pathogens. If a field is populated exclusively by genetically identical individuals, such as single-cross hybrids or clones, then each plant is vulnerable in exactly the same way to the same pathogen, be it a virus, fungus, bacterium, or nematode.[19] Such a field is an ideal genetic habitat for the proliferation of precisely those strains or mutants of pathogens that thrive and feed on this particular cultivar. The uniform habitat, especially one in which plants are crowded, exerts a natural-selection pressure, as it were, that favors such pathogens. Given the right seasonal conditions for the pathogen to multiply (temperature, humidity, wind, and so on), the classic conditions for the geometric progression of an epidemic are in place.[20]

In contrast, diversity is the enemy of epidemics. In a field with many species of plants, only a few individuals are likely to be susceptible to a given pathogen, and they are likely to be widely scattered. The mathematical logic of the epidemic is broken.[21] A monocropped field, as the National Research Council report noted, increases vulnerability appreciably inasmuch as all members of the same plant species share much of their genetic inheritance. But where a field is populated by many genetically diverse landraces of a given species, the risk is vastly reduced. Any agricultural practice that increases diversity over time and space, such as crop rotation or mixed cropping on a farm or in a region, acts as a barrier to the spread of epidemics.

The modern regime of pesticide use, which has arisen over the past fifty years, must be seen as an *integral* feature of this genetic vulnerability, not as an unrelated scientific breakthrough. It is precisely because hybrids are so uniform and hence disease prone that quasi-heroic measures have to be taken to control the environment in which they are grown. Such hybrids are analogous to a human patient with a compromised immune system who must be kept in a sterile field lest an opportunistic infection take hold. The sterile field, in this case, has been established by the blanket use of pesticides.[22]

Corn, as the most widely planted crop in the United States (85 million acres in 1986)[23] and the first one to be hybridized, has provided nearly ideal conditions for insect, disease, and weed buildup. Pesticide use is correspondingly high. Corn accounts for one-third of the total market for herbicides and one-quarter of the market for insecticides.[24] One of the long-term effects, which is readily predictable according to the theory of natural selection, has been the emergence of resistant strains among insects, fungi, and weeds, necessitating either larger doses or a new set of chemical agents. Some pathogens, again predictably, have developed what is termed "cross-resistance" to a whole class of pesticides.[25] As more generations of the pathogen are exposed to the pesticide, the likelihood that resistant strains will emerge is correspondingly greater. Above and beyond the troubling consequences of pesticide use for the organic matter in the soil, groundwater quality, human health, and the ecosystem, pesticides have exacerbated some existing crop diseases while creating new ones.[26]

Just prior to the corn leaf blight in the South in 1970, 71 percent of all acreage in corn was planted to only six hybrids. The specialists investigating the blight stressed the pressures of mechanization and product uniformity that led to a radically narrower genetic crop base. "*Uniformity*," the report asserted, "is the key word."[27] Most of the hybrids had been developed by the male-sterile method using "Texas cytoplasm." It was this uniformity that was attacked by the fungus *Helminthosporium maydis;* those hybrids created without Texas cytoplasm suffered only trivial damage. The pathogen was not new; in its report, the National Research Council committee imagined that it was probably in existence when Squanto showed the Pilgrims how to plant corn. While *H. maydis* may have from time to time produced more virulent strains, "American corn was *too variable* to give the new strain a very good foothold."[28] What was new was the vulnerability of the host.

The report went on to document the fact that "most major crops are impressively uniform genetically and impressively vulnerable [to epidemics]."[29] Exotic germ plasm from a rare Mexican landrace proved to be the solution to breeding new hybrids that were less susceptible to the blight. In this and many other cases, it was only the genetic diversity created by a long history of landrace development by nonspecialists that provided a way out.[30] Like the formal order of the planned section of Brasília or collectivized agriculture, modern, simplified, and standardized agriculture depends for its existence on a "dark twin" of informal practices and experience on which it is, ultimately, parasitic.

The Catechism of High-Modernist Agriculture

The model and promise of American agricultural modernism was absolutely hegemonic in the three decades from 1945 to 1975. It was the prevailing "export model." Hundreds of irrigation and dam projects modeled roughly on the Tennessee Valley Authority (TVA) were begun; many large and highly capitalized agricultural schemes were inaugurated with great fanfare; and thousands of advisers were dispatched. There was a continuity in personnel as well as in ideas. Economists, engineers, agronomists, and planners who had served in the TVA, the U.S. Department of Agriculture, or the Department of the Treasury moved to the United Nations, the Food and Agriculture Organization, or USAID, bringing their experience and ideas with them. A combination of American political, economic, and military hegemony, the promise of loans and assistance, concerns about world population and food supply, and the great productivity of American agriculture made for a degree of self-confidence in the American model that is hard to overestimate.

A few skeptics like Rachel Carson were beginning to question the model, but they were greatly outnumbered by a chorus of visionaries who saw an unlimited and brilliant future ahead. Typical of the optimism was an article by James B. Billard entitled "More Food for Our Multiplying Millions: The Revolution in American Agriculture," which appeared in a 1970 issue of *National Geographic*.[31] Its vision of the farm of the future, reproduced here in figure 34, was not an idle fantasy; it was, we are told, drawn "with the guidance of U.S. Department of Agriculture specialists." Billard's text is one long paean to mechanization, scientific marvels, and huge scale. For all the technical wizardry, he envisions a process of simplification of the landscape and centralization of command. Fields will be larger, with fewer trees, hedges, and roads; plots may be "several miles long and a hundred yards wide"; "weather control" will prevent hailstorms and tornadoes; atomic energy will "level hills" and make irrigation water from seawater; satellites, sensors, and airplanes will spot plant epidemics while the farmer sits in his control tower.

At the operational level, the credo of American agriculture for export incorporated the same fundamental convictions. Both the exporters and the vast majority of their eager clients were committed to the following truths: the superior technical efficiency of large-scale farms, the importance of mechanization to save labor and break technical bottlenecks, the superiority of monocropping and hybrids over polycropping and landraces, and the advantages of high-input agriculture, including commercial fertilizers and pesticides. Above all, they believed in large, integrated, planned projects rather than piecemeal improvements, partly because the large, capital-intensive schemes could be planned as nearly pure technical exercises, rather like the design of the Soviet collective farm that was invented in a Chicago hotel room. The greater the industrial content of a scheme and the more its environment could be made uniform (through controlled irrigation and nutrients, the use of tractors and combines, the development of flat fields), the less was left to chance.[32] Local soils, local landscape, local labor, local implements, and local weather appeared to be almost irrelevant to the prepackaged projects. At the same time, schemes conceived along these lines emphasized the technical expertise of the planners, the possibility of central control, and, not least, a "module" that could be redeployed to almost any locale. For local elites anxious to have a modern show project over which they could preside, the advantages were also obvious.

The lamentable fate of the vast majority of these projects, whether private or public, is by now a matter of record.[33] They failed in most

34. Illustration of the farm of the future, painted by Davis Meltzer "with the guidance of U.S. Department of Agriculture specialists," from a 1970 issue of *National Geographic*. The caption details the farm of the early twenty-first century: "Grainfields stretch like fairways and cattle pens resemble high-rise apartments. . . . Attached to a modernistic farmhouse, a bubble-topped control tower hums with a computer, weather reports, and a farm-price ticker tape. A remote-controlled tiller-combine glides across the 10-mile-long wheat field on tracks that keep the heavy machine from compacting the soil. Threshed grain, funneled into a pneumatic tube beside the field, flows into storage elevators rising close to a distant city. The same machine that cuts the grain prepares the land for another crop. A similar device waters neighboring strips of soybeans as a jet-powered helicopter sprays insecticides.

"Across a service road, conical mills blend feed for beef cattle, fattening in multilevel pens that conserve ground space. Tubes carry the feed to be mechanically distributed. A central elevator transports the cattle up and down, while a tubular side drain flushes wastes to be broken down for fertilizer. Beside the farther pen, a processing plant packs beef into cylinders for shipment to market by helicopter and monorail. Illuminated plastic domes provide controlled environments for growing high-value crops such as strawberries, tomatoes, and celery. Near a distant lake and recreation area, a pumping station supplies water for the vast operation."

cases despite lavish credit subsidies and strong administrative backing. While each failure had its own peculiarities, the level of abstraction at which most projects were conceived was fatal. Imported faith and abstraction prevailed, as we shall see, over close attention to the local context.

Modernist Faith Versus Local Practices

We can explore the contrast between imported faith and local context by juxtaposing several tenets of the catechism of high-modernist agriculture with the local practices that appeared to violate them. And as we shall see, contrary to contemporary expectations, these practices turned out to be scientifically sound and in some cases superior to the program of farming being urged or imposed by the agricultural reformers.

Monoculture and Polyculture

Nothing better illustrates the myopic credo of high-modernist agriculture, originating in temperate zones and brought to the tropics, than its nearly unshakable faith in the superiority of monoculture over the practice of polyculture found in much of the Third World.

To take West African indigenous farming systems as an example, colonial agricultural specialists encountered what seemed to them to be an astonishingly diverse regime of polycropping, with as many as four crops (not to mention subspecies) in the same field simultaneously.[34] A fairly representative instance of what met their eyes is depicted in figure 35. The visual effect, to Western eyes, was one of sloppiness and disorder. Given their visual codification of modern agricultural practice, most specialists knew, without further empirical investigation, that the apparent disorder of the crops was a symptom of backward techniques; it failed the visual test of scientific agriculture. Campaigns to replace polyculture with pure-stand planting were pushed with equal fervor by colonial officials and, after independence, by their local successors.

We have gradually come to understand a quite specific logic of *place*—in particular, tropical soils, climate, and ecology—that helps to explain the functions of polyculture. The diversity of species naturally occurring in a tropical setting is, other things being equal, consistently greater than the diversity of species in a temperate setting. An acre of tropical forest will have far more species of plants, although fewer individuals of each species, than will an acre of temperate woodland. Thus unmanaged nature in temperate climates *looks* more or-

35. Construction of stick bunds across incipient gullies
in a Sierra Leone rice field

derly because it is less diverse, and this may play a role in the visual
culture of Westerners.[35] In favoring polyculture, the tropical cultivator
also imitates nature in his techniques of cultivation. Polyculture, like
the tropical forest itself, plays an important role in protecting thin soils
from the erosive effects of wind, rain, and sunlight. Furthermore, the
seasonality of tropical agriculture is governed more by the timing of
rains than by temperature. For this reason, a variety of polycropping
strategies allows farmers to hedge their bets about the rains, holding
the soil with drought-resistant crops and interspersing among them
crops that can take best advantage of the rains. Finally, the creation of
a uniform, controlled farming environment is intrinsically more difficult in a tropical setting than in a temperate one, and, where popula-

tion densities are low, the labor requirements of extensive terracing or irrigation are uneconomic in the strict neoclassical sense of the word.

Here one may recall Jane Jacobs's important distinction between visual orderliness on one hand and functional working order on the other. The city desk of a newspaper, a rabbit's intestines, or the interior of an aircraft engine may certainly look messy, but each one reflects, sometimes brilliantly, an order related to the function it performs. In such instances the apparent surface disarray obscures a more profound logic. Polyculture was a floral variant of such order. Only a very few colonial specialists managed to peer behind the visual confusion to its logic. One of them was Howard Jones, a mycologist in Nigeria, who wrote in 1936:

> [To the European] the whole scheme seems . . . laughable and ridiculous, and in the end he would probably conclude that it is merely foolish to crowd different plants together in this childish way so that they may choke one another. Yet if one looks at it more closely there seems a reason for everything. The plants are not growing at random, but have been planted at proper distances on hillocks of soil arranged in such a way that when rain falls it does not waterlog the plants, nor does it pour off the surface and wash away the fine soil. . . . The soil is always occupied and is neither dried up by the sun nor leached out by the rain, as it would be if it were left bare. . . . This is but one of many examples that might be given that should warn us to be very cautious and thorough before we pass judgement upon native agriculture. The whole method of farming and outlook of the farmer are so entirely new to us that we are strongly tempted to call it foolish from an instinctive conservatism.[36]

Elsewhere in the tropical world, a few astute observers were uncovering a different agricultural logic. A striking example of visual order versus working order was provided by Edgar Anderson, on the basis of his botanical work in rural Guatemala. He realized that what appeared to be overgrown, "riotous" dump heaps that no Westerner would have taken for gardens exhibited, on closer inspection, an exceptionally efficient and well-thought-out order. Anderson sketched one of these gardens (figures 36 and 37), and his description of the logic he discerned in it is worth quoting at length.

> Though at first sight there seems little order, as soon as we started mapping the garden, we realized that it was planted in fairly definite crosswise rows. There were fruit trees, native and European in great variety: annonas, cherimoyas, avocados, peaches, quinces, plums, a fig, and a few coffeebushes. There were giant cacti grown for their fruit. There was a large plant of rosemary, a plant of rue, some poinsettias, and a fine semiclimbing tea rose. There was a whole row of the native domesticated hawthorn, whose fruits like yellow, doll-size apples, make a de-

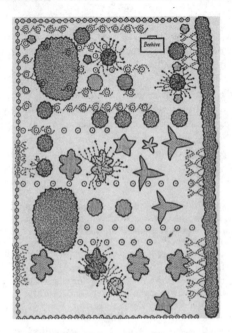

36. Edgar Anderson's drawing of an orchard
garden in Santa Lucia, Guatemala

licious conserve. There were two varieties of corn, one well past bearing and now serving as a trellis for climbing string beans which were
just coming into season, the other, a much taller sort, which was tas-
seling out. There were specimens of a little banana with smooth wide
leaves which are the local substitute for wrapping paper, and are also
used instead of cornhusks in cooking the native variant of hot tamales.
Over it all clambered the luxuriant vines of the various cucurbits. Chayote, when finally mature, has a large nutritious root weighing several
pounds. At one point there was a depression the size of a small bathtub
where a chayote root had recently been excavated; this served as a
dump heap and compost for the waste from the house. At one end of the
garden was a small beehive made from boxes and tin cans. In terms of
our American and European equivalents, the garden was a vegetable
garden, an orchard, a medicinal garden, a dump heap, a compost heap,
and a beeyard. There was no problem of erosion though it was at the top
of a steep slope; the soil surface was practically all covered and apparently would be during most of the year. Humidity would be kept during
the dry season and plants of the same sort were so isolated from one another by intervening vegetation that pests and diseases could not readily
spread from plant to plant. The fertility was being conserved; in addi-

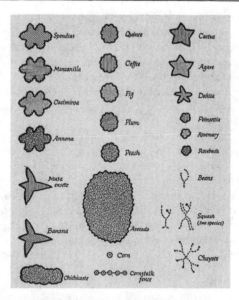

37. In his drawing of an orchard garden in
Santa Lucia, Anderson used glyphs that identify
not only the plants but also their general categories. Circular glyphs indicate fruit trees of
European origin (plum, peach); rounded, irregular glyphs indicate fruit trees of American origin (manzanilla). Dotted lines stand for climbing vegetables, small circles for subshrubs,
large stars for succulents, and wedge-shaped
figures for plants in the banana family. The narrow mass seen at the right side of figure 36 represents a hedge of chichicaste, a shrub used by
the Mayas.

tion to the waste from the house, mature plants were being buried in between the rows when their usefulness was over.

It is frequently said by Europeans and European Americans that
time means nothing to an Indian. This garden seemed to me to be a
good example of how the Indian, when we look more than superficially
into his activities, is budgeting his time more efficiently than we do.
The garden was in continuous production but was taking only a little
effort at any one time: a few weeds pulled when one came down to pick
the squashes, corn and bean plants dug in between the rows when the
last of the climbing beans were picked, and a new crop of something
else planted above them a few weeks later.[37]

Like the micrologic of the Guatemalan garden, the logic of West African polycropping systems, long dismissed as being primitive, has finally been recognized. In fact, they came under investigation partly as a reaction against the many monocropping schemes that miscarried. The advantages were often evident even at the level of narrow productivist outcomes; and once other goals such as sustainability, conservation, and food security were considered, their advantages seemed especially striking.

Various forms of polyculture are the norm in 80 percent of West Africa's farmland.[38] Given what we now know, this should occasion little surprise. Intercropping systems are best adapted to soils of low fertility, which characterize much of West Africa. Their use produces greater gains in yield on such soils than on soils of high fertility.[39] One reason seems to be that optimal planting densities are greater in intercropping than in monocropping, and the resulting crowding appears, for reasons that are poorly understood but may have to do with root fungi interactions, to improve the performance of each cultivar. Crowding at the later stage of cropping also helps to suppress weeds, which are otherwise a major constraint in tropical farming. Since the mixture of cultivars usually combines grains and legumes (maize and sorghum, for example, with cowpeas and groundnuts), each crop has complementary nutritional needs and rooting systems that extract nutrients from different levels in the soil.[40] In the case of relay cropping, it appears that the residues of the first crop gathered benefit the remaining crop. The diversity of cultivars on the same field also has a beneficial effect on the health of the crops and hence on yields. Mixed crops and the scattering of particular cultivars limit the habitat of various pests, diseases, and weeds that otherwise might build up to devastating proportions, as they do on monocropped plots.[41] In fact, two specialists who were very much out of step with the agronomic establishment of the 1930s and 1940s went so far as to suggest that "the systematic study of mixed cropping and other native practices might lead to comparatively minor modifications in Yoruba and other forms of agriculture, which might in the aggregate do more to increase crop production and soil fertility than revolutionary changes to green manuring or mixed farming."[42]

The multistoried effect of polyculture has some distinct advantages for yields and soil conservation. "Upper-story" crops shade "lower-story" crops, which are selected for their ability to thrive in the cooler soil temperature and increased humidity at ground level. Rainfall reaches the ground not directly but as a fine spray that is absorbed with less damage to soil structure and less erosion. The taller crops often serve as a useful windbreak for the lower crops. Finally, in mixed or relay cropping, a crop is in the field at all times, holding the soil together and reducing the leaching effects that sun, wind, and rain exert, particularly on fragile land. Even if polyculture is not to be preferred on the grounds of immediate yield, there is much to recommend it in terms of sustainability and thus long-term production.

Our discussion of mixed cropping has thus far dealt only with the narrow issues of yield and soil conservation. It has overlooked the cultivators themselves and the various other ends that they seek by using such techniques. The most significant advantage of intercropping, Paul Richards claims, is its great flexibility, "the scope [it] offers for a range of combinations to match individual needs and preferences, local conditions, and changing circumstances within each season and from season to season."[43] Farmers may polycrop in order to avoid labor bottlenecks at planting and at harvest.[44] Growing many different crops is also an obvious way to spread risks and improve food security. Cultivators can reduce the danger of going hungry if they sow, instead of only one or two cultivars, crops of long and short maturity, crops that are drought resistant and those that do well under wetter conditions, crops with different patterns of resistance to pests and diseases, crops that can be stored in the ground with little loss (such as cassava), and crops that mature in the "hungry time" before other crops are gathered.[45] Finally, and perhaps most important, each of these crops is embedded in a distinctive set of social relations. Different members of the household are likely to have different rights and responsibilities with respect to each crop. The planting regimen, in other words, is a reflection of social relations, ritual needs, and culinary tastes; it is not just a production strategy that a profit-maximizing entrepreneur took straight out of the pages of a text in neoclassical economics.

The high-modernist aesthetic and ideology of most colonial agronomists and their Western-trained successors foreclosed a dispassionate examination of local cultivation practices, which were regarded as deplorable customs for which modern, scientific farming was the corrective. A critique of such hegemonic ideas comes, if it comes at all, not from within, but typically from the margins, where the intellectual point of departure and operating assumptions, as was the case with Jacobs, are substantially different. Thus the case for the rationality of mixed cropping has largely come from rogue figures outside the establishment.

Perhaps the most striking of these figures was Albert Howard (later Sir Albert), an agricultural researcher who worked under local patronage for more than three decades in India. He was known chiefly for the Indore process, a scientific procedure of making humus from organic wastes, and unlike most Western agronomists, he was an avid observer of forest ecology and indigenous practices. Concerned above all with soil fertility and sustainable agriculture, Howard observed that the natural diversity of the forest and local polycropping practices were both successful means of maintaining or increasing soil health and fertility. Soil fertility was a matter of not simply chemical composition but also structural properties: the soil's tilth (or crumb structure), its degree of aeration, its moisture-holding power, and the "fungus bridge" (the mycorrhizal association) necessary to humus creation.[46] Some but not all elements in this complex soil interaction could be precisely measured, while others could be recognized by a practiced observer but not readily measured. Howard undertook elaborate experiments in humus production, soil structure, and plant response and was able to show field-trial yield results superior to those achieved by standard Western practices. His main concern, however, was not with how many bushels of wheat or maize could be gotten from an acre as with the health and quality of the crops and soil over the long haul.

The case for polyculture has worked its way back to the West, although it remains one voiced by only a tiny minority. Rachel Carson, in her revolutionary book *Silent Spring*, published in 1962, traced the destructive use of massive doses of pesticides and herbicides to mono-cropping itself. The problem with insects, she explained, resulted from the "devotion of immense acreage to a single crop. Such a system set the stage for explosive increases in specific insect populations. Single crop farming does not take advantage of the principles by which nature works, it is agriculture as an engineer might conceive it to be. Nature has introduced great variety into the landscape, but man has displayed passion for simplifying it. . . . One important check is a limit on the amount of suitable habitat for each species."[47] Just as Howard believed that monoculture had contributed to the loss of soil fertility and its corrective, the growing use of chemical fertilizers (260 pounds per acre in the United States in 1970), so Carson argued that monoculture spawned the exploding population of pests and its corrective, the massive application of insecticides—a cure that turned out to be worse than the disease.

For these and other reasons, there are at least faint indications that some forms of polycropping might be suitable for Western farmers as well as Africans.[48] This is not the place to attempt to demonstrate the superiority of polyculture over monoculture, nor am I qualified to do so. There is no single, context-free answer to this issue, for answers would depend on any number of variables, including the goals sought, the crops sown, and the microsettings in which they were planted.

What I have tried to demonstrate, however, is that polyculture, even on the narrow production-oriented grounds favored by Western agronomy, merited empirical examination as one among many agricultural strategies. That it was instead dismissed summarily by all but a handful of rogue agronomists is a tribute to the power both of imperialist ideology and of the visual aesthetic of agricultural high modernism.

The case of polyculture also raises an issue relevant to both agricultural practice and social structure, an issue that we will ponder at greater length in the remainder of this book: *the resilience and durability of diversity*. Whatever its other virtues or demerits, polyculture is a more stable, more easily sustainable form of agriculture than monocropping. It is more likely to produce what economists call Hicksian income: income that does not undermine factor endowments, which will permit that income flow to continue indefinitely into the future. Polyculture is, at the same time, more supple and adaptable. That is, it is more easily able to absorb stress and damage without being devastated. Elegant research has recently shown that, at least up to a point, the more cultivars that a given plot has, the more productive and resilient it is.[49] Polyculture, as we have seen, is more resistant to the insults of weather and pests, not to mention more generous in the improvements it effects in the soil. Even if monoculture could be shown to always give superior yields in the short run, polyculture might still be considered to have decisive long-term advantages.[50] The evidence from forestry has some application to agriculture as well: monocropped forests like those in Germany and Japan have led to ecological problems so severe that restoration ecology has been called to the rescue in order to reestablish something approaching the earlier diversity (in insects, flora, and fauna) necessary to the health of the forest.[51]

Here it is worth noting the strong parallel between the case for diversity in cultivation and forestry and the case that Jacobs made for diversity in urban neighborhoods. The more complex the neighborhood, she reasoned, the better it will resist short-term shocks in business conditions and market prices. Diversity, by the same token, provides many potential growth points which can benefit from new opportunities. A highly specialized neighborhood, by contrast, is like a gambler placing all his bets on one turn of the roulette wheel. If he wins, he wins big; if he loses, he may lose everything. For Jacobs, of course, a key point about the diversity of a neighborhood is the *human* ecology it fosters. The variety of locally available goods and services and the complex human networks that it makes possible, the foot traffic that promotes safety, the visual interest that an animated and convenient neighborhood provides—all interact to make such a location's advantages cumulative.[52] The diversity and complexity that cause systems of flora to become more durable and resilient work, at another level apparently, to cause human communities to become more nimble and satisfactory.

Permanent Fields Versus Shifting Cultivation

Most West African farmers practiced some form of shifting cultivation.[53] Variously called slash-and-burn cultivation, swiddening, and rotational bush fallow, shifting cultivation involves the temporary cultivation of a field cleared by cutting and burning most of the vegetation. After being worked for a few years, the field is abandoned for a new plot. Eventually, when new growth has restored the original field to something like its original fertility, it is cultivated again. Polycropping and minimum tillage were often combined with shifting cultivation.

Like polycropping, shifting cultivation, as we shall see, turns out to be a rational, efficient, and sustainable technique under the soil, climate, and social conditions where it is generally practiced. Polycropping and shifting cultivation are almost invariably associated. Harold Conklin's early, detailed, and still unsurpassed account of shifting cultivation in the Philippines noted that, for a newly cleared plot, the *average* number of cultivars in a single season was between forty and sixty.[54] At the same time, shifting cultivation is an exceptionally complex and hence quite illegible form of agriculture from the perspective of a sovereign state and its extension agents. The fields themselves are "fugitive," going in and out of cultivation at irregular intervals—hardly promising material for a cadastral map. The cultivators themselves, of course, are often fugitive as well, moving periodically to be near their new clearings. Registering or monitoring such populations, let alone turning them into easily assessable taxpayers, is a Sisyphean task.[55] The project of the state and the agricultural authorities, as we saw in the Tanzanian case, was to replace this illegible and potentially seditious space with permanent settlements and permanent (preferably monocropped) fields.

Shifting cultivation also gave offense to agricultural modernizers of whatever race, because it violated in almost every respect their understanding of what modern agriculture *had* to look like. "Early attitudes to shifting cultivation were almost entirely negative," Richards notes. "It was a bad system: exploitative, untidy, and misguided."[56] The finely adapted logic of shifting cultivation depended on disturbing the landscape and ecology as little as possible and mimicking, where it could, many of the symbiotic associations of local plants. This meant that such fields looked far more like unimproved nature than the neatly manicured, rectilinear fields that most agricultural officers were used to.

The ecological caution of shifting cultivation, in other words, was the reason behind the appearances that so offended development officials.

Rotational bush fallow had a good many other advantages that were rarely appreciated. It upheld the physical properties of upland and hill soils which, once destroyed, were difficult to restore. The rotation itself, where land was abundant, ensured the long-run stability of the practice. Shifting cultivators rarely removed large trees or stumps—a custom that limited erosion and helped the soil structure but that struck agricultural officials as sloppy and unsightly. With some exceptions, swidden plots were cultivated by hoe or dibble stick rather than plowed. To Westernized agronomists, it appeared that the farmers were merely "scratching the surface" of their soils out of a deplorable ignorance or sloth. Where they encountered farming systems involving deep plowing and monocropping, they believed they had encountered a more advanced and industrious population.[57] The burning of the brush accumulated in clearing a new swidden was also condemned as wasteful. After a time, however, both shallow cultivation and burning were found to be highly beneficial; the former preserved the soil, especially in areas of high rainfall, while the latter reduced pest populations and provided valuable nutrients to the crop. Experiments showed, in fact, that burning the brush *in* the field (rather than hauling it off) contributed to better yields, as did a carefully timed burn.[58]

To someone trained to a Western perspective, the total effect of such cultivation practices had "backwardness" written all over it—heaps of brush waiting to be burned on unplowed, half-cleared fields littered with stumps and planted with several interspersed crops, none of them sown in straight rows. And yet, as the hard evidence accumulated, it was clear that appearances were deceiving, even in productionist terms. As Richards concludes, "The proper test for any practice was whether it worked in the environment concerned, not whether it looked 'advanced' or 'backward.' Testing requires carefully controlled input-output trials. If 'shallow' cultivation on 'partially cleared' land gives better returns relative to the inputs expended than rival systems, and these results can be sustained over time, then the technique is a good one, irrespective of whether it was invented yesterday or a thousand years ago."[59] Lost in the early blanket condemnations of shifting cultivation was the realization that the practice was deployed in a highly discriminating way by African cultivators. Most farmers combined permanent bottomland cultivation of some kind with swidden cultivation of the more fragile hillsides, uplands, or forests. Rather than not knowing any better, as was often assumed, most shifting cultivators were familiar with a range of cropping techniques among which they selected with care.

Fertilizer Versus Fertility

> The best fertilizer on any farm is the footsteps of the owner.
> —Confucius

Commercial fertilizers have often been touted as magical inoculations for improving poor soils and raising yields; extension agents have routinely referred to fertilizers and pesticides as medicine for the soil. The actual results have often been disappointing. Two major reasons for the disappointment are directly relevant to our larger argument.

First, recommendations for fertilizer applications are inevitably gross simplifications. Their applicability to any *particular* field is questionable, since a map of soil classes is likely to overlook an enormous degree of microvariation between and within fields. The conditions under which fertilizers are applied, the "dosage," the soil structure, the crops for which they are intended, and the weather immediately prior and subsequent to their application can all greatly influence their uptake and effect. As Richards observes, the unavoidable variation by farm and field "requires a more open-ended approach, with, in all probability, farmers doing much of the necessary experimentation for themselves."[60]

Second, fertilizer formulas suffer from an analytical narrowness. The formulas themselves derive from the work of a remarkable German scientist, Justus Freiherr von Liebig, who, in a classic manuscript published in 1840, identified the main chemical nutrients present in the soil and to whom we still owe the current standard fertilizer recipe (N, P, K). It was a brilliant scientific advance, with far-reaching and usually beneficial results. Where it tended to get into trouble, however, was when it posed as "imperial" knowledge—when it was touted as the way in which all soil deficiencies could be remedied.[61] As Howard and others have painstakingly shown, there are a range of intervening variables—including the physical structure of the soil, aeration, tilth, humus, and the fungus bridge—that greatly influence plant nutrition and soil fertility.[62] Chemical fertilizers can in fact so thoroughly oxidize beneficial organic matter as to destroy its crumb structure and contribute to a progressive alkalization and a loss of fertility.[63]

The details are less important than the larger point: an effective soil science must not stop at chemical nutrients; it must encompass elements of physics, bacteriology, entomology, and geology, and that is at a minimum. Ideally, then, a practical approach to fertilizers requires, simultaneously, a general, interdisciplinary knowledge, which a single specialist is unlikely to have, *and* attention to the particularity of a given field, which only the farmer is likely to have. A procedure that blends a purely chemical nutrient perspective with soil classification grids and that leaves the particular field far behind is a recipe for ineffectiveness or even disaster.

A History of "Unauthorized" Innovation

For most colonial officials and their successors, high-modernist commitments led them to form inaccurate assumptions about indigenous agriculture and blinded them to its dynamism. Far from being timeless, static, and rigid, indigenous agricultural practices were constantly being revised and adapted. Some of this plasticity was part of a broad repertoire of techniques that could be adjusted, for example, to different patterns of rainfall, soils, pitches of land, market opportunities, and labor supplies. Most African cultivators were typically utilizing more than one cultivation technique during a season and knew many more that might come in handy. When entirely novel cultivars from the New World became available, they were adopted with alacrity where appropriate. Thus maize, cassava, potatoes, chiles, and a variety of New World pulses and gourds were incorporated into many African planting regimens.[64]

The history of "on-farm" experimentation, selection, and adaptation was, of course, a very old story indeed, both in Africa and elsewhere. Ethnobotany and paleobotany have been able to trace in some historical detail how hybrids and variants of, for example, the main Old World grains or New World maize were selected and propagated for a host of different uses and growing conditions. The same observation holds true for those plants that are vegetatively propagated—that is, propagated by cuttings rather than by seeds.[65]

On a strictly dispassionate view, more specialists would have concluded that there were many grounds for considering every African farm as something of a small-scale experimental station. It stands to reason that any community of cultivators who must wrest their living from a stingy and variable environment will rarely overlook the opportunity to improve their security and food supply. The limits to local knowledge must also be emphasized. Indigenous cultivators knew their own environment and its possibilities remarkably well. But they of course lacked the knowledge that such tools of modern science as the microscope, aerial photography, and scientific plant breeding could provide. They often lacked, as did many cultivators elsewhere, the technology or the access to technology that make, say, large-scale irrigation schemes and highly mechanized agriculture possible. Like peasants in the Mediterranean Basin, China, and India, they were capable of damaging their ecosystem, even if low population densities had thus far spared them from making this mistake.[66] But if most agricultural specialists had appreciated how much the indigenous farmer *did* know, had appreciated her practical, experimental temper and willingness to adopt new crops and techniques when they met local needs, such specialists would have concluded, with Robert Chambers, that "indigenous agricultural knowledge, despite being ignored or overridden by consultant experts, is the single largest knowledge resource not yet mobilized in the development enterprise."[67]

The Institutional Affinities of High-Modernist Agriculture

The willful disdain for local competence shown by most agricultural specialists was not, I believe, simply a case of prejudice (of the educated, urban, and Westernized elite toward the peasantry) or of the aesthetic commitments implicit in high modernism. Rather, official attitudes were also a matter of institutional privilege. To the degree that the cultivators' practices were presumed reasonable until proven otherwise, to the degree that specialists might learn as much from the farmer as vice versa, and to the degree that specialists had to negotiate with farmers as political equals, would the basic premise behind the officials' institutional status and power be undermined. The unspoken logic behind most of the state projects of agricultural modernization was one of consolidating the power of central institutions and diminishing the autonomy of cultivators and their communities vis-à-vis those institutions. Every new material practice altered in some way the existing distribution of power, wealth, and status; and the agricultural specialists' claims to be neutral technicians with no institutional stake in the outcome can hardly be accepted at face value.[68]

The centralizing effects of Soviet collectivization and ujamaa villages were perfectly obvious. So are those of large irrigation projects, where authorities decide when to release the water, how to distribute it, and what water fees to charge, or of agricultural plantations, where the workforce is supervised as if it were in a factory setting.[69] For colonialized farmers, the effect of such centralization and expertise was a radical de-skilling of the cultivators themselves. Even in the context of family farms and a liberal economy, this was in fact the utopian prospect held up by Liberty Hyde Bailey, a plant breeder, apostle of agricultural science, and the chairman of the Country Life Commission under Theodore Roosevelt. Bailey declared, "There will be established in the open country plant doctors, plant breeders, soil experts, health experts, pruning and spraying experts, forest experts, recreation experts, market experts, . . . [and] housekeeping experts, . . . [all of whom are] needed for the purpose of giving special advice and direction."[70] Bailey's future was one organized almost entirely by a managerial elite: "Yet we are not to think of society as founded wholly on small separate tracts, of 'family farms,' occupied by persons who live merely in contentment; this would mean that all landsmen would be essentially laborers. We need to hold on the land many persons who possess large powers of organization, who are managers, who can handle affairs in a bold way: it would be fatal to the best social and spiritual results if such persons could find no adequate opportunities on the land and were forced into other occupations."[71]

In spite of these hopeful pronouncements and intentions, if one examines carefully many of the agricultural innovations of the twentieth century—innovations that seemed purely technical and hence neutral —one cannot but conclude that many of them created commercial and political monopolies that inevitably diminished the autonomy of the farmer. The revolution in hybrid seeds, particularly corn, had this effect.[72] Since hybrids are either sterile or do not breed "true," the seed company that has bred the parents of the hybrid-cross has valuable property in hybrid seed, which it can sell every year, unlike the open-pollinated varieties which the farmer can select himself.[73]

A similar but not identical centralizing logic applied to the high-yielding varieties (HYVs) of wheat, rice, and maize developed over the past thirty years. Their enormous impact on yields (an impact that varied widely by crop and growing conditions) depended on combining a massive response to nitrogen application with short, tough stalks that prevented lodging. Realizing their potential yield required abundant water (usually via irrigation), large applications of commercial fertilizer, and the periodic application of pesticides. Mechanization of field preparation and harvesting was also promoted. As with hybrids, the lack of biological diversity in the fields meant that each generation of HYVs was likely to succumb to infestations of fungus, rust, or insects, necessitating the purchase of new seeds *and* new pesticides (as the insects built up resistance). The resulting biological arms race, which plant breeders and chemists believe that they can continue to win, is one that puts the cultivator increasingly in the hands of public and private specialists. As with the truly democratic aspects of Nyerere's policies, those elements of research and policy that might threaten the position of a managerial elite tended either not to be explored at all or, if explored, to be "selected against" in policy implementation.

The Simplifying Assumptions of Agricultural Science

> This attempt at total control is an invitation to disorder. And the rule seems to
> be that the more rigid and exclusive is the specialist's boundary, and the
> stricter the control within it, the more disorder rages around it. One can take
> a greenhouse and grow summer vegetables in the wintertime, but in doing so
> one creates a vulnerability to the weather and to the possibility of failure
> where none existed before. The control by which a tomato plant lives through
> January is much more problematic than the natural order by which an oak
> tree or a titmouse lives through January.
> —Wendell Berry, *The Unsettling of America*

Most of the elements of state development programs have not been
merely the whims of powerful elites. Even villagization in Tanzania had
long been the subject of apparently sound agroeconomic analysis.
Schemes for the introduction of such new crops as cotton, tobacco,
groundnuts, and rice as well as plans for mechanization, irrigation,
and fertilizer regimens had been preceded by lengthy technical studies
and field trials. Why, then, have such a large number of these schemes
failed to deliver anything like the results foreseen for them? A closely
related question, which we will address in the next chapter, is why so
many successful changes in agricultural practices and production have
been pioneered, not by the state, but by the autonomous initiative of
cultivators themselves.

The Isolation of Experimental Variables

The record shows, it seems to me, that a substantial part of the problem lies in the systematic and necessary limitations of scientific work
whenever the ultimate purpose of that work is practical adoption by a
diverse set of practitioners working in a large variety of conditions.
That is, some of the problems lie deeper than the institutional temptations to central control, the pathologies of administration, or the penchant for aesthetically satisfying but uneconomic show projects. Even
under the best of circumstances, the laboratory results and the data
from the experimental plots of research stations are a long country
mile from the human and natural environments where they must ultimately find a home.

The normal procedure in scientific agricultural research has historically been to focus almost exclusively on crop-by-crop experiments
designed to test the impact of variations in inputs on yields. More recently, other variables have come under scrutiny. Thus experiments
might test yields under different soil and moisture conditions or determine which hybrids resisted lodging or ripened in a way that facili-

tated machine harvesting. Ecologically conscious research has often proceeded in the same fashion: by isolating one by one the variables that might contribute, say, to biological resistance of a certain variety of fruit to a particular pest.

The isolation of a very few variables—ideally just two, while controlling all others—is a key tenet of experimental science.[74] As a procedure, it is both valuable and necessary to scientific work. Only by radically simplifying the experimental situation is it possible to guarantee unambiguous, verifiable, impersonal, and universal results.[75] As a pioneer in chaos theory has put it: "There is a fundamental presumption in physics that the way you understand the world is that you keep isolating its ingredients until you understand the stuff you think is truly fundamental. Then you presume that the other things you don't understand are details. The assumption is that there are a small number of principles that you can discern by looking at things in their pure state—this is the truly analytic notion—and somehow you put these together in some more complicated ways when you want to solve more *dirty* problems. *If you can.*"[76] In agricultural research, controlling for all possible variables except those under experimental scrutiny required normalizing assumptions about such things as weather, soils, and landscapes, not to mention normalizing assumptions, often implicit, about farm size, labor availability, and the desires of cultivators. "Test-tube research," of course, most closely approximated the ideal of controls.[77] Even the experimental plot on a research station, however, was itself a radical simplification. It maximized the degree of control "within a small and highly simplified enclosure" and ignored the rest, leaving it "totally out of control."[78]

It is easy to see how monoculture and attention to quantitative yields would fit most comfortably within this paradigm. Monoculture eliminates all other cultivars that might complicate the design, while concern with quantitative yields avoids the thorny measurement problems that would arise if a particular quality or taste were the objective. The science of forestry is easiest when one is interested only in the commercial wood from a single species of tree. The science of agriculture is easiest when it is a question of the most efficient way of getting as many bushels as possible of one hybrid of maize from a "normalized" acre.

A progressive loss of experimental control occurs when one moves from the laboratory to the research plot on an experimental station and then to field trials on actual farms. Richards notes the unease such a move aroused among researchers in West Africa, who were anxious about making their research more practical yet concerned about any relaxing of experimental conditions. After discussing how the farms selected for trials ought to be relatively homogeneous so that they would respond in uniform ways to the experimental results, the researchers went on to lament the experimental control that they they lost by leaving the research station. "It may be difficult," they wrote, "to plant at all locations within a few days and almost impossible to find farm plots of uniform soil." They continued, "Other types of *interference*, such as pest attacks or bad weather, may affect some treatments and not others."[79] This is, Richards explains, a "salutary reminder of one of the reasons why 'formal' scientific research procedures on experimental stations, with the stress on controlling all variables except the one or two under direct investigation, 'miss the point' as far as many small-holders are concerned. The main concern of farmers is how to cope with these complex interactions and unscheduled events. From the scientist's point of view (particularly in relation to the need to secure clear-cut results for publication), on-farm experimentation poses a tough challenge."[80]

To the extent that science is obliged to deal simultaneously with the complex interactions of many variables, it begins to lose the very characteristics that distinguish it as modern science. Nor does the accumulation of many narrow experimental studies add up to the same thing as a single study of such complexity. This is not, I must repeat, a case against the experimental techniques of modern scientific research. Any extensive, on-farm research study that did not reduce the complexity of interactions might be able to show, as farmers can, that a set of practices produced "good results": say, high yields. But it would not be able to isolate the key factors responsible for this result. The case that I am making instead recognizes the power and utility of scientific work, within its domain, *and* recognizes its limitations in dealing with the kinds of problems for which its techniques are ill suited.

Blind Spots

Returning once again to the case of polyculture, we can see why agronomists might have scientific as well as aesthetic and institutional grounds for opposing polycropping. Complex forms of intercropping introduce *too many variables* into simultaneous play to offer much chance of unambiguous experimental proof of causal relations. We know that certain polycultural techniques, particularly those combining nitrogen-fixing legumes with grains, are quite productive, but we know little about the precise interactions that bring about these results.[81] And we find problems in teasing out causation even when we confine our attention to the single dependent variable of quantitative yields.[82] If we relax this restriction of focus and begin to consider a wider range of dependent variables (outcomes), such as soil fertility, interactions with livestock (fodder, manuring), compatibility with family labor supply, and so on, the difficulties of comparison rapidly become intractable to scientific method.

The nature of the scientific problem here is strongly analogous to that of complexity in physical systems. The elegantly simple formulas of Newton's laws of mechanics make it relatively easy to calculate the orbits of two heavenly bodies once we know their respective masses and the distance between them. Add one more body, however, and the calculation of orbits resulting from the interaction becomes far more complex. When there are ten bodies interacting (this is the *simplified* version of our solar system),[83] no orbits ever exactly repeat themselves, and there is no way to predict the long-term state of the system. As each new variable is introduced, the number of ramifying interactions to be taken into account grows geometrically.

It does not stretch the facts too far, I think, to claim that scientific agricultural research has an elective affinity with agricultural techniques that lie within reach of its powerful methods. Maximizing the yields of pure-stand crops is one technique where its power can be used to best advantage. Insofar as its institutional power has permitted, agricultural agencies, like scientific foresters, have tended to simplify their environments in ways that make them more amenable to their system of knowledge. The forms of agriculture that conformed to their modernist aesthetic and their politico-administrative interests also happened to fit securely within the perimeter of their professional scientific vocation.[84]

What of the "disorder" outside the realm of the experimental design? Extra-experimental interactions can in fact prove beneficial when they strengthen the desired effect.[85] There is no a priori reason for anticipating what their effects might be; what is significant is that they lie wholly outside the experimental model.

Occasionally, however, these effects have been both important and potentially threatening. A striking example from the years between 1947 and 1960 was the massive, worldwide use of pesticides, the most infamous of which was DDT. DDT was sprayed to kill mosquito populations and thereby reduce the many diseases that the pests carry. The experimental model was largely confined to determining the dosage concentrations and application conditions required for eradicating mosquito populations. Within its field of vision, the model was successful; DDT did kill mosquitos and dramatically reduced the incidence of endemic malaria and other diseases.[86] It also had, as we slowly became aware, devastating ecological effects, as residues were absorbed by organisms all along the food chain, of which humans are of course also a part. The consequences of the use of DDT and other pesticides on soil, water, fish, insects, birds, and fauna were so intricate that we have not yet gotten to the bottom of them.

Weak Peripheral Vision

Part of the problem was that the side effects were constantly ramifying. A first-order effect—say, the decline or disappearance of a local insect population—led to changes in flowering plants, which changed the habitat for other plants and for rodents, and so on. Another part of the problem was that the effects of pesticides on other species were examined only under experimental conditions. Yet the application of DDT was under *field* conditions, and as Carson pointed out, scientists had no idea what the interactive effects of pesticides were when they were mixed with water and soil and acted upon by sunlight.

That awareness of these interaction effects came from *outside* the scientific paradigm itself is both interesting and, I think, diagnostic. It began, in particular, when people gradually came to realize that the songbird population had suffered a radical decline. Public alarm at what was *not* happening anymore outside their kitchen windows led, eventually (through scientific research), to a tracing of how DDT concentrations in the organs of birds led to fragile eggshells and reproductive failure. This finding in turn stimulated a host of related inquiries into the effects of pesticides and ultimately to legislation banning the use of DDT. In this case, as in others, the power of the scientific paradigm was achieved partly by its exclusion of extra-experimental variables that have often circled back, as it were, to take their revenge.

The logic of agroeconomic analysis of farming efficiency and profits also wins its power by a comparable restriction of the field of focus. Its tools are used to best advantage in examining the microeconomics of the farm as a firm. On the basis of its necessary simplifying assumptions about factor costs, inputs, weather, labor use, and prices, it can show how profitable or unprofitable it might be to use a particular piece of machinery, to buy irrigation equipment, or to raise one crop rather than another. Studies of this kind and also of marketing have tended to demonstrate the economies of scale achievable by large, highly capitalized, and highly mechanized operations. Outside this narrow perspective are hundreds of considerations that are necessarily bracketed, in a manner similar to that used in experimental science. But here, in agroeconomic analysis, the human agents adopting this view have the political capacity, in the short run at least, to make certain that they are not held economically responsible for the larger "extra-firm" consequences of their logic. The pattern in agriculture in the United States was clearly outlined by a rogue economist testifying to Congress in 1972.

> Only in the past decade has serious attention been given to the fact that the large agricultural firm is . . . able to achieve benefits by externalizing certain costs. The disadvantages of large scale operation fall largely outside the decision-making framework of the large farm firm. Problems of waste disposal, pollution control, added burdens on public service, deterioration of rural social structures, impairment of the tax base, and the political consequences of a concentration of economic power have typically not been considered as costs of large scale, by the firm. They are unquestionably costs to the larger community.
>
> In theory, large scale operation should enable the firm to bring a wide range of both costs and benefits within its internal decision-making framework. In practice the economic and political power that accompanies large scale provides constant temptation to the large firm to take the benefits and pass on the costs.[87]

In other words, although the business analysts of the agricultural firms have weak peripheral vision, the political clout that such firms possess both individually and collectively can help them avoid being blindsided.

Shortsightedness

Nearly all studies purporting to evaluate decisions of interest to farmers are experiments that last one or at most a few seasons. Implicitly, the logic behind a research design of this kind is that the long-run effects will not contradict the short-run findings. The question of the time horizon of research is directly relevant even to those for whom the maximization of yields is the holy grail. Unless they are exclusively interested in immediate yields, no matter what the consequences, their attention must be directed to the issue of sustainability or to Hicksian income. Perhaps the most significant practical division is thus not between those who would design agricultural policy with cultural and social goals in mind (such as the preservation of the family farm, the landscape, or diversity) and those who want to maximize production and profit, but rather between productionists with a short view and productionists with a long view. After all, concern about soil erosion and water supply was motivated less often by regard for the environment than by regard for the sustainability of current production.

The relatively short-run orientation of crop studies and farm economics works to exclude even those long-run results of interest to the productionists. Many of the claims for polyculture, for example, assert its superiority over the long haul as a system of production. A poly-cropping trial of twenty or more years, as Stephen Marglin has suggested, might well reach conclusions that are quite different from those derived from a trial that lasts a season or two.[88] It is not at all implausible that the process of open pollination and selection by farmers, as opposed to hybridization, might have developed cultivars roughly equal in yield to the best hybrids and superior to them in many other respects, including profitability.[89] The paper profits of scientific, mono-cropped forests, we now realize, were achieved at considerable cost to the long-term health and productivity of the forest. One would have supposed that since most farms are family enterprises, there would have been more studies of cropping and firm economics that took as their analytical unit of time the entire family cycle of one generation.[90]

Nothing in the logic of the scientific method itself seems to require that a short-run perspective prevail; rather, such a perspective seems to be a response to institutional and perhaps commercial pressures. On the other hand, the need to isolate a few variables while assuming everything else constant and the bracketing of interaction effects that lie outside the experimental model are very definitely inscribed in scientific method. They are a condition of the formidable clarity it achieves within its field of vision. Taken together, the parts of the landscape occluded by actual scientific practice—the blind spots, the periphery, and the long view—also constitute a formidable portion of the real world.

The Simplifying Practice of Scientific Agriculture

Some Yields Are More Equal Than Others

Modern agricultural research commonly proceeds as if yields, per unit of scarce inputs, were the central concern of the farmer. The assumption is enormously convenient; like the commercial wood of scientific forestry, the generic, homologous, uniform commodities thus derived create the possibility both of quantitative comparisons between the yield of different cultivation techniques and of aggregate statistics. The familiar tabulations of acres planted, yields per acre, and total production from year to year are usually the decisive measure of success in a development program.

But the premise that all rice, all corn, and all millet are "equal," however useful, is simply not a plausible assumption about any crop unless it is *purely* a commodity for sale in the market.[91] Each subspecies of grain has distinctive properties, not just in how it grows but in its qualities as a grain once harvested. In some cultures, certain varieties of rice are grown for use in certain distinctive dishes; other varieties of rice may be used only for specific ritual purposes or in the settlement of local debts. Some of the complex considerations that go into distinguishing one rice from another in terms of their cooking properties alone can be appreciated from Richards's observations about how the considerations are weighed in Sierra Leone.

> A phrase like "it cooks badly" is often a catch-all for a range of properties connected with storage, preparation and consumption, going well beyond subjective questions of "taste." Is the variety concerned well-adapted to local food processing techniques? Is it readily peeled, milled, and pounded? How much water and fuel does it require in cooking? How long does it keep, prior to cooking and once cooked? Mende women claim that improved swamp rices are much less palatable than the harder "upland" rices when served up a second time. With the right kind of rice, it is possible to cut down the number of times it is necessary to cook during busy periods on the farm. Since cooking sometimes takes up to 3–4 hours per day (including the time taken to husk rice, prepare a fire and collect water) this is a factor of no small importance when labour is short.[92]

So far, we have considered only the husked grain. What if we broaden our view to take in the rest of the plant? At once we see that there is a great deal more to be harvested from a plant than its seed grains. Thus a Central American peasant may not be interested only in the number and size of the corn kernels she harvested. She may also be interested in using the cobs for fodder and scrub brushes; the husk and leaves for wrappers, thatch, and fodder; and the stalks as trellises for climbing beans, as fodder, and as temporary fencing. The fact that Central American farmers know of many more maize varieties than do their counterparts in the Corn Belt of the United States is partly related to the uses to which different varieties are put. Maize may also be sold in the market for any of these purposes and thus prized for qualities other than its kernels. The same story could, of course, be told about virtually any widely grown cultivar. Its various parts from various stages of growth may come in handy as twine, vegetable dyes, medicinal poultices, greens to eat raw or to cook, packaging material, bedding, or items for ritual or decorative purposes.

Even from a commercial point of view, then, the plant is not simply its grain. Nor are all grains of all subspecies and hybrids of maize and rice equal. The yield of seeds by weight or volume may therefore be only one of many ends—and perhaps not the most important one—for a cultivator. But once scientific agriculture or plant breeding begins to introduce this enormous range of value and uses into its own calculations, it is once again in the Newtonian dilemma of the ten heavenly bodies. And even if it were able to represent some of this complexity in its models, these usages are subject to change without notice.

Experimental Plots Versus Actual Fields

All environments, as we noted earlier, are intractably local. There is always what we might call the translation problem in converting the generic, standardized High Church Latin which emanates from labs and experimental stations into the vernacular of the local parish. Standardized solutions to field preparation, planting schedules, and fertilizer requirements always have to be adjusted when they are applied to, say, a stony, low-lying, north-facing field which has just grown two crops of oats. Agricultural scientists at research stations and extension agents are very much aware of this translation problem, as are specialists in any applied science. The question is always how to discover and convey findings so that they will be helpful to farmers. As long as the findings or solutions are not simply imposed, the farmer must decide if they meet his needs.

Like cadastral maps, the experimental plots of agricultural research stations cannot begin to represent the diversity and variability of farmers' fields. The researchers must operate on the basis of standard, normal-range assumptions about soil, field preparation, weeding, rainfall, temperature, and so on, whereas each farmer's field is a unique concatenation of circumstances, actions, and events, some of which are knowable in advance (soil composition) and some of which are out of anyone's hands (the weather). The *interactions* among these and other variables are at least as important as the status of each; thus the effects of an early monsoon on rocky soil that has just been weeded are different from those of an early monsoon on waterlogged land that has not been weeded.

The averages and normalizations of experimental work obscure the fact that an average weather year or a standard soil is a statistical fiction. As Wendell Berry puts it:

> The industrial version of agriculture has it that farming brings the farmer annually, over and over again, to the same series of problems, to each one of which there is always the same generalized solution, and therefore, that industry's solution can be simply and safely substituted for his solution. But that is false. On a good farm, because of weather and other so-called variables, neither the annual series of problems nor any of the problems individually is ever quite the same two years running. The good farmer (like the artist, the quarterback, the statesman)

must be master of many possible solutions, one of which he must choose under pressure and apply with skill in the right place at the right time.[93]

Soil, although it is not as capriciously variable day by day as the weather, is often exceptionally variable within the same field. The essential simplifications of agricultural science require, first, that soil be sorted into a small number of categories based on acidity, nitrogen levels, and other qualities. For analyzing the soil of a single field, the practice is to gather bits of soil from several parts of the field and to combine them in the sample to be analyzed so that it will represent an average. This procedure implicitly recognizes the substantial variation in soil quality over a given field. The recommended fertilizer application may therefore not be right for *any* part of the field, but compared to applications derived from other formulas, it will be "less wrong," on average, for the field as a whole. Once again, Berry cautions us against these generalizations: "Most farms, even most fields, are made up of different kinds of soil patterns and soil sense. Good farmers have always known this and have used the land accordingly; they have been careful students of the natural vegetation, soil depth, and structure, slope and drainage. They are not appliers of generalizations, theoretical or methodological or mechanical."[94] When, to the complexity and variation of the soil conditions, we add the practice of polyculture, the obstacles to a successful application of a general formula become virtually insurmountable. The knowledge we do have of the limits on some plants' tolerance of temperature and moisture does not ensure that they will necessarily thrive within these limits. The typical plant is "awfully finicky about just where and when it will grow, under exactly what conditions it will germinate," as Edgar Anderson explains. "The vastly more intricate business of which plants they will and will not tolerate as neighbors and under what conditions, has never been looked into except in a preliminary way for a few species."[95]

Indigenous farmers are exceptionally alert to microfeatures of terrain and environment that are important to cultivation. Two examples from Richards's analysis of West Africa will serve to illustrate the small details that are simply too minute to be visible within a standardizing grid. Among the bewildering variety of small-scale, local irrigation practices, Richards classifies at least eleven different kinds, some with subvariations. All depend directly on locally specific details of topography, soil, flooding, rainfall, and so on, with the type of irrigation used depending on whether the area is a seasonally flooded delta, saucer-shaped depression with poor drainage, or an inland valley swamp. These small "schemes," which take advantage of the existing possibilities of the landscape, are a far cry from vast engineered schemes in which no effort is spared to modify the landscape in conformity with the engineering plan.

Richards's second example shows how West African farmers used a rather simple but ingenious choice in what strain of rice to plant to help them cope with a local pest. Mende farmers on one area of Sierra Leone had, against the textbook advice on the varieties of rice to be preferred, selected a variant of rice with long awns (beard or bristles) and glumes (bracts). The textbook reasoning was probably that such varieties were lower yielding or that the awns and glumes would simply add more chaff that would have to be winnowed after threshing. The farmers' reasoning was that the long awns and glumes discouraged birds from eating the bulk of their rice before it ever made it to the threshing floor. These details about microirrigation and the damage caused by birds are vital for local cultivators, but such details do not and cannot appear on the high-flying mapping of modern agricultural planning.

Many critics of scientific agriculture have claimed not only that it has systematically favored large-scale, production-oriented monoculture but that its research findings are of at best limited use, since all agriculture is local. Howard argued for a fundamentally different practice, basing it on two premises. The first was that experimental plots could not yield helpful results.

> Small plots and farms are very different things. It is impossible to manage a small plot as a self-contained unit in the same way as a good farm is conducted. The essential relation between livestock and the land is lost; there are no means of maintaining the fertility of the soil by suitable rotations as is the rule in good farming. The plot and the farm are obviously out of relation; the plot does not even represent the field in which it occurs. A collection of field plots cannot represent the agricultural problem they set out to investigate. . . . What possible advantage therefore can be obtained by the application of higher mathematics to a technique which is so fundamentally unsound?[96]

Howard's second premise is that many of the most important indications of a farm and a crop's health are *qualitative:* "Can a mutually interacting system like the crop and the soil, for example, dependent on a multitude of factors which are changing from week-to-week and year-to-year, ever be made to yield quantitative results corresponding to the precision of mathematics?"[97] As Howard sees it, the danger is that the narrow, experimental, and exclusively quantitative approach will succeed in completely driving out the other forms of local knowledge and judgment possessed by most cultivators.

But Howard and others, it seems to me, miss the most important abstraction of experimental work in scientific agriculture. How can we define how useful this research is until we know the ends to which cultivators will put it? Useful for what? It is at the level of human agency where scientific agriculture constructs its greatest abstraction: the creation of a stock character, the Everyman cultivator, who is interested only in realizing the greatest yields at the least cost.

Fictional Farmers Versus Real Farmers

Not only are the weather, the crops, and the soil complex and variable; the farmer is, too. Season by season and frequently day by day, millions of cultivators are pursuing an innumerable variety of complicated goals. These goals and the shifting mix between them defy any simple model or description.

Profitable production of one or more major crops, the usual standard of agricultural research, is obviously one purpose shared by most cultivators. It is instructive, nevertheless, to observe how deeply mediated this goal is by other purposes that may indeed usurp it altogether. The complexities I suggest below merely scratch the surface.

Each farm family has its unique endowment of land, skills, tools, and labor, which greatly constrain how it farms. Consider only one aspect of labor supply: a "labor-rich" farm with many able-bodied young workers has options in growing labor-intensive crops, in planting schedules, and in developing artisan sidelines that are not easily available to "labor-poor" farms. Furthermore, the same family farm will go through several stages in the course of a family cycle of development.[98] Farmers who migrate out for wage work during part of the year may plant crops of early or late maturity or crops requiring little care in order to accommodate their migratory schedule.

As we saw earlier, a particular crop's profit may be tied to more than just its yield in grain and the cost of producing it. The stubble of a crop may be crucial as fodder for livestock or waterfowl. A crop may be vital because of what it does to the soil in rotation with other crops or how it assists another crop with which it is interplanted. A crop may be less important for its grain that for what it supplies, in raw material, for artisanal production, whether that material is sold in the market or used at home. Families who live close to the subsistence line may choose their crops, not on the basis of their profitability, but on the basis of how steady their yields are and whether they can be eaten if their market price plunges.

The complexities thus far introduced could, at least in principle, be accommodated within a drastically modified, neoclassical notion of economic maximization, even though it would be too elaborate to model easily. Once we add such considerations as aesthetics, rituals, taste, and social and political considerations, this is no longer the case. There are any number of perfectly rational but noneconomic reasons for wanting to grow a certain crop in a certain way, whether because one wishes to maintain cooperative relations with neighbors or because a particular crop is linked to group identity. Such cultural habits are perfectly compatible with commercial success, as the experience of the Amish, Mennonites, and Hutterites demonstrates. As long as we are pointing to the high level of abstraction of "the farm family" for whom scientific agricultural research does its work, we should note that, in much of the world, an understanding of the practices in use on almost any farm will require distinguishing the purposes of the various members of the family. Each family enterprise is, on closer inspection, a partnership—albeit typically unequal—with its own internal politics.

The units of "farmer" and "farm community" are, finally, every bit as intricate and fluid as the weather, soil, and landscape. Mapping them is even more problematic than, say, analyzing the soil. The reason, I think, is that while the farmer's expertise may occasionally fail him in assessing his own soil, we will not doubt the farmer's expertise in knowing his own mind and interests.[99]

Just as the buzzing complexity and plasticity of customary land tenure practices cannot be satisfactorily represented in the straitjacket of modern freehold property law, so the complex motives and goals of cultivators and the land they farm cannot be effectively portrayed by the standardizations of scientific agriculture. The schematic representations so important for experimental work can and have produced important new knowledge, which, suitably adapted, has been incorporated into most agricultural routines. But such abstractions, again like those of freehold tenure, are powerful misrepresentations that usually circle back to influence reality. They operate, at a minimum, to generate research and findings most applicable to farms that meet the description of their schematization: large, monocropped, mechanized, commercial farms producing solely for the market. In addition, this standardization is typically linked to public policy in the form of tax incentives, loans, price supports, marketing subsidies, and, significantly, handicaps imposed on enterprises that do not fit the schematization, which systematically operate to nudge reality toward the grid of its observations. The effect is nothing like the shock therapy of the campaigns for Soviet collectivization or ujamaa villages, which relied more on sticks than carrots. But over the long haul such a powerful grid can, and does, change the landscape.

Two Agricultural Logics Compared

If the logic of actual farming is one of an inventive, practiced response to a highly variable environment, the logic of scientific agriculture is, by contrast, one of adapting the environment as much as possible to its centralizing and standardizing formulas. Thanks to the pioneering work of Jan Douwe van der Ploeg, it is possible to spell out how this logic works for potato cultivation in the Andes.[100]

Van der Ploeg calls indigenous potato cultivation in the Andes a "craft."[101] The cultivator begins with an exceptionally diverse local ecology and aims at both successfully adapting to it and gradually improving it. Andean farmers' skills have allowed them to achieve results that are quite respectable in terms of narrow productionist goals and extraordinarily so in terms of reliability of yields and sustainability.

The typical farmer cultivates anywhere from twelve to fifteen distinct parcels as well as other plots on a rotating basis.[102] Given the great variety of conditions on each plot (altitude, soil, history of cultivation, slope, orientation to wind and sun), each field is unique. The very idea of a "standard field" in this context is an empty abstraction. "Some fields contain only one cultivar, others between two and ten, sometimes interplanted in the same row or with each in its own row."[103] Each cultivar is a well-placed bet in its niche. The variety of cultivars makes for local experimentation with new crosses and hybrids, each of which is tested and exchanged among farmers, and the many landraces of potatoes thus developed have unique characteristics that become well known. From the appearance of a new variety to its substantial use in the fields takes at least five or six years. Each season is the occasion for a new round of prudent bets, with last season's results in terms of yield, disease, prices, and response to changed plot conditions having been carefully weighed. These farms are market-oriented experiment stations with good yields, great adaptability, and reliability. Perhaps more important, they are not just producing crops; they are reproducing farmers and communities with plant breeding skills, flexible strategies, ecological knowledge, and considerable self-confidence and autonomy.

Compare this "craft-based" potato production with the inherent logic of scientific agriculture. The process begins with the definition of an ideal plant type. "Ideal" is defined mainly, but not only, in terms of yields. Professional plant breeders then begin synthesizing the strains that might combine to form a new genotype with the desired characteristics. Then, and only then, are the plant strains grown in experimental plots in order to determine the conditions under which the potential of the new genotype will be realized. The basic procedure is exactly the reverse of Andean craft production, where the cultivator *begins* with the plot, its soil, and its ecology and then selects or develops varieties that will likely thrive in this setting. The variety of cultivars in such a community is in large part a reflection of the variety of both local needs and ecological conditions. In scientific potato growing, by contrast, the point of departure is the new cultivar or genotype, in service of which every effort is made to transform and homogenize field conditions so that the field meets the genotype's specific requirements.

The logic of beginning with an ideal genotype and then transforming nature to accord with its growing conditions has some predictable consequences. Extension work essentially becomes the attempt to remake the farmer's field to suit the genotype. This usually requires the application of nitrogen fertilizer and pesticides, which must be purchased and applied at the right moment. It usually also requires a watering regimen that in many cases only irrigation can possibly satisfy.[104] The timing of all operations for this genotype (planting, cultivating, fertilizer spreading, and so forth) are spelled out carefully. The logic of the process—a logic not even remotely realized on the ground—is to transform the farmers into "standard" farmers growing the required genotype on similar soils and leveled fields and according to the instructions printed right on the seed packages, applying the same fertilizers, pesticides, and amounts of water. It is a logic of homogenization and the virtual elimination of local knowledge. To the degree that this homogenization is successful, the genotype will likely succeed in terms of production levels in the short run. Conversely, to the degree that such homogenization is impossible, the genotype will fail.

Once the job of the agricultural specialist is defined as one of raising all farmers' plots to the uniform condition that will realize the new cultivar's promise, there is no further need to attend to the great variety of conditions—some of which are unalterable—on actual farmers' fields. Rather than have the facts on the ground muddy a simple, unitary research issue, it was more convenient to try to impose a research abstraction on the fields (and lives) of farmers. Given the intractable ecological variety of the Andes, this was a nearly fatal step.[105] Rarely have agricultural specialists asked themselves, as did the Russian S. P. Fridolin well before the revolution, whether they might not be working from the wrong angle: "He realized that his work was actually harming the peasants. Instead of learning what local conditions were and *then* making agricultural practice fit these conditions better, he had been trying to 'improve' local practice so that it would conform to abstract standards."[106] It is little wonder that scientific agriculture tends to favor the creation of large artificial practices and environments—irrigation schemes, large and leveled fields, the application of fertilizer by formula, greenhouses, pesticides—all of which allow a homogenization and control of nature within which "ideal" experimental conditions for its genotypes can be maintained.

There is, I think, a larger lesson here. An explicit set of rules will take you further when the situation is cut-and-dried. The more static and one-dimensional the stereotype, the less the need for creative interpretation and adaptation. In the Andes, van der Ploeg implies, the "rules" attached to the new potato were so restrictive that they could never be successfully translated to the great variety of local farming vernaculars. One of the major purposes of state simplifications, collectivization, assembly lines, plantations, and planned communities alike is to strip down reality to the bare bones so that the rules will in fact explain more of the situation and provide a better guide to behavior. To the extent that this simplification can be imposed, those who make the rules *can* actually supply crucial guidance and instruction. This, at any rate, is what I take to be the inner logic of social, economic, and productive de-skilling. If the environment can be simplified down to the point where the rules do explain a great deal, those who formulate the rules and techniques have also greatly expanded their power. They have, correspondingly, diminished the power of those who do not. To the degree that they do succeed, cultivators with a high degree of autonomy, skills, experience, self-confidence, and adaptability are replaced by cultivators following instructions. Such reduction in diversity, movement, and life, to recall Jacobs's term, represents a kind of social "taxidermy."

The new potato genotype, as van der Ploeg shows, usually fails, if not immediately, within three or four years. Unlike the ensemble of indigenous varieties, the new cultivar thrives within a narrower band of environmental conditions. *Many* things, in other words, must go right for the new cultivar to produce well, and if *any* of these things goes wrong (too much hot weather, late delivery of fertilizer, and so forth), the yields suffer dramatically. Within a few years the new genotypes "become incapable of generating even low levels of production."[107]

In practice, however, the vast majority of Andean cultivators are neither purely traditional cultivators nor mindless followers of the scientific specialists. They are, instead, crafting unique amalgams of strategies that reflect their aims, their resources, and their local conditions. Where the new potatoes seem to fit their purposes, they may plant some, but they may interplant them with other cultivars and may substitute dung, or plow in green manure (alfalfa, clover), rather than apply the standard fertilizer package. They are constantly inventing and experimenting with different rotations, timing, and weeding techniques. But because of the very particularity of these thousands of "infield experiments" and the specialists' studied inattention to them, they are illegible, if not invisible, to scientific research. Farmers, being polytheists when it comes to agricultural practice, are quick to seize whatever seems useful from the epistemic work of formal science. But the researchers, trained as monotheists, seem all but incapable of absorbing the informal experimental results of practice.

Conclusion

The great confidence that high-modernist agriculture has inspired among its practitioners and partisans should not surprise us. It *is* associated with unparalleled agricultural productivity in the West and with the power and prestige of the scientific and industrial revolutions. Little wonder, then, that the tenets of high modernism, as talismans of the true faith, should have been carried throughout the world uncritically and indeed with the conviction that they lighted the way to agricultural progress.[108] I believe that this uncritical, and hence unscientific, trust in the artifacts and techniques of what became codified as scientific agriculture was responsible for its failures. The logical companion to a complete faith in a quasi-industrial model of high-modernist agriculture was an often explicit contempt for the practices of actual cultivators and what might be learned from them. Whereas a scientific spirit would have counseled skepticism *and* dispassionate inquiry into these practices, modern agriculture as a blind faith preached scorn and summary dismissal.

Actual cultivators in West Africa and elsewhere should more accurately have been understood as lifelong experimenters conducting infield seasonal trials, the results of which they incorporated into their ever-evolving repertoire of practices. Inasmuch as these experimenters were and are surrounded by hundreds or thousands of other local experimenters with whom they share research findings and the knowledge of generations of earlier research as codified in folk wisdom, they could be said to have instant access to the popular equivalent of an impressive research library. Now it is also undeniably the case that they carry out most of their research without the proper experimental controls and are therefore prone to drawing false inferences from their findings. They are also limited by what they can observe; microprocesses only visible in the laboratory necessarily escape them. Nor is it clear that the ecological logic that seems to work well on a single farm over the long haul will at the same time produce sustainable aggregate results for an entire region.

That said, it is also the case, however, that West African cultivators have at their disposal a lifetime of careful, local observation and the fine-grained knowledge of the locality that no research scientist can hope to duplicate for the same terrain. And let us not fail to note what kind of experimenters these are. Their lives and the lives of their families depend directly on the outcomes of their field experiments. Given these important positional advantages, one would have imagined that agricultural scientists would have paid attention to what these farmers did know. It was their failure to do so, Howard claims, that constitutes the great shortcoming of modern scientific agriculture: "The approach to the problems of farming must be made from the field, not from the laboratory. The discovery of the things that matter is three quarters of the battle. In this the observant farmer and labourer, who have spent their lives in close contact with nature, can be of greatest help to the investigator. The views of the peasantry in all countries are worthy of respect; there is always good reason for their practices; in matters like the cultivation of mixed crops they themselves are still the pioneers."[109] Howard credits most of his own findings about soil, humus, and root action to a careful observation of indigenous farming practice. And he is rather disdainful of agricultural specialists who "do not have to take their own advice"—that is, who have never had to see their own crop through from planting to harvest.[110]

Why, then, the *unscientific* scorn for practical knowledge? There are at least three reasons for it, as far as I can tell. The first is the "professional" reason mentioned earlier: the more the cultivator knows, the less the importance of the specialist and his institutions. The second is the simple reflex of high modernism: namely, a contempt for history and past knowledge. As the scientist is always associated with the modern and the indigenous cultivator with the past that modernism will banish, the scientist feels that he or she has little to learn from that quarter. The third reason is that practical knowledge is represented and codified in a form uncongenial to scientific agriculture. From a narrow scientific view, *nothing* is known until and unless it is proven in a tightly controlled experiment. Knowledge that arrives in any form other than through the techniques and instruments of formal scientific procedure does not deserve to be taken seriously. The imperial pretense of scientific modernism admits knowledge only if it arrives through the aperture that the experimental method has constructed for its admission. Traditional practices, codified as they are in practice and in folk sayings, are seen presumptively as not meriting attention, let alone verification.

And yet, as we have seen, cultivators have devised and perfected a host of techniques that do work, producing desirable results in crop production, pest control, soil preservation, and so forth. By constantly observing the results of their field experiments and retaining those methods that succeed, the farmers have discovered and refined practices that work, without knowing the precise chemical or physical reasons why they work. In agriculture, as in many other fields, "practice has long preceded theory."[111] And indeed some of these practically successful techniques, which involve a large number of simultaneously interacting variables, may never be fully understood by the techniques of science. We turn, then, to a closer examination of practical knowledge, a kind of knowledge that high modernism has ignored to its peril.

Part 4

The Missing Link

9 Thin Simplifications and Practical Knowledge: Mētis

> No battle—Tarutino, Borodino, or Austerlitz—takes place as those who planned it anticipated. That is an essential condition.
> —Tolstoy, *War and Peace*

We have repeatedly observed the natural and social failures of thin, formulaic simplifications imposed through the agency of state power. The utilitarian commercial and fiscal logic that led to geometric, monocropped, same-age forests also led to severe ecological damage. Where the formula had been applied with the greatest rigor, it eventually became necessary to attempt to restore much of the forest's original diversity and complexity—or rather, to create a "virtual" forest that would mimic the robustness and durability of the "prescientific" forest.

The planned "scientific city," laid out according to a small number of rational principles, was experienced as a social failure by most of its inhabitants. Paradoxically, the failure of the designed city was often averted, as was the case in Brasília, by practical improvisations and illegal acts that were entirely outside the plan. Just as the stripped-down logic behind the scientific forest was an inadequate recipe for a healthy, "successful" forest, so were the thin urban-planning schemata of Le Corbusier an inadequate recipe for a satisfactory human community.

Any large social process or event will inevitably be far more complex than the schemata we can devise, prospectively or retrospectively, to map it. Lenin had every reason, as a would-be head of the vanguard party, to emphasize military discipline and hierarchy in the revolutionary project. After the October Revolution, the Bolshevik state authorities had every reason, once again, to exaggerate the central, all-seeing role of the party in bringing the revolution about. And yet we know—and Lenin and Luxemburg knew—that the revolution had been a close call, relying more on the improvisations, missteps, and strokes of luck that Tolstoy described in *War and Peace* than on the precision of a parade-ground drill.

The thin simplifications of agricultural collectivization and centrally planned production have met a comparable fate, whether on the collective farms of the former Soviet Union or in the ujamaa villages of Nyerere's Tanzania. Here again, the schemes that did not collapse altogether managed to survive thanks largely to desperate measures either not envisaged or else expressly prohibited by the plan. Thus an informal economy developed in Russian agriculture, operating on tiny private plots and and the "theft" of time, equipment, and commodities from the state sector and supplying most of the dairy products, fruit, vegetables, and meat in the Russian diet.[1] Thus the forcibly resettled Tanzanians successfully resisted collective production and drifted back to sites more suitable for grazing and cultivation. At times, the price of an unyielding imposition of state simplifications on agrarian life and production—Stalin's forced collectivization or China's Great Leap Forward—was famine. As often as not, however, state officials recoiled before the abyss and came to tolerate, if not condone, a host of informal practices that in fact underwrote the survival of the official scheme.

These rather extreme instances of massive, state-imposed social engineering illustrate, I think, a larger point about formally organized social action. In each case, the necessarily thin, schematic model of social organization and production animating the planning was inadequate as a set of instructions for creating a successful social order. By themselves, the simplified rules can never generate a functioning community, city, or economy. Formal order, to be more explicit, is always and to some considerable degree parasitic on informal processes, which the formal scheme does not recognize, without which it could not exist, and which it alone cannot create or maintain.

This homely insight has long been of great tactical value to generations of trade unionists who have used it as the basis of the work-to-rule strike. In a work-to rule action (the French call it *grève du zèle*), employees begin doing their jobs by meticulously observing every one of the rules and regulations and performing only the duties stated in their job descriptions. The result, fully intended in this case, is that the work grinds to a halt, or at least to a snail's pace. The workers achieve the practical effect of a walkout while remaining on the job and following their instructions to the letter. Their action also illustrates pointedly how actual work processes depend more heavily on informal understandings and improvisations than upon formal work rules. In the long work-to-rule action against Caterpillar, the large equipment manufacturer, for example, workers reverted to following the inefficient procedures specified by the engineers, knowing they would cost the company valuable time and quality, rather than continuing the more expeditious practices they had long ago devised on the job.[2] They were relying on the tested assumption that working strictly by the book is necessarily less productive than working with initiative.

This perspective on social order is less an analytical insight than a sociological truism. It does offer, however, a valuable point of departure for understanding why authoritarian, high-modernist schemes are potentially so destructive. What they ignore—and often suppress—are precisely the practical skills that underwrite any complex activity. My aim in this chapter is to conceptualize these practical skills, variously called know-how (*savoir faire* or *arts de faire*),[3] common sense, experience, a knack, or *mētis*. What are these skills? How are they created, developed, and maintained? What is their relation to formal epistemic knowledge? I hope to show that many forms of high modernism have replaced a valuable collaboration between these two dialects of knowledge with an "imperial" scientific view, which dismisses practical know-how as insignificant at best and as dangerous superstitions at worst. The relation between scientific knowledge and practical knowledge is, as we shall see, part of a political struggle for institutional hegemony by experts and their institutions. Taylorism and scientific agriculture are, on this reading, not just strategies of production, but also strategies of control and appropriation.

Mētis: The Contours of Practical Knowledge

Following the illuminating studies of Marcel Detienne and Jean-Pierre Vernant, we can find in the Greek concept of mētis a means of comparing the forms of knowledge embedded in local experience with the more general, abstract knowledge deployed by the state and its technical agencies.[4] Before elaborating the concept and its use, we will turn to a brief example in order to illustrate the vernacular character of local knowledge and ground the discussion that follows.

When the first European settlers in North America were wondering when and how to plant New World cultivars, such as maize, they turned to the local knowledge of their Native American neighbors for help. They were told by Squanto, according to one legend (Chief Massasoit, according to another), to plant corn when the oak leaves were the size of a squirrel's ear.[5] Embedded in this advice, however folkloric its ring today, is a finely observed knowledge of the succession of natural events in the New England spring. For Native Americans it was this *orderly* succession of, say, the skunk cabbage appearing, the willows beginning to leaf, the red-wing blackbird returning, and the first hatch of the mayfly that provided a readily observable calendar of spring. While the timing of these events might be earlier or later in a given year and while the pace of their succession might be more drawn out or accelerated, the *sequence* of the events was almost never violated. As a rule of thumb, it was a nearly foolproof formula for avoiding a frost. We almost certainly distort Squanto's advice, as the colonists perhaps did, by reducing it to a single observation. Everything we know about indigenous technical knowledge suggests that it relies on an accumulation of many partly redundant signals. If other indications did not confirm the oak-leaf formula, a prudent planter might delay further.

Compare this advice to that based on more universalistic units of measurement. A typical local edition of *The Farmer's Almanac* is a case in point. It may suggest planting corn after the first full moon in May or after a specified date, such as May 20. In New England, at any rate, this advice would require considerable adjustment by latitude and altitude. A date that would serve for southern Connecticut would not suit Vermont; a date that worked in the valleys would not be right for the hills (especially the north-facing slopes); a date that worked near the coast would not work inland. And the almanac's date is almost certainly a fail-safe date, since the worst thing that could happen to an almanac publisher would be to have his or her advice lead to a crop failure. As a result of this commercial caution, some valuable growing time may have been lost in the interest of certainty.[6]

The Native American maxim, by contrast, is vernacular and local, keyed to common features of the local ecosystem; it inquires about oak leaves *in this place*, and not oak leaves in general. Despite its specificity, it travels remarkably well. It can be deployed successfully anywhere in temperate North America where there are oak trees and squirrels. The precision provided by the observed sequence almost certainly gains a few days of growing time while not appreciably raising the risk of planting before a hard frost.

Practical knowledge like Squanto's can, of course, be translated into more universalistic scientific terms. A botanist might observe that the first growth of oak leaves is made possible by rising ground and ambient temperatures, which also assure that maize will grow and that the probability of a killing frost is negligible. The mean soil temperature at a given depth might do just as well. Along these lines, the early nineteenth-century mathematician, Adolph Quetelet, turned his scientific eye to the mundane problem of when the lilacs would bloom in Brussels. He concluded, after much rigorous observation, that the lilacs burst into bloom "when the sum of the squares of the mean daily temperature since the last frost added up to (4264C) squared."[7] Knowledge this certainly is! Given the techniques for making the required observations, it is probably quite accurate. But it is hardly practical. Quetelet's playful formula alerts us to a hallmark of most practical, local knowledge: it is as economical and accurate as it needs to be, no more and no less, for addressing the problem at hand.

One hesitates before introducing yet another unfamiliar term, such as "mētis," into this discussion. In this case, however, "mētis" seems to better convey the sorts of practical skills that I have in mind than do such plausible alternatives as "indigenous technical knowledge," "folk wisdom," "practical skills," techne, and so on.[8]

The concept comes to us from the ancient Greeks. Odysseus was frequently praised for having mētis in abundance and for using it to outwit his enemies and make his way home. Mētis is typically translated into English as "cunning" or "cunning intelligence." While not wrong, this translation fails to do justice to the range of knowledge and skills represented by mētis. Broadly understood, mētis represents a wide array of practical skills and acquired intelligence in responding to a constantly changing natural and human environment. Odysseus's mētis was in evidence, not only in his deceiving of Circe, the Cyclops, and Polyphemus and in binding himself to the mast to avoid the Sirens, but also in holding his men together, in repairing his ship, and in improvising tactics to get his men out of one tight spot after another. The emphasis is both on Odysseus's ability to adapt successfully to a constantly shifting situation *and* on his capacity to understand, and hence outwit, his human and divine adversaries.

All human activities require a considerable degree of mētis, but some activities require far more. To begin with skills that require adapting to a capricious physical environment, the acquired knowledge of how to sail, fly a kite, fish, shear sheep, drive a car, or ride a bicycle relies on the capacity for mētis. Each of these skills requires hand-eye coordination that comes with practice and a capacity to "read" the waves, the wind, or the road and to make the appropriate adjustments. One powerful indication that they all require mētis is that they are exceptionally difficult to teach apart from engaging in the activity itself. One might imagine trying to write down explicit instructions on how to ride a bicycle, but one can scarcely imagine that such instructions would enable a novice to ride a bicycle on the first try. The maxim "Practice makes perfect" was devised for such activities as this, inasmuch as the continual, nearly imperceptible adjustments necessary for riding a bicycle are best learned by having to make them. Only through an acquired "feel" for balanced motion do the required adjustments become automatic.[9] No wonder that most crafts and trades requiring a touch or feel for implements and materials have traditionally been taught by long apprenticeships to master craftsmen.

There is no doubt that some individuals seem to get the hang of a particular skill and master it more quickly than most other people. But beyond this ineffable difference (which often spells the difference between competence and genius), riding a bike, sailing, fishing, shearing sheep, and so on can be learned through practice. Since every road, wind, stream, and sheep is different and continually changing, the best practitioner, like Odysseus, will have had experience under many different conditions. If your life depended on your ship coming through rough weather, you would surely prefer a successful captain with long experience to, say, a brilliant physicist who had analyzed the natural laws of sailing but who had never actually sailed a vessel.

Those specialists who deal with emergencies and disasters are also exemplary of mētis. Firefighters, rescue squads, paramedics, mine-disaster teams, doctors in hospital emergency rooms, crews that repair downed electrical lines, teams that extinguish fires in oil fields, and, as we shall see, farmers and pastoralists in precarious environments must respond quickly and decisively to limit damage and save lives. Although there are rules of thumb that can be and are taught, each fire or accident is unique, and half the battle is knowing which rules of thumb to apply in which order and when to throw the book away and improvise.

Red Adair's team, which has been hired worldwide to cap well-head fires, was a striking and diagnostic case. Before the Gulf War of 1990, his was the only team with any appreciable "clinical" experience, and he could set his own price. Each fire presented new problems and required an inspired mixture of experience and improvisation. We can imagine, at almost opposite ends of a spectrum, Adair on one hand and a minor clerk performing highly repetitive steps on the other. Adair's job cannot, by definition, be reduced to a routine. He must *begin* with the unpredictable—an accident, a fire—and then devise the techniques and equipment (from an existing repertoire, to be sure, but one invented largely by him) required to extinguish that fire and cap that well.[10] The clerk, by contrast, deals with a predictable, routinized environment that can often be ordered in advance and down to the smallest detail. Adair cannot simplify his environment in order to apply a cookie-cutter solution.

The examples thus far introduced have been mostly concerned with the relation between people and their physical environment. But mētis equally applies to human interaction. Think of the complex physical activities that require constant adjustment to the movement, values, desires, or gestures of others. Boxing, wrestling, and fencing require instant, quasi-automatic responses to an opponent's moves, which can be learned only through long practice of the activity itself. Here the element of deception enters as well. The successful boxer will learn to feint a move in order to provoke a response of which he can then take advantage. If we move from physical contests to such cooperative activities as dancing, music, or lovemaking, a similar practiced responsiveness born of experience is essential. Many sports combine both the cooperative and the competitive aspects of mētis. A soccer player must learn not only the moves of his or her teammates but also which *team* moves and fakes will deceive their opponents. Such skills, it is important to note, are both generic and particular; while each player may be more or less skilled at different facets of the game, each team has its particular combination of skills, its "chemistry," and each contest with an opposing team represents a challenge that is in some ways unique.[11]

On a much bigger, higher-stakes canvas, war diplomacy and politics more generally are mētis-laden skills. The successful practitioner, in each case, tries to shape the behavior of partners and opponents to his own ends. Unlike the sailor, who can adjust to the wind and the waves but not influence them directly, the general and the politician are in constant interaction with their counterparts, each of whom is trying to outfox the other. Adapting quickly and well to unpredictable events—both natural events, such as the weather, and human events, such as the enemy's move—and making the best out of limited resources are the kinds of skills that are hard to teach as cut-and-dried disciplines.

The necessarily implicit, experiential nature of mētis seems central. A simple experiment in implicit learning conducted by the philosopher Charles Peirce may help to convey something of the process. Peirce had people lift two weights and judge which of the two was heavier. At first, their discrimination was rather crude. But as they practiced for long periods, they became able to distinguish accurately quite minute differences in weight. They could not pinpoint what it was that they sensed or felt, but their actual capacity to discriminate grew enormously. Peirce took the results as evidence for a kind of subliminal communication via "faint sensations" between people. For our purposes, however, it illustrates a rudimentary kind of knowledge that can be acquired only by practice and that all but defies being communicated in written or oral form apart from actual practice.[12]

Surveying the range of examples that we have touched on, we can venture some preliminary generalizations about the nature of mētis and about where it is relevant. Mētis is most applicable to broadly similar but never precisely identical situations requiring a quick and practiced adaptation that becomes almost second nature to the practitioner. The skills of mētis may well involve rules of thumb, but such rules are largely acquired through practice (often in formal apprenticeship) and a developed feel or knack for strategy. Mētis resists simplification into deductive principles which can successfully be transmitted through book learning, because the environments in which it is exercised are so complex and nonrepeatable that formal procedures of rational decision making are impossible to apply. In a sense, mētis lies in that large space between the realm of genius, to which no formula can apply, and the realm of codified knowledge, which can be learned by rote.

The Art of the Locality

Why are the rules of thumb that can be derived from any skilled craft still woefully inadequate to its practice? Artists or cooks, Michael Oakeshott has noted, may in fact write about their art and try to boil it down to technical knowledge, but what they write represents not much of what they know but rather only that small part of their knowledge that can be reduced to exposition. Knowing a craft's shorthand rules is a very long way from its accomplished performance: "These rules and principles are mere abridgements of the activity itself; they do not exist in advance of the activity, they cannot properly be said to govern it and they cannot provide the impetus of the activity. A complete mastery of the principles may exist alongside a complete inability to pursue the activity to which they refer, for the pursuit of the activity does not consist in the application of these principles; and even if it did, the knowledge of how to apply them (the knowledge of actually pursuing the activity) is not given in a knowledge of them."[13]

Knowing how and when to apply the rules of thumb *in a concrete situation* is the essence of mētis. The subtleties of application are important precisely because mētis is most valuable in settings that are mutable, indeterminant (some facts are unknown), and particular.[14] Although we shall return to the question of indeterminacy and change, here I want to explore further the localness and particularity of mētis.

In seamanship, the difference between the more general knowledge of navigation and the more particular knowledge of piloting is instructive. When a large freighter or passenger liner approaches a major port, the captain typically turns the control of his vessel over to a local pilot, who brings it into the harbor and to its berth. The same procedure is followed when the ship leaves its berth until it is safely out into the sea-lanes. This sensible procedure, designed to avoid accidents, reflects the fact that navigation on the open sea (a more "abstract" space) is the more general skill, while piloting a ship through traffic in a particular port is a highly contextual skill. We might call the art of piloting a "local and situated knowledge." What the pilot knows are local tides and currents along the coast and estuaries, the unique features of local wind and wave patterns, shifting sandbars, unmarked reefs, seasonal changes in microcurrents, local traffic conditions, the daily vagaries of wind patterns off headlands and along straits, how to pilot in these waters at night, not to mention how to bring many different ships safely to berth under variable conditions.[15] Such knowledge is particular, by definition; it can be acquired only by local practice and experience. Like a bird or an insect that has adapted brilliantly to a narrow ecological niche, the pilot knows *one* harbor. Much of his knowledge would be irrelevant if he were suddenly transposed to a different port.[16] Despite the rather narrow context of this knowledge, it is agreed by captains, harbormasters, and, not least, those who insure maritime commerce against losses that the pilot's knowledge of a particular port must prevail. The pilot's experience is *locally superior* to the general rules of navigation.

Mark Twain's classic *Life on the Mississippi* reflects at great length on the knowledge acquired by riverboat pilots. Part of that knowledge consists of rules of thumb about surface features that may signal shallows, currents, or other navigational hazards. Much of it, however, consists of a quite specific familiarity with their particular stretch of the Mississippi at different seasons and water levels—knowledge that could have been gained in that particular place only through experience. Although there is something that might properly be called a knowledge of rivers in general, it is a quite thin and unsatisfactory knowledge when it comes to making a particular trip on a particular river. A native pilot is no less necessary on a given river than a native tracker for a given jungle or a local guide in Bruges or in the medina of an ancient Arab city.

The practice and experience reflected in mētis is almost always *local*. Thus a guide on mountain climbing may be best at Zermatt, which she has scaled often; an airplane pilot best on Boeing 747s, on which he was trained; and the orthopedic surgeon best at knees, where her surgical experience has given her a certain expertise. It is not entirely clear how much of these experts' mētis would be transferable if they were suddenly shifted to Mont Blanc, DC3s, and hands.

Every instance of the application of a given skill will require specific adjustments for local conditions. For a weaver, each new supply of yarn or thread handles differently. For a potter, a new supply of clay "works" differently. Long experience with different materials will have the effect of making such adjustments quasi-automatic. The specificity of knowledge goes even deeper, in the sense that each loom or potter's wheel has its own distinctive qualities, which an artisan comes to know and appreciate (or work around). Every general knowledge that is actually applied, then, requires some imaginative translation. A consummate knowledge of looms in general does not translate directly into the successful operation of this particular loom with its peculiarities of design, use, woods, and repairs. To speak of the art of one loom, the art of one river, the art of one tractor, or the art of one automobile is not preposterous; it is to point to the size and importance of the gap between general knowledge and situated knowledge.

We might reasonably think of situated, local knowledge as being *partisan* knowledge as opposed to generic knowledge. That is, the holder of such knowledge typically has a passionate interest in a particular outcome. An insurer of commercial shipping for a large, highly capitalized maritime firm can afford to rely on probability distributions for accidents. But for a sailor or captain hoping for a safe voyage, it is the outcome of the single event, a single trip, that matters. Mētis is the ability and experience necessary to influence the outcome—to improve the odds—in a particular instance.

The state simplifications and utopian schemes we have examined in earlier chapters all concern activities that are carried out in spatially and temporally unique settings. While something can indeed be said about forestry, revolution, urban planning, agriculture, and rural settlement in general, this will take us only so far in understanding *this* forest, *this* revolution, *this* farm. All farming takes place in a unique space (fields, soil, crops) and at a unique time (weather pattern, season, cycle in pest populations) and for unique ends (this family with its needs and tastes). A mechanical application of generic rules that ignores these particularities is an invitation to practical failure, social disillusionment, or most likely both. The generic formula does not and cannot supply the local knowledge that will allow a successful translation of the necessarily crude general understandings to successful, nuanced, local applications. The more general the rules, the more they require in the way of translation if they are to be locally successful. Nor is it simply a matter of the captain or navigator realizing at what point his rules of thumb are inferior to the intimate local knowledge of the pilot. Rather, it is a matter of recognizing that the rules of thumb themselves are largely a codification derived from the actual practices of sailing and piloting.

One last analogy may help to clarify the relationship between general rules of thumb and mētis. Mētis is not merely the specification of local values (such as the local mean temperature and rainfall) made in order to successfully apply a generic formula to a local case. Taking language as a parallel, I believe that the rule of thumb is akin to formal grammar, whereas mētis is more like actual speech. Mētis is no more derivative of general rules than speech is derivative of grammar. Speech develops from the cradle by imitation, use, trial and error. Learning a mother tongue is a stochastic process—a process of successive, self-correcting approximations. We do not begin by learning the alphabet, individual words, parts of speech, and rules of grammar and then trying to use them all in order to produce a grammatically correct sentence. Moreover, as Oakeshott indicates, a knowledge of the rules of speech by themselves is compatible with a complete inability to speak intelligible sentences. The assertion that the rules of grammar are derivative of the practice of actual speech is nearer to the truth. Modern language training that aims at competence in speaking recognizes this and begins with simple speech and rote repetition in order to imprint pattern and accent while leaving the rules of grammar implicit, or else introducing them later as a way of codifying and summarizing practical mastery.

Like language, the mētis or local knowledge necessary to the successful practice of farming or pastoralism is probably best learned by daily practice and experience. Like serving a long apprenticeship, growing up in a household where that craft is continually practiced often represents the most satisfactory preparation for its exercise. This kind of socialization to a trade may favor the conservation of skills rather than daring innovation. But any formula that excludes or suppresses the experience, knowledge, and adaptability of mētis risks incoherence and failure; learning to speak coherent sentences involves far more than merely learning the rules of grammar.

The Relation with Episteme and Techne

For the Greeks and particularly for Plato, episteme and techne represented knowledge of an order completely different from mētis.[17] Technical knowledge, or techne, could be expressed precisely and comprehensively in the form of hard-and-fast rules (*not* rules of thumb), principles, and propositions. At its most rigorous, techne is based on logical deduction from self-evident first principles. As an ideal type, it radically differs from mētis in terms of how it is organized, how it is codified and taught, how it is modified, and the analytical precision it exhibits.

Where mētis is contextual and particular, techne is universal. In the logic of mathematics, ten multiplied by ten equals one hundred everywhere and forever; in Euclidean geometry, a right angle represents ninety degrees of a circle; in the conventions of physics, the freezing point of water is always zero degrees centigrade.[18] Techne is settled knowledge; Aristotle wrote that techne "came into being when from many notions gained from experience, a universal judgement about a group of similar things arises."[19] The universality of techne arises from the fact that it is organized analytically into small, explicit, logical steps and is both decomposable and verifiable. This universality means that knowledge in the form of techne can be taught more or less completely as a formal discipline. The rules of techne provide for theoretical knowledge that may or may not have practical applications. Finally, techne is characterized by impersonal, often quantitative precision and a concern with explanation and verification, whereas mētis is concerned with personal skill, or "touch," and practical results.

If the description of techne as an ideal or typical system of knowledge resembles the self-image of modern science, that is no accident. The actual *practice* of science, however, is something else again.[20] The rules of techne are the specification of how knowledge is to be codified, expressed, and verified, *once* it has been discovered. No rules of techne or episteme can explain scientific invention and insight. Discovering a mathematical theorem requires genius and perhaps mētis; the proof of the theorem, however, must follow the tenets of techne.[21] Thus the systematic and impersonal rules of techne facilitate the production of knowledge that can be readily assembled, comprehensively documented, and formally taught, but they cannot by themselves add to that knowledge or explain how it came into being.[22]

Techne is characteristic, above all, of self-contained systems of reasoning in which the findings may be logically derived from the initial assumptions. To the degree that the form of knowledge satisfies these conditions, to that degree is it impersonal, universal, and completely impervious to context. But the context of mētis, as Detienne and Vernant emphasize, is characteristically "situations which are transient, shifting, disconcerting and ambiguous, situations which do not lend themselves to precise measurement, exact calculation, or rigorous logic."[23] Nussbaum shows convincingly how Plato attempted, especially in the *Republic*, to transform the realm of love—a realm that almost by definition is one of contingency, desire, and impulse—into a realm of techne or episteme.[24] Plato regarded mundane love as subject to the lower appetites, and he hoped to purge it of these base instincts so that it could more closely resemble the philosopher's pure search for truth.

The superiority of pure reasoning, especially scientific and mathematical logic, lay in the fact that it was "pure of pain, maximally stable, and directed at the truth." The objects of such reasoning "are eternally what they are regardless of what human beings do and say."[25] What one loved, or *should* love, Plato claimed, was not the beloved himself but rather the pure forms of unalloyed beauty reflected in the beloved.[26] Only in this way could love remain straight and rational, free of the appetites.

The spheres of human endeavor that are freest of contingency, guesswork, context, desire, and personal experience—and thus free of mētis—hence came to be perceived as man's highest pursuits. They are the philosopher's work. One can see why, on the strength of such criteria, Euclidean geometry, mathematics, some self-contained forms of analytical philosophy, and perhaps music are considered to be among the purest of pursuits.[27] Unlike the natural sciences and concrete experiments, these disciplines exist as realms of pure thought, untouched by the contingencies of the material world. They begin in the mind or on a blank sheet of paper. The Pythagorean theorem, $a^2 + b^2 = c^2$, is true for all right triangles everywhere and forever.

A recurrent theme of Western philosophy and science, including social science, has been the attempt to reformulate systems of knowledge in order to bracket uncertainty and thereby permit the kind of logical deductive rigor possessed by Euclidean geometry.[28] In the natural sciences, the results have been revolutionary. Where philosophy and the human sciences are concerned, the efforts have been just as persistent but the results far more ambiguous. Descartes's famous episteme "I think, therefore I am" mimicked the first step in a mathematical proof and was an "answer to the disorder that threatened to undo society."[29] The aim of Jeremy Bentham and the utilitarians was, through their calculus of pleasure and pain (hedonism), to reduce the study of ethics to a pure natural science, to an examination of "every circumstance by which an individual can be influenced, being remarked and inventoried, nothing . . . left to chance, caprice, or unguided discretion, everything being surveyed and set down in dimension, number, weight, and measure."[30]

Even chance (*tuche*) itself, which techne was designed to master, was eventually, thanks to statistics and probability theory, transformed into a singular fact that might enter the formulas of techne. Risk, providing it could be assigned a known probability, became a fact like any other, whereas uncertainty (where the underlying probabilities are not known) still lay outside techne's reach.[31] The intellectual "career" of risk and uncertainty is indicative of many fields of inquiry in which the realm of analysis was reformulated and narrowed to exclude elements that could not be quantified and measured but could only be judged. Better put, techniques were devised to isolate and domesticate those aspects of key variables that might be expressed in numbers (a nation's wealth by gross national product, public opinion by poll numbers, values by psychological inventories). Neoclassical economics, for example, has undergone a transformation along these lines. Consumer preferences are first taken as a given and then counted, in order to bracket taste as a major source of uncertainty. Invention and entrepreneurial activity are treated as exogenous and cast outside the perimeter of the discipline as too intractable to submit to measurement and prediction.[32] The discipline has incorporated calculable risk while exiling those topics where genuine uncertainty prevails (ecological dangers, shifts in taste).[33] As Stephen Marglin shows, "the emphasis on self-interest, calculation, and maximization in economics" are classical examples of "self-evident postulates" and reflect "more an ideological commitment to the superiority of episteme than a serious attempt to unravel the complexities and mysteries of human motivation and behavior."[34]

The logic of such reformulations is analogous to the experimental practice and self-imposed boundaries of modern scientific agriculture. By constricting its field of inquiry, it gained enormously in precision and scientific power at the possible expense of irrelevance or unpleasant surprises from beyond its artificial perimeters.[35] Techne is most suitable to activities "that have a singular end or goal, an end that is specifiable apart from the activity itself, and one susceptible to quantitative measurement."[36] Thus the problem most successfully addressed by scientific agriculture is how to grow the largest number of bushels of a crop at the least cost per acre, as revealed through one-variable-at-a-time trials conducted on experimental plots. Issues of farming life and community, family needs, long-term soil structure, ecological diversity, and sustainability are either difficult to incorporate or excluded altogether. Formulas of efficiency, production functions, and rational action are specifiable only when the ends sought are simple, sharply defined, and hence measurable.

The problem, as Aristotle recognized, is that certain practical choices cannot, "even in principle, be adequately and completely captured in a system of universal rules."[37] He singled out navigation and medicine as two activities in which the practical wisdom of long experience is indispensable to superior performance. They were mētis-laden activities in which responsiveness, improvisation, and skillful, successive approximations were required. If Plato can be credited, Socrates deliberately refrained from writing down his teachings, because he believed that the activity of philosophy belonged more to mētis than to episteme or techne. A written text, even if it takes the form of a philosophical dialogue, is a cut-and-dried set of codified rules. An oral dialogue, by contrast, is alive and responsive to the mutuality of the participants, reaching a destination that cannot be specified in advance. Socrates evidently believed that the interaction between teacher and students that we now call the Socratic method, and not the resulting text, *is* philosophy.[38]

Practical Knowledge Versus Scientific Explanation

Only by grasping the potential achievement and range of mētis is it possible to appreciate the valuable knowledge that high-modernist schemes deprive themselves of when they simply impose their plans. One major reason why mētis is denigrated, particularly in the hegemonic imperium of scientific knowledge, is that its "findings" are practical, opportune, and contextual rather than integrated into the general conventions of scientific discourse.

We have seen the idiosyncracies of mētis at work in the historical vernaculars of measurement of area, weight, and volume. The aim was always to achieve a local purpose or to express an important local feature (such as "a farm of two cows") rather than to accommodate some universal unit of measurement. Like Squanto's maxim, such vernacular measures apparently often conveyed more information than an abstract measure could. They certainly conveyed information that was more *locally* relevant. It was just this local, practical index, which varied from place to place, that ensured that mētis would be confusing, incoherent, and unassimilable for purposes of statecraft.

The classification of flora follows much the same logic among indigenous people. What matters is local use and value. Thus the categories into which various plants are sorted follow a logic of practical use: good for making soup, good for making twine, helpful in healing cuts, effective for settling an upset stomach, poisonous for cattle, useful for weaving our cloth, favored by rabbits as food, good for making fences, and so on. This knowledge is never static, however; it is constantly being expanded through practical experimentation. And the categories into which floral reality is divided are clearly not the occasionally invisible Linnaean botanical categories favored by scientific researchers.[39]

The litmus test for mētis is practical success. Did the navigator make the trip safely? Did Odysseus's stratagems outwit the Cyclops? Did the poultice cure the boil? Was the farmer's harvest abundant? If a technique works effectively and repeatedly for the purpose intended, the practitioners of mētis do not pause long to ask why and how it worked, to define the precise mechanism of cause and effect. Their intent is not to contribute to a wider body of knowledge but to solve the concrete problems they face. This does not mean that the practitioners of mētis do not invent new solutions. They most decidedly do. Until quite recently virtually all the improvements in agriculture have come from the field rather than from industry or science. What it does mean, however, is that the innovations of mētis will typically represent a recombination (*bricolage*, to use Lévi-Strauss's term)[40] of existing elements; farmers did not invent the tractor to solve their problems of traction power.[41] By the same token, the bricolage of practical knowledge has often produced complex techniques—such as polycropping and soil-building strategies—that work admirably but that science has not (yet?) understood.

The power of practical knowledge depends on an exceptionally close and astute observation of the environment. It should by now be rather obvious why traditional cultivators like Squanto are such consummate observers of their environment, but the reasons bear repeating in the context of a comparison with scientific knowledge. First, these cultivators have a vital, direct stake in the results of close observation. Unlike the research scientist or extension agent who does not have to take her own advice, the peasant is the immediate consumer of his own conclusions. Unlike the typical modern-day farmer, the peasant has no outside experts to rely on beyond his experienced neighbors; he must make decisions based on what he knows.

Second, the poverty or marginal economic status of many of these cultivators is itself, I would argue, a powerful impetus to careful observation and experimentation. Consider the hypothetical case of two fishermen, both of whom must make their living from a river. One fisherman lives by a river where the catch is stable and abundant. The other lives by a river where the catch is variable and sparse, affording only a bare and precarious subsistence. The poorer of the two will clearly have an immediate, life-and-death interest in devising new fishing techniques, in observing closely the habits of fish, in the careful siting of traps and weirs, in the timing and signs of seasonal runs of different species, and so forth.

Nor should we forget that the peasant cultivator or pastoralist lives year in and year out in the field of observation. He or she will likely know things that neither an absentee cultivator nor a research scientist would ever notice.[42] Finally, as mentioned in the previous chapter, such a cultivator is always a member of a community that serves as a living, oral reference library for observations, practices, and experiments—a body of knowledge that an individual could never amass alone.

The experimental temper of "prescientific" peoples, often impelled by mortal threats, resulted in many important, efficacious discoveries. South American Indians discovered that chewing the bark of the cinchona tree was an effective remedy for malaria, without knowing that its active ingredient was quinine or why it worked. Westerners knew that certain foods consumed in the early spring, such as rhubarb, could relieve the symptoms of wintertime scurvy, without knowing anything about Vitamin C. The mold from certain breads was used to stem infections long before the isolation of penicillin.[43] According to Anil Gupta, roughly three-quarters of the modern pharmacopoeia are derivatives of traditionally known medicines.[44] Even in the absence of remedies, people often knew what measures would lessen their chances of contracting a dreaded contagious disease. The Londoners in Daniel Defoe's *Journal of the Plague Year* knew that moving to the country or, failing that, sealing oneself up in one's rooms vastly improved one's chances of surviving the bubonic plague of 1665.[45] Knowing, as we now do, that the vectors of the plague were the fleas carried by rats, we can appreciate why these strategies often worked, but Defoe's contemporaries hit on these effective solutions even though they thought that the plague was caused by vapors.

A most striking illustration of practice preceding science is the widespread use of variolation to check the spread of smallpox long before Sir William Jenner's heralded development of vaccination in 1798. The story, which Frédérique Apffel Marglin analyzes in impressive detail, is valuable because it demonstrates how purely mētis skills led to a form of inoculation that mimicked or presaged what is justifiably seen as a great milestone in scientific medicine.[46] Let me make it clear that the last thing I intend here is a defense of traditional medicine vis-à-vis modern medical research and experimental method.[47] What this account does highlight, however, is how frequently local knowledge, trial and error, or what we might more generously call the stochastic method have produced practical solutions without benefit of scientific method.

By at least the sixteenth century, the technique of variolation was widely practiced in India, the Middle East, Europe, and China. The practice consisted of using human smallpox matter, scratched into the skin or inhaled, which gave the recipient a mild, rarely fatal case of smallpox. "Fresh" smallpox matter—from the pustules or scabs of someone with an active infection contracted in the usual way—was never used. The inoculation was typically made with attenuated matter saved from those who had had mild cases during last year's epidemic or with matter taken from the pustules of those who had been inoculated the previous year. Dosage could be regulated according to the size and age of the patient.

The principle behind variolation, the same principle that forms the basis of homeopathy, reflected a much older practice. Inoculation in one form or another was widely practiced well before the rise of modern medicine. In India, variolation was carried out by ritual specialists and was thoroughly integrated with the worship of the goddess Sithala.[48] In other societies, its cultural setting was no doubt different, although the actual procedures were remarkably parallel.

Jenner's discovery of vaccination using cowpox matter was therefore not entirely novel. A young girl had told him that she was protected against smallpox because she had already had cowpox. Jenner, following this lead, inoculated his own children with cowpox matter and observed that they showed no reaction to a subsequent smallpox vaccination. Vaccination was, of course, a great advance over variolation. Because it used live smallpox matter, variolation induced a mild but active case that was contagious, and 1 to 3 percent of those so treated died from the treatment, a ratio that nonetheless compared favorably with the one or two in six who perished in an epidemic. Jenner's technique used killed virus, thus avoiding contagion, and his vaccination had a remarkably low iatrogenic rate: only one in a thousand died of the vaccination itself. His achievement is rightly celebrated, but it is important to recognize that "Jennerian vaccination was not an abrupt break with the past, but the direct descendant and heir of inoculation."[49]

Variolation, though hardly to be preferred to vaccination, was an impressive accomplishment of practical prescientific medicine. The principle of inoculation had long been grasped, and, one imagines, a great many practitioners in affected communities were trying to develop a successful technique. Once the efficacy of a new treatment was established, the news must have traveled faster than any epidemic and quickly displaced less successful preventative measures. There is no magic here. The ingredients of such practical knowledge are simple: a pressing need (in this case, a matter literally of life and death), a few promising leads that worked in analogous contexts (inoculation), a vast army of freelance experimenters willing to try almost anything,[50] time to "simmer" (as the experimenters and their clients observed the results of various stratagems through successive epidemics), and the sharing (through chains of communication) of the experimental results. As long as it didn't require an electron microscope, it would in fact be surprising if such a combination of passionate interest, close observation, large numbers of amateur specialists trying different possibilities, and the time necessary for trial and error did not produce many novel solutions to practical problems. The variolators before Jenner were not unlike the polycropping cultivators described by Paul Richards. They had devised, not just stumbled upon, something that worked, without quite knowing exactly why it worked. While this increased their risk of drawing false inferences from what they saw, it did not diminish the practical achievements of their bricolage.

Mētis, with the premium it places on practical knowledge, experience, and stochastic reasoning, is of course not merely the now-superseded precursor of scientific knowledge. It is the mode of reasoning most appropriate to complex material and social tasks where the uncertainties are so daunting that we must trust our (experienced) intuition and feel our way. Albert Howard's description of water management in Japan offers an instructive example: "Erosion control in Japan is like a game of chess. The forest engineer, after studying his eroding valley, makes his first move, locating and building one or more check dams. He waits to see what Nature's response is. This determines the forest engineer's next move, which may be another dam or two, an increase in the former dam, or the construction of side retaining walls. Another pause for observation, the next move is made, and so on, until erosion is checkmated. The operations of natural forces, such as sedimentation and re-vegetation, are guided and used to the best advantage to keep down costs and to obtain practical results. *No more is attempted than Nature has already done in the region.*"[51] The engineer in Howard's account recognizes implicitly that he is dealing with "an art of one valley." Each prudent, small step, based on prior experience, yields new and not completely predictable effects that become the point of departure for the next step. Virtually any complex task involving many variables whose values and interactions cannot be accurately forecast belongs to this genre: building a house, repairing a car, perfecting a new jet engine, surgically repairing a knee, or farming a plot of land.[52] Where the interactions involve not just the material environment but social interaction as well—building and peopling new villages or cities, organizing a revolutionary seizure of power, or collectivizing agriculture—the mind boggles at the multitude of interactions and uncertainties (as distinct from calculable risks).

More than thirty-five years ago, in recognition of the refractory complexity of ambitious social policy, Charles Lindblom coined the memorable expression "the science of muddling through."[53] The phrase was meant to capture the spirit of a practical approach to large-scale policy problems that could not be completely understood, let alone comprehensively addressed. Models of public administration, Lindblom complained, implicitly assumed a synoptic mastery of a policy initiative, when in practice, knowledge was both limited and fragmentary, and means could never be neatly separated from goals. His characterization of actual policy practice emphasized a piecemeal approach of limited comparisons, a sequence of trials and errors followed by revised trials, reliance on past experience, and "disjointed incrementalism."[54] Albert Hirschman has made the same point, rather more metaphorically, by comparing social policy to house building: "The architect of social change can never have a reliable blueprint. Not only is each house he builds different from any other that was built before, but it necessarily uses new construction materials and even experiments with untested principles of stress and structure. Therefore what can be most usefully conveyed by the builders of one house is an understanding of the experience that made it at all possible to build under these trying circumstances."[55]

Taken together, Lindblom's and Hirschman's positions amount to a well-reasoned strategic retreat from the ambition to comprehensive, rational planning. If we can make allowances for the social-science jargon, the concepts behind such terms as "bounded rationality" (rather than "synoptic mastery") and "satisficing" (rather than "maximizing"), terms invented to describe a world working by educated guesswork and rules of thumb, sound very much like mētis.

Learning Beyond the Book

A step-by-step "muddling through" approach would seem to be the only prudent course in a field like erosion management or public policy implementation, where surprises are all but guaranteed. The fact that in these cases the level of uncertainty and hence of potential disaster can be reduced by breaking down the process into more manageable steps does *not* imply that any novice could then take charge. On the contrary, only someone with wide experience will be able to interpret the results of and reactions to an initial step in order to determine the next step. One would want hydrologists and policy managers who had been surprised many times and have had many successes behind them. Their repertoire of responses would be larger, their judgment in reading the environment surer, their sense of what surprises might await them more accurate. Once again, some of their competence could be interpreted and taught, but much of it would remain implicit—a sixth sense that comes with long practice. At the risk of trying to pinpoint the ineffable, I want to suggest how important such knowledge is and how difficult it is to translate it into codified form.[56]

Mētis knowledge is often so implicit and automatic that its bearer is at a loss to explain it.[57] A staple of early medical training, I have been told, is the story of a physician who, at the turn of the century, had a spectacularly high success rate in diagnosing syphilis in its early stages. Laboratory tests confirmed his diagnoses, but he himself did not know precisely what it was that he detected in the physical exams that led him to his conclusions. Intrigued by his success, hospital administrators asked two other doctors to closely observe his examination of patients over several weeks and to see if they could spot what he was picking up. At long last, they and the doctor realized that he was unconsciously registering the patients' slight eye tremor. The eye tremor then became a universally recognized symptom of syphilis. Although this insight could be codified, what is instructive here is that it could have been achieved only through close observation and long clinical experience and that, even before then, it could have been known subliminally.

Any experienced practitioner of a skill or craft will develop a large repertoire of moves, visual judgments, a sense of touch, or a discriminating gestalt for assessing the work as well as a range of accurate intuitions born of experience that defy being communicated apart from practice. A few brief examples will help to convey the subtlety and nuance of this knowledge. In Indonesia, older Bugis sea captains, sound asleep below decks, will awaken the moment there is a change in direction, weather, current, or some combination of the three. As the ocean's waves change amplitude or begin striking the ship from a different direction, a captain immediately senses the change through the resulting slight alterations in the roll and pitch of the ship.

In the days when a case of diphtheria in town was still an occasion for quarantining the patient at home, a doctor was taking a young medical student along with him on his rounds. When they had been admitted to the front hall of a quarantined house but before they had seen the patient, the older man paused and said, "Stop. Smell the odor! Never forget this smell; this is the smell of a house with diphtheria."[58] Another doctor once told me that, after seeing thousands of infants at a busy clinic, he believed that he could tell with a high degree of accuracy, just by looking, whether an infant was seriously ill and needed immediate attention. He couldn't quite put his finger on the exact visual cue that informed his judgment, but he supposed that it was some combination of complexion, the expression of the eyes, body tone, and animation. Albert Howard once again makes a persuasive case for the "practiced eye": "An experienced farmer can tell the health of the soil and the quality of the humus by the plants—their vigor, their growth, the profuse roots, the 'glow' of health. . . . The same is true for the

health of animals on good land." Indeed, he continues, "it is not necessary to weigh or measure them. A glance on the part of the successful
grazier, or a butcher accustomed to deal with high class animals, is
sufficient to tell him whether all is well or whether there is something
wrong with the soil or the management of the animals, or both."[59]

What is the status of such insight or intuition? We might call these
skills the "tricks of the trade" (in the nondeceptive sense) that most
"crafty" practitioners acquire.[60] Notice that virtually all the experienced
judgments described in these anecdotes could be verified by tests and
measurements. Diphtheria can be detected in the laboratory, a child's
anemia can be verified by blood tests, and the Bugis sea captain can go
on deck to confirm the shift in the wind. It is doubtless reassuring to
those who have both the intuition and access to formal measurement
to know that their judgment can be checked. But the epistemic alternative to mētis is far slower, more laborious, more capital intensive,
and not always decisive. When rapid judgments of high (not perfect)
accuracy are called for, when it is important to interpret early signs that
things are going well or poorly, then there is no substitute for mētis. In
the case of the experienced doctor, in fact, it is mētis that informs a decision about whether tests are needed and, if so, which tests.

Even the part of mētis that can be conveyed by rules of thumb is the
codification of practical experience. The boiling down of maple sap
into syrup is a tricky business. If one goes too far, the sap will boil over.
The stopping point can be determined by a thermometer or by a hy-
drometer (which indicates specific gravity). But those with experience
look for the mass of small bubbles that forms on the surface of the sap
just before it begins to boil over—a visual rule of thumb that is far easier to use. Achieving the insight, however, *requires* that, at least once,
the syrup maker make a mistake and go too far. Chinese recipes, it has
always amused me, often contain the following instruction: "Heat the
oil until it is *almost* smoking." The recipes assume that the cook has
made enough mistakes to know what oil looks like just before it begins
smoking. The rule of thumb for maple syrup and for oil are, by definition, the rules of experience.

Those who do not have access to scientific methods and laboratory
verification have often relied on mētis to develop rich knowledge systems that are remarkably accurate. Traditional navigation skills before
the eras of sextants, magnetic compasses, charts, and sonar are a case
in point. I refer again to the Bugis in this context, because their skills
have been so brilliantly documented by Gene Ammarell.[61] In the absence of formal tide tables, the Bugis have elaborated a thoroughly reliable scheme for forecasting rising and falling tides, the direction of

currents, and the relative strength of tides—all of which are vitally important to their sailing plans and safety.[62] Calculating on the basis of time of day, the number of days into the lunar cycle, and the monsoon season, the Bugis captain holds in his head a system that provides all the accurate information he needs about tides. From an astronomer's perspective, it seems odd that the scheme makes no reference to the angle of declination of the moon. But since the monsoon is directly related to the declination of the moon, it serves effectively as a proxy. The cognitive map of the Bugis captain can be reconstructed in written form, as Ammarell has done, for illustrative purposes, but it was learned orally and by informal apprenticeship among the Bugis. Given the complexity of the phenomena it is meant to address, the system for evaluating and predicting tides is elegantly simple and eminently effective.

The Dynamism and Plasticity of Mētis

The term "traditional," as in "traditional knowledge"—a term that I have carefully avoided—is a misnomer, sending all the wrong signals.[63] In the mid–nineteenth century, explorers in West Africa stumbled upon groups growing maize, a New World grain, as their main staple. Although it was unlikely that the West Africans had been growing maize for longer than two generations, its cultivation was already surrounded by elaborate rituals and myths about a maize goddess or spirit who had given them the first kernels. What was striking was both the alacrity with which they had adopted maize and the speed with which they had integrated it into their traditions.[64] The apparent spread of variolation across four continents is a further instance of how widely and how rapidly "traditional peoples" will embrace techniques that solve vital problems. Examples could be multiplied. Sewing machines, matches, flashlights, kerosene, plastic bowls, and antibiotics are only a tiny sample of the products that solved vital problems or eliminated great drudgery and were thus readily accepted.[65] Practical efficacy is, as we have noted, the key test of mētis knowledge, and all these products passed with flying colors.

The point that I am making would hardly need emphasis or elaborate illustration except for the fact that a certain understanding of science, modernity, and development has so successfully structured the dominant discourse that all other kinds of knowledge are regarded as backward, static traditions, as old wives' tales and superstitions. High modernism has needed this "other," this dark twin, in order to rhetorically present itself as the antidote to backwardness.[66] The binary opposition also comes from a history of competition between the institutions and personnel that sprang up around these two forms of knowledge. Modern research institutions, agricultural experiment stations, sellers of fertilizer and machinery, high-modernist city planners, Third World developers, and World Bank officials have, to a considerable degree, made their successful institutional way in the world by the systematic denigration of the practical knowledge that we have called mētis.

Their characterization could not, in this context, be further from the truth. Mētis, far from being rigid and monolithic, is plastic, local, and divergent.[67] It is in fact the idiosyncrasies of mētis, its contextualness, and its fragmentation that make it so permeable, so open to new ideas. Mētis has no doctrine or centralized training; each practitioner has his or her own angle. In economic terms, the market for mētis is often one of nearly perfect competition, and local monopolies are likely to be broken by innovation from below and outside. If a new technique works, it is likely to find a clientele.

In his defense of traditionalism against rationalism, Michael Oakeshott emphasizes the pragmatism of real, existing traditions: "The big mistake of the rationalist—though it is not inherent in the method—is to assume that 'tradition,' or what is better called 'practical knowledge,' is rigid, fixed and unchanging—in fact it is 'preeminently fluid.' "[68] Tradition, in part because of its local variation, is pliable and dynamic. "No traditional way of behavior, no traditional skill ever remains fixed," he says elsewhere. "Its history is one of continual change."[69] The changes are likely to be small and gradual (incrementalism) rather than sudden and discontinuous.

It is worth emphasizing the degree to which oral cultures, as opposed to written cultures, may avoid the rigidity of orthodoxy. Because an oral culture has no textual reference point for marking deviations, its religious myths, rituals, and folklore are likely to drift. The tales and traditions currently in circulation vary with the speaker, the audience, and local needs. Having no yardstick like a sacred text to measure the degree of drift from its Ur-tradition, such a culture can change greatly over time and simultaneously think of itself as remaining faithful to tradition.[70]

Perhaps the best analogy for a society's stock of mētis is its language. Yes, there are rules of thumb for expression: clichés, formulas of politeness, customs for swearing, and conventional conversations. But unless there is a central committee of grammarians with draconian police powers, the language is always being added to as new expressions and novel combinations are invented and puns and irony undermine old formulas. Under great pressure and rapid change, the language may change rather dramatically and new hybrids arise, but for the people who speak it, it remains recognizably their language. Influence over the direction of a language is never equally distributed, but innovation comes from far and wide, and if others find a particular innovation useful or apposite, they will adopt it as part of *their* language. In language as in mētis, seldom is the name of an innovator remembered, and this, too, helps to make the result a joint, mutual product.

The Social Context of Mētis and Its Destruction

While doing fieldwork in a small village in Malaysia, I was constantly struck by the breadth of my neighbors' skills and their casual knowledge of local ecology. One particular anecdote is representative. Growing in the compound of the house in which I lived was a locally famous mango tree. Relatives and acquaintances would visit when the fruit was ripe in the hope of being given a few fruits and, more important, the chance to save and plant the seeds next to their own house. Shortly before my arrival, however, the tree had become infested with large red ants, which destroyed most of the fruit before it could ripen. It seemed nothing could be done short of bagging each fruit. Several times I noticed the elderly head of household, Mat Isa, bringing dried nipah palm fronds to the base of the mango tree and checking them. When I finally got around to asking what he was up to, he explained it to me, albeit reluctantly, as for him this was pretty humdrum stuff compared to our usual gossip. He knew that small black ants, which had a number of colonies at the rear of the compound, were the enemies of large red ants. He also knew that the thin, lancelike leaves of the nipah palm curled into long, tight tubes when they fell from the tree and died. (In fact, the local people used the tubes to roll their cigarettes.) Such tubes would also, he knew, be ideal places for the queens of the black ant colonies to lay their eggs. Over several weeks he placed dried nipah fronds in strategic places until he had masses of black-ant eggs beginning to hatch. He then placed the egg-infested fronds against the mango tree and observed the ensuing week-long Armageddon. Several neighbors, many of them skeptical, and their children followed the fortunes of the ant war closely. Although smaller by half or more, the black ants finally had the weight of numbers to prevail against the red ants and gain possession of the ground at the base of the mango tree. As the black ants were not interested in the mango leaves or fruits while the fruits were still on the tree, the crop was saved.

This successful field experiment in biological controls presupposes several kinds of knowledge: the habitat and diet of black ants, their egg-laying habits, a guess about what local material would substitute as movable egg chambers, and experience with the fighting proclivities of red and black ants. Mat Isa made it clear that such skill in practical entomology was quite widespread, at least among his older neighbors, and that people remembered something like this strategy having worked once or twice in the past. What is clear to me is that no agricultural extension official would have known the first thing about ants, let alone biological controls; most extension agents were raised in town and in any case were concerned entirely with rice, fertilizer, and loans. Nor would most of them think to ask; they were, after all, the experts, trained to instruct the peasant. It is hard to imagine this knowledge being created and maintained except in the context of lifelong observation and a relatively stable, multigenerational community that routinely exchanges and preserves knowledge of this kind.

One purpose of this illustration is to alert us to the social conditions necessary for the reproduction of comparable practical knowledge. These social conditions, at a minimum, would seem to require a community of interest, accumulated information, and ongoing experimentation. Occasionally there are formal institutions that seem almost perfectly tailored to the collection and exchange of practical information, such as the *veillées* of nineteenth-century France. The veillée, as its name implies, was a traditional pattern of gathering practiced by farm families during winter evenings, often in barns to take advantage of the warmth generated by the livestock and thus save on fuel. With no agenda save sociability and economy, the gatherings amounted to local assemblies where opinions, stories, agricultural news, advice, gossip, and religious or folk tales were exchanged while the participants shelled nuts or embroidered. Given the fact that each member there possessed a lifetime of interested observation and practice in which every family paid for the consequences of its agricultural decisions, the veillée was an unheralded daily seminar on practical knowledge.

This brings us squarely to two of the great ironies of mētis. The first is that mētis is not democratically distributed. Not only does it depend on a touch or a knack that may not be common, but access to the experience and practice necessary for its acquisition may be restricted. Artisan guilds, gifted craftsmen, certain classes, religious fraternities, entire communities, and men in general often treat some forms of knowledge as a monopoly they are reluctant to share. Better stated, the availability of such knowledge to others depends greatly on the social structure of the society and the advantages that a monopoly in some forms of knowledge can confer.[71] In this respect mētis is not unitary, and we should perhaps speak of metises, recognizing its nonhomo-geneity. The second irony is that, however plastic and receptive mētis is, some forms of it seem to depend on key elements of preindustrial life for their elaboration and transmission. Communities that are marginal to markets and to the state are likely to retain a high degree of mētis; they have no choice, as they have to rely disproportionately on the knowledge and materials at hand. If, while shopping at the local store or visiting at the farmers' association, Mat Isa had found a cheap pesticide that would have finished off the red ants, I don't doubt that he would have used it.

Some forms of mētis are disappearing every day.[72] As physical mobility, commodity markets, formal education, professional specialization, and mass media spread to even the most remote communities, the social conditions for the elaboration of mētis are undermined. One could, with great justice, welcome a great many of these extinctions of local knowledge. Once matches become widely available, why would anyone want to know, except as a matter of idle curiosity, how to make fire with flint and tinder? Knowing how to scrub clothes on a washboard or on a stone in the river is undoubtedly an art, but one gladly abandoned by those who can afford a washing machine. Darning skills were similarly lost, without much nostalgia, when cheap, machine-made stockings came on the market. As the older Bugis seamen say, "These days, with charts and compasses, *anyone* can steer."[73] And why not? The production of standardized knowledge has made certain skills more broadly—more democratically—available, as they are no longer the preserve of a guild that may refuse admission or insist on a long apprenticeship.[74] Much of the world of mētis that we have lost is the all but inevitable result of industrialization and the division of labor. And much of this loss was experienced as a liberation from toil and drudgery.

But it would be a serious error to believe that the destruction of mētis was merely the inadvertent and necessary by-product of economic progress. The destruction of mētis and its replacement by standardized formulas legible only from the center is virtually inscribed in the activities of both the state and large-scale bureaucratic capitalism. As a "project," it is the object of constant initiatives which are never entirely successful, for no forms of production or social life can be made to work by formulas alone—that is, without mētis. The logic animating the project, however, is one of control and appropriation. Local knowledge, because it is dispersed and relatively autonomous, is all but unappropriable. The reduction or, more utopian still, the elimination of mētis and the local control it entails are preconditions, in the case of the state, of administrative order and fiscal appropriation and, in the case of the large capitalist firm, of worker discipline and profit.

The subordination of mētis is fairly obvious in the development of mass production in the factory. A comparable de-skilling process is, I believe, more compelling and, given the intractable obstacles to complete standardization, ultimately less successful in agricultural production.

As Stephen Marglin's early work has convincingly shown, capitalist profit requires not only efficiency but the *combination* of efficiency and control.[75] The crucial innovations of the division of labor at the sub-product level and the concentration of production in the factory represent the key steps in bringing the labor process under unitary control. Efficiency and control might coincide, as in the case of the mechanized spinning and weaving of cotton. At times, however, they might be unrelated or even contradictory. "Efficiency at best creates a *potential* profit," notes Marglin. "Without control the capitalist cannot realize that profit. Thus organizational forms which enhance capitalist control may increase profits and find favor with capitalists even if they affect productivity and efficiency adversely. Conversely, more efficient ways of organizing production which reduce capitalist control may end up reducing profits and being rejected by capitalists."[76] The typical structure of artisanal production was often an impediment to efficiency. But it was nearly *always* an obstacle to capitalist profits. In the "putting-out" system in textiles that prevailed before factory organization, cottage workers had control over the raw material, could set the pace of the work, and could increase their return by various stratagems that were difficult to monitor. The crucial advantage of the factory, from the boss's point of view, was that he could more directly fix the hours and the intensity of the work and control the raw materials.[77] To the degree that efficient production could still be organized on an artisanal basis (such as early woolen manufacturing and silk ribbon weaving, according to Marglin), to that degree was it difficult for the capitalist to appropriate the profits of a dispersed craft population.

The genius of modern mass-production methods, Frederick Taylor, saw the issue of destroying mētis and turning a resistant, quasi-autonomous, artisan population into more suitable units, or "factory hands," with great clarity. "Under scientific management . . . the managers assume . . . the burden of gathering together all of the traditional knowledge which in the past has been possessed by the workmen and then of classifying, tabulating, and reducing this knowledge to rules, laws, formulae. . . . Thus all of the planning which under the old system was done by the workmen, must of necessity under the new system be done by management in accordance with the law of science."[78]

In the Taylorized factory, only the factory manager had the knowledge and command of the whole process, and the worker was reduced to the execution of a small, often minute, part of the overall process. The result was often remarkably efficient, as in the early Ford plants; it was always, however, a great boon to control and profit.[79]

The utopian dream of Taylorization—a factory in which every pair of hands was more or less reduced to automatic movements, on the model of programmed robots—was unrealizable. Not that it wasn't tried. David Noble has described the well-funded attempt to make machine tools through numerical controls because it promised "emancipation from the human worker."[80] Its ultimate failure came precisely because the system had designed out mētis—the practical adjustments that an experienced worker would make to compensate for slight changes in material, temperatures, the wear on or irregularities in the machine, mechanical malfunction, and so forth. As one operator said, "Numerical controls are supposed to be like magic, but all you can do automatically is produce scrap."[81] This conclusion could be generalized. In a brilliant ethnography of the work routines of machine operators whose jobs appeared to have been thoroughly de-skilled, Ken Kusterer has shown how the workers nevertheless had to develop individual skills that were absolutely necessary to successful production but that could never be reduced to formulas a novice could immediately use. One machine operator, whose job was classified as "unskilled," drew an analogy between performing his job and driving a car: "Cars are basically the same but every car is different. . . . At first when you're learning, you just learn rules about driving. But as you get to know how to drive, you get a feel for the car you're driving—you know, things like how it feels at different speeds, how well the brakes work, when it's going to overheat, how to start it when it's cold. . . . Then if you think about old cars like these machines, been running three shifts for twenty years, some of them, like maybe you've got a car with no horn, that wants to turn right when you hit the brake, that don't start right unless you pump the gas in a certain way—then maybe you see what it's like trying to run these old machines they've got down here."[82]

Taylorization has its analogue in agricultural production as well, an analogue with a far longer and more variegated history. In agriculture, as in manufacturing, the mere efficiency of a form of production is not sufficient to ensure the appropriation of taxes or profits. Independent smallholder agriculture may, as we have noted, be the most efficient way to grow many crops. But such forms of agriculture, although they may present possibilities for taxation and profit when their products are bulked, processed, and sold, are relatively illegible and hard to control. As is the case with autonomous artisans and petit-bourgeois shopkeepers, monitoring the commercial fortunes of small-fry farms is an administrative nightmare. The possibilities for evasion and resistance are numerous, and the cost of procuring accurate, annual data is high, if not prohibitive.[83]

A state mainly concerned with appropriation and control will find sedentary agriculture preferable to pastoralism or shifting agriculture. For the same reasons, such a state would generally prefer largeholding to smallholding and, in turn, plantation or collective agriculture to both. Where control and appropriation are the overriding considerations, only the last two forms offer direct control over the workforce and its income, the opportunity to select cropping patterns and techniques, and, finally, direct control over the production and profit of the enterprise. Although collectivization and plantation agriculture are seldom very efficient, they represent, as we have seen, the most legible and hence appropriable forms of agriculture.

The large capitalist agricultural producer faces the same problem as the factory owner: how to transform the essentially artisanal or mētis knowledge of farmers into a standardized system that will allow him greater control over the work and its intensity. The plantation was one solution. In colonial countries, where able-bodied men were pressed into service as gang labor, the plantation represented a kind of private collectivization, inasmuch as it relied on the state for the extramarket sanctions necessary to control its labor force. More than one plantation sector has made up what it lacked in efficiency by using its political clout to secure subsidies, price supports, and monopoly privileges.

The control made possible by the plantation, not to mention the collective farm, has proved, with few exceptions, to entail such high costs in supervision, rigidity, and overhead as to be inefficient. Now that plantation agriculture has been discredited, some of the newer alternatives devised to replicate its control and standardization are instructive, as they indicate the functional similarity that may lie behind different forms.[84] The invention of contract farming worldwide is just one noteworthy example.[85] When chicken farmers realized that huge, centralized operations for raising fryers not only were inefficient but posed serious disease and environmental problems, they devised a kind of high-tech putting-out system.[86] The large firm contracts with a farmer to supply him with chicks and then to buy back (after six weeks or so) a certain number of chickens meeting their standards. The farmer, for his part, is obliged to construct and pay for a building that meets corporate specifications and to feed, water, and medicate the chickens with rations supplied by the corporation and according to their precise timetable. An inspector frequently verifies compliance. For the corporation, the advantages are enormous: it risks no capital except what is invested in the birds; it needs no land of its own; its management expenses are small; it achieves uniform product standards; and, not least, it can fail to renew a contract or change the price paid after each round at no cost to itself.

The logic, although not the form, is the same as on the plantation. Given its national or international market, what the corporation requires is absolute, guaranteed uniformity of product and a stable supply.[87] The need to administer the production of uniform fryers in many different localities requires an optic of standardization and aggregation. As we saw in the case of scientific forestry, this is not merely a question of inventing measures that accurately reflect the facts on the ground and that can be conveyed to administrators. It is, above all, a question of changing the environment so that it is more standardized to begin with. Only the standardized breeding, the building constructed to specifications, the fixed formula for feed, and the mandatory feeding schedule—all disciplined by the contract—make it possible for a single specialist to inspect one hundred poultry farms raising fryers for, say, Kentucky Fried Chicken, and to ensure that the variation is minimal. One can visualize his handy checklist. The purpose of contract farming is not to understand farms and adapt to them; rather, it is to transform farms and farm labor at the outset so that they fit the grid of the contract.

For farmers who sign up, as long as the contracts are rolled over, there are profits to be made, although at considerable risk. The contracts are short term, the work schedules detailed, and the set-up and supplies mandatory. The contract farmers are in theory small-business entrepreneurs, but aside from the fact that they risk their land and buildings, they have not much more control over their working day than do assembly-line workers.

The Case Against Imperial Knowledge

> They said . . . that he was so devoted to Pure Science . . . that he would rather have people die by the right therapy than be cured by the wrong.
> —Sinclair Lewis, *Arrowsmith*

The argument that I have been venturing is not a case against high modernism or state simplifications per se or, to be sure, against epistemic knowledge per se. Our ideas about citizenship, public-health pro-

grams, social security, transportation, communication, universal public education, and equality before the law are all powerfully influenced
by state-created, high-modernist simplifications. I will go further and
say that the *initial* land reforms in Bolshevik Russia and in postrevolutionary China were state-abetted simplifications that effectively en-
franchised millions who had lived in virtual serfdom. Epistemic knowledge, though never separate in its practice from mētis, has provided us
with a knowledge of the world that, for all its darker aspects, few of us
would want to surrender.

What has proved to be truly dangerous to us and to our environment, I think, is the *combination* of the universalist pretensions of epistemic knowledge and authoritarian social engineering. Such a combination has been at work in city planning, in Lenin's view of revolution
(but not his practice), in collectivization in the Soviet Union, and in villagization in Tanzania. The combination is implicit in the logic of scientific agriculture and explicit in its colonial practice. When schemes
like these come close to achieving their impossible dreams of ignoring
or suppressing mētis and local variation, they all but guarantee their
own practical failure.

Universalist claims seem inherent in the way in which rationalist
knowledge is pursued. Although I am no philosopher of knowledge,
there seems to be no door in this epistemic edifice through which mētis
or practical knowledge could enter on its own terms. It is this *imperialism* that is troubling. As Pascal wrote, the great failure of rationalism
is "not its recognition of technical knowledge, but its *failure* to recognize any other."[88] By contrast, mētis does not put all its eggs in one basket; it makes no claim to universality and in this sense is pluralistic. Of
course, certain structural conditions can thwart this imperialism of epistemic claims. Democratic and commercial pressures sometimes oblige
agricultural scientists to premise their work on practical problems as
defined by farmers. During the Meiji Restoration, three-person technical teams began by investigating farmers' innovations and then taking
them back to the laboratory to perfect them. The construction workers
who refused to leave Brasília as planned or the disillusioned ujamaa
villagers who fled from their settlements to some degree undid the
plans made for them. Such resistance, however, comes from outside the
paradigm of epistemic knowledge itself. When someone like Albert
Howard, himself a meticulous scientist, recognizes the "art" of farming and the nonquantifiable ways of knowing, he steps outside the
realm of codified, scientific knowledge.

Authoritarian high-modernist states in the grip of a self-evident
(and usually half-baked) social theory have done irreparable damage

to human communities and individual livelihoods. The danger was compounded when leaders came to believe, as Mao said, that the people were a "blank piece of paper" on which the new regime could write. The utopian industrialist Robert Owen had the same vision for the factory town New Lanark, although on a civic rather than national level: "Each generation, indeed each administration, shall see unrolled before it the blank sheet of infinite possibility, and if by chance this tabula rasa had been defaced by the irrational scribblings of tradition-ridden ancestors, then the first task of the rationalist must be to scrub it clean."[89]

What conservatives like Oakeshott miss, I think, is that high modernism has a natural appeal for an intelligentsia and a people who may have ample reason to hold the past in contempt.[90] Late colonial modernizers sometimes wielded their power ruthlessly in transforming a population that they took to be backward and greatly in need of instruction. Revolutionaries have had every reason to despise the feudal, poverty-stricken, inegalitarian past that they hoped to banish forever, and sometimes they have also had a reason to suspect that immediate democracy would simply bring back the old order. Postindependence leaders in the nonindustrial world (occasionally revolutionary leaders themselves) could not be faulted for hating their past of colonial domination and economic stagnation, nor could they be faulted for wasting no time or democratic sentimentality on creating a people that they could be proud of. Understanding the history and logic of their commitment to high-modernist goals, however, does not permit us to overlook the enormous damage that their convictions entailed when combined with authoritarian state power.

10 Conclusion

They would reconstruct society on an imaginary plan, much like the astronomers for their own calculation would make over the system of the universe.
—Pierre-Joseph Proudhon, *on the utopian socialists*

Yet a man who uses an imaginary map, thinking that it is a true one, is likely to be worse off than someone with no map at all; for he will fail to inquire whenever he can, to observe every detail on his way, and to search continuously with all his senses and all his intelligence for indications of where he should go.
—E. F. Schumacher, *Small Is Beautiful*

The great high-modernist episodes that we have examined qualify as tragedies in at least two respects. First, the visionary intellectuals and planners behind them were guilty of hubris, of forgetting that they were mortals and acting as if they were gods. Second, their actions, far from being cynical grabs for power and wealth, were animated by a genuine desire to improve the human condition—a desire with a fatal flaw. That these tragedies could be so intimately associated with optimistic views of progress and rational order is in itself a reason for a searching diagnosis. Another reason lies in the completely ecumenical character of the high-modernist faith. We encounter it in various guises in colonial development schemes, planned urban centers in both the East and the West, collectivized farms, the large development plans of the World Bank, the resettlement of nomadic populations, and the management of workers on factory floors.

If such schemes have typically taken their most destructive human and natural toll in the states of the former socialist bloc and in revolutionary Third World settings, that is surely because there authoritarian state power, unimpeded by representative institutions, could nullify resistance and push ahead. The ideas behind them, however, on which their legitimacy and appeal depended, were thoroughly Western. Order and harmony that once seemed the function of a unitary God had been replaced by a similar faith in the idea of progress vouchsafed by scientists, engineers, and planners. Their power, it is worth remembering, was least contested at those moments when other forms of coordination had failed or seemed utterly inadequate to the great tasks at hand: in times of war, revolution, economic collapse, or newly won independence. The plans that they hatched bore a family resemblance to the schemes of legibility and standardization devised by the absolutist kings of the seventeenth and eighteenth centuries. What was wholly new, however, was the magnitude of both the plans for the wholesale transformation of society and the instruments of statecraft —censuses, cadastral maps, identity cards, statistical bureaus, schools, mass media, internal security apparatuses—that could take them farther along this road than any seventeenth-century monarch would have dreamed. Thus it has happened that so many of the twentieth century's political tragedies have flown the banner of progress, emancipation, and reform.

We have examined in considerable detail how these schemes have failed their intended beneficiaries. If I were asked to condense the reasons behind these failures into a single sentence, I would say that the progenitors of such plans regarded themselves as far smarter and farseeing than they really were and, at the same time, regarded their subjects as far more stupid and incompetent than *they* really were. The remainder of this chapter is devoted to expanding on this cursory judgment and advancing a few modest lessons.

"It's Ignorance, Stupid!"

> The mistake of our ancestors was to think that they were "the last number," but since numbers are infinite, they could not be the last number.
> —Eugene Zamiatin, *We*

The maxim that serves as the heading for this section is not simply suitable for bumper stickers mimicking the insider slogan of Bill Clinton's 1992 presidential campaign, "It's the economy, stupid!" It is meant to call attention to how routinely planners ignore the radical contingency of the future. How rare it is to encounter advice about the future which *begins* from a premise of incomplete knowledge. One small exception—a circular on nutrition published by the health clinic at Yale University, where I teach—will underscore its rarity. Normally, such circulars explain the major food groups, vitamins, and minerals known to be essential for balanced nutrition and advise a diet based on these categories. This circular, however, noted that many new, essential elements of proper nutrition had been discovered in the past two decades and that many more elements will presumably be identified by researchers in the decades ahead. Therefore, *on the basis of what they did not know*, the writers of this piece recommended that one's diet be as varied as possible, on the prudent assumption that it would contain many of these yet unidentified essentials.

Social and historical analyses have, almost inevitably, the effect of diminishing the contingency of human affairs. A historical event or state of affairs simply *is* the way it is, often appearing determined and necessary when in fact it might easily have turned out to be otherwise. Even a probabilistic social science, however careful it may be about establishing ranges of outcomes, is apt to treat these probabilities, for the sake of analysis, as solid facts. When it comes to betting on the future, the contingency is obvious, but so is the capacity of human actors to influence this contingency and help to shape the future. And in those cases where the bettors thought that they knew the shape of the future by virtue of their grasp of historical laws of progress or scientific truth, whatever awareness they retained of the contingency seemed to dissolve before their faith.

And yet each of these schemes, as might also have been predicted, was largely undone by a host of contingencies beyond the planners' grasp. The scope and comprehensiveness of their plans were such that they would have had indeterminate outcomes even if their historical laws and the attendant specification of variables and calculations had been correct. Their temporal ambitions meant that although they might, with some confidence, guess the immediate consequences of their moves, no one could specify, let alone calculate, the second- or third-order consequences or their interaction effects. The wild cards in their deck, however, were the human and natural events outside their models—droughts, wars, revolts, epidemics, interest rates, world consumer prices, oil embargoes. They could and did, of course, attempt to adjust and improvise in the face of these contingencies. But the magnitude of their initial intervention was so great that many of their missteps could not be righted. Stephen Marglin has put their problem succinctly: If "the only certainty about the future is that the future is uncertain, if the only sure thing is that we are in for surprises, then no amount of planning, no amount of prescription, can deal with the contingencies that the future will reveal."[1]

There is a curiously resounding unanimity on this point, and on no others, between such right-wing critics of the command economy as Friedrich Hayek and such left-wing critics of Communist authoritarianism as Prince Peter Kropotkin, who declared, "It is impossible to legislate for the future." Both had a great deal of respect for the diversity of human actions and the insurmountable difficulties in successfully coordinating millions of transactions. In a blistering critique of failed development paradigms, Albert Hirschman made a comparable case, calling for "a little more 'reverence for life,' a little less strait-jacketing of the future, a little more allowance for the unexpected—and a little less wishful thinking."[2]

One might, on the basis of experience, derive a few rules of thumb that, if observed, could make development planning less prone to disaster. While my main goal is hardly a point-by-point reform of development practice, such rules would surely include something along the following lines.

Take small steps. In an experimental approach to social change, presume that we cannot know the consequences of our interventions in advance. Given this postulate of ignorance, prefer wherever possible to take a small step, stand back, observe, and then plan the next small move. As the biologist J. B. S. Haldane metaphorically described the advantages of smallness: "You can drop a mouse down a thousand-yard mineshaft; and on arriving at the bottom, it gets a slight shock and walks away. A rat is killed, a man broken, a horse splashes."[3]

Favor reversibility. Prefer interventions that can easily be undone if they turn out to be mistakes.[4] Irreversible interventions have irreversible consequences.[5] Interventions into ecosystems require particular care in this respect, given our great ignorance about how they interact. Aldo Leopold captured the spirit of caution required: "The first rule of intelligent tinkering is to keep all the parts."[6]

Plan on surprises. Choose plans that allow the largest accommodation to the unforeseen. In agricultural schemes this may mean choosing and preparing land so that it can grow any of several crops. In planning housing, it would mean "designing in" flexibility for accommodating changes in family structures or living styles. In a factory it may mean selecting a location, layout, or piece of machinery that allows for new processes, materials, or product lines down the road.

Plan on human inventiveness. Always plan under the assumption that those who become involved in the project later will have or will develop the experience and insight to improve on the design.

Planning for Abstract Citizens

The power and precision of high-modernist schemes depended not only on bracketing contingency but also on standardizing the subjects of development. Some standardization was implicit even in the noblest goals of the planners. The great majority of them were strongly committed to a more egalitarian society, to meeting the basic needs of its citizens (especially the working class), and to making the amenities of a modern society available to all.

Let us pause, however, to consider the kind of human subject for whom all these benefits were being provided. This subject was singularly abstract. Figures as diverse as Le Corbusier, Walther Rathenau, the collectivizers of the Soviet Union, and even Julius Nyerere (for all his rhetorical attention to African traditions) were planning for generic subjects who needed so many square feet of housing space, acres of farmland, liters of clean water, and units of transportation and so much food, fresh air, and recreational space. Standardized citizens were uniform in their needs and even interchangeable. What is striking, of course, is that such subjects—like the "unmarked citizens" of liberal theory—have, for the purposes of the planning exercise, no gender, no tastes, no history, no values, no opinions or original ideas, no traditions, and no distinctive personalities to contribute to the enterprise. They have none of the particular, situated, and contextual attributes that one would expect of any population and that we, as a matter of course, always attribute to elites.

The lack of context and particularity is not an oversight; it is the necessary first premise of any large-scale planning exercise. To the degree that the subjects can be treated as standardized units, the power of resolution in the planning exercise is enhanced. Questions posed within these strict confines can have definitive, quantitative answers. The same logic applies to the transformation of the natural world. Questions about the volume of commercial wood or the yield of wheat in bushels permit more precise calculations than questions about, say, the quality of the soil, the versatility and taste of the grain, or the well-being of the community.[7] The discipline of economics achieves its formidable resolving power by transforming what might otherwise be considered qualitative matters into quantitative issues with a single metric and, as it were, a bottom line: profit or loss.[8] Providing one understands the heroic assumptions required to achieve this precision and the questions that it cannot answer, the single metric is an invaluable tool. Problems arise only when it becomes hegemonic.

What is perhaps most striking about high-modernist schemes, despite their quite genuine egalitarian and often socialist impulses, is how little confidence they repose in the skills, intelligence, and experience of ordinary people. This is clear enough in the Taylorist factory, where the logic of work organization is to reduce the factory hands' contribution to a series of repetitive, if practiced, movements—operations as machinelike as possible. But it is also clear in collectivized farms, ujamaa villages, and planned cities, where the movements of the populace have been to a large degree inscribed in the designs of these communities. If Nyerere's aspirations for cooperative state farming were frustrated, it was not because the plans had failed to integrate a scheme of cooperative labor. The more ambitious and meticulous the plan, the less is left, theoretically, to chance and to local initiative and experience.

Stripping Reality to Its Essentials

The quantitative technologies used to investigate social and economic life work best if the world they aim to describe can be remade in their image.
—Theodore M. Porter, *Trust in Numbers*

If the facts—that is, the behavior of living human beings—are recalcitrant to such an experiment, the experimenter becomes annoyed and tries to alter the facts to fit the theory, which, in practice, means a kind of vivisection of societies until they become what the theory originally declared that the experiment should have caused them to be.
—Isaiah Berlin, *"On Political Judgment"*

The clarity of the high-modernist optic is due to its resolute singularity. Its simplifying fiction is that, for any activity or process that comes under its scrutiny, there is only one thing going on. In the scientific forest there is only commercial wood being grown; in the planned city there is only the efficient movement of goods and people; in the housing estate there is only the effective delivery of shelter, heat, sewage, and water; in the planned hospital there is only the swift provision of professional medical services. And yet both we and the planners know that each of these sites is the intersection of a host of interconnected activities that defy such simple descriptions. Even something as apparently monofunctional as a road from *A* to *B* can at the same time function as a site for leisure, social intercourse, exciting diversions, and enjoying the view *between A* and *B*.[9]

For any such site, it is helpful to imagine two different maps of activity. In the case of a planned urban neighborhood, the first map consists of a representation of the streets and buildings, tracing the routes that the planners have provided for the movements between workplaces and residences, the delivery of goods, access to shopping, and so on. The second map consists of tracings, as in a time-lapse photograph, of all the *unplanned* movements—pushing a baby carriage, window shopping, strolling, going to see a friend, playing hopscotch on the sidewalk, walking the dog, watching the passing scene, taking shortcuts between work and home, and so on. This second map, far more complex than the first, reveals very different patterns of circulation. The older the neighborhood, the more likely that the second map will have nearly superseded the first, in roughly the same way that planned, suburban Levittowns have, after fifty years, become thoroughly different settings from what their designers envisioned.

If our inquiry has taught us anything, it is that the first map, taken alone, is misrepresentative and indeed nonsustainable. A same-age, monocropped forest with all the debris cleared is in the long run an ecological disaster. No Taylorist factory can sustain production without the unplanned improvisations of an experienced workforce. Planned Brasília is, in a thousand ways, underwritten by unplanned Brasília. Without at least some of the diversity identified by Jacobs, a stripped-down public housing project (like Pruitt-Igoe in Saint Louis or Cabrini Green in Chicago) will fail its residents. Even for the limited purposes of a myopic plan—commercial timber, factory output—the one-dimensional map will simply not do. As with industrial agriculture and its dependency on landraces, the first map is possible only because of processes lying outside its parameters, which it ignores at its peril.

Our inquiry has also taught us that such maps of legibility and control, especially when they are backed by an authoritarian state, *do* partly succeed in shaping the natural and social environment after their image. To the degree that such thin maps do manage to impress themselves on social life, what kind of people do they foster? Here I would argue that just as the monocropped, same-age forest represents an impoverished and unsustainable ecosystem, so the high-modernist urban complex represents an impoverished and unsustainable social system.

Human resistance to the more severe forms of social straitjacketing prevents monotonic schemes of centralized rationality from ever being realized. Had they been realized in their austere forms, they would have represented a very bleak human prospect. One of Le Corbusier's plans, for example, called for the segregation of factory workers and their families in barracks along the major transportation arteries. It was a theoretically efficient solution to transportation and production problems. If it had been imposed, the result would have been a dispiriting environment of regimented work and residence without any of the animation of town life. This plan had all the charm of a Taylorist scheme where, using a comparable logic, the efficient organization of work was achieved by confining the workers' movements to a few repetitive gestures. The cookie-cutter design principles behind the layout of the Soviet collective farm, the ujamaa village, or the Ethiopian resettlement betray the same narrowness of vision. They were designed, above all, to facilitate the central administration of production and the control of public life.

Almost all strictly functional, single-purpose institutions have some of the qualities of sensory-deprivation tanks used for experimental purposes. At the limit, they approach the great social control institutions of the eighteenth and nineteenth centuries: asylums, workhouses, prisons, and reformatories. We have learned enough of such settings to know that over time they can produce among their inmates a characteristic institutional neurosis marked by apathy, withdrawal, lack of initiative and spontaneity, uncommunicativeness, and intractability. The neurosis is an accommodation to a deprived, bland, monotonous, controlled environment that is ultimately stupifying.[10]

The point is simply that high-modernist designs for life and production tend to diminish the skills, agility, initiative, and morale of their intended beneficiaries. They bring about a mild form of this institutional neurosis. Or, to put it in the utilitarian terms that many of their partisans would recognize, these designs tend to reduce the "human capital" of the workforce. Complex, diverse, animated environments contribute, as Jacobs saw, to producing a resilient, flexible, adept population that has more experience in confronting novel challenges and taking initiative. Narrow, planned environments, by contrast, foster a less skilled, less innovative, less resourceful population. This population, once created, would ironically have been exactly the kind of human material that would in fact have needed close supervision from above. In other words, the logic of social engineering on this scale was to produce the sort of subjects that its plans had assumed at the outset.

That authoritarian social engineering failed to create a world after its own image should not blind us to the fact that it did, at the very least, damage many of the earlier structures of mutuality and practice that were essential to mētis. The Soviet kolkhoz hardly lived up to its expectations, but by treating its workforce more like factory hands than farmers, it did destroy many of the agricultural skills the peasantry had possessed on the eve of collectivization. Even if there was much in the earlier arrangements that ought to have been abolished (local tyrannies based on class, gender, age, and lineage), a certain institutional autonomy was abolished as well. Here, I believe, there is something to the classical anarchist claim—that the state, with its positive law and central institutions, undermines individuals' capacities for autonomous self-governance—that might apply to the planning grids of high modernism as well. Their own institutional legacy may be frail and evanescent, but they may impoverish the local wellsprings of economic, social, and cultural self-expression.

The Failure of Schematics and the Role of Mētis

> Everything is said to be under the leadership of the Party. No one is in charge
> of the crab or the fish, but they are all alive.
> —Vietnamese villager, *Xuan Huy village*

Not long after the decisive political opening in 1989, in what was then
still the Soviet Union, a congress of agricultural specialists was convened to consider reforms in agriculture. Most participants were in
favor of breaking up the collectives and privatizing the land in the hope
of recreating a modern version of the private sector that had thrived in
the 1920s and that Stalin had destroyed in 1930. And yet they were
nearly unanimous in their despair over what three generations had
done to the skills, initiative, and knowledge of the kolkhozniki. They
compared their situation unfavorably to that of China, where a mere
twenty-five years of collectivization had, they imagined, left much of
the entrepreneurial skill of the peasantry intact. Suddenly a woman
from Novosibirsk scolded them: "How do you think the rural people
survived sixty years of collectivization in the first place? If they hadn't
used their initiative and wits, they wouldn't have made it through!
They may need credit and supplies, but there's nothing wrong with
their initiative."[11]

Despite the manifold failures of collectivization, it seems, the kolkhozniki had found ways and means to at least get by. We should not
forget in this context that the first response to collectivization in 1930
was determined resistance and even rebellion. Once that resistance
was broken, the survivors had little choice but to comply outwardly.
They could hardly make the rural command economy a success, but
they could do what was necessary to meet minimal quotas and ensure
their own economic survival.

An indication of the kinds of improvisations both tolerated and required may be inferred from an astute case study of two East German
factories before the Wall came down in 1989.[12] Each factory was
under great pressure to meet production quotas—on which their all-
important bonuses depended—in spite of old machinery, inferior raw
materials, and a lack of spare parts. Under these draconian conditions,
two employees were indispensable to the firm, despite their modest
place in the official hierarchy. One was the jack-of-all-trades who improvised short-term solutions to keep machinery running, to correct or
disguise production flaws, and to make raw materials stretch further.
The second was a wheeler-dealer who located and bought or bartered
for spare parts, machinery, and raw material that could not be obtained
through official channels in time. To facilitate the wheeler-dealer's

work, the factory routinely used its funds to stock up on such valued nonperishable goods as soap powder, cosmetics, quality paper, yarn, good wine and champagne, medicines, and fashionable clothes. When it seemed that the plant would fall short of the quota because it lacked a key valve or machine tool, these knowledgeable dealers would set off across the country, their small Trabant autos jammed with barter goods, to secure what was needed. Neither of these roles was provided for in the official table of organization, and yet the survival of the factory depended more on their skills, wisdom, and experience than on those of any other employee. A key element in the centrally planned economy was underwritten, always unofficially, by mētis.

Cases like the one just described are the rule, not the exception. They serve to illustrate that the formal order encoded in social-engineering designs inevitably leaves out elements that are essential to their actual functioning. If the factory were forced to operate only within the confines of the roles and functions specified in the simplified design, it would quickly grind to a halt. Collectivized command economies virtually everywhere have limped along thanks to the often desperate improvisation of an informal economy wholly outside its schemata.

Stated somewhat differently, all socially engineered systems of formal order are in fact subsystems of a larger system on which they are ultimately dependent, not to say parasitic. The subsystem relies on a variety of processes—frequently informal or antecedent—which alone it cannot create or maintain. The more schematic, thin, and simplified the formal order, the less resilient and the more vulnerable it is to disturbances outside its narrow parameters. This analysis of high modernism, then, may appear to be a case for the invisible hand of market coordination as opposed to centralized economies. An important caution, however, is in order. The market is itself an instituted, formal system of coordination, despite the elbow room that it provides to its participants, and it is therefore similarly dependent on a larger system of social relations which its own calculus does not acknowledge and which it can neither create nor maintain. Here I have in mind not only the obvious elements of contract and property law, as well as the state's coercive power to enforce them, but antecedent patterns and norms of social trust, community, and cooperation, without which market exchange is inconceivable. Finally, and most important, the economy is "a subsystem of a finite and nongrowing eco-system," whose carrying capacity and interactions it must respect as a condition of its persistence.[13]

It is, I think, a characteristic of large, formal systems of coordination that they are accompanied by what appear to be anomalies but on closer inspection turn out to be integral to that formal order. Much of

this might be termed "mētis to the rescue," although for people ensnared in schemes of authoritarian social engineering that threaten to
do them in, such improvisations bear the mark of scrambling and des-
peration. Many modern cities, and not just those in the Third World,
function and survive by virtue of slums and squatter settlements whose
residents provide essential services. A formal command economy, as
we have seen, is contingent on petty trade, bartering, and deals that are
typically illegal. A formal economy of pension systems, social security,
and medical benefits is underwritten by a mobile, floating population
with few of these protections. Similarly, hybrid crops in mechanized
farm operations persist only because of the diversity and immunities of
antecedent landraces. In each case, the nonconforming practice is an
indispensable condition for formal order.

A Case for Mētis-Friendly Institutions

The invention of scientific forestry, freehold tenure, planned cities, collective farms, ujamaa villages, and industrial agriculture, for all their
ingeniousness, represented fairly simple interventions into enormously
complex natural and social systems. After being abstracted from systems whose interactions defied a total accounting, a few elements were
then made the basis for an imposed order. At best, the new order was
fragile and vulnerable, sustained by improvisations not foreseen by its
originators. At worst, it wreaked untold damage in shattered lives, a
damaged ecosystem, and fractured or impoverished societies.

This rather blanket condemnation must be tempered, especially in
the case of social systems, by at least four considerations. First, and
most important, the social orders they were designed to supplant were
typically so manifestly unjust and oppressive that almost any new order
might seem preferable. Second, high-modernist social engineering usually came cloaked in egalitarian, emancipatory ideas: equality before
the law, citizenship for all, and rights to subsistence, health, education,
and shelter. The premise and great appeal of the high-modernist credo
was that the state would make the benefits of technological progress
available to all its citizens.

The two remaining reasons for tempering our condemnation of
such schemes have less to do with their potentially destructive consequences than with the capacity of ordinary human actors to modify
them or, in the end, to bring them down. Where functioning representative institutions were at hand, some accommodation was inevitable.
In their absence, it is still remarkable how the dogged, day-to-day re-

sistance of thousands of citizens forced the abandonment or restructuring of projects. Given sufficient time and leeway, of course, any high-modernist plan will be utterly remade by popular practice. Soviet collective farms, the most draconian case, were finally brought down as much by the dispirited work and resistance of the kolkhozniki as by the political shifts in Moscow.

Without denying the incontestable benefits either of the division of labor or of hierarchical coordination for some tasks, I want to make a case for institutions that are instead multifunctional, plastic, diverse, and adaptable—in other words, institutions that are powerfully shaped by mētis. The fact that those ensnared in confining systems of formal order seem constantly to be working, in their own interest, to make the systems more versatile is one indication of a common process of "social domestication." A second indication is the social magnetism of autonomy and diversity as seen, for example, in the popularity of Jacobs's mixed-use neighborhoods and in the continued attraction of self-employment.

Diversity and certain forms of complexity, apart from their attractiveness, have other advantages. In natural systems, we know, these advantages are manifold. Old-growth forests, polycropping, and agriculture with open-pollinated landraces *may* not be as productive, in the short run, as single-species forests and fields or identical hybrids. But they are demonstrably more stable, more self-sufficient, and less vulnerable to epidemics and environmental stress, needing far less in the way of external infusions to keep them on track. Every time we replace "natural capital" (such as wild fish stocks or old-growth forests) with what might be called "cultivated natural capital" (such as fish farms or tree plantations), we gain in ease of appropriation and in immediate productivity, but at the cost of more maintenance expenses and less "redundancy, resiliency, and stability."[14] If the environmental challenges faced by such systems are both modest and predictable, then a certain simplification might also be relatively stable.[15] Other things being equal, however, the less diverse the cultivated natural capital, the more vulnerable and nonsustainable it becomes. The problem is that in most economic systems, the external costs (in water or air pollution, for example, or the exhaustion of nonrenewable resources, including a reduction in biodiversity) accumulate long before the activity becomes unprofitable in a narrow profit-and-loss sense.

A roughly similar case can be made, I think, for human institutions —a case that contrasts the fragility of rigid, single-purpose, centralized institutions to the adaptability of more flexible, multipurpose, decentralized social forms. As long as the task environment of an institution remains repetitive, stable, and predictable, a set of fixed routines may prove exceptionally efficient. In most economies and in human affairs generally, this is seldom the case, and such routines are likely to be counterproductive once the environment changes appreciably. The long-term survival of certain human institutions—the family, the small community, the small farm, the family firm in certain businesses—is something of a tribute to their adaptability under radically changing circumstances. They are by no means infinitely adaptable, but they have weathered more than one prediction of their inevitable demise. The small family farm, by virtue of its flexible labor (including the exploitation of its children), its capacity to shift into new crops or livestock, and its tendency to diversify its risks, has managed to persist in competitive economies when many huge, highly leveraged, mechanized, and specialized corporate and state farms have failed.[16] In a sector of the economy where local knowledge, quick responses to weather and crop conditions, and low overhead (smallness) are more important than in, say, large industry, the family farm has some formidable advantages.

Even in huge organizations, diversity pays dividends in stability and resilience. A one-product city like the Stalinist steel-making jewel of Magnitogorsk is vulnerable when its technology is superseded and more specialty products are required, whereas a nonspecialized city with a host of industries and a diverse labor force can weather greater shocks. Within the most industrialized economies, it is still striking that complex and often low-income subsistence strategies, self-provisioning, and working off the books are both widespread and essential, although they are nearly invisible in most forms of economic accounting.[17] Much has also been made of the rather complex family firms in Emilia-Romagna, Italy, which have thrived for generations in an extremely competitive world textile market by virtue of networks of mutuality, adaptability, and a highly skilled and committed workforce. The family firms are at the same time embedded in a much-studied local society that is several centuries deep in associational life and civic skills.[18] These firms and the dense, diverse societies upon which they depend have increasingly seemed less like archaic survivals and more like forms of enterprise ideally suited to postindustrial capitalism. Even within the narrow confines of market competitiveness in liberal industrial societies, the case for polyvalent, adaptive, small units is stronger than any high modernist of the 1920s could possibly have imagined.

Once we measure such polyvalent institutions by broader criteria, moreover, the case becomes even more powerful. Much of the argument at this level comes back to the question posed earlier: what kind of person does this sort of institution foster? No one has established the link between economic enterprise and political skills better than Thomas Jefferson in his celebration of the yeoman farmer. The autonomy and the skills required in independent farming, Jefferson believed, helped to nurture a citizen with a habit of responsible decision making, enough property to avoid social dependence, and a tradition of reasoning and negotiation with his fellow citizens. The yeomanry was, in short, an ideal training ground for democratic citizenship.

To any planned, built, or legislated form of social life, one may apply a comparable test: to what degree does it promise to enhance the skills, knowledge, and responsibility of those who are a part of it? On narrower institutional grounds, the question would be how deeply that form is marked by the values and experience of those who compose it. The purpose in each case would be to distinguish "canned" situations that permit little or no modification from situations largely open to the development and application of mētis.

A brief example comparing war memorials may be helpful. The Vietnam Memorial in Washington, D.C., is surely one of the most successful war memorials ever built, if one is to judge by the quantity and intensity of the visits it receives. Designed by Maya Lin, the memorial consists simply of a gently undulating site marked (not dominated) by a long, low, black marble wall listing the names of the fallen. The names are listed neither alphabetically nor by military unit but chronologically, in the order in which they fell—thus grouping those who had fallen on the same day in the same engagement.[19] No larger claim is made about the war either in prose or in sculpture—which is hardly surprising, in view of the stark political cleavages the war still inspires.[20] What is most remarkable, however, is the way that the Vietnam Memorial works for those who visit it, particularly those who come to pay their respects to the memory of a comrade or loved one. They touch the names incised on the wall, make rubbings, and leave artifacts and mementos of their own—everything from poems and a woman's high-heeled shoe to a glass of champagne and a poker hand of a full house, aces high. So many of these tributes have been left, in fact, that a museum has been created to house them. The scene of many people together at the wall, touching the names of particular loved ones who fell in the same war, has moved observers regardless of their position on the war itself. I believe that a great part of the memorial's symbolic power is its capacity to honor the dead with an openness that allows visitors to impress upon it their own meanings, their own histories, their own memories. The memorial virtually requires participation in order to complete its meaning. Although one would not compare it to a Rorschach test, the memorial nevertheless does achieve its meaning as much by what citizens bring to it as by what it imposes.

Compare the Vietnam Memorial to a very different American war memorial: the sculpture depicting the raising of the American flag at the summit of Mount Suribachi on Iwo Jima in World War II. Moving in its own right, referring as it does to the final moment of a victory gained at an enormous cost in lives, the Iwo Jima statue is manifestly heroic. Its patriotism (symbolized by the flag), its reference to conquest, its larger-than-life scale, and its implicit theme of unity in victory leave little room for wondering what is expected from the viewer. Given the virtual unanimity with which that war was, and is, viewed in the United States, it is hardly surprising that the Iwo Jima memorial should be monumental and explicit about its message. Although not exactly "canned," the Iwo Jima site is more symbolically self-sufficient, as are most war memorials. Visitors can stand in awe, gazing on an image that through photographs and sculpture has become a virtual icon for the War in the Pacific, but they receive its message rather than completing it.[21]

An institution, social form, or enterprise that takes much of its shape from the evolving mētis of the people engaged in it will thereby enhance their range of experience and skills. Following the advice of the saying "Use it or lose it," the mētis-friendly institution both uses and renews a valuable public good. As an exclusive litmus test for all social forms, this is clearly insufficient. All social forms are "artificially" constructed to serve some human purpose. Where that purpose is narrow, simple, and invariable over time, it may well be that codified, hierarchical routines are adequate and possibly the most efficient in the short run. Even in such cases, however, we should be aware of the human costs of stultifying routines and the likely resistance to rote performance.

Whenever, on the contrary, the quality of the institution and its product depends on engaging the enthusiastic participation of its people, then such a litmus test makes sense. In the case of housing, for example, its success cannot be severed from the opinions of its users. Housing planners that take as a given the variety of human tastes and the inevitable (but unpredictable) changes in the shape of families will accommodate that variation from the outset by providing flexible building designs and adjustable floor plans. Developers of neighborhoods, by the same token, will promote the sort of diversity and complexity that will help to ensure their vitality and durability. Above all, those with planning and zoning powers will not see their task as one of making sure that neighborhoods hold, through thick and thin, to their designed forms. One can imagine many types of institutions—schools, parks, playgrounds, civic associations, business enterprises, families, even planning bodies—that might well be evaluated through the same lens.

A good many institutions in liberal democracies already take such a form and may serve as exemplars for fashioning new ones. One could say that democracy itself is based on the assumption that the mētis of its citizenry should, in mediated form, continually modify the laws and policies of the land. Common law, as an institution, owes its longevity to the fact that it is not a final codification of legal rules, but rather a set of procedures for continually adapting some broad principles to novel circumstances. Finally, that most characteristic of human institutions, language, is the best model: a structure of meaning and continuity that is never still and ever open to the improvisations of all its speakers.

Notes

Chapter 1: Nature and Space

1. Henry E. Lowood, "The Calculating Forester: Quantification, Cameral Science, and the Emergence of Scientific Forestry Management in Germany," in Tore Frangsmyr, J. L. Heilbron, and Robin E. Rider, eds., *The Quantifying Spirit in the Eighteenth Century* (Berkeley: University of California Press, 1991), pp. 315–42. The following account is largely drawn from Lowood's fine analysis.

2. The most striking exception was the royal attention to the supply of "noble game" (e.g., deer, boars, foxes) for the hunt and hence to the protection of its habitat. Lest one imagine this to be a quaint premodern affectation, it is worth recalling the enormous social importance of the hunt to such recent "monarchs" as Erich Honeker, Nicolae Ceaușescu, Georgy Zhuvkov, Władysław Gomułka, and Marshal Tito.

3. John Evelyn, *Sylva, or A Discourse of Forest Trees* (London, 1664, 1679), p. 118, cited in John Brinckerhoff Jackson, *A Sense of Place, a Sense of Time* (New Haven: Yale University Press, 1994), pp. 97–98.

4. Ramachandra Guha reminds me that the verb "ignore" is inadequate here, for the state typically sought to control, regulate, and extinguish those practices that interfered with its own management policies. For much of my (admittedly limited) early education in the history of forestry, I am grateful to Ramachandra Guha and his two books, *The Unquiet Woods: Ecological Change and Peasant Resistance in the Himalaya* (Berkeley: University of California Press, 1989), and, with Madhav Gadgil, *This Fissured Land: An Ecological History of India* (Delhi: Oxford University Press, 1992). For an evocative and wide-ranging exploration of the changing cultural meaning of the forest in the West, see Robert Pogue Harrison, *Forests: The Shadow of Civilization* (Chicago: University of Chicago Press, 1992).

5. Harrison, *Forests*, p. 121.

6. This last is a kind of twist on the Heisenberg principle. Instead of altering the phenomenon observed through the act of observation, so that the pre-observation state of the phenomenon is unknowable in principle, the effect of (interested) obser-

vation in this case is to alter the phenomenon in question over time so that it, in fact, more closely resembles the stripped down, abstract image the lens had revealed.

7. See Keith Tribe, *Governing Economy: The Reformation of German Economic Discourse, 1750–1840* (Cambridge: Cambridge University Press, 1988). The more general process of codifying the principles of state administration in seventeenth- and eighteenth-century Europe is examined by Michel Foucault under the (misleading) heading of "police state" (from *Polizeiwissenschaft*) in his lectures on "governmentality," delivered at the Collège de France. See Graham Burchell, Colin Gordon, and Peter Miller, eds., *The Foucault Effect: Studies in Governmentality* (London: Harvester Wheatsheaf, 1991), especially chap. 4.

8. In the late seventeenth century, Jean-Baptiste Colbert had extensive plans to "rationalize" forest administration in order both to prevent poaching and to generate a more reliable revenue yield. To this end, Etienne Dralet's *Traité du régime forestier* proposed regulated plots (*tire-aire*) "so that the growth is regular and easy to guard." Despite these initiatives, nothing much came of it in France until 1820, when the new German techniques were imported. See Peter Sahlins, *Forest Rites: The War of the Demoiselles in Nineteenth-Century France*, Harvard Historical Studies no. 115 (Cambridge: Harvard University Press, 1994.

9. ·Lowood, "The Calculating Forester," p. 338.

10. Various techniques were tried, including cutting an actual tree into bits and then compressing them to find the volume of the tree, and putting wood in a barrel of known volume and adding measured amounts of water to calculate the volume of the barrel *not* occupied by the wood (ibid., p. 328).

11. The utilitarian framework could, in principle, have been used to emphasize some other calculable "end" of the forest—e.g., game populations, mast-quality timber, or grazing acreage. Where several agencies superintending the forest have conflicting utilitarian agendas, the result can be incoherence and room for the local population to maneuver. See the fine study by K. Sivaramakrishnan, "Forests, Politics, and Governance in Bengal, 1794–1994" (Ph.D. diss., Department of Anthropology, Yale University, 1996).

12. I was tempted to add that, with regard to the use of forests, the view of the state might be longer and broader than that of private firms, which can, and have, plundered old-growth forests and then sold their acreage or surrendered it for back taxes (e.g., the "cutover" in the Upper Midwest of the United States at the turn of the century). The difficulty is that in cases of war or a fiscal crisis, the state often takes an equally shortsighted view.

13. Lowood, "The Calculating Forester," p. 341. See also Harrison, *Forests*, pp. 122–23.

14. The recent cloning of tree stock to produce genetically uniform members of a given species is a yet more dramatic step in the direction of uniformity and control.

15. One of the innovations such experimentation gave rise to was "financial rotation." Close attention to annual rates of growth over the life of a pure stand and the surer knowledge about timber yields enabled foresters to calculate precisely the point at which the added value of another year of growth was exceeded by the added value (minus the amortized cost of earlier felling and replanting) of new growth. The precision was, of course, predicated on the comparisons made possible by the assumption of homogeneous units of timber and market prices.

16. The term "redesigned" is adopted from Chris Maser's valuable book, *The Redesigned Forest* (San Pedro: R. and E. Miles, 1988). Much of his argument can be inferred from the oppositions he emphasizes in the headings of the early sections: "Nature designed a forest as an experiment in unpredictability. . . . We are trying to

design a regulated forest"; "Nature designed a forest of long-term trends. . . . We are trying to design a forest of short-term absolutes"; "Nature designed a forest with diversity. . . . We are designing a forest with simplistic uniformity"; "Nature designed a forest with interrelated processes. . . . We are trying to design a forest based on isolated products" (p. vii).

17. See, for example, Honoré de Balzac's *Les paysans* (Paris: Pleiades, 1949); E. P. Thompson, *Whigs and Hunters: The Origin of the Black Act* (New York: Pantheon, 1975); Douglas Hay, "Poaching on Cannock Chase," in Douglas Hay et al., eds., *Albion's Fatal Tree* (New York: Pantheon, 1975); and Steven Hahn, "Hunting, Fishing, and Foraging: Common Rights and Class Relations in the Postbellum South," *Radical History Review* 26 (1982): 37–64. For an apposite German case, see one of Karl Marx's first published articles linking the theft of wood to the business cycle and unemployment in the Rhineland: reported in Peter Linebaugh, "Karl Marx, the Theft of Wood, and Working-Class Composition: A Contribution to the Current Debate," *Crime and Social Justice*, Fall-Winter 1976, pp. 5–16.

18. The results of three rotations might require as much as two hundred years, or the working lives of perhaps six foresters, to observe. Compare this with, say, the results of three rotations of maize, which would require only three years. For most contemporary forests, the results of the third rotation are not yet in. In forest experimentation, the experimental period easily stretches well beyond a single lifetime. See Maser, *The Redesigned Forest*.

19. There was within Germany a debate between the utilitarian outlook I have described and an anti-utilitarian, anti-Manchester School stream of thought represented by, among others, Karl Geyer, an exponent of the *Mischwald* and natural regeneration. But the short-run success of the utilitarians ensured that their view became the hegemonic "export model" of German scientific forestry. I am grateful to Arvid Nelson for this information and for sharing his deep knowledge about the history of forest policy in Germany. In 1868, Deitrich Brandes, the German chief of colonial India's forests, proposed a plan that would have encouraged community forests as well as state production forests, but the first part of his plan was vetoed by British administrators. The interests of state officials, it appears, tended to select out of the mixed heritage of German forestry those elements most favorable to legibility, management, and revenue.

20. Pinchot toured Prussian and Swiss forests after his studies in Nancy. Carl Schenk, the founder of the first forestry school in the United States, was a German immigrant trained in German universities, and Bernhard Fernow, the chief of the federal government's forestry division from 1886 to 1898 (before Pinchot), was a graduate of the Prussian Forest Academy at Meunden. I am grateful to Carl Jacoby for this information.

21. For a detailed and analytically searching account of colonial forest policy in India, see Sivaramakrishnan, "Forests, Politics, and Governance in Bengal." In chap. 6 he shows how three principles of scientific forestry—that pure stands of commercial timber did better than mixed stands, that fire was a destructive factor to be avoided, and that grazing or firewood collecting could only threaten the forest management program—were overthrown by accumulating evidence in India.

22. Richard Plochmann, *Forestry in the Federal Republic of Germany*, Hill Family Foundation Series (Corvallis: Oregon State University School of Forestry, 1968), pp. 24–25; quoted in Maser, *The Redesigned Forest*, pp. 197–98. The elided sentences, for those interested in the specific interactions, continue: "A spruce stand may serve as an example. Our spruce roots are normally very shallow. Planted on former hardwood soil, the spruce roots could follow the deep root channels of the former hardwoods in the first generation. But in the second gen-

eration the root systems turned shallow on account of progressive soil compaction. As a result, the available nutrient supply for the trees became smaller. The spruce stand could profit from the mild humus accumulated in the first generation by the hardwoods, but it was not able to produce a mild humus itself. Spruce litter rots much more slowly than broadleaf litter and is much more difficult for the fauna and flora of the upper soil layer to decompose. Therefore a raw humus developed in most cases. Its humic acids started to leach the soil under our humid climate and impoverished the soil fauna and flora. This caused an even poorer decomposition and a faster development of raw humus." Plochmann points out that the process in pine plantations is roughly similar. I have confirmed this pattern with David Smith of Yale's School of Forestry and Environmental Studies, author of *The Practice of Silviculture*, an important reference on modern forestry techniques. For a similar account of how the techniques of scientific forestry, particularly its aversion to fire and its preference for monoculture, negatively affected forest health and production, see Nancy Langston, *Forest Dreams, Forest Nightmares: The Paradox of Old Growth in the Inland West* (Seattle: University of Washington Press, 1995).

23. "When snags are removed from short-rotation stands, 10% of the wildlife species (excluding birds) will be eliminated; 29% of the wildlife species will be eliminated when both snags and fallen trees (logs) are removed from intensively managed young growth forests. As pieces are continually removed from the forest with the notion of the simplistic uniformity that is termed 'intensive timber management,' we come closer to the ultimate simplistic view of modern forestry—the plantation or 'Christmas tree farm'" (Maser, *The Redesigned Forest*, p. 19).

24. The key step in this process seems to be the below-ground, symbiotic fungus-root structures (mycorrhizal association) studied closely by Sir Albert Howard. See chapter 7.

25. Some of the pests in question included the "pine looper moth, pine beauty, pine moth, Nun moth, saw flies, bark beetles, pine needle cast fungus, pine bluster rust, honey fungus, red rot" (Maser, *The Redesigned Forest*, p. 78).

26. For a brief description of these practices, see Rachel Carson, *Silent Spring* (Boston: Houghton Mifflin, 1962, 1987). Carson praised these advances because they seemed to herald the use of biological controls rather than pesticides.

27. The untoward consequences of engineering a forest in order to maximize the production of a single commodity is by now a worldwide experience. After World War II, Japan adopted a policy of replacing many of the forests that had been plundered for fuelwood and building materials with a single species: the Japanese cedar, selected for its rapid growth and commercial value. Now it is clear that the miles of tall, slender, uniform cedars have caused heavy soil erosion and landslides, have reduced the water table, and are easily felled by storms. They allow little sunlight to filter through to the forest floor and provide little protection or food for fauna. For urban Japanese, the chief short-term inconvenience of the cedars is their seasonal massive release of pollen, which triggers severe allergic responses. But allergies are just the most manifest symptom of the deeper consequences of such radical simplification. See James Sterngold, "Japan's Cedar Forests Are a Man-Made Disaster," *New York Times*, January 17, 1995, pp. C1, C10.

28. Maser, *The Redesigned Forest*, pp. 54–55. The "commodity" in question in a great many contemporary forests is not wood per se but pulp for making paper. This has led, in turn, to the genetic engineering of species and cloned stock that will produce the ideal quality and quantity of pulp.

29. In the context of welfare economics, the practice of scientific forestry was able to externalize a large number of costs to the community at large which did not

appear on its own balance sheet: e.g., soil depletion, loss of water retention capacity and water quality, reduction of game, and loss of biodiversity.

30. Plochmann, *Forestry in the Federal Republic of Germany*, p. 25. There are, of course, naturally occurring pure stands of timber, usually in constrained ecological conditions, including, diagnostically, those found on severely degraded sites. For a range of views on this issue, see Matthew J. Kelty, Bruce C. Larson, and Chadwick D. Oliver, eds., *The Ecology and Silviculture of Mixed-Species Forests: A Festschrift for David W. Smith* (Dordrecht and Boston: Kluwer Academic Publishing, 1992).

31. Nancy Langston has a more global assessment: "Everyone who has ever tried to fix the forests has ended up making them worse" (*Forest Dreams, Forest Nightmares*, p. 2).

32. The brief description that follows is drawn largely from James B. Collins, *Fiscal Limits of Absolutism: Direct Taxation in Early Seventeenth-Century France* (Berkeley: University of California Press, 1988).

33. P. M. Jones, *The Peasantry in the French Revolution* (Cambridge: Cambridge University Press, 1988), p. 17.

34. Collins, *Fiscal Limits of Absolutism*, pp. 201, 204. It was precisely this capacity for evading taxes that gave the fiscal regime a degree of unintended (from the top, at least) flexibility and helped states to avoid even more rebellion in the troubled seventeenth century.

35. J. L. Heilbron notes that in 1791 an English colonel in the militia obliged the Scottish clergy to send him inventories of their population by threatening to quarter troops in their parish (introduction to Tore Frangsmyr, J. L. Heilbron, and Robin E. Rider, eds., *The Quantifying Spirit in the Eighteenth Century* [Berkeley: University of California Press, 1991], p. 13).

36. This assumes that the crown wanted to maximize its proceeds in the long run. It was and is common, of course, for regimes in political or military crises to mortgage their futures by squeezing as much as possible from their forests or their subjects. See, in this context, the superb analytical synthesis of Charles Tilly, *Coercion, Capital, and European States, A.D. 990–1992* (Oxford: Blackwell, 1990), who stresses the influence of preparation for war and war-making in state formation and describes the transition from "tributary" states to states that extract directly from citizens.

37. Witold Kula, *Measures and Men*, trans. R. Szreter (Princeton: Princeton University Press, 1986).

38. J. L. Heilbron, "The Measure of Enlightenment," in Tore Frangsmyr, J. L. Heilbron, and Robin E. Rider, eds., *The Quantifying Spirit in the Eighteenth Century* (Berkeley: University of California Press, 1991), pp. 207–8.

39. For an illuminating discussion along these lines, see Arjun Appadurai, "Measurement Discourse in Rural Maharastra," in Appadurai et al., *Agriculture, Language, and Knowledge in South Asia: Perspectives from History and Anthropology* (forthcoming).

40. Ibid., p. 14.

41. The same motive was at work in the folk categories of stratification used by Javanese villagers: the *Kekurangans* (those-who-have-less-than-enough) and the *Kecukupans* (those-who-have-enough). See Clifford Geertz, *Agricultural Involution* (Berkeley: University of California Press, 1963).

42. What was seen as customary might not have had a very long pedigree. It was always in the interests of at least one party, who feared a disadvantageous renegotiation, to treat the existing arrangement as fixed and sacrosanct.

43. Occasionally, the balance of power might swing in the other direction. See,

in this connection, the evidence for a long decline in tithe payments in France: Emmanuel LeRoi Ladurie and Joseph Gay, *Tithe and Agrarian History from the Fourteenth Century to the Nineteenth Century: An Essay in Comparative History*, trans. Susan Burke (Cambridge: Cambridge University Press, 1982), p. 27.

44. Kula, *Measures and Men*, p. 150. In Lower Burma in the 1920s and '30s, the landlord's paddy basket for receiving tenants' rent in kind was nicknamed "the cartbreaker" (James C. Scott, *The Moral Economy of the Peasant: Rebellion and Subsistence in Southeast Asia* [New Haven: Yale University Press, 1976], p. 71).

45. The famous iron *toise* of Paris, for example, was set in one of the walls of the Grand Chatelet; see Ken Alder, "A Revolution Made to Measure: The Political Economy of the Metric System in France," in Norton W. Wise, ed., *Values of Precision* (Princeton: Princeton University Press, 1995), p. 44.

46. Marsenne, in the seventeenth-century spirit of exactitude, calculated that a striked boisseau held 172,000 grains of wheat, whereas a heaped measure held 220,160 (Kula, *Measures and Men*, p. 172). The advantage with oats, a larger grain, is less.

47. Ibid., pp. 73–74. As with the other challenges to customary measures, this one provoked municipal authorities and the populace to insist on weighing and measuring, in this case bakers' loaves, to prevent such practices.

48. Ibid., pp. 98–99.

49. Ibid., p. 173.

50. It was, in fact, the active evasion of regions that were fiscally hard-pressed that provided the "drag" or gyroscope that often prevented an ill-considered tax claim from provoking an actual resistance.

51. As Ken Alder points out, the absence of a central authority that could impose standardization does not seem to have impeded the growth of national markets in Britain, Germany, or the United States ("A Revolution Made to Measure," p. 62). Mobility and economic growth alone seem to produce common standards of exchange. For a more general historical treatment, see Frank J. Swetz, *Capitalism and Arithmetic: The New Math of the Fifteenth Century* (La Salle, Ill.: Open Court, 1987).

52. Quoted in Kula, *Measures and Men*, pp. 203–4.

53. Alder, "A Revolution Made to Measure," p. 48.

54. Ibid., p. 54.

55. Ibid., p. 56. The meter was only one shell in a barrage of measurement reforms. For a time, there was a concerted effort to divide the day into ten hours of one hundred minutes, with each minute containing one hundred seconds, as well as an initiative to create a duodecimal, or base-twelve, system of numbers.

56. Ibid., pp. 122–23.

57. I believe that the recent impassioned debate in France about whether Muslim schoolgirls should be allowed to wear head scarves in class was about preserving this tradition of the unmarked citizen in secular education.

58. Alder, "A Revolution Made to Measure," p. 211.

59. As Tony Judt has astutely noted, the difference between citizens' rights as established by revolutionary decrees and natural or individual rights is that the former are in principle contingent on the state and its law and hence revocable by statute, whereas the latter are in principle unabridgeable. See Judt, *Past Imperfect: French Intellectuals, 1944–1956* (Berkeley: University of California Press, 1992).

60. The revolutionary conception of citizenship in France swept away the legal impediments under which the Jewish community had labored. Wherever French armies penetrated after the Revolution and in the Napoleonic conquests, their arrival was accompanied by the extension of full citizenship to Jews. See Pierre Birn-

baum and Ira Katznelson, eds., *Paths of Emancipation: Jews, States, and Citizenship* (Princeton: Princeton University Press, 1995).

61. Gianfranco Poggi, *The Development of the Modern State: A Sociological Introduction* (Stanford: Stanford University Press, 1978), p. 78. For all the advance in human rights that equal citizenship carried with it, it is worth recalling that this momentous step also undercut the intermediary structures between the state and the citizen and gave the state, for the first time, direct access to its subjects. Equal citizenship implied not only legal equality and universal male suffrage but also universal conscription, as those mobilized into Napoleon's armies were shortly to discover. From the heights of the state, the society below increasingly appeared as an endless series of nationally equal *particuliers* with whom it dealt in their capacity as subjects, taxpayers, and potential military draftees.

62. Quoted in Kula, *Measures and Men*, p. 286.

63. As E. P. Thompson wrote in *Whigs and Hunters: The Origin of the Black Act* (New York: Pantheon, 1975): "During the eighteenth century one legal decision after another signaled that the lawyers had become converted to notions of absolute property ownership, and that (wherever the least doubt could be found) the law abhorred the messy complexities of coincident use-right" (p. 241).

64. The *code civil* did not deal with agriculture explicitly, with one exception: it specified guidelines for tenant farming (*fermage*), in recognition of the wealthy and influential large tenants in the Paris basin and to the north. I am grateful to Peter Jones for bringing to my attention the study on which this brief discussion is based: Serge Aberdam, *Aux origines du code rural, 1789–1900: Un siècle de débat* (n.d., but probably 1978–80).

65. "En resumé, la ligne genérale du projet de 1807 est de refuser toute specificité au droit rural en ramenant, autant que possible, les rapports socieux a la campagne à la forme d'authorité légale que la bourgeoisie projette sur l'ensemble de la population" (In brief, the general policy of the proposal of 1807 is to deny any particularity to rural law, placing rural social relations as much as possible in the context of the legal authority that the bourgeoisie applied to the population as a whole [my translation]; ibid., p. 19).

66. No such political scruples were in evidence in the colonies, where administrative convenience and commercial logic prevailed over popular opinion and practice. See, for example, the fine case study by Dennis Galvan, "Land Pawning as a Response to the Standardization of Tenure," chap. 4 of "The State Is Now Master of Fire: Peasant Lore, Land Tenure, and Institutional Adaptation in the Siin Region of Senegal" (Ph.D. diss., Department of Political Science, University of California, Berkeley, 1996).

67. Ibid., p. 18.

68. Ibid., p. 22.

69. In colonial Vietnam, the head tax, or capitation, was levied on whole communities on the basis of their presumed population. If the sum were not remitted, the police would come and hold an auction of whatever they could seize (e.g., water buffalos, furniture, jewelry) until they had the required sum. This system gave the village notables, who owned most of the goods worth seizing, an incentive to make sure that the taxes were remitted on time.

70. This generalization also has validity for modern socialist forms of collective farming. A considerable amount of farmland, for example, "disappeared" from the books when Hungary's collective farms were created; see Istvan Rev, "The Advantages of Being Atomized: How Hungarian Peasants Coped with Collectivization," *Dissent* 34 (Summer 1987): 335–49. In China, after the deadly Great Leap Forward, many collective farms systematically hid production from central authorities

in the interest of local survival; see Daniel Kelliher, *Peasant Power in China* (New Haven: Yale University Press, 1992).

71. Cadastral surveys might also be undertaken by aristocratic holders of large fiefs who were convinced that they could thereby uncover taxable land and subjects who had hitherto eluded them.

72. Both the Danish and Norwegian examples are from the valuable historical analysis in Roger J. P. Kain and Elizabeth Baigent, *The Cadastral Map in the Service of the State: A History of Property Mapping* (Chicago: University of Chicago Press, 1992), p. 116.

73. The great efficiency of the Hutterite grain farmers in the northern Plains states and Canada is but one of many pieces of conflicting evidence. For more, see George Yaney, *The Urge to Mobilize: Agrarian Reform in Russia* (Urbana: University of Illinois Press, 1982), pp. 165–69.

74. A contemporary example from Mexico can be found in a fine analysis by Sergio Zendejas in "Contested Appropriation of Governmental Reforms in the Mexican Countryside: The *Ejido* as an Arena of Confrontation of Political Practices," in Sergio Zendejas and Pieter de Vries, eds., *Rural Transformation as Seen from Below: Regional and Local Perspectives from Western Mexico* (La Jolla, Calif.: Center for U.S.-Mexican Studies, University of California, San Diego, 1997). As Zendejas shows, the ejido system emerging from the Mexican revolution has had the effect of depriving the state of a great deal of knowledge about agricultural patterns, house lots, or village common-land tenure in most of the twenty-eight thousand ejidos in the country. Michoacán villagers have regarded a national program to survey, register, and title every plot of rural land as a prelude to the individualization of property rights, the division of the common lands, and the imposition of property taxes, and they have therefore resisted having their lands measured. Under the changes made to article 27 of the constitution, which envisions a national, freehold land market, their fears have proven justified. It has not been a question of establishing local land markets; as one villager said, "Haven't we always been selling and renting [ejido] parcels with or without certificates?" It has been, rather, a question of creating a regional and national market for land, backed by state power. To do this, the first task of the state has been to make legible a tenure landscape that the local autonomy achieved by the revolution had helped make opaque. See also, in this context, Luin Goldring, *Having One's Cake and Eating It, Too: Selective Appropriation of Ejido Reform in an Urbanizing Ejido in Michoacán* (forthcoming).

75. Here I am guilty of conveying a false sense of uniformity. In fact, there were a host of land arrangements, even in "black earth" Russia, and many villages did not redistribute land (Yaney, *The Urge to Mobilize*, p. 169).

76. Ibid., p. 212.

77. Yaney points out that Mennonite land that was interstripped was just as productive as Mennonite land that was organized into consolidated farms (ibid., p. 160).

78. And not always in such newly settled lands, inasmuch as *group* land settlement, with common property and against the government's wishes, was also common.

79. Ibid., chaps. 7 and 8. The Peasant Bank, under great pressure to loan money to poor peasants, inadvertently encouraged the older allotment system. The bank needed collateral that it could seize in the event of default, but poorer peasants farming allotment land had no fixed land that could serve as security. Faced with this quandary, the bank found itself loaning to whole villages or to groups of peasants farming adjacent, identifiable plots. It is worth noting that, like the modern tax system, the modern credit system requires a legible property regime for its functioning.

80. Ibid., pp. 412–42.

81. Orlando Figes, *Peasant Russia, Civil War: The Volga Countryside in Revolution, 1917–1921* (Oxford: Clarendon Press, 1989), chap. 6, "The Rural Economy Under War Communism."

82. Before comprehensive cadastral surveys, some land was open to all and belonged to no one, though social arrangements might regulate its use. With the first cadastral map, such land was generally designated as state land. All land was accounted for; everything not owned privately became the property of the state.

83. Kain and Biagent, *The Cadastral Map*, p. 33. Seas, rivers, and wastes were to be omitted since they did not bear revenue. The whole operation was guided by a manual entitled *Mode d'arpentage pour l'impôt foncier.*

84. Quoted in ibid., p. 5.

85. In a Third World setting, as Peter Vandergeest points out, a cadastral or land-use map using global positioning technology allows experts to formulate land-use policies and rules without having the inconvenience of visiting the terrain itself ("Mapping Resource Claims, or, The Seductive Appeal of Maps: The Use of Maps in the Transformation of Resource Tenure," paper presented at a meeting of the Association for the Study of Common Property, Berkeley, June 1996).

86. The land itself occasionally moves, due to landslides, erosion, avulsion, and accretion. For an interesting account of property law as it tries to deal with the "mobility" of its subject, see Theodore Steinberg, *Slide Mountain, or The Folly of Owning Nature* (Berkeley: University of California Press, 1995).

87. In an earlier work, I examined this problem in some detail in its Southeast Asian context. See Scott, *The Moral Economy of the Peasant*, chap. 4.

88. In 1785 Austria's Franz Joseph had to choose between using net income or gross income as a basis for land taxation. Gross income was chosen because it was far simpler (e.g., average crop per unit of land × units of land × average grain price = gross income). It was necessary to sacrifice accuracy and fairness to create a procedure that was administratively feasible. See Kain and Biagent, *The Cadastral Map*, p. 193.

89. Ibid., p. 59.

90. Issue of mineral rights and mineral income from subsoil deposits was a significant exception to this generalization.

91. Eugen Weber, *Peasants into Frenchmen: The Modernization of Rural France, 1870–1914* (Stanford: Stanford University Press, 1976), p. 156.

92. For a brilliant analysis of the process of "permanent settlement" in India and its intellectual roots, see Ranajit Guha, *A Rule of Property for Bengal: An Essay on the Idea of Permanent Settlement* (Paris: Mouton, 1963). As Guha notes, the existing system of tenure that the British colonial rulers encountered in the eighteenth century was completely mystifying: "At every step they came up against quasi-feudal rights and obligations which defied any attempt at interpretation in familiar western terms. The hieroglyphics of Persian estate-accounts baffled them. It was only a part of the difficulty that they could not easily master the languages in which the ancient and medieval texts relating to the laws of property were written; for tradition recorded only in memory and customs embedded in a variety of local usages wielded an authority equal to that of any written code" (p. 13).

93. For a remarkably thoughtful and thorough examination of how the colonial legal code transformed land-dispute settlement, land tenure, and social structure, see Sally Falk Moore, *Social Facts and Fabrications: "Customary" Law on Mount Kilimanjaro, 1880–1980* (Cambridge: Cambridge University Press, 1986).

94. The combination of a complete cadastral register, freehold tenure, and a national market in land makes for a level of legibility that is as advantageous to the land speculator as it is to the tax collector. Commoditization in general, by denom-

inating all goods and services according to a common currency, makes for what Tilly has called the "visibility [of] a commercial economy." He writes, "In an economy where only a small share of goods and services are bought and sold, a number of conditions prevail: collectors of revenue are unable to observe or evaluate resources with any accuracy, [and] many people have claims on any particular resource" (*Coercion, Capital, and European States*, pp. 89, 85).

95. The equality was, of course, purely areal. See Kain and Biagent, *The Cadastral Map*, p. 225. Colbert's Forest Code of 1667 was also the first coherent attempt to codify forest space in France along sharp Cartesian lines. In this connection, see Sahlins, *Forest Rites*, p. 14.

96. In Malaysia, Chinese are legally barred from owning certain kinds of agricultural land. To get around this barrier, a Chinese man will register land in the name of a Malay confederate. To ensure that the confederate does not attempt to exercise his formal property rights, he will simultaneously sign loan papers worth far more than the property, with the Chinese man named as creditor.

97. Revolutionary legislation in France, rather than abolishing tithes outright, attempted to phase them out with temporary "tithe redemption payments." Popular defiance was so massive and intractable that the payments were finally abandoned. See James C. Scott, "Resistance Without Protest and Without Organization: Peasant Opposition to the Islamic *Zakat* and the Christian Tithe," *Comparative Study in Society and History* 29, no. 3 (1987): 417–52.

98. Ian Hacking, *The Taming of Chance* (Cambridge: Cambridge University Press, 1990), p. 17. Petty, a student of Hobbes, conducted the survey with an eye to accurate assessments of value and productivity. His theory of political economy can be found in *Political Arithmetik, or A Discourse Concerning the Value of Lands, People, Buildings* . . . (1691).

99. The fiction that North American and Australian landscapes were essentially empty, which in turn meant that they were not being used as a factor of production in market exchange, was the basis on which such lands were "redesignated." This is a fiction that joins the Highland Clearances and the expropriation of land from Native Americans, New Zealand Maoris, Australian native peoples, Argentine indigenous peoples, and so on.

100. Heilbron, introduction to *The Quantifying Spirit in the Eighteenth Century*, p. 17.

101. Theodore M. Porter, *Trust in Numbers: The Pursuit of Objectivity in Science and Public Life* (Princeton: Princeton University Press, 1995), p. 22. Porter shows convincingly how "mechanical objectivity" has served as a means for bureaucracies, especially in democracies where expert judgment and expertise are always suspected of masking self-serving motives, to create an impersonal set of decision rules at once seemingly democratic and neutral.

102. Quoted in Kain and Biagent, *The Cadastral Map*, p. 320.

103. Students of these matters will perhaps wonder why I have not dealt with the simplification of time. The rationalization and commoditization of linear time in work and administration do indeed form a companion story, which I did not take up here because it would have made this chapter too long and because it has already been imaginatively treated by, among others, E. P. Thompson in "Time, Work, Discipline, and Industrial Capitalism," *Past and Present* 38 (December 1967). For a fine survey, see Ronald Aminzade, "Historical Sociology and Time," *Sociological Methods and Research* 20, no. 3 (May 1992): 456–80.

104. Heilbron, introduction to *The Quantifying Spirit in the Eighteenth Century*, pp. 22–23.

105. Hacking, *The Taming of Chance*, p. 145. Napoleon avoided conducting a

census after 1806 for fear that its results would show the catastrophic impact that his wars had had on the French population.

Chapter 2: Cities, People, and Language

1. As one might expect, independent towns were likely to privilege local knowledge far more than royal towns, which were designed with administrative and military order in mind.

2. The Casbah's illegibility, however, was not insurmountable. The FLN's resistance there was eventually broken, although at great long-run political cost, by determined police work, torture, and networks of local informers.

3. The inability of many U.S. municipal authorities to effectively govern inner cities has prompted attempts to bring back the "cop on the beat" in the form of "community policing." The purpose of community policing is to create a cadre of local police who are intimately familiar with the physical layout of the community and especially the local population, whose assistance is now judged vital to effective police work. Its aim is to turn officials who had come to be seen as outsiders into insiders.

4. I am grateful to Ron Aminzade for sending me the explanatory notes (*mémoires*) meant to accompany two of the maps the military officials had prepared as part of this *haute reconnaissance* in the city of Toulouse in 1843. They come from the *Archives de l'Armée, Paris*, dossier MR 1225. They note the streets or terrain that would be difficult to traverse, watercourses that might impede military movement, the attitude of the local population, the difficulty of their accents, the locations of markets, and so on.

5. René Descartes, *Discourse on Method*, trans. Donald A. Cress (Indianapolis: Hackett, 1980), p. 6, quoted in Harrison, *Forests*, pp. 111–12.

6. Lewis Mumford, *The City in History: Its Origins, Its Transformations, and Its Prospects* (New York: Harcourt Brace Jovanovich, 1961), p. 364.

7. Ibid., p. 387.

8. Quoted in ibid., p. 369.

9. Thomas More's utopian cities, for example, were to be perfectly uniform, so that "he who knows one of the cities will know them all, so exactly alike are they, except where the nature of the ground prevents" (More's *Utopia*, quoted in ibid., p. 327).

10. Saint Petersburg is the most striking example of the planned utopian capital, a metropolis that Dostoyevsky called the "most abstract and premeditated city in the world." See Marshall Berman, *All That Is Solid Melts into Air: The Experience of Modernity* (New York: Penguin, 1988), chap. 4. The Babylonians, Egyptians, and, of course, the Romans built "grid-settlements." Long before the Enlightenment, right angles were seen as evidence of cultural superiority. As Richard Sennett writes, "Hippodamus of Miletus is conventionally thought the first city builder to conceive of these grids as expressions of culture; the grid expressed, he believed, the rationality of civilized life. In their military conquests the Romans elaborated the contrast between the rude and formless camps of the barbarians and their own military forts, or castra" (*The Conscience of the Eye: The Design and Social Life of Cities* [New York: Norton, 1990], p. 47).

11. Well, almost. There are a few streets—among them Lincoln, Archer, and Blue Island—that follow old Indian trails and thus deviate from the geometric logic.

12. It may have occurred to the reader that certain grid sections of upper Manhattan and Chicago are, despite their formal order, essentially ungoverned and

dangerous. No amount of formal order can overcome massive countervailing factors such as poverty, crime, social disorganization, or hostility toward officials. As a sign of the illegibility of such areas, the Census Bureau acknowledges that the number of uncounted African-Americans was six times the number of uncounted whites. The undercount is politically volatile since census figures determine the number of congressional seats to which a state is entitled.

13. See the mind-opening book by the geographer Yi-Fu Tuan, *Dominance and Affection: The Making of Pets* (New Haven: Yale University Press, 1984).

14. Denis Cosgrove, "The Measure of America," in James Corner and Alex S. MacLean, eds., *Taking Measures Across the American Landscape* (New Haven: Yale University Press, 1996), p. 4. Mercator maps had, of course, accustomed people to the projection of vast, miniaturized landscapes on a flat plane.

15. Mumford, *The City in History*, p. 422.

16. The plan created not only a more legible fiscal space but also the fortunes of the small coterie who used their inside knowledge of the plan to profit from real-estate speculation.

17. There was an older, quasi-planned, baroque city bequeathed to Paris by her absolutist rulers, especially those prior to Louis XIV, who for his part chose to lavish his planning on a "new space," Versailles.

18. As Mark Girouard notes, the plan included public facilities and institutions such as parks (notably the huge Bois de Boulogne), hospitals, schools, colleges, barracks, prisons, and a new opera house (*Cities and People: A Social and Architectural History* [New Haven: Yale University Press, 1985], p. 289). Roughly a century later, against greater odds, Robert Moses would undertake a similar retrofit of New York City.

19. Quoted in John Merriman, "Baron Haussmann's Two Cities" (typescript, p. 8), later published in French as chap. 9 of Merriman's *Aux marges de la ville: Faubourgs et banlieues en France, 1815–1871* (Paris: Seuil, 1994). This part of my discussion is greatly indebted to Merriman's careful account. Unless otherwise indicated, all translations are mine.

20. Mumford writes, "Were not the ancient medieval streets of Paris one of the last refuges of urban liberties? No wonder that Napoleon III sanctioned the breaking through of narrow streets and culs-de-sac and the razing of whole quarters to provide wide boulevards. It was the best possible protection against assault from within" (*The City in History*, pp. 369–70).

21. Quoted in Louis Girard, *Nouvelle histoire de Paris: La deuxième république et le second empire, 1848–1870* (Paris, 1981), p. 126. Cited in Merriman, *Aux marges de la ville*, p. 15. The parallels with the later *ceinture rouge*, the leftist working-class suburbs ringing Paris, are striking. Soweto and other black townships in South Africa under apartheid, although established explicitly for the purposes of segregation, also became illegible, subversive spaces from the perspective of the authorities.

22. Since the planners lacked a reliable map of the city, the first step was to build temporary wooden towers in order to achieve the triangulation necessary for an accurate map. See David H. Pinkney, *Napoleon III and the Rebuilding of Paris* (Princeton: Princeton University Press, 1958), p. 5.

23. Quoted in Jeanne Gaillard, *Paris, la ville, 1852–1870* (Paris, 1979), p. 38, cited in Merriman, *Aux marges de la ville*, p. 10.

24. Ibid., pp. 8–9.

25. Ibid., p. 9. Translation by Merriman.

26. Pinkney, *Napoleon III*, p. 23. A commonplace of demographic history has been that urban populations in Western Europe, beset with epidemics and generally high mortality, did not successfully reproduce themselves until well into the

nineteenth century; the growth of cities came largely from in-migration from the healthier countryside. Although this position has been challenged, the evidence for it is still convincing. See the judicious synthesis and assessment by Jan de Vries, *European Urbanization, 1500–1800* (Cambridge: Harvard University Press, 1984), pp. 175–200.

27. Pinkney, *Napoleon III*, chap. 2.

28. Merriman, *Aux marges de la ville*, pp. 7–8. See also T. J. Clark, *The Painting of Modern Life: Paris in the Art of Manet and His Followers* (Princeton: Princeton University Press, 1984), p. 35. Louis Napoleon's and Haussmann's mania for straight lines was the butt of many jokes. A character in a play by Edmond About, for instance, dreams of the day when the Seine itself will be straightened, because, as he says, "its irregular curve is really rather shocking" (quoted in Clark, *The Painting of Modern Life*, p. 35).

29. Pinkney, *Napoleon III*, p. 93.

30. Clark, *The Painting of Modern Life*, p. 66. For a superb analysis of how tidy Orientalist expositions depicting Old Cairo, the peasant village, and so on gave Arab visitors to Paris a completely new way of seeing their society, see Timothy Mitchell, *Colonizing Egypt* (Berkeley: University of California Press, 1991), especially chaps. 1–3.

31. Gaillard, *Paris, la ville*, p. 568, quoted in Merriman, *Aux marges de la ville*, p. 20.

32. David Harvey, *Consciousness and the Urban Experience* (Baltimore: Johns Hopkins University Press, 1985), p. 165, quoted in Merriman, *Aux marges de la ville*, p. 12. See also David Harvey, *The Urban Experience* (Baltimore: Johns Hopkins University Press, 1989), which covers much of the same ground.

33. Jacques Rougerie, *Paris libre, 1871* (Paris, 1971), p. 19, quoted in Merriman, *Aux marges de la ville*, p. 27.

34. Merriman, *Aux marges de la ville*, p. 28.

35. Ibid., p. 30.

36. I owe this astute observation about *The Witness* to Benedict Anderson. More generally, his analysis of the census and the map as totalizing classificatory grids, particularly in colonial settings, has greatly influenced my thinking here. See Anderson, *Imagined Comunities: Reflections on the Origin and Spread of Nationalism* (London: Verso, 1983), and also the remarkable book by Thongchai Winichakul, *Siam Mapped: A History of the Geo-Body of a Nation* (Honolulu: University of Hawaii Press, 1994).

37. See, for example, William E. Wormsley, "Traditional Change in Imbonggu Names and Naming Practices," *Names* 28 (1980): 183–94.

38. The adoption of permanent, inherited patronyms went far, but not the whole way. How is a state to associate a name, however unique and unambiguous, with an individual? Like identity cards, social security numbers, and pass systems, names require that the citizenry cooperate by carrying them and producing them on the demand of an official. Cooperation is secured in most modern state systems by making a clear identity a prerequisite for receiving entitlements; in more coercive systems, harsh penalties are exacted for failure to carry identification documents. If, however, there is widespread defiance, individuals will either fail to identify themselves or use false identities. The ultimate identity card, then, is an ineradicable mark on the body: a tattoo, a fingerprint, a DNA "signature."

39. I am especially grateful to Bill Jenner and Ian Wilson of the Australian National University and to Paul Smith of Haverford College for their generous advice about China. The Qin and Han administrative plans for population registration were ambitious, but how completely their goals were realized in practice remains

an important question. Jenner contends that the goals were largely realized, whereas Alexander Woodside claims that slippage must have been considerable.

40. See, for example, W. J. F. Jenner, "Freedom and Backwardness: Europe and China," paper delivered at "Ideas of Freedom in Asia," Humanities Research Centre, Australian National University, July 4–6, 1994; and Patricia Ebrey, "The Chinese Family and the Spread of Confucian Values," in Gilbert Rozman, ed., *The East Asian Region: Confucian Heritage and Its Modern Adaptation* (Princeton: Princeton University Press, 1991), pp. 45–83.

41. Ebrey, "The Chinese Family," pp. 55–57.

42. Ibid., p. 59.

43. To my knowledge, Iceland is the only European nation that had not adopted permanent surnames by the late twentieth century.

44. This account of the Florentine census is drawn entirely from David Herlihy and Christiane Klapisch-Zuber, *Tuscans and Their Families: A Study of the Florentine Catasto of 1427* (New Haven: Yale University Press, 1985).

45. The matter of age, like the matter of landholding, was a vastly different concept in the state's hands than it was in popular practice. See ibid., pp. 162–69. In local practice, exact ages were unimportant. Approximate ages and birth order (e.g., oldest son, youngest son) were more useful; in the catasto this is reflected by the tendency to declare ages in units of five or ten years (e.g., thirty-five, forty, forty-five, fifty, and sixty years). For the state, however, exact age was important for several reasons. The age of "fiscal adulthood" as well as liability for conscription was eighteen, and, beyond age sixty, one was no longer responsible for capitation taxes. As one might expect, there was a demographically improbable clustering of declarations just below age eighteen and just above sixty. Like the surname, the designation of age, in the strict, linear, chronological sense, originates as a state project.

46. In the West, women, domestic servants, and tied laborers were typically the last to adopt surnames (and to be given the vote), because they were legally subsumed as minors in the charge of the male head of family.

47. Other surnames referring to fathers are not quite so obvious. Thus the name "Victor Hugo" would originally have meant simply "Victor, son of Hugo."

48. I am indebted to Kate Stanton, an astute research assistant, for her background research on this issue.

49. See C. M. Matthews, *English Surnames* (London: Weidenfeld and Nicolson, 1966), pp. 35–48.

50. As Matthews notes, "The humble peasant with only one virgate of land was as anxious to claim it by right of being his father's eldest son as the rich man inheriting a large estate. The land could be claimed and awarded only at the Manorial Court, being held 'by copy of the Court Roll' [that is, being a copyhold], which meant that the life tenant's name was inscribed there on permanent record. This system provided a direct incentive to men to keep the same surname that had been put down on the roll for their father and grandfather" (ibid., p. 44). And given the vagaries of the mortality rate in fourteenth-century England, younger sons might want to keep the name as well, just in case.

51. In historical documents one can occasionally glimpse a moment when a permanent surname seems to gel. Under Henry VIII in the early sixteenth century, for example, a Welshman who appeared in court was asked for his name, and he answered, in the Welsh fashion, "Thomas Ap [son of] William, Ap Thomas, Ap Richard, Ap Hoel, Ap Evan Vaughan." He was scolded by the judge, who instructed him to "leave the old manner, . . . whereupon he after called himself Moston, according to the name of his principal house, and left that name to his posteritie" (William Camden, *Remains Concerning Britain*, ed. R. D. Dunn [1605; Toronto:

373 Notes to Pages 68-71

University of Toronto Press, 1984], p. 122). This "administrative" last name almost certainly remained unknown to Thomas's neighbors.

52. See the classic study by Rodney Hilton, *Bond Men Made Free: Medieval Peasant Movements and the English Rising of 1381* (New York: Viking Press, 1977), pp. 160-64.

53. I am particularly grateful to Rosanne Ruttan, Otto van den Muijzenberg, Harold Conklin, and Charles Bryant for putting me on the track of the Philippine case. The key document is Domingo Abella, ed., *Catalogo alfabetico de Apellidos* (Manila: National Archives, 1973). See also the short account in O. D. Corpuz, *The Roots of the Filipino Nation*, vol. 1 (Quezon City: Aklahi Foundation, 1989), pp. 479-80. For a perceptive analysis of naming and identity formation among the Karo-Batak of colonial East Sumatra, see Mary Margaret Steedly, "The Importance of Proper Names: Language and 'National' Identity in Colonial Karoland," *American Ethnologist* 23, no. 3 (1996): 447-75.

54. For nearly three hundred years, the Spanish calendar for the Philippines had been one day ahead of the Spanish calendar, because Magellan's expedition had not, of course, adjusted for their westward travel halfway around the globe.

55. Abella, *Catalogo alfabetico de Apellidos*, p. viii.

56. Ibid., p. vii.

57. As if the Filipinos did not have perfectly adequate oral and written genealogical schemes to achieve the same end.

58. Abella, *Catalogo alfabetico de Apellidos*, p. viii.

59. For the best treatment of permanent patronyms in France and their relation to state-building, see the insightful book by Anne Lefebvre-Teillard, *Le nom: Droit et histoire* (Paris: Presses Universitaires de France, 1990). She examines the process whereby state officials, both administrative and judicial, gradually authorized certain naming practices and limited the conditions under which names might be changed. The civil registers, along with the *livret de famille* (family pass book), established toward the end of the nineteenth century, became important tools for police administration, conscription, civil and criminal justice, and elections monitoring. The standard opening line of an encounter between a policeman and a civilian—"Vos papiers, Monsieur"—dates from this period. Having experienced the "blinding" of the administration caused by the destruction of civil registers in the burning of the Hôtel de Ville (city hall) and the Palais de Justice at the end of the Commune in 1871, officials took care to keep duplicate registers.

60. Robert Chazon, "Names: Medieval Period and Establishment of Surnames," *Encyclopedia Judaica* (Jerusalem and Philadelphia: Keter Publishers and Coronet Books, 1982), 12:809-13. In the 1930s the Nazis passed a series of "name decrees" whose sole purpose was to distinguish what they had determined as the Jewish population from the Gentile population. Jews who had Aryan-sounding names were required to change them (or to add "Israel" or "Sarah"), as were Aryans who had Jewish-sounding names. Lists of approved names were compiled, and contested cases were submitted to the Reich Office for Genealogical Research. Once the administrative exercise was complete, a person's name alone could single out him or her for deportation or execution. See Robert M. Rennick, "The Nazi Name Decrees of the Nineteen Thirties," *Journal of the American Name Society* 16 (1968): 65-88.

61. Turkey, for example, adopted surnames only in the 1920s as a part of Ataturk's modernization campaign. Suits, hats (rather than fezzes), permanent last names, and modern nationhood all fit together in Ataturk's scheme. Reze Shah, the father of the deposed Shah, ordered all Iranians to take the last name of their town of residence in order to rationalize the country's family names. Ali Akbar Rafsan-

jani thus means Ali Akbar from Rafsanjan. Although this system has the advantage of designating the homes of the generation that adopted it, it certainly doesn't clarify much locally in Rafsanjan. It may well be that the state is particularly concerned with monitoring those who are mobile or "out of place."

62. Dietary laws that all but preclude commensality are also powerful devices for social exclusion. If one were designating a set of cultural rules in order to wall off a group from surrounding groups, making sure its members cannot easily speak to or eat with others is a splendid beginning.

63. This is true despite the fact, as Benedict Anderson insightfully points out, that the "national past" is so often fitted with a bogus pedigree.

64. Eugen Weber, *Peasants into Frenchmen: The Modernization of Rural France, 1870–1914* (Stanford: Stanford University Press, 1976), chap. 6. Weber points out that in the last twenty-five years of the nineteenth century, fully half of the Frenchmen reaching adulthood had a native tongue other than French. See Peter Sahlins's remarkable book *Boundaries: The Making of France and Spain in the Pyrenees* (Berkeley: University of California Press, 1989) for a discussion of French language policy at its periphery. Although administrative official languages have a lineage that goes back to at least the sixteenth century, the imposition of a national language in other spheres comes in the mid-nineteenth century at the earliest.

65. For an illuminating analytical account of this process, see Abram de Swaan, *In Care of the State* (Oxford: Polity Press, 1988), especially chap. 3, "The Elementary Curriculum as a National Communication Code," pp. 52–117.

66. Weber, *Peasants into Frenchmen*, p. 73.

67. Quoted in ibid., p. 113.

68. Ibid., p. 197.

69. For a careful depiction of the geography of standard market areas, see G. William Skinner, *Marketing and Social Structure in Rural China* (Tucson: Association of Asian Studies, 1975).

70. Much of the following material on the centralization of transport in France comes from the fine survey by Cecil O. Smith, Jr., "The Longest Run: Public Engineers and Planning in France," *American Historical Review* 95, no. 3 (June 1990): 657–92. See also the excellent discussion and comparison of the Corps des Ponts et des Chaussées with the U.S. Army Corps of Engineers in Theodore Porter, *Trust in Numbers: The Pursuit of Objectivity in Science and Public Life* (Princeton: Princeton University Press, 1995), chap. 6.

71. Weber, *Peasants into Frenchmen*, p. 195.

72. There were continual debates over various plans: their cost, their commercial viability, and their military efficacy. Some of this history can be found in François Caron, *Histoire de l'exploitation d'un grand réseau: La compagnie des chemins de fer du Nord* (Paris: Mouton, 1973), and Louis-Maurice Jouffroy, *L'ère du rail* (Paris: A. Colin, 1953). I thank Ezra Suleiman for his bibliographical help.

73. The technical affinity of rail travel to straight lines and exact timetables becomes, along with "streamlining," an important aesthetic in modernism generally.

74. Smith, "The Longest Run," pp. 685–71. Smith claims that the Legrand Star meant that many reservists being mustered for World War I had to funnel through Paris, whereas, under a more decentralized rail plan, there would have been far more direct routes to the front: "Some reservists in Strasbourg [were] journeying via the capital to don their uniforms in Bordeaux before returning to fight in Alsace." General Von Möltke observed that he had six different rail lines for moving troops from the North German Confederation to the war zone between the Moselle and the Rhine, while French troops coming to the front had to detrain at Strasbourg or Metz, with the Vosges mountains in between. Finally, and perhaps most

important, once Paris was surrounded, the Legrand Star was left headless. After the war, the high command insisted on building more transverse lines to correct the deficiency.

75. See Ian Hacking, *The Emergence of Probability: A Philosophical Study of Early Ideas About Probability, Induction, and Statistical Inference* (Cambridge: Cambridge University Press, 1975).

76. I am extraordinarily grateful to the City Museum of Amsterdam for providing a copy of the map reproduced in this book as figure 13 and, above all, for staging the fine and unsparing exhibition "Hungerwinter and Liberation in Amsterdam" and the accompanying catalogue, *Here, back when . . .* (Amsterdam: City Museum, 1995).

77. *Here, back when . . .*, p. 10.

78. Since, as we know best from the case of Anne Frank, a good many citizens were willing to hide Jews in the city and the countryside, deportation as a systematic administrative exercise eventually failed. As the Jewish population became increasingly opaque to the authorities, they were increasingly forced to rely on Dutch collaborators who became their local trackers.

79. Even when these facts appear dynamic, they are usually the result of multiple static observations through time that, through a "connect the dots" process, give the appearance of continuous movement. In fact, what actually happened between, say, observation A and observation B remains a mystery, which is glossed over by the convention of merely drawing a straight line between the two data points.

80. This is the way that Benedict Anderson puts it in *Imagined Communities*, p. 169.

81. I am grateful to Larry Lohmann for insisting to me that officials are not necessarily any more abstract or narrow of vision in their representation of reality than laypeople are. Rather, the facts that they need are facts that serve the interests and practices of their institutional roles. He would have preferred, I think, that I drop the term "simplification" altogether, but I have resisted.

82. There are at least three problems here. The first is the hegemony of the categories. How does one classify someone who usually works for relatives, who may sometimes feed him, let him use some of their land as his own, or pay him in crops or cash? The sometimes quite arbitrary decisions about how to classify such cases are obscured by the final result, in which only the prevailing categories appear. Theodore Porter notes that officials in France's Office of National Statistics report that even trained coders will code up to 20 percent of occupational categories differently (*Trust in Numbers*, p. 41). The goal of the statistical office is to ensure the maximum reliability among coders, even if the conventions applied to achieve it sacrifice something of the true state of affairs. The second problem, to which we shall return later, is how the categories and, more particularly, the state power behind the categories shape the data. For example, during the recession in the United States in the 1970s, there was some concern that the official unemployment rate, which had reached 13 percent, was exaggerated. A major reason, it was claimed, was that many nominally unemployed were working "off the books" in the informal economy and were not reporting their income or employment for fear of being taxed. One could say then and today that the fiscal system had provoked an off-stage reality that was designed to stay out of the data bank. The third problem is that those who collect and assemble the information may have special interests in what the data show. During the Vietnam War the importance of body counts and pacified villages as a measure of counterinsurgency success led commanders to produce inflated figures that pleased their superiors—in the short run—but increasingly bore little relation to the facts on the ground.

83. The goal is to get rid of intersubjective variability on the part of the census takers or coders. And that requires standard, mechanical procedures that leave no room for personal judgment. See Porter, *Trust in Numbers*, p. 29.

84. Charles Tilly, *Coercion, Capital, and European States, A.D. 990–1992* (Oxford: Blackwell, 1990), p. 100.

85. Indicative of this tendency in scientific forestry is the substantial literature on "optimum control theory," which is imported from management science. For an application and bibliography, see D. M. Donnelly and D. R. Betters, "Optimum Control for Scheduling Final Harvest in Even-Aged Forest Stands," *Forest Ecology and Management* 46 (1991): 135–49.

86. The caricature is not so far-fetched that it does not capture the lyrical utopianism of early advocates of state sciences. I quote the father of Prussian statistics, Ernst Engel: "In order to obtain an accurate representation, statistical research accompanies the individual through his entire earthly existence. It takes account of his birth, his baptism, his vaccination, his schooling and the success thereof, his diligence, his leave of school, his subsequent education and development, and, once he becomes a man, his physique and his ability to bear arms. It also accompanies the subsequent steps of his walk through life; it takes note of his chosen occupation, where he sets up his household and his management of the same, if he saved from the abundances of his youth for his old age, if and when and at what age he marries and whom he chooses as his wife—statistics look after him when things go well for him and when they go awry. Should he suffer shipwreck in his life, undergo material, moral, or spiritual ruin, statistics take note of the same. Statistics leave a man only after his death—after it has ascertained the precise age of his death and noted the causes that brought about his end" (quoted in Ian Hacking, *The Taming of Chance* [Cambridge: Cambridge University Press, 1990], p. 34). One could hardly ask for a more complete list of early nineteenth-century state interests and the paper trail that it generated.

87. Tilly, echoing the colonial theme, describes much of this process within the European nation-state as the replacement of indirect rule with direct rule (*Coercion, Capital, and European States*, pp. 103–26).

88. Donald Chisholm, *Coordination Without Hierarchy: Informal Structures in Multiorganizational Systems* (Berkeley: University of California Press, 1989), p. 10.

89. This process is best described by Benedict Anderson: "Guided by its [the colonial state's] imagined map, it organized the new educational, juridical, public-health, police and immigration bureaucracies it was building on the principle of ethno-racial hierarchies which were, however, always understood in terms of parallel series. The flow of subject populations through the mesh of differential schools, courts, clinics, police stations and immigration offices created 'traffic-habits' which in time gave real social life to the state's earlier fantasies" (*Imagined Communities*, p. 169). A related argument about the cultural dimension of state-building in England can be found in Philip Corrigan and Derek Sayer, *The Great Arch: English State Formation as Cultural Revolution* (Oxford: Blackwell, 1991).

Chapter 3: Authoritarian High Modernism

1. My colleague Paul Landau recalls the story by Borges in which a king, unhappy at maps that do not do justice to his kingdom, finally insists on a map with a scale of one-to-one. When complete, the new map exactly covers the existing kingdom, submerging the real one beneath its representation.

2. A commonplace example may help. One of the ordinary frustrations of the

modern citizen, even in liberal democracies, is the difficulty of representing his unique case to a powerful agent of a bureaucratic institution. But the functionary operates with a simplified grid designed to cover all the cases that she confronts. Once a decision has been made as to which "bin" or "pigeonhole" the case falls into, the action to be taken or the protocol to be followed is largely cut-and-dried. The functionary endeavors to sort the case into the appropriate category, while the citizen resists being treated as an instance of a category and tries to insist, often unsuccessfully, that his unique case be examined on its singular merits.

3. I have borrowed the term "high modernism" from David Harvey, *The Condition of Post-Modernity: An Enquiry into the Origins of Social Change* (Oxford: Basil Blackwell, 1989). Harvey locates the high-water mark of this sort of modernism in the post-World War II period, and his concern is particularly with capitalism and the organization of production. But his description of high modernism also works well here: "The belief 'in linear progress, absolute truths, and rational planning of ideal social orders' under standardized conditions of knowledge and production was particularly strong. The modernism that resulted was, as a result, 'positivistic, technocratic, and rationalistic' at the same time as it was imposed as the work of an elite avant-garde of planners, artists, architects, critics, and other guardians of high taste. The 'modernization' of European economies proceeded apace, while the whole thrust of international politics and trade was justified as bringing a benevolent and progressive 'modernization process' to a backward Third World" (p. 35).

4. For case studies of "public entrepreneurs" in the United States, see Eugene Lewis's study of Hyman Rickover, J. Edgar Hoover, and Robert Moses, *Public Entrepreneurs: Toward a Theory of Bureaucratic Political Power: The Organizational Lives of Hyman Rickover, J. Edgar Hoover, and Robert Moses* (Bloomington: Indiana University Press, 1980).

Monnet, like Rathenau, had experience in economic mobilization during World War I, when he helped organize the transatlantic supply of war material for Britian and France, a role that he resumed during World War II. By the time he helped plan the postwar integration of French and German coal and steel production, he had already had several decades of experience in supranational management. See François Duchene, *Jean Monnet: The First Statesman of Interdependence* (New York: Norton, 1995).

5. I will not pursue the argument here, but I think Nazism is best understood as a reactionary form of modernism. Like the progressive left, the Nazi elites had grandiose visions of state-enforced social engineering, which included, of course, extermination, expulsion, forced sterilization, and selective breeding and which aimed at "improving" genetically on human nature. The case for Nazism as a virulent form of modernism is made brilliantly and convincingly by Zygmunt Bauman in *Modernity and the Holocaust* (Oxford: Oxford University Press, 1989). See also, along the same lines, Jeffrey Herf, *Reactionary Modernism: Technology, Culture, and Politics in Weimar and the Third Reich* (Cambridge: Cambridge University Press, 1984), and Norbert Frei, *National Socialist Rule in Germany: The Führer State, 1933–1945*, trans. Simon B. Steyne (Oxford: Oxford University Press, 1993).

6. I am grateful to James Ferguson for reminding me that reactionary high-modernist schemes are about as ubiquitous as progressive variants.

7. This is not by any means meant to be a brief for conservatism. Conservatives of many stripes may care little for civil liberties and may resort to whatever brutalities seem necessary to remain in power. But their ambitions and hubris are much more limited; their plans (in contrast to those of reactionary modernists) do not necessitate turning society upside down to create new collectivities, new family and group loyalties, and new people.

8. Václav Havel, address given at Victoria University, Wellington, New Zealand, on March 31, 1995, reprinted in the *New York Review of Books* 42, no. 11 (June 22, 1995): 36.

9. Quoted in Zygmunt Bauman, *Socialism: The Active Utopia* (New York: Holmes and Meier, 1976), p. 11.

10. For an enlightening discussion of the intellectual lineage of authoritarian environmentalism, see Douglas R. Weiner, "Demythologizing Environmentalism," *Journal of the History of Biology* 25, no. 3 (Fall 1992): 385–411.

11. See Michael Adas's *Machines as the Measure of Men: Science, Technology, and Ideologies of Western Dominance* (Ithaca: Cornell University Press, 1989) and Marshall Berman's *All That Is Solid Melts into Air: The Experience of Modernity* (New York: Penguin, 1988). What is new in high modernism, I believe, is not so much the aspiration for comprehensive planning. Many imperial and absolutist states have had similar aspirations. What are new are the administrative technology and social knowledge that make it plausible to imagine organizing an entire society in ways that only the barracks or the monastery had been organized before. In this respect, Michel Foucault's argument, in *Discipline and Punish: The Birth of the Prison*, trans. Alan Sheridan (New York: Vintage Books, 1977), is persuasive.

12. Here I want to distinguish between advances in scientific knowledge and inventions (many of which occurred in the eighteenth century or earlier) and the massive transformations that scientific inventions wrought in daily material life (which came generally in the nineteenth century).

13. Witold Kula, *Measures and Men*, trans. R. Szreter (Princeton: Princeton University Press, 1986), p. 211.

14. Quoted in Ian Hacking, *The Taming of Chance* (Cambridge: Cambridge University Press, 1990), p. 38. A few years later, the Jacobins were, one could argue, the first to attempt to actually engineer happiness by transforming the social order. As Saint-Just wrote, "The idea of happiness is new in Europe." See Albert O. Hirschman, "Rival Interpretations of Market Society: Civilizing, Destructive, or Feeble," *Journal of Economic Literature* 20 (December 1982): 1463–84.

15. I am greatly indebted to James Ferguson, whose perceptive comments on an early draft of the book pointed me in this direction.

16. See, for example, Graham Buschell, Colin Gordon, and Peter Miller, eds., *The Foucault Effect: Studies in Governmentality* (London: Harvester Wheatsheaf, 1991), chap. 4.

17. Hacking, *The Taming of Chance*, p. 105. Hacking shows brilliantly how a statistical "average" metamorphosed into the category "normal," and "normal," in turn, into a "normative" standard to be achieved by social engineering.

18. By now, a great deal of historical research has made crystal clear how widespread throughout the West was the support for eugenic engineering. The belief that the state must intervene to protect the races' physical and mental characteristics was common among progressives and animated a well-nigh international social movement. By 1926, twenty-three of the forty-eight U.S. states had laws permitting sterilization.

19. See Gareth Stedman-Jones, *Languages of Class: Studies in English Working-Class History, 1832–1982* (Cambridge: Cambridge University Press, 1983). It is important to recognize that, among Western powers, virtually all the initiatives associated with the "civilizing missions" of colonialism were preceded by comparable programs to assimilate and civilize their own lower-class populations, both rural and urban. The difference, perhaps, is that in the colonial setting officials had greater coercive power over an objectified and alien population, thus allowing for greater feats of social engineering.

20. For a science-fiction account of the attempt to create a "technocratic and objective man" who would be free of "nature," see C. S. Lewis, *That Hideous Strength: A Modern Fairy Tale for Grown-Ups* (New York: Macmillan, 1946).

21. There is the interesting and problematic case of the "wild" garden, in which the precise shape of "disorder" is minutely planned. Here it is a matter of an aesthetic plan, designed to have a certain effect on the eye—an attempt to copy untended nature. The paradox is just as intractable as that of a zoo designed to mimic nature—intractable, that is, until one realizes that the design does not extend to allowing the critters to eat one another!

22. Karl Marx, from the *Communist Manifesto*, quoted in Berman, *All That Is Solid Melts into Air*, p. 95.

23. The airplane, having replaced the locomotive, was in many respects the defining image of modernity in the early twentieth century. In 1913, the futurist artist and playwright Kazimir Malevich created the sets for an opera entitled *Victory over the Sun*. In the last scene, the audience heard from offstage a propeller's roar and shouts announcing that gravity had been overcome in futurist countries. Le Corbusier, Malevich's near contemporary, thought the airplane was the reigning symbol of the new age. For the influence of flight, see Robert Wohl, *A Passion for Wings: Aviation and the Western Imagination, 1908–1918* (New Haven: Yale University Press, 1996).

24. The Jacobins intended just such a fresh start, starting the calendar again at "year one" and renaming the days and months according to a new, secular system. To signal its intention to create a wholly new Cambodian nation, the Pol Pot regime began with "year zero."

25. Quoted in Harvey, *The Condition of Post-Modernity*, p. 99.

26. In this section, the masculine personal pronoun is less a convention than a choice made with some deliberation. See Carolyn Merchant, *The Death of Nature: Women, Ecology, and the Scientific Revolution* (San Francisco: Harper, 1980).

27. See, for example, Margaret M. Bullitt, "Toward a Marxist Theory of Aesthetics: The Development of Socialist Realism in the Soviet Union," *Russian Review* 35, no. 1 (January 1976): 53–76.

28. Baruch Knei-Paz, "Can Historical Consequences Falsify Ideas? Or, Karl Marx After the Collapse of the Soviet Union." Paper presented to Political Theory Workshop, Department of Political Science, Yale University, New Haven, November 1994.

29. Raymond Aron's prophetic dissent, *The Opium of the Intellectuals*, trans. Terence Kilmartin (London: Secker and Warburg, 1957), is a key document in this context.

30. The larger, the more capital-intensive, and the more centralized the schemes, the greater their appeal in terms of power and patronage. For a critique of flood-control projects and World Bank projects in this context, see James K. Boyce, "Birth of a Megaproject: Political Economy of Flood Control in Bangladesh," *Environmental Management* 14, no. 4 (1990): 419–28.

31. Harvey, *The Condition of Post-Modernity*, p. 12.

32. See Charles Tilly's important theoretial contribution in *Coercion, Capital, and European States, A.D. 990–1992* (Oxford: Blackwell, 1990).

33. A civil war, as in the Bolshevik case, may be the price of consolidating the revolutionaries' power.

34. White-settler colonies (e.g., South Africa, Algeria) and anti-insurgency campaigns (e.g., Vietnam, Algeria, Afghanistan) have carried out huge population removals and forced resettlements. In most such cases, however, even the pretense that the comprehensive social planning was for the welfare of the affected populations has been paper-thin.

35. Here I am particularly indebted to the discussion of George Yaney, *The Urge to Mobilize: Agrarian Reform in Russia* (Urbana: University of Illinois Press, 1982), pp. 448–62.

36. Anson Rabinbach, *The Human Motor: Energy, Fatigue, and the Origins of Modernity* (Berkeley: University of California Press, 1992), pp. 260–71. In 1907, long before the war, Rathenau and a number of architects and political leaders had founded Deutsche Werkbund, which was devoted to fostering technical innovation in industry and the arts.

37. See Gregory J. Kasza, *The Conscription Society: Administered Mass Organizations* (New Haven: Yale University Press, 1995), especially chap. 1, pp. 7–25.

38. Rabinbach, *The Human Motor*, p. 290.

39. For recent assessments of the evolution of technology and production in the United States, see Nathan Rosenberg, *Perspectives on Technology* (Cambridge: Cambridge University Press, 1976); Rosenberg, *Inside the Black Box: Technology and Economics* (New York: Cambridge University Press, 1982); and Philip Scranton, *Figured Tapestry: Production, Markets, and Power in Philadelphia, 1885–1942* (New York: Cambridge University Press, 1989).

40. See the inventive article by Ernest J. Yanorella and Herbert Reid, "From 'Trained Gorilla' to 'Humanware': Repoliticizing the Body-Machine Complex Between Fordism and Post-Fordism," in Theodore R. Schatzki and Wolfgang Natter, eds., *The Social and Political Body* (New York: Guildford Press, 1996), pp. 181–219.

41. Rabinbach, *The Human Motor*, p. 272. Rabinbach is here paraphrasing the conclusions of a seminal article by Charles S. Maier, "Between Taylorism and Technocracy: European Ideologies and the Vision of Industrial Productivity in the 1920s," *Journal of Contemporary History* 5, no. 2 (1970): 27–63.

42. Thorstein Veblen was the best-known social scientist expounding this view in the United States. Literary versions of this ideology are apparent in Sinclair Lewis's *Arrowsmith* and Ayn Rand's *Fountainhead*, works from very different quadrants of the political spectrum.

43. Rabinbach, *The Human Motor*, p. 452. For Rathenau's writings, see, for example, *Von kommenden Dingen* (Things to come) and *Die Neue Wirtschaft* (The new economy), the latter written after the war.

44. Walther Rathenau, *Von kommenden Dingen* (1916), quoted in Maier, "Between Taylorism and Technocracy," p. 47. Maier notes that the apparent harmony of capital and labor in wartime Germany was achieved at the cost of an eventually ruinous policy of inflation (p. 46).

45. Michael Adas, *Machines as the Measure of Men: Science, Technology, and Ideologies of Western Dominance* (Ithaca: Cornell University Press, 1989), p. 380. Sheldon Wolin, in *Politics and Vision: Continuity and Innovation in Western Political Thought* (Boston: Little, Brown, 1960), provides an extensive list of like-minded thinkers spanning the political spectrum, from fascists and nationalists at one end to liberals, social democrats, and communists at the other, and hailing from France, Germany, Austria-Prussia (the Prussian Richard von Moellendorf, a close associate of Rathenau and a publicist for a managed postwar economy), Italy (Antonio Gramsci on the left and fascists Masimo Rocca and Benito Mussolini on the right), and Russia (Alexej Kapitonovik Gastev, the "Soviet Taylor").

46. V. I. Lenin, *The Agrarian Programme of Social-Democracy in the First Russian Revolution, 1905–1907*, 2nd rev. ed. (Moscow: Progress Publishers, 1954), p. 195, written September 28, 1917 (first emphasis only added).

47. Leon Smolinski, "Lenin and Economic Planning," *Studies in Comparative Communism* 2, no. 1 (January 1969): 99. Lenin and Trotsky were explicit, Smolinski claims, about how electric centrals would create a farm population depen-

dent on the center and thus make state control of agricultural production possible (pp. 106–7).

48. Lenin, *Works* (Moscow, 1972), 27:163, quoted in Ranier Traub, "Lenin and Taylor: The Fate of 'Scientific Management' in the (Early) Soviet Union," trans. Judy Joseph, in *Telos* 34 (Fall 1978): 82–92 (originally published in *Kursbuch* 43 [1976]). The "bard" of Taylorism in the Soviet Union was Alexej Kapitonovik Gastev, whose poetry and essays waxed lyrical about the possibilities of a "union" between man and machine: "Many find it repugnant that we want to deal with human beings as a screw, a nut, a machine. But we must undertake this as fearlessly as we accept the growth of trees and the expansion of the railway network" (quoted in ibid., p. 88). Most of the labor institutes were closed and their experts deported or shot in the Stalinist purges of the 1930s.

49. Lenin, "The Immediate Tasks of the Soviet Government," *Izvestia*, April 28, 1918, cited in Maier, "Between Taylorism and Technocracy," p. 51 n. 58.

50. Graham Burchell, Colin Gordon, and Peter Miller, *The Foucault Effect: Studies in Governmentality*, with two lectures by and an interview with Michel Foucault (London: Wheatsheaf, 1991), p. 106.

51. This point has been made forcefully and polemically in the twentieth century by Friedrich Hayek, the darling of those opposed to postwar planning and the welfare state. See, especially, *The Road to Serfdom* (Chicago: University of Chicago Press, 1976).

Chapter 4: The High-Modernist City

1. I am particularly grateful to Talja Potters for her perceptive comments on a first draft of this chapter.

2. Le Corbusier's entry in the 1927 design competition for the palace of the League of Nations won first prize, but his design was never built.

3. For this period, see Jean-Louis Cohen, *Le Corbusier and the Mystique of the USSR: Theories and Projects for Moscow, 1928–1936* (Princeton: Princeton University Press, 1992).

4. For an excellent analysis of modernity and the American city, see Katherine Kia Tehranian, *Modernity, Space, and Power: The American City in Discourse and Practice* (Cresskill, N.J.: Hampton Press, 1995).

5. Le Corbusier (Charles-Edouard Jeanneret), *The Radiant City: Elements of a Doctrine of Urbanism to Be Used as the Basis of Our Machine-Age Civilization*, trans. Pamela Knight (New York: Orion Press, 1964). The original French edition is *La ville radieuse: Eléments d'une doctrine d'urbanisme pour l'équipement de la civilisation machiniste* (Boulogne: Editions de l'Architecture d'Aujourd'hui, 1933). The following analysis draws heavily on both.

6. Le Corbusier, *The Radiant City*, p. 220.

7. Like many high modernists, Le Corbusier had a romance with the airplane. He wrote: "It is as an architect and town planner . . . that I let myself be carried off on the wings of an airplane, make use of the bird's-eye view, of the view from the air. . . . The eye now sees in substance what the mind could only subjectively conceive. [The view from the air] is a new function added to our senses; it is a new standard of measurement; it is the basis of a new sensation. Man will make use of it to conceive new aims. Cities will arise out of their ashes" (quoted in James Corner and Alex S. MacLean, *Taking Measures Across the American Landscape* [New Haven: Yale University Press, 1996], p. 15).

8. Le Corbusier, *The Radiant City*, p. 322 (emphasis added).

9. Ibid. p. 121.

10. Robert Fishman, *Urban Utopias of the Twentieth Century: Ebenezer Howard, Frank Lloyd Wright, and Le Corbusier* (New York: Basic Books, 1977), p. 186.

11. Le Corbusier, *The Radiant City*, p. 134.

12. Ibid., pp. 82–83 (first emphasis added, second emphasis in original).

13. From Le Corbusier's "When the Cathedrals Were White," trans. Francis Hyslop, quoted in Richard Sennett, *The Conscience of the Eye: The Design and Social Life of Cities* (New York: Norton, 1990), p. 169. For an account of Le Corbusier's yearlong visit to America in 1935, see Mardges Bacon, *Le Corbusier in America: Travels in the Land of the Timid* (forthcoming). Le Corbusier failed to win the commissions he sought in America, apparently because, even at the frontier, urban planners were put off by his demolition-based schemes.

14. Le Corbusier, *The Radiant City*, p. 123 (emphasis in original).

15. For an accessible introduction to the fractal logic of living processes, see James Gleick, *Chaos: Making a New Science* (New York: Penguin, 1988).

16. Le Corbusier, *The Radiant City*, p. 178. In his actual buildings, however, Le Corbusier's practice was far more varied.

17. Ibid., pp. 22–23. It was ironically fitting that his never-built design for the palace of the League of Nations—at the time, the most universal of institutions—had won first prize.

18. Ibid., p. 46.

19. Ibid., pp. 29–30. For a convincing argument that rigid, functionally specific zoning laws lie behind failed communities and suburban sprawl in the United States today, see James Howard Kunstler, "Home from Nowhere," *Atlantic Monthly,* September 1996, pp. 43–66.

20. Lawrence Vale, *Architecture, Power, and National Identity* (New Haven: Yale University Press, 1992), p. 109.

21. Le Corbusier, *The Radiant City*, p. 71.

22. One alternative to such simplification is to be guided by the tastes of the end user or consumer. Do people want to live here? Do current residents like living there? These criteria are not to be confounded with market criteria, which also ask whether people can afford it.

23. I write "Le Corbusier's doctrine" because in practice his buildings were neither low in cost nor efficient in function. The actual buildings, however, were also rather more interesting than his theoretical doctrines.

24. Le Corbusier, *The Radiant City*, p. 7.

25. Le Corbusier, quoted in Fishman, *Urban Utopias*, p. 193 (emphasis added).

26. Le Corbusier, *La ville radieuse*, pp. 178–79 (my translation).

27. Le Corbusier, quoted in Fishman, *Urban Utopias*, p. 208.

28. Compare this spatial representation of social and political order with the city plan Plato outlines in *The Laws:* an acropolis at the center, concentric rings of the urban core, an artisan (noncitizen) suburb, and the the inner and outer rings of the cultivated area. The "pie" is divided into twelve segments that form the basis for the recruitment and annual rotation of the guard force. See Pierre Vidal-Naquet, "A Study in Ambiguity: Artisans in the Platonic City," chap. 11 of *The Black Hunter: Forms of Thought and Forms of Society in the Greek World,* trans. Andrew Szegedy-Maszak (Baltimore: Johns Hopkins University Press, 1986), pp. 224–45.

29. The urban-planning genius's search for the autocrat who will give him the power to realize his vision was also evident in the career of Walter Christaller, the great German geographer and originator of central place theory. He lent his services to the Nazi regime "in order to give advice about the creation of a hierarchical order of urban settlements for the newly won Polish territories." It was a chance

to implement his theory of hexagonal market areas and town placement on a flat plain. After the war he joined the Communist Party, "for his hope was that an authoritarian regime would use its power to relocate war-devastated cities according to an optimal pattern as demanded by central place theory." It was a classic case of the attempt to *impose* what had begun as a simplified analytical description of the economics of location. Hans Carol, "Geographica: Walter Christaller, a Personal Memoir," *Canadian Geographer* 14, no. 1 (1970): 67–69. I am grateful to Otto van den Muijzenberg for this reference.

30. Le Corbusier, *The Radiant City*, p. 181.

31. Ibid., p. 154 (emphasis added).

32. I try to be exceptionally cautious in using such loaded terms as "fascism," but I think this one is justified here. When Le Corbusier writes of the beauty of the Parthenon, the celebration of violence is just beneath the surface. "Remember the Parthenon," he writes. "Remember its clarity, its clear lines, its intensity, its economy, its *violence*, remember its great cry in the midst of that landscape created by grace and *terror*. Strength and purity" (ibid., p. 187 [emphasis added]). Le Corbusier also has the tendency, as we shall presently see, to dehumanize his opponents and the urban poor: "Everything depends upon the wisdom of the plans. . . . I am talking here of a society that has already provided itself with a planned economy and swept away all the *parasites* present in the society we know today" (p. 73 [emphasis added]).

33. Mumford condemns for its similar hubris the spirit of baroque planning, which, to a twentieth-century eye, seems far less expansive. In his commentary on the passage from Descartes (quoted in chapter 1), Mumford contrasts two orders of thinking: the organic and the mechanical. "The first springs out of the total situation, the other simplifies the facts of life for the sake of an artful system of concepts, more dear to the mind than life itself. One works cooperatively with the 'materials of others,' perhaps guiding them, but first acknowledging their existence and understanding their purpose; the other, that of the baroque despot, insisting on his law, his order, his society, is imposed by a single professional authority, working under his command" (*The City in History: Its Origins, Its Transformations, and Its Prospects* [New York: Harcourt Brace Jovanovich, 1961], p. 394). The appeal of a centrally conceived city over a city grown up largely by unplanned accretions stemmed not necessarily from an *esprit géométrique*, as it did with Descartes; the planned city was seen to demonstrate royal power and to be more healthful, even in the seventeenth century. Thus John Evelyn, recently back from European exile with Charles II, wrote that London was "a city consisting of a wooden, northern, and *inartificial* congestion of houses, some of its principal streets so narrow, as there is nothing more deformed and unlike the prospect of it at a distance, and its *assymmetrie* within the walls" (quoted in Mark Jenner, "The Politics of London Air: John Evelyn's *Fumifugium* and the Restoration," *Historical Journal* 38, no. 3 [1995]: 542 [emphasis added]).

34. Quoted in Fishman, *Urban Utopias*, p. 213.

35. Le Corbusier was a member of Redressment Français, a circle of industrialists linked to the right. Regarding this connection and especially Le Corbusier's work in the Soviet Union, see Cohen, *Le Corbusier and the Mystique of the USSR*.

36. Le Corbusier, *The Radiant City*, p. 131 (emphasis in original). He continued, "The power of calculation is such that the imprudent might be tempted to raise altars to it forthwith, and worship it."

37. Le Corbusier was particularly proud of the transparency and line of this building, which, like many of his buildings in the 1920s, was set up on pilings (*pilotis*). Describing it, he wrote, "Appreciate the entirely new and formidable virtues of

this architecture; the impeccable line of the substructure. The building resembles an object in a window display, *and it is perfectly legible*" (Le Corbusier, "Les Techniques sont l'assiette même du lyricisme: Elles ouvrent un nouveau cycle de l'architecture," in *Précisions sur un état présent de l'architecture et de l'urbanisme* [Paris, 1930], quoted in Cohen, *Le Corbusier and the Mystique of the USSR*, p. 77 [emphasis added]).

38. In the end, Le Corbusier was bitter about his Soviet experience: "On several occasions I have been asked to draw up plans of cities for the Soviet Union; unfortunately it was all hot air. I am extremely sorry about this. . . . I have studied the basic social truths in such depth that I have been the first to create, in a natural way, THE GREAT CLASSLESS CITY, harmonious and joyful. It sometimes pains me to think that in the USSR I am resisted for reasons that to me do not appear to be valid" (quoted in Cohen, *Le Corbusier and the Mystique of the USSR*, p. 199).

39. Quoted in ibid., p. 109. In justifying the linear rigor of his Moscow plans, Le Corbusier wrote, "curved lines constitute paralysis, and the winding path is the path of donkeys" (quoted in ibid., p. 15).

40. Quoted in ibid., p. 93 (emphasis in original). Like so much of *The Radiant City*, this passage reflects Le Corbusier's constant appeal to the political authorities who alone can give substance to his plans.

41. See Colin Rowe, *The Architecture of Good Intentions: Towards a Possible Retrospect* (London: Academy Editions, 1995), for a discussion of Le Corbusier and the concept of the sublime.

42. Le Corbusier, quoted in ibid., p. 152.

43. Le Corbusier, quoted in Fishman, *Urban Utopias*, p. 177 (emphasis added).

44. Le Corbusier, *The Radiant City*, p. 116.

45. Ibid., p. 138.

46. Ibid., p. 176.

47. Ibid., p. 120. Baroque city planners also recognized that narrow streets posed a danger to the state. See Mumford's comment about the Neapolitan king Ferrante's fear of dark and crooked streets (*The City in History*, p. 348).

48. Le Corbusier, *The Radiant City*, p. 120. In a whimsical footnote Le Corbusier imagines a monument in bronze with Louis XIV, Napoleon I, and Napoleon III joining hands in the foreground and a smiling Colbert and Haussmann, also holding hands, in the background. With their free hands the three in the foreground raise a scroll bearing the admonition, "Keep at it, for God's sake."

49. Ibid., p. 27.

50. Ibid., p. 187.

51. Ibid., p. 185.

52. Ibid., p. 70. The influence of Fordism and Taylorism are evident here, too. See David Harvey, *The Condition of Post-Modernity: An Enquiry into the Origins of Social Change* (Oxford: Basil Blackwell, 1989), pp. 35–44. Le Corbusier was, after his first two decades of professional work, firmly associated with purism and constructivism. For constructivists, the most efficient shape of an object was the ideal shape; decorative touches were forbidden, as they only detracted from the pure beauty of functional design. The design of a house conceived in this spirit would begin from the inside, with its function and the available materials determining its shape and look. Despite his ideological commitments, Le Corbusier was always concerned with the painterly line of his designs, which he associated with classical or natural forms. In his later years, he forbade the use of the word "functionalism" in his studio. For discussions of Le Corbusier's early designs and intellectual milieu, see Russel Walden, ed., *The Open Hand: Essays on Le Corbusier* (Cambridge: MIT Press, 1975), especially the selections by Charles Jencks, Anthony Sutcliffe, and Mary Patricia May Sekler.

53. Le Corbusier, *The Radiant City*, p. 121.

54. Ibid., p. 128 (emphasis added). Curiously enough, when compared to Le Corbusier's grand schemes, his smaller projects seem to have been more successful, both aesthetically and practically. In particular, his small Chapel of Notre Dame du Haut at Ronchamp is considered a brilliant achievement, and his early houses at La Chaux-de-Fonds are much admired for decorative features that he later renounced.

55. James Holston, *The Modernist City: An Anthropological Critique of Brasília* (Chicago: University of Chicago Press, 1989).

56. Brazil has something of a history of making ambitious plans to claim the interior and then seeing them come to grief. In 1972, the trans-Amazonian highway was opened amid much fanfare (and ecological concern); by the late 1980s, much of the road was overgrown and impassible.

57. Quoted in Lawrence J. Vale, *Architecture, Power, and National Identity* (New Haven: Yale University Press, 1992), p. 125.

58. Holston, *The Modernist City*, pp. 113–19.

59. Ibid., p. 115.

60. Compare this tradition with the intention of Le Corbusier, who wrote, "Cafes and places of recreation will no longer be the fungus which eats up the pavements of Paris. We must kill the street" (*Towards a New Architecture*, trans. Frederick Etchells [New York: Praeger, 1959], pp. 56–59).

61. See Holston's interesting analysis in *The Modernist City*, pp. 119–36.

62. Ibid., pp. 105–7. I take the liberty of translating *convivencia* as "conviviality" rather than "sociality," as it seems more faithful to the point that Holston's informant is trying to make (p. 105).

63. Ibid., pp. 24–26.

64. Ibid., p. 24.

65. There are, of course, some things that residents *do* like about living in Brasília: the government facilities, the high standard of living, and the fact that it is a safe environment for children.

66. Ibid., p. 163.

67. Ibid., p. 171. The freestanding small house could also be merely a representational convention that gets established early in childhood.

68. See Holston's interesting analysis of how the superquadra apartment design eliminates the most public or social space of the traditional Brazilian dwelling, the *copa*, in ibid., pp. 177–80.

69. Ibid., p. 149. See also Kevin Lynch, *The Image of the City* (Cambridge: MIT Press, 1960). Lynch's concept of "imageability" has more to do with how a place or neighborhood can be "pictured" by its inhabitants than the legibility it might have to a planner or administrator. The two forms of order might often, as Holston reminds us, be negatively correlated.

70. Holston, *The Modernist City*, p. 209.

71. Quoted in ibid., p. 210.

72. My information about Chandigarh comes from the following sources: Ravi Kalia, *Chandigarh: In Search of an Identity* (Carbondale: Southern Illinois University Press, 1987), and three articles in Russell Walden, ed., *The Open Hand: Essays on Le Corbusier* (Cambridge: MIT Press, 1977): Maxwell Fry, "Le Corbusier at Chandigarh," pp. 351–63; Madhu Sarin, "Chandigarh as a Place to Live In," pp. 375–411; and Stanislaus von Moos, "The Politics of the Open Hand: Notes on Le Corbusier and Nehru at Chandigarh," pp. 413–57.

73. Punjabi politicians also embraced the project, seeing it as compensation for the loss of Lahore, the pre-partition capital of the Punjab, a focus of Mogul power,

and capital of the Sikh kingdom of Ranjit Singh. I'm grateful to Ramachandra Guha for this information.

74. As Maxwell Fry describes it, Le Corbusier was preoccupied at the time with the visual effects of buildings in large spaces. He had brought with him a plan of the grand axis that joined the Louvre to the Arc de Triomphe via the Champs Elysées and tried to work out "the farthest extension of grandeur comprehensible, at a single view," in the new setting. See Fry, "Le Corbusier at Chandigarh," p. 357.

75. Sarin, "Chandigarh as a Place to Live In," p. 386.

76. See, for example, the book published a decade and a half earlier by Percival Goodman and Paul Goodman, *Communitas: Means of Livelihood and Ways of Life* (New York: Vintage Books, 1947), which touches on many of the same themes found in Jacobs's work but which promotes decentralization and appropriate technology.

77. In New York City, Jacobs was seen as a prominent enemy of the master builder Robert Moses.

78. On the other hand, Jacobs had a great deal of knowledge about architecture. She was married to an architect and had worked her way up from newspaper and editing jobs to become associate editor of the journal *Architectural Forum*.

79. An interesting parallel case from the same time period is Rachel Carson's *Silent Spring* (Boston: Houghton Mifflin, 1962). Carson began her influential attack on the profligate use of insecticides by asking a homely but powerful question: "Where have all the songbirds gone?"

80. Jane Jacobs, *The Death and Life of Great American Cities* (New York: Vintage Books, 1961), p. 15.

81. Ibid., p. 376. The early constructivist Le Corbusier would not have disavowed this view as a matter of principle, but as a matter of practice he was always greatly concerned with the sculptural properties of an urban plan or a single building—sometimes with brilliant results, as in Notre-Dame-du-Haut, Ronchamp (1953).

82. A useful critique of current zoning practice may be found in James Howard Kunstler, "Home from Nowhere," *Atlantic Monthly*, September 1996, pp. 43–66.

83. Jacobs, *Death and Life*, p. 375. This seems especially reasonable so long as the disciplined works of art one is talking about are those of a Josef Albers rather than a Jackson Pollock. In this connection, it is useful to recall that Le Corbusier began as an artist and never stopped painting.

84. Ibid., p. 437.

85. Ibid., pp. 31–32. The recent social science literature on social trust and social capital, demonstrating the economic costs of their absence, signals that this homely truth is now a subject of formal inquiry. It is important to specify that Jacobs's point about "eyes on the street" assumes a rudimentary level of community feeling. If the eyes on the street are hostile to some or all members of the community, as Talja Potters has reminded me, public security is not enhanced.

86. Ibid., pp. 38–40. It is worth noting that the linchpin of this informal surveillance and social order is the fast-disappearing and much maligned petite bourgeoisie.

87. Ibid., pp. 59–62.

88. Ibid., pp. 60–61. Jacobs offers a catalogue of nonreimbursed services provided by a typical candy-store proprietor in the course of a single morning, acknowledging that many of these small services allow the shopkeeper to further "entangle" his or her clientele.

89. Ibid., p. 56 (emphasis in original).

90. Ibid., pp. 84–88. Jacobs quotes a 1928 regional planning report on recre-

ation, which noted that only about one-fourth of the population whose ages ranged from five to fifteen years actually played in playgrounds, which could not compete with city streets that were "teeming with life and adventure."

91. In the modern home, if the kitchen also has a television, its status as the most heavily used room in the home is likely to be without competition. Talja Potters, a Dutch colleague, tells me that in working-class apartments built in Holland between 1920 and 1970, the dimensions of the kitchen were deliberately minimized so that laborers would be obliged to dine and socialize in the living room, like decent middle-class people.

92. Jacobs's chapter "The Need for Small Blocks" is a model of her mode of analysis. See *Death and Life*, pp. 178–86.

93. Ibid., p. 222.

94. Jacobs, in addition to holding several jobs, was a wife and mother in the 1950s.

95. In explaining why children often prefer to play on sidewalks rather than in playgrounds, Jacobs writes: "Most city architectural designers are men. Curiously, they design and plan to exclude men as part of normal, daytime life wherever people live. In planning residential life, they aim at filling the presumed daily needs of impossibly vacuous housewives and preschool tots. They plan, in short, strictly for matriarchal societies" (*Death and Life*, p. 83).

96. Ibid., pp. 372–73 (emphasis in original). Compare Jacobs's critique with Mumford's criticism of baroque city planning as being "ruthless, one-sided, noncooperative, . . . [and] indifferent to the slow, complex interactions, the patient adjustments and modifications, through trial and selection, which mark more organic methods of city development" (*The City in History*, p. 350).

97. Jacobs, *Death and Life*, p. 289. For an extensive analysis of the process of economic diversification, see Jacobs's later book, *The Economy of Cities* (New York: Random House, 1970). Carol Rose, the legal theorist, makes the interesting point that the visual representations of property—fences, walls, hedges, windows, gates—function as a rhetoric of a static and timeless property that ignores historical change. See Rose, *Property and Persuasion: Essays in the History, Theory, and Rhetoric of Ownership* (Boulder: Westview Press, 1994), especially chap. 9, "Seeing Property," pp. 267–303.

98. Jacobs, *Death and Life*, p. 287.

99. Ibid., p. 391. The echoes of such influential anarchist thinkers as Pierre-Joseph Proudhon and Peter Kropotkin reverberate in this passage. I do not know whether Jacobs intended these resonances, which may have come from the work of Paul Goodman. But what is missing is a recognition that, in the absence of state-based urban planning, large commercial and speculative interests are transforming the urban landscape every day. The effect of her argument is to "naturalize" the unplanned city by treating it as the consequence of thousands of small and notionally equal acts.

100. Ibid., p. 737.

101. Some small components of buildings have of course been mass produced for a long time, from standard lumber stock, Sheetrock, and shingles to flooring and, most famously, nails. Sears and Roebuck home kits were available as early as the 1890s.

102. Where performance is critical—say, in an army—this logic is superseded by other criteria. Thus soldiers will typically have different-sized boots that fit well but haircuts that are identical.

103. Jacobs, *Death and Life*, p. 241.

104. Ibid., p. 238. The caveat, "and only when," may be a rare recognition by Ja-

cobs that, in the absence of extensive planning in a liberal economy, the asymmetrical market forces which shape the city are hardly democratic.

105. Ibid., p. 241.

106. For an elaboration of this argument applied to urban design, see Michel de Certeau, *The Practice of Everyday Life* (Arts de faire: La pratique du quotidien), trans. Steven Rendall (Berkeley: University of California Press, 1984). Another analogy that may be made in this context is to the market, along the lines developed by Friedrich Hayek. The problem that I see with this analogy is that the market in the modern sense is not synonymous with "spontaneous social order," but rather had to be imposed by a coercive state in the nineteenth century, as Karl Polanyi has convincingly shown. Hayek's description of the development of common law is, I believe, somewhat closer to the mark. In any event, city, market, and common law are all creators of historical power relations that are neither "natural" nor creative of "spontaneous social order." In her telling critique of planning, Jacobs is frequently tempted to naturalize the unplanned city rather as Hayek naturalizes the market.

107. Ibid., p. 138.

108. Some of Jacobs's insights appear to be behind the early stages of recuperation in a few blighted sections of New York City's South Bronx, once a synonym for the worst in urban decay. A combination of refurbishing existing buildings and apartments, promoting mixed-use development and urban homesteading, making small loans more readily available, and keeping to a modest scale appears to have facilitated the creation of viable neighborhoods.

109. Quoted in ibid., pp. 336–37. Tankel's plea appeared in a symposium called "The Architecture Forum" in June 1957.

110. See Lisa Redfield Peattie, *Planning, Rethinking Ciudad Guayana* (Ann Arbor: University of Michigan Press, 1987).

111. Jacobs, *Death and Life*, p. 195.

Chapter 5: The Revolutionary Party

1. V. I. Lenin, *What Is to Be Done? Burning Questions of Our Movement* (New York: International Publishers, 1929), p. 82.

2. Quoted in Robert Conquest, "The Somber Monster," *New York Review of Books*, June 8, 1995, p. 8. We also know that Lenin was an admirer of another utopian work, Tommaso Campanella's *City of the Sun*, which describes a religious utopia whose design includes strong pedagogical and didactic features for shaping the minds and souls of its citizens.

3. The metaphors of the classroom and the barracks were in keeping with Lenin's reputation in the party, where his comrades referred to him as "the German" or "Herr Doktor," alluding not so much to his time in Zurich or the assistance he received from Germany but simply to "his tidiness and self-discipline" (Conquest, "The Somber Monster").

4. Lenin, *What Is to Be Done?* p. 80.

5. Ibid., p. 84 (emphasis added).

6. Ibid., p. 161 (emphasis added).

7. Ibid., p. 114. Lenin is here referring to the Social Democrats in Germany, whom he regards as far more advanced than their Russian counterparts. See also p. 116, where Lenin asserts, "No movement can be durable without a stable organization of leaders to maintain continuity." This issue was debated anew in practically every socialist movement. We see it in the writings of the Italian Communist

and theoretician Antonio Gramsci, who basically shared Lenin's opinion on this matter. Rosa Luxemburg, as we shall see, also addressed the issue and reached very different conclusions.

8. Ibid., p. 162.

9. Ibid., p. 95.

10. Ibid., p. 15.

11. Quoted in ibid., p. 40. It is possible, Lenin remarks in a footnote (p. 41), for workers to rise into the intelligentsia and thereby play a role in creating socialist ideology. "But," he adds, "they take part not as workers, but as socialist theoreticians like Proudhon and Weitling."

12. Ibid., p. 33.

13. Ibid., p. 41.

14. Ibid., p. 151 (emphasis added). Lenin is writing specifically here about the newspaper *Iskra*, an organ of the vanguard party.

15. Ibid., pp. 120–21.

16. Ibid., p. 122 (emphasis in original).

17. See, for example, Kathy E. Ferguson, "Class Consciousness and the Marxist Dialectic: The Elusive Synthesis," *Review of Politics* 42, no. 4 (October 1986): 504–32.

18. Lenin, *What Is to Be Done?* p. 129.

19. Ibid., p. 121 (emphasis added).

20. "Agitation" is another diagnostic word in this context. It conjures up still waters that move only when "agitated" by an outside agent.

21. In the Tenth Party Congress in 1921, while troops under Trotsky were crushing a genuine proletarian revolt against Bolshevik autocracy, Bukharin and others condemned the "petit-bourgeois infection" that had spread from the peasantry to parts of the working class. See Paul Averich, *Kronstadt, 1921* (Princeton: Princeton University Press, 1970), chap. 3, especially pp. 129–30.

22. When it came to preventing actual disease and infection, Lenin took it on himself to ensure that the Kremlin was a clean, germ-free environment by writing its sanitary regulations himself. He instructed, for example, that "all those arriving (by train) shall before entering their accommodation take a bath and hand their dirty clothes to the disinfector at the baths. . . . Anyone refusing to obey the sanitary regulations will be expelled from the Kremlin at once and tried for causing social harm." From Dimitri Volkogonov, *Lenin: Life and Legacy*, trans. Harold Shukman (London: Harper Collins, 1995), cited in Robert Service, "The First Master Terrorist," *Times Literary Supplement*, January 6, 1995, p. 9.

23. Lenin, *What Is to Be Done?* p. 79 (emphasis added).

24. See Bruce M. Garver, *The Young Czech Party, 1874–1901, and the Emergence of a Multi-Party System* (New Haven: Yale University Press, 1978), p. 117. Peter Rutland tells me that such displays were by no means confined to political movements with authoritarian ideologies but were part of a view of machine precision and coordination from above that was applied to physical culture and shared by nationalist, bourgeois, and democratic movements, too. The tradition of coordinated "mass movement" survives, of course, in marching-band parades seen during halftimes of college football games in the United States. For more on the machine as a metaphor for social movements, see Chap. 6.

25. Nicolae Ceaușescu's nearly built Palace of the Republic in Bucharest contained many design features along these lines. The legislative assembly hall had tiered balconies encircling Ceaușescu's "hydraulically lifted podium, and the palace's six hundred clocks were all centrally set from a console in Ceaușescu's suite (*New York Times*, December 5, 1991, p. 2). Lenin, in contrast, was always opposed

to any cult of personality; the party itself was to be the conductor of the revolution-ary orchestra.

26. Even so, it should be noted, neither Le Corbusier nor Lenin was of a steady, methodical, bureaucratic temperament.

27. Hannah Arendt, *On Revolution* (New York: Viking, 1965).

28. E. H. Carr, *The Bolshevik Revolution, 1917–1923*, vol. 1 (Harmondsworth: Penguin, 1966), p. 36; Lenin quoted on p. 80. Carr extends this judgment to all par-ties in the February Revolution: "The revolutionary parties played no direct part in the making of the revolution. They did not expect it, and were at first somewhat nonplussed by it. The creation at the moment of the revolution of a Petrograd So-viet of Workers' Deputies was a spontaneous act of groups of workers without cen-tral direction. It was a revival of the Petersburg Soviet which had played a brief but glorious role in the revolution of 1905" (p. 81).

29. See, for example, ibid.; Sheila Fitzpatrick, *The Russian Revolution* (Oxford: Oxford University Press, 1982); and Marc Ferro, *The Bolshevik Revolution: A Social History of the Russian Revolution*, trans. Norman Stone (London: Routledge and Kegan Paul, 1980).

30. The best Russian depiction of this situation is in Tolstoy's brilliant analysis of battle during the Napoleonic campaign in Russia in *War and Peace* (New York: Simon and Schuster, 1942), pp. 713, 874, 921, 988. See also John Keegan, *The Face of Battle* (New York: Viking Press, 1976).

31. The role of autonomous action in driving the revolution forward even after October 1917 was recognized by Lenin when he said, in 1918, "Anarchist ideas have now taken on living form." See Daniel Guérin, *Anarchism: From Theory to Practice*, trans. Mary Klopper (New York: Monthly Review Press, 1970), p. 85. Much of the early Bolshevik legislation, Guérin notes, was the ex post facto legalization of autonnous actions and practices.

32. See the illuminating, detailed study, based on rich archival material, by Or-lando Figes: *Peasant Russia, Civil War: The Volga Countryside in Revolution, 1917–1921* (Cambridge: Cambridge University Press, 1996).

33. Milovan Djilas, *The New Class* (New York: Praeger, 1957), p. 32.

34. I am indebted to Peter Perdue for having pointed this out to me. Djilas makes much the same point (ibid.).

35. The official story, even though it may partly shape collective memory, cannot entirely supplant the individual and collective experiences of those who actually par-ticipated in the revolutionary process. For those who have no personal recollection and who thus come to the revolution via the schoolbook or patriotic speech, however, the official story will prevail unless there is another conflicting source of information.

36. This is the point of the ditty "For want of a nail the shoe was lost; for want of a shoe the horse was lost; for want of a horse the messenger was lost; for want of a message the battle was lost; for want of a victory a kingdom was lost . . ." (John M. Merriman, ed., *For Want of a Horse: Choice and Chance in History* [Lexington, Mass.: S. Greens Press, 1985]).

37. It is exceptionally rare to find any historical account that stresses the con-tingencies. The very exercise of producing an account of a past event virtually re-quires an often counterfactual neatness and coherence. Anyone who has ever read a newspaper account of an event in which he or she participated will recognize this phenomenon. Consider, too, the fact that a person who commits murder, say, or who takes his own life by jumping off a bridge will thereafter be known as the per-son who shot so-and-so or the person who jumped off such-and-such bridge. The events of that person's life will be reread in light of that ending, with an air of in-evitability being given to an act that may have been highly contingent.

38. In the case of the Bolshevik Revolution, it was also necessary that the official narrative include a genuinely popular mass movement of which the Bolsheviks eventually assumed leadership. Marxist historiography required a militant, revolutionary proletariat. This was an aspect of the February and October events that did not have to be invented. What had to be written out of the account, however, was the ferocious struggle between the new state apparatus on one hand and the autonomous soviets and peasantry on the other.

39. Lenin, quoted in Averich, *Kronstadt, 1921*, p. 160. I believe that Lenin is consciously copying Luxemburg here, although I have no direct proof. One can find a precedent for this in Lenin's momentary euphoria about the 1905 revolution: "Revolutions are the festival of the oppressed and the exploited. . . . At no other time are the masses of the people in a position to come forward so actively as creators of a new social order as at the time of revolution. At such times, the people are capable of performing miracles" (from "Two Tactics of Social Democracy," quoted by Richard Stites, *Revolutionary Dreams: Utopian Vision and Experimental Life in the Russian Revolution* [New York: Oxford University Press, 1989], p. 42).

40. V. I. Lenin, *State and Revolution* (New York: International Publishers, 1931), p. 23 (emphasis in original). Note that those who are to be "guided" by force are not the bourgeoisie, the enemies of the revolution, but the exploited classes, with the exception of the proletariat, for whom coercion will be unnecessary.

Lest one imagine that the state coercion to be applied would be decided democratically by the proletariat or its representatives, Lenin makes it clear just after the revolution that, as Leszek Kolakowski puts it, "the point about the dictatorship of the proletariat . . . is the absolute power, constrained by no laws, based on sheer, direct violence. And he said that there would be no freedom and no democracy (those were his very words) until the complete victory of Communism all over the world" ("A Calamitous Accident," *Times Literary Supplement*, November 6, 1992, p. 5).

41. Lenin, *State and Revolution*, pp. 23–24.

42. Ibid., p. 38 (emphasis in original).

43. Ibid., p. 83 (emphasis added).

44. Lenin, "The Immediate Tasks of the Soviet Government," March-April 1918, quoted in Carmen Claudin-Urondo, *Lenin and the Cultural Revolution*, trans. Brian Pearce (Sussex: Harvester Press, 1977), p. 271. It is worth noting the brief naturalistic imagery associated with "public-meeting democracy" here, as it is almost certainly borrowed from Rosa Luxemburg's work.

45. See David Harvey, *The Condition of Post-Modernity: An Enquiry into the Origins of Cultural Change* (Oxford: Basil Blackwell, 1989), p. 126. Harvey groups Lenin, Ford, Le Corbusier, Ebenezer Howard, and Robert Moses as modernists.

46. In fact, of course, there is no rationally efficient solution to any problem of this kind that ignores human subjectivity. An efficient production design depends vitally on the positive response of the workforce. The autoworkers who hated the "efficient" mass-assembly line in Lordsville, Ohio, responded by working so sloppily that they made it an inefficient assembly line.

47. Lenin, *State and Revolution*, pp. 84–85 (emphasis in original). Marx, Engels, and Lenin used the term "lumpen" proletariat to designate all those marginals who had escaped working-class discipline. Their contempt for lumpen elements was boundless and echoes the quasi-racist attitude of Victorian elites toward the "undeserving" poor.

48. Stites, *Revolutionary Dreams*, p. 32.

49. V. I. Lenin, *The Agrarian Question and the Critics of Marx*, 2nd rev. ed. (Moscow: Progress Publishers, 1976). Lenin's basic position on agriculture had been worked out long before in his 1889 book, *The Development of Capitalism in*

392 Notes to Pages 164–67

Russia. That book, however, had predicted a spontaneous development of capitalism in the countryside that had not occurred to anything like the extent he had forecast. For an important revisionist work on Marx's analysis of rural Russia, see Teodor Shanin, ed., *Late Marx and the Russian Road: Marx and the Peripheries of Capitalism* (New York: Monthly Review Press, 1983).

50. Ibid., p. 45.

51. V. I. Lenin, *The Agrarian Programme of Social Democracy in the First Russian Revolution, 1905–1907*, 2nd rev. ed. (Moscow: Progress Publishers, 1977), p. 70.

52. The German and Austrian schools of empirical household surveys of farm operations were very influential at the turn of the century. The great Russian economist in this tradition was A. V. Chayanov. A careful scholar, a partisan of small property (he wrote a utopian novel of his own), and a Soviet official, he was arrested by the Stalinist police in 1932 and is believed to have been executed in 1936. Pyotr Maslov was another contemporary Russian exponent of small-farm efficiency and intensification who disputed Lenin's position.

53. Lenin, *The Agrarian Question*, p. 86.

54. Ibid.

55. For an extensive treatment, see Jonathan Coppersmith, *The Electrification of Russia, 1880–1926* (Ithaca: Cornell University Press, 1992); and Kendall Bailes, *Technology and Society Under Lenin and Stalin: Origins of the Soviet Technical Intelligentsia* (Princeton: Princeton University Press, 1978). H. G. Wells, following a visit to the Soviet Union, wrote glowingly of his conversation with Lenin in October 1920: "For Lenin, who like a good orthodox Marxist denounces all 'Utopians,' has succumbed at last to a Utopia, the Utopia of the electricians" (*Russia in the Shadows* [New York: George H. Doran, 1921], p. 158).

56. Lenin, *The Agrarian Question*, p. 46. It is easy today to forget how breathtaking electricity was for those experiencing it for the first time. As Vladimir Mayakovsky was reported to have said, "After electricity, I lost interest in nature" (Stites, *Revolutionary Dreams*, p. 52). In fact, for all the activities mentioned by Lenin, the tractor, as a moveable power source without transmission lines, has proven more practical than electricity.

57. From Lenin's report to the Eighth Congress of Soviets (December 22, 1920), at the founding of the State Commission on the Electrification of Russia (GOELRO). Quoted in Robert C. Tucker, ed., *The Lenin Anthology* (New York: Norton, 1975), p. 494.

58. The centralization that electrification makes possible also sets the stage for large-scale power failures and brownouts. The practice of this technical centralization is often in stark, if not comic, contrast to its utopian promise. See, for an illuminating example from the Philippines under Marcos, Otto van den Muijzenberg, "As Bright Lights Replace the Kingke: Some Sociological Aspects of Rural Electrification in the Philippines," in Margaret M. Skutsch et al., eds., *Towards a Sustainable Development* (forthcoming).

59. As might be expected, the analogy between the light of electricity and the "enlightenment" of the narod was often evoked in Soviet rhetoric, combining, as it were, the Bolshevik technical project with its cultural project. Lenin wrote, "To the non-Party peasant masses electric light is an 'unnatural' light; but what we consider unnatural is that the peasants and workers should have lived for hundreds and thousands of years in such backwardness, poverty and oppression under the yoke of the landowners and the capitalists. . . . What we must now try is to convert every electric power station we build into a stronghold of enlightenment to be used to make the masses electricity-conscious" (quoted in Tucker, *The Lenin Anthology*, p. 495).

60. Figes, *Peasant Russia, Civil War*, p. 67.

61. Nor did he abandon his belief in the role of violence in ensuring party rule. In 1922, when religious believers in provincial Shuya openly demonstrated against the seizure of church treasures, Lenin argued for massive retaliation. "The more of them we manage to shoot the better," he declared. "Right now we have to teach this public a lesson so that for several decades they won't even dare think of resisting" (quoted in John Keep, "The People's Tsar," *Times Literary Supplement*, April 7, 1995, p. 30).

62. Quoted in Averich, *Kronstadt, 1921*, p. 224 (emphasis added).

63. Rosa Luxemburg, "Mass-Strike, Party, and Trade Unions" and "Organizational Questions of Russian Social Democracy," in Dick Howard, ed., *Selected Political Writings of Rosa Luxemburg* (New York: Monthly Review Press, 1971), pp. 223–70, 283–306; and Luxemburg, "The Russian Revolution," trans. Bertram D. Wolfe, in Mary-Alice Waters, ed., *Rosa Luxemburg Speaks* (New York: Pathfinder Press, 1970), pp. 367–95. It is interesting to speculate how much of Luxemburg's faith would have remained had she actually come to power in Germany. What is clear, however, is that her view when she was out of power is radically different from Lenin's view when he was out of power.

64. Elzbieta Ettinger suggests that one likely source of Luxemburg's faith in the wisdom of ordinary workers was her love of the great Polish nationalist poet, Adam Mickiewicz, who celebrated the insight and creativity of ordinary Poles. See *Rosa Luxemburg: A Life* (Boston: Beacon Press, 1986), pp. 22–27.

65. Luxemburg, "Mass-Strike, Party, and Trade Unions," p. 229. Despite Luxemburg's dismissive reference to anarchism, her views overlap considerably with an anarchist view of the independent, creative role of ordinary actors in a revolution. See, for example, G. D. Maximoff, ed., *The Political Philosophy of Bakunin: Scientific Anarchism* (New York: Free Press, 1953), p. 289, in which Bakunin's view of the limitations of leadership by a central committee prefigures Luxemburg's own modest opinion of a central committee's role.

66. This way of analyzing working-class movements grew directly out of Luxemburg's research for her 1898 doctoral thesis at the University of Zurich, "The Industrial Development of Poland." See J. P. Nettl, *Rosa Luxemburg*, vol. 1 (London: Oxford University Press, 1966).

67. Luxemburg, "Mass-Strike, Party, and Trade Unions," p. 236.

68. Luxemburg was something of an aesthetic free spirit as well. Continually scolded by her lover and comrade, Leo Jogiches, for her petit-bourgeois tastes and desires, she defended the value of a private life while devoting herself to the revolution. Her élan is nicely captured by her advice on the design of the Spartacist newspaper *Die Rote Fahne* (The red banner): "I do not think a newspaper should be symmetrical, trimmed like an English lawn. . . . Rather, it should be somewhat untamed, like a wild orchard, should bristle with life and shine with young talents" (quoted in Ettinger, *Rosa Luxemburg*, p. 186).

69. Luxemburg, "Organizational Questions," p. 291 (emphasis added).

70. "An awakening of the revolutionary energy of the working class in Germany can never again be called forth in the spirit of the guardianship methods of the German Social Democracy of late-lamented memory. . . . [The awakening of revolutionary energy could be effected] only by an insight into all the fearful seriousness, all the complexity of the tasks involved, only as a result of political maturity and independence of spirit, only as a result of *a capacity for critical judgment on the part of the masses, which capacity was systematically killed by the social democracy for decades under various pretexts*" (Luxemburg, "The Russian Revolution," pp. 369–70; emphasis added).

71. Luxemburg, "Mass-Strike, Party, and Trade Unions," p. 236.

72. Ibid., p. 237.

73. Ibid., p. 241.

74. Ibid., pp. 241–42.

75. Luxemburg, "Organizational Questions," p. 306.

76. Luxemburg, "The Russian Revolution," p. 389. By constantly stressing the ethical and idealistic side of the working class, Luxemburg probably underestimated the importance of bread-and-butter concerns. Such concerns could as easily, in 1917 at least, lead to revolutionary action as to narrow trade unionism. Neither she nor Lenin had the respect for working-class materialism to be found, for example, in Orwell's *Road to Wigan Pier* or *Down and Out in Paris and London*. While Lenin treated the workers as truant schoolboys constantly in need of monitoring and instruction, Luxemburg probably missed, among other things, their proclivities for nationalism and their occasional timorousness.

77. Ibid., p. 390. The reference to a textbook is not mocking; what strikes a contemporary observer of turn-of-the-century socialism is how extraordinarily bookish and pedagogical it was. The classroom metaphor prevailed in socialist thought, and formal instruction was the norm. Luxemburg spent much of her career meeting classes and grading papers at the higher party school of the SDP.

78. Ibid. (emphasis added). Compare this with the approach of the Italian anarchist Errico Malatesta, who in 1907 stated in *Anarchy* that even if rule by beneficent authoritarian socialists were possible, it "would immensely diminish [productive force], because the government would restrict initiative to the few" (quoted in Irving Louis Horowitz, *The Anarchists* [New York: Dell, 1964], p. 83).

79. Luxemburg, "The Russian Revolution," p. 391.

80. Ibid.

81. Kollontay, unlike so many other dissidents, was not murdered or sent to the labor camps. She survived in a series of ceremonial and ambassadorial posts taken with the implicit understanding that she muzzle her criticism. See Beatrice Farnsworth, *Alexandra Kollontai: Socialism, Feminism, and the Bolshevik Revolution* (Stanford: Stanford University Press, 1980).

82. Alexandra Kollontai, *Selected Writings of Alexandra Kollontai*, trans. Alix Holt (London: Allison and Busby, 1977), p. 178. Kollontay's essay "The Workers' Opposition," from which this quotation is taken, reprints a translation made in 1921 since the original Russian essay could not be found.

83. Ibid., p. 183. The issue of the autonomy of the family was another matter. Kollontay urged Soviet mothers to think of their children not as "mine" or "yours" but as "our children, those of the Communist state."

84. Ibid., p. 182 (emphasis in original).

85. Ibid., p. 185.

86. Ibid., pp. 191, 188, 190.

87. Ibid., p. 187.

88. Ibid., pp. 187, 160.

Introduction to Part 3

1. Pierre-Joseph Proudhon, "Q'est-ce que c'est la propriété?" quoted in Daniel Guerin, *Anarchism: From Theory to Practice*, trans. Mary Klopper (New York: Monthly Review Press, 1970), pp. 15–16.

2. It may be more accurate to say that societies are likely to exhibit not only the purposes and activities of their members (including, of course, their resistance) but

also traces of many previous state "projects," each of which has laid down its particular geological stratum.

3. The phrase comes from the title of Norbert Elias's great work, *The Civilizing Process*, vol. 1 of *The History of Manners*, trans. Edmund Jephcott (New York: Pantheon, 1982), but it applies also, as we shall see, to the self-descriptions of the "modernizers" outside the West who have implemented these schemes. See also Elias's *Power and Civility*, the second volume of *The History of Manners*.

4. See *Von Thünen's Isolated State* (1966), trans. Carla M. Wartenberg (Oxford: Pergamon Press), and G. William Skinner, *Marketing and Social Structure in China* (Tucson: Association of Asian Studies, 1975). Walter Christaller was the founder of central place theory. That theory, elaborated in his thesis at the University of Erlangen in 1932, forms the premise of Skinner's work.

5. Waterborne movement was far easier than overland movement, so proximity was measured less by physical distance, abstractly measured, than by "travel time." As these kingdoms had a tradition of long-distance trade, they were thus interested in appropriation, often by tribute relations, of not only grain and manpower but also valuable goods, such as gems, precious metals, medicines, and resins, that were profitable and manageable for trade conducted over long distances.

6. An illustration of this is found in the following admonition directed to King Narathihapate from Queen Saw, taken from *The Glass Palace Chronicle of the Kings of Burma*, trans. Pe Maung Tin and G. H. Luce (London: Oxford University Press, 1923), p. 177: "'Consider the state of the realm. Thou hast no folk or people, no host of countrymen and countrywomen around thee. . . . Thy countrymen and countrywomen tarry and will not enter thy kingdom. They fear thy domination; for thou, O King Alaung, art a hard master.'"

The classic analysis of the phenomenon in Southeast Asia may be found in Michael Adas, "From Avoidance to Confrontation: Peasant Protest in Pre-Colonial and Colonial Southeast Asia," *Comparative Studies in Society and History* 23, no. 2 (1981): 217–47. Coastal and riverine populations could be said to have "voted with their oars."

7. The problem of population flight was hardly unique to Southeast Asia. In the late fourteenth and fifteenth centuries, after the Black Plague had reduced the population of Western Europe by nearly one-third, the nobility faced a serious problem in attracting serfs on favorable terms now that they could so easily flee to land that had been abandoned by those felled by the plague. Slave states with open frontiers have always been vulnerable on this score; in the pre-Civil War United States, escaping slaves could head to the North, Canada, or the "free states" of the West. In Russia, the majority of czarist decrees addressed the subject of runaway serfs. In general, wherever there is an open frontier, unfree forms of labor are difficult to sustain unless sufficient coercion can be mobilized to contain the population.

8. This logic works best for inland (*kraton*-style) kingdoms. It breaks down whenever there are strategic locations that function as natural monopolies or choke points and control of which can serve as a basis for appropriation. I have in mind the control of river mouths (the *hulu-hilir* distinction in the Malay world), straits, mountain passes, or deposits of vital resources.

9. Abstracting from the Southeast Asian case, one might say that state formation is abetted by concentrated, intensive cultivation, a population who produces a consistent surplus and who finds it costly to leave (having had, for example, high sunk-costs in field creation and water control), who produce goods that, if bulky (such as food), can be stored and moved easily (such as grain) and that have relatively high value per unit volume and weight.

10. Those who dwell in such spaces, of course, saw the matter differently, con-

trasting their freedom, mobility, and honor, to the bondage of those under the thumb of the court. An evocative and evenhanded Afghan proverb captures the distinction: "Taxes ate the valleys; honor ate the hills."

11. One of the best ways to conjure up such places is to ask where runaway serfs and slaves repaired to and where Maroon communities of fugitive slaves established themselves. Such places were nonstate spaces, which the authorities tried to efface if possible. In the United States, a telling example is the enormous effort made in the postbellum South to eliminate the large commons on which free blacks could eke out an independent existence and to drive the blacks into the labor market, often to work for their former masters. Most freed slaves preferred to make a precarious living by farming, fishing, hunting, trapping, and grazing a few animals on open land over the subordination of permanent wage labor. A series of fencing and trespassing laws, hunting and trapping prohibitions, grazing restrictions, vagrancy laws, and so on were, as Steven Hahn has shown, designed to eliminate this nonwage labor (and nonstate) space. See Hahn, "Hunting, Fishing, and Foraging: Common Rights and Class Relations in the Post-Bellum South," *Radical History Review* 26 (1982): 37–64.

12. Lest this seem geographically determinist, let me emphasize that human agency plays a large role in creating and maintaining a nonstate space. At the limit, even parts of great cities may come to be nonstate spaces when the state essentially cedes control to a rebellious or resistant population.

13. A goal related to dispossessing the Meratus of "their" forest was to make the land more easily available for inclusion in state logging and revenue plans.

14. Anna Lowenhaupt Tsing, *In the Realm of the Diamond Queen: Marginality in an Out-of-the-Way Place* (Princeton: Princeton University Press, 1993), pp. xiii, 28, 41.

15. Ibid., pp. 48, 93.

16. I recall seeing such settlements in the Philippine provinces of Tarlac and Pangasinan, where each house displayed, in large letters on the front near the steps, the names and ages of all the family members who slept there, allowing security forces on their nightly patrols to more easily identify any unauthorized visitors.

17. Once it is cut, sugarcane must be crushed quickly in order to avoid losses through evaporation and fermentation. The need for a large crushing mill (often called a sugar "central," for good reason), problems relating to transportation of the cane, and the great bulk reduction through processing provide a kind of natural bottleneck that allows the mill owner to control production directly or else through tied contracts. Compared to coffee, tobacco, tea, rubber, or palm oil, sugarcane is unique in this advantage to centralized production.

18. The difficulties of recruiting Malays, who were independent cultivators, to work on the estates proved insurmountable, and thus it seemed more convenient to import Indian and Chinese laborers for the growing estate labor force. This fact alone favored plantations unless the colonizers were willing to risk the political dangers of creating a class of imported yeomen to compete with the Malays for land. Elsewhere, there were other solutions to creating a legible sphere of appropriation. On Java, the Culture System required the village, in lieu of taxes, to plant an export crop every so often on village lands. Where it was vital to force an economically independent peasantry into wage labor or plantation work, a universal, annual head tax payable in cash was often found to be useful.

19. Thus the morally obtuse but sociologically correct observation by Samuel Huntington during the Vietnam War: the massive bombing of the countryside and the subsequent creation of huge refugee settlements on the outskirts of major cities

provided many advantages to those who wanted to influence and mobilize the electorate. Those in the camps, he reasoned, were more easily manipulable than those still living in their rural communities. The implicit but macabre logic was impeccable; the more bombs rained on the countryside, the greater the opportunities for the United States and its allies in Saigon to dominate any peaceful electoral competition that followed. From Huntington, "Getting Ready for Political Competition in South Vietnam," paper presented at the Southeast Asia Development Advisory Group of the Asia Society, circa 1970.

I believe that this logic of social demobilization is the key element in the commonly observed fact that, at the beginning of industrialization, the declining rural community is often more likely to be a source of collective protest than is the newly constituted proletariat, notwithstanding standard Marxist reasoning to the contrary. Resettlement, whether forced or unforced, often eliminates a prior community and replaces it with a temporarily disaggregated mass of new arrivals. It is ironically just such a population that may, for the time being, more closely resemble the "potatoes in a sack" than the peasantry of the *bocage* described by Marx in *The Eighteenth Brumaire*.

Chapter 6: Soviet Collectivization, Capitalist Dreams

1. The best source for a discussion about Soviet high modernism is probably Richard Stites, *Revolutionary Dreams: Utopian Vision and Experimental Life in the Russian Revolution* (New York: Oxford University Press, 1989). Its generous bibliography appears to cover most of the available sources.

2. This inference, we know, is not a distortion of the doctrines of liberalism. J. S. Mill, whose credentials as a liberal son of the Enlightenment are not in doubt, considered backwardness a sufficient justification for placing authoritarian powers in the hands of a modernizer. See Ernest Gellner, "The Struggle to Catch Up," *Times Literary Supplement*, December 9, 1994, p. 14. For a more detailed argument along these lines, see also Jan P. Nederveen Pieterse and Bhikhu Parekh, eds., *The Decolonization of the Imagination: Culture, Knowledge, and Power* (London: Zed Press, 1995).

3. Stites, *Revolutionary Dreams*, p. 19. Engels expressed his disdain for Communist utopian schemes like these by calling them "barracks Communism."

4. One could say that Catherine the Great, being Prussian born and an avid correspondent with several of the Encyclopedists, including Voltaire, came by her mania for rational order honestly.

5. Sheila Fitzpatrick, *The Russian Revolution* (Oxford: Oxford University Press, 1982), p. 119. The term "gigantomania" was, I believe, also in use in the Soviet Union. The ultimate failure of most of the USSR's great schemes is in itself an important story, the significance of which was captured epigrammatically by Robert Conquest, who observed that "the end of the Cold War can be seen as the defeat of Magnitogorsk by Silicon Valley" ("Party in the Dock," *Times Literary Supplement*, November 6, 1992, p. 7). For an industrial, cultural, and social history of Magnitogorsk, see Stephen Kotkin, *Magnetic Mountain: Stalinism as a Civilization* (Berkeley: University of California Press, 1995).

6. An interesting parallel can be seen in the French countryside following the Revolution, when campaigns called for "de-Christianization" and offered associated secular rituals.

7. Stites, *Revolutionary Dreams*, p. 119. See also Vera Sandomirsky Dunham, *In Stalin's Time: Middle-Class Values in Soviet Fiction* (Cambridge: Cambridge

University Press, 1976), for how, under Stalin, this austerity was transformed into opulence.

8. Stites, "Festivals of the People," chap. 4 of *Revolutionary Dreams*, pp. 79–97.

9. Ibid., p. 95. Through Sergey Eisenstein's films, these public theatrical reenactments are the visual images that remain embedded in the consciousness of many of those who were not participants in the actual revolution.

10. Composers and filmmakers were also expected to be "engineers of the soul."

11. Quoted in Stites, *Revolutionary Dreams*, p. 243.

12. Lenin, almost certainly influenced by another of his favorite books, Campanella's *City of the Sun*, wanted public sculptures of revolutionaries, complete with inspiring inscriptions, to be erected throughout the city: a propaganda of monuments. See Anatoly Lunacharsky, "Lenin and Art," *International Literature* 5 (May 1935): 66–71.

13. Stites, *Revolutionary Dreams*, p. 242.

14. This entire section is based on chaps. 2, 4, and 6 of a remarkable forthcoming book by Deborah Fitzgerald, *Yeoman No More: The Industrialization of American Agriculture*, to which I am greatly indebted. The chapter and page numbers that follow refer to the draft manuscript.

15. Ibid., chap. 2, p. 21.

16. As many commentators have emphasized, this redesigning of work processes wrested the control of production from skilled artisans and laborers and placed it in the hands of management, whose ranks and prerogatives grew as the labor force was "de-skilled."

17. Around 1920, much of the market for agricultural machinery made by U.S. manufacturers was not in the United States, where farm sizes were still relatively small, but outside the country, in such places as Canada, Argentina, Australia, and Russia, where farms were considerably larger. Fitzgerald, *Yeoman No More*, chap. 2, p. 31.

18. For a fascinating and more complete account of the Campbell enterprise, see "The Campbell Farm Corporation," chap. 5, ibid. It's worth adding here that the economic depression for agriculture in the United States began at the end of World War I, not in 1930. The time was thus ripe for bold experimentation, and cost of buying or leasing land was cheap.

19. Wheat and flax are, in the terminology developed later in this chapter, "proletarian" crops as opposed to "petit-bourgeois" crops.

20. Fitzgerald, *Yeoman No More*, chap. 4, pp. 15–17.

21. See above, nn. 14 and 18.

22. Another such farm, and one with direct links to New Deal experimentation in the 1930s, was the Fairway Farms Corporation. Founded in 1924 by M. L. Wilson and Henry C. Taylor, both of whom were trained in institutional economics at the University of Wisconsin, the corporation was designed to turn landless farmers into scientific, industrial farmers. The capital for the new enterprise came, through intermediaries, from John D. Rockefeller. "Fair Way" Farms would become the model for many of the New Deal's more ambitious agricultural programs as Wilson, Taylor, and many of their progressive colleagues in Wisconsin moved to influential positions in Washington under Roosevelt. A more searching account of the connection is in Jess Gilbert and Ellen R. Baker, "Wisconsin Economists and New Deal Agricultural Policy: The Legacy of Progressive Professors" (unpublished paper, 1995). The 1920s were a fertile time for agricultural experimentation, partly because the economic slump for agricultural commodities after World War I prompted policy initiatives designed to alleviate the crisis.

23. Fitzgerald, *Yeoman No More*, chap. 4, pp. 18–27. For an account of indus-

trial farming in Kansas and its link to the ecological disaster known as the dust bowl, see Donald Worster, *Dust Bowl: The Southern Plains in the 1930s* (New York: Oxford University Press, 1979).

24. Fitzgerald, *Yeoman No More*, chap. 4, p. 33. The plan's outline can be found in Mordecai Ezekial and Sherman Johnson, "Corporate Farming: The Way Out?" *New Republic*, June 4, 1930, pp. 66–68.

25. Michael Gold, "Is the Small Farmer Dying?" *New Republic*, October 7, 1931, p. 211, cited in Fitzgerald, *Yeoman No More*, chap. 2, p. 35.

26. Ibid., chap. 6, p. 13. See also Deborah Fitzgerald, "Blinded by Technology: American Agriculture in the Soviet Union, 1928–1932," *Agricultural History* 70, no. 3 (Summer 1996): 459–86.

27. Enthusiastic visitors included the likes of John Dewey, Lincoln Steffens, Rexford Tugwell, Robert LaFollette, Morris Llewellyn Cooke (at the time the foremost exponent of scientific management in the United States), Thurman Arnold, and, of course, Thomas Campbell, who called the Soviet experiment "the biggest farming story the world has ever heard." Typical of the praise for Soviet plans for a progressive, modernized rural life was this appraisal by Belle LaFollette, the wife of Robert LaFollette: "If the Soviets could have their way, all land would be cultivated by tractors, all the villages lighted by electricity, each community would have a central house serving for the purpose of school, library, assembly hall, and theatre. They would have every convenience and advantage which they plan for the industrial workers in the city" (quoted in Lewis S. Feuer, "American Travelers to the Soviet Union, 1917–1932: The Formation of a Component of New Deal Ideology," *American Quarterly* 14 [Spring 1962]: 129). See also David Caute, *The Fellow Travellers: Intellectual Friends of Communism*, rev. ed. (New Haven: Yale University Press, 1988).

28. Feuer, "American Travelers to the Soviet Union," pp. 119–49, cited in Fitzgerald, *Yeoman No More*, chap. 6, p. 4.

29. Fitzgerald, *Yeoman No More*, chap. 6, p. 6.

30. Ibid., p. 37.

31. Ibid., p. 14.

32. Ibid., p. 39 (emphasis added).

33. Quoted in Robert Conquest, *The Harvest of Sorrow: Soviet Collectivization and the Terror-Famine* (New York: Oxford University Press, 1986), p. 232. An even more explicit recognition that this was a "war" appears in this statement by M. M. Khateyevich: "A ruthless struggle is going on between the peasantry and our regime. It's a struggle to the death. This year was a test of our strength and their endurance. It took a famine to show them who was master here. It has cost millions of lives, but the collective farm system is here to stay, we've won the war" (quoted in ibid., p. 261).

34. The so-called Great Leap Forward in China was at least as deadly and may be analyzed in comparable terms. I have chosen to concentrate on Soviet Russia largely because events there occurred some thirty years before the Great Leap Forward and hence have received much more scholarly attention, especially during the past seven years, when the newly opened Russian archives have greatly expanded our knowledge. For a recent popular account of the Chinese experience, see Jasper Becker, *Hungry Ghosts: China's Secret Famine* (London: John Murray, 1996).

35. In cases where yields were high among state farms and show projects, they were typically achieved with such costly inputs of machinery, fertilizers, pesticides, and herbicides that the results were economically irrational.

36. For an exceptionally perceptive account of collectivization and its results,

see Moshe Lewin, *The Making of the Soviet System: Essays in the Social History of Interwar Russia* (New York: Pantheon, 1985), especially part 2, pp. 89–188.

37. I use the term "lumpen" here to designate a huge floating population of great variety and shifting occupations. Although Marx and Lenin always used the term scornfully, implying both criminal tendencies and political opportunism, I intend no such denigration.

38. Stalin, it is now believed, was personally responsible for drafting in August 1932 a secret decree branding all those who withheld grain, now declared to be "sacred and untouchable" state property, as "enemies of the people" and ruling that they should be summarily arrested and shot. The same Stalin, at the Second Congress of Outstanding Kolkhozniks in 1935, championed the retaining of adequate private plots: "The majority of kolkhozniks want to plant an orchard, cultivate a vegetable garden or keep bees. The kolkhozniks want to live a decent life, and for that this 0.12 hectares is not enough. We need to allocate a quarter to half a hectare, and even as much as one hectare in some districts" (quoted in Sheila Fitzpatrick, *Stalin's Peasants: Resistance and Survival in the Russian Village After Collectivization* [New York: Oxford University Press, 1995], pp. 73, 122).

39. Ibid., p. 432.

40. Orlando Figes, "Peasant Aspirations and Bolshevik State-Building in the Countryside, 1917–1925," paper presented at the Program in Agrarian Studies, Yale University, New Haven, April 14, 1995, p. 24. Figes also links these views to socialist tracts that date from at least the 1890s and that pronounced the peasantry doomed by economic progress (p. 28).

41. R. W. Davies, *The Socialist Offensive: The Collectivisation of Soviet Agriculture, 1929–1930* (London: Macmillan, 1980), p. 51.

42. Conquest, *Harvest of Sorrow*, p. 43.

43. Also, the collapse of urban enterprises, which would normally have supplied consumer goods and farm implements to the rural areas, meant that there was less incentive for the peasantry to sell grain in order to make purchases in the market.

44. See Orlando Figes's remarkably perceptive and detailed book, *Peasant Russia, Civil War: The Volga Countryside in Revolution, 1917–1921* (Oxford: Clarendon Press, 1989). Even near revolutions create a similar vacuum. Following the 1905 revolution, it took the czarist government nearly two years to reassert its control over the countryside.

45. The relative unity of the village was itself enhanced by the revolutionary process. The richest landlords had left or been burned out, and the poorest, landless families had typically gotten some land. As a result, the villagers were more socioeconomically similar and therefore more likely to respond similarly to external demands. Since many of the independent farmers were pressured to return to the commune, they were now dependent on the entire village for their household's allotment of the communal lands. Thus it is not hard to understand why, in those instances where the kombedy was an instrument of Bolshevik policy, it faced determined opposition from the more representative village soviet. "One government official from Samara Province claimed, with conscious irony, that the conflicts between the kombedy and the Soviets represented the main form of 'class struggle' in the rural areas during this period" (ibid., p. 197). In the larger villages, some support for Bolshevik agrarian plans could be found among educated youth, schoolteachers, and veterans who had become Bolsheviks while serving with the Red Army during World War I or the civil war (and who might have imagined themselves occupying leading roles in the new collective farms). See Figes, "Peasant Aspirations and Bolshevik State-Building."

46. There was also a tendency to hide income from craft, artisanal, and trading sidelines as well as "garden" crops. During this same period, it should be added, insufficient resources—manpower, draft animals, manure, and seed—meant that some of the arable either could not be planted or could only produce yields that were far lower than usual.

47. Yaney, *The Urge to Mobilize*, pp. 515–16. For Yaney, the continuity in aspirations from what he terms "messianic social agronomists" under the czarist regime to the Bolshevik collectivizers was striking. In a few cases, they were the same people.

48. Figes, *Peasant Russia, Civil War*, p. 250.

49. Hunger and flight from the towns had reduced the number of urban industrial workers from 3.6 million in 1917 to no more than 1.5 million in 1920 (Fitzpatrick, *The Russian Revolution*, p. 85).

50. Figes, *Peasant Russia, Civil War*, p. 321.

51. Quoted in Fitzpatrick, *Stalin's Peasants*, p. 39.

52. In theory, at least, the most "advanced" were the state farms—the proletarian, industrial, collective farms in which workers were paid wages and no private plots were allowed. These farms also received the bulk of state investment in machinery in the early years. For production statistics, see Davies, *The Socialist Offensive*, p. 6.

53. Ibid., pp. 82–113.

54. Fitzpatrick, *Stalin's Peasants*, p. 4.

55. Conquest, *Harvest of Sorrow*, p. 183.

56. Andrei Platonov, *Chevengur*, trans. Anthony Olcott (Ann Arbor: Ardis, 1978).

57. M. Hindus, *Red Breed* (London, 1931), quoted in Davies, *The Socialist Offensive*, p. 209.

58. Davies, *The Socialist Offensive*, p. 205.

59. The size of collective farms remained enormous, even by American standards, throughout the Soviet period. Fred Pryor calculates that in 1970 the average state farm comprised more than 100,000 acres, while the average collective farm comprised over 25,000 acres. The state farms were greatly favored in access to inputs, machinery, and other subsidies. See Frederick Pryor, *The Red and the Green: The Rise and Fall of Collectivized Agriculture in Marxist Regimes* (Princeton: Princeton University Press, 1992), table 7, p. 34.

60. Fitzgerald, *Stalin's Peasants*, p. 105.

61. Ibid., pp. 105–6. One imagines that the soils and existing cropping patterns were also ignored.

62. As the Bolsheviks explained, "The kolkhozy are the *only* means by which the peasantry can escape from poverty and darkness" (Davies, *The Socialist Offensive*, p. 282). Perhaps the best visual images of the culturally transforming properties of electricity, machinery, and collectivization are found in Sergey Eisenstein's film *The General Line*, a veritable technological romance set in rural Russia. The film masterfully conveys the utopian aspirations of high modernism by contrasting the plodding dark narod with his horse and scythe with images of electric cream separators, tractors, mowing machines, engines, skyscrapers, engines, and airplanes.

63. Fitzpatrick, *Stalin's Peasants*, p. 194.

64. Ibid., pp. 306–9.

65. For an account of how an even more extreme version of regional specialization was imposed on the Chinese countryside, in violation of local soil and climatological conditions, see Ralph Thaxton, *Salt of the Earth: The Political Origins of Peasant Protest and Communist Revolution in China* (Berkeley: University of California Press, forthcoming).

66. Figes, *Peasant Russia, Civil War*, p. 304. The analogy took concrete form in

many of the early revolts against collectivization, during which the peasantry destroyed all the records of labor dues, crop deliveries, debts, and so on, just as they had under serfdom.

67. Conquest, *Harvest of Sorrow*, p. 152.

68. The resemblances to serfdom are spelled out in some detail in Fitzgerald, *Stalin's Peasants*, pp. 128–39. For a careful and informed discussion of serfdom and comparisons to slavery, see Peter Kolchin, *Unfree Labor: American Slavery and Russian Serfdom* (Cambridge: Harvard University Press, 1987).

69. For an astute account by a Soviet journalist and human rights campaigner in the 1980s, indicating that the basic pattern had not greatly changed, see Lev Timofeev, *Soviet Peasants, or The Peasants' Art of Starving*, trans. Jean Alexander and Alexander Zaslavsky, ed. Armando Pitassio and Alexander Zaslavsky (New York: Telos Press, 1985).

70. I am persuaded by the historical accounts that characterize the mir as the peasantry's adaptation to a gentry and state that treated it as a collective unit for the purposes of taxation, conscription, and some forms of servile dues. The periodic redivision of land among the households ensured that all had the means of paying their share of the head taxes, which were levied on the commune collectively. That is, the relative solidarity of the Russian repartitional commune is itself a result of a distinct history of relations with overlords. This claim is perfectly compatible with the fact that such solidarity, once in place, can serve other purposes, including resistance.

71. Fitzgerald, *Stalin's Peasants*, p. 106 (emphasis added).

72. I am immensely grateful to my colleague Teodor Shanin and his research teams, who are conducting comparative work on more than twenty collective farms, for making available to me the maps and photographs for this chapter. Particular thanks to Galya Yastrebinskaya and Olga Subbotina for the photograph of the older village of Utkino, founded in 1912 and located twenty miles from the city of Vologda.

73. Notice that the old-style houses that were not moved (legend reference 12) are themselves laid out on roughly equal plots along the main road. I do not know whether there were administrative reasons behind these forms in the eighteenth century, when the village was founded, or whether the original pioneers themselves laid out the grid. How the older houses that have been relocated were originally disposed is also a mystery.

74. The same logic, of course, applied to industry, in which large units are favored over small factories or artisanal production. As Jeffrey Sachs has observed: "Central planners had no desire to coordinate the activities of hundreds or thousands of small firms in a sector if one large firm could do the job. A standard strategy, therefore, was to create one giant firm wherever possible" (*Poland's Jump into the Market Economy* [Cambridge: Cambridge University Press, 1993]). In the context of the Soviet economy, the largest industrial unit was the huge steel complex at Magnitogorsk. It is now a stunning example of an industrial and ecological ruin. See also Kotkin, *Magnetic Mountain*.

75. For a more extensive treatment of the ecological effects of Soviet agriculture, see Murray Feshbach, *Ecological Disaster: Cleaning Up the Hidden Legacy of the Soviet Regime* (New York: 1995), and Ze'ev Wolfson (Boris Komarov), *The Geography of Survival: Ecology in the Post-Soviet Era* (New York: M. E. Sharpe, 1994).

76. I worked for six weeks in 1990 on a cooperative (ex-collective) farm in eastern Germany, on the Mecklenburg Plain, not too far from Neubrandenburg. The local officials were exceptionally proud of their world-class yields per hectare in rye and potatoes with high starch content grown for industrial uses. It was clear, however, that as an economic matter, the market cost of the inputs (labor, machin-

ery, and fertilizer) needed to produce these yields made this enterprise an inefficient producer by any cost accounting standard.

77. There is no doubt that a number of bureaucratic "pathologies" amplified the disaster of Soviet collectivization. They include the tendency of administrators to concentrate on specified, quantifiable results (e.g., grain yields, tons of potatoes, tons of pig iron) rather than on quality and the fact that long chains of specialization and command shielded many officials from the larger consequences of their behavior. Also, the difficulty of making officials accountable to their clientele, as opposed to their superiors, meant that the pathology of group "commandism," on one hand, or individual corruption and self-serving, on the other, were rampant. Highmodernist schemes in revolutionary, authoritarian settings like that of the Soviet Union are thus likely to go off the rails more easily and remain off the rails far longer than in a parliamentary setting.

78. The rush toward collectivization was momentarily halted by Stalin's famous "Dizzy with Success" speech of March 1930, which prompted many to leave the collectives; however, it was not long before the pace of collectivization resumed. In order to have enough capital for rapid industrialization, 4.8 million tons of grain were exported in 1930 and 5.2 million tons in 1931, helping to set the stage for the famine of the years immediately following. See Lewin, *The Making of the Soviet System*, p. 156.

79. Compare this with Bakunin's forecast of what state socialism would amount to: "They will concentrate all of the powers of government in strong hands, because the very fact that the people are ignorant necessitates strong, solicitous care by the government. They will create a single state bank, concentrating in its hands all the commercial, industrial, agricultural, and even scientific producers, and they will divide the masses of people into two armies—industrial and agricultural armies under the direct command of the State engineers who will constitute the new privileged scientific-political class" (quoted in W. D. Maximoff, *The Political Philosophy of Bakunin: Scientific Anarchism* [New York: Free Press, 1953], p. 289).

80. The term "elective affinity" comes from Max Weber's analysis of the relation between capitalist norms and institutions on one hand and Protestantism on the other. His argument is not one of direct causation but of "fit" and symbiosis.

81. See books 4 and 5 in vol. 2 of Gabriel Ardant, *Théorie sociologique de l'impôt* (Paris: CEVPEN, 1965).

82. Quoted in Michel Crozier, *The Bureaucratic Phenomenon* (Chicago: University of Chicago Press, 1964), p. 239. As Abram de Swaan has noted, "The nineteenth-century school regime does reveal some unmistakable similarities with the factory regime of that time: standardization, formalization and the imposition of punctuality and discipline were paramount in both" (*In Care of the State*, p. 61).

83. For a detailed account of the relationship between the private plot and the collective just prior to 1989, see Timofeev, *Soviet Peasants, or The Peasants' Art of Starving*.

Chapter 7: Compulsory Villagization in Tanzania

1. Julius Nyerere claimed that over 9 million people had been moved to ujamaa villages, but since a good many of these villages were administrative fictions and others had preexisting population bases that were probably included in the self-congratulatory government statistics, a more modest figure is probably closer to the truth. See Goran Hyden, *Beyond Ujamaa in Tanzania: Underdevelopment and an Uncaptured Peasantry* (Berkeley: University of California Press, 1980), p. 130 n. 2.

2. During his presidency, Nyerere visited almost every socialist-bloc state. For an enlightening survey of Marxism-inspired development plans throughout the Third World, see Forrest D. Colburn, *The Vogue of Revolution in Poor Countries* (Princeton: Princeton University Press, 1994).

3. For a searching critique focusing on the returns to scale and to mechanization in agriculture in five such projects, see Nancy L. Johnson and Vernon W. Ruttan, "Why Are Farms So Small?" *World Development* 22, no. 5 (1994): 691–706.

4. These influences were quite direct, as we have noted, for many of the personnel in the Food and Agriculture Organization, the International Bank for Reconstruction and Development, the World Bank, and development agencies from the United Nations were American economists, agronomists, engineers, and bureaucrats.

5. See, for example, Lionel Cliffe and Griffiths L. Cunningham, "Ideology, Organization, and the Settlement Experience of Tanzania," in Lionel Cliffe and John S. Saul, eds., *Policies*, vol. 2 of *Socialism in Tanzania: An Interdisciplinary Reader* (Nairobi: East African Publishing House, 1973), pp. 131–40.

6. Lionel Cliffe, "Nationalism and the Reaction to Enforced Agricultural Change in Tanganyika During the Colonial Period," in Lionel Cliffe and John S. Saul, eds., *Politics*, vol. 1 of *Socialism in Tanzania: An Interdisciplinary Reader* (Nairobi: East African Publishing House, 1973), pp. 18, 22. For a brilliant treatment of peasant-state relations, see Steven Feierman, *Peasant Intellectuals: Anthropology and History in Tanzania* (Madison: University of Wisconsin Press, 1990).

7. William Beinert, "Agricultural Planning and the Late Colonial Technical Imagination: The Lower Shire Valley in Malawi, 1940–1960," in *Malawi: An Alternative Pattern of Development*, proceedings of a seminar held at the Centre of African Studies, University of Edinburgh, May 14 and 25, 1984 (Edinburgh: Centre of African Studies, University of Edinburgh, 1985), pp. 95–148.

8. Ibid., p. 103.

9. Such schemes often included, as Beinert explains, "storm drains, contour bunding, ridging, protection of stream banks, compulsory grass fallows, restorative crops and eventually a full system of rotational strip cropping" (ibid., p. 104).

10. There is nothing odd about this displacement, which occurs almost unconsciously. The "look" of agriculture is stamped with specific, historically contingent features that tend to be forgotten in practice until one's visual expectations are upset. When, for example, I first visited northern Bohemia before 1989, I was taken aback by huge collectivized maize fields that extended two or three miles, unbroken by fences or lines of trees. I realized that my visual expectations about the countryside included the physical evidence of small private properties: tree lines, fences, smaller and more irregular plots, the physical features of independent farmsteads. (Had I grown up in, say, Kansas, I would not have been quite so surprised.)

11. Beinert, "Agricultural Planning," p. 113.

12. For an exceptionally perceptive account of the differences between the geography of traditional, chiefly power and the Cartesian logic of colonial planning in southern Africa, see Isable Hofmyer, *They Spend Their Lives as a Tale That Is Told* (Portsmouth, N.H.: Heinemann, 1994).

13. Ibid., pp. 138–39.

14. For a sampling of accounts, see J. Phillips, *Agriculture and Ecology in Africa* (London: Faber and Faber, 1959); F. Samuel, "East African Groundnut Scheme," *United Empire* 38 (May–June 1947): 133–40; S. P. Voll, *A Plough in Field Arable* (London: University Presses of New England, 1980); Alan Wood, *The Groundnut Affair* (London: Bodley Head, 1950); Johnson and Ruttan, "Why Are Farms So Small?"

pp. 691–706; Andrew Coulson, "Agricultural Policies in Mainland Tanzania," *Review of African Political Economy* 10 (September–December 1977): 74–100.

15. Coulson, "Agricultural Policies in Mainland Tanzania," p. 76.

16. Johnson and Ruttan, "Why Are Farms So Small?" p. 694. Samuel's motto notwithstanding, the scheme was designed to employ a workforce of thirty-two thousand Africans.

17. Permanent settlement was also a keystone of colonial health and veterinary policy in Tanganyika. See, in this context, Kirk Arden Hoppe, "Lords of the Flies: British Sleeping Sickness Policies as Environmental Engineering in the Lake Victoria Region, 1900–1950," Working Papers in African Studies no. 203 (Boston: Boston University African Studies Center, 1995).

18. Goran Hyden, *Beyond Ujamaa in Tanzania* (London: Heineman, 1980).

19. During the independence struggle and immediately afterward, peasants tore down the terraces that they had been ordered to build and refused to destock or to dip their cattle. See Andrew Coulson, *Tanzania: A Political Economy* (Oxford: Clarendon Press, 1982), p. 117.

20. From "President's Inaugural Address" (December 10, 1962), in Julius K. Nyerere, *Freedom and Unity: A Selection from Writings and Speeches, 1952–1965* (London: Oxford University Press, 1967), p. 184. I owe much of my early appreciation for the Tanzanian material to Joel Gao Hiza's exceptionally perceptive senior essay in anthropology, "The Repetition of 'Traditional' Mistakes in Rural Development: Compulsory Villagization in Tanzania," April 1993, and to his invaluable bibliographic assistance. He was unfailingly generous in sharing his analytical judgment and his command of the literature.

21. Julius K. Nyerere, "Socialism and Rural Development" (September 1967), in Nyerere, *Freedom and Socialism: A Selection from Writings and Speeches, 1965–1967* (Dar es Salaam: Oxford University Press, 1968), p. 365. It is worth noting here that the abolition of individual freehold title shortly after independence was one of the legal preconditions for forced villagization, as, in Nyerere's words, "all land now belong[ed] to the nation" (p. 307). Nyerere justified this move in terms of African traditions of "communal ownership," thus eliding the difference between communal ownership and state ownership.

22. Quoted in Coulson, *Tanzania*, p. 237 (emphasis added).

23. One imagines that Nyerere had a powerful visual image of what a "proper" village should look like—its layout, tractors crisscrossing communal fields, a clinic, a school, a government service center, small village industries, and perhaps, looking ahead, electric engines and lights. Where did this image come from? From Russia, China, the West?

24. Quoted in Nyerere, *Freedom and Socialism*, p. 356.

25. Ibid. (emphasis added).

26. Quoted from the 1961 World Bank report (p. 19), in Coulson, *Tanzania*, p. 161.

27. Cliffe and Cunningham, "Ideology, Organization, and the Settlement Experience," p. 135. The authors omit the actual location and name of the village, almost certainly for political reasons. Although I have no way of proving it, I would guess that this Xanadu was close to the capital at Dar es Salaam so that officials could visit and admire it.

28. By the contemporary standards of rule in neighboring states like Ethiopia, Uganda, South Africa, Mozambique, and Zaire, Nyerere's Tanzania was paradise itself. Nevertheless, TANU routinely suborned the legal system or circumvented it altogether. The Preventive Detention Act of 1962 provided no safeguards against flagrant abuse. In early 1964, after an army mutiny, it was used liberally to round

up about five hundred opponents of the regime, most of whom had no connection to the conspiracy. In addition to the Preventive Detention Act, the regime also had frequent recourse to a number of authoritarian colonial laws. See, in this connection, Cranford Pratt, *The Critical Phase in Tanzania, 1945–1968: Nyerere and the Emergence of a Socialist Strategy* (Cambridge: Cambridge University Press, 1976), pp. 184–89.

29. Jannik Boesen, Birgit Storgaard Madsen, and Tony Moody, *Ujamaa: Socialism from Above* (Uppsala: Scandinavian Institute of African Studies, 1977), p. 38. The reference is to the Makazi Mapya settlement program prior to 1969 in the West Lake region.

30. Ibid., p. 77.

31. See Cliffe and Cunningham, "Ideology, Organization, and the Settlement Experience," pp. 137–39; Lionel Cliffe, "The Policy of Ujamaa Vijijini and the Class Struggle in Tanzania," in Cliffe and John S. Saul, eds., *Policies*, vol. 2 of *Socialism in Tanzania: An Interdisciplinary Reader* (Nairobi: East African Publishing House, 1973), pp. 195–211; and Coulson, "Agricultural Policies in Mainland Tanzania," pp. 74–100. The last-mentioned article is a splendid synthetic treatment of rural policy in Tanzania.

32. Cliffe and Cunningham, "Ideology, Organization, and the Settlement Experience," p. 139.

33. Coulson, "Agricultural Policies in Mainland Tanzania," p. 91.

34. Nyerere made the order in a speech delivered via radio, and the content of his speech is instructive. He reminded his audience of "all that the TANU Government had done for the people after the Arusha Declaration: abolishing the poll tax, abolishing primary school fees, building permanent, clean water supplies in the villages, expanding the number of health clinics and dispensaries in the rural areas, increasing primary school facilities. He then went on to ask what the peasants had done in return for these favors. In answering that question, President Nyerere suggested that they had done virtually nothing. They had remained idle and evaded their responsibility to make a contribution to the country's socialist development. He concluded his speech by saying that he knew he could not turn people into socialists by force, but what his government could do was to ensure that everybody lived in village. He said he wanted that to be done before the end of 1976" (Hyden, *Beyond Ujamaa in Tanzania*, p. 130).

35. The stage had already been set when, in early October, the Sixteenth Biennial Conference of TANU ended with an urgent call to the government to "map village areas" with a view to making the ujamaa village movement national rather than relying on local initiative (*Daily News* [Dar es Salaam], October 2, 1973). Accordingly, there were calls in the next months for land officers and professional surveyors to train local cadres in the simpler techniques of surveying so that they could lay out new villages (*Daily News* [Dar es Salaam], January 30, 1974). "Frontal" approaches to ujamaa villages, however, had been urged from at least 1969 by TANU, the Ministry of Rural Development, and the second five-year plan. See Bismarck U. Mwansasu and Cranford Pratt, *Towards Socialism in Tanzania* (Buffalo: University of Toronto Press, 1979), p. 98.

36. Quoted in Coulson, "Agricultural Policies in Mainland Tanzania," p. 74. See also Juma Volter Mwapachu, "Operation Planned Villages in Rural Tanzania: A Revolutionary Strategy of Development," *African Review* 6, no. 1 (1976): 1–16. The discourse begs for closer analysis. The subject of the last two sentences is the impersonal actor "the State" or "Tanzania," represented in practice, of course, by Nyerere and the TANU elite. In the context of coercion the linguistic fiction of choice is still

maintained. Finally, using the phrase "life of death" to describe the lives most Tanzanians are leading elevates Nyerere and the party to the role of saviors raising their people from the dead, as Jesus did with Lazarus.

37. See Dean E. McHenry, Jr., *Tanzania's Ujamaa Villages: The Implementation of a Rural Development Strategy*, Research Series no. 39 (Berkeley: Berkeley Institute of International Studies, 1979), p. 136; Mwapachu, "Operation Planned Villages"; Katabaro Miti, *Whither Tanzania?* (New Delhi: Ajanta, 1987), pp. 73-89.

38. In the antiseptic terminology of the 1961 World Bank report, "When people move to new areas, they are likely to be more receptive of change than when they remain in their familiar surroundings" (quoted in Coulson, *Tanzania*, p. 75). This was presumably the psychological premise behind forced settlement. I was told by a World Bank official that early in the campaign to transplant thousands of Javanese on the outer islands of Indonesia, it was thought better to move them by airplane rather than by boat, which would have been cheaper, because their first experience of flight would suitably disorient them and convey to them the revolutionary and permanent nature of their relocation.

39. Quoted in Coulson, *African Socialism in Practice: The Tanzanian Experience* (Nottingham: Spokesman, 1979), pp. 31-32.

40. Helge Kjekhus, "The Tanzanian Villagization Policy: Implementation Lessons and Ecological Dimensions, *Canadian Journal of African Studies* 11 (1977): 282, cited in Rodger Yaeger, *Tanzania: An African Experiment*, 2nd ed. (Boulder: Westview Press, 1989), p. 62.

41. A. P. L. Ndabakwaje, Student Report, University of Dar es Salaam, 1975, quoted in McHenry, *Tanzania's Ujamaa Villages*, pp. 140-41. In one celebrated case, a cultivator who was incensed that his land was being seized for a new village replied in kind by shooting and killing the regional commissioner. See B. C. Nindi, "Compulsion in the Implementation of Ujamaa," in Norman O'Neill and Kemal Mustafa, eds., *Capitalism, Socialism, and the Development Crisis in Tanzania* (Avebury: Aldershot, 1990), pp. 63-68, cited in Bruce McKim, "Bureaucrats and Peasants: Ujamaa Villagization in Tanzania, 1967-1976" (term paper, Department of Anthropology, Yale University, April 1993), p. 14.

42. For a forthright account, under the circumstances, of the fear and suspicion surrounding the forced movement to new villages, see P. A. Kisula, "Prospects of Building Ujamaa Villages in Mwanza District," (Ph.D. diss., Department of Political Science, University of Dar es Salaam, 1973). I am grateful to David Sperling for bringing this paper to my attention. In many areas, flight from ujamaa villages was closely monitored by the security forces.

43. Ibid., p. 134. One could argue that it is far easier to impose high-modernist schemes of transformation on a population that is somehow constructed as "the other" than on a group that is part of "us." This would help to explain why villagization was imposed first in poor areas such as Kigoma and Dodoma and why it went particularly hard on the pastoral Maasai.

44. Quoted in Coulson, *African Socialism in Practice*, p. 66.

45. Ibid.

46. Sally Falk Moore, *Social Facts and Fabrications: "Customary" Law on Kilimanjaro, 1880-1980* (Cambridge: Cambridge University Press, 1986), p. 314.

47. Here, incidentally, is where I think Goran Hyden's otherwise interesting book misses the boat altogether. The resistance of the Tanzanian peasantry seems less a consequence of some age-old "economy of affection" than a rational response to painful memories of the dire consequences of many state schemes, most of which had miscarried.

48. Elsewhere, in Tanga for example, there are cases of "Potemkin villages" being created for a Nyerere visit and dismantled later. See Hyden, *Beyond Ujamaa in Tanzania*, pp. 101–8.

49. Mwapachu, "Operation Planned Villages," quoted in Coulson, *African Socialism in Practice*, p. 121.

50. Henry Bernstein, "Notes on State and the Peasantry: The Tanzanian Case," *Review of African Political Economy* 21 (May–September 1981): 57.

51. Jannik Boesen, quoted in Coulson, *Tanzania*, p. 254.

52. Boesen, Madsen, and Moody, *Ujamaa*, p. 165.

53. Coulson, "Agricultural Policies in Mainland Tanzania," p. 88 (emphasis added).

54. See Phil Raikes, "Eating the Carrot and Wielding the Stick: The Agricultural Sector in Tanzania," in Jannik Boesen et al., *Tanzania: Crisis and Struggle for Survival* (Uppsala: Scandinavian Institute of African Studies, 1986), p. 119. Unfavorable price and currency movements meant that a five-fold increase in the volume of imports from 1973 to 1975 now represented a *thirty-fold* increase in value.

55. Here the key is perhaps the difference between subsistence production and production for the market. I am grateful to Bruce McKim for emphasizing that the macroeconomic incentives for market production were minimal. Producer prices, which were set by the state marketing boards, were all but confiscatory, and in any case the shops contained few goods on which the proceeds could have been spent.

56. The intention of this law, which had a long colonial history, was to force the peasantry into planting crops that did well under arid conditions, thus lowering the government's food relief expenditures during times of famine.

57. The system of cotton cultivation in Mozambique was a draconian model of this policy. The Portuguese made great efforts to concentrate the population (*concentraçaoes*) so that officials or concessionaires could enforce cotton cultivation and delivery. In one variant, plots were marked off by surveyors, and every family was assigned a plot. The scheme was enforced by a system in which personalized passes indicated whether their bearers had acquitted their cotton quotas for the year; those found in default could be arrested, beaten, or sent off as draft labor to the dreaded sisal plantations. For an exceptionally detailed and comprehensive account, see Allen Isaacman, *Cotton Is the Mother of Poverty: Peasants, Work, and Rural Struggle in Colonial Mozambique, 1938–1961* (Portsmouth, N.H.: Heinemann, 1996).

58. Officials aspired to control not only production but also consumption. In mid–1974 in the Dodoma district, for example, all private retail trade in essential food items was banned in favor of the monopoly formed by the state's consumer cooperative societies and Ujamaa shops. See "Only Co-ops Will Sell Food in Dodoma," *Daily News* (Dar es Salaam), June 6, 1974. This move was probably provoked by the losses experienced by "official" shops, which were usually run by party cadres and lower-level officials. It would be surprising if such a monopoly over retail trade in food ever became much more than an aspiration.

59. Boesen, Madsen, and Moody, *Ujamaa*, p. 105.

60. Graham Thiele, "Villages as Economic Agents: The Accident of Social Reproduction," in R. G. Abrahams, ed., *Villagers, Villages, and the State in Modern Tanzania*, Cambridge African Monograph Series, no. 4 (Cambridge: Cambridge University Press, 1985), pp. 81–109.

61. For early examples of these figures for five crops, see Boesen, Madsen, and Moody, *Ujamaa*, p. 102.

62. Graham Thiele, "Villages as Economic Agents," pp. 98–99. See also Don Hassett, "The Development of Village Co-operative Enterprise in Mchinga II Village, Lindi Region," in Abrahams, *Villagers, Villages*, pp. 16–54.

63. Thus Ndugu Lyander, the regional part secretary for the Kilombero district along the Great Uhuru Railway (built with Chinese assistance), reminded the people that each family must cultivate its two assigned acres, warning them (in language suggestive of the resistance that he was meeting) "that action will be taken against anyone who does not have a farm and no excuses will be entertained" ("100,000 Move to Uhuru Line Villages," *Daily News* [Dar es Salaam], October 28, 1974).

64. Bernstein, "Notes on State and the Peasantry," p. 48.

65. Ibid. Bernstein points out astutely that the Tanzanian state faced an imposing fiscal crisis at the time. The growth of the state budget and personnel had for a long time outpaced the growth of the economy and of government revenues, including foreign exchange. The effort to regiment the peasant economy in the hope of both raising production and increasing state revenues was virtually the only alternative available.

66. There had also been considerable growth in parastatal corporations where production was carried out by wage labor. A good many of these corporations took to farming (grains, sugar, and fodder for dairy cows). These operations, especially the sugar parastatal plantations, were large and capital intensive, as were the nationalized sisal and tea plantations.

67. Quoted in Coulson, *Tanzania*, p. 255.

68. Ibid., p. 161.

69. Ibid., p. 92.

70. Ibid., p. 158.

71. Nyerere, "Broadcast on Becoming Prime Minister" (May 1961), in Nyerere, *Freedom and Unity*, p. 115.

72. Coulson, "Agricultural Policies in Mainland Tanzania," p. 76.

73. As might well be expected, the aftermath of ujamaa villagization has seen a huge number of land disputes between settlements, individuals, and kin groups — disputes with important environmental consequences. See the excellent analysis by Achim von Oppen, "Bauern, Boden, und Baeume: Landkonflikte und ihre Bedeutung fuer Ressourcenschutz in tanzanischen Doerfern nach *Ujamaa*," *Afrika-Spectrum* (February 1993).

74. Boesen, Madsen, and Moody, *Ujamaa*, p. 115.

75. Phil Raikes, "Coffee Production in West Lake Region, Tanzania," Institute for Development Research, Copenhagen, Paper A.76.9 (1976), p. 3, quoted in Coulson, "Agricultural Policies in Mainland Tanzania," p. 80. See also Phil Raikes, "Eating the Carrot and Wielding the Stick," pp. 105–41.

76. Boesen, Madsen, and Moody, *Ujamaa*, p. 67.

77. James De Vries and Louise P. Fortmann, "Large-scale Villagization: Operation Sogeza in Iringa Region," in Coulson, *African Socialism in Practice*, p. 135.

78. The apt phrase is from Bernstein, "Notes on State and the Peasantry," p. 59.

79. Mwapachu, "Operation Planned Villages," p. 117 (emphasis added).

80. Neither in Nyerere's speeches at this time nor in official reports in the press were such numbers often linked to indices of rural transformation such as mortality rates, income, consumption, etc. See Jannik Boesen, "Tanzania: From Ujamaa to Villagization," in Mwansasu and Pratt, *Towards Socialism in Tanzania*, p. 128.

81. Quoted in Coulson, *African Socialism in Practice*, p. 65. The relentless emphasis on quantitative achievements was echoed in the newspapers: so many people moved to new villages, so many new villages formed, so many acres of crops sown, such and such a percentage of a district rehoused, so many plots of land allocated, etc. See, for example, typical articles in *Daily News* [Dar es Salaam]: "14,133 Move into Villages in Chjunya," February 19, 1974; "Two Months After Op-

eration Arusha: 13,928 Families Move into Ujamaa Villages," October 21, 1974; "Iringa: Settling the People into Planned Villages," April 15, 1975.

Nyerere did not, as had Stalin, make a "Dizzy with Success" speech and call a temporary halt in villagization. On the other hand, Tanzanian villagization was not nearly as brutal. Nyerere continued on in this speech to explain again how this concentration of population would permit the delivery of social services "necessary to a life of dignity."

82. Coulson, *Tanzania*, pp. 320–31.

83. For a powerfully argued parallel case, see James Ferguson, *The Anti-Politics Machine: "Development," Depoliticization, and Bureaucratic Power in Lesotho* (Cambridge: Cambridge University Press, 1990). Ferguson concludes that "the 'development' apparatus in Lesotho is not a machine for eliminating poverty that is incidentally involved with the state bureaucracy; it is a machine for reinforcing and expanding the exercise of bureaucratic state power, which incidentally takes 'poverty' as its point of entry" (pp. 255–56). In Tanzania, there were still more important ways in which the official classes gained power, including the displacement of the Asian trading minority as buyers of rural produce and in retailing, as well as the nationalization of trade and industry in general. It is indicative that the size of the government's budget and the number of state employees increased at rates well above the rate of economic growth until the mid-1970s, when a fiscal crisis prevented any further expansion.

84. In a stingy landscape, to stay put is suicide and to move is the condition of survival. See, for an extended and poetic case along these lines, Bruce Chatwin, *The Songlines* (London: Cape, 1987).

85. M. L. Ole Parkipuny, "Some Crucial Aspects of the Maasai Predicament," in Coulson, *African Socialism in Practice*, chap. 10, pp. 139–60.

86. See, for example, Raikes, "Eating the Carrot and Wielding the Stick": "Many policies rest on assumptions about agricultural 'modernization' held in common by the Tanzanian Government and its anti-socialist critics, while no small proportion of policy has been carried over (with or without change) from the colonial period" (p. 106). See also the brilliant analysis of the application of the World Bank development paradigm to Lesotho in Ferguson, *The Anti-Politics Machine*, which also discusses World Bank plans for villagization in Lesotho.

87. Ron Aminzade (personal communication, September 22, 1995) claims that Nyerere's continued popularity, despite the failures of villagization, may be partly due to the ways in which resettlement and other national policies have worked to erode hierarchies of age and gender, thus improving the relative position of younger people and of women.

88. The pace of villagization slowed precipitously in late 1974, when a drought that reduced the harvest by 50 percent followed on the heels of poor harvests from the preceding two years. It is difficult to specify the extent to which villagization and mandated cultivation exacerbated the food-supply shortage. Tanzania was, at any rate, obliged to import unprecedented amounts of foodstuffs at precisely the time when the costs of foreign oil and machinery had skyrocketed. Although the food shortage made many peasants more willing to move in exchange for food rations, they were less willing to hand over the food that they had grown to the state marketing boards. Under the straitened circumstances, large-scale social experimentation was shelved. See Hyden, *Beyond Ujamaa in Tanzania*, pp. 129–30, 141, 146, and Deborah Bryceson, "Household, Hoe, and Nation: Development Policies of the Nyerere Era," in Michael Hodd, ed., *Tanzania After Nyerere* (London: Pinter, 1988), pp. 36–48.

89. Much of the surplus-producing population of Tanzania has the decided tac-

tical advantage of living near the country's borders, making smuggling in both directions a ready option.

90. Here again, for the best source on the copying of administrative structures, development plans, and economic organization among Marxist regimes, see Colburn, *The Vogue of Revolution,* especially chaps. 4 and 5, pp. 49–77.

91. Quoted in Girma Kebbede, *The State and Development in Ethiopia* (Englewood, N.J.: Humanities Press, 1992), p. 23.

92. See the remarkably detailed and insightful report by Cultural Survival: Jason W. Clay, Sandra Steingraber, and Peter Niggli, *The Spoils of Famine: Ethiopian Famine Policy and Peasant Agriculture,* Cultural Survival Report 25 (Cambridge, Mass.: Cultural Survival 1988), especially chap. 5, "Villagization in Ethiopia," pp. 106–35. As an empire, the Ethiopian state had a long tradition of military settlements and colonization which continued under Mengistu in the forced migration of populations from the north into the lands of the Oromo in the south.

93. Ibid., pp. 271, 273.

94. John M. Cohen and Nils-Ivar Isaksson, "Villagization in Ethiopia's Arsi Region," *Journal of Modern African Studies* 25, no. 3 (1987): 435–64. These figures are a bit fishy. As each village was planned for a notional one thousand inhabitants, it looks as if they multiplied the number of villages by the mandated population, adding perhaps a few additional inhabitants to account for officials. Cohen and Isaksson were more inclined to take the regime at its word than were Clay and his colleagues at Cultural Survival.

95. Ibid., p. 449.

96. A similar geometrical meticulousness was followed in Pol Pot's Cambodia. Walls of earth were thrown up to make long, straight canals, eliminating irregular paddies and creating hectare squares of riceland. Concentration of population, forced labor, the prohibition of foraging or departure, the control of food rations, and executions were carried to an extreme rarely seen in Ethiopia. See Ben Kiernan, *The Pol Pot Regime: Race, Power, and Genocide in Cambodia Under the Khmer Rouge, 1975–1979* (New Haven: Yale University Press, 1996), chap. 5.

97. Clay, Steingraber, and Niggli, *The Spoils of Famine,* p. 121. Like the Soviet Union, Ethiopia had a separate category of state farms that were run on the basis of hired labor and were, at least initially, very highly mechanized. They were expected to produce a supply of major grains and export crops that would be under direct control of the government. "In the late 1970s, as a result of the slow voluntary move toward collectivization, the government began to identify for future state farms, flat, fertile areas for mechanized agriculture. The clearing of residents off such areas so that they could be used to produce directly for the state appears to be a primary reason for the villagization in Bale" (ibid., p. 149).

98. Ibid., pp. 190–92, 204.

99. The roots of this program can be traced to a 1973 World Bank report "that recommended the relocation of peasants from northern areas suffering from high population pressure, soil erosion, and deforestation," although it was termed a policy response to famine in 1984–85 (Cohen and Isaksson, "Villagization in Ethiopia's Arsi Region," p. 443). Something of the logic of social control behind these schemes can be found in the fine paper by Donald Donham, "Conversion and Revolution in Maale, Ethiopia," Program in Agrarian Studies, Yale University, New Haven, December 1, 1995.

100. See, especially, Kebbede, *The State and Development,* pp. 5–102, and Clay, Steingraber, and Niggli, *The Spoils of Famine,* passim.

101. Clay, Steingraber, and Niggli, *The Spoils of Famine,* p. 23.

102. As one farmer told Clay, "There are six kinds of sorghum I plant: two red

kinds, two white kinds that are intermediate and ripen very fast. There are also types we eat while the fruit is still green. There are five kinds of teff and three kinds of corn: red, orange, and white. Each is planted according to its season, and each has its own time to plant" (ibid., p. 23).

103. Ibid., p. 55.

104. Food aid was, in turn, used to round up people for resettlement and, when resettled, to hold them there. A standard technique of the Dergue was to announce a time and place for food distribution and then ship off the crowd that assembled.

105. An extreme version of this visual codification can be seen in Ceauşmescu's Romania, where hundreds of villages were destroyed in order to make room for nonfunctioning towns with "modern apartment flats" (easier to control) and where the countryside was divided up into zones of strict agricultural specialization as if it were a single enterprise with its own division of labor. The regime termed the entire exercise "systematization." Perhaps the best treatment is to be found in Katherine Verdery, *What Was Socialism and What Comes Next* (Princeton: Princeton University Press, 1996), especially chap. 6, pp. 133–67.

106. But even here, see Donald Worster, *The Dust Bowl: The Southern Plains in the 1930s* (New York: Oxford University Press, 1979).

107. John Berger, *Ways of Seeing* (London, 1992), p. 16, quoted in Martin Jay, *Downcast Eyes: The Denigration of Vision in Twentieth-Century French Thought* (Berkeley: University of California Press, 1993). For a useful collection on the issue of modernity and vision, see also David Michael Levin, ed., *Modernity and the Hegemony of Vision* (Berkeley: University of California Press, 1993).

108. For a more elaborate argument along these lines, see James C. Scott, *Domination and the Arts of Resistance: Hidden Transcripts* (New Haven: Yale University Press, 1990), pp. 45–69.

109. Zygmunt Bauman, in *Modernity and the Holocaust* (Oxford: Oxford University Press, 1989), makes the same point with regard to the "gardening metaphor," which he sees as characteristic of modernist thought in general and Nazi racial policies in particular.

110. This point is made exceptionally well, both empirically and analytically, in Sally Falk Moore, *Social Facts and Fabrications*, especially chap. 6.

111. See, in this connection, the classic article arguing that our modest degree of knowledge about the likely consequences of any major policy initiative makes a strategy of "crab-wise" adjustments, which can be undone without great damage, the more prudent course: Charles E. Lindblom, "The Science of Muddling Through," *Public Administration Review* 19 (Spring 1959): 79–88. A follow-up article published twenty years later, "Still Muddling, Not Yet Through," may be found in Lindblom, *Democracy and the Market System* (Oslo: Norwegian University Presses, 1979), pp. 237–59.

112. Proponents of this view forget or ignore, I think, the fact that in order to do its work, the market requires its own vast simplifications in treating land (nature) and labor (people) as factors of production (commodities). This, in turn, can and has been profoundly destructive of human communities and of nature. In a sense, the simplification of the scientific forest compounds the simplification of scientific measurement and the simplification made possible by the commercial market for wood. Karl Polanyi's classic, *The Great Transformation* (Boston: Beacon Press, 1957), is still perhaps the best case against pure market logic.

113. I am aware that the binary distinction between "artificial" and "natural" is ultimately untenable when it comes to things like languages and communities. By "artificial," I mean languages and communities that are planned centrally and at a single stroke, as it were, as opposed to communities that grow by accretion.

114. See J. C. O'Connor, *Esperanto, the Universal Language: The Student's Complete Text Book* (New York: Fleming H. Revell, 1907); and Pierre Janton, *Esperanto Language, Literature, and Community*, trans. Humphrey Tonkin et al. (Albany: State University of New York Press, 1973). By "universal," of course, Esperanto's proponents meant, in fact, "European."

115. See, in this context, Susan Stewart, *On Longing: Narratives of the Miniature, the Gigantic, the Souvenir* (Baltimore: Johns Hopkins University Press, 1984).

116. For a remarkable account of a Soviet theme park, Exhibition of the Achievements of the People's Economy, which was erected in 1939, see Jamey Gambrell, *Once upon an Empire: The Soviet Paradise* (New Haven: Yale University Press, forthcoming). For two accounts of an Indonesian analog (*Taman-Mini*, or "mini-park") built according to the inspiration of Mrs. Soeharto, the wife of Indonesia's president since 1965, after she visited Disneyland, see John Pemberton, "Recollections from 'Beautiful Indonesia' (Somewhere Beyond the Postmodern)," *Public Culture* 6 (1994): 241–62; and Timothy C. Lindsey, "Concrete Ideology: Taste, Tradition, and the Javanese Past in New Order Public Space," in Virginia Matheson Hooker, ed., *Culture and Society in New Order Indonesia* (Kuala Lumpur: Oxford University Press, 1993), pp. 166–82.

117. In another example of the exemplum being mistaken for reality, during the disastrous Great Leap Forward in the late 1950s, Mao Tse-tung's subordinates set up elaborate, deceptive tableaux of healthy peasants and bumper crops along the route that his train would follow.

118. Yi-fu Tuan, *Dominance and Affection: The Making of Pets* (New Haven: Yale University Press, 1984).

119. Lawrence Vale, *Architecture, Power, and National Identity* (New Haven: Yale University Press, 1992), p. 90.

120. One political advantage of a new capital is precisely that it does not belong to any existing community. Founding a new capital avoids certain delicate, if not explosive, choices that would otherwise have to be made. By the same logic, English became the national language of India because it was the only widely spoken language that did not belong exclusively to any particular traditional community. It *did* belong, however, to India's English-speaking intelligentsia, which was enormously privileged when its "dialect" became the national language. The United States and Australia, with no urban past to transcend, created planned capitals that represented a vision of progress and order and that were, not incidentally, in stark contrast to indigenous settlement practices.

121. Vale, *Architecture, Power, and National Identity*, p. 293.

122. Ibid., p. 149.

123. Coulson, "Agricultural Policies in Mainland Tanzania," p. 86.

124. For a fine description of the Mozambique case, see chap. 7 of Isaacman, *Cotton Is the Mother of Poverty*.

125. Quoted in Coulson, "Agricultural Policies in Mainland Tanzania," p. 78. The document goes on to stress how important it is to separate the good, industrious cultivators from the bad, lazy ones. One wonders whether the Latin American revolutionary strategy of *focos*, or creating small insurrectionary enclaves (and elaborated by Regis DeBray in the 1960s), shares an intellectual lineage with "focal-point" strategies in development work.

126. Pauline Peters, "Transforming Land Rights: State Policy and Local Practice in Malawi," paper presented at the Program in Agrarian Studies, Yale University, New Haven, February 19, 1993.

127. Birgit Müller, unpublished paper, 1990.

128. Kate Xiao Zhou, *How the Farmers Changed China: Power of the People* (Boulder: Westview Press, 1996).

129. The large gap that thus develops between an inevitably thin authoritarian high-modernist social fiction and the informal, "deviant" practices that cannot be openly avowed but that are its necessary complement is diagnostically characteristic. Although we shall return to this theme, here it is relevant to recall that the hypocrisy, cynicism, and comedy generated by the gulf between the official pieties of a mendacious public sphere and the practices necessary to the reproduction of daily life often become the raw material for such a society's finest literature, poetry, and song.

Chapter 8: Taming Nature

1. For persuasive evidence that even the most apparently pristine forests are in part the product of human agency practiced over centuries, see, for example, Darryl Posey, "Indigenous Management of Tropical Forest Eco-Systems: The Case of the Kayapo Indians of the Brazilian Amazon," *Agroforestry Systems* 3 (1985): 139–58; Susanna Hecht, Anthony Anderson, and Peter May, "The Subsidy from Nature: Shifting Cultivation, Successional Palm Forests, and Rural Development," *Human Organization* 47, no. 1 (1988): 25–35; J. B. Alcorn, "Huastec Noncrop Resource Management: Implications for Prehistoric Rain Forest Management," *Human Ecology* 9, no. 4 (1981): 395–417; and Christine Padoch, "The Woodlands of Tae: Traditional Forest Management in Kalimantan," in William Bentley and Marcia Gowen, eds., *Forest Resources and Wood Based Biomass Energy as Rural Development Assets* (New Delhi: Oxford and IBH, 1995).

2. For marketed crops in a fully commercialized system, profit maximization would rarely be precisely the same as crop-volume maximization. Where labor was scarce, cultivators would be more concerned about maximizing the crop return per unit of labor, whereas if land was scarce, the return per acre would be the focus.

3. Paul Richards, *Indigenous Agricultural Revolution: Ecology and Food Production in West Africa* (London: Unwin Hyman, 1985), p. 160; in this chapter I rely heavily on this brilliant book. Richards is committed to scientific agricultural research but insists that it examine, without prejudice, the existing practices of African farmers and that it reflect the actual problems and goals of local cultivators.

4. The specifically structural and institutional interests that lead to agricultural policies favoring state power, urban consumption, and elite economic interests have been spelled out persuasively by Robert Bates in *Markets and States in Tropical Africa: The Political Basis of Agricultural Policies* (Los Angeles: University of California Press, 1981). My analysis deals with the deeper sources of policy error lying outside Bates's political-economy field of vision.

5. Jack R. Harlan, *Crops and Man*, 2nd ed. (Madison, Wis.: American Society of Agronomy, Crop Science Society of America, 1992), p. 5.

6. For the major grains—all in the family of grasses—this has led to a kind of symbiotic mimicry. Each major grain has in the same family one or more lookalike "obligate weeds," which thrive under precisely the same field conditions as the cultivar but which shatter their hardy seeds early and thus reseed themselves in the cultivated field.

7. Harlan, *Crops and Man*, p. 127 (emphasis in original).

8. In a Malay village where I carried out fieldwork for two years, each of the older cultivators knew of roughly eighty varieties of rice by name and by its properties.

9. In fact, the clearing or field is itself a powerful selector for resistance. Even if the cultivator were to randomly choose the seed stock for the next season or, for that matter, leave the crop standing in the field to reseed itself, the resistance of next year's crop will increase, in a phenomenon called field resistance. Whichever landraces (including random crosses and mutants) do best *over time* against pests, adverse weather, and so on will contribute, willy-nilly, more of their seed to the subsequent season's crop. See Harlan, *Crops and Man*, pp. 117–33.

10. "Probably, the total genetic change achieved by farmers over the millennia was far greater than that achieved by the last hundred or two years of more systematic, science-based efforts" (Norman Simmonds, *Principles of Crop Improvement* [New York: Longman, 1979], cited by Jack Ralph Kloppenberg, Jr., *First the Seed: The Political Economy of Plant Biotechnology, 1492–2000* [Cambridge: Cambridge University Press, 1988], p. 185). As will be apparent, I am much indebted to Kloppenberg's fine analysis throughout much of this chapter.

11. James Boyce, "Biodiversity and Traditional Agriculture: Toward a New Policy Agenda—a Pre-Proposal" (unpublished paper, January 1996). See also Boyce, "The Environmental Impact of North-South Trade: A Political Economy Approach," Working Paper 1996–3, Department of Economics, University of Massachusetts, Amherst, 1996. Actually, the relation between modern varieties and traditional agriculture is one of dependence rather than complementarity. Traditional agriculture does not require modern agriculture as a condition of its existence, whereas modern agriculture would appear to depend on the genetic capital of the landraces. On this basis, Boyce argues for in situ preservation (as opposed to storage in seed banks) and development of landraces by protecting traditional cultivators in these centers.

12. Eye appeal has depended on aesthetic values that have often diverged markedly from matters of yields, taste, and even profitability. In the American tradition of awarding prizes to fruits, vegetables, and livestock entered in competition at agricultural fairs, first prize has generally gone to the ideal ear of corn or the ideal pig despite the fact that they might be economically inferior in terms of profitability. Of course, if a buyer was willing to pay a sufficient "aesthetic premium" for the ideal pig, then aesthetics and profit might coincide. See Kloppenberg, *First the Seed*, p. 96.

13. Ibid., p. 117. The following two observations are also based on the same passage.

14. R. E. Webb and W. M. Bruce, "Redesigning the Tomato for Mechanized Production," in *Science for Better Living: Yearbook of Agriculture, 1968* (Washington: United States Department of Agriculture, 1968), p. 104, cited in ibid., p. 126. Kloppenberg continues, "Hybrids were particularly attractive to the vegetable industry, and spinach, carrots, cucumbers, and the brassicas (cabbage, cauliflower, etc.) have been hybridized and redesigned to permit non-selective, once-over, machine harvesting" (ibid.). It is worth noting that, quite apart from the harvest, the mechanical cultivating, sorting, and packing of some crops had earlier influenced crop selection and breeding.

15. Ibid., p. 127.

16. Jim Hightower et al., *Hard Tomatoes, Hard Times*, Final Report of the Task Force on the Land Grant College Complex of the Agribusiness Accountability Project (Cambridge: Schenkman, 1978).

17. Committee on Genetic Vulnerability of Major Crops, Agricultural Board, Division of Biology and Agriculture, United States National Research Council, *Genetic Vulnerability of Major Crops* (Washington: National Academy of Sciences, 1972), p. 21.

18. Ibid., p. 12.

19. Another effect of genetic uniformity is to make the entire population of plants also vulnerable to the same environmental stresses.

20. The first scientist to work out the mathematical model of plant epidemics was van der Plank. See Committee on Genetic Vulnerability of Major Crops, *Genetic Vulnerability of Major Crops*, pp. 28–32.

21. The same logic, of course, holds true for human diseases. Other things being equal, scattered populations are healthier than concentrated populations. Urban populations in Western Europe did not successfully reproduce themselves until at least the nineteenth century; they depended on being demographically replenished from the comparatively healthy population in the countryside. For the epidemiological reasons behind the association of diversity and dispersion with health and the association of bio-uniformity and concentration with high mortality, see Alfred Crosby, *Ecological Imperialism: The Biological Expansion of Europe, 900–1900* (New York: Cambridge University Press, 1988), and Mark Ridley, "The Microbes' Opportunity," *Times Literary Supplement*, January 13, 1995, pp. 6–7. The logic of dispersion during epidemics was recognized long before anyone understood the causes or vectors of major epidemic diseases. See, for example, Daniel Defoe, *A Journal of the Plague Year* (1722; Harmondsworth: Penguin, 1966).

22. Well, not quite. As we have learned, the profligate use of antibiotics on humans and pesticides on crops runs up against the problem that the pathogens, which are the target of the attack, often adapt and mutate, through selection pressures, faster than the human and plant defenses do. For this reason, new generations of pesticides must be created to keep one jump ahead of the pathogens, and infectious diseases such as tuberculosis and cholera, once thought extinct, have returned in more virulent strains. See, in this context, Randolph M. Nesse and George C. Williams, *Evolution and Healing: The New Science of Darwinian Medicine* (London: Weidenfeld and Nicolson, 1995).

23. David Pimentel and Lois Levitan, "Pesticides: Amounts Applied and Amounts Reaching Pests," *BioScience* 36, no. 2 (February 1986): 87.

24. Kloppenberg, *First the Seed*, pp. 118–19. Worldwide, cotton and high-yielding varieties of rice absorb the largest share of pesticides.

25. Once again, there are striking parallels in human epidemics with the development of resistant strains of viral and bacterial diseases and resistant vectors of disease. See John Wargo's discussion of malaria and its carrier, the *Anopheles* mosquito, in *Our Children's Toxic Legacy: How Science and Law Fail to Protect Us from Pesticides* (New Haven: Yale University Press, 1996), pp. 15–42.

26. "The extensive use of herbicides has not been without its costs. Of forty-five iatrogenically (i.e., caused by our use of pesticides) induced diseases of crop plants, thirty were found to be caused by herbicides" (Kloppenberg, *First the Seed*, p. 247). The literature also abounds with cases of insecticides and other agents having indirect but equally devastating consequences. In 1995, for example, the massive application of malathion to control the boll weevil in Texas also killed many beneficial insects, thereby touching off an explosion of army worms who ate most of the beet crop. See "Where Cotton's King, Trouble Reigns," *New York Times*, October 9, 1995, p. A10, and Sam Howe Verhovek, "In Texas, an Attempt to Swat an Old Pest Stirs a Revolt," *New York Times*, January 24, 1996, p. A10.

27. Committee on Genetic Vulnerability of Major Crops, *Genetic Vulnerability of Major Crops*, p. 6.

28. Ibid., p. 7 (emphasis added).

29. Ibid., p. 1. To take a minor crop, of the peas planted commercially in 1969, 96 percent were in only two varieties. A small dress rehearsal for the corn blight of 1970 could have been witnessed in the case of oats. A "miracle oat," Victoria, was

bred to resist all forms of crown rust fungus. It was planted throughout the country in 1940 and, in 1946, succumbed to a devastating epidemic. Because oats by that time were not as widely planted as earlier in the century, the disaster was not much reported.

30. For an impressive listing of such instances, see Kloppenberg, *First the Seed*, p. 168.

31. James B. Billard, "More Food for Multiplying Millions: The Revolution in American Agriculture," with photographs by James R. Blair and a painting of the farm of the future by Davis Meltzer, *National Geographic* 137, no. 2 (February 1970): 147–85. This article is the subject of a scathing critique by Wendell Berry in *The Unsettling of America: Culture and Agriculture* (San Francisco: Sierra Club Books, 1977), chap. 5. It is remarkable how little of the article, as an "informed" fantasy, holds up from the vantage point of 1997. The revolution in biotechnology and recombinant DNA transfer, surely the most important change in agriculture, is hardly a speck on its horizon, nor are the problems of genetic vulnerability and pesticide use.

32. See Albert O. Hirschman, *Development Projects Observed* (Washington: Brookings Institution, 1967).

33. For a fine analysis of five such schemes (four of them private and one public, namely, the Tanganyika groundnuts scheme of 1947), see Nancy L. Johnson and Vernon W. Ruttan, "Why Are Farms So Small?" *World Development* 22, no. 5 (1994): 691–706.

34. Richards, *Indigenous Agricultural Revolution*, pp. 63–116. In this discussion I shall use the terms "polycropping" and "mixed cropping" interchangeably. Intercropping is a form of polycropping in which a second cultigen in planted between rows of the first. Relay cropping refers to a sequence of crops that overlap in the field and is thus also a form of polyculture.

35. The more stringent the climate, the less the biodiversity. As one approaches the tundra, the number of species of trees, mammals, and insects diminishes. The same, of course, applies to the climatic zones created by successively higher elevations in mountainous terrains.

36. Quoted in Paul Richards, "Ecological Change and the Politics of African Land Use," *African Studies Review* 26, no. 2 (June 1983): 40. Richards also quotes Dudley Stamp, who at about the same time wrote enthusiastically about the wider applicability of African techniques for combating soil erosion: "A recent tour of Nigeria has convinced the writer that the native farmer has already evolved a scheme of farming which cannot be bettered in principle even if it can be improved in detail and that, as practised in some areas, this scheme affords almost complete protection against soil erosion and loss of fertility. It may be that the African has thus a contribution to make towards the solution of the great soil erosion problems in other regions" (p. 23).

37. Edgar Anderson, *Plants, Man, and Life* (Boston: Little, Brown, 1952), pp. 140–41. It goes without saying that the gardens Anderson is describing are so diverse in part because the villagers in question wish to grow many of the foods needed for subsistence rather than paying for them in the market. The point, however, is the plan behind the visual disorder.

38. Richards, *Indigenous Agricultural Revolution*, p. 63.

39. Ibid., p. 70.

40. Most traditional cropping systems, whether polyculture or crop rotation, combine a grain and a legume in this fashion.

41. Richards, *Indigenous Agricultural Revolution*, pp. 66–70.

42. H. C. Sampson and E. M. Crowther, "Crop Production and Soil Fertility

Problems," *West Africa Commission, 1938–1939: Technical Reports*, part 1 (London: Leverhulme Trust, 1943), p. 34, cited in ibid., p. 30. Mixed *cropping* (polyculture) must not be confused with mixed *farming*, which indicates a farm producing a variety of crops (each typically on its own plot) and livestock on the European smallholder model.

43. Richards, "Ecological Change and the Politics of African Land Use," p. 27.

44. This is just one example of how the choice of technique is influenced by the factor endowments of the farmer—a large consideration, but by no means the only one.

45. Strictly speaking, many of these advantages could also be obtained by planting many tiny parcels to single cultivars. What would be lost are the specific advantages of polycropping mentioned earlier.

46. "Mycorrhizal association" refers to the symbiotic relation between the mycelium of certain fungi and the roots of a seed plant.

47. Rachel Carson, *Silent Spring* (1962; Boston: Houghton Mifflin, 1987), p. 10.

48. Organic farmers have occasionally opted for mixed cropping as a way of avoiding the heavy use of fertilizers and insecticides. The most common obstacle to certain (not all) forms of polyculture is that they are too labor intensive in a context where labor is the scarce factor of production. It is hard to know how much of this labor intensiveness is the result of the fact that virtually all machine implements have been designed with monoculture exclusively in mind. One pioneer, Wes Jackson, has demonstrated that, over a three-year period and in production terms alone, polyculture can outperform monoculture. The fact that the gains to polyculture are greater in the second and third years suggests that the interaction effects between the two crops are responsible for the performance (Jackson, "Becoming Native to This Place," paper presented at the Program in Agrarian Studies, Yale University, New Haven, November 18, 1994). Jackson, like Howard, is primarily concerned with developing a form of agriculture that will preserve or enhance its soil capital. Such preservation is less urgent in stable bottomland but vital in ecological zones with fragile soils (e.g., hillsides and uplands). The polycropping of perennials seems particularly suitable to achieving this end.

49. Comparative experimental studies of prairie ecologies have confirmed Darwin's original premise that more diverse ecosystems are more productive and resilient. Ecologists at the University of Minnesota compared 147 one-hundred-square-foot plots sown with different numbers of randomly chosen grass species. "The more species a plot had, the greater its biomass of plants and the more nitrogen it had taken up in its increased growth"; "the fewer the species, the sparser the growth and the greater the amount of nitrogen leaching out of upper soil layers." After a drought, the plots with the larger number of species returned more rapidly to full productivity than did the plots with fewer species. Productivity increased dramatically with each species added up to ten species, and each species added thereafter offered much less to overall productivity. In the long run, it has been theorized, additional species might prove vital in protecting the ecosystem against extremes of weather or pest infestations. See Carol Kaesuk Yoon, "Ecosystem's Productivity Rises with Diversity of Its Species," *New York Times*, March 5, 1996, p. C4.

50. These advantages might include, on the cost side, lower expenditures for such inputs as fertilizers and pesticides.

51. Those who investigate the order that lies behind seemingly turbulent natural systems (clouds, water flows, air turbulence, epidemics, etc.) have come to contrast what they call fractal systems with linear systems. The key difference of relevance to us is the flexibility and sturdiness of fractal processes, which can survive perturbations and function over a wide range of frequencies—a quality com-

mon to many biological processes. In contrast, linear processes, once they are knocked off the rails, continue to veer off on the new tangent, never to return to the original equilibrium range. Polyculture, in just this sense, has a greater tolerance of disturbances.

52. Up to a point. Jacobs shows how a neighborhood's success can have effects on property values that will undermine some uses and will eventually transform the place. There is no equilibrium in Jacobs's view, only a cycle that begins repeatedly in different parts of a city.

53. Shifting cultivation is also common throughout much of Southeast Asia and Latin America.

54. Harold C. Conklin, *Hanunoo Agriculture: A Report on an Integral System of Shifting Cultivation in the Philippines* (Rome: Food and Agriculture Organization of the United Nations, 1957), p. 85. One cannot come away from Conklin's meticulous account without a sense of awe at the breadth of knowledge and skills of these cultivators.

55. And that, of course, was part of the reason why such populations often remained in, or fled to, non-state spaces.

56. Richards, *Indigenous Agricultural Revolution*, p. 50. Richards continues: "The Parliamentary Under-Secretary of State for the Colonies, W. G. A. Ormsby-Gore, summed up the attitude of the day when noting that in Sierra Leone, for example, 'the natural forest has been ruthlessly destroyed to find virgin soil for the cultivation of "hill" or "land" rice'" (pp. 50–51).

57. Ibid., p. 42.

58. See ibid., chap. 2. Richards concludes: "From the point of view of fertilization, modern soil science confirms the validity of the forest farmer's emphasis on ash and the savannah farmer's emphasis on 'manure' and 'compost'" (p. 61). For an excellent analysis of the techniques of burning in Honduras, see Kees Jansen, "The Art of Burning and the Politics of Indigenous Agricultural Knowledge," paper presented at a congress entitled "Agrarian Questions: The Politics of Farming Anno 1995," May 22–24, 1995, Wageningen, The Netherlands.

59. Richards, *Indigenous Agricultural Revolution*, p. 43. In this context Richards is accepting the premise that the only test is market efficiency, providing that it is sustainable.

60. Ibid., p. 61.

61. Liebig did believe that his formula could cure all soil problems.

62. Among the many experiments that Howard conducted were elaborate trials of "green manuring" (the plowing under of a nitrogen-fixing, leguminous crop prior to the planting of a grain crop), which showed that its effect depended greatly on these other variables as well as the right timing and the amount of moisture in the soil in order to promote the chemical reactions (first aerobic and then anaerobic) necessary for the production of more humus. See Sir Albert Howard, *An Agricultural Testament* (London: Oxford University Press, 1940).

63. Alkalization occurs as well with the salts left behind in the course of intensive irrigation. Growers in those areas of the Imperial Valley in California suffering from alkalization have had to install drainage tiles at shorter and shorter intervals over the years in order to prevent the buildup from reaching ruinous proportions.

64. Rice, an Old World plant, had come much earlier and been adapted. Although a perennial, rice is planted as if it were an annual.

65. Just how deep this history is, is reflected in the fact that modern man has added no important domesticated species of plant or animal in the last four thousand years. This story can be followed in Carl O. Sauer, *Agricultural Origins and Dispersals* (New York: American Geographical Society, 1952). Sauer relies heavily

on an important work by the pioneer Russian scientist in this area, N. I. Vavilov: *The Origin, Variation, Immunity, and Breeding of Cultivated Plants*, trans. K. Starr Chester, vol. 13, nos. 1–6, of *Chronica botanica* (1949–50). Potatoes are a good example of a plant that must be vegetatively propagated by cuttings.

66. There are exceptions, one of which seems to be the ecologically devastated northern part of Ethiopia and Eritrea. It is worth adding that neither does the record of the industrialized world in soil erosion, pollution or exhaustion of groundwater, and global warming represent an edifying example of foresight.

67. Robert Chambers, *Rural Development: Putting the Last First* (London: Longman, 1983), quoted in Richards, *Indigenous Agricultural Revolution*, p. 40. There is a case to be made for Howard's claim that "agricultural revolutions" are always acts of autonomous farmers rather than states. From the agricultural revolution in Britain that laid the groundwork for industrialization to the broad adoption of such new crops as cocoa, tobacco, and maize in Africa, Howard's generalization rings true. It does not hold true, however, for large-scale irrigation projects or for the more recent, research-driven breeding of high-yielding varieties of wheat, rice, and maize. These state-sponsored innovations typically have powerful implications for centralization.

68. James Ferguson, *The Anti-Politics Machine: "Development," Depoliticization, and Bureaucratic Power in Lesotho* (Cambridge: Cambridge University Press, 1990). Ferguson shows brilliantly how the institutional power of international and national development agencies depends vitally on their representing their activities as neutral interventions by scientific specialists.

69. It might be objected that, in the case of large irrigation works, a centralized logic is mandatory for the apportionment of water rights between upstream and downstream users. The fact is that quite large irrigation systems have been successfully organized for hundreds of years without centralized political authorities exercising coercive powers. For a remarkable study showing how such a system worked and how it was nearly destroyed by the "simplifications" imposed by hydrological experts and agronomists from the Asian Development Bank, see J. Steven Lansing, *Priests and Programmers: Technologies of Power in the Engineered Landscape of Bali* (Princeton: Princeton University Press, 1991). Also useful is Elinor Ostrom, *Governing the Commons: The Evolution of Institutions for Collective Action* (Cambridge: Cambridge University Press, 1990).

70. Quoted in Stephen A. Marglin, "Farmers, Seedsmen, and Scientists: Systems of Agriculture and Systems of Knowledge" (unpublished paper, May 1991, revised March 1992). Marglin's account is an astute analysis of the ecological and institutional consequences of scientific agriculture. His analysis of knowledge systems has strong parallels with my own analysis of mētis in chapter 8. We each independently discovered the value of using concepts of knowledge from Greek philosophy to distinguish practical knowledge from deductive knowledge. I have found his discussion helpful and clarifying. Marglin's analysis of American agricultural practice is usefully read along with Deborah Fitzgerald, *Yeomen No More: The Industrialization of American Agriculture* (forthcoming).

71. Marglin, "Farmers, Seedsmen, and Scientists," p. 7.

72. The term "hybrid" has changed in meaning. Originally, it referred to any cross; now it refers only to crosses between two inbred "pure" lines.

73. Marglin notes the close collaboration between the U.S. Department of Agriculture and the large seed companies, which helped the latter achieve dominance in maize hybrids. The same dominance is less likely for wheat and rice, which are self-pollinating. Improved yields for these crops are achieved with new varieties which are genetically stable. Marglin, "Farmers, Seedsmen, and Scientists," p. 17.

74. Since such control is only approximated in most real experiments, every experiment is followed by a great deal of discussion about the "extraneous variables," or variables other than those singled out by the experimental design, which might have produced the findings. The findings in such cases are ambiguous until a subsequent experiment controls the rogue variables.

75. Marglin, "Farmers, Seedsmen, and Scientists," p. 5.

76. Mitchell Feigenbaum, quoted in James Gleick, *Chaos: Making a New Science* (New York: Penguin, 1988), p. 185.

77. Experimental laboratory science is necessarily carried out using a standardized and purified nature (e.g., purified reagents from catalogues) and man-made instruments of observation. The reliable manipulation of such objects makes for successful experiments and a certain level of self-vindication in laboratory practice. See Theodore M. Porter, *Trust in Numbers: The Pursuit of Objectivity in Science and Public Life* (Princeton: Princeton University Press, 1995), chap. 1. See also Ian Hacking, "The Self-Vindication of the Laboratory Sciences," in Andrew Pickering, ed., *Science as Practice and Culture* (Chicago: University of Chicago Press, 1992), pp. 29–64.

78. Berry, *The Unsettling of America*, pp. 70–71. There is no reason, in principle, why the dependent variable of greatest interest cannot be, say, nutritional value, the timing of tillering, taste, or hardiness. But the research is more manageable when the variable of interest is less subjective and more easily quantifiable.

79. D. S. Ngambeki and G. F. Wilson, "Moving Research to Farmers' Fields," International Institute of Tropical Agriculture Research Briefs, 4:4, 1, 7–8, quoted in Richards, *Indigenous Agricultural Revolution*, p. 143.

80. Richards, *Indigenous Agricultural Revolution*, p. 143.

81. Sauer, *Agricultural Origins and Dispersals*, pp. 62–83.

82. In addition to the difficulties in finding the "active" cause among many possibilities, such a study of polycropping would have to find and justify a formula for comparing different combinations of yields. Assuming the same costs, which is superior: a yield of two hundred bushels of lima beans and three hundred bushels of corn, or a yield of three hundred bushels of lima beans and two hundred bushels of corn? Does one arrive at a common denominator by using market prices (which would mean the answer would vary week by week and year by year), caloric content, overall nutritive value, or some other measure? The difficulties rapidly pile up.

83. That is, this is a version of the solar system that discounts all the various moons, asteroids, nearby stars, and so on.

84. Writing in 1977, Wendell Berry rhetorically asked the U.S. Department of Agriculture: "Where are the control plots which test the various systems of soil management? Where are the performance figures for present-day small farms using draft animals, small scale technologies, and alternative energy sources? Where are the plots kept free of agricultural chemicals? If these exist, then they are the best-kept secrets of our time. But if they do not exist, whence comes the scientific authority of scientific agriculture? Without appropriate controls, one has no proof; one does not, in any respectable sense, have an experiment" (*The Unsettling of America*, p. 206). Since that time, such comparisons have been made, with many of the results reported in a USDA study on organic farming entitled *Report and Recommendations on Organic Farming*, prepared by the U.S. Department of Agriculture Team on Organic Farming (Washington: USDA, 1980). The parallels with the West African story are striking. In each case certain practices were deemed not to be worth investigating, partly because they and their practitioners were presumed to be backward and inefficient. Only when the anomalies and long-run consequences of mainstream doctrines became apparent were such practices examined carefully.

85. Aspirin, for example, which has long been used to alleviate headaches, has turned out to have a number of other beneficial effects that were discovered only recently.

86. With hindsight, one could still argue that, in terms of a cost-benefit analysis, the reduction in disease was so valuable that it outweighed any harm caused to the environment. But that is not the point. The point is that the costs in this case were *outside* the experimental model and could not have been assessed in any event.

87. Philip M. Raup, University of Minnesota, testifying before the U.S. Senate Small Business Committee (March 1, 1972), quoted in Wendell Berry, *The Unsettling of America*, p. 171.

88. Marglin, "Farmers, Seedsmen, and Scientists," pp. 33–38.

89. See, for example, Kloppenberg, *First the Seed*, chap. 5. Harlan, *Crops and Man*, p. 129, reports that a selection of barley left in the field as seed stock over a trial of sixty years produced 95 percent of the yield that plant breeders would have been able to achieve and were almost certainly hardier and more disease resistant strains of barley.

90. The classic study of the family development cycle is A. V. Chayanov, *The Theory of Peasant Economy*, introduction by Teodor Shanin (Madison: University of Wisconsin Press, 1986). One of the policy arguments for the stable family farm as an institution is that it is more likely than a capitalist firm to have an intergenerational interest in maintaining or improving the quality of the land and environment. The same logic has traditionally been deployed to argue that many forms of sharecropping and tenancy lead to destructive practices.

91. Even if all such grains were equal in the marketplace, each variety would still have unique labor requirements, growing characteristics, and resistances that would make an important difference to the growers.

92. Richards, *Indigenous Agricultural Revolution*, p. 124.

93. Wendell Berry, "Whose Head Is the Farmer Using? Whose Head Is Using the Farmer?" in Wes Jackson, Wendell Berry, and Bruce Coleman, eds., *Meeting the Expectations of the Land: Essays in Sustainable Agriculture and Stewardship* (San Francisco: North Point Press, 1984), quoted in Marglin, "Farmers, Seedsmen, and Scientists," p. 32.

94. Berry, *The Unsettling of America*, p. 87. I do not consider myself to be a good farmer in Berry's sense of the term, but in a three-acre sheep pasture on my small farm, I can recognize at least six different soil conditions from the patterns of vegetation alone. Four of them seem directly related to drainage, while two of them seem to reflect slope, sunlight, and the continued influence of past use.

95. Anderson, *Plants, Man, and Life*, p. 146.

96. Howard, *An Agricultural Testament*, pp. 185–86.

97. Ibid., p. 196.

98. See Chayanov, *The Theory of Peasant Economy*, pp. 53–194.

99. At least we can be sure that he is the best expert when it comes to his own interests, whether he is entirely sure of them or not.

100. Jan Douwe van der Ploeg, "Potatoes and Knowledge," in Mark Hobart, ed., *An Anthropological Critique of Development* (London: Routledge, 1993), pp. 209–27. I thank Stephen Gudeman for bringing this work to my attention.

101. Compare the term "craft" with the term "mētis," which is elaborated in chapter 9.

102. One can see why the logic of scientific agriculture would make extension agents the implacable enemies of multiple plots and multiple cultivars. Together they place far too many variables in play for scientific method to model.

103. Van der Ploeg, "Potatoes and Knowledge," p. 213.

104. In a larger sense, irrigation, standard fertilizer applications, greenhouses, cloud seeding, and hybridization and cloning represent the decision to adapt the climate and environment to the crop rather than the crop to the environment. These are what Vernon W. Ruttan has called "land substitutes." See "Constraints on the Design of Sustainable Systems of Agricultural Production," *Ecological Economics* 10 (1994): 209–19.

105. Some agricultural environments lend themselves to abstract treatment more easily than others. Well-watered bottomlands with rich soils not subject to erosion *can* be treated more homogeneously without great immediate harm, whereas fragile, semiarid hillsides subject to sheet and gully erosion need to be treated with great care.

106. Yaney, *The Urge to Mobilize*, p. 445.

107. Van der Ploeg, "Potatoes and Knowledge," p. 222. The author does not specify the precise reasons for the decline. It is possible that the strongly recommended monocropping of the new variety encourages the buildup of pest populations and disease, that it depletes the soil of vital nutrients or damages its structural properties, or that the genotype loses its vigor over two or three generations.

108. The talisman of vitamins offers something of a parallel. The discovery of their existence and their role in health was an important breakthrough, but they are now taken by masses of people, most of whom may not need them, in one-size-fits-all dosages, rather in the way some of our ancestors felt protected by wearing garlands of garlic around their necks.

109. Howard, *An Agricultural Testament*, p. 221.

110. Ibid., p. 160. Richards, *Indigenous Agricultural Revolution*, concurs, writing, "No student should expect to be able to advise farmers on changes in their farming practices until he or she has a firm grasp of the issues from the participant's point of view. No one expects a pilot to captain a plane on the basis of textbook knowledge alone. Why should a farmer expect to 'hand over the controls' to an advisor who, in all probability, has never before piloted a farm 'for real'?" (p. 157).

111. Howard, *An Agricultural Testament*, p. 116.

Chapter 9: Thin Simplifications and Practical Knowledge

1. See Lev Timofeev, *Soviet Peasants, or The Peasants' Art of Starving*, trans. Jean Alexander and Victor Zaslavsky, ed. Armando Pitassio and V. Zaslavsky (New York: Telos Press, 1985), for a penetrating discussion of the private-plot economy. An exception to the generalization about meat may have been beef, but supplies of pork, lamb, and chicken were largely provided from private plots or other sources outside of the state marketing channels.

2. See Louis Uchitelle, "Decatur," *New York Times*, June 13, 1993, p. C1.

3. Michel de Certeau, *The Practice of Everyday Life* (Arts de faire: Le pratique du quotidien), trans. Steven Rendall (Berkeley: University of California Press, 1984). See also Jacques Rancière, *The Names of History: On the Poetics of Knowledge*, trans. Hassan Melehy (Minneapolis: University of Minnesota Press, 1994).

4. Marcel Detienne and Jean-Pierre Vernant, *Cunning Intelligence in Greek Culture and Society*, trans. Janet Lloyd (Atlantic Highlands, N.J.: Humanities Press, 1978), originally published in French as *Les ruses d'intelligence: La mētis des grecs* (Paris: Flammarion, 1974).

5. The version of the story that I know appears not to specify the species of oak, whether white, red, burr, or other variety, or the species of squirrel, which was pre-

sumably the common gray squirrel. For the Native Americans, the context must have served to specify such details as these.

6. I am ignoring, in my treatment of the almanac's advice, the fact that European settlers quickly developed their own comparable rules of thumb, and like farmers everywhere, they were paying close attention to what other cultivators were doing. One usually does not want to be the first to plow and plant, nor does one want to be the last.

7. Quoted in Ian Hacking, *The Taming of Chance* (Cambridge: Cambridge University Press, 1990), p. 62. Note that even in Quetelet's formula, the calculations must begin with an unpredictable event: the "last frost." Since the date of the last frost can be known only in retrospect, Quetelet's formula fails as a useful guide for action.

8. Such terms as "indigenous technical knowledge" and "folk wisdom" seem to me to confine this knowledge to "traditional" or "backward" peoples, whereas I want to emphasize how these skills are implicit in the most modern of activities, whether on the factory floor or in a research laboratory. "Local knowledge" and "practical knowledge" are better, but both terms seem too circumscribed and static to capture the constantly changing, dynamic aspect of mētis.

The term descends to us from Greek mythology. Mētis, the first bride of Zeus, had tricked Cronos into swallowing an herb that caused him to regurgitate Zeus's elder brothers, whom Cronos feared would rise against him. Zeus in turn swallowed Mētis, thereby incorporating all her intelligence and wiles, before she could give birth to Athena. Athena was then born from Zeus's thigh.

9. The difference between the first halting, awkward steps of a toddler and the gait of a child who has been walking for a year is a measure of the complexity and "on-the-job training" necessary to master such an apparently simple skill.

10. During the Gulf War, teams with little experience were hired from all over the world to cope with an unprecedented number of fires. A great many new techniques were tried, and much new field experience gained. One team hit on the use of a mounted jet engine (as opposed to dynamite or water) to literally blow out the fire at the wellhead, as if it were a candle on a birthday cake.

11. It is in part this aspect of team sports that often makes the outcomes nontransitive. That is, team A may routinely beat team B, and team B may routinely beat team C, but because of the particular *relation* of skills between teams A and C, team C may often beat team A.

12. Taoism emphasizes precisely this kind of knowledge and skill. Compare Peirce's observation with that of Chuang Tzu: "Cook Ting laid down his knife and replied. What I care about is the Way, which goes beyond skill. When I first began cutting up oxen, all I could see was the ox itself. After three years I no longer saw the whole ox. And now—now I go at it by spirit and don't look with my eyes. Perception and understanding have come to a stop and the spirit moves where it wants. I go along with the natural makeup, strike in the big hollows, guide the knife through the big openings, and follow things as they are. So I never touch the smallest ligament or tendon, much less a joint" (*Chuang Tzu: Basic Writings*, trans. Burton Watson [New York: Columbia University Press, 1964], p. 47).

13. Michael Oakeshott, *Rationalism in Politics and Other Essays* (New York: Basic Books, 1962). As a conservative thinker in the Burkean sense of the term, Oakeshott tends to be an apologist for whatever the past has bequeathed to the present in terms of power, privilege, and property. On the other hand, his criticism of purely rationalist schemes for the design of human life and his understanding of the contingency of practice are astute and telling.

14. Martha C. Nussbaum, *The Fragility of Goodness: Luck and Ethics in Greek Tragedy and Philosophy* (Cambridge: Cambridge University Press, 1986), p. 302.

Nussbaum is concerned particularly with the differences between moral systems that allow for the passions and attachments of human life and closed, self-sufficient moral systems that achieve "moral safety and rational power" at the expense of a fully human life. Plato, depending upon how one interprets the *Symposium*, is an exemplar of the latter, and Aristotle an exemplar of the former.

15. I am greatly indebted for this distinction to the brilliant doctoral thesis of Gene Ammarell, "Bugis Navigation" (Ph.D. diss., Department of Anthropology, Yale University, 1994). Ammarell's analysis of traditional Bugis navigation techniques is the most compelling understanding of indigenous technical knowledge that I have encountered.

16. Compare the pilot's knowledge with this observation, from Bruce Chatwin's *Songlines* (London: Jonathan Cape, 1987): "The dry heart of Australia . . . was a jigsaw of microclimates, of different minerals in the soil and different plants and animals. A man raised in one part of the desert would know its flora and fauna backwards. He knew which plant attracted game. He knew his water. He knew where there were tubers underground. In other words, by *naming* all the 'things' in his territory, he could always count on survival. . . . But if you took him blindfolded to another country, . . . he might end up lost and starving" (p. 269).

17. In what follows I am heavily indebted to the discussions of Nussbaum, *The Fragility of Goodness*, and to Stephen A. Marglin, "Losing Touch: The Cultural Conditions of Worker Accommodation and Resistance," in Frédérique Apffel Marglin and Stephen A. Marglin, eds., *Dominating Knowledge: Development, Culture, and Resistance* (Oxford: Clarendon, 1990), pp. 217–82. Marglin's argument has been elaborated in two subsequent papers: "Farmers, Seedsmen, and Scientists: Systems of Agriculture and Systems of Knowledge" (unpublished paper, May 1991, revised March 1992); and "Economics and the Social Construction of the Economy," in Stephen Gudeman and Stephen A. Marglin, eds., *People's Ecology, People's Economy* (forthcoming). Readers of both texts will note the disparity between Nussbaum's and Marglin's uses of the term "techne." For Nussbaum, techne is analogous to episteme, at least through the work of Plato, and both are sharply distinguished from mētis or practical knowledge. Marglin uses the word "techne" ("T/Knowledge") in much the same way that I use "mētis," and he distinguishes it sharply from "episteme" ("E/Knowledge)"). I have elected to adopt the terminology of the classicist Nussbaum, who convinces me that her usage has a far stronger grounding in the original texts of Plato and Aristotle. Support for Nussbaum's understanding comes also from Pierre Vidal-Naquet: "As G. Cambiano justly [correctly] observes, in the Platonic view, *episteme, dynamis, and techne* comprise a system of concepts that mutually reinforce one another," he writes. "*The Republic*, for example, puts under the control of mathematics a unit composed of *technai, dianoiai,* and *epistemai:* skills, intellectual processes, and sciences" (*The Black Hunter: Forms of Thought and Forms of Society in the Greek World*, trans. Andrew Szegedy-Maszak [Baltimore: Johns Hopkins Press, 1986], p. 228). Even so, those who are familiar with Marglin's argument will note how, in drawing formal comparisons, I have relied on his contrasts while not using his terms.

18. As I recall, this holds only at sea level, as with the standard temperature for water's boiling point. The constant is, then, a universal convention and does in fact vary by altitude.

19. Quoted in Nussbaum, *The Fragility of Goodness*, p. 95.

20. There is a large and rapidly growing literature on the practice or ethnomethodology of science, particularly laboratory science. Most of this literature emphasizes the difference between actual scientific practice on one hand and its codified form (in articles and lab reports, for example) on the other. For an intro-

duction to this literature, see Bruno Latour, *Science in Action: How to Follow Scientists and Engineers Through Society* (Cambridge: Harvard University Press, 1987); Ian Hacking, "The Self-Vindication of the Laboratory Sciences," in Andrew Pickering, ed., *Science as Practice and Culture* (Chicago: University of Chicago Press, 1992), pp. 29–64; and Andrew Pickering, "From Science as Knowledge to Science as Practice," ibid., pp. 1–26. See also Pickering, "Objectivity and the Mangle of Practice," in Allan Megill, ed., *Rethinking Objectivity* (Durham: Duke University Press, 1994), pp. 109–25.

21. Marglin, "Losing Touch," p. 234.

22. In many ways the most searching philosophical treatment of these issues is found in Michael Polanyi, *Personal Knowledge: Towards a Post-Critical Philosophy* (Chicago: University of Chicago Press, 1958).

23. Detienne and Vernant, *Cunning Intelligence*, pp. 3–4.

24. Nussbaum, *The Fragility of Goodness*, chaps. 5 and 6.

25. Ibid., p. 238.

26. I use "himself" because Plato is talking about what he considered to be the highest form of love: that between men and boys.

27. Music is, in a sense, pure form, but Plato was deeply suspicious of music's emotional appeal and in fact believed that the ideal republic should ban certain modes of music.

28. An important critique of social science might well take this observation as a point of departure. Borrowing the prestige of scientific language and methods from the biological sciences, many social scientists have envisioned and tried to effect an objective, precise, and strictly replicable set of techniques—a set of techniques that gives impartial and quantitative answers. Thus most forms of formal policy analysis and cost-benefit analysis manage, through heroic assumptions and an implausible metric for comparing incommensurate variables, to produce a quantitative answer to thorny questions. They achieve impartiality, precision, and replicability at the cost of accuracy. A brief and persuasive case along these lines can be found in Theodore M. Porter, "Objectivity as Standardization: The Rhetoric of Impersonality in Measurement, Statistics, and Cost-Benefit Analysis," in Allan Megill, ed., *Rethinking Objectivity* (Durham: Duke University Press, 1994), pp. 197–237.

29. Marglin, "Farmers, Seedsmen, and Scientists," p. 46.

30. Jeremy Bentham, *Pauper Management Improved*, cited in Nussbaum, *The Fragility of Goodness*, p. 89.

31. See Hacking, *The Taming of Chance*. Warren Weaver long ago distinguished between what he termed "disorganized complexity," which could be dealt with through statistical techniques that captured average outcomes, and "organized complexity" (including, most notably, organic systems), which could not yield to such techniques because the complexity of their nonrandom, systemic relationships prevents us from fully understanding first-order effects of an intervention, let alone second- or third-order effects ("Science and Complexity," *American Scientist* 36 [1948]: 536–44).

32. Marglin, "Economics and the Social Construction of the Economy," pp. 44–45.

33. But while the focus has narrowed in economics, the reach has grown. Witness the efforts of William D. Nordhaus to treat such ecological issues as global warming with an often spurious precision. See Nordhaus, "To Slow or Not to Slow: The Economics of the Greenhouse Effect," *Economic Journal*, July 1991, pp. 920–37.

34. Marglin, "Economics and the Social Construction of the Economy," p. 31. Marglin also describes and critiques the attempts *within* the boundaries of epistemic economics to deal with such issues as public goods, sustainability, and un-

certainty. Friedrich Hayek himself was a skeptic: "The delusion that advancing theoretical knowledge places us everywhere increasingly in a position to reduce complex interconnections to ascertainable particular facts often leads to new scientific errors. . . . Such errors are largely due to an arrogation of pretended knowledge, which in fact no one possesses and which even the advance of science is not likely to give us" (*Studies in Philosophy, Economics, and Politics* [Chicago: University of Chicago Press, 1967], p. 197).

35. At its most extreme, this strategy is analogous to that of tracking body counts during the Vietnam War—a technique that offered at least one precise measure, it was thought, for military progress.

36. Nussbaum, *The Fragility of Goodness*, p. 99.

37. Ibid., p. 302.

38. Ibid., p. 125. Thus in the *Phaedrus*, Socrates, speaking through Plato, deplores the invention of writing and claims that books cannot reply to questions. He argues for the organic unity of a work of art, one whose arguments and style should take into account the prospective audience. In his *Seventh Letter*, Plato writes that his deepest teachings are not written. See R. B. Rutherford, *The Art of Plato: Ten Essays in Platonic Interpretation* (London: Duckworth, 1996).

39. See Harold Conklin, *Hanunoo Agriculture: A Report on an Integral System of Shifting Cultivation in the Philippines* (Rome: Food and Agriculture Organization of the United Nations, 1957).

40. Claude Lévi-Strauss, *La pensée sauvage* (Paris: Plon, 1962).

41. Once the tractor became available (especially the tractor with power take-off, or PTO), however, it was imaginatively adapted by farmers and mechanics to serve purposes its inventors had never imagined.

42. Later in this chapter I offer, as anecdotal evidence of this truism, an account about how a Malaysian villager rid a mango tree of an infestation of red ants.

43. Gladys L. Hobby, *Penicillin: Meeting the Challenge* (New Haven: Yale University Press, 1985).

44. Anil Gupta, paper presented at a congress entitled "Agrarian Questions: The Politics of Farming Anno 1995," May 22–24, 1995, Wageningen, The Netherlands. The fact that in the past two or three decades research laboratories have begun to inventory and analyze large numbers of traditional medicines is an indication of the rich capital of findings which mētis has bequeathed to modern medicine and pharmacology. For questions of property rights in such products, see Jack Ralph Kloppenberg, Jr., *First the Seed: The Political Economy of Plant Biotechnology, 1492–2000* (Cambridge: Cambridge University Press, 1988).

45. Daniel Defoe, *Journal of the Plague Year* (1722; Harmondsworth: Penguin, 1966). It is worth noting that these stratagems were more practical for the rich than for the poor. The result was that, far from being indiscriminate, the plague wreaked its greatest havoc among poor Londoners.

46. Frédérique Apffel Marglin, "Smallpox in Two Systems of Knowledge," in Marglin and Marglin, *Dominating Knowledge*, pp. 102–44.

47. There are different models of scientific medicine as well, some of which require a fundamentally different optic than standard allopathic practice. Thus Darwinian medicine looks at the adaptive functions of what are otherwise seen as pathological conditions. One example is morning sickness, which occurs for many women during the first trimester of pregnancy and which is thought to be an adaptive rejection of foods, particularly of fruits and vegetables, that are most likely to carry toxins harmful to the fetus. Another example is fever during the course of ordinary influenza or a cold, which is thought to be an adaptive mechanism for triggering elements of the immune system to combat infection. To the

degree that the Darwinian perspective is correct, it forces us to ask what the beneficial or, more precisely, the adaptive functions of a medical condition might be. Surely, a view of plant disease from this angle might lead to novel insights. For an accessible introduction, see Randolph M. Nesse and George C. Williams, *Evolution and Healing: The New Science of Darwinian Medicine* (London: Weidenfeld and Nicolson, 1995).

48. Much of F. A. Marglin's account is concerned with the undoubtedly well-intended but coercive efforts made by the British to suppress variolation and to substitute vaccination, as well as the popular resistance to these efforts. Marglin implies that the British pretty quickly succeeded in replacing variolation with vaccination, but Sumit Guha, an Indian colleague who has also studied these matters, believes that it is unlikely that the British had either the personnel or the power to stamp out variolation so quickly.

49. Donald R. Hopkins, *Princes and Peasants: Smallpox in History* (Chicago: University of Chicago Press, 1983), p. 77, cited in Marglin, "Losing Touch," p. 112. For the scientific career of vaccination and its application to anthrax and rabies, see Gerald L. Geison, *The Private Science of Louis Pasteur* (Princeton: Princeton University Press, 1995).

50. There were literally thousands of competitors for cures and preventatives, as there always are with diseases that seem incurable.

51. Albert Howard, *An Agricultural Testament* (London: Oxford University Press, 1940), p. 144 (emphasis in original). Howard is paraphrasing here a work by Lowdermilk, and although Howard provides no reference, I believe he is referring to A. W. C. Lowdermilk, who visited Basutoland in 1949 and whose papers are at Yale University's Sterling Memorial Library.

52. For the case of jet engines, the performance of which "remains notoriously uncertain in the development process" and which have to be adjusted by engineers with long experience after pilots conduct in-flight testing, see Nathan Rosenberg, *Inside the Black Box: Technology and Economics* (New York: Cambridge University Press, 1982), especially pp. 120–41. Rosenberg makes it clear that the limits of scientific methodology in this case have to do with the impossibility of anticipating the interactive consequences of the enormous number of independent variables (including different technologies) at work in a jet engine. See also Kenneth Arrow, "The Economics of Learning by Doing," *Review of Economic Studies*, June 1962, pp. 45–73.

53. Charles E. Lindblom, "The Science of Muddling Through," *Public Administration Review* 19 (Spring 1959): 79–88. Twenty years after this article appeared, Lindblom extended the argument in another article with a catchy title: "Still Muddling, Not Yet Through." See Lindblom, *Democracy and the Market System* (Oslo: Norwegian University Press, 1988), pp. 237–59.

54. Lindblom, "Still Muddling, Not Yet Through."

55. Albert O. Hirschman, "The Search for Paradigms as a Hindrance to Understanding," *World Politics* 22 (April 1970): 243.

56. Implicit knowledge is almost a staple of discourse in the philosophy of knowledge and in the psychology of cognition. See, for example, Gilbert Ryle, *Concept of the Mind* (New York: Barnes and Noble, 1949), whose distinction between "knowing how" and "knowing that" mimics my distinction between mētis and episteme, and Jerome Bruner, *On Knowing: Essays for the Left Hand* (Cambridge: Belknap Press, Harvard University Press, 1962).

57. A great basketball move may be diagrammed and even taught, but the ability to make that same move in the traffic and rush of a real game is, alas, another thing altogether.

58. A similar story tells of a man dying in a Chicago hospital of a disease that the physicians could not diagnose. Although they knew that the man's trips abroad meant that he could have been suffering from a tropical ailment, their tests and researches were to no avail. One day, an experienced doctor from India was simply walking through the ward with a colleague on his way to an appointment when he stopped, sniffed the air, and said, "There's a bloke here with X" (I don't recall the name of the disease). He was correct, but unfortunately the patient was too far gone to be saved.

59. Howard, *An Agricultural Testament*, pp. 29–30.

60. Marglin has noted how the word "crafty" brings the idea of experienced knowledge of a craft together with the concept of "cunning" connoted by "mētis." See "Economics and the Social Construction of the Economy," p. 60.

61. Bugis sailors are exceptionally astute observers of their environment at sea and have assembled a large array of signs to forecast weather, wind, landfall, and tides. The dominant color of rainbows carries meaning: yellow means more rain, blue means more wind. A morning rainbow in the northwest signals the beginning of the western monsoon. The slaty-breasted rail's call, if it is a buzzing "kech, kech, kech," means a change in the wind. When raptors soar very high, rain is no more than two days away. Many of these reliable associations could perhaps be explained more "scientifically," but they have served as rapid, accurate, and occasionally life-saving signals for generations.

62. Ammarell, "Bugis Navigation," chap. 5, pp. 220–82.

63. An alternative, the subject of a growing literature, is the term "indigenous knowledge" or "indigenous technical knowledge." Although I have nothing against this term per se, inasmuch as it points to the skills and experience already in the possession of the subjects of development schemes, it has come in some hands to connote something self-contained, completely sufficient, and intractably opposed to modern scientific knowledge, when in fact it is constantly changing through experimentation and through contact with the outside. For two exceptionally perceptive critiques of the term, see Akil Gupta, "The Location of 'the Indigenous' in Critiques of Modernity," Ninety-First Annual Meeting of the American Anthropological Association, San Francisco, December 2–6, 1992, and Arun Agrawal, "Indigenous and Scientific Knowledge," *Indigenous Knowledge and Development Monitor* 4, no. 1 (April 1996): 1–11, and the commentary following it. See also Agrawal, "Dismantling the Divide Between Indigenous and Scientific Knowledge," *Development and Change* 26, no. 3 (1995): 413–39.

64. For a general argument along these line, see Eric Hobsbawm and T. O. Ranger, *The Invention of Tradition* (New York: Cambridge University Press, 1983). Although Hobsbawm and Ranger are largely concerned with traditions "invented" by elites to legitimate their rule and legitimacy, their general point about the nonantiquity of many so-called traditions is well taken.

65. I do not deal here with such related issues as how readily people abandon habits and norms that are perhaps closer to the center of their self-identity: death rituals, religious beliefs, ideas about friendship, and so on. One of the most curious and important aspects of adaptation, however, is that the poor and marginal are often in the vanguard of innovations that do not require a lot of capital. This is not at all surprising when one considers that, for the poor, a gamble often makes sense if their current practices are failing them. Occasionally, when a whole community or a culture experiences an overwhelming sense of powerlessness and its categories no longer make sense of the world, such gambles take on millennial tones, with new prophets arising to proclaim the way forward. The colonial conquest of preindustrial peoples, the German Peasant War at the time of the Reformation, the English Civil War, and the French Revolution seem to belong in this category.

66. James Ferguson, *The Anti-Politics Machine: "Development," Depoliticization, and Bureaucratic Power in Lesotho* (Cambridge: Cambridge University Press, 1990).

67. See Arturo Escobar's elaboration of the concept of hybridization in Marglin and Gudeman, *People's Economy, People's Ecology*.

68. Oakeshott, "Rationalism in Politics," in *Rationalism in Politics*, p. 31.

69. Oakeshott, "The Tower of Baal," in *Rationalism in Politics*, p. 64.

70. If innovation in such societies must be represented as compatible with tradition in order to gain acceptance, this is another reason for the plasticity of tradition.

71. Access to codified, epistemic knowledge is also sharply restricted by such markers as wealth, gender, social position, and region in developed countries as well. The difference is that, in principle, in developed societies the secrets of medicine, science, engineering, ecology, and so on are open secrets, available to all to use and modify.

72. It goes without saying that new forms of mētis are constantly being created. Computer hacking would fall into this category. Mētis, it should be quite clear, is ubiquitous in modern and in less modern societies alike, and perhaps the crucial difference is that, compared to preindustrial societies, modern societies are particularly reliant on codified, epistemic knowledge, usually conveyed through formal instruction.

73. Ammarell, "Bugis Navigation," p. 372.

74. There is little doubt that many apprenticeships were longer than necessary for training a young craftsmen and were a thinly disguised form of indentured labor designed to increase the profits of an oligopoly of master craftsmen.

75. The desire for control over the work process is not merely a short-term prerequisite to capturing profits; it is crucial to the capacity of managers to transform the work process from above for adapting to the market and meeting the demands of their superiors. Ken C. Kusterer calls management control over the production process the "steerability" of a firm. See Kusterer, *Know-How on the Job: The Important Working Knowledge of "Unskilled" Workers* (Boulder: Westview Press, 1978).

76. Marglin, "Losing Touch," p. 220.

77. Ibid., p. 222. But as the capitalists were shortly to discover, one advantage of the putting-out system was a diminished exposure to large-scale industrial strikes and equipment breakdowns.

78. Taylor, quoted in ibid., p. 220 n. 3.

79. As Marglin notes, "Only a recapitulation of workers' knowledge in the form of an episteme to which management alone had access would provide a firm basis for managerial control" (ibid., p. 247).

80. David F. Noble, *Forces of Production: A Social History of Automation* (New York: Oxford Press, 1984), p. 250, quoted in ibid., p. 248.

81. Noble, *Forces of Production*, p. 277, quoted in Marglin, "Losing Touch," p. 250.

82. Quoted in Kusterer, *Know-How on the Job*, p. 50.

83. This is why, before the income tax, the administrators of the older systems of taxation found it easiest to assess taxes by relying solely on the more permanent fact of land or real property ownership.

84. A branch of social theory called principal-agent analysis is devoted to the various techniques by which one person can be persuaded to do another person's bidding. As one might imagine, its most immediate applications have been in management science.

85. Michael J. Watts, "Life Under Contract: Contract Farming, Agrarian Restructuring, and Flexible Accumulation," in Michael J. Watts and Peter O. Little, eds., *Living Under Contract: Contract Farming and Agrarian Transformation in Sub-*

Saharan Africa (Madison: University of Wisconsin Press, 1974), pp. 21–77. See also Allan Pred and Michael J. Watts, *Reworking Modernity: Capitalism and Symbolic Discontent* (New Brunswick: Rutgers University Press, 1992).

86. The system with fryers also involved farms that specialized in hatching and caring for chicks and farms that grew certain elements of the feed. Contract farming for vegetables is widespread in the Third World and has recently been extended to the raising of pigs.

87. The uniformity is achieved at the outset, of course, by means of scientific breeding.

88. Quoted in Oakeshott, "Rationalism in Politics," p. 20 (emphasis added).

89. Quoted in ibid., p. 5.

90. It is in fact impossible for most modern readers to take in the vast complacency with which Oakeshott regards what the past has bequeathed to him in its habits, practices, and morals without wondering if Jews, women, the Irish, and the working class in general might not feel as blessed by the deposit of history as did this Oxford don.

Chapter 10: Conclusion

1. Stephen A. Marglin, "Economics and the Social Construction of the Economy," in Stephen Gudeman and Stephen Marglin, eds., *People's Ecology, People's Economy* (forthcoming).

2. Albert O. Hirschman, "The Search for Paradigms as a Hindrance to Understanding," *World Politics* 22 (April 1970): 239. Elsewhere Hirschman takes social science in general to task in much the same fashion: "But after so many failed prophecies, is it not in the interest of social science to embrace complexity, be it at some sacrifice of its claim to predictive power?" ("Rival Interpretations of Market Society: Civilizing, Destructive, or Feeble?" *Journal of Economic Literature* 20 [December 1982]: 1463–84).

3. Quoted in Roger Penrose, "The Great Diversifier," a review of Freeman Dyson, *From Eros to Gaia*, in the *New York Review of Books*, March 4, 1993, p. 5.

4. Like all rules of thumb, this rule is not absolute. It could be waived, for example, if catastrophe seems imminent and quick decisions are essential.

5. This is, I believe, the strongest argument against capital punishment for those who are not opposed to it on other grounds.

6. Aldo Leopold, quoted in Donald Worster, *Nature's Economy*, 2nd ed. (New York: Cambridge University Press, 1994), p. 289.

7. The typical social science solution to this sort of issue is to turn it into a quantitative exercise by, say, asking citizens to assess the well-being of the community on a predetermined scale.

8. "Everything becomes crystal clear after you have reduced reality to one—one only—of its thousand aspects. You know what to do. . . . There is at the same time the perfect measuring rod for the degree of success or failure. . . . The point is that the real strength of the theory of private enterprise lies in its ruthless simplification, which fits so admirably into the mental patterns created by the phenomenal successes of science. The strength of science too derives from its 'reduction' of reality to one or another of its many aspects, primarily the reduction of quality to quantity" (E. F. Schumacher, *Small Is Beautiful: A Study of Economics as if People Mattered* [London: Blond and Briggs, 1973], pp. 272–73).

9. See John Brinckerhoff Jackson, *A Sense of Place, a Sense of Time* (New Haven: Yale University Press, 1994), p. 190.

10. For this insight I am much indebted to Colin Ward's *Anarchy in Action* (London: Freedom Press, 1988), pp. 110–25.

11. Personal notes from the first congress of the Agrarian Scientists' Association, "Agrarian Reform in the USSR," held in Moscow, June 24–28, 1991.

12. Birgit Müller, *Toward an Alternative Culture of Work: Political Idealism and Economic Practices in a Berlin Collective Enterprise* (Boulder: Westview Press, 1991), pp. 51–82.

13. Herman E. Daly, "Policies for Sustainable Development," paper presented at the Program in Agrarian Studies, Yale University, New Haven, February 9, 1996, p. 4.

14. Ibid., pp. 12–13. Daly adds, "In the limit, all other species become cultivated natural capital, bred, managed at the smaller population size to make more room for humans and their furniture. Instrumental values such as redundancy, resiliency, stability, sustainability, would be sacrificed, along with the intrinsic value of life enjoyment by sentient human species, in the interests of 'efficiency' defined as anything that increases the human scale" (p. 13).

15. I am grateful to my colleague Arun Agrawal for emphasizing this point.

16. The classic elaboration of this argument, empirically grounded in many case studies, may be found in Robert M. Netting, *Smallholders, Householders: Farm Families and the Ecology of Intensive, Sustainable Agriculture* (Stanford: Stanford University Press, 1993).

17. See the important book by Enzo Mingione, *Fragmented Societies: A Sociology of Economic Life Beyond the Market Paradigm*, trans. Paul Goodrick (Oxford: Basil Blackwell, 1991).

18. Robert Putnam, *Making Democracy Work: Civic Traditions in Modern Italy* (Princeton: Princeton University Press, 1993).

19. This ordering of the names of the dead, which was insisted on by Maya Lin, caused quite a controversy at the time the memorial was built.

20. Near the site of the Vietnam Memorial is the statue of a small squad of soldiers carrying a wounded comrade. This statue was the original proposal by a good many veterans' organizations who had opposed the present wall as a fitting monument.

21. For an imaginative application of a comparable logic to the subject of children's playgrounds, see "Play as an Anarchist Parable," chap. 10 in Ward, *Anarchy in Action*, pp. 88–94.

Sources for Illustrations

Figure 1. Photograph from P. Mark S. Ashton Collection. Courtesy of P. Mark S. Ashton.

Figure 2. Photograph by Angelo Lomeo. Courtesy of Bullaty Lomeo Photographers.

Figures 3–6. From George Yaney, *The Urge to Mobilize: Agrarian Reform in Russia, 1861–1930* (Urbana: University of Illinois Press, 1982), pp. 147, 149, 148, 150. Copyright 1982 by the Board of Trustees of the University of Illinois. Used by permission of the University of Illinois.

Figure 7. Photograph by Alex S. MacLean, from James Corner and MacLean, *Taking Measures Across the American Landscape* (New Haven: Yale University Press, 1996), p. 51. Courtesy of Alex S. MacLean, Landslides.

Figure 8. From Mark Girouard, *Cities and People: A Social and Architectural History* (New Haven: Yale University Press, 1985), p. 91. Courtesy of the city of Bruges.

Figure 9. Map from the Chicago Historical Society. Used by permission of the Chicago Historical Society.

Figure 10. Map from A. Alphand, *Les promenades de Paris*, 2 vols. (Paris, 1867–73), plates 11 and 12.

Figure 13. Photograph of map from the exhibition "Hungerwinter and Liberation in Amsterdam," Amsterdam Historical Museum, 1995. Courtesy of the Amsterdam Historical Museum.

Figures 14–17. From Le Corbusier, *The Radiant City*, trans. Pamela Knight (1933; New York: Orion Press, 1964), pp. 204, 220, 225, 149.

Figure 18. Plan by Lucio Costa, reprinted in Lawrence Vale, *Architecture, Power, and National Identity* (New Haven: Yale University Press, 1992), p. 118.

Figures 19–26. Photographs by James Holston. From Holston, *The Modernist City: An Anthropological Critique of Brasília* (Chicago: University of Chicago Press, 1989), pp. 100, 102, 132, 313. For figure 23, photograph by Abril Imagens/Carlos Fenerich. Courtesy of James Holston.

Figure 27. Photograph from Ravi Kalia, *Chandigarh: In Search of an Identity* (Carbondale: Southern Illinois University Press, 1987), p. 97. Copyright 1987 by

433

the Board of Trustees, Southern Illinois University. Used by permission of the Trustees of Southern Illinois University.

Figures 28–30. Plan and photograph courtesy of Teodor Shanin.

Figure 31. Jannik Boesen, Birgit Storgaard Madsen, and Tony Moody, *Ujamaa: Socialism from Above* (Uppsala: Scandinavian Institute of African Studies, 1977), p. 178. Used by permission of the publishers.

Figure 32. John M. Cohen and Nils-Ivar Isaksson, "Villagization in Ethiopia's Arsi Region," *Journal of Modern African Studies* 15, no. 3 (1987): 450. Reproduced by permission of Cambridge University Press.

Figure 33. Jason W. Clay, Sandra Steingraber, and Peter Niggli, *The Spoils of Famine: Ethiopian Famine Policy and Peasant Agriculture*, Cultural Survival Report no. 25 (Cambridge, Mass.: Cultural Survival, 1988), p. 248. Used by permission of Cultural Survival, Inc.

Figure 34. Painting by Davis Meltzer, from James B. Billard, "The Revolution in American Agriculture," with illustrations by James R. Blair, *National Geographic* 137, no. 2 (February 1970): 184–85. Used by permission of Davis Meltzer/National Geographic Image Collection.

Figure 35. Photograph from Paul Richards, *Indigenous Agricultural Revolutions: Ecology and Food Production in West Africa* (London: Unwin Hyman, 1985), plate 3. Courtesy of Paul Richards.

Figures 36–37. Drawings from Edgar Anderson, *Plants, Man, and Life* (Boston: Little, Brown, 1952), pp. 138–39. Used by permission of the Missouri Botanical Garden.

Index